MW00774931

THEOCRITUS
MOSCHUS
BION

LCL 28

THEOCRITUS
MOSCHUS
BION

EDITED AND TRANSLATED BY

NEIL HOPKINSON

HARVARD UNIVERSITY PRESS

CAMBRIDGE, MASSACHUSETTS
LONDON, ENGLAND
2015

Library of Congress Control Number 2014947085
CIP data available from the Library of Congress

ISBN 978-0-674-99644-1

*Composed in ZephGreek and ZephText by
Technologies 'N Typography, Merrimac, Massachusetts.
Printed on acid-free paper and bound by
The Maple-Vail Book Manufacturing Group*

CONTENTS

CONTENTS

INTRODUCTION

THEOCRITUS

External evidence for Theocritus' life[1] tells us little that could not have been inferred from his poetry. His parents were Praxagoras and Philinna. He was from Syracuse in Sicily (*Idd.* 11.7, 28.16). *Idyll* 16 asks for patronage from Hiero II, tyrant of Syracuse circa 271 to 216 BC. *Idylls* 14, 15, and 17 are set in the reign of Ptolemy II Philadelphus, king of Egypt circa 283 to 246. *Idylls* 15 and 17 speak of Queen Arsinoe, consort of Philadelphus circa 278 to 270; *Idyll* 17 is a eulogy of the king. *Idylls* 4, 5, 6, and 11 are set in Sicily, 7 on Cos in the eastern Aegean (an island favored by Ptolemy as his birthplace), and 15 and 17 in Ptolemy's capital city, Alexandria. It has been inferred from these few facts that Theocritus composed some of his pastoral poems in Sicily, failed in his appeal to Hiero, moved to Cos, succeeded in his appeal to Ptolemy, and took up residence at Alexandria. But he may, for all we know to the contrary, have moved freely between the western and eastern Mediterranean areas.

Ptolemy patronized scholarship and the arts. He founded the Alexandrian library and went to great lengths to collect rare manuscripts; and he established the Mu-

[1] See pp. 2–7.

seum, or Temple of the Muses, a sort of institute for writers, scholars, and researchers. Apollonius of Rhodes was librarian there circa 270 to 245, and Callimachus compiled an enormous catalog of its holdings; the recherché learned details in their poetry are a product of their extensive reading as scholars. They also composed works in prose on a variety of learned topics. Although Theocritus' poetry is not obtrusively learned, the song of Simichidas in *Idyll* 7 shows that he was familiar with the erudition of the avant-garde. In composing short poems in a variety of literary dialects and meters, and in treating at times unepic subject matter in the epic hexameter, he adopts the aesthetic of small-scale, carefully crafted work developed a generation earlier by Philitas,[2] espoused most prominently by Callimachus, and adopted or adapted in various ways by contemporary writers of epigram, by Aratus in his elegant poem on astronomy, and by Herodas in his humorously unedifying dramatic vignettes of daily life in iambic meter.

Theocritus composed hymns, encomia formal and informal, and poems inspired by shepherds' songs, by magic ritual, and by mundane characters from popular drama. Some poems have a contemporary setting; others refer to or are set in a mythic past. *Idyll* 16 has characteristics of begging songs. *Idyll* 22, a celebration of the twin Dioscuri, contains a passage of stichomythia (repartee in a series of single lines) unique in epic-style narrative. *Idyll* 24, on the babyhood and youth of Heracles, incorporates a lullaby. *Idylls* 28 to 31 are in Aeolic meters and dialect in the man-

---

[2] *Id.* 7.35–48 praises Philitas and the epigrammatist Asclepiades and deprecates grandiose attempts to rival Homer.

ner of Sappho and Alcaeus. The epigrams are composed in a variety of rhythms. The *Syrinx* is a pattern poem in the shape of a panpipe.

Theocritus is best known for poems set in the countryside. Most of these are dialogues, and some feature dialogue's formal complement, the singing contest. Earlier poetry had country scenes: the hospitable pig-keeper Eumaeus is an important figure in the *Odyssey;* in the *Theogony* Hesiod says he encountered the Muses while pasturing his sheep, and in the *Works & Days* he gives precepts for farmers; Dicaeopolis, hero of Aristophanes' *Acharnians,* feels nostalgia for his farm; epigrams of Anyte and Leonidas of Tarentum treat rustic themes. But none of these is a close precedent for Theocritus' original combination of lyric tone with epic meter and Doric dialect,[3] or for his creation of an idealized and evocatively described pastoral landscape whose lovelorn inhabitants, presided over by the Nymphs, Pan, and Priapus, use song as a natural mode of expression.[4] It is likely enough that the idea for singing contests came to him from real shepherds'

[3] The most notable metrical feature is the so-called bucolic diaeresis, a word break, often reinforced by a sense pause, after a dactylic fourth foot in the hexameter (exemplified by *Id.* 1.1–6); this rhythm came to be seen as characteristic of pastoral poetry. Both meter and dialect vary subtly from poem to poem. *Idyll* 11, perhaps because it is a Cyclopean performance, is less metrically polished than the other pastorals. The hymns and encomia are closer to the refined metrics of Callimachus.

[4] Recurrent names (Adonis, Amaryllis, Comatas, Daphnis, Polyphemus and Galatea, Tityrus) enhance the effect of an enclosed world, even if in some cases the names seem not always to refer to the same character.

songs and that he chose Doric because that was the dialect of his native Sicily.[5] Indeed, he may have seen himself as part of a tradition of specifically Sicilian poetry. We know that the Sicilian lyric poet Stesichorus of Himera (7th/6th c. BC) celebrated Daphnis, who is a prominent figure in *Idyll* 1. Epicharmus, probably of Syracuse, composed a *Cyclops* (Frr. 70–72 K-A), which may have influenced *Idylls* 6 and 11, and an *Amycus* (Frr. 6–8 K-A; cf. *Id.* 22); Theocritus celebrated him in an epigram (18). Sophron, another fifth-century Syracusan, wrote dramatic pieces in rhythmical prose and with an urban setting. He is said by the scholia (ancient commentators) to have been a source for *Idylls* 2 and 15, and he may have influenced the pastoral poems too.

MOSCHUS AND BION

Little is known of Moschus and Bion, second and third in the canon of bucolic poets (Theoc. T 1). Moschus was a literary scholar from Syracuse who flourished in the mid-second century BC. Fragments of his bucolic poems survive, but the *Europa* is his only extant complete work. Bion, who flourished some fifty years later, was from Phlossa, near Smyrna on the coast of Asia Minor. A poem commemorating him states that he died from poison (see p. 479, n. 24). His bucolic poems too survive only in frag-

---

[5] A Byzantine essay (pp. 2–3 Wendel), based on much earlier sources, places the origin of pastoral poetry in Laconia or at Sicilian country festivals of Artemis; but Artemis is conspicuous by her absence in Theocritus' works.

ments,[6] though the extant *Lament for Adonis* is set in the countryside. Both poets will have treated the theme of love in a pastoral setting.

LATER PASTORAL

By including in the *Idylls* references to the famous singers Daphnis and Comatas, Theocritus gives the impression that pastoral poetry already has a distinguished history. The genre was developed, in ways now hardly possible to determine, by Moschus and Bion, and introduced into Latin by Virgil in his book of ten *Eclogues* (ca. 40 BC). Some of these are modeled closely on Theocritus, but in the first poem Virgil signals a new direction for pastoral: the countryside is threatened by confiscations of land, and only Octavian (the future Augustus) has it in his power to grant security. Virgil thus introduces contemporary issues, treated by Theocritus only in nonpastoral poems (*Idd.* 14–17), into the bucolic world. A second innovation is his setting of two of the *Eclogues* in an idealized Arcadia.

Of the seven *Eclogues* of Calpurnius Siculus (1st c. AD), three are concerned with Nero and his court. In the late third century Nemesianus composed four nonpolitical pastoral poems derivative from Virgil, Ovid, and Calpurnius.

Longus' prose pastoral romance *Daphnis & Chloe* (2nd/3rd c. AD) owes much (including the name of its hero) to Theocritus.

---

[6] Unless Fr. 13 is a complete poem.

Virgil's fourth *Eclogue* hails the birth of a child that heralds a new Golden Age. The European tradition of pastoral was much influenced by this poem, which many took to foretell the birth of Christ. The Adoration of the Shepherds and the image of Christ as shepherd of his people led medieval poets to employ pastoral motifs. In the Renaissance, some writers emulated what they took to be the rustic realism and unadorned style of Theocritus, others the refined artistry of Virgil. Among the best-known works composed in the pastoral mode may be mentioned the ten Latin eclogues of Mantuan (late 15th c.), entitled *Adulescentia,* which included love poems and religious allegory; the *Arcadia* of Sannazaro (1480s), in alternating Italian prose and verse, with its melancholy and lovelorn narrator who wanders the countryside listening to shepherds' songs; Sidney's *Arcadia* (ca. 1572–1586), a prose romance of chivalry and adventure inspired also by Heliodorus' *Aethiopica* (3rd/4th c. AD) and by Longus; Spenser's *Shepheardes Calender* (1579), whose twelve eclogues, each in a different meter, employ archaizing Chaucerian language and spelling to treat, among other topics, love, theology, and Queen Elizabeth; Tasso's verse-drama *Aminta* (1573), set in the time of Alexander the Great; Guarini's tragicomedy *Il pastor fido* (1585); the brief lyric evocations of country life in Herrick's *Hesperides* (1648); and Milton's *Comus* (1634). Notable versions of the pastoral lament, inspired by the song of Daphnis in *Idyll* 1 and by the *Epitaphia* for Bion and Adonis, are Milton's *Lycidas* (1637), Shelley's *Adonais* (1821), and Arnold's *Thyrsis* (1866).

THE TEXT

It is uncertain how the poems of Theocritus and the other bucolic poets were "published." They may at first have been recited, then circulated, individually. It has been suggested that the ten *Eclogues* of Virgil are inspired by a ten-poem Thecritean bucolic collection, but there is no evidence for this; and the fact that the manuscripts vary in the order in which they present the *Idylls* suggests that Theocritus himself left no collected edition.[7] The scholar Artemidorus of Tarsus gathered together the bucolic poems, and perhaps others, in the first century BC (T 9), and his son Theon composed a commentary on Theocritus that probably formed the basis of the extant ancient scholia. *Idylls* 1–18 are preserved in more than 180 medieval manuscripts, 19–30 (and Moschus and Bion) in a much smaller number. Lines from some *Idylls* also exist on scraps of papyrus manuscripts dating from the second to the sixth centuries AD. These have some readings not attested in any medieval manuscript; textual variants must have existed from an early date. There is considerable disagreement in the manuscripts between Ionic and Doric dialectal forms in some poems. It is possible that Theoc-

---

[7] The traditional order of Theocritus' poems, which is followed here, goes back to the edition of Stephanus in his *Poetae Graeci principes heroici carminis et alii nonnulli* (1566). The manuscripts and papyri order the poems in various ways, *Idyll* 1 being almost always placed first. Although there would be advantages in arranging the poems by genre or theme and in separating the genuine from the spurious, to change the established order now would produce more inconvenience than benefit.

ritus took particular care over his choice between such forms, but the manuscripts are not reliable enough for us to be able to discover much about his principles.

Thirty *Idylls* (εἰδύλλια) and twenty-seven epigrams are ascribed to Theocritus in surviving medieval manuscripts.[8] A papyrus has preserved scraps of a thirty-first poem, and we have a short quotation from the lost *Berenice*. The end of *Idyll* 24 and the beginning of *Idyll* 27 are missing in the medieval manuscripts, and there may have been other major losses, now undetectable.

Almost all the fragments of Bion and Moschus are preserved by the anthologist Stobaeus (5th c. AD). *Runaway Love, Europa, The Epitaph for Bion, Megara, The Epitaph for Adonis, The Wedding Song of Achilles and Deidamia, Adonis Dead,* and the pseudo-Theocritean *Idylls* 19, 20, 21, 23, 25, and 27 are preserved in manuscripts that also include poems of Theocritus. There may have existed an independent collection of works by later bucolic poets; part of it may have been copied into some of Theocritus' manuscripts, and Stobaeus may have made his excerpts while it was still complete. All this is however uncertain.

The pattern poems and Theocritus' epigrams are preserved in some bucolic manuscripts and in the *Palatine Anthology,* a collection of epigrams made in the Byzantine period.

For reports of manuscript readings, the present edition is based on those of A. S. F. Gow (OCT, 1952) and C. Gallavotti (3rd ed., 1993) and on published reports of the

---

[8] Whether Theocritus or a later editor called the poems idylls is unclear, as is the meaning of the term: suggestions include "little poems," "little types," and "vignettes."

papyri. In choice of readings, Gow's text is the more judicious. For the *Europa* and for Bion, the editions of Bühler and Reed have been consulted. In the brief apparatus criticus on each page of Greek text, the following abbreviations are used:

M   reading of all medieval manuscripts
m   reading of some of the medieval manuscripts
pap.   reading given by a papyrus
schol. reading recorded in the scholia
v.l.   variant reading (*varia lectio*) recorded in the
        scholia

Of conjectures made by scholars since the Renaissance, only those adopted into the text are mentioned in the apparatus; a few more are discussed in the notes. There has not been space to record dialectal conjectures and corrections, especially in the Aeolic poems.

For Theocritus' poems, a variety of titles appear in the manuscripts and in citations. Which, if any, of these were supplied by Theocritus himself is not known:

> *Idyll* 1, Θύρσις (ἢ) ᾠδή, "Thyrsis" or "Song"
> *Idyll* 2, Φαρμακεύτρια (-ιαι), "The Sorceress/The Sorceresses"
> *Idyll* 3, Κῶμος, "The Serenade"; Ἀμαρυλλίς, "Amaryllis"; Αἰπόλος, "The Goatherd"; Κωμαστής, "The Serenader"; Αἰπολικόν, "The Goatherd's Performance"
> *Idyll* 4, Νομεῖς, "Herdsmen"; Βουκολιασταί, "The Bucolic Singers"; Εἰς Κορύδωνα, "To Corydon"; Φιλαλήθης, "The Lover of Truth"; Βάττος, "Battus"; Αἴγων, "Aegon"

Idyll 5, Αἰπολικὸν (καὶ) ποιμενικόν, "Goatherd's Performance (and) Shepherd's Performance"

Idyll 6, Βουκολιασταί, "The Bucolic Singers"; Δαμοίτας καὶ Δάφνις, "Damoetas and Daphnis"

Idyll 7, Θαλύσια, "The Harvest Festival"; Τὰ εἰς Κομάταν Θαλύσια, "The Harvest Festival, Addressed to Comatas"; Λυκίδας, "Lycidas"; Ἐαρινοὶ ὁδοιπόροι, "A Springtime Saunter"

Idyll 8, Βουκολιασταί, "The Bucolic Singers"; Δάφνις καὶ Μενάλκας, "Daphnis and Menalcas"

Idyll 10, Ἐργατίναι ἢ Θερισταί, "The Laborers" or "The Reapers"

Idyll 11, Κύκλωψ καὶ (ἡ) Γαλάτεια, "The Cyclops and Galatea"/"The Cyclops" or "Galatea"

Idyll 12, Ἀίτης, "The Beloved Boy"

Idyll 13, Ὕλας, "Hylas"

Idyll 14, Αἰσχίνας καὶ Θυώνιχος, "Aeschinas and Thyonichus"

Idyll 15, Συρακόσιαι ἢ Ἀδωνιάζουσαι, "The Women from Syracuse" or "The Women at the Festival of Adonis"; Γοργὼ καὶ Πραξινόα, "Gorgo and Praxinoa"

Idyll 16, Χάριτες ἢ Ἱέρων, "The Graces" or "Hiero"

Idyll 17, Ἐγκώμιον εἰς Πτολεμαῖον, "Encomium of Ptolemy"; Ἔπαινος Πτολεμαίου, "Praise of Ptolemy"

Idyll 18, Ἑλένης ἐπιθαλάμιος, "Wedding Song for Helen"; Ἐπιθαλάμιος Ἑλένης καὶ Μενελάου, "Wedding Song for Helen and Menelaus"; Ἐγκώμιον Ἑλένης, "Encomium of Helen"

Idyll 19, Κηριοκλέπτης, "The Honey Thief"

Idyll 20, Βουκολίσκος, "The Naïve Cowherd"

THE TRANSLATION

J. M. Edmonds' Loeb translation was published in 1912. Edmonds, by his own admission a member of the "fain/twain school," was taken to task by reviewers for using archaic and dialectal words such as "skilly," "knaggy," "lith," and "transmewed." He rendered the shepherds' songs into a sort of ballad meter and *Idyll* 15 into "colloquial suburban" because "the chief characters so closely resemble the average educated Englishwoman" (p. xxvi). In this way he

---

[9] Obscure; presumably related to the Lenaea, a Bacchic festival.

tried to reproduce the protean combinations of stately epic meter, Doric dialect, lowly subject matter, and recherché vocabulary characteristic of Theocritus in particular.

The present translation is less ambitious. It aims to be literal enough to help those with some Greek to construe and understand the original, and also to provide a modestly idiomatic version for the Greekless.

ABBREVIATIONS

A&A	*Antike und Abendland*
AJPh	*American Journal of Philology*
BCH	*Bulletin de correspondance hellénique*
CA	*Collectanea Alexandrina,* ed. J. U. Powell (Oxford, 1925)
ClAnt	*Classical Antiquity*
CQ	*Classical Quarterly*
CR	*Classical Review*
CSCA	*California Studies in Classical Antiquity*
EGM	*Early Greek Mythography,* ed. R. L. Fowler (Oxford, 2000–2013)
FGH	*Die Fragmente der griechischen Historiker* (Leipzig, 1923–)
GIF	*Giornale italiano di filologia*
GLP	*Select papyri III: Literary Papyri: Poetry,* ed. D. L. Page (LCL 360, Cambridge, MA, 1941)
GRBS	*Greek, Roman and Byzantine Studies*
HE	*The Greek Anthology: Hellenistic Epigrams,* eds. A. S. F. Gow and D. L. Page (Cambridge, 1965)
IG	*Inscriptiones Graecae,* ed. A. Kirchoff et al. (Berlin, 1873–)
IGUR	*Inscriptiones Graecae urbis Romae,* ed. L. Moretti (Rome, 1968–1979).

ABBREVIATIONS

JHS	*Journal of Hellenic Studies*
K	*Flavii Philostrati quae supersunt*, ed. C. L. Kayser (Zurich, 1844)
K-A	*Poetae comici Graeci*, eds. R. Kassel and C. Austin (Berlin, 1983–2001)
LIMC	*Lexicon iconographicum mythologiae classicae* (Zurich, 1981–1997)
MD	*Materiali e discussioni per l'analisi dei testi classici*
MH	*Museum Helveticum*
M-W	*Fragmenta Hesiodea*, eds. R. Merkelbach and M. L. West (Oxford, 1967)
PCPhS	*Proceedings of the Cambridge Philological Society*
PMG	*Poetae melici Graeci*, ed. D. L. Page (Oxford, 1962)
QUCC	*Quaderni urbinati di cultura classica*
RBPh	*Revue belge de philologie et d'histoire*
RCCM	*Rivista di cultura classica e medioevale*
RFIC	*Rivista di filologia e di istruzione classica*
RhM	*Rheinisches Museum*
SEG	*Supplementum epigraphicum Graecum* (Leiden, 1923–)
SH	*Supplementum Hellenisticum*, eds. H. Lloyd-Jones and P. Parsons (Oxford, 1982)
TAPhA	*Transactions of the American Philological Association*

GENERAL BIBLIOGRAPHY

HISTORICAL BACKGROUND

Bugh, G. R., ed. *The Cambridge Companion to the Hellenistic World.* Cambridge, 2006.

Erskine, A., ed. *A Companion to the Hellenistic World.* Oxford, 2003.

Fraser, P. M. *Ptolemaic Alexandria.* Oxford, 1972.

Hazzard, R. A. *Imagination of a Monarchy: Studies in Ptolemaic Propaganda.* Toronto, 2000.

Shipley, G. *The Greek World after Alexander, 323–30 BC.* London, 2000.

Walbank, F. W., A. E. Astin, M. W. Frederikson, and R. M. Ogilvie, eds. *The Cambridge Ancient History² VII 1: The Hellenistic World.* Cambridge, 1984.

HELLENISTIC POETRY

Baumbach, M., and S. Bär. *Brill's Companion to Greek and Latin Epyllion and Its Reception.* Leiden, 2012.

Bing, P. *The Well-read Muse: Present and Past in Callimachus and the Hellenistic Poets.* Göttingen, 1988.

Burton, J. B. *Theocritus's Urban Mimes. Mobility, Gender, and Patronage.* Berkeley, 1995.

Clauss, J. J., and M. Cuypers, eds. *A Companion to Hellenistic Literature.* Oxford, 2010.

Effe, B. *Theokrit und die griechische Bukolik*. Darmstadt, 1986.

Fantuzzi, M., and R. Hunter. *Tradition and Innovation in Hellenistic Poetry*. Cambridge, 2004.

Goldhill, S. *The Poet's Voice*. Cambridge, 1991.

Griffiths, F. T. *Theocritus at Court*. Leiden, 1979.

Gutzwiller, K. *Studies in the Hellenistic Epyllion*. Königstein, 1981.

Harder, M. A., R. F. Regtuit, and G. C. Wakker, eds. *Theocritus*. Groningen, 1996.

———. *Genre in Hellenistic Poetry*. Groningen, 1998.

Hopkinson, N. *A Hellenistic Anthology*. Cambridge, 1988.

Hunter, R. *Theocritus and the Archaeology of Greek Poetry*. Cambridge, 1996.

———. *Theocritus: A Selection*. Cambridge, 1999.

Hutchinson, G. O. *Hellenistic Poetry*. Oxford, 1988.

Meincke, W. *Untersuchungen zu den enkomiastischen Gedichten Theokrits*. PhD diss., Kiel, 1965.

Morrison, A. D. *The Narrator in Archaic Greek and Hellenistic Poetry*. Cambridge, 2007.

Payne, M. E. *Theocritus and the Invention of Fiction*. Cambridge, 2007.

Segal, C. *Poetry and Myth in Ancient Pastoral*. Princeton, 1981.

Zanker, G. *Realism in Alexandrian Poetry: A Literature and Its Audience*. London, 1987.

SOME EDITIONS AND COMMENTARIES

Ahrens, H. L. 2 vols. Leipzig, 1855–1859. Text of Th., B., M.

Cholmeley, R. J. 2nd ed. London, 1919. Text and comm. on Th. and *Megara*.

Dover, K. J. London, 1971. Text and comm. on Th. *Idd.* 1–7, 10, 11, 13–16, 18, 22, 24, 26, 28, Epigrr. 4, 17–19, 21–22.

Fritzsche, A. T. H. 2nd ed. Leipzig, 1870. Text of Th.

Gallavotti, C. 3rd ed. Rome, 1993. Text of Th., B., M., etc.

Gow, A. S. F. 2 vols. 2nd ed. Cambridge, 1952. Text, trans., and comm. on Th.

————. OCT, Oxford, 1952. Text of Th., B. M., etc.

Hopkinson, N. (above). Text and comm. on *Idd.* 2, 10, 11, 28, M. *Europa*, B. *Epit. Ad.*, Fr. 13.

Hunter. R. *Selection.* Text and comm. on *Idd.* 1, 3, 4, 6, 7, 10, 11, 13.

Kirsten, R. *Junge Hirten und alte Fischer: die Gedichte 27, 20 und 21 des Corpus Theocriteum.* Berlin, 2007.

Latte, K. Iserlohn, 1948. Text of Th. *Idd.* 1–18, 22, 24, 26, 28–31, Epigr., Fr.

Legrand, Ph. E. 2 vols. Budé, Paris, 1925–1927. Text, French trans., and notes on Th., B., M., etc.

Meineke, A. 3rd ed., Berlin, 1856. Text and comm. on Th., B., M.

Monteil, P. Paris, 1968. Text and comm. on Th. *Idd.* 2, 5, 7, 11, 15.

von Wilamowitz-Moellendorf, U. OCT, Oxford, 1905. Text of Th., B., M., etc.

————. *Die Textgeschichte der griechischen Bukoliker.* Berlin, 1906. On the manuscript tradition.

Vox, O. UTET, Turin, 1997. Text, trans., and notes on Th.

THE SCHOLIA

Dickey, E. *Ancient Greek Scholarship.* Oxford, 2007, 63–65.

Gow, A. S. F. *Comm.,* 1.lxxx–lxxxiv.

Wendel, C. *Scholia in Theocritum vetera.* Leipzig, 1914.

————. *Überlieferung und Entstehung der Theokrit-Scholien*. Berlin, 1920.

DIALECT

Abbenes, J. G. J. "The Doric of Theocritus." In *Theocritus*, Harder-Regtuit-Wakker, 1–17.

Arena, R. "Studi sulla lingua di Teocrito." *Bolletino del centro di studi filologici e linguistici siciliani* 4 (1956): 5–27; 6 (1957): 42–86.

Darms, G. "Die Ionismen des papyrus Antinoe in der Pharmakeutria des Theokrit." *Glotta* 59 (1981): 165–208.

Dover, K. J. *Comm.*, xxvii–xlv.

Gow, A. S. F. *Comm.*, 1.lxxii–lxxx.

Hunter, R. *Selection*, 22–26.

Monteil, P. *Comm.*, 23–48.

Ruijgh, C. J. "La Dorien de Théocrite: dialecte cyrénien d' Alexandrie et d'Égypte." *Mnemosyne* ser. 4, 37 (1984): 56–88.

Stanford, W. B. "On the Zeta/Sigma-Delta Variation in the Dialect of Theocritus: A Literary Approach." *Proceedings of the Irish Academy* 67 (1968): 1–8.

Turrioni, A. "Osservazioni sul lessico degli Idilli dorici di Teocrito." *ASNP* ser. 2.32 (1963): 212–24.

METER

Dover, K. J. *Comm.*, xxii–xxvii.

Fantuzzi, M. "Variazioni sull'esametro in Teocrito." In *Struttura e storia dell' esametro Greco*, edited by M.

Fantuzzi and R. Pretagostini, 1.220–64. Rome, 1995–1996.

Hunter, R. *Archaeology,* 29–31.

West, M. L. *Greek Metre.* Oxford, 1982, 150–59.

PASTORAL

Alpers, P. *What Is Pastoral?* Chicago, 1996.

Empson, W. *Some Versions of Pastoral.* London, 1935.

Ettin, A. V. *Literature and the Pastoral.* New Haven, 1994.

Fantuzzi, M., and Th. Papanghelis. *Brill's Companion to Greek and Latin Pastoral.* Leiden, 2006.

Gutzwiller, K. *Theocritus' Pastoral Analogies: The Formation of a Genre.* Madison, WI, 1991.

Haber, J. *Pastoral and the Poetics of Self-contradiction.* Cambridge, 1994.

Halperin, D. M. *Before Pastoral: Theocritus and the Ancient Tradition of Bucolic Poetry.* Yale, 1983.

Hunter, R. *A Study of Daphnis & Chloe.* Cambridge, 1983.

Kegel-Brinkgreve, E. *The Echoing Woods: Bucolic and Pastoral from Theocritus to Wordsworth.* Amsterdam, 1990.

Paschalis, M., ed. *Pastoral Palimpsests: Essays in the Reception of Theocritus and Virgil.* Rethymnon, 2007.

Patterson, A. M. *Pastoral and Ideology: Virgil to Valéry.* Oxford, 1988.

Rosenmeyer, T. G. *The Green Cabinet: Theocritus and the European Pastoral Lyric.* Berkeley, 1969.

Skoie, M., and S. Bjornstad-Velasquez, eds. *Pastoral and the Humanities: Arcadia Re-inscribed.* Exeter, 2006.

Stanzel, K.-H. *Liebende Hirten: Theokrits Bukolik und die alexandrinische Poesie.* Stuttgart, 1995.

Williams, R. *The Country and the City.* London, 1973.

THEOCRITUS

TESTIMONIA

1 *Suda* s.v. Θεόκριτος, θ 166

Θεόκριτος, Χῖος, ῥήτωρ, μαθητὴς Μητροδώρου τοῦ Ἰσοκρατικοῦ. ἔγραψε Χρείας· ἀντεπολιτεύσατο δὲ Θεοπόμπῳ τῷ ἱστορικῷ. φέρεται αὐτοῦ ἱστορία Λιβύης καὶ ἐπιστολαὶ θαυμάσιαι. ἔστι καὶ ἕτερος Θεόκριτος, Πραξαγόρου καὶ Φιλίννης, οἱ δὲ Σιμίχου· Συρακούσιος, οἱ δέ φασι Κῷον· μετῴκησε δὲ ἐν Συρακούσαις. οὗτος ἔγραψε τὰ καλούμενα Βουκολικὰ ἔπη Δωρίδι διαλέκτῳ. τινὲς δὲ ἀναφέρουσιν εἰς αὐτὸν καὶ ταῦτα· Προιτίδας, Ἐλπίδας, Ὕμνους, Ἡρωΐνας, Ἐπικήδεια μέλη, ἐλεγείας καὶ ἰάμβους, ἐπιγράμματα. ἰστέον δὲ ὅτι τρεῖς γεγόνασι Βουκολικῶν ἐπῶν ποιηταί, Θεόκριτος οὑτοσί, Μόσχος Σικελιώτης καὶ Βίων ὁ Σμυρναῖος, ἔκ τινος χωριδίου καλουμένου Φλώσσης.

2 Vit. Theoc., pp. 1.4–2.3 Wendel

a Θεόκριτος ὁ τῶν βουκολικῶν ποιητὴς Συρακούσιος ἦν τὸ γένος, ὡς αὐτός φησι "Σιμιχίδα, πᾷ δὴ τὸ μεσαμέριον πόδας ἕλκεις"; ἔνιοι δὲ τὸ "Σιμιχίδα" ἐπώνυ-

TESTIMONIA

1 *Suda* s.v. Theocritus

Theocritus of Chios, orator, pupil of Metrodorus the Isocratean. He composed *Anecdotes* and was a political opponent of the historian Theopompus. There exists a history of Africa by him, and *Extraordinary Letters*.

There is another Theocritus, son of Praxagoras and Philinna (or of Simichus, according to some), a Syracusan (or a Coan who moved to Syracuse). He composed the so-called *Bucolics* in Doric dialect. Some credit him with *The Daughters of Proetus*, *Hopes*, hymns, *Heroines*, laments, lyric poems,[1] elegies, iambics, and epigrams.

Note that there are three bucolic poets: Theocritus, Moschus of Sicily, and Bion of Smyrna, from a place called Phlossa.

[1] Or, perhaps, "laments in lyric meter."

2 *Life of Theocritus*

a Theocritus the bucolic poet was a Syracusan by birth, as he himself says: "Simichidas, where are you going on foot in the middle of the day?"[1] Some say that Simichidas

[1] *Id.* 7.21.

μον εἶναι λέγουσι—δοκεῖ γὰρ σιμὸς εἶναι τὴν πρόσ-
οψιν—πατέρα δ᾽ ἐσχηκέναι Πραξαγόραν καὶ μητέρα
Φιλίναν. ἀκουστὴς δὲ γέγονε Φιλητᾶ καὶ Ἀσκληπιά-
δου, ὧν μνημονεύει. ἤκμασε δὲ κατὰ Πτολεμαῖον τὸν
ἐπικληθέντα ⟨Φιλάδελφον τὸν Πτολεμαίου τοῦ ἐπι-
κληθέντος⟩ Λάγου. περὶ δὲ τὴν τῶν βουκολικῶν ποί-
ησιν εὐφυὴς γενόμενος πολλῆς δόξης ἐπέτυχε. κατὰ
γοῦν τινας Μόσχος καλούμενος Θεόκριτος ὠνομά-
σθη.

b ἰστέον, ὅτι ὁ Θεόκριτος ἐγένετο ἰσόχρονος τοῦ τε
Ἀράτου καὶ τοῦ Καλλιμάχου καὶ τοῦ Νικάνδρου· ἐγέ-
νετο δὲ ἐπὶ τῶν χρόνων Πτολεμαίου τοῦ Φιλαδέλφου.

Σιμίχου Ahrens: -ίδου vel -ίδα M   Φιλάδελφον—ἐπι-
κληθέντος suppl. Wendel post Ahrens: κατὰ τὸν Πτ. τὸν (ἐπι)
κλ. Λαγωόν (Λάγων) M (Λάγου postulaverat G. Dindorf)

3 Choerob. in Theodos. Can., GG IV.1, p. 333.10–11
Hilgard

Φιλητᾶς ὁ διδάσκαλος Θεοκρίτου

Φιλητᾶς Bernhardy: Φιλίππας, Φιλητὸς codd.

4 Σ Id. 4 Arg. (p. 135.4–5 Wendel)

Θεόκριτος δέ . . . κατὰ τὴν ρκδ′ Ὀλυμπιάδα ἤκμαζεν.

4

was a given name—he seems to have been snub-nosed (*simos*)—and that his father was Praxagoras, his mother Philina. He was a pupil of Philetas and Asclepiades, of whom he makes mention.[2] He flourished in the reign of Ptolemy Philadelphus,[3] son of Ptolemy the son of Lagus. He had a genius for bucolic poetry and gained great fame. According to some, he was called Moschus and given the name Theocritus.[4]

b Note that Theocritus was a contemporary of Aratus, Callimachus and Nicander.[5] He lived in the reign of Ptolemy Philadelphus.

[2] See on *Id.* 7.40.

[3] 282–246 BC.

[4] Perhaps because of his fame; Theocritus means "chosen of god."

[5] Aratus (ca. 315–ca. 245 BC) wrote the *Phaenomena*, a didactic poem on astronomy. Callimachus was a contemporary, but the didactic poet Nicander is now thought to have lived a century or more later.

3 Choeroboscus, scholia on Theodosius' *Canones*

Philitas, teacher of Theocritus.

4 Scholiast on *Idyll* 4

Theocritus flourished in the 124th Olympiad.[1]

[1] 284–281 BC.

5 Σ *Syrinx* Arg. (ibid., p. 336.13–14)

ὁ γοῦν Θεόκριτος τὸ γένος Συρηκόσιος ἤκμασεν ἐπὶ Πτολεμαίου τοῦ Φιλαδέλφου.

6 Σ *Id.* 7 Arg. (ibid., p. 76.15–18)

τὰ δὲ πράγματα διάκεινται ἐν Κῷ. ἐπιδημήσας γὰρ ὁ Θεόκριτος τῇ νήσῳ καθ᾽ ὃν χρόνον εἰς Ἀλεξάνδρειαν πρὸς Πτολεμαῖον ἐπορεύετο, φίλος κατέστη Φρασιδάμῳ καὶ Ἀντιγένει Λυκωπέως υἱοῖς.

7 Σ *Id.* 15 Arg. (ibid., p. 305.14–15)

διαγράφει δὲ ὁ Θεόκριτος ἐπιδημήσας ἐν Ἀλεξανδρείᾳ χαριζόμενος τῇ βασιλίδι.

8 *Anth. Pal.* 9.434

   Ἄλλος ὁ Χῖος, ἐγὼ δὲ Θεόκριτος ὃς τάδ᾽ ἔγραψα
     εἷς ἀπὸ τῶν πολλῶν εἰμὶ Συρακοσίων,
   υἱὸς Πραξαγόραο περικλειτᾶς τε Φιλίννας·
     Μοῦσαν δ᾽ ὀθνείαν οὔτιν᾽ ἐφελκυσάμαν.

5 Scholiast on *The Panpipe*

Theocritus, a Syracusan by birth, flourished in the reign of Ptolemy Philadelphus.

6 Scholiast on *Idyll* 7

The setting is Cos. Living on the island at the time when he used to go to visit Ptolemy, Theocritus became friendly with Lycopeus' sons Philodamus and Antigenes.[1]

  [1] See *Id.* 7.3–4.

7 Scholiast on *Idyll* 15

Theocritus describes the scene as an inhabitant of Alexandria and in such a way as to please the queen.[1]

  [1] Arsinoe: cf. *Id.* 15.22–24, 109–11.

8 *Anth. Pal.* 9.434[1]

The Chian is another man,[2] but I, Theocritus, who wrote these poems, am one of the great populace of Syracuse,[3] the son of Praxagoras and renowned Philinna; and the Muse I have adopted is no alien.[4]

  [1] This poem is attributed to Theocritus in the manuscript, but it is much more likely to be by an editor of his poems.
  [2] Probably Theocritus the Chian, a famous sophist (cf. T 1), but possibly Homer, who is called "the Chian" at *Id.* 7.47.
  [3] The tone is probably one of pride; but εἷς ἀπὸ τῶν πολλῶν, "one of many," may be self-disparaging.
  [4] I.e., "my poetry is as Sicilian as I am," or, perhaps, "I have not imitated another poet" (Homer, if he is "the Chian").

9 *Anth. Pal.* 7.262

> βουκολικαὶ Μοῖσαι σποράδες ποκά, νῦν δ᾽ ἅμα πᾶσαι
> ἐντὶ μιᾶς μάνδρας, ἐντὶ μιᾶς ἀγέλας.

10 Quint. 10.1.55

admirabilis in suo genere Theocritus, sed musa illa rustica et pastoralis non forum modo verum ipsam etiam urbem reformidat.

11 Man. 2.39–42

> quin etiam ritus pastorum et Pana sonantem
> in calamos Sicula memorat tellure creatus,
> nec silvis silvestre canit perque horrida motus
> rura serit dulces Musamque inducit in aulas.

12 Gell. *NA* 9.9.4–11

sicuti nuperrime aput mensam cum legerentur utraque simul *Bucolica* Theocriti et Vergilii, animadvertimus reliquisse Vergilium, quod Graecum quidem mire quam suave est, verti autem neque debuit neque potuit. sed enim, quod substituit pro eo, quod omiserat, non abest, quin iucundius lepidiusque sit:

9 Artemidorus the scholar, *Anth. Pal.* 7.262 = *Epigr.* 26

The Muses of country song were once scattered, but now they are all together in one pen, in one flock.[1]

---

[1] By Artemidorus of Tarsus, an Alexandrian scholar of the first century BC, who it seems made a collection of bucolic poetry. His son Theon wrote a commentary on Theocritus (*Etym. Magn.* 144.55). See p. xiii.

10 Quintilian, *The Orator's Education*

Theocritus is admirable in his own kind, but this rural, pastoral Muse shuns not only the forum but the city itself.[1]

---

[1] Quintilian is thinking only of Theocritus' pastoral poetry.

11 Manilius, *Astronomica*

Then the ways of shepherds and Pan piping upon his reeds are told by a son of Sicily's isle: to the woods he sings a more than woodland strain, sows tender emotions over the rugged countryside, and brings the Muse to the farmstead.

12 Gellius, *Attic Nights*

For example, when very recently the *Bucolics* of Theocritus and Virgil were being read together at table, we perceived that Virgil had omitted something that in the Greek is, to be sure, wonderfully pleasing, but neither could nor ought to have been translated. But what he has substituted for that omission is almost more charming and graceful. Theocritus writes:

βάλλει καὶ μάλοισι τὸν αἰπόλον ἁ Κλεαρίστα
τὰς αἶγας παρελᾶντα καὶ ἁδύ τι ποππυλιάζει,—
malo me Galatea petit, lasciva puella,
et fugit ad salices et se cupit ante videri.

illud quoque alio in loco animadvertimus caute omissum,
quod est in Graeco versu dulcissimum:

Τίτυρ᾽ ἐμὶν τὸ καλὸν πεφιλημένε, βόσκε τὰς
αἶγας
καὶ ποτὶ τὰν κράναν ἄγε, Τίτυρε· καὶ τὸν
ἐνόρχαν,
τὸν Λιβυκὸν κνάκωνα, φυλάσσεο μή τυ κορύψῃ.

quo enim pacto diceret: τὸ καλὸν πεφιλημένε, verba
hercle non translaticia, sed cuiusdam nativae dulcedinis?
hos igitur reliquit et cetera vertit non infestiviter, nisi quod
"caprum" dixit, quem Theocritus ἐνόρχαν appellavit—
auctore enim M. Varrone is demum Latine "caper" dicitur,
qui excastratus est—:

Tityre, dum redeo, brevis est via, pasce capellas
et potum pastas age, Tityre, et inter agendum
occursare capro, cornu ferit ille, caveto.

And Clearista pelts the goatherd with apples as he drives his flock by her, and she whistles to him sweetly.[1]

Virgil has:

Galatea, cheeky girl, pelts me with apples, runs in among the willow trees, and hopes I see her first.

Also in another place I notice that what was very sweet in the Greek was prudently omitted. Theocritus writes:

Tityrus, my dear friend, feed my goats and take them to the spring, Tityrus; and watch out for the billy goat, the tawny Libyan one, in case he butts you.[2]

But how could Virgil reproduce τὸ καλὸν πεφιλημένε (my dear friend), words that, by heaven, defy translation, but have a certain native charm? He therefore omitted that expression and translated the rest very cleverly, except in using *caper* for Theocritus' ἐνόρχας; for, according to Marcus Varro, a goat is called *caper* in Latin only after he has been castrated. Virgil's version is:

Tityrus, until I return—I'll not be long—feed my goats, and once they are fed, Tityrus, take them for a drink. But as you go take care not to go near the billy goat—he butts!

[1] *Id.* 5.88–89.
[2] *Id.* 3.3–5.

13 Plin. *HN* 28.19

hinc Theocriti apud Graecos, Catulli apud nos proximeque Vergili incantamentorum amatoria imitatio.

14 Serv. *Comm. in Verg. Buc. praef.*

ille enim ubique simplex est, hic necessitate compulsus aliquibus locis miscet figuras, quas perite plerumque etiam ex Theocriti versibus facit, quos ab illo dictos constat esse simpliciter.

15 Serv. ibid.

adhibetur autem ad carmen bucolicum, quod debet quarto pede terminare partem orationis. qui pes si sit dactylus, meliorem efficit versum ut "vos patriae finis et dulcia." primus etiam pes secundum Donatum et dactylus esse debet et terminare partem orationis ut "Tityre." quam legem Theocritus vehementer observat, Vergilius non adeo; ille enim in paucis versibus ab ista ratione deviavit, hic eam in paucis secutus est.

13 Pliny, *Natural History*

And so Theocritus among the Greeks, Catullus and quite recently Virgil among ourselves, have represented love charms in their poems.[1]

[1] The reference is to *Idyll* 2 and Virg. *Ecl.* 8. There are no similar passages in Catullus; either Pliny has misremembered or the name should be changed (*Calvi* Unger).

14 Servius, *Commentary on Virgil's* Eclogues

Theocritus is everywhere straightforward, whereas in places Virgil is obliged to combine figures of speech. This he does skillfully for the most part, using as source material lines of Theocritus that are unarguably straightforward in diction.

15 Servius, ibid.

A further point concerning bucolic poetry is that there should be a sense break after the fourth foot. If that foot is a dactyl, the effect is better (e.g., *nos patriae finis et dulcia*).[1] According to Donatus the first foot, too, should be a dactyl and should be followed by a break in the sense (e.g., *Tityre*). Theocritus observes this rule strictly, but Virgil does not;[2] Theocritus deviates from it only occasionally, while Virgil observes it rarely.

[1] Virg. *Ecl.* 1.3, "I ‹am leaving› my native land and my dear ‹fields›." This example does not in fact include a sense break after the fourth foot. On the so-called bucolic diaeresis, see p. ix n. 3.

[2] Referring to the bucolic diaeresis, not to Donatus' rule.

IDYLL 1

Thyrsis and an unnamed goatherd elaborately compliment each other's musical ability. The goatherd promises an ivy-wood cup, which he describes at length, if Thyrsis will perform his famous song about the death of Daphnis. Thyrsis does so and receives his reward.

Although there is no evidence that Theocritus designed this poem to begin a collection (see p. xiii), its concern with the origins and nature of bucolic poetry is evident. The opening courtesies (ll. 1–11), full of alliteration, assonance, and parallel expressions, suggest that bucolic emerges from and complements the sounds of nature; at the close, reference to the rutting billy goat evokes earthier concerns after the mythical narrative of Daphnis. The cup of ivy wood (27–56) is a bucolic equivalent of the Iliadic Shield of Achilles (18.478–608), on which were depicted the whole cosmos and diverse aspects of human life. The third scene on the cup, a young boy plaiting a cage for tuneful crickets, represents a metaphor for poetic composition. Whereas in several of the bucolic poems two songs are set out for evaluation, here the song of Thyrsis is formally equated with a product in a different medium; the cup, song, and idyll, it is implied, share the same aesthetic. Pan and Priapus, gods absent from the Homeric poems, preside over a world in which love, song, and art combine in a novel way. Moreover, Thyrsis has been promised not only the ivy-wood cup but also an opportunity to milk the best nanny goat. The equivalence of song, cup, and milk is typical of the limited, faux-naïf aesthetic of bucolic verse. Theocritus is probably alluding, too, to the well-known etymologizing of the word "tragedy" from tragos *(billy goat) and* ôdê *(song): he presents a new sort of "goat song" that treats song, art, desire, and myth in a country setting.*

Thyrsis' masterpiece, which is punctuated by a refrain evocative of folk song, tells of the love and the death of Daphnis. The sixth-century Sicilian poet Stesichorus is said by one source to have sung about Daphnis, and another connects Daphnis' death with the origins of bucolic song (Diod. Sic. 4.84, Ael. VH 10.18). Theocritus' account is mysteriously allusive—perhaps deliberately so, but more likely because we do not know the version of the myth that he is following. His other reference to the story appears to have Daphnis dying of unrequited love for a certain Xenea (Id. 7.72–77), but here the words of Priapus suggest that "the girl" is not reluctant (81–94). It seems that here at any rate Daphnis has taken a vow of chastity; that would account for Aphrodite's anger (96) and for Daphnis' defiance (100–103). His death, too, is mysterious: he "went to the stream," and the "eddying water" is said to have "washed over" or "engulfed" him (140–41). "Going to the stream" is not elsewhere a euphemism for death, and rivers in the underworld are not elsewhere said to engulf the dead; rather, they have to be crossed. It seems likely, therefore, that the allusion is to suicide in a pool, perhaps a pool belonging to a Naiad whom Daphnis loves but has forsworn. (Most other known versions of the story have him blinded as punishment for infidelity: Diod. Sic.

and Aelian locc. citt.; Parth. Amat. narr. 29; schol. Theoc. 8.93; Serv. on Virg. Ecl. 5.20).

The lamenting of the natural world in sympathy with Daphnis' death (the so-called pathetic fallacy) is a thematic link with the world of bucolic poetry evoked by the opening dialogue. His death, however, is not typical of the power of Eros in the bucolic poems. It contrasts pointedly with the earthy remonstrances of Priapus, and with the goats' imminent mating with which the idyll closes. But it is out of that death that bucolic poetry seems to arise when Daphnis passes his pipes to Pan.

Criticism

Cairns, F. "Theocritus' First Idyll: The Literary Programme." *WS* 97 (1984): 89–113.

Halperin, *Before Pastoral,* 161–89.

Hunter, *Selection,* 60–107.

Ogilvie, R. M. "The Song of Thyrsis." *JHS* 82 (1962): 106–10.

Segal, C. "Death by Water: A Narrative Pattern in Theocritus." *Hermes* 102 (1974): 20–38 = *Poetry and Myth,* 47–65.

———. "'Since Daphnis Dies': The Meaning of Theocritus' First Idyll." *MH* 31 (1974): 1–22 = *Poetry and Myth,* 25–46.

Williams, F. J. "Theocritus, *Idyll* i 81–91." *JHS* 89 (1969): 121–23.

Zuntz, G. "Theocritus 1.95f." *CR* 10 (1960): 37–40.

1

Ἁδύ τι τὸ ψιθύρισμα καὶ ἁ πίτυς, αἰπόλε, τήνα,
ἁ ποτὶ ταῖς παγαῖσι, μελίσδεται, ἁδὺ δὲ καὶ τύ
συρίσδες· μετὰ Πᾶνα τὸ δεύτερον ἆθλον ἀποισῇ.
αἴ κα τῆνος ἕλῃ κεραὸν τράγον, αἶγα τὺ λαψῇ·
5 αἴ κα δ' αἶγα λάβῃ τῆνος γέρας, ἐς τὲ καταρρεῖ
ἁ χίμαρος· χιμάρῳ δὲ καλὸν κρέας, ἔστε κ' ἀμέλ-
ξῃς.

ΑΙΠΟΛΟΣ

ἅδιον, ὦ ποιμήν, τὸ τεὸν μέλος ἢ τὸ καταχές
τῆν' ἀπὸ τᾶς πέτρας καταλείβεται ὑψόθεν ὕδωρ.
αἴ κα ταὶ Μοῖσαι τὰν οἶδα δῶρον ἄγωνται,
10 ἄρνα τὺ σακίταν λαψῇ γέρας· αἰ δέ κ' ἀρέσκῃ
τήναις ἄρνα λαβεῖν, τὺ δὲ τὰν ὄιν ὕστερον ἀξῇ.

ΘΥΡΣΙΣ

λῇς ποτὶ τᾶν Νυμφᾶν, λῇς, αἰπόλε, τεῖδε καθίξας,
ὡς τὸ κάταντες τοῦτο γεώλοφον αἵ τε μυρῖκαι,
συρίσδεν; τὰς δ' αἶγας ἐγὼν ἐν τῷδε νομευσῶ.

13 αἵ τε Heinsius: ᾇτε M

IDYLL 1

THYRSIS

A sweet thing is the whispered music of that pine by the springs, goatherd, and sweet is your piping, too; after Pan you will take the second prize. If he should choose the horned goat, you will have the she-goat, and if he has the she-goat as his prize, the kid falls to you.[1] The flesh of a kid is good before you milk her.[2]

GOATHERD

Sweeter is the outpouring of your song, shepherd, than that cascade teeming down from the rock up above. If the Muses should take the sheep as their gift, you will have a stall-fed lamb, and if they would like to have a lamb, you will be next and take away the sheep.

THYRSIS

Are you willing, by the Nymphs, are you willing to sit down here, goatherd, where this mound slopes down and the tamarisks are growing, to play your pipe? I will look after your goats meanwhile.

[1] Lit., "flows to you"; *chimaros* (young female goat) may pun on *cheimarrhos* (mountain torrent).
[2] If eaten before she is old enough to have given birth.

ΑΙΠΟΛΟΣ

15 οὐ θέμις, ὦ ποιμήν, τὸ μεσαμβρινὸν οὐ θέμις ἄμμιν
   συρίσδεν. τὸν Πᾶνα δεδοίκαμες· ἦ γὰρ ἀπ' ἄγρας
   τανίκα κεκμακὼς ἀμπαύεται· ἔστι δὲ πικρός,
   καί οἱ ἀεὶ δριμεῖα χολὰ ποτὶ ῥινὶ κάθηται.
   ἀλλὰ τὺ γὰρ δή, Θύρσι, τὰ Δάφνιδος ἄλγε' ἀείδες
20 καὶ τᾶς βουκολικᾶς ἐπὶ τὸ πλέον ἵκεο μοίσας,
   δεῦρ' ὑπὸ τὰν πτελέαν ἐσδώμεθα τῶ τε Πριήπω
   καὶ τᾶν κρανίδων κατεναντίον, ᾇπερ ὁ θῶκος
   τῆνος ὁ ποιμενικὸς καὶ ταὶ δρύες. αἰ δέ κ' ἀείσῃς
   ὡς ὅκα τὸν Λιβύαθε ποτὶ Χρόμιν ᾇσας ἐρίσδων,
25 αἶγά τέ τοι δωσῶ διδυματόκον ἐς τρὶς ἀμέλξαι,
   ἃ δύ' ἔχοισ' ἐρίφως ποταμέλγεται ἐς δύο πέλλας,
   καὶ βαθὺ κισσύβιον κεκλυσμένον ἁδέι κηρῷ,
   ἀμφῶες, νεοτευχές, ἔτι γλυφάνοιο ποτόσδον.
   τῶ ποτὶ μὲν χείλη μαρύεται ὑψόθι κισσός,
30 κισσὸς ἑλιχρύσῳ κεκονιμένος· ἁ δὲ κατ' αὐτόν
   καρπῷ ἕλιξ εἰλεῖται ἀγαλλομένα κροκόεντι.
   ἔντοσθεν δὲ γυνά, τι θεῶν δαίδαλμα, τέτυκται,

---

3 Lit., "bitter anger is always sitting at his nostril"—an angry
snorting, perhaps.

4 I.e., a statue of Priapus, a phallic deity who protected crops
and orchards. His cult originated in Lampsacus on the Helles-
pont.

5 Or possibly Κρανιάδων (the Nymphs of the springs [= their
statues]).

6 Originally from Libya, perhaps; but it may be implied that
he traveled specially for the competition.

7 The cup is a pastoral equivalent for a vessel of painted pot-

GOATHERD

It is not right, shepherd, it is not right for us to pipe at midday. We are in fear of Pan, who at that time is weary from hunting and takes his rest. He has a short temper, and his bitter anger is always ready to well up.[3] But you, Thyrsis, are able to sing about the sufferings of Daphnis, and you have truly great distinction in country song. Let us sit down here under the elm, facing Priapus[4] and the springs,[5] where that shepherd's seat is, and the oak trees. If you will sing as you sang when you competed with Chromis from Libya,[6] I will let you milk three times a goat that has given birth to twins; even with two kids to feed, she is milked into two pails besides. I will give you a deep cup, too, sealed with sweet wax, two-handled, newly made, still fragrant from its chiseling.[7] High up on the rim winds ivy, ivy speckled with gold-flowers; and along it twines the tendril making a fine show of its yellow fruit.[8] Inside, with more than human artistry, is carved a woman

tery or chased silver; it is called *kissubion*, with reference either to its being made of ivy wood (*kissos*) or to the ivy with which it is decorated (29–31). How the interwoven ivy and helichryse relate to the three scenes, and how the acanthus can be spread "all over" (55), is unclear. Possibly acanthus decorates the base and ivy rises from there in three places, defining three panels, and winds round the rim. "Inside" (32) is usually taken to mean "inside the framing ivy," not "inside the cup," although having three scenes on the outside of a two-handled cup seems unexpected.

[8] The wordplay ἑλιχρύσῳ, ἕλιξ, εἱλεῖται suggests that the "tendril" belongs to the helichryse (gold flower), but it must belong to the ivy. If (as an ancient lexicon states) ἑλίχρυσος can mean the ivy's own flower, then the frame is more conventional, but "along it" is awkward.

ἀσκητὰ πέπλῳ τε καὶ ἄμπυκι· πὰρ δέ οἱ ἄνδρες
καλὸν ἐθειράζοντες ἀμοιβαδὶς ἄλλοθεν ἄλλος
35 νεικείουσ᾽ ἐπέεσσι· τὰ δ᾽ οὐ φρενὸς ἅπτεται αὐτᾶς·
ἀλλ᾽ ὅκα μὲν τῆνον ποτιδέρκεται ἄνδρα γέλαισα,
ἄλλοκα δ᾽ αὖ ποτὶ τὸν ῥιπτεῖ νόον· οἱ δ᾽ ὑπ᾽ ἔρωτος
δηθὰ κυλοιδιόωντες ἐτώσια μοχθίζοντι.
τοῖς δὲ μετὰ γριπεύς τε γέρων πέτρα τε τέτυκται
40 λεπράς, ἐφ᾽ ᾇ σπεύδων μέγα δίκτυον ἐς βόλον ἕλκει
ὁ πρέσβυς, κάμνοντι τὸ καρτερὸν ἀνδρὶ ἐοικώς.
φαίης κεν γυίων νιν ὅσον σθένος ἐλλοπιεύειν,
ὧδέ οἱ ᾠδήκαντι κατ᾽ αὐχένα πάντοθεν ἶνες
καὶ πολιῷ περ ἐόντι· τὸ δὲ σθένος ἄξιον ἄβας.
45 τυτθὸν δ᾽ ὅσσον ἄπωθεν ἁλιτρύτοιο γέροντος
περκναῖσι σταφυλαῖσι καλὸν βέβριθεν ἀλωά,
τὰν ὀλίγος τις κῶρος ἐφ᾽ αἱμασιαῖσι φυλάσσει
ἥμενος· ἀμφὶ δέ νιν δύ᾽ ἀλώπεκες, ἁ μὲν ἀν᾽ ὄρχως
φοιτῇ σινομένα τὰν τρώξιμον, ἁ δ᾽ ἐπὶ πήρᾳ
50 πάντα δόλον τεύχοισα τὸ παιδίον οὐ πρὶν ἀνησεῖν
φατὶ πρὶν ἢ ἀκράτιστον ἐπὶ ξηροῖσι καθίξῃ.
αὐτὰρ ὅγ᾽ ἀνθερίκοισι καλὰν πλέκει ἀκριδοθήραν
σχοίνῳ ἐφαρμόσδων· μέλεται δέ οἱ οὔτε τι πήρας
οὔτε φυτῶν τοσσῆνον ὅσον περὶ πλέγματι γαθεῖ.
55 παντᾷ δ᾽ ἀμφὶ δέπας περιπέπταται ὑγρὸς ἄκανθος,
αἰπολικὸν θάημα· τέρας κέ τυ θυμὸν ἀτύξαι.

46 περκναῖσι Briggs: .]ε[pap.: πυρναίαις M   51 v.
corruptus

---

[9] Love has stopped them sleeping.

arrayed with a cloak and headband. By her, two men with fine heads of hair are contending in speech, one from each side; but she is unimpressed, and she at one time gives one of them a smiling glance, then turns her attention to the other, while they labor in vain, their eyes long dark-rimmed from love.[9] Near them are carved an old fisherman and a rugged rock, on which the old man energetically gathers his big net for a cast. He is the very image of effort: you would say that he was fishing with all the strength of his limbs, so much do the sinews bulge all over his neck, gray haired though he is; his strength is worthy of youth. A short distance from the sea-worn old man is a vineyard with a fine load of purple grapes. A little boy is on guard there, sitting on the drystone wall. Near him are two foxes; one goes among the vine rows and plunders the grapes that are ready to eat, while the other uses all its guile to get his knapsack, and is determined not to leave the boy alone until he has only dry bread left for his breakfast.[10] He meanwhile is weaving a fine trap for grasshoppers[11] by linking together rushes and stalks of asphodel, and his care for his knapsack and vines is much less than the pleasure he takes in his plaiting. All around the cup is spread pliant acanthus. It is a wonderful product of the pastoral world,[12] a marvel to amaze your mind. As

[10] Or, perhaps, "until it has raided his breakfast bread." One of these is probably the sense intended; but the transmitted text cannot be translated satisfactorily, and none of the suggested emendations is convincing.

[11] Grasshoppers and crickets were kept for their song (cf. *Anth. Pal.* 7.189, 190, 192–95, 197–98).

[12] Or, "a marvel for a goatherd to behold."

τῷ μὲν ἐγὼ πορθμῆι Καλυδνίῳ αἶγά τ' ἔδωκα
ὦνον καὶ τυρόεντα μέγαν λευκοῖο γάλακτος·
οὐδέ τί πω ποτὶ χεῖλος ἐμὸν θίγεν, ἀλλ' ἔτι κεῖται
60 ἄχραντον. τῷ κά τυ μάλα πρόφρων ἀρεσαίμαν
αἴ κά μοι τύ, φίλος, τὸν ἐφίμερον ὕμνον ἀείσῃς.
κοὔτι τυ κερτομέω. πόταγ', ὠγαθέ· τὰν γὰρ ἀοιδάν
οὔ τί πα εἰς Ἀίδαν γε τὸν ἐκλελάθοντα φυλαξεῖς.

ΘΥΡΣΙΣ
Ἄρχετε βουκολικᾶς, Μοῖσαι φίλαι, ἄρχετ' ἀοιδᾶς.

65 Θύρσις ὅδ' ὦξ Αἴτνας, καὶ Θύρσιδος ἁδέα φωνά.
πᾷ ποκ' ἄρ' ἦσθ', ὅκα Δάφνις ἐτάκετο, πᾷ ποκα,
Νύμφαι;
ἦ κατὰ Πηνειῶ καλὰ τέμπεα, ἢ κατὰ Πίνδω;
οὐ γὰρ δὴ ποταμοῖο μέγαν ῥόον εἴχετ' Ἀνάπω,
οὐδ' Αἴτνας σκοπιάν, οὐδ' Ἄκιδος ἱερὸν ὕδωρ.

70 ἄρχετε βουκολικᾶς, Μοῖσαι φίλαι, ἄρχετ' ἀοιδᾶς.

τῆνον μὰν θῶες, τῆνον λύκοι ὠρύσαντο,
τῆνον χὠκ δρυμοῖο λέων ἔκλαυσε θανόντα.

57 καλυδνίῳ schol. v. l.: καλυδωνίῳ M

24

payment I gave the ferryman from Calydna[13] a goat and a great cheese made from white milk. It has never yet touched my lips; it still lies unused. I would very gladly give you the pleasure of owning it, dear friend, if you will perform that beautiful song for me. Come on, my good fellow; you can't keep singing in Hades,[14] where memory is undone.

THYRSIS

Begin, dear Muses, begin the pastoral song.

Thyrsis of Etna am I, and sweet is the voice of Thyrsis.
     Where were you, Nymphs, where were you while Daphnis pined away? Were you in the lovely valleys of Peneius or of Pindus?[15] Certainly you were not at home by the great stream of the Anapus River, or the peak of Etna, or the sacred waters of Acis.[16]

Begin, dear Muses, begin the pastoral song.

For him the jackals howled, and the wolves too; for his death even the forest lion grieved aloud.

---

[13] Calydna is an island northwest of Cos. The manuscripts have "Calydonian"; Calydon, however, is at the western end of the Gulf of Corinth.

[14] Lit., "you can't retain your song as far as Hades."

[15] The Pindus range covers the central part of northern Greece, and the Peneius flows through it in a famously beautiful valley called Tempe, which might be supposed to be a haunt of country nymphs. Similarly, at the beginning of the *Odyssey*, Poseidon has left Olympus to visit the Ethiopians (Hom. *Od.* 1.22).

[16] Anapus, Acis: rivers near Syracuse in Sicily.

ἄρχετε βουκολικᾶς, Μοῖσαι φίλαι, ἄρχετ᾽ ἀοιδᾶς.

πολλαί οἱ πὰρ ποσσὶ βόες, πολλοὶ δέ τε ταῦροι,
75 πολλαὶ δὲ δαμάλαι καὶ πόρτιες ὠδύραντο.

ἄρχετε βουκολικᾶς, Μοῖσαι φίλαι, ἄρχετ᾽ ἀοιδᾶς.

ἦνθ᾽ Ἑρμᾶς πράτιστος ἀπ᾽ ὤρεος, εἶπε δὲ "Δάφνι,
τίς τυ κατατρύχει; τίνος, ὠγαθέ, τόσσον ἔρασαι;"

ἄρχετε βουκολικᾶς, Μοῖσαι φίλαι, ἄρχετ᾽ ἀοιδᾶς.

80 ἦνθον τοὶ βοῦται, τοὶ ποιμένες, ᾠπόλοι ἦνθον·
πάντες ἀνηρώτευν τί πάθοι κακόν. ἦνθ᾽ ὁ Πρίηπος
κἤφα "Δάφνι τάλαν, τί τὺ τάκεαι; ἁ δέ τυ κώρα
πάσας ἀνὰ κράνας, πάντ᾽ ἄλσεα ποσσὶ φορεῖται—

ἄρχετε βουκολικᾶς, Μοῖσαι φίλαι, ἄρχετ᾽ ἀοιδᾶς—

85 ζάτεισ᾽· ἆ δύσερώς τις ἄγαν καὶ ἀμήχανος ἐσσί.
βούτας μὲν ἐλέγευ, νῦν δ᾽ αἰπόλῳ ἀνδρὶ ἔοικας.
ᾠπόλος, ὅκκ᾽ ἐσορῇ τὰς μηκάδας οἷα βατεῦνται,
τάκεται ὀφθαλμὼς ὅτι οὐ τράγος αὐτὸς ἔγεντο.

ἄρχετε βουκολικᾶς, Μοῖσαι φίλαι, ἄρχετ᾽ ἀοιδᾶς.

90 καὶ τὺ δ᾽ ἐπεί κ᾽ ἐσορῇς τὰς παρθένος οἷα γελᾶντι,
τάκεαι ὀφθαλμὼς ὅτι οὐ μετὰ ταῖσι χορεύεις."

82 τυ Fritzsche: τι m: τοι m

IDYLL 1

Begin, dear Muses, begin the pastoral song.

At his feet many cows, many bulls, many heifers and many calves made lament.

Begin, dear Muses, begin the pastoral song.

First to arrive was Hermes, from the mountain. "Daphnis," he said, "who is tormenting you? Whence this great passion, my friend?"

Begin, dear Muses, begin the pastoral song.

The oxherds came, the shepherds and the goatherds came, and they all asked what was troubling him. Priapus came, and said, "Poor Daphnis, why are you pining away? The girl is wandering by every spring and every grove—

Begin, dear Muses, begin the pastoral song—

"searching for you. Ah, you are simply a hopeless lover[17] and quite at a loss what to do. You used to be called an oxherd, but now you are acting like a goatherd. When he sees the nanny goats being mounted, the goatherd weeps his eyes away regretting that he wasn't born a goat.

Begin, dear Muses, begin the pastoral song.

"And you, when you see how the girls laugh, weep your eyes away just because you're not dancing with them."

---

[17] Translation of the word δύσερως ("unlucky," "hopeless," "obsessive" in love) will depend on what version of the story Theocritus is taken to be following: see p. 16.

τὼς δ' οὐδὲν ποτελέξαθ' ὁ βουκόλος, ἀλλὰ τὸν αὐτῶ
ἆννε πικρὸν ἔρωτα, καὶ ἐς τέλος ἆννε μοίρας.

ἄρχετε βουκολικᾶς, Μοῖσαι, πάλιν ἄρχετ' ἀοιδᾶς.

95   ἦνθέ γε μὰν ἀδεῖα καὶ ἁ Κύπρις γελάοισα,
λάθρη μὲν γελάοισα, βαρὺν δ' ἀνὰ θυμὸν ἔχοισα,
κεῖπε "τύ θην τὸν Ἔρωτα κατεύχεο, Δάφνι, λυγιξεῖν·
ἦ ῥ' οὐκ αὐτὸς Ἔρωτος ὑπ' ἀργαλέω ἐλυγίχθης";

ἄρχετε βουκολικᾶς, Μοῖσαι, πάλιν ἄρχετ' ἀοιδᾶς.

100 τὰν δ' ἄρα χὠ Δάφνις ποταμείβετο· "Κύπρι βαρεῖα,
Κύπρι νεμεσσατά, Κύπρι θνατοῖσιν ἀπεχθής,
ἤδη γὰρ φράσδη πάνθ' ἄλιον ἄμμι δεδύκειν;
Δάφνις κἠν Ἀίδα κακὸν ἔσσεται ἄλγος Ἔρωτι.

ἄρχετε βουκολικᾶς, Μοῖσαι, πάλιν ἄρχετ' ἀοιδᾶς.

105 οὐ λέγεται τὰν Κύπριν ὁ βουκόλος; ἕρπε ποτ' Ἴδαν,
ἕρπε ποτ' Ἀγχίσαν· τηνεὶ δρύες ἠδὲ κύπειρος,
αἱ δὲ καλὸν βομβεῦντι ποτὶ σμάνεσσι μέλισσαι.

106–7 ἠδὲ ... αἱ δὲ Meineke: ὧδε ... ὧδε M

---

18 The tone of Aphrodite's speech and of Daphnis' reply sug-
gests that they are enemies; but then why would Aphrodite laugh
only "inwardly," and why finally does she wish to save Daphnis
(138–39)? It is possible to translate "pretending to be very angry"
or "displaying heavy grief," but these too are difficult in context.
Perhaps she pretends to mock but is secretly favorable to him (cf.
95–96).

The oxherd made no reply, but bore his bitter love, bore it right up to the end of his days.

Begin, Muses, begin again the pastoral song.

Cypris came too, laughing with delight, laughing inwardly and nursing heavy anger,[18] and she said, "Daphnis, you boasted[19] that you would get the better of[20] Love, but has cruel Love not got the better of you?"

Begin, Muses, begin again the pastoral song.

Daphnis in turn replied to her, "Cruel Cypris, spiteful Cypris, Cypris hateful to mortals, do you think, then, that all my suns are set already? Even in Hades Daphnis will be a source of bitter grief for Love.[21]

Begin, Muses, begin again the pastoral song.

"Isn't there the story that by an oxherd Cypris was—?[22] Get away to Ida, get away to Anchises. Oak trees and galingale are there, and the bees buzz sweetly around their hives.[23]

[19] Or, "vowed."

[20] A metaphor from a wrestling hold.

[21] Because famously undefeated by him.

[22] He refrains from a coarse word. Aphrodite fell in love with Anchises, a wellborn Trojan who tended his herds on Mt. Ida. Their son was Aeneas. The story is told in the *Homeric Hymn to Aphrodite.*

[23] I.e., it is a good place for a tryst (cf. *Hom. Hymn Aphr.* 264ff.). Daphnis may be making a sly allusion to a story that the pair were stung by bees (cf. Plut. *Quaest. Nat.* Fr. 36 [Loeb 426]).

ἄρχετε βουκολικᾶς, Μοῖσαι, πάλιν ἄρχετ' ἀοιδᾶς.

ὡραῖος χὤδωνις, ἐπεὶ καὶ μῆλα νομεύει
110   καὶ πτῶκας βάλλει καὶ θηρία πάντα διώκει.

ἄρχετε βουκολικᾶς, Μοῖσαι, πάλιν ἄρχετ' ἀοιδᾶς.

αὖτις ὅπως στασῇ Διομήδεος ἆσσον ἰοῖσα,
καὶ λέγε 'τὸν βούταν νικῶ Δάφνιν, ἀλλὰ μάχευ μοι.'

ἄρχετε βουκολικᾶς, Μοῖσαι, πάλιν ἄρχετ' ἀοιδᾶς.

115   ὦ λύκοι, ὦ θῶες, ὦ ἀν' ὤρεα φωλάδες ἄρκτοι,
χαίρεθ'· ὁ βουκόλος ὔμμιν ἐγὼ Δάφνις οὐκέτ' ἀν'
      ὕλαν,
οὐκέτ' ἀνὰ δρυμώς, οὐκ ἄλσεα. χαῖρ', Ἀρέθοισα,
καὶ ποταμοὶ τοὶ χεῖτε καλὸν κατὰ Θύβριδος ὕδωρ.

ἄρχετε βουκολικᾶς, Μοῖσαι, πάλιν ἄρχετ' ἀοιδᾶς.

120 Δάφνις ἐγὼν ὅδε τῆνος ὁ τὰς βόας ὧδε νομεύων,
Δάφνις ὁ τὼς ταύρως καὶ πόρτιας ὧδε ποτίσδων.

Begin, Muses, begin again the pastoral song.

"Adonis, too, is the right age for you: he herds his sheep, kills hares, and hunts wild animals of every sort.[24]

Begin, Muses, begin again the pastoral song.

"Why not go and take a stand near Diomedes again, and say, 'I am the conqueror of Daphnis the oxherd; come and fight me, then'?[25]

Begin, Muses, begin again the pastoral song.

"Farewell, you wolves, jackals and bears in your mountain caves. I, Daphnis the oxherd, shall no longer be found in your forests, no longer be found in your groves and woods. Farewell, Arethusa, and you rivers that pour your fair waters down Thybris.[26]

Begin, Muses, begin again the pastoral song.

"I am the famous Daphnis who herded his cows here, Daphnis who watered here his bulls and calves.

[24] Aphrodite's favorite, Adonis, was gored to death by a wild boar: see pp. 504–17. Daphnis may be speaking with malice, knowing that Adonis is already dead, or with prophetic irony; lines 105–7 and 112–13 suggest the former.

[25] In the fifth book of the *Iliad*, Aphrodite intervenes in the fighting and is wounded and mocked by Diomedes (335–430).

[26] Arethusa: a famous spring at Syracuse. Thybris: unidentified; probably a mountain or valley in the same area.

ἄρχετε βουκολικᾶς, Μοῖσαι, πάλιν ἄρχετ' ἀοιδᾶς.

ὦ Πὰν Πάν, εἴτ' ἐσσὶ κατ' ὤρεα μακρὰ Λυκαίω,
εἴτε τύγ' ἀμφιπολεῖς μέγα Μαίναλον, ἔνθ' ἐπὶ νᾶσον
125 τὰν Σικελάν, Ἑλίκας δὲ λίπε ῥίον αἰπύ τε σᾶμα
τῆνο Λυκαονίδαο, τὸ καὶ μακάρεσσιν ἀγητόν.

λήγετε βουκολικᾶς, Μοῖσαι, ἴτε λήγετ' ἀοιδᾶς.

ἔνθ', ὦναξ, καὶ τάνδε φέρευ πακτοῖο μελίπνουν
ἐκ κηρῶ σύριγγα καλὸν περὶ χεῖλος ἑλικτάν·
130 ἦ γὰρ ἐγὼν ὑπ' Ἔρωτος ἐς Ἅιδαν ἕλκομαι ἤδη.

λήγετε βουκολικᾶς, Μοῖσαι, ἴτε λήγετ' ἀοιδᾶς.

νῦν ἴα μὲν φορέοιτε βάτοι, φορέοιτε δ' ἄκανθαι,
ἁ δὲ καλὰ νάρκισσος ἐπ' ἀρκεύθοισι κομάσαι,
πάντα δ' ἄναλλα γένοιτο, καὶ ἁ πίτυς ὄχνας ἐνείκαι,
135 Δάφνις ἐπεὶ θνάσκει, καὶ τὰς κύνας ὤλαφος ἕλκοι,
κἠξ ὀρέων τοὶ σκῶπες ἀηδόσι γαρύσαιντο."

129 καλὸν Fritzsche: -ὰν M

---

[27] Greek invocations are typically exhaustive. Lycaeus and
Maenalus are mountains in Arcadia, the area with which Pan
was most closely associated. "The peak of Helice" and "the lofty
tomb of Lycaon's grandson" are probably references to these two
places: Helice, also known as Callisto, was daughter of Lycaon
and had her tomb on Mt. Maenalus (Paus. 8.35.8), as did Arcas,
grandson of Lycaon (Paus. 8.9.3–4). The gods' admiration prob-
ably means that several of them had sanctuaries there.

[28] Or, "sweet sounding and made of compacted wax." The
Greek syrinx of this period was usually rectangular; all the reeds

Begin, Muses, begin again the pastoral song.

"O Pan, Pan, whether you are on the high mountains of Lycaeus or are ranging over great Maenalus,[27] come to the island of Sicily and leave the peak of Helice and that lofty tomb of the descendant of Lycaon which even the blessed gods admire.

Cease, Muses, come cease the pastoral song.

"Come, lord, and accept this pipe, smelling sweetly of honey from its compacted wax[28] and with a good binding around its lip; for I am now being haled away by Love to Hades.

Cease, Muses, come cease the pastoral song.

"Now you brambles may bear violets, and you thorns may do the same, and the fair narcissus may bloom on the juniper, and everything may be changed, and pears can grow on the pine tree, since Daphnis is dying. Let the deer tear apart the hounds, and let the screech owls from the mountains rival nightingales."[29]

were of the same length, each being plugged with wax at a different point. Wax could be used also to help bind the reeds together.

[29] This final reversal ought to be owls' acquiring a song more beautiful than that of nightingales, but the word translated "rival" (γηρύσαιντο) really means "sing to"; and the emphatic ἐξ ὀρέων (from the mountains) is difficult. If it were replaced by a phrase meaning "in broad daylight," owls and nightingales would be united in a different sort of reversal; but that would remove the emphasis on singing, which seems to be the reason why Daphnis, the singer *par excellence*, concludes as he does: now that he is dead, inferior rivals may come to the fore.

λήγετε βουκολικᾶς, Μοῖσαι, ἴτε λήγετ' ἀοιδᾶς.

χὢ μὲν τόσσ' εἰπὼν ἀπεπαύσατο· τὸν δ' Ἀφροδίτα
ἤθελ' ἀνορθῶσαι· τά γε μὰν λίνα πάντα λελοίπει
140 ἐκ Μοιρᾶν, χὢ Δάφνις ἔβα ῥόον. ἔκλυσε δίνα
τὸν Μοίσαις φίλον ἄνδρα, τὸν οὐ Νύμφαισιν ἀπε-
χθῆ.

λήγετε βουκολικᾶς, Μοῖσαι, ἴτε λήγετ' ἀοιδᾶς.

καὶ τὺ δίδου τὰν αἶγα τό τε σκύφος, ὥς κεν ἀμέλξας
σπείσω ταῖς Μοίσαις. ὦ χαίρετε πολλάκι, Μοῖσαι,
145 χαίρετ'· ἐγὼ δ' ὔμμιν καὶ ἐς ὕστερον ἅδιον ᾀσῶ.

ΑΙΠΟΛΟΣ

πλῆρές τοι μέλιτος τὸ καλὸν στόμα, Θύρσι, γένοιτο,
πλῆρες δὲ σχαδόνων, καὶ ἀπ' Αἰγίλω ἰσχάδα τρώ-
γοις
ἀδεῖαν, τέττιγος ἐπεὶ τύγα φέρτερον ᾄδεις.
ἠνίδε τοι τὸ δέπας· θᾶσαι, φίλος, ὡς καλὸν ὄσδει·
150 Ὡρᾶν πεπλύσθαι νιν ἐπὶ κράναισι δοκησεῖς.
ὧδ' ἴθι, Κισσαίθα· τὺ δ' ἄμελγέ νιν. αἱ δὲ χίμαιραι,
οὐ μὴ σκιρτασῆτε, μὴ ὁ τράγος ὔμμιν ἀναστῇ.

---

30 On Daphnis' mysterious death, see p. 16.

31 These lines, though not part of Thyrsis' song, sound like the conclusion of a hymn (cf. *Id.* 17.135–37).

32 Several traditional stories told how poets were fed by bees (cf. *Id.* 7.80–85), symbolizing the sweetness of their song. The Attic deme Aegilia was famous for its figs (Ath. 14.652e–f). The

34

Cease, Muses, come cease the pastoral song.

With these words he ended. Aphrodite wanted to raise him up, but all the thread granted him by the Fates had run out, and Daphnis went to the stream. The eddying water engulfed the man dear to the Muses,[30] the man by no means unwelcome to the Nymphs.

Cease, Muses, come cease the pastoral song.

Now give me the goat and the bowl so that I can milk her and make a libation to the Muses. Farewell, Muses, many farewells. Some other time I will sing you a yet sweeter song.[31]

GOATHERD

May your fair mouth be filled with honey, Thyrsis, and with honeycomb, and may you have sweet figs from Aegilus to eat, for your song is better than the cicada's.[32] Look, here is the cup. See how fragrant it is: you would think it had been dipped in the spring of the Hours.[33] Come here, Cissaetha; you can milk her now. And as for you nanny goats—don't be so frisky, in case the billy will have to see to you.[34]

cicada was nature's unrivaled songster: cf. Pl. *Phdr.* 258e–259d; Callim. Fr. 1.34.

[33] Not known from elsewhere; perhaps metaphorical. The Hours are goddesses of springtime, and here they bestow fresh beauty.

[34] Lit., "in case the billy goat gets up for you" (to put them in good order but also, it is implied, to mate with them).

IDYLL 2

Simaetha has been abandoned by her lover Delphis. In the
first section of the poem (1–63), she performs magic rites.
In the second section (64–162), having sent away her ser-
vant Thestylis, she tells the Moon the story of her pas-
sion—how she first saw Delphis, how she began to sicken
for love, how she summoned him to her house, his smooth
talk, their lovemaking, and his ultimate betrayal. In the
closing lines (163–66), she bids farewell to the Moon in a
tone of quiet resignation.

Simaetha's social status and the reason for her unusual
lack of a legal guardian are not made clear. She is able to
act independently, but the results have not been happy.
Delphis has exploited her love and abandoned her, as she
seems to realize (112, 138). In the morning she intends to
confront him; her magic and her narrative, which take
place during the night, are substitutes for that direct ac-
tion and are each punctuated by a refrain that perhaps
evokes the repetitive chanting of spells. Her various ac-
tions seem intended partly to attract Delphis and partly to
punish him (23–26, 58), and they represent her entangled
emotions of anger and love. These emotions are no less
strong than the passions once felt by Medea and Circe
(15–16); in another age, and in a different type of poetry,
Simaetha could have been a heroine of epic or tragedy.

IDYLL 2

*The "downgrading" is typically Hellenistic. She is made to
speak in language that veers between the mundane and the
elevated; her narrative is dignified with poetic epithets and
similes, and she addresses the gods in a style evocative of
epic grandeur.*

*The scholia tell us that the name Thestylis and her mis-
sion with the herbs (59–62) are borrowed from a mime of
Sophron; this may have been* The Female Exorcists *(Ταὶ
γυναῖκες αἱ τὰν θεόν φαντι ἐξελᾶν, Frr. 3–9 K-A; Page,*
GLP *no. 73, pp. 328–31).*

Criticism

Ankarloo, B., and S. Clark. *Witchcraft and Magic in Eu-
rope.* Philadelphia, 1999.

Dickie, M. W. "Who Practised Love-Magic in Antiquity
and in the Late Roman World?" *CQ* 50 (2000): 563–83.

Goldhill, *Poet's Voice*, 261–72.

Graf, F. *Magic in the Ancient World.* Cambridge, MA,
175–85.

Griffiths, F. T. "Poetry as *Pharmakon* in Theocritus' *Idyll*
2." In *Arktouros: Hellenic Studies Presented to Bernard
M. W. Knox on the Occasion of His 65th Birthday,* ed-
ited by G. W. Bowersock, W. Burkert, and M. C. Put-
nam, 1.81–88. Berlin, 1979.

Hopkinson, *Hellenistic Anthology*, 154–66.

Hordern, J. H. "Love Magic and Purification in Sophron,
PSI 1214a, and Theocritus." *CQ* 52 (2002): 164–73.

Segal, C. "Space, Time and Imagination in Theocritus'
Second *Idyll*." *CSCA* 16 (1985): 103–19.

2

Πᾷ μοι ταὶ δάφναι; φέρε, Θεστυλί. πᾷ δὲ τὰ φίλτρα;
στέψον τὰν κελέβαν φοινικέῳ οἰὸς ἀώτῳ,
ὡς τὸν ἐμὸν βαρὺν εὖντα φίλον καταδήσομαι ἄνδρα,
ὅς μοι δωδεκαταῖος ἀφ' ὦ τάλας οὐδὲ ποθίκει,
5 οὐδ' ἔγνω πότερον τεθνάκαμες ἢ ζοοὶ εἰμές,
οὐδὲ θύρας ἄραξεν ἀνάρσιος. ἦ ῥά οἱ ἀλλᾷ
ᾤχετ' ἔχων ὅ τ' Ἔρως ταχινὰς φρένας ἅ τ' Ἀφρο-
δίτα.
βασεῦμαι ποτὶ τὰν Τιμαγήτοιο παλαίστραν
αὔριον, ὥς νιν ἴδω, καὶ μέμψομαι οἷά με ποιεῖ.
10 νῦν δέ νιν ἐκ θυέων καταδήσομαι. ἀλλά, Σελάνα,
φαῖνε καλόν· τὶν γὰρ ποταείσομαι ἄσυχα, δαῖμον,
τᾷ χθονίᾳ θ' Ἑκάτᾳ, τὰν καὶ σκύλακες τρομέοντι
ἐρχομέναν νεκύων ἀνά τ' ἠρία καὶ μέλαν αἷμα.
χαῖρ', Ἑκάτα δασπλῆτι, καὶ ἐς τέλος ἄμμιν ὀπάδει,
15 φάρμακα ταῦτ' ἔρδοισα χερείονα μήτε τι Κίρκας
μήτε τι Μηδείας μήτε ξανθᾶς Περιμήδας.

IDYLL 2

Where are my laurel leaves?[1] Bring them, Thestylis.
Where are my potions? Circle the bowl[2] with finest scarlet
sheep's wool so that I can bind fast my lover, who is a heavy
trouble to me. The wretch has not even come near for
twelve days, and he doesn't know whether I am living or
dead: he has not even knocked at my door, he is so cruel.
Certainly Love and Aphrodite have gone off somewhere
else with his fickle heart. I shall go tomorrow to Timagetus'
wrestling school to see him, and I shall reproach him for
treating me so. But for now I shall bind him with fire
spells. Cast a fair light, Moon: to you I shall chant softly,
goddess, and to Hecate in the underworld, at whom even
dogs tremble[3] when she comes among the tombs of the
dead and the black blood.[4] Hail, dread Hecate, and keep
with me to the end, making these drugs of mine no less
powerful than those of Circe or Medea or fair-haired Peri-
mede.[5]

---

[1] These and the wool are probably to ward off evil.

[2] For a libation (cf. 43).

[3] Dogs were sacrificed to Hecate.

[4] Perhaps the blood of victims sacrificed at tombs.

[5] A powerful witch ξανθὴν Ἀγαμήδην (fair-haired Agamede)
is mentioned in the *Iliad* (11.740). Theocritus may have misre-
membered the name, or he may refer to an alternative form un-
known to us, or represent Simaetha as misremembering.

Ἴυγξ, ἕλκε τὺ τῆνον ἐμὸν ποτὶ δῶμα τὸν ἄνδρα.

ἄλφιτά τοι πρᾶτον πυρὶ τάκεται. ἀλλ' ἐπίπασσε,
Θεστυλί. δειλαία, πᾷ τὰς φρένας ἐκπεπότασαι;
20 ἦ ῥά γέ θην, μυσαρά, καὶ τὶν ἐπίχαρμα τέτυγμαι;
πάσσ' ἅμα καὶ λέγε ταῦτα· "τὰ Δέλφιδος ὀστία
πάσσω."

ἴυγξ, ἕλκε τὺ τῆνον ἐμὸν ποτὶ δῶμα τὸν ἄνδρα.

Δέλφις ἔμ' ἀνίασεν· ἐγὼ δ' ἐπὶ Δέλφιδι δάφναν
αἴθω· χὠς αὕτα λακεῖ μέγα καππυρίσασα
25 κἠξαπίνας ἄφθη κοὐδὲ σποδὸν εἴδομες αὐτᾶς,
οὕτω τοι καὶ Δέλφις ἐνὶ φλογὶ σάρκ' ἀμαθύνοι.

27 ἴυγξ, ἕλκε τὺ τῆνον ἐμὸν ποτὶ δῶμα τὸν ἄνδρα.

33 νῦν θυσῶ τὰ πίτυρα. τὺ δ', Ἄρτεμι, καὶ τὸν ἐν Ἅιδα
κινήσαις ἀδάμαντα καὶ εἴ τί περ ἀσφαλὲς ἄλλο—
35 Θεστυλί, ταὶ κύνες ἄμμιν ἀνὰ πτόλιν ὠρύονται·
ἁ θεὸς ἐν τριόδοισι· τὸ χαλκέον ὡς τάχος ἄχει.

20 θην pap.: τοι M
28–32 post 42 habent papp., m

40

Magic wheel, draw that man to my house.[6]

First barley grains are melted in the fire. Scatter them on, Thestylis. Where have your wits flown off to, you wretch? Have I become an object of scorn to you too,[7] then, you vile girl? Scatter it on, and at the same time say, "I scatter the bones of Delphis."

Magic wheel, draw that man to my house.

Delphis has caused me distress; against Delphis I burn this laurel. As it crackles loudly when set on fire and from it we do not see even ash remaining, just so may Delphis' flesh waste in flame.[8]

Magic wheel, draw that man to my house.

Now I shall burn the bran. You, Artemis, who can move the adamant of Hades[9] and anything else as firmly fixed— Thestylis, the dogs are howling for us in the town: the goddess is at the crossroads—[10] clash the bronze quick as you can.[11]

---

[6] The *iynx*, a wooden disk or wheel made to spin by alternately loosening and tightening a cord passed through two holes near the center. It was used to attract or recapture a lover.

[7] As well as to her lover, Delphis.

[8] Consumed by the fires of love.

[9] The gates of Hades, made of adamant (Virg. *Aen.* 6.552).

[10] Hecate was goddess of the crossroads.

[11] Apotropaic, to ward off the dangerous power she has invoked.

ἶυγξ, ἕλκε τὺ τῆνον ἐμὸν ποτὶ δῶμα τὸν ἄνδρα.

ἠνίδε σιγῇ μὲν πόντος, σιγῶντι δ᾽ ἀῆται·
ἁ δ᾽ ἐμὰ οὐ σιγῇ στέρνων ἔντοσθεν ἀνία,
40 ἀλλ᾽ ἐπὶ τήνῳ πᾶσα καταίθομαι ὅς με τάλαιναν
ἀντὶ γυναικὸς ἔθηκε κακὰν καὶ ἀπάρθενον ἦμεν.

ἶυγξ, ἕλκε τὺ τῆνον ἐμὸν ποτὶ δῶμα τὸν ἄνδρα.

28 ὡς τοῦτον τὸν κηρὸν ἐγὼ σὺν δαίμονι τάκω,
29 ὣς τάκοιθ᾽ ὑπ᾽ ἔρωτος ὁ Μύνδιος αὐτίκα Δέλφις.
30 χὠς δινεῖθ᾽ ὅδε ῥόμβος ὁ χάλκεος ἐξ Ἀφροδίτας,
31 ὣς τῆνος δινοῖτο ποθ᾽ ἁμετέραισι θύραισιν.

32 ἶυγξ, ἕλκε τὺ τῆνον ἐμὸν ποτὶ δῶμα τὸν ἄνδρα.

43 ἐς τρὶς ἀποσπένδω καὶ τρὶς τάδε, πότνια, φωνῶ·
εἴτε γυνὰ τήνῳ παρακέκλιται εἴτε καὶ ἀνήρ,
45 τόσσον ἔχοι λάθας ὅσσον ποκὰ Θησέα φαντί
ἐν Δίᾳ λασθῆμεν ἐυπλοκάμω Ἀριάδνας.

ἶυγξ, ἕλκε τὺ τῆνον ἐμὸν ποτὶ δῶμα τὸν ἄνδρα.

ἱππομανὲς φυτόν ἐστι παρ᾽ Ἀρκάσι, τῷ δ᾽ ἔπι πᾶσαι
καὶ πῶλοι μαίνονται ἀν᾽ ὤρεα καὶ θοαὶ ἵπποι·

---

[12] Epiphanies are often said to be accompanied by a supernatural silence.

[13] He is from Myndia, a town on the coast of Caria, almost opposite the island of Cos. This fact, together with the reference

Magic wheel, draw that man to my house.

Look, still is the sea and still are the breezes;[12] but the pain in my heart is not still. The whole of me is burning for the man who made me disgraced—wretch that I am—and no longer a virgin, instead of his wife.

Magic wheel, draw that man to my house.

As I with the goddess's aid melt this wax, so may Myndian Delphis[13] melt at once with love. And as this bronze rhombos[14] turns round by the power of Aphrodite, so may he turn to and fro about my door.

Magic wheel, draw that man to my house.

Three times I pour a libation and three times, lady, I utter these words: whether it is a woman who lies with him or a man, may he have so much forgetfulness of them as they say Theseus on Dia had of Ariadne with her lovely tresses.[15]

Magic wheel, draw that man to my house.

Hippomanes is a plant which grows among the Arcadians, and in the mountains all the foals and swift horses are mad

to the sea (38) and the mention of Philinus, a famous Coan athlete (115), suggests that Cos may be the imagined setting.

[14] The bull roarer, a piece of wood or metal which hums loudly when spun at the end of a length of cord.

[15] Dia is another name for Naxos, where Theseus abandoned Ariadne, who had fled with him from Crete after helping him to kill the Minotaur, her half brother (Catull. 64.76–264).

50 ὡς καὶ Δέλφιν ἴδοιμι, καὶ ἐς τόδε δῶμα περάσαι
μαινομένῳ ἴκελος λιπαρᾶς ἔκτοσθε παλαίστρας.

ἶυγξ, ἕλκε τὺ τῆνον ἐμὸν ποτὶ δῶμα τὸν ἄνδρα.

τοῦτ᾽ ἀπὸ τᾶς χλαίνας τὸ κράσπεδον ὤλεσε Δέλφις,
ὠγὼ νῦν τίλλοισα κατ᾽ ἀγρίῳ ἐν πυρὶ βάλλω.
55 αἰαῖ Ἔρως ἀνιαρέ, τί μευ μέλαν ἐκ χροὸς αἷμα
ἐμφὺς ὡς λιμνᾶτις ἅπαν ἐκ βδέλλα πέπωκας;

ἶυγξ, ἕλκε τὺ τῆνον ἐμὸν ποτὶ δῶμα τὸν ἄνδρα.

σαύραν τοι τρίψασα κακὸν ποτὸν αὔριον οἰσῶ.
Θεστυλί, νῦν δὲ λαβοῖσα τὺ τὰ θρόνα ταῦθ᾽ ὑπόμα-
ξον
60 τᾶς τήνω φλιᾶς καθ᾽ ὑπέρτερον ᾇς ἔτι καὶ νύξ,
62 καὶ λέγ᾽ ἐπιτρύζοισα "τὰ Δέλφιδος ὀστία μάσσω."

ἶυγξ, ἕλκε τὺ τῆνον ἐμὸν ποτὶ δῶμα τὸν ἄνδρα.

Νῦν δὴ μώνα ἐοῖσα πόθεν τὸν ἔρωτα δακρύσω;
65 ἐκ τίνος ἄρξωμαι; τίς μοι κακὸν ἄγαγε τοῦτο;
ἦνθ᾽ ἁ τωὐβούλοιο καναφόρος ἄμμιν Ἀναξώ

59 ἀπόμορξον schol. v.l.
60 νύξ Bücheler: νῦν pap., M
61 ἐκ θυμῶ δέδεμαι. ὃ δέ μευ λόγον οὐδένα ποιεῖ fere m:
om. pap., m
62 ἐπιτρύζοισα pap., schol. v.l.: ἐπιφθύζοισα M   μάσσω
Ahlwardt: πάσσω M: καίω pap.

for it;[16] just so may I see Delphis, just so may he come to this house from the glossy wrestling school,[17] like a man made mad.

Magic wheel, draw that man to my house.

From his cloak Delphis lost this fringe, which I now shred and cast into the wild fire.[18] Ah, cruel Love, why, like a leech from the marsh, have you fastened on me and drunk all the black blood from my body?

Magic wheel, draw that man to my house.

Tomorrow I will crush a lizard and take it to him, an evil drink. Thestylis, take these herbs now and knead them over his threshold while it is still night,[19] and say in a whisper, "I knead the bones of Delphis."[20]

Magic wheel, draw that man to my house.

And now that I am alone, from what point shall I lament my love? Where should I start? Who brought me this trouble? Our Anaxo, daughter of Eubulus, went as a bas-

[16] The name of this unidentified plant is compounded from "horse" and "mad."

[17] Glossy because of the oil with which athletes anointed themselves; cf. 79, 102.

[18] Destruction of bodily tokens (especially hair and nails) was thought to affect by "sympathy" the body itself.

[19] A line has been interpolated here (". . . while I am still bound to him in my heart; but he takes no notice of me") as a result of "night" ($\nu\acute{\upsilon}\xi$) at the end of line 60 being corrupted to "now" ($\nu\upsilon\nu$). [20] So that his bones will ache with desire.

ἄλσος ἐς Ἀρτέμιδος, τᾷ δὴ τόκα πολλὰ μὲν ἄλλα
θηρία πομπεύεσκε περισταδόν, ἐν δὲ λέαινα.

φράζεό μευ τὸν ἔρωθ' ὅθεν ἵκετο, πότνα Σελάνα.

70   καί μ' ἁ Θευμαρίδα Θρᾷσσα τροφός, ἁ μακαρῖτις,
ἀγχίθυρος ναίοισα κατεύξατο καὶ λιτάνευσε
τὰν πομπὰν θάσασθαι· ἐγὼ δέ οἱ ἁ μεγάλοιτος
ὡμάρτευν βύσσοιο καλὸν σύροισα χιτῶνα
κἀμφιστειλαμένα τὰν ξυστίδα τὰν Κλεαρίστας.

75   φράζεό μευ τὸν ἔρωθ' ὅθεν ἵκετο, πότνα Σελάνα.

ἤδη δ' εὖσα μέσαν κατ' ἀμαξιτόν, ᾇ τὰ Λύκωνος,
εἶδον Δέλφιν ὁμοῦ τε καὶ Εὐδάμιππον ἰόντας·
τοῖς δ' ἦς ξανθοτέρα μὲν ἑλιχρύσοιο γενειάς,
στήθεα δὲ στίλβοντα πολὺ πλέον ἢ τύ, Σελάνα,
80   ὡς ἀπὸ γυμνασίοιο καλὸν πόνον ἄρτι λιπόντων.

φράζεό μευ τὸν ἔρωθ' ὅθεν ἵκετο, πότνα Σελάνα.

χὠς ἴδον, ὡς ἐμάνην, ὥς μοι πυρὶ θυμὸς ἰάφθη
δειλαίας, τὸ δὲ κάλλος ἐτάκετο. οὐκέτι πομπᾶς

67 τόκα Casaubon: ποκα pap., M
82 πυρὶ pap., coni. Taylor: περὶ M
83 οὐκέτι pap.: κοὐδέ τι m

---

21 It was a great honor for girls to be selected to carry baskets
containing the sacred objects in ritual processions.

ket bearer[21] to the grove of Artemis, in whose honor at that time many animals were paraded, and among them a lioness.[22]

Note, lady Moon, whence came my love.

And Theumaridas' Thracian nurse,[23] now among the blessed, who was a near neighbor, had begged and pleaded with me to see the show; and I most unluckily accompanied her wearing a fair long linen dress and wrapping myself in Clearista's cloak.[24]

Note, lady Moon, whence came my love.

And when I was already halfway along the road, where Lycon's place is,[25] I saw Delphis and Eudamippus going along together.[26] Their beards were blonder than the gold flower and their chests gleamed much more than you, Moon, because they had just left the fair exercise of the gymnasium.

Note, lady Moon, whence came my love.

And when I saw them I was seized with madness, and my wretched heart was caught with fire, and my beauty wasted

[22] As goddess of the hunt, Artemis was associated with wild animals.

[23] Thrace was a source of slaves.

[24] Borrowed for the day.

[25] Perhaps a farm.

[26] Festivals were a rare opportunity for women to appear in public and for potential lovers to see them. Here the normal gender roles are reversed.

τήνας ἐφρασάμαν, οὐδ' ὡς πάλιν οἴκαδ' ἀπῆνθον
85 ἔγνων, ἀλλά μέ τις καπυρὰ νόσος ἐξεσάλαξεν,
κείμαν δ' ἐν κλιντῆρι δέκ' ἄματα καὶ δέκα νύκτας.

φράζεό μευ τὸν ἔρωθ' ὅθεν ἵκετο, πότνα Σελάνα.

καί μευ χρὼς μὲν ὁμοῖος ἐγίνετο πολλάκι θάψῳ,
ἔρρευν δ' ἐκ κεφαλᾶς πᾶσαι τρίχες, αὐτὰ δὲ λοιπά
90 ὀστί' ἔτ' ἦς καὶ δέρμα. καὶ ἐς τίνος οὐκ ἐπέρασα,
ἢ ποίας ἔλιπον γραίας δόμον ἅτις ἐπᾷδεν;
ἀλλ' ἦς οὐδὲν ἐλαφρόν, ὁ δὲ χρόνος ἄνυτο φεύγων.

φράζεό μευ τὸν ἔρωθ' ὅθεν ἵκετο, πότνα Σελάνα.

χοὔτω τᾷ δώλᾳ τὸν ἀλαθέα μῦθον ἔλεξα·
95 "εἰ δ' ἄγε, Θεστυλί, μοι χαλεπᾶς νόσω εὑρέ τι μᾶχος.
πᾶσαν ἔχει με τάλαιναν ὁ Μύνδιος· ἀλλὰ μολοῖσα
τήρησον ποτὶ τὰν Τιμαγήτοιο παλαίστραν·
τηνεὶ γὰρ φοιτῇ, τηνεὶ δέ οἱ ἁδὺ καθῆσθαι.

φράζεό μευ τὸν ἔρωθ' ὅθεν ἵκετο, πότνα Σελάνα.

100 κἠπεί κά νιν ἐόντα μάθῃς μόνον, ἄσυχα νεῦσον,
κεἴφ' ὅτι 'Σιμαίθα τυ καλεῖ', καὶ ὑφαγέο τεῖδε."
ὣς ἐφάμαν· ἁ δ' ἦνθε καὶ ἄγαγε τὸν λιπαρόχρων

85 ἐξεσάλαξεν pap., schol. v.l.: ἐξαλάπαξεν M

48

away.[27] I no longer took notice of that procession, and I had no idea how I got home again, but a burning fever shook me, and I lay on my bed ten days and ten nights.

Note, lady Moon, whence came my love.

Often my skin would become as pale as fustic,[28] and all the hair began to fall from my head,[29] and only my skin and bones were left. To whose house did I not go? What old enchantress did I leave unvisited? But it was no light matter, and flying time moved on.

Note, lady Moon, whence came my love.

So I gave the slave girl a true account: "Come, Thestylis, find some cure for my hard suffering. Myndian Delphis has me in his power completely. Go and wait by Timagetus' wrestling school: there he attends, and there he likes to sit.

Note, lady Moon, whence came my love.

"And when you find him alone, nod to him discreetly and say, 'Simaetha calls you,' and lead him here." So I said; and she went and brought sleek-skinned Delphis to my house.

---

[27] These symptoms, and those of lines 106–8, are probably inspired by a famous passage of Sappho: "When I look at you for a moment, I no longer have power to speak . . . straightaway a subtle flame has stolen beneath my flesh . . . my tongue is silent . . . a cold sweat holds me" (Fr. 31.7–16 Campbell).

[28] A shrub from which yellow dye was made.

[29] Apparently a symptom of extreme desire: Hes. Fr. 133; Virg. *Ecl.* 6.51.

εἰς ἐμὰ δώματα Δέλφιν· ἐγὼ δέ νιν ὡς ἐνόησα
ἄρτι θύρας ὑπὲρ οὐδὸν ἀμειβόμενον ποδὶ κούφῳ—

105 φράζεό μευ τὸν ἔρωθ' ὅθεν ἵκετο, πότνα Σελάνα—

πᾶσα μὲν ἐψύχθην χιόνος πλέον, ἐκ δὲ μετώπω
ἱδρώς μευ κοχύδεσκεν ἴσον νοτίαισιν ἐέρσαις,
οὐδέ τι φωνῆσαι δυνάμαν, οὐδ' ὅσσον ἐν ὕπνῳ
κνυζεῦνται φωνεῦντα φίλαν ποτὶ ματέρα τέκνα·
110 ἀλλ' ἐπάγην δαγῦδι καλὸν χρόα πάντοθεν ἴσα.

φράζεό μευ τὸν ἔρωθ' ὅθεν ἵκετο, πότνα Σελάνα.

καί μ' ἐσιδὼν ὥστοργος ἐπὶ χθονὸς ὄμματα πάξας
ἕζετ' ἐπὶ κλιντῆρι καὶ ἑζόμενος φάτο μῦθον·
"ἦ ῥά με, Σιμαίθα, τόσον ἔφθασας, ὅσσον ἐγώ θην
115 πρᾶν ποκα τὸν χαρίεντα τράχων ἔφθασσα Φιλῖνον,
ἐς τὸ τεὸν καλέσασα τόδε στέγος ἢ 'μὲ παρῆμεν.

φράζεό μευ τὸν ἔρωθ' ὅθεν ἵκετο, πότνα Σελάνα.

ἦνθον γάρ κεν ἐγώ, ναὶ τὸν γλυκὺν ἦνθον Ἔρωτα,
ἢ τρίτος ἠὲ τέταρτος ἐὼν φίλος αὐτίκα νυκτός,
120 μᾶλα μὲν ἐν κόλποισι Διωνύσοιο φυλάσσων,
κρατὶ δ' ἔχων λεύκαν, Ἡρακλέος ἱερὸν ἔρνος,
πάντοθι πορφυρέαισι περὶ ζώστραισιν ἑλικτάν.

---

30 She takes this to be a sign of modesty; but he is preparing
his disingenuous speech.

And when I saw him just crossing the threshold of my door
with his light foot—

Note, lady Moon, whence came my love—

the whole of me became much colder than snow, and
sweat like damp dews ran from my forehead, and I could
say nothing, not even as much as children whimper in their
sleep, crying to their own dear mother: my fair body be-
came stiff, just like a doll.

Note, lady Moon, whence came my love.

And when he saw me the faithless man fixed his eyes on
the ground[30] and sat on the bed and, sitting down, said,
"Indeed, Simaetha, when you called me to this house of
yours you were ahead of me only by as much as I outran
the graceful Philinus the other day.[31]

Note, lady Moon, whence came my love.

"I would have come, by sweet Love I would have come
with two or three friends as soon as it was night,[32] keeping
safe in my lap the apples of Dionysus,[33] and wearing a
garland of white poplar on my head, the holy plant of Her-
acles, wound all round with purple bands.[34]

[31] See on line 29. Delphis is boastful.
[32] He would have come in the *kômos,* a noisy revel through
the streets ending at the mistress' door with a plea for admission
(cf. *Id.* 3) and placing of garlands from the wearer's head.
[33] Perhaps so called because Dionysus was patron of drinkers
at the symposium, starting point for *kômoi.*
[34] This type of garland was associated with Heracles, patron
of athletics (see Gow's note).

φράζεό μευ τὸν ἔρωθ' ὅθεν ἵκετο, πότνα Σελάνα.

καί κ', εἰ μέν μ' ἐδέχεσθε, τάδ' ἦς φίλα (καὶ γὰρ
    ἐλαφρός
125   καὶ καλὸς πάντεσσι μετ' ἠιθέοισι καλεῦμαι),
εὗδόν τ', εἴ κε μόνον τὸ καλὸν στόμα τεῦς ἐφίλησα·
εἰ δ' ἄλλα μ' ὠθεῖτε καὶ ἁ θύρα εἴχετο μοχλῷ,
πάντως κα πελέκεις καὶ λαμπάδες ἦνθον ἐφ' ὑμέας.

φράζεό μευ τὸν ἔρωθ' ὅθεν ἵκετο, πότνα Σελάνα.

130   νῦν δὲ χάριν μὲν ἔφαν τᾷ Κύπριδι πρᾶτον ὀφείλειν,
καὶ μετὰ τὰν Κύπριν τύ με δευτέρα ἐκ πυρὸς εἵλευ,
ὦ γύναι, ἐσκαλέσασα τεὸν ποτὶ τοῦτο μέλαθρον
αὔτως ἡμίφλεκτον· Ἔρως δ' ἄρα καὶ Λιπαραίω
πολλάκις Ἀφαίστοιο σέλας φλογερώτερον αἴθει·

135   φράζεό μευ τὸν ἔρωθ' ὅθεν ἵκετο, πότνα Σελάνα.

σὺν δὲ κακαῖς μανίαις καὶ παρθένον ἐκ θαλάμοιο
καὶ νύμφαν ἐφόβησ' ἔτι δέμνια θερμὰ λιποῖσαν
ἀνέρος." ὣς ὁ μὲν εἶπεν· ἐγὼ δέ νιν ἁ ταχυπειθής
χειρὸς ἐφαψαμένα μαλακῶν ἔκλιν' ἐπὶ λέκτρων·
140   καὶ ταχὺ χρὼς ἐπὶ χρωτὶ πεπαίνετο, καὶ τὰ πρόσωπα
θερμότερ' ἦς ἢ πρόσθε, καὶ ἐψιθυρίσδομες ἁδύ.

124 κ' . . . μ' hoc ordine pap., coni. Ahrens: μ' . . . κ' M
128 κα Ahrens: καὶ pap., M
138 νιν Gow: μιν pap.: οἱ M

IDYLL 2

Note, lady Moon, whence came my love.

"And if you had received me, that would have been pleasant—for I am called nimble and handsome among all the young men—and I would have slept happy if I had only kissed your fair mouth; but if you had rejected me and kept your door closed with a bar, by every means axes and torches would have come against you.[35]

Note, lady Moon, whence came my love.

"But as it is I say thanks are due to Cypris;[36] and, after Cypris, you next have saved me from the fire, lady, by summoning me, quite half-consumed, to this house of yours. Often Love kindles a blaze more fiery than does Hephaestus on Lipari.[37]

Note, lady Moon, whence came my love.

"With dire madness he rouses the girl from her bedroom and makes the bride leave her husband's bed while it is still warm."[38] So he spoke. Too swift to believe him, I caught him by the hand and laid him on the soft bed; quickly body warmed to body, our faces grew hotter than before, and we whispered sweetly. The main thing was

[35] A traditional threat of the *kômastês*.

[36] Aphrodite, born on Cyprus (Hes. *Theog.* 190–200).

[37] One of the Lipari islands northeast of Sicily was a volcano thought to be Hephaestus' forge (Thuc. 3.88.2–3).

[38] To meet a lover.

ὡς καί τοι μὴ μακρὰ φίλα θρυλέοιμι Σελάνα,
ἐπράχθη τὰ μέγιστα, καὶ ἐς πόθον ἤνθομες ἄμφω.
κοὔτε τι τῆνος ἐμὶν ἀπεμέμψατο μέσφα τό γ᾽ ἐχθές,
145 οὔτ᾽ ἐγὼ αὖ τήνῳ. ἀλλ᾽ ἦνθέ μοι ἅ τε Φιλίστας
μάτηρ τᾶς ἁμᾶς αὐλητρίδος ἅ τε Μελιξοῦς
σάμερον, ἁνίκα πέρ τε ποτ᾽ ὠρανὸν ἔτραχον ἵπποι
Ἀῶ τὰν ῥοδόεσσαν ἀπ᾽ ὠκεανοῖο φέροισαι,
κεἶπέ μοι ἄλλα τε πολλὰ καὶ ὡς ἄρα Δέλφις ἔραται.
150 κεῖτε νιν αὖτε γυναικὸς ἔχει πόθος εἴτε καὶ ἀνδρός,
οὐκ ἔφατ᾽ ἀτρεκὲς ἴδμεν, ἀτὰρ τόσον· αἰὲν Ἔρωτος
ἀκράτω ἐπεχεῖτο καὶ ἐς τέλος ᾤχετο φεύγων,
καὶ φάτο οἱ στεφάνοισι τὰ δώματα τῆνα πυκαξεῖν.
ταῦτά μοι ἁ ξείνα μυθήσατο, ἔστι δ᾽ ἀλαθής.
155 ἦ γάρ μοι καὶ τρὶς καὶ τετράκις ἄλλοκ᾽ ἐφοίτη,
καὶ παρ᾽ ἐμὶν ἐτίθει τὰν Δωρίδα πολλάκις ὄλπαν·
νῦν δέ τε δωδεκαταῖος ἀφ᾽ ὧτέ νιν οὐδὲ ποτεῖδον.
ἦ ῥ᾽ οὐκ ἄλλο τι τερπνὸν ἔχει, ἁμῶν δὲ λέλασται;
νῦν μὰν τοῖς φίλτροις καταδήσομαι· αἱ δ᾽ ἔτι κά με
160 λυπῇ, τὰν Ἀίδαο πύλαν, ναὶ Μοίρας, ἀραξεῖ·
τοῖά οἱ ἐν κίστᾳ κακὰ φάρμακα φαμὶ φυλάσσειν,
Ἀσσυρίω, δέσποινα, παρὰ ξείνοιο μαθοῖσα.

142 ὡς pap., m: χὡς m   καί m: κά m: κεν pap.   θρυλέ-
οιμι M: θρέοιμ᾽ ω pap.: θρυλέωμι Hermann
144 τό γ᾽ Ahrens: τοδ᾽ pap.: τύγ᾽ m: τοι m
148 ῥοδοεσσαν pap.: ῥοδόπαχυν M
153 πυκαξεῖν Edmonds: -άσδεν M: -ασθην pap.
159 μὰν pap., m: μὲν m   κα με pap., coni. Ahrens: κήμὲ M

done, and we both came to our desire. And until yesterday, at least, he had no cause to complain at me, nor I at him. But today, as the steeds of rosy Dawn were carrying her up from the ocean and galloping skywards,[39] the mother of our piper Philista and of Melixo came to me and told me many things, and in particular that Delphis is in love. She said she did not know for sure whether desire for a man or for a woman occupies him, but just this much, that he was always toasting Love in unmixed wine[40] and that at last he ran off quickly[41] and said that he would go to garland a house.[42] This is what the woman told me, and she tells the truth: in the past he would visit me three or four times a day and would often leave with me his Dorian oil flask,[43] but now it is the twelfth day since I even saw him. Has he some other delight, and forgotten me? Now I shall bind him with my charms; but if he still gives me trouble he shall knock at Death's door, by the Fates;[44] such evil drugs, I say, I keep in my box, which I learned about, Queen Moon, from an Assyrian stranger.[45]

[39] Dawn, Helios, Selene, and Night (cf. 165–66) were all conceived of as traveling across the sky in horse-drawn chariots.

[40] I.e., he kept drinking strong toasts to an unnamed person.

[41] From the symposium.

[42] See on line 119.

[43] As a pledge of his return; cf. on line 51. "Dorian" may refer to a shape of flask; but since the usual word is not *olpa* but *lēkythos*, the phrase may imply "what the Dorians call an *olpa*" (cf. 18.45).

[44] If he will not knock at mine.

[45] The Babylonians were famous practitioners of magic.

ἀλλὰ τὺ μὲν χαίροισα ποτ᾽ ὠκεανὸν τρέπε πώλως,
πότνι᾽· ἐγὼ δ᾽ οἰσῶ τὸν ἐμὸν πόθον ὥσπερ ὑπέσταν.
165 χαῖρε, Σελαναία λιπαρόθρονε, χαίρετε δ᾽ ἄλλοι
ἀστέρες, εὐκάλοιο κατ᾽ ἄντυγα Νυκτὸς ὀπαδοί.

164 πόθον pap., m: πόνον m

But farewell! Turn your steeds toward the ocean, lady; and I will bear my desire as I have borne it till now.[46] Hail, Selene of the gleaming throne; and hail, you other stars, attendants at the chariot of quiet Night.

[46] Or, "as I have undertaken to endure it."

IDYLL 3

*A goatherd sings a serenade outside the cave of Amaryllis.
The first word of the poem,* kômasdô, *points the humor of
the situation: the* kômos, *an urban convention (see on* Id.
*2.118), is here transferred to the country, and the song of
the locked-out lover, or* paraclausithyron, *is performed not
before a bolted door (as for example in* Id. *23) but in front
of a cave's mouth. It falls into short stanzas. The tone is
naïve, with country lore and homely detail. In the second
part the goatherd tries to raise the tone by associating
himself with characters from myth who succeeded in love.
His listing of these aligns his performance with so-called
catalog poems on erotic themes, such as the* Leontion *of
Hermesianax (Frr. 1–5 Lightfoot) and the* Erotes *of Pha-
nocles (CA pp. 106–9). After this, the closing lines are
bathetic.*

Criticism

Fantuzzi, M. "Mythological Paradigms in the Bucolic Po-
      etry of Theocritus." *PCPhS* 41 (1995): 22–27.
Hunter, *Selection,* 107–29.
Payne, *Invention of Fiction,* 60–67.

3

Κωμάσδω ποτὶ τὰν Ἀμαρυλλίδα, ταὶ δέ μοι αἶγες
βόσκονται κατ᾽ ὄρος, καὶ ὁ Τίτυρος αὐτὰς ἐλαύνει.
Τίτυρ᾽, ἐμὶν τὸ καλὸν πεφιλημένε, βόσκε τὰς αἶγας,
καὶ ποτὶ τὰν κράναν ἄγε, Τίτυρε· καὶ τὸν ἐνόρχαν,
5 τὸν Λιβυκὸν κνάκωνα, φυλάσσεο μή τυ κορύψῃ.

ᾮ χαρίεσσ᾽ Ἀμαρυλλί, τί μ᾽ οὐκέτι τοῦτο κατ᾽
ἄντρον
παρκύπτοισα καλεῖς, τὸν ἐρωτύλον; ἦ ῥά με μισεῖς;
ἦ ῥά γέ τοι σιμὸς καταφαίνομαι ἐγγύθεν ἦμεν,
νύμφα, καὶ προγένειος; ἀπάγξασθαί με ποησεῖς.
10 ἠνίδε τοι δέκα μᾶλα φέρω· τηνῶθε καθεῖλον
ὧ μ᾽ ἐκέλευ καθελεῖν τύ· καὶ αὔριον ἄλλα τοι οἰσῶ.
θᾶσαι μάν. θυμαλγὲς ἐμὶν ἄχος. αἴθε γενοίμαν
ἁ βομβεῦσα μέλισσα καὶ ἐς τεὸν ἄντρον ἱκοίμαν,
τὸν κισσὸν διαδὺς καὶ τὰν πτέριν ᾇ τυ πυκάσδει.
15 νῦν ἔγνων τὸν Ἔρωτα· βαρὺς θεός· ἦ ῥα λεαίνας
μαζὸν ἐθήλαζεν, δρυμῷ τέ νιν ἔτραφε μάτηρ,

---

[1] It is possible, but unlikely, that Tityrus is not a name but a word for a he-goat, which the speaker goes on to warn about a rival; cf. the Cyclops' address to his ram at Hom. *Od.* 9.447–60.

[2] Libya was famous for its flocks (Hom. *Od.* 4.85–89; Hdt. 4.189).

IDYLL 3

I'm going to serenade Amaryllis. My goats are grazing on the hill, and Tityrus is in charge of them.[1] Tityrus, my dear friend, feed my goats and take them to the spring, Tityrus; and watch out for the billy goat, the tawny Libyan one,[2] in case he butts you.

Charming Amaryllis,[3] why don't you peep out any longer from your cave and invite me in—me, your sweetheart? Do you hate me?

Do I look snub-nosed close up, my girl, and is my beard too full?[4] You'll make me go hang myself.

Look, I'm bringing you ten apples; I've gathered them from the place you told me to gather them, and tomorrow I'll bring some more.[5]

Just look; there's such pain in my heart. If only I could turn into a buzzing bee and come into your cave through the ivy and fern that hide you!

Now I know what love is: he's a cruel god. Truly he was suckled by a lioness, and his mother gave birth to him in

---

[3] The scene changes to outside Amaryllis' cave.

[4] He looks like a goat.

[5] An apple symbolizes love, but this goatherd seems to think they are for eating.

ὅς με κατασμύχων καὶ ἐς ὀστίον ἄχρις ἰάπτει.

ὦ τὸ καλὸν ποθορεῦσα, τὸ πᾶν λίθος, ὦ κυάνοφρυ
νύμφα, πρόσπτυξαί με τὸν αἰπόλον, ὥς τυ φιλήσω.
20 ἔστι καὶ ἐν κενεοῖσι φιλήμασιν ἀδέα τέρψις.

τὸν στέφανον τῖλαί με κατ' αὐτίκα λεπτὰ ποησεῖς,
τόν τοι ἐγών, Ἀμαρυλλὶ φίλα, κισσοῖο φυλάσσω,
ἀμπλέξας καλύκεσσι καὶ εὐόδμοισι σελίνοις.

ὤμοι ἐγών, τί πάθω, τί ὁ δύσσοος; οὐχ ὑπακούεις.

25 τὰν βαίταν ἀποδὺς ἐς κύματα τηνῶ ἀλεῦμαι,
ὧπερ τὼς θύννως σκοπιάζεται Ὄλπις ὁ γριπεύς·
καἴ κα μὴ 'ποθάνω, τό γε μὰν τεὸν ἀδὺ τέτυκται.

ἔγνων πρᾶν, ὅκα μοι, μεμναμένῳ εἰ φιλέεις με,
οὐδὲ τὸ τηλέφιλον ποτεμάξατο τὸ πλατάγημα,
30 ἀλλ' αὕτως ἁπαλῷ ποτὶ πάχεϊ ἐξεμαράνθη.

εἶπε καὶ Ἀγροιὼ τἀλαθέα κοσκινόμαντις,

---

31 ἀγροιὼ M: ἁ γραία Heinsius

---

6 An echo of Patroclus' words to Achilles: "It was the gray sea
and the harsh cliffs that bore you, your heart is so cruel" (Hom.
Il. 16.33–35).

7 Unexpected in this context of praise. There is a variant,
ἄπαν λίπος (all-shining), which would provide a compliment (cf.
Id. 2.102 λιπαρόχρων) and perhaps, together with "glances," a
reference to Amaryllis' name, which means "Dazzler."

8 "Empty," because given as a mere favor; or because not
leading further.

a thicket:[6] he's making me smolder with love and torturing me deep in my bones.

Dark-browed girl with beautiful glances, all stonyhearted,[7] embrace me, your goatherd, so that I can kiss you. There is a sweet pleasure even in empty kisses.[8]

You will make me shred this garland into little pieces straightaway, the garland of ivy that I am wearing for you; I wove into it rosebuds and fragrant celery.[9]

Ah! What will become of me? I'm so wretched. You're not listening.

I'll take off my cloak and leap into the waves at the place where Olpis the fisherman looks out for the tuna;[10] and even if I don't die,[11] at any rate your pleasure will certainly be achieved.

I realized this the other day. I was wondering if you loved me, and the smack didn't make the love-in-absence stick: it shriveled away uselessly on my smooth forearm.[12]

Agroeo, too, the sieve diviner,[13] who was cutting grass

[9] The leaves of wild celery were popular for garlands.
[10] Shoals of fish are spotted by a lookout, who gesticulates to the boats; cf. Opp. *Hal.* 3.631–40.
[11] Or (with δή) "if I should die."
[12] Reference to a form of divination. You were lucky in love if the petal stuck to the forearm when applied with a smack.
[13] Probably small objects such as beans or bones were shaken in a sieve and omens taken from their arrangement, as with tealees today.

ἁ πρᾶν ποιολογεῦσα παραιβάτις, οὔνεκ' ἐγὼ μέν
τὶν ὅλος ἔγκειμαι, τὺ δέ μευ λόγον οὐδένα ποιῇ.

ἦ μάν τοι λευκὰν διδυματόκον αἶγα φυλάσσω,
35 τάν με καὶ ἁ Μέρμνωνος ἐριθακὶς ἁ μελανόχρως
αἰτεῖ· καὶ δωσῶ οἱ, ἐπεὶ τύ μοι ἐνδιαθρύπτῃ.

ἅλλεται ὀφθαλμός μευ ὁ δεξιός· ἆρά γ' ἰδησῶ
αὐτάν; ᾀσεῦμαι ποτὶ τὰν πίτυν ὧδ' ἀποκλινθείς,
καί κέ μ' ἴσως ποτίδοι, ἐπεὶ οὐκ ἀδαμαντίνα ἐστίν.

40 Ἱππομένης, ὅκα δὴ τὰν παρθένον ἤθελε γᾶμαι,
μᾶλ' ἐν χερσὶν ἑλὼν δρόμον ἄννεν· ἁ δ' Ἀταλάντα
ὡς ἴδεν, ὡς ἐμάνη, ὡς ἐς βαθὺν ἅλατ' ἔρωτα.

τὰν ἀγέλαν χὠ μάντις ἀπ' Ὄθρυος ἆγε Μελάμ-
        πους
ἐς Πύλον· ἁ δὲ Βίαντος ἐν ἀγκοίναισιν ἐκλίνθη
45 μάτηρ ἁ χαρίεσσα περίφρονος Ἀλφεσιβοίας.

τὰν δὲ καλὰν Κυθέρειαν ἐν ὤρεσι μῆλα νομεύων
οὐχ οὕτως Ὤδωνις ἐπὶ πλέον ἄγαγε λύσσας,
ὥστ' οὐδὲ φθίμενόν νιν ἄτερ μαζοῖο τίθητι;

---

14 And therefore yields copious milk.

15 Evidently a lucky sign (because on the right).

16 Atalanta's suitors had to compete with her in a footrace, and
those who lost were killed by her father. Hippomenes dropped
irresistible golden apples, given him by a god, to delay her
(Hes. Frr. 72–76 M-W; Callim. Fr. 412). The goatherd, himself
equipped with apples (10–11), refers (if "them" rather than "him"
is to be understood as object of "saw") to a version of the myth in
which the apples themselves inspired her with love (cf. Philitas
Fr. 17 Lightfoot).

alongside me the other day, spoke truly when she said I was besotted with you but that you make no account of me.

I am keeping for you a white goat that has had twins;[14] Mermon's swarthy serving girl begs me for it—and I shall give it her, since you play hard to get.

My right eye is twitching:[15] am I to see her, then? I'll sing here resting against this pine tree, and perhaps she'll take notice of me, since she's not made of adamant.

Hippomenes, when he wished to marry the girl, ran the race with apples in his hands, and as soon as Atalanta saw them she leaped deep in love.[16]

The seer Melampus, too, brought the herd from Othrys to Pylos; and the graceful mother of wise Alphesiboea was laid in Bias' embrace.[17]

Did not Adonis, as he pastured his flock on the hills, drive fair Cytherea to such frenzy that she holds him to her breast even in death?[18]

[17] Bias loved Pero, daughter of Nereus of Pylos, whose price for his daughter's hand was recovery of his cattle, stolen by Phlyacus. Melampus, Bias' brother, recovered them from Mt. Othrys in Thessaly, and Bias married Pero, who bore Alphesiboea, "Cattle bringer" (Hom. *Od.* 11.281–97, 15.230–38; Pherec. *FGH* 3 F 33; ps.-Apollod. *Bibl.* 1.9.12). [18] On Adonis, the young lover of Aphrodite (Cytherea), whose death and rebirth were celebrated annually, see *Id.* 15.100–144 and Bion's *Lament* (pp. 504–17). The goatherd probably refers to the familiar tableau of the dying Adonis in Aphrodite's arms (Bion, ll. 40–42).

ζαλωτὸς μὲν ἐμὶν ὁ τὸν ἄτροπον ὕπνον ἰαύων
50 Ἐνδυμίων· ζαλῶ δέ, φίλα γύναι, Ἰασίωνα,
ὃς τόσσων ἐκύρησεν, ὅσσ' οὐ πευσεῖσθε, βέβαλοι.

Ἀλγέω τὰν κεφαλάν, τὶν δ' οὐ μέλει. οὐκέτ' ἀείδω,
κεισεῦμαι δὲ πεσών, καὶ τοὶ λύκοι ὧδέ μ' ἔδονται.
ὡς μέλι τοι γλυκὺ τοῦτο κατὰ βρόχθοιο γένοιτο.

I envy Endymion, who slumbers undisturbed for ever;[19]
and I envy Iasion, dear lady, whose fate was of a kind that
you who are not initiates will never know.[20]

My head is aching, but you don't care. My song is ended.
I shall die where I fall, and the wolves will devour me just
so. May that be as sweet as honey in your throat.

[19] Endymion was usually said to be a hunter but was some-
times said to have pastured flocks (Serv. on Virg. *Geo.* 3.391). The
Moon sent him to sleep so that she could kiss him at will (schol.
ad loc.).

[20] Iasion, a Cretan shepherd loved by Demeter, was according
to some accounts killed by Zeus with a thunderbolt (Hom. *Od.*
5.125; Hes. *Theog.* 969–74). Here it is implied that he is con-
nected with a mystery cult of the goddess (cf. Diod. Sic. 5.49.4,
5.48.4–5).

IDYLL 4

*This poem is a dialogue between Battus, whose conversa-
tion is spiced with irony and cynicism, and the literal-
minded Corydon. Its themes have something in common
with* Idyll 1: *the effect on the pastoral world of an oxherd
singer's absence, the survival of song, the closing reaf-
firmation of earthy sexuality. Unlike in* Idyll 1, *however,
the pastoral world is here open to external influences:
Aegon is drawn away to compete at Olympia, and the lat-
est songs by Glauce and Pyrrhus are performed in the
countryside.*

The setting is near Croton, in the south of Italy.

Criticism

Hunter, *Selection*, 129–44.
Segal, C. "Theocritean Criticism and the Interpretation of
the Fourth Idyll." *Ramus* 1 (1972): 1–25 = *Poetry and
Myth*, 85–109.

4

ΒΑΤΤΟΣ
Εἰπέ μοι, ὦ Κορύδων, τίνος αἱ βόες; ἦ ῥα Φιλώνδα;

ΚΟΡΤΔΩΝ
οὔκ, ἀλλ' Αἴγωνος· βόσκειν δέ μοι αὐτὰς ἔδωκεν.

ΒΑΤΤΟΣ
ἦ πᾴ ψε κρύβδαν τὰ ποθέσπερα πάσας ἀμέλγες;

ΚΟΡΤΔΩΝ
ἀλλ' ὁ γέρων ὑφίητι τὰ μοσχία κἠμὲ φυλάσσει.

ΒΑΤΤΟΣ
5 αὐτὸς δ' ἐς τίν' ἄφαντος ὁ βουκόλος ᾤχετο χώραν;

ΚΟΡΤΔΩΝ
οὐκ ἄκουσας; ἄγων νιν ἐπ' Ἀλφεὸν ᾤχετο Μίλων.

ΒΑΤΤΟΣ
καὶ πόκα τῆνος ἔλαιον ἐν ὀφθαλμοῖσιν ὀπώπει;

ΚΟΡΤΔΩΝ
φαντί νιν Ἡρακλῆι βίην καὶ κάρτος ἐρίσδειν.

---

1 Probably Aegon's father, as the scholia suggest.

2 The river at Olympia. Milon of Croton was a famous sixth-century Olympic wrestler. Theocritus seems to have chosen the name for its athletic associations or for its links with Croton; the poem is not set in the distant past.

IDYLL 4

BATTUS

Tell me, Corydon, whose cows are these? Do they belong
to Philondas?

CORYDON

No, to Aegon. He gave me them to pasture.

BATTUS

I daresay you milk them all on the quiet in the evening?

CORYDON

No, the old man[1] puts their calves under them and keeps
his eye on me.

BATTUS

And their master the oxherd, which country has he disap-
peared to?

CORYDON

Haven't you heard? Milon has gone off with him to the
Alpheus.[2]

BATTUS

And when has he ever set eyes on oil?[3]

CORYDON

They say he's a match for Heracles in strength and might.

[3] Oil with which athletes anointed themselves (cf. *Id.* 2.51, 79,
156).

THEOCRITUS

ΒΑΤΤΟΣ

κἤμ᾽ ἔφαθ᾽ ἁ μάτηρ Πολυδεύκεος ἦμεν ἀμείνω.

ΚΟΡΥΔΩΝ

10 κᾤχετ᾽ ἔχων σκαπάναν τε καὶ εἴκατι τουτόθε μῆλα.

ΒΑΤΤΟΣ

πείσαι κα Μίλων καὶ τὼς λύκος αὐτίκα λυσσῆν.

ΚΟΡΥΔΩΝ

ταὶ δαμάλαι δ᾽ αὐτὸν μυκώμεναι αἵδε ποθεῦντι.

ΒΑΤΤΟΣ

δείλαιαί γ᾽ αὗται, τὸν βουκόλον ὡς κακὸν εὗρον.

ΚΟΡΥΔΩΝ

ἦ μὰν δείλαιαί γε, καὶ οὐκέτι λῶντι νέμεσθαι.

ΒΑΤΤΟΣ

15 τήνας μὲν δή τοι τᾶς πόρτιος αὐτὰ λέλειπται
τὠστία. μὴ πρῶκας σιτίζεται ὥσπερ ὁ τέττιξ;

11 κα Ahrens: κε m: τοι m

---

[4] One of the twin Dioscuri, famous for his boxing (cf. *Id.* 22.27–134).

[5] According to the scholia, digging was a part of training. The sheep are for him to eat while he trains. Athletes were proverbial for gluttony (cf. 33–34; Ath. 10.412d–414d).

[6] It is not clear whether this refers to Milon's powers of persuasion (though persuading wolves to go mad seems a modest feat) or to the fact that the loss of twenty sheep is equivalent to a raid by wolves, so that Milon might as well have driven them rabid in the first place.

IDYLL 4

BATTUS

Yes; and my mother used to say I was better than Poly-
deuces.[4]

CORYDON

And he's gone taking his shovel and twenty sheep from
here.[5]

BATTUS

Milon could even persuade wolves to go mad in an in-
stant.[6]

CORYDON

The heifers are lowing and longing for him.[7]

BATTUS

Well they *are* wretched. What a poor herdsman they've
found![8]

CORYDON

Wretched they certainly are, and they don't want to graze
any more.

BATTUS

In fact the calf has just bones left. Does she feed on dew
like a cicada?[9]

---

[7] Corydon believes the animals are grieving (cf. 1.74–75; *Epit. Bion.* 23–24), but Battus will imply that their lowing has a more mundane explanation.

[8] Battus criticizes Aegon for leaving, but also perhaps Corydon for neglecting his duties.

[9] The cicada was generally believed to eat nothing but dew (Hes. [*Sc.*] 393–97; Arist. *Hist. an.* 532b13, 556b16, *Part. an.* 682a25; Callim. Fr. 1.34).

ΚΟΡΤΔΩΝ

οὐ Δᾶν, ἀλλ' ὅκα μέν νιν ἐπ' Αἰσάροιο νομεύω
καὶ μαλακῶ χόρτοιο καλὰν κώμυθα δίδωμι,
ἄλλοκα δὲ σκαίρει τὸ βαθύσκιον ἀμφὶ Λάτυμνον.

ΒΑΤΤΟΣ

20 λεπτὸς μὰν χὠ ταῦρος ὁ πυρρίχος. αἴθε λάχοιεν
τοὶ τῶ Λαμπριάδα, τοὶ δαμόται ὅκκα θύωντι
τᾷ Ἥρᾳ, τοιόνδε· κακοχράσμων γὰρ ὁ δᾶμος.

ΚΟΡΤΔΩΝ

καὶ μὰν ἐς στομάλιμνον ἐλαύνεται ἔς τε τὰ Φύσκω,
καὶ ποτὶ τὸν Νήαιθον, ὅπᾳ καλὰ πάντα φύοντι,
25 αἰγίπυρος καὶ κνύζα καὶ εὐώδης μελίτεια.

ΒΑΤΤΟΣ

φεῦ φεῦ βασεῦνται καὶ ταὶ βόες, ὦ τάλαν Αἴγων,
εἰς Ἀίδαν, ὅκα καὶ τὺ κακᾶς ἠράσσαο νίκας,
χἀ σῦριγξ εὐρῶτι παλύνεται, ἅν ποκ' ἐπάξα.

ΚΟΡΤΔΩΝ

οὐ τήνα γ', οὐ Νύμφας, ἐπεὶ ποτὶ Πῖσαν ἀφέρπων
30 δῶρον ἐμοί νιν ἔλειπεν· ἐγὼ δέ τις εἰμὶ μελικτάς,
κεὖ μὲν τὰ Γλαύκας ἀγκρούομαι, εὖ δὲ τὰ Πύρρω.

22 κακοφράσμων m, Meineke

10 Lit., "No, by Earth." 11 The river that flowed through
Croton (Str. 6.1.12; Ov. *Met.* 15.53–59).

12 I.e., they deserve to make the goddess displeased, and a
thin sacrificial animal is likely to do that. The details are obscure.
Lampriadas may be the hero who gives his name to the deme

CORYDON

Certainly not.[10] Sometimes I pasture her by the Aesarus[11]
and give her a bundle of soft hay, and sometimes she gam-
bols in the dense shade of Mt. Latymnum.

BATTUS

That reddish-colored bull is thin, too. If only Lampriadas'
people could be allotted one like that when the demesmen
sacrifice to Hera! That deme is a bad one.[12]

CORYDON

And yet he's driven to the salt lake and to Physcus' place[13]
and to the Neaethus,[14] where good fodder of every kind
grows—restharrow, fleabane, and fragrant balm.

BATTUS

Oh dear! Your cattle, too, will be gone to Hades, wretched
Aegon, because you, too, are lusting after a miserable vic-
tory; and the pipe you once made is spotted with mold.

CORYDON

Oh no it isn't, by the Nymphs, for as he was going off to
Pisa[15] he left it me as a gift. I'm quite a singer; I strike up
songs of Glauce and Pyrrhus pretty well,[16] and I sing the

(local division of a city, here Croton). The allotting probably re-
fers to division of sacrificial meat among the participants.

[13] The scholia say Physcus is a mountain; they may be right
("the area around Mt. Physcus").

[14] A river north of Croton (Str. 6.1.12).   [15] Poets often
use the nearby town of Pisa as a synonym for Olympia.

[16] Glauce of Chios, a well-known lyre player and singer, is said
to have been connected with Ptolemy II (Ael. *NA* 8.11; Plin. *HN*
10.51); Corydon is proud of his up-to-date repertoire. Pyrrhus is
probably another contemporary.

αἰνέω τάν τε Κρότωνα—"Καλὰ πόλις ἅ τε Ζάκυνθος
. . ."—

καὶ τὸ ποταῷον τὸ Λακίνιον, ᾇπερ ὁ πύκτας
Αἴγων ὀγδώκοντα μόνος κατεδαίσατο μάζας.
35 τηνεὶ καὶ τὸν ταῦρον ἀπ' ὤρεος ἆγε πιάξας
τᾶς ὁπλᾶς κῆδωκ' Ἀμαρυλλίδι, ταὶ δὲ γυναῖκες
μακρὸν ἀνάυσαν, χὠ βουκόλος ἐξεγέλασσεν.

ΒΑΤΤΟΣ

ὦ χαρίεσσ' Ἀμαρυλλί, μόνας σέθεν οὐδὲ θανοίσας
λασεύμεσθ'· ὅσον αἶγες ἐμὶν φίλαι, ὅσσον ἀπέσβης.
40 αἰαῖ τῶ σκληρῶ μάλα δαίμονος ὅς με λελόγχει.

ΚΟΡΔΩΝ

θαρσεῖν χρή, φίλε Βάττε· τάχ' αὔριον ἔσσετ' ἄμει-
νον.
ἐλπίδες ἐν ζωοῖσιν, ἀνέλπιστοι δὲ θανόντες,
χὠ Ζεὺς ἄλλοκα μὲν πέλει αἴθριος, ἄλλοκα δ' ὕει.

ΒΑΤΤΟΣ

θαρσέω. βάλλε κάτωθε τὰ μοσχία· τᾶς γὰρ ἐλαίας
τὸν θαλλὸν τρώγοντι, τὰ δύσσοα.

ΚΟΡΔΩΝ

45   σίτθ', ὁ Λέπαργος,
σίτθ', ἁ Κυμαίθα, ποτὶ τὸν λόφον. οὐκ ἐσακούεις;
ἡξῶ, ναὶ τὸν Πᾶνα, κακὸν τέλος αὐτίκα δωσῶν,

---

17 The chief town of the island of Zacynthus, off the northwest
coast of the Peloponnese. It is not quite clear where Corydon's
quotation begins and ends. With the punctuation given here, he

praises of Croton—"Zacynthus is a fair city . . ."[17]—and of the Lacinian sanctuary that faces the dawn, where Aegon the boxer ate up eighty loaves all by himself.[18] And it was there that he brought the bull from the mountain, grabbing it by the hoof,[19] and gave it to Amaryllis. The women gave a great scream, and the oxherd laughed.

BATTUS

Lovely Amaryllis, you alone we shall not forget, even now that you are dead: you were as dear to me as my goats when your life was extinguished. Oh, what a cruel fate is my lot![20]

CORYDON

Take heart, Battus my friend; tomorrow things may be better. While there's life there's hope; it's the dead who have none. Zeus sometimes gives fine weather, sometimes rain.

BATTUS

I do take heart. Drive the calves up here; they're nibbling the olive shoots, the wretched things.

CORYDON

Hey, Lepargus! Hey, Cymaetha! Go toward the hill, do you hear? If you don't move away from there I'll come straight

gives a brief snatch from an introduction that will have built up to Croton's being the fairest city of all.

[18] A famous temple of Hera at Lacinium, southeast of Croton (Livy 24.3.3–7); athletes would compete at its festivals. For their gluttony cf. line 10.   [19] The famous Milon (see on line 6) is said to have performed a similar feat (Ael. *VH* 12.22).

[20] In these lines again Battus speaks with a portentous irony wasted on Corydon.

εἰ μὴ ἄπει τουτῶθεν. ἴδ᾽ αὖ πάλιν ἅδε ποθέρπει.
αἴθ᾽ ἧς μοι ῥοικόν τι λαγωβόλον, ὥς τυ πάταξα.

BATTOΣ

50 θᾶσαί μ᾽, ὦ Κορύδων, ποττῶ Διός· ἁ γὰρ ἄκανθα
ἁρμοῖ μ᾽ ὧδ᾽ ἐπάταξ᾽ ὑπὸ τὸ σφυρόν. ὡς δὲ βαθεῖαι
τἀτρακτυλλίδες ἐντί. κακῶς ἁ πόρτις ὄλοιτο·
εἰς ταύταν ἐτύπην χασμεύμενος. ἦ ῥά γε λεύσσεις;

KORTΔΩΝ

ναὶ ναί, τοῖς ὀνύχεσσιν ἔχω τέ νιν· ἅδε καὶ αὐτά.

BATTOΣ

55 ὁσσίχον ἐστὶ τὸ τύμμα, καὶ ἁλίκον ἄνδρα δαμάσδει.

KORTΔΩΝ

εἰς ὄρος ὄκχ᾽ ἔρπῃς, μὴ νήλιπος ἔρχεο, Βάττε·
ἐν γὰρ ὄρει ῥάμνοι τε καὶ ἀσπάλαθοι κομόωντι.

BATTOΣ

εἶπ᾽ ἄγε μ᾽, ὦ Κορύδων, τὸ γερόντιον ἦ ῥ᾽ ἔτι μύλλει
τήναν τὰν κυάνοφρυν ἐρωτίδα τᾶς ποκ᾽ ἐκνίσθη;

KORTΔΩΝ

60 ἀκμάν γ᾽, ὦ δείλαιε· πρόαν γε μὲν αὐτὸς ἐπενθών
καὶ ποτὶ τᾷ μάνδρᾳ κατελάμβανον ἁμὸς ἐνήργει.

BATTOΣ

εὖ γ᾽, ὤνθρωπε φιλοῖφα. τό τοι γένος ἢ Σατυρίσκοις
ἐγγύθεν ἢ Πάνεσσι κακοκνάμοισιν ἐρίσδει.

49 τὺ Hermann: τὸ m: τὸ m   57 κάκτοι pap., schol. v.l.

___

21 Lit., "a hare hitter," a stick originally used like a boomerang
for throwing; cf. Id. 7.128.

over and put an end to you, by Pan. Look, she's coming
back again! I wish I'd a stick[21] to get you with.

BATTUS

Look at me, Corydon, for heaven's sake: a thorn has just
got me below the ankle. How densely these spindle thorns
grow![22] A curse on that heifer! I was pricked when I gaped
after her. Can you see it?

CORYDON

Yes, yes; I have it in my nails: here it is.

BATTUS

Such a little wound to fell a big man like me!

CORYDON

When you walk in the mountains don't go barefoot, Battus;
buckthorn and spiny shrubs grow on the mountains.[23]

BATTUS

Now tell me, Corydon, is the old man[24] still grinding that
dark-browed charmer who once tickled his fancy?[25]

CORYDON

Of course he still is, my poor chap.[26] Just the other day I
came across him while he was at it by the cattle pens.

BATTUS

Well done, old lecher! Your sort are not far behind the race
of Satyrs and ugly-legged Pans.

[22] Or, perhaps, "How long they are!" This seems to be a spe-
cies of thistle used as a spindle (Theophr. *Hist. pl.* 6.4.6; Diosc.
3.93).   [23] Condescending humor, treating Battus like an
ignorant child.

[24] Probably Aegon's father (cf. 4).

[25] Continuing the metaphor of thorns from above.

[26] Showing pity and contempt for Battus' ignorance.

IDYLL 5

Comatas the goatherd and Lacon the shepherd bicker and
mock each other. They resolve to have a singing contest but
argue at length even over where it should take place. They
appoint the woodcutter Morson as judge and perform al-
ternating couplets until Comatas is declared the winner.
In the closing lines Comatas celebrates his victory and
warns the billy goat not to mount the females.

The servile status of Comatas and Lacon is matched by
the coarseness of their conversation. If Idyll 1 showed how
bucolic song can complement the sounds of nature, this
poem demonstrates that contests in singing can arise natu-
rally out of, or be a formal complement to, everyday rep-
artee. The closing sexual threat is a variation on the theme
of human sexuality found in their bickering and also in the
contest; and it aligns the structure of the poem with Idylls
1 and 4.

No reason is given for Comatas' victory, which is an-
ticipated in lines 136–37. It has been suggested that Mor-
son judges Lacon's responses, or his final response, to
be somehow inadequate; but he seems to perform well
enough, especially since he is at a disadvantage in having
to respond to themes set by Comatas. Perhaps it is suffi-
cient to say that by speaking first in the dialogue and sing-

ing first in the contest, Comatas is able to maintain the advantage he has throughout the poem.

The setting is near Thurii, in the south of Italy.

Criticism

Crane, G. "Realism in the Fifth Idyll of Theocritus." *TAPhA* 118 (1998): 107–22.

Hutchinson, *Hellenistic Poetry*, 146–47, 171–72, 188–89.

ΚΟΜΑΤΑΣ

Αἶγες ἐμαί, τῆνον τὸν ποιμένα, τὸν Συβαρίταν,
φεύγετε, τὸν Λάκωνα· τό μευ νάκος ἐχθὲς ἔκλεψεν.

ΛΑΚΩΝ

οὐκ ἀπὸ τᾶς κράνας; σίττ', ἀμνίδες· οὐκ ἐσορῆτε
τόν μευ τὰν σύριγγα πρόαν κλέψαντα Κομάταν;

ΚΟΜΑΤΑΣ

5   τὰν ποίαν σύριγγα; τὺ γάρ ποκα, δῶλε Σιβύρτα,
ἐκτάσω σύριγγα; τί δ' οὐκέτι σὺν Κορύδωνι
ἀρκεῖ τοι καλάμας αὐλὸν ποππύσδεν ἔχοντι;

ΛΑΚΩΝ

τάν μοι ἔδωκε Λύκων, ὠλεύθερε. τὶν δὲ τὸ ποῖον
Λάκων ἀγκλέψας ποκ' ἔβα νάκος; εἰπέ, Κομάτα·
10   οὐδὲ γὰρ Εὐμάρᾳ τῷ δεσπότᾳ ἦς τοι ἐνεύδειν.

ΚΟΜΑΤΑΣ

τὸ Κροκύλος μοι ἔδωκε, τὸ ποικίλον, ἀνίκ' ἔθυσε
ταῖς Νύμφαις τὰν αἶγα· τὺ δ', ὦ κακέ, καὶ τόκ'
       ἐτάκευ
βασκαίνων, καὶ νῦν με τὰ λοίσθια γυμνὸν ἔθηκας.

4 πρόαν Briggs: πρώαν Μ

IDYLL 5

COMATAS

You goats, keep away from that shepherd from Sybaris, that Lacon. Yesterday he stole my goatskin cloak.

LACON

Won't you come away from the spring? Come by, you lambs; don't you see Comatas,[1] who stole my panpipe yesterday?

COMATAS

What panpipe? Did you, a slave of Sibyrtas, ever own a panpipe? Isn't it enough for you any longer to toot on a straw whistle with Corydon?

LACON

The one Lycon gave me, Mr. Freeman.[2] But what goatskin of yours did Lacon ever steal and make off with? Tell me that, Comatas! Not even your master Eumaras had one to sleep in.

COMATAS

The one Crocylus gave me, the dappled one, when he sacrificed that goat to the Nymphs. You were consumed with envy then, you scoundrel, and now finally you've left me naked.

---

[1] Comatas is the name of a mythical goatherd whose story is alluded to at *Id.* 7.78–89; but see p. ix n. 4.

[2] Lit., "O freeman," ironical counterpoint to "slave" (5).

ΛΑΚΩΝ

οὐ μαὐτὸν τὸν Πᾶνα τὸν ἄκτιον, οὐ τέ γε Λάκων
15 τὰν βαίταν ἀπέδυσ᾽ ὁ Καλαιθίδος· ἢ κατὰ τήνας
τᾶς πέτρας, ὤνθρωπε, μανεὶς εἰς Κρᾶθιν ἁλοίμαν.

ΚΟΜΑΤΑΣ

οὐ μάν, οὐ ταύτας τὰς λιμνάδας, ὠγαθέ, Νύμφας,
αἴτε μοι ἵλαοί τε καὶ εὐμενέες τελέθοιεν,
οὔ τευ τὰν σύριγγα λαθὼν ἔκλεψε Κομάτας.

ΛΑΚΩΝ

20 αἴ τοι πιστεύσαιμι, τὰ Δάφνιδος ἄλγε᾽ ἀροίμαν.
ἀλλ᾽ ὦν αἴ κα λῇς ἔριφον θέμεν, ἔστι μὲν οὐδέν
ἱερόν, ἀλλά γέ τοι διαείσομαι ἔστε κ᾽ ἀπείπῃς.

ΚΟΜΑΤΑΣ

ὗς ποτ᾽ Ἀθαναίαν ἔριν ἤρισεν. ἠνίδε κεῖται
ὤριφος· ἀλλ᾽ ἄγε καὶ τύ τιν᾽ εὔβοτον ἀμνὸν ἔρειδε.

ΛΑΚΩΝ

25 καὶ πῶς, ὦ κίναδος τύ, τάδ᾽ ἔσσεται ἐξ ἴσω ἄμμιν;
τίς τρίχας ἀντ᾽ ἐρίων ἐποκίξατο; τίς δὲ παρεύσας
αἰγὸς πρατοτόκοιο κακὰν κύνα δήλετ᾽ ἀμέλγειν;

17 οὐ ταύτας Reiske: οὔτ᾽ αὐτὰς m: οὐδ᾽ αὐτὰς m: fort. οὐκ
αὐτὰς (cf. 14)
22 ἀλλ᾽ ἄγε m (cf. 24)
24 τιν᾽ Fritzsche: τὸν M
25 κίναδος τύ Wordsworth: κιναδεῦ fere M

IDYLL 5

LACON

By Pan of the shore himself,[3] I, Lacon, son of Calaethis,[4]
did not strip you of your cloak. If I did, my good man, may
I go mad and leap from that rock into the Crathis.[5]

COMATAS

By these Nymphs of the lake—and may they be kind and
propitious to me—I, Comatas, did not steal away with
your pipe.

LACON

May I have the sufferings of Daphnis if I believe you.[6] But
if you would like to wager a kid—not a big stake, after
all[7]—then I'll compete with you in song until you give in.

COMATAS

A pig once challenged Athena.[8] There: the kid is my stake;
now you put forward a fat lamb.

LACON

And how will that be fair, you trickster? Who shears hair
instead of wool? Who wants to milk a wretched dog when
a goat is at hand which has just given birth for the first
time?

---

[3] Perhaps a reference to a nearby shrine rather than to a formal cult title.

[4] If this is a woman's name, Lacon is trying to be dignified while revealing that he does not know who his father is.

[5] A river near Sybaris (Hdt. 5.45.1; Paus. 7.25.11).

[6] See *Id.* 1.66–145.

[7] Lit., "it's nothing sacred," a proverbial expression (schol.).

[8] More usually this proverb refers to those who claim to be able to teach their betters (Festus *Gloss. Lat.* p. 408 L.).

ΚΟΜΑΤΑΣ

ὅστις νικασεῖν τὸν πλατίον ὡς τὺ πεποίθεις,
σφὰξ βομβέων τέττιγος ἐναντίον. ἀλλὰ γὰρ οὔτι
30 ὤριφος ἰσοπαλής τοι, ἴδ᾽ ὁ τράγος οὗτος· ἔρισδε.

ΛΑΚΩΝ

μὴ σπεῦδ᾽· οὐ γάρ τοι πυρὶ θάλπεαι. ἅδιον ᾀσῇ
τεῖδ᾽ ὑπὸ τὰν κότινον καὶ τἄλσεα ταῦτα καθίξας.
ψυχρὸν ὕδωρ τουτεὶ καταλείβεται· ὧδε πεφύκει
ποία, χἀ στιβὰς ἅδε, καὶ ἀκρίδες ὧδε λαλεῦντι.

ΚΟΜΑΤΑΣ

35 ἀλλ᾽ οὔτι σπεύδω· μέγα δ᾽ ἄχθομαι εἰ τύ με τολμῇς
ὄμμασι τοῖς ὀρθοῖσι ποτιβλέπεν, ὅν ποκ᾽ ἐόντα
παῖδ᾽ ἔτ᾽ ἐγὼν ἐδίδασκον. ἴδ᾽ ἀ χάρις ἐς τί ποχ᾽ ἔρπει·
θρέψαι καὶ λυκιδεῖς, θρέψαι κύνας, ὥς τυ φάγωντι.

ΛΑΚΩΝ

καὶ πόκ᾽ ἐγὼν παρὰ τεῦς τι μαθὼν καλὸν ἢ καὶ
    ἀκούσας
40 μέμναμ᾽, ὦ φθονερὸν τὺ καὶ ἀπρεπὲς ἀνδρίον αὔτως;

ΚΟΜΑΤΑΣ

ἁνίκ᾽ ἐπύγιζόν τυ, τὺ δ᾽ ἄλγεες· αἱ δὲ χίμαιραι
αἵδε κατεβληχῶντο, καὶ ὁ τράγος αὐτὰς ἐτρύπη.

33 τηνεὶ m
37 ποχ᾽ ἔρπει Meineke: ποθέρπει M

COMATAS

Who? A man who is as confident as you are that he will
beat his neighbor, just like a wasp buzzing against a ci-
cada.[9] But since the kid doesn't seem a fair bet to you,
look, here's the billy goat. Start the contest!

LACON

Don't hurry; you're not on fire. You'll sing more sweetly
here, sitting under the wild olive and these trees. Here
cool water drips down; here is grass, and a natural couch,
and here the grasshoppers are chirping.

COMATAS

I'm not in a hurry; but I'm annoyed that you dare to look
me in the face, me who used to teach you when you were
still a boy. See what a good turn comes to at last: rear wolf
cubs, rear dogs, and they'll eat you up.[10]

LACON

And when do I remember ever learning or even hearing
anything good from you, you simply envious and foul little
fellow?

COMATAS

When I was buggering you, and you were in pain; and
these sheep were bleating at you, and the ram mounted
them.

[9] I.e., a person mistakenly confident of winning. The cicada's
song was proverbially tuneful (Callim. Fr. 1. 29–30).

[10] Apparently a reference to proverbial thanklessness. What
form the proverb took is unclear; the dogs seem anticlimactic
after wolf cubs.

ΛΑΚΩΝ

μὴ βάθιον τήνω πυγίσματος, ὑβέ, ταφείης.
ἀλλὰ γὰρ ἔρφ᾽, ὧδ᾽ ἔρπε, καὶ ὕστατα βουκολιαξῇ.

ΚΟΜΑΤΑΣ

45 οὐχ ἐρψῶ τηνεί. τουτεὶ δρύες, ὧδε κύπειρος,
ὧδε καλὸν βομβεῦντι ποτὶ σμάνεσσι μέλισσαι,
ἔνθ᾽ ὕδατος ψυχρῶ κρᾶναι δύο, ταὶ δ᾽ ἐπὶ δένδρει
ὄρνιχες λαλαγεῦντι, καὶ ἁ σκιὰ οὐδὲν ὁμοία
τᾷ παρὰ τίν· βάλλει δὲ καὶ ἁ πίτυς ὑψόθε κώνοις.

ΛΑΚΩΝ

50 ἦ μὰν ἀρνακίδας τε καὶ εἴρια τεῖδε πατησεῖς,
αἴ κ᾽ ἔνθῃς, ὕπνω μαλακώτερα· ταὶ δὲ τραγεῖαι
ταὶ παρὰ τὶν ὄσδοντι κακώτερον ἢ τύ περ ὄσδεις.
στασῶ δὲ κρατῆρα μέγαν λευκοῖο γάλακτος
ταῖς Νύμφαις, στασῶ δὲ καὶ ἁδέος ἄλλον ἐλαίω.

ΚΟΜΑΤΑΣ

55 αἰ δέ κε καὶ τὺ μόλῃς, ἁπαλὰν πτέριν ὧδε πατησεῖς
καὶ γλάχων᾽ ἀνθεῦσαν· ὑπεσσεῖται δὲ χιμαιρᾶν
δέρματα τᾶν παρὰ τὶν μαλακώτερα τετράκις ἀρνᾶν.
στασῶ δ᾽ ὀκτὼ μὲν γαυλὼς τῷ Πανὶ γάλακτος,
ὀκτὼ δὲ σκαφίδας μέλιτος πλέα κηρί᾽ ἐχοίσας.

57 ἀρνᾶν Ahrens: -ῶν M, pap.

IDYLL 5

LACON

May you be buried no deeper than you buggered me, you hunchback![11] But come over here, and you'll be competing for the last time.[12]

COMATAS

I'll not come over there. Here are oak trees, here is galingale, here the bees buzz sweetly round the hives. Two springs of cool water are here, and the birds chatter in the trees, and the shade isn't at all like yours; and the pine tree drops down its cones from above.[13]

LACON

Truly you will be treading here, if you come, on lambskins and on fleeces softer than sleep. Your goatskins there smell worse than you do yourself. And I'll set up a large bowl of white milk for the Nymphs, and another of sweet oil.

COMATAS

But if *you* come here, you will be treading on soft fern and flowering pennyroyal, and goatskins will be spread four times softer than your lambskins there. And I'll set up eight pails of milk for Pan, with combs full of honey.[14]

---

[11] Comatas ingeniously turns the insult to his advantage by both implying that Lacon is underendowed and hoping that in death he will be dug up and eaten by wild animals.

[12] I.e., after being so soundly defeated you will not want to compete again.

[13] The kernels are edible: Ath. 2.57b; Plin. *HN* 15.35.

[14] They rival each other in exaggerated piety; each tries to entice the other with the hope of a share in these offerings.

ΛΑΚΩΝ

60 αὐτόθε μοι ποτέρισδε καὶ αὐτόθε βουκολιάσδευ·
τὰν σαυτῶ πατέων ἔχε τὰς δρύας. ἀλλὰ τίς ἄμμε,
τίς κρινεῖ; αἴθ᾽ ἔνθοι ποχ᾽ ὁ βουκόλος ὧδε Λυκώπας.

ΚΟΜΑΤΑΣ

οὐδὲν ἐγὼ τήνω ποτιδεύομαι· ἀλλὰ τὸν ἄνδρα,
αἰ λῇς, τὸν δρυτόμον βωστρήσομες, ὃς τὰς ἐρείκας
65 τήνας τὰς παρὰ τὶν ξυλοχίζεται· ἔστι δὲ Μόρσων.

ΛΑΚΩΝ

βωστρέωμες.

ΚΟΜΑΤΑΣ

τὺ κάλει νιν.

ΛΑΚΩΝ

ἴθ᾽ ὦ ξένε, μικκὸν ἄκουσον
τεῖδ᾽ ἐνθών· ἄμμες γὰρ ἐρίσδομες, ὅστις ἀρείων
βουκολιαστάς ἐστι. τὺ δ᾽, ὠγαθέ, μήτ᾽ ἐμέ, Μόρσων,
ἐν χάριτι κρίνῃς, μήτ᾽ ὧν τύγα τοῦτον ὀνάσῃς.

ΚΟΜΑΤΑΣ

70 ναί, ποτὶ τᾶν Νυμφᾶν, Μόρσων φίλε, μήτε Κομάτᾳ
τὸ πλέον ἰθύνῃς, μήτ᾽ ὧν τύγα τῷδε χαρίξῃ.
ἅδε τοι ἁ ποίμνα τῶ Θουρίω ἐστὶ Σιβύρτα,
Εὐμάρα δὲ τὰς αἶγας ὁρῇς, φίλε, τῶ Συβαρίτα.

ΛΑΚΩΝ

μὴ τύ τις ἠρώτη, ποττῶ Διός, αἴτε Σιβύρτα
75 αἴτ᾽ ἐμόν ἐστι, κάκιστε, τὸ ποίμνιον; ὡς λάλος ἐσσί.

IDYLL 5

LACON

Compete from where you are, and perform your pastoral song from there; tread your own way and keep to your oak trees. But who will be our judge? I wish Lycopas the ox-herd would come this way!

COMATAS

I have no need of him; but, if you like, let's shout for that fellow, the woodsman, who's cutting heath there near you. It's Morson.

LACON

Let's shout for him.

COMATAS

You call him.

LACON

Come, my friend, come over here and listen for a while. We are competing to see who is better at pastoral singing. And Morson, my good fellow, don't give your verdict to please me, or on the other hand give this man the benefit.

COMATAS

Yes, dear Morson, by the Nymphs, don't give an advantage to Comatas, or on the other hand favor this man. This is the flock of Sibyrtas of Thurii, and here, my friend, you see the goats of Eumaras of Sybaris.

LACON

Did anyone ask you, for god's sake, whether the flock is Sibyrtas' or my own, you rascal? What a prattler you are!

ΚΟΜΑΤΑΣ

βέντισθ' οὗτος, ἐγὼ μὲν ἀλαθέα πάντ' ἀγορεύω
κοὐδὲν καυχέομαι· τύγα μὰν φιλοκέρτομος ἐσσί.

ΛΑΚΩΝ

εἶα λέγ', εἴ τι λέγεις, καὶ τὸν ξένον ἐς πόλιν αὖθις
ζῶντ' ἄφες· ὦ Παιάν, ἦ στωμύλος ἦσθα, Κομᾶτα.

ΚΟΜΑΤΑΣ

80 ταὶ Μοῖσαί με φιλεῦντι πολὺ πλέον ἢ τὸν ἀοιδόν
Δάφνιν· ἐγὼ δ' αὐταῖς χιμάρως δύο πρᾶν ποκ'
ἔθυσα.

ΛΑΚΩΝ

καὶ γὰρ ἔμ' Ὡπόλλων φιλέει μέγα, καὶ καλὸν αὐτῷ
κριὸν ἐγὼ βόσκω· τὰ δὲ Κάρνεα καὶ δὴ ἐφέρπει.

ΚΟΜΑΤΑΣ

πλὰν δύο τὰς λοιπὰς διδυματόκος αἶγας ἀμέλγω,
καί μ' ἁ παῖς ποθορεῦσα "τάλαν," λέγει, "αὐτὸς
85   ἀμέλγεις;"

ΛΑΚΩΝ

φεῦ φεῦ, Λάκων τοι ταλάρως σχεδὸν εἴκατι πληροῖ
τυρῶ, καὶ τὸν ἄναβον ἐν ἄνθεσι παῖδα μολύνει.

ΚΟΜΑΤΑΣ

βάλλει καὶ μάλοισι τὸν αἰπόλον ἁ Κλεαρίστα
τὰς αἶγας παρελᾶντα καὶ ἁδύ τι ποππυλιάσδει.

---

15 I.e., don't be the death of him with your talking (cf. *Id.*
15.88).

16 God of healing, invoked to avert the danger to Morson's life.

IDYLL 5

COMATAS

My good man, everything I say is true, and I'm not boasting. You just like to quarrel.

LACON

Speak then, if you have anything to say, and let our guest go back to town still alive.[15] By Paean,[16] how chattersome you are, Comatas!

COMATAS[17]

The Muses love me much more than Daphnis the singer; I sacrificed two nanny goats to them the other day.

LACON

Yes, and I am a great favorite of Apollo, and I am rearing a fine ram for him: the Carnea will soon be here.[18]

COMATAS

Of the goats that I milk, all but two have had twins, and my girl looks at me and says, "You poor thing, are you milking alone?"[19]

LACON

Good heavens! Lacon fills almost twenty baskets with cheese, and he screws the young lad among the flowers.

COMATAS

And Clearista pelts the goatherd[20] with apples[21] as he drives his flock by her, and she whistles to him sweetly.

[17] The contest begins here.

[18] A yearly festival of Apollo celebrated in the autumn with sacrifices of horned animals (Paus. 3.13.4).

[19] She offers to join him, admiring his rustic prosperity.

[20] I.e., me myself. Clearista is presumably the girl mentioned in line 85.   [21] Tokens of Love.

ΛΑΚΩΝ

90 κἠμὲ γὰρ ὁ Κρατίδας τὸν ποιμένα λεῖος ὑπαντῶν
ἐκμαίνει· λιπαρὰ δὲ παρ' αὐχένα σείετ' ἔθειρα.

ΚΟΜΑΤΑΣ

ἀλλ' οὐ συμβλήτ' ἐστὶ κυνόσβατος οὐδ' ἀνεμώνα
πρὸς ῥόδα, τῶν ἄνδηρα παρ' αἱμασιαῖσι πεφύκει.

ΛΑΚΩΝ

οὐδὲ γὰρ οὐδ' ἀκύλοις ὀρομαλίδες· αἲ μὲν ἔχοντι
95 λεπτὸν ἀπὸ πρίνοιο λεπύριον, αἲ δὲ μελιχραί.

ΚΟΜΑΤΑΣ

κἠγὼ μὲν δωσῶ τᾷ παρθένῳ αὐτίκα φάσσαν,
ἐκ τᾶς ἀρκεύθω καθελών· τηνεὶ γὰρ ἐφίσδει.

ΛΑΚΩΝ

ἀλλ' ἐγὼ ἐς χλαῖναν μαλακὸν πόκον, ὁππόκα πέξω
τὰν οἶν τὰν πέλλαν, Κρατίδᾳ δωρήσομαι αὐτός.

ΚΟΜΑΤΑΣ

100 σίττ' ἀπὸ τᾶς κοτίνω, ταὶ μηκάδες· ὧδε νέμεσθε,
ὡς τὸ κάταντες τοῦτο γεώλοφον αἵ τε μυρῖκαι.

94 ὀμομαλίδες Asclepiades ap. schol.
101 αἵ τε Xylander: ἆιτε M

94

LACON

Yes, and Cratidas drives me, the shepherd, mad with desire when he smoothly comes to meet me[22] and his hair moves brightly to and fro on his neck.

COMATAS

But the briar and anemone are not to be compared with roses that grow in beds by the wall.

LACON

Nor are wild apples to be compared with acorns. From the holm oak the acorn gets a thin rind, but the apples are honey sweet.[23]

COMATAS

I shall soon give my girl a dove, catching it in the juniper bush; that's where it perches.

LACON

And I, when I shear the black ewe, shall present its soft fleece unasked to Cratidas to make a cloak.

COMATAS

Hey, come away from that wild olive, my kids.[24] Browse here by this sloping hill with the tamarisks.

[22] "Smoothly": when applied to an attractive boy, the adjective λειός would usually mean "smooth-skinned"; but in combination with "comes to meet," a meaning nearer "affably" seems more suitable.

[23] The point of the comparison is unclear. Comatas was comparing Clearista with Cratidas, but Lacon seems to continue only the botanical theme.

[24] Comatas must suddenly address his kids, but he fits his call within the framework of the contest. Lacon must respond in kind.

ΛΑΚΩΝ

οὐκ ἀπὸ τᾶς δρυός, οὗτος ὁ Κώναρος ἅ τε Κιναίθα;
τουτεὶ βοσκησεῖσθε ποτ᾽ ἀντολάς, ὡς ὁ Φάλαρος.

ΚΟΜΑΤΑΣ

ἔστι δέ μοι γαυλὸς κυπαρίσσινος, ἔστι δὲ κρατήρ,
105 ἔργον Πραξιτέλευς· τᾷ παιδὶ δὲ ταῦτα φυλάσσω.

ΛΑΚΩΝ

χἀμῖν ἐστι κύων φιλοποίμνιος ὃς λύκος ἄγχει,
ὃν τῷ παιδὶ δίδωμι τὰ θηρία πάντα διώκειν.

ΚΟΜΑΤΑΣ

ἀκρίδες, αἳ τὸν φραγμὸν ὑπερπαδῆτε τὸν ἁμόν,
μή μευ λωβάσησθε τὰς ἀμπέλος· ἐντὶ γὰρ αὖαι.

ΛΑΚΩΝ

110 τοὶ τέττιγες, ὁρῆτε τὸν αἰπόλον ὡς ἐρεθίζω·
οὕτω κὔμμες θην ἐρεθίζετε τὼς καλαμευτάς.

ΚΟΜΑΤΑΣ

μισέω τὰς δασυκέρκος ἀλώπεκας, αἳ τὰ Μίκωνος
αἰεὶ φοιτῶσαι τὰ ποθέσπερα ῥαγίζοντι.

ΛΑΚΩΝ

καὶ γὰρ ἐγὼ μισέω τὼς κανθάρος, οἳ τὰ Φιλώνδα
115 σῦκα κατατρώγοντες ὑπανέμιοι φορέονται.

109 αὖαι m: ἆβαι m: ἄζαι, αὐταί schol. vv. ll.
115 ποτέονται m

96

IDYLL 5

LACON

Won't you come away from the oak tree, Conarus and Cinaetha? Feed here toward the east, where Phalarus is.[25]

COMATAS

I have a pail of cypress wood, and a bowl made by Praxiteles;[26] and I am keeping them for my girl.

LACON

And *I* have a dog devoted to his flock who can throttle wolves, and I am presenting him to my lad for hunting game of all sorts.

COMATAS

Locusts that hop over our fence, don't harm my vines, for they are dried up.[27]

LACON

Cicadas, see how I am provoking the goatherd. Just so do you provoke the reapers.[28]

COMATAS

I detest the foxes with their bushy tails that constantly come in the evening and plunder Micon's vines.[29]

LACON

Yes, and I detest the wind-borne beetles that nibble the figs of Philondas.

[25] Presumably the name of a ram, "Whitehead," "Patch."

[26] A famous Athenian sculptor, who never made any such item.   [27] I.e., not worth eating.

[28] Since the cicada's song was generally admired, the meaning is probably that the reapers are provoked to sing their work songs even louder (cf. *Id.* 10).

[29] Cf. *Id.* 1.48–51.

ΚΟΜΑΤΑΣ

ἦ οὐ μέμνασ', ὅκ' ἐγώ τυ κατήλασα, καὶ τὺ σεσαρώς
εὖ ποτεκιγκλίζευ καὶ τᾶς δρυὸς εἴχεο τήνας;

ΛΑΚΩΝ

τοῦτο μὲν οὐ μέμναμ'· ὅκα μάν ποκα τεῖδέ τυ δήσας
Εὐμάρας ἐκάθηρε, καλῶς μάλα τοῦτό γ' ἴσαμι.

ΚΟΜΑΤΑΣ

120 ἤδη τις, Μόρσων, πικραίνεται· ἦ οὐχὶ παρῆσθεν;
σκίλλας ἰὼν γραίας ἀπὸ σάματος αὐτίκα τίλλοις.

ΛΑΚΩΝ

κἠγὼ μὰν κνίζω, Μόρσων, τινά· καὶ τὺ δὲ λεύσσεις.
ἐνθὼν τὰν κυκλάμινον ὄρυσσέ νυν ἐς τὸν Ἄλεντα.

ΚΟΜΑΤΑΣ

Ἱμέρα ἀνθ' ὕδατος ῥείτω γάλα, καὶ τὺ δέ, Κρᾶθι,
125 οἴνῳ πορφύροις, τὰ δέ τοι σία καρπὸν ἐνείκαι.

ΛΑΚΩΝ

ῥείτω χἀ Συβαρῖτις ἐμὶν μέλι, καὶ τὸ πότορθρον
ἁ παῖς ἀνθ' ὕδατος τᾷ κάλπιδι κηρία βάψαι.

ΚΟΜΑΤΑΣ

ταὶ μὲν ἐμαὶ κύτισόν τε καὶ αἴγιλον αἶγες ἔδοντι,
καὶ σχῖνον πατέοντι καὶ ἐν κομάροισι κέονται.

---

30 Morson needs to avert the malice coming from Lacon.
Squills had apotropaic powers (Plin. *HN* 20.101; Theophr. *Char.*
16.13; cf. on Theoc. *Id.* 7.107).

31 Apotropaic: Plin. *HN* 25.115. A river of the same name on
Cos is mentioned at *Id.* 7.1.

COMATAS

Don't you remember the time I took you from behind, and you grimaced and waggled your rump and held fast to that oak tree?

LACON

That I do not remember, but I do know very well that Eumaras tied you up here and gave you a thrashing.

COMATAS

Someone's getting cross, Morson; or didn't you notice? Go at once and gather squills from an old woman's tomb.[30]

LACON

Indeed I too am irritating someone, Morson; you see it yourself. Go to the Haleis now and dig up cyclamen.[31]

COMATAS

Let Himera flow with milk instead of water, and may you, Crathis, become red with wine, and may you bear fruit.[32]

LACON

And for me let Sybaris flow with honey;[33] and at dawn may my girl dip with her pitcher into honeycomb instead of water.

COMATAS

My goats feed on tree medick and goatwort; they tread mastich underfoot, and lie down on arbutus.

---

[32] A series of *adynata,* or impossibilities. Himera is probably a spring, source of the river Himeras. The Crathis was a river near Sybaris. Comatas perhaps implies that these things are more likely to happen than that he should be losing his temper.

[33] Probably the source of the river Sybaris, which flowed near the city of the same name.

ΛΑΚΩΝ

130 ταῖσι δ᾽ ἐμαῖς ὀίεσσι πάρεστι μὲν ἁ μελίτεια
φέρβεσθαι, πολλὸς δὲ καὶ ὡς ῥόδα κισθὸς ἐπανθεῖ.

ΚΟΜΑΤΑΣ

οὐκ ἔραμ᾽ Ἀλκίππας, ὅτι με πρᾶν οὐκ ἐφίλησε
τῶν ὤτων καθελοῖσ᾽, ὅκα οἱ τὰν φάσσαν ἔδωκα.

ΛΑΚΩΝ

ἀλλ᾽ ἐγὼ Εὐμήδευς ἔραμαι μέγα· καὶ γὰρ ὅκ᾽ αὐτῷ
135 τὰν σύριγγ᾽ ὤρεξα, καλόν τί με κάρτ᾽ ἐφίλησεν.

ΚΟΜΑΤΑΣ

οὐ θεμιτόν, Λάκων, ποτ᾽ ἀηδόνα κίσσας ἐρίσδειν,
οὐδ᾽ ἔποπας κύκνοισι· τὺ δ᾽, ὦ τάλαν, ἐσσὶ φιλεχθής.

ΜΟΡΣΩΝ

παύσασθαι κέλομαι τὸν ποιμένα. τὶν δέ, Κομᾶτα,
δωρεῖται Μόρσων τὰν ἀμνίδα· καὶ τὺ δὲ θύσας
140 ταῖς Νύμφαις Μόρσωνι καλὸν κρέας αὐτίκα πέμψον.

ΚΟΜΑΤΑΣ

πεμψῶ, ναὶ τὸν Πᾶνα. φριμάσσεο, πᾶσα τραγίσκων
νῦν ἀγέλα· κἠγὼν γὰρ ἴδ᾽ ὡς μέγα τοῦτο καχαξῶ
καττῶ Λάκωνος τῶ ποιμένος, ὅττι ποκ᾽ ἤδη
ἀνυσάμαν τὰν ἀμνόν· ἐς ὠρανὸν ὔμμιν ἀλεῦμαι.
145 αἶγες ἐμαί, θαρσεῖτε, κερουχίδες· αὔριον ὔμμε
πάσας ἐγὼ λουσῶ Συβαρίτιδος ἔνδοθι λίμνας.
οὗτος ὁ λευκίτας ὁ κορυπτίλος, εἴ τιν᾽ ὀχευσεῖς
τᾶν αἰγῶν, φλασσῶ τυ, πρὶν ἢ ἐμὲ καλλιερῆσαι

146 κράνας m

100

IDYLL 5

LACON

There is balm for my sheep to graze on, and the eglantine
blooms in abundance, like roses.

COMATAS

I do not love Alcippe, because the other day she did not
take me by the ears and kiss me when I gave her the
dove.[34]

LACON

But *I* am much in love with Eumedes; and when I gave
him the panpipe he gave me a fine kiss.

COMATAS

It's not right, Lacon, for jays to compete against nightin-
gales or hoopoes against swans; but you, you wretch, just
love to quarrel.[35]

MORSON

I order the shepherd to stop. Comatas, it's to you that
Morson awards the lamb. Sacrifice it to the Nymphs and
send a good piece of meat to Lacon at once.

COMATAS

So I shall, by Pan. Snort now, all my flock of kids: look how
much I'll be laughing at the shepherd Lacon, because at
last I've won the lamb. I'll leap you a leap as high as the
sky. Courage, my horned goats! Tomorrow I shall wash you
all in the lake of Sybaris. Hey you, the white butting ram,
if you cover one of the nanny goats before I've sacrificed

---

[34] Hence his partiality for Clearista.
[35] The swan, sacred to Apollo, was reputed to sing beautifully
just before its death (Pl. *Phd.* 84e3–85b9; Callim. Fr. 1.39–40).

ταῖς Νύμφαις τὰν ἀμνόν. ὃ δ᾽ αὖ πάλιν. ἀλλὰ γε-
    νοίμαν,
150 αἰ μή τυ φλάσσαιμι, Μελάνθιος ἀντὶ Κομάτα.

my lamb to the Nymphs, I'll castrate you![36] He's at it again!
If I don't smash your balls, may I be Melanthius instead
of Comatas.[37]

[36] An amusing extension of ritual purity. Normally it was the
person sacrificing who abstained from sexual intercourse.

[37] Odysseus took revenge on the disloyal goatherd Melanthius
by mutilating and killing him (Hom. *Od.* 22.475–77); in particular,
his genitals were cut off.

IDYLL 6

This poem presupposes, and forms a sequel to, Idyll 11, *a
love song of the Cyclops Polyphemus addressed to the sea
nymph Galatea. The Cyclops of* Idyll 11 *gains through
song a palliation for his suffering, but his suffering sets the
tone. In this poem, a singing contest between Daphnis and
Damoetas, the first song reproves Polyphemus for being
backward in love, but the second, sung in the character
of Polyphemus himself, triumphantly justifies his seeming
naïveté and reveals that his neglect of Galatea is in fact an
ingenious strategy. Because the Cyclops' reply is Damoe-
tas' part of the singing contest, the ingenuity is also his:
he shows himself able to respond more than adequately
to Daphnis' challenge. Whether the Cyclops is justifiably
confident in his strategy is less clear. A tradition proba-
bly known to Theocritus told of a son of Polyphemus and
Galatea (Timaeus, FGH 566 F 69). However, the emphasis
on seeing, seeming, and self-delusion, which these songs
share with* Idyll 11, *suggests that Polyphemus' blinding by
Odysseus will be a fitting complement to his lack of insight
and his blindness to the truth.*

If Idyll 5 *depicts one extreme of bucolic competition, this
poem represents the other. The second song does not stand
in opposition to the first, but subtly modifies it. The herds-
men's driving their flocks to the same spot contrasts with*

the bickering over a place to sit in Idyll 5, *and the result of the contest is a harmonious equality. The subject of the two songs, a Homeric shepherd perhaps not far removed in time from the singers and affected by the universal passion of* erôs, *fuses myth, literature, and the bucolic world.*

In the Odyssey *Polyphemus is a savage and solitary one-eyed herdsman. In the fifth and fourth centuries he was a popular subject in drama; Euripides' satyr-play* Cyclops *exploits the humorous potential of Homer's narrative. Polyphemus' love for Galatea was first celebrated in a famous lyric poem, now lost, by Philoxenus in about 400 BC (PMG 815–24; vol. 5, pp. 154–65 Campbell).*

Criticism

Bernsdorff, H. "Polyphem und Daphnis: Zu Theokrits sechsten Idyll." *Philologus* 138 (1994): 38–51.

Bowie, E. "Frame and framed in Theocritus Poems 6 and 7." In Harder, Regtuit, Wakker, *Theocritus*, 91–100.

Cusset, C. *Cyclopodie: édition critique et commenté de l'Idylle VI de Théocrite.* Lyon, 2011.

Fantuzzi and Hunter, *Tradition and Innovation*, 149–51.

Hunter, *Selection*, 243–61.

Hutchinson, *Hellenistic Poetry*, 183–87.

Payne, *Invention of Fiction*, 94–100.

Reed, J. D. "Idyll 6 and the Development of Bucolic after Theocritus." In Clauss and Cuypers, *Companion*, 238–50.

6

ΔΑΜΟΙΤΑΣ ΚΑΙ ΔΑΦΝΙΣ

Δαμοίτας χὠ Δάφνις ὁ βουκόλος εἰς ἕνα χῶρον
τὰν ἀγέλαν ποκ', Ἄρατε, συνάγαγον· ἦς δ' ὁ μὲν
   αὐτῶν
πυρρός, ὁ δ' ἡμιγένειος· ἐπὶ κράναν δέ τιν' ἄμφω
ἑσδόμενοι θέρεος μέσῳ ἄματι τοιάδ' ἄειδον.
5 πρᾶτος δ' ἄρξατο Δάφνις, ἐπεὶ καὶ πρᾶτος ἔρισδεν.

ΔΑΦΝΙΣ

βάλλει τοι, Πολύφαμε, τὸ ποίμνιον ἁ Γαλάτεια
μάλοισιν, δυσέρωτα καὶ αἰπόλον ἄνδρα καλεῦσα·
καὶ τύ νιν οὐ ποθόρησθα, τάλαν τάλαν, ἀλλὰ κάθη-
   σαι
ἁδέα συρίσδων. πάλιν ἅδ', ἴδε, τὰν κύνα βάλλει,
10 ἅ τοι τᾶν ὀίων ἕπεται σκοπός· ἁ δὲ βαΰσδει
εἰς ἅλα δερκομένα, τὰ δέ νιν καλὰ κύματα φαίνει

---

1 χὠ m: καὶ m   7 καὶ Meineke: τὸν M

---

1 The definite article ὁ implies that this is the famous Daphnis
of *Id.* 1.
2 Or "herds," poetic singular for plural. But their being joint
custodians of a single herd better suits the complementary nature
of their songs and their lack of rivalry (42–46).

IDYLL 6

Damoetas and Daphnis the oxherd[1] once brought their herd[2] together to the same place, Aratus.[3] One of them had a downy face, the other a beard half-grown. One summer noon they both sat down at a spring and sang as follows. Daphnis first began, since he first made the challenge.

DAPHNIS

Galatea is pelting your flock with apples,[4] Polyphemus; she calls you a laggardly lover and a goatherd. And you have no regard for her, you poor wretch, but sit piping sweetly. Again—look!—she is pelting the dog that follows you to watch your sheep;[5] it is barking as it looks in the sea, and the fair waves reflect it as it runs along the gently

[3] Probably to be identified with Aratus the Coan friend of Simichidas in *Id.* 7, who is advised to give up pursuing the boy Philinus (98–127). How this poem relates to his affairs is not made explicit, but there is some similarity between Simichidas' advice to Aratus and that of Daphnis to Polyphemus here. There seems to be no good reason to identify this Aratus with the well-known astronomical poet.

[4] Tokens of love: cf. *Idd.* 3.10, 5.88, 11.10. There is wordplay here: $\mu\hat{a}\lambda o\nu$ means "sheep" as well as "apple."

[5] Homer's uncivilized Polyphemus has no dog.

ἄσυχα καχλάζοντος ἐπ' αἰγιαλοῖο θέοισαν.
φράζεο μὴ τᾶς παιδὸς ἐπὶ κνάμαισιν ὀρούσῃ
ἐξ ἁλὸς ἐρχομένας, κατὰ δὲ χρόα καλὸν ἀμύξῃ.
15 ἃ δὲ καὶ αὐτόθε τοι διαθρύπτεται· ὡς ἀπ' ἀκάνθας
ταὶ καπυραὶ χαῖται, τὸ καλὸν θέρος ἁνίκα φρύγει,
καὶ φεύγει φιλέοντα καὶ οὐ φιλέοντα διώκει,
καὶ τὸν ἀπὸ γραμμᾶς κινεῖ λίθον· ἦ γὰρ ἔρωτι
πολλάκις, ὦ Πολύφαμε, τὰ μὴ καλὰ καλὰ πέφανται.

20   Τῷ δ' ἐπὶ Δαμοίτας ἀνεβάλλετο καὶ τάδ' ἄειδεν.

ΔΑΜΟΙΤΑΣ

εἶδον, ναὶ τὸν Πᾶνα, τὸ ποίμνιον ἁνίκ' ἔβαλλε,
κού μ' ἔλαθ', οὐ τὸν ἐμὸν τὸν ἕνα γλυκύν, ᾧ
      ποθορῷμι
ἐς τέλος (αὐτὰρ ὁ μάντις ὁ Τήλεμος ἐχθρ' ἀγορεύων
ἐχθρὰ φέροι ποτὶ οἶκον, ὅπως τεκέεσσι φυλάσσοι)·
25 ἀλλὰ καὶ αὐτὸς ἐγὼ κνίζων πάλιν οὐ ποθόρημι,
ἀλλ' ἄλλαν τινὰ φαμὶ γυναῖκ' ἔχεν· ἃ δ' ἀίοισα
ζαλοῖ μ', ὦ Παιάν, καὶ τάκεται, ἐκ δὲ θαλάσσας
οἰστρεῖ παπταίνοισα ποτ' ἄντρα τε καὶ ποτὶ ποίμνας.

---

22 ποθορῷμι Heinsius: -ῶμαι m: -ημαι m

---

6 Lit., "moves the stone from the line," a proverbial expression. In the board game *pesseia,* moving a counter from the "sacred line" (the middle one of five) was a last resort.

7 The Homeric Polyphemus, by contrast, says, "We Cyclopes care nothing for aegis-bearing Zeus or for the other gods, since we are much superior to them" (*Od.* 9.275–76). At *Id.* 11.29 Polyphemus swears by Zeus.

plashing shore. Take care that it doesn't jump at the girl's legs as she comes out of the sea and doesn't scratch her fair skin. Even from there she is flirting with you: fickle as dry thistledown when fair summer parches it, she flees him who loves her and pursues him who does not, trying every move.[6] Truly, Polyphemus, ugly things often seem fair to love.

After him Damoetas played a prelude and began to sing in this way:

DAMOETAS

By Pan,[7] I saw her when she was pelting my flock, and she did not escape my notice—no, by my sweet single eye, which I hope will see me through to the end of my life.[8] (Let Telemus the prophet take home the foul fate he utters for me, and keep it for his children.)[9] But I myself, too, teasing her in turn, pay her no attention, but claim to have another woman; and hearing this she is jealous, by Paean,[10] and mopes, and is in a frenzy as she gazes on my caves and flocks from the sea. As for the dog, I whistled it

[8] Lit., "by which may I see to the end."

[9] At *Od.* 9.507–16 Polyphemus remembers that a seer called Telemus had predicted that Odysseus would blind him; but the turning of the prediction against Telemus' own family is inspired by *Od.* 2.178–79, where the suitor Eurymachus says to the prophet Halitherses, "Go home and prophesy to your children, in case something bad happens to them in the future."

[10] See *Id.* 5.79n. Here the cry is probably one of triumph rather than an appeal for protection from any malicious effects of Galatea's jealousy.

σίξα δ' ὑλακτεῖν νιν καὶ τᾷ κυνί· καὶ γὰρ ὅκ' ἤρων,
30 αὐτᾶς ἐκνυζεῖτο ποτ' ἰσχία ῥύγχος ἔχοισα.
ταῦτα δ' ἴσως ἐσορεῦσα ποεῦντά με πολλάκι πεμψεῖ
ἄγγελον. αὐτὰρ ἐγὼ κλαξῶ θύρας, ἔστε κ' ὀμόσσῃ
αὐτά μοι στορεσεῖν καλὰ δέμνια τᾶσδ' ἐπὶ νάσω·
καὶ γάρ θην οὐδ' εἶδος ἔχω κακὸν ὥς με λέγοντι.
35 ἦ γὰρ πρᾶν ἐς πόντον ἐσέβλεπον, ἦς δὲ γαλάνα,
καὶ καλὰ μὲν τὰ γένεια, καλὰ δέ μευ ἁ μία κώρα,
ὡς παρ' ἐμὶν κέκριται, κατεφαίνετο, τῶν δέ τ' ὀδό-
    ντων
λευκοτέραν αὐγὰν Παρίας ὑπέφαινε λίθοιο.
ὡς μὴ βασκανθῶ δέ, τρὶς εἰς ἐμὸν ἔπτυσα κόλπον·
40 ταῦτα γὰρ ἁ γραία με Κοτυτταρὶς ἐξεδίδαξε.

42 Τόσσ' εἰπὼν τὸν Δάφνιν ὁ Δαμοίτας ἐφίλησε·
χὢ μὲν τῷ σύριγγ', ὃ δὲ τῷ καλὸν αὐλὸν ἔδωκεν.
αὔλει Δαμοίτας, σύρισδε δὲ Δάφνις ὁ βούτας·
45 ὠρχεῦντ' ἐν μαλακᾷ ταὶ πόρτιες αὐτίκα ποίᾳ.
νίκη μὲν οὐδάλλος, ἀνήσσατοι δ' ἐγένοντο.

29 σίξα Ruhnken: σίγα fere M
36 δέ μευ Ahrens: δέ μοι m: δ' ἐμὶν m
38 αὐγὰ λευκοτέρα Fritzsche (λ. α. iam Meineke): -αν
-ὰν M   41 (= 10.16) om. m

11 Or, less likely, "when I was in love with her, it would whimper <as it rested> with its snout in its flank" (taking αὐτᾶς with ἤρων).
12 The commonplace of the locked-out lover (cf. *Id.* 3). In the *Odyssey* Polyphemus' door is a huge rock, which serves to lock *in*

to bark at her; for when *I* was the lover it would whine and lay its snout right in her lap.[11] Perhaps, when she sees me keep behaving in this way, she will send a messenger. But I shall lock my doors [12] until she swears that she will make my fair bed herself upon this island.[13] Indeed, even my looks are not so bad as they say. The other day, when there was a calm, I was looking into the sea, and in my judgment my beard seemed fair, and fair my single eye, and it[14] reflected the gleam of my teeth whiter than Parian marble.[15] But to avert bad luck I spat in my breast three times, as the old woman Cottytaris had taught me.[16]

After that Damoetas kissed Daphnis; he gave him a pan-pipe, and Daphnis gave Damoetas a flute. Damoetas began to play his flute, and Daphnis his pipe; and the calves at once began to frolic in the soft grass. Neither was victorious; each was undefeated.

Odysseus and his men (9.240–43). Here the plural θύρας (doors) perhaps suggests a more civilized entrance.

[13] I.e., until she formally agrees to be his bedfellow.

[14] Text perhaps corrupt. To understand "the sea" as subject of the verb is awkward; and ὑπέφαινε may be from κατεφαίνετο above.

[15] Marble from Paros was valued for its whiteness: Pind. *Nem.* 4.81; Hor. *Carm.* 1.19.6.

[16] For apotropaic spitting, common in ritual, cf. 7.127, Theophr. *Char.* 16.15, Tib. 1.2.54; three is a magic number. Divine anger can be aroused by boasting and conceit (Pl. *Phd.* 95b5–6); but here there may be a reference to the idea that seeing one's own reflection can bring on a dangerous narcissistic self-absorption (cf. Plut. *Mor.* 682b–c = Euphor. Fr. 189 Lightfoot). The name Cottytaris is to be linked with the Thracian goddess Cotys or Cottyto.

IDYLL 7

This poem is set on the island of Cos and is narrated by a poet called Simichidas. While traveling with friends from the town to a harvest festival in the country, he encounters Lycidas, another poet. A dialogue between the two concludes with Lycidas presenting Simichidas with a throwing stick in acknowledgment of his talent. Each then performs a song. Lycidas' song wishes bon voyage to the boy Ageanax—provided that he first grants the poet his favors—and imagines that once he departs Lycidas will relax at a country party and listen to Tityrus performing a song about the old-time poet Comatas, who was imprisoned in a chest and fed on honey by bees. Simichidas' song treats the love of his friend Aratus for a boy called Philinus; he prays Pan to grant his desire and humorously threatens the god with punishment if he will not do so. The idyll concludes with a long and sensuous description of the harvest celebrations given by Phrasidamus and Antigenes.

This is a tantalizingly complex poem. There are references to real persons and specific places on the island of Cos, but the identity of the two poets is made mysterious. It is tempting to identify the narrator Simichidas ("son of Simichus") with Theocritus, especially if the Aratus mentioned here (98) is the same as the addressee of Idyll 6; but Theocritus' father is said to have been Praxagoras (T 1–2,

*pp. 2–5). Possibly Simichidas is a nickname for which we
have no other evidence (cf. Sicelidas for Asclepiades in l.
40). Lycidas is enigmatic. Although he is explicitly said to
be a goatherd (13), there are hints that his sudden appear-
ance is a sort of epiphany. The time is midday, when gods
tend to be abroad (cf. Id. 1.15–17); his laughter (19–20,
42, 128) and his rank smell (16) allude to the joviality and
fragrance of divinities in literature; and his gift of a stick
to Simichidas evokes the Muses' gift of a staff to Hesiod as
token of his investiture as a poet at the beginning of the
Theogony. There is probably a reference, too, to the poet
Archilochus' encounter with the Muses as he drove a cow
to town (SEG XV 517 = T 3 Gerber). If (in spite of l. 13)
Lycidas is to be understood as a god in disguise, then the
most likely candidate is Apollo, who as Apollo Nomios was
associated with herdsmen, and who had a Coan shrine at
Pyxa, Lycidas' destination (130–31). In that case the god
of poetry himself would be shown acknowledging Simich-
idas' work and approving the aesthetic of short, unpreten-
tious, and refined poetry advocated by Callimachus and
practiced by Theocritus (see p. viii).*

*The structure of the poem is familiar: two songs are set
within a frame of dialogue and description. Readers are
left to evaluate the merits of each. There are hints that, like
Idyll 1, the poem enacts the origins, or presents two ele-
ments, of pastoral poetry: Simichidas is from the town,
Lycidas from the country, and their meeting gives way to
a lush description of a rural festival that combines learned
allusion with the sights and sounds of nature—the town
poet is treating country themes. It has also been plausibly
suggested that the poem contains allusions to works by
Philitas of Cos, an important forerunner of the Hellenistic*

poets, who is explicitly praised by Simichidas (40). At any rate, it suggests an etiology of bucolic poetry and implies an association with the symposium (63ff.). The mythical poet Comatas, once imprisoned in a chest and fed by bees in recognition of the sweetness of his song, provides a further possible origin for the genre.

Criticism

Arnott, W. G. "The Mound of Brasilas and Theocritus' Seventh *Idyll*." *QUCC* 32, n.s. 3 (1979): 99–106.

Bowie, E. L. "Theocritus' Seventh *Idyll*, Philetas and Longus." *CQ* 35 (1985): 67–91.

Goldhill, *Poet's Voice*, 225–40.

Hunter, *Selection*, 144–99.

Ott, U. "Theokrits 'Thalysien' und ihre literarische Vorbilder." *RhM* 115 (1972): 134–49.

Payne, *Invention of Fiction*, 114–45.

Puelma, M. "Die Dichterbegegnung in Theokrits 'Thalysien.'" *MH* 17 (1960): 144–64.

Seeck, G. A. "Dichterische Technik in Theokrits 'Thalysien' und die Theorie der Hirtendichtung." In ΔΩΡΗΜΑ *Hans Diller zum 70. Geburtstag,* edited by K. Vourveris and A. D. Skiadas, 195–209. Athens, 1975.

Segal, C. "Theocritus' Seventh Idyll and Lycidas." *WS* 87 (1974): 20–76 = *Poetry and Myth,* 110–66.

Williams, F. J. "A Theophany in Theocritus." *CQ* 21 (1971): 136–45.

Ἧς χρόνος ἁνίκ' ἐγών τε καὶ Εὔκριτος εἰς τὸν
    Ἅλεντα
εὕρπομες ἐκ πόλιος, σὺν καὶ τρίτος ἄμμιν Ἀμύντας.
τᾷ Δηοῖ γὰρ ἔτευχε θαλύσια καὶ Φρασίδαμος
κἀντιγένης, δύο τέκνα Λυκωπέος, εἴ τί περ ἐσθλὸν
5 χαῶν τῶν ἐπάνωθεν ἀπὸ Κλυτίας τε καὶ αὐτῶ
Χάλκωνος, Βούριναν ὃς ἐκ ποδὸς ἄννε κράναν
εὖ ἐνερεισάμενος πέτρᾳ γόνυ· ταὶ δὲ παρ' αὐτάν
αἴγειροι πτελέαι τε ἐύσκιον ἄλσος ὕφαινον
χλωροῖσιν πετάλοισι κατηρεφέες κομόωσαι.
10 κοὔπω τὰν μεσάταν ὁδὸν ἄνυμες, οὐδὲ τὸ σᾶμα
ἁμῖν τὸ Βρασίλα κατεφαίνετο, καί τιν' ὁδίταν
ἐσθλὸν σὺν Μοίσαισι Κυδωνικὸν εὕρομες ἄνδρα,
οὔνομα μὲν Λυκίδαν, ἦς δ' αἰπόλος, οὐδέ κέ τίς νιν
ἠγνοίησεν ἰδών, ἐπεὶ αἰπόλῳ ἔξοχ' ἐῴκει.
15 ἐκ μὲν γὰρ λασίοιο δασύτριχος εἶχε τράγοιο
κνακὸν δέρμ' ὤμοισι νέας ταμίσοιο ποτόσδον,
ἀμφὶ δέ οἱ στήθεσσι γέρων ἐσφίγγετο πέπλος

---

5 ἐπάνωθεν Reiske: ἔτ' ἀν- M   7 εὖ pap., coni. Her-
mann: εὖ γ' M   8 ὕφαινον Heinsius: ἔφαινον M

---

1 They are walking from Cos town westward to "the Haleis,"
a village or a river in the deme of that name, which had a sanctu-
ary of Demeter.

IDYLL 7

Some time ago Eucritus and I were on our way from town to the Haleis, and Amyntas made a third with us.[1] Phrasidamus and Antigenes were preparing a harvest festival for Demeter, the two sons of Lycopeus, noble, if anyone is, among men illustrious on account of their descent from Clytia and Chalcon himself,[2] who by setting his knee firmly against a rock made the fountain Bourina spring up beneath his foot. Nearby, poplars and elms wove a shady grove with their green foliage arching above.

We had not yet reached the midpoint of our journey, and the tomb of Brasilas had not come in sight, when thanks to the Muses we encountered a fine man of Cydonia.[3] Lycidas was his name, and he was a goatherd; at a glance no one could have mistaken him, for he looked very much like a goatherd. Over his shoulders he was wearing the tawny skin of a thick-haired, shaggy goat smelling of fresh rennet,[4] round his breast an old cloak was tied with a broad

[2] I.e., Phrasidamus and Antigenes are from a venerable family. Clytia was daughter of Merops, an early hero of Cos; she married Eurypylus, a son of Poseidon, and bore him Chalcon and Antagoras, according to the scholia. The story of the spring's creation, not known from elsewhere, is of a common etiological type (cf. Hippocrene), but why the pressure of Chalcon's knee is emphasized is not clear.   [3] Perhaps a place on Cos. The best-known Cydonia was in Crete.   [4] A pungent extract from calves' stomachs used for curdling milk.

ζωστῆρι πλακερῷ, ῥοικὰν δ' ἔχεν ἀγριελαίω
δεξιτερᾷ κορύναν. καί μ' ἀτρέμας εἶπε σεσαρώς
20 ὄμματι μειδιόωντι, γέλως δέ οἱ εἴχετο χείλευς·
"Σιμιχίδα, πᾷ δὴ τὺ μεσαμέριον πόδας ἕλκεις,
ἁνίκα δὴ καὶ σαῦρος ἐν αἱμασιαῖσι καθεύδει,
οὐδ' ἐπιτυμβίδιοι κορυδαλλίδες ἠλαίνοντι;
ἦ μετὰ δαῖτ' ἄκλητος ἐπείγεαι, ἤ τινος ἀστῶν
25 λανὸν ἔπι θρῴσκεις; ὥς τοι ποσὶ νισσομένοιο
πᾶσα λίθος πταίοισα ποτ' ἀρβυλίδεσσιν ἀείδει."
τὸν δ' ἐγὼ ἀμείφθην· "Λυκίδα φίλε, φαντί τυ πάντες
ἦμεν συρικτὰν μέγ' ὑπείροχον ἔν τε νομεῦσιν
ἔν τ' ἀματήρεσσι. τὸ δὴ μάλα θυμὸν ἰαίνει
30 ἀμέτερον· καίτοι κατ' ἐμὸν νόον ἰσοφαρίζειν
ἔλπομαι. ἁ δ' ὁδὸς ἅδε θαλυσιάς· ἦ γὰρ ἑταῖροι
ἀνέρες εὐπέπλῳ Δαμάτερι δαῖτα τελεῦντι
ὄλβω ἀπαρχόμενοι· μάλα γάρ σφισι πίονι μέτρῳ
ἁ δαίμων εὔκριθον ἀνεπλήρωσεν ἀλωάν.
35 ἀλλ' ἄγε δή, ξυνὰ γὰρ ὁδὸς ξυνὰ δὲ καὶ ἀώς,
βουκολιασδώμεσθα· τάχ' ὥτερος ἄλλον ὀνασεῖ.
καὶ γὰρ ἐγὼ Μοισᾶν καπυρὸν στόμα, κἠμὲ λέγοντι
πάντες ἀοιδὸν ἄριστον· ἐγὼ δέ τις οὐ ταχυπειθής,
οὐ Δᾶν· οὐ γάρ πω κατ' ἐμὸν νόον οὔτε τὸν ἐσθλὸν
40 Σικελίδαν νίκημι τὸν ἐκ Σάμω οὔτε Φιλίταν

28 ἦμεν Wilamowitz: ἔμμεν(αι) M
40 Φιλίταν Croenert: -ήταν M

---

5 Its crest was reminiscent of the floral decoration on grave-
stones, and a fable accounted for this with the story that it buried

belt, and in his right hand he held a crooked club of wild olive. With a twinkle in his eye he grinned complacently, and laughter hung about his lips as he said to me, "Simichidas, where are you going on foot in the middle of the day, when even the lizard sleeps in the walls and the tomb-crested[5] larks are not about? Are you hurrying to gate-crash a dinner, or rushing off to some citizen's store of wine? As your feet go along all the pebbles are ringing as they strike against your boots."

"Lycidas my friend," I replied, "everyone among the herdsmen and reapers says that you are far and away the most eminent piper, and it gladdens my heart to hear it; and yet in my own opinion I think I can rival you. It's to a harvest festival that we are traveling. Some friends of mine are arranging a feast for fair-robed Demeter as an offering of firstfruits from their copious stores; the goddess has filled their threshing floors with good grain in rich measure. But come, since we are traveling the same road at the same time, let's perform bucolic songs, and maybe each of us will benefit the other. I myself am a clear voice of the Muses, and everyone says I'm an excellent singer—not that I'm quick to believe them, by Zeus; in my own opinion I'm not yet a match in song for the great Sicelidas from Samos, or for Philitas,[6] but compete with them like

its father in its head (cf. Ar. *Av.* 472–75). But the epithet may in fact mean "tomb-haunting": cf. lines 10–11.

[6] Sicelidas: another name for Asclepiades, an older contemporary of Theocritus, who wrote lyric poetry now lost and epigrams, several of which are preserved in the *Greek Anthology*. Philitas: a poet and scholar, born about 340, who was tutor to the young Ptolemy Philadelphus and composed learned poetry, including elegiacs to his mistress Bittis.

ἀείδων, βάτραχος δὲ ποτ' ἀκρίδας ὥς τις ἐρίσδω."
ὣς ἐφάμαν ἐπίταδες· ὁ δ' αἰπόλος ἁδὺ γελάσσας,
"τάν τοι," ἔφα, "κορύναν δωρύττομαι, οὕνεκεν ἐσσί
πᾶν ἐπ' ἀλαθείᾳ πεπλασμένον ἐκ Διὸς ἔρνος.
45   ὥς μοι καὶ τέκτων μέγ' ἀπέχθεται ὅστις ἐρευνῇ
ἶσον ὄρευς κορυφᾷ τελέσαι δόμον Ὠρομέδοντος,
καὶ Μοισᾶν ὄρνιχες ὅσοι ποτὶ Χῖον ἀοιδόν
ἀντία κοκκύζοντες ἐτώσια μοχθίζοντι.
ἀλλ' ἄγε βουκολικᾶς ταχέως ἀρξώμεθ' ἀοιδᾶς,
50   Σιμιχίδα· κἠγὼ μέν–ὅρη, φίλος, εἴ τοι ἀρέσκει
τοῦθ' ὅτι πρᾶν ἐν ὄρει τὸ μελύδριον ἐξεπόνασα.

Ἔσσεται Ἀγεάνακτι καλὸς πλόος ἐς Μιτυλήναν,
χὥταν ἐφ' ἑσπερίοις Ἐρίφοις νότος ὑγρὰ διώκῃ
κύματα, χὠρίων ὅτ' ἐπ' ὠκεανῷ πόδας ἴσχει,
55   αἴ κα τὸν Λυκίδαν ὀπτεύμενον ἐξ Ἀφροδίτας
ῥύσηται· θερμὸς γὰρ ἔρως αὐτῶ με καταίθει.
χαλκυόνες στορεσεῦντι τὰ κύματα τάν τε θάλασσαν
τόν τε νότον τόν τ' εὖρον, ὃς ἔσχατα φυκία κινεῖ,

---

7 Probably in order to provoke Lycidas to a contest rather than
to conciliate him.   8 Lit., "with a sweet laugh"; but the ex-
pression usually refers to derisive laughter.

9 Referring to Simichidas' honest appraisal of his own talent
(39–41). Zeus as god of the weather controls the shape of trees as
they grow.

10 Probably what is now called Mt. Dikeo, the highest part of
the chain of mountains visible on the travelers' left.

11 Homer; the poet of the *Homeric Hymn to Apollo* "lives in
rocky Chios" (172). In these two images, and in line 51 ("little
song . . . worked hard at"), Lycidas is seen to be allying himself
with the aesthetic of small-scale, finely crafted poetry advocated

a frog against crickets." I chose my words carefully;[7] and with a laugh[8] the goatherd said, "I present you with this stick of mine, because you are a sapling molded for truth by Zeus.[9] I very much dislike the builder who strives to produce a house as high as Mt. Oromedon[10] and those cocks of the Muses who vainly struggle to crow in rivalry with the Chian bard.[11] But come, let's begin our bucolic songs at once, Simichidas, and I[12]—see, my friend, whether you like this little song which I worked hard at the other day on the hill.

"'Ageanax shall have a good voyage to Mitylene[13] both when the Kids appear at evening and the south wind drives before it the waves of the sea and when Orion's feet touch the ocean,[14] if only he will rescue Lycidas from his roasting by Aphrodite: a hot love for him is burning me up. The halcyons[15] will smooth the sea, its waves, the south wind and the east wind that stirs up the seaweed in its

most memorably by Callimachus (e.g., *Hymn* 2.105; *Epigr.* 27.3–4; *Aet.* Fr. 1).

[12] He is about to speak proudly of his composition but checks himself.   [13] Ageanax is due to sail, when the weather is propitious, from Cos to Mitylene on Lesbos, a distance of nearly two hundred miles. Poems wishing bon voyage were common, and came later to be termed *propemptika*.

[14] The Kids (*Haedi*) and Orion are associated with storms (e.g., Aratus *Phaen.* 158, 300–310; Hor. *Carm.* 3.1.28, 1.28.21), and the times indicated here are in late October or November. Lycidas' point is that Ageanax will have a safe voyage even if he sails at the worst time, provided that he "rescues" Lycidas first.

[15] Halcyons were believed to be able to calm the sea during the "halcyon days," fourteen days around the winter solstice, when they tended their floating nests (Arist. *Hist. an.* 542b4–17).

ἀλκυόνες, γλαυκαῖς Νηρηΐσι ταί τε μάλιστα
60 ὀρνίχων ἐφίληθεν, ὅσοις τέ περ ἐξ ἁλὸς ἄγρα.
Ἀγεάνακτι πλόον διζημένῳ ἐς Μιτυλήναν
ὥρια πάντα γένοιτο, καὶ εὔπλοος ὅρμον ἵκοιτο.
κἠγὼ τῆνο κατ᾽ ἆμαρ ἀνήτινον ἢ ῥοδόεντα
ἢ καὶ λευκοΐων στέφανον περὶ κρατὶ φυλάσσων
65 τὸν Πτελεατικὸν οἶνον ἀπὸ κρατῆρος ἀφυξῶ
πὰρ πυρὶ κεκλιμένος, κύαμον δέ τις ἐν πυρὶ φρυξεῖ.
χἀ στιβὰς ἐσσεῖται πεπυκασμένα ἔστ᾽ ἐπὶ πᾶχυν
κνύζᾳ τ᾽ ἀσφοδέλῳ τε πολυγνάμπτῳ τε σελίνῳ.
καὶ πίομαι μαλακῶς μεμναμένος Ἀγεάνακτος
70 αὐταῖς ἐν κυλίκεσσι καὶ ἐς τρύγα χεῖλος ἐρείδων.
αὐλησεῦντι δέ μοι δύο ποιμένες, εἷς μὲν Ἀχαρνεύς,
εἷς δὲ Λυκωπίτας· ὁ δὲ Τίτυρος ἐγγύθεν ᾀσεῖ
ὥς ποκα τᾶς Ξενέας ἠράσσατο Δάφνις ὁ βούτας,
χὤς ὄρος ἀμφεπονεῖτο καὶ ὡς δρύες αὐτὸν ἐθρήνευν
75 Ἱμέρα αἵτε φύοντι παρ᾽ ὄχθαισιν ποταμοῖο,
εὖτε χιὼν ὥς τις κατετάκετο μακρὸν ὑφ᾽ Αἷμον
ἢ Ἄθω ἢ ῥοδόπαν ἢ Καύκασον ἐσχατόωντα.

60 ὅσοις Greverus: -αις M   62 εὔπλοος Schaefer: -ον M
70 αὐταῖς ἐν Valckenaer (ἐν αὐταῖς schol.): αὐταῖσιν M

16 Lit., "those whose prey is from the sea."
17 Ptelea: perhaps a place on Cos.
18 Lit., "cubit-deep."   19 Text uncertain; lit., "having remembrance of Ageanax in my very cups."
20 Probably Coan place-names, though the only known Acharnae is a deme in Attica.   21 The Himeras is a river in Sicily. On the myth of Daphnis see p. 16. Stesichorus, the sixth-century poet who sang about him, was from the town of Himera.

lowest depths—the halcyons, birds dearest to the sea-
green Nereids and to fishermen.[16] Ageanax wants to set
sail to Mitylene; may everything be in his favor, and may
he reach the harbor after a good voyage. On that day I shall
garland my head with dill or roses or white stocks and draw
Ptelean[17] wine from the bowl as I lie by the fire while
someone roasts beans for me there. I shall have a couch
knee-deep[18] with fleabane, asphodel and curly-leafed cel-
ery, and I shall drink in comfort as I toast Ageanax with
each cup[19] and drain each to the dregs. Two shepherds will
play the pipes for me, one from Acharnae, the other from
Lycope,[20] and close by them Tityrus will sing how Daphnis
the oxherd once loved Xenea, and how the mountains la-
mented for him and the oak trees that grow on the banks
of the river Himeras sang his dirge[21] as he wasted away
like snow under Haemus or Athos or Rhodope or furthest
Caucasus.[22] He will sing[23] how the goatherd was once en-

[22] Haemus and Rhodope: the highest mountains in the Balkan
range (Str. 7.5.1). Athos: the most prominent peak in the northern
Aegean region.

[23] The remainder of Lycidas' song seems to presuppose more
knowledge than we have. It deals with two further founding fig-
ures of country song, the unnamed "goatherd" (78) and Comatas.
An ancient commentary records the tale of an unnamed south
Italian shepherd who sacrificed some of his master's sheep to
the Muses and was punished by being shut in a chest; two months
later the chest was opened and the shepherd found safe and well,
feeding on honeycomb (Lycos of Rhegium, *FGH* 570 F 7). Why
Comatas too was enclosed in a box (83–84) is entirely mysterious.
(On another view the goatherd and Comatas are the same person,
and "you too" means "you, like Daphnis," Daphnis according to
one tradition having been exposed as an infant and perhaps fed
by bees; this seems less likely.)

ἀσεῖ δ᾽ ὥς ποκ᾽ ἔδεκτο τὸν αἰπόλον εὐρέα λάρναξ
ζωὸν ἐόντα κακαῖσιν ἀτασθαλίαισιν ἄνακτος,
80   ὥς τέ νιν αἱ σιμαὶ λειμωνόθε φέρβον ἰοῖσαι
κέδρον ἐς ἁδεῖαν μαλακοῖς ἄνθεσσι μέλισσαι,
οὕνεκά οἱ γλυκὺ Μοῖσα κατὰ στόματος χέε νέκταρ.
ὦ μακαριστὲ Κομᾶτα, τύ θην τάδε τερπνὰ πεπόνθεις·
καὶ τὺ κατεκλάσθης ἐς λάρνακα, καὶ τὺ μελισσᾶν
85   κηρία φερβόμενος ἔτος ὥριον ἐξεπόνασας.
αἴθ᾽ ἐπ᾽ ἐμεῦ ζωοῖς ἐναρίθμιος ὤφελες ἦμεν,
ὥς τοι ἐγὼν ἐνόμευον ἀν᾽ ὥρεα τὰς καλὰς αἶγας
φωνᾶς εἰσαΐων, τὺ δ᾽ ὑπὸ δρυσὶν ἢ ὑπὸ πεύκαις
ἁδὺ μελισδόμενος κατεκέκλισο, θεῖε Κομᾶτα."

90   Χὢ μὲν τόσσ᾽ εἰπὼν ἀπεπαύσατο· τὸν δὲ μέτ᾽
            αὖθις
κἠγὼν τοῖ᾽ ἐφάμαν· "Λυκίδα φίλε, πολλὰ μὲν ἄλλα
Νύμφαι κἠμὲ δίδαξαν ἀν᾽ ὥρεα βουκολέοντα
ἐσθλά, τά που καὶ Ζηνὸς ἐπὶ θρόνον ἄγαγε φάμα·
ἀλλὰ τόγ᾽ ἐκ πάντων μέγ᾽ ὑπείροχον, ᾧ τυ γεραίρειν
95   ἀρξεῦμ᾽· ἀλλ᾽ ὑπάκουσον, ἐπεὶ φίλος ἔπλεο Μοίσαις.

Σιμιχίδα μὲν Ἔρωτες ἐπέπταρον· ἦ γὰρ ὁ δειλός
τόσσον ἐρᾷ Μυρτοῦς ὅσον εἴαρος αἶγες ἔρανται.
Ὦρατος δ᾽ ὁ τὰ πάντα φιλαίτατος ἀνέρι τήνῳ

---

24 Poets sometimes speak as if bees bring blossoms to the hive
(e.g., Ov. *Met.* 13.928), though here the meaning must be that he
was fed on honey, derived from flowers. Poets who sing sweetly
are often said to have been fed by bees as children (cf. Paus.
9.23.2 on Pindar).

closed alive in a great chest thanks to his king's wicked impiety, and how the blunt-nosed bees came from the meadows to the fragrant coffer of cedarwood to feed him on tender flowers[24] because the Muse had poured sweet nectar on his lips. Blessed Comatas, you have experienced these pleasures; you too were shut in a chest; you too were fed on honeycomb and labored hard in the year's springtime.[25] If only you had been counted among the living in my day, so that I could have herded your fine goats in the hills and listened to your voice as you sat making sweet music under the oaks or pines, divine Comatas.'"

With that he concluded, and in response I said, "Lycidas my friend, the Muses have taught me too many good songs as I tended my herd in the hills, and their reputation may even have reached the throne of Zeus;[26] but by far the most notable is this one, which in tribute to you I shall now begin. Listen, then, since you are a favorite of the Muses.[27]

"'The Loves sneezed for Simichidas:[28] he, poor thing, loves Myrto as much as goats love the spring. But Aratus,[29]

[25] Or, perhaps, "through the seasons of the year."

[26] Fame is commonly said to "reach the sky" (e.g., Hom. *Od.* 9.20), but here there is a reference also to Ptolemy Philadelphus, who was born on Cos and favored the island (*Id.* 17.56–76).

[27] I.e., as a poet yourself you will better appreciate my efforts.

[28] Sneezes were taken as omens (cf. Catull. 45.16), and here it seems to be implied that the omen is favorable: although he is a "poor thing," as all lovers are, Simichidas suffers less than Aratus.

[29] Probably to be identified with the addressee of *Id.* 6.

παιδὸς ὑπὸ σπλάγχνοισιν ἔχει πόθον. οἶδεν
 Ἄριστις,
100 ἐσθλὸς ἀνήρ, μέγ' ἄριστος, ὃν οὐδέ κεν αὐτὸς ἀείδειν
Φοῖβος σὺν φόρμιγγι παρὰ τριπόδεσσι μεγαίροι,
ὡς ἐκ παιδὸς Ἄρατος ὑπ' ὀστίον αἴθετ' ἔρωτι.
τόν μοι, Πάν, Ὁμόλας ἐρατὸν πέδον ὅστε λέλογχας,
ἄκλητον τήνοιο φίλας ἐς χεῖρας ἐρείσαις,
105 εἴτ' ἔστ' ἆρα Φιλῖνος ὁ μαλθακὸς εἴτε τις ἄλλος.
κεἰ μὲν ταῦτ' ἔρδοις, ὦ Πὰν φίλε, μήτι τυ παῖδες
Ἀρκαδικοὶ σκίλλαισιν ὑπὸ πλευράς τε καὶ ὤμως
τανίκα μαστίζοιεν, ὅτε κρέα τυτθὰ παρείη·
εἰ δ' ἄλλως νεύσαις, κατὰ μὲν χρόα πάντ' ὀνύχεσσι
110 δακνόμενος κνάσαιο καὶ ἐν κνίδαισι καθεύδοις·
εἴης δ' Ἠδωνῶν μὲν ἐν ὤρεσι χείματι μέσσῳ
Ἕβρον πὰρ ποταμὸν τετραμμένος ἐγγύθεν Ἄρκτω,
ἐν δὲ θέρει πυμάτοισι παρ' Αἰθιόπεσσι νομεύοις
πέτρᾳ ὕπο Βλεμύων, ὅθεν οὐκέτι Νεῖλος ὁρατός.
115 ὔμμες δ' Ὑετίδος καὶ Βυβλίδος ἁδὺ λιπόντες

---

30 Lit., "in his guts."

31 Punning on his name: *aristos* = "best."

32 I.e., the god would welcome Aristis' performing at a musical competition at the Pythian Games.

33 It may be implied that Aristis has composed a lyric poem on the subject. 34 In northern Thessaly. It is not linked with Pan in any extant writers; but Simichidas is indulging in obscure learning (cf. 106–8).

35 Reference to an otherwise unattested Arcadian ritual of whipping a statue of Pan when meat (from hunting or perhaps from sacrificial victims) is scarce. The threats that follow are of a

that man's dearest friend in every way, has desire for a boy
deep down in his heart.[30] Aristis, best of men,[31] a real
gentleman, whom Apollo himself would not begrudge to
play the lyre beside his tripods,[32] knows that Aratus is
burning in his very bones with love for a boy.[33] Pan, you
who have as your portion the lovely plain of Homole,[34] do
please make him go of his own accord and press him into
Aratus' open arms, whether it is indeed the soft Philinus
that he loves or someone else. If you do this, dear Pan,
then may Arcadian boys never flog your flanks and shoul-
ders with squills when meat is scarce.[35] But if you refuse,
may you be bitten[36] so that you scratch yourself all over
with your nails and sleep in a bed of nettles; in midwinter
may you live turned toward the river Hebrus on the moun-
tain of the Edonians, near the pole, but in summer may
you pasture your flocks among the furthest Ethiopians
beneath the rock of the Blemyes, where the Nile can no
longer be seen.[37] But you Loves, rosy as apples, leave the

type common in surviving magical papyri, but they are self-con-
sciously learned in keeping with Simichidas' style and humorously
out of proportion with the supposed offense.

[36] Presumably by insects.

[37] A learned wish for Pan's maximum discomfort: he will be in
the coldest place in winter and in the hottest in summer. The Edo-
nians lived in Macedonia and Thrace; the Hebrus flows through
modern Bulgaria and is the border between Greece and Turkey.
The Ethiopians ("Burned Men"; "most remote of men," Hom.
Od. 1.23) live close to the sun; the Blemyes are here taken to be
in the extreme southern desert, though in fact they lived further
north (Eratosth. ap. Str. 17.1.2). Their "rock" is not mentioned
elsewhere. The source of the Nile was a matter for endless spec-
ulation.

νᾶμα καὶ Οἰκοῦντα, ξανθᾶς ἕδος αἰπὺ Διώνας,
ὦ μάλοισιν Ἔρωτες ἐρευθομένοισιν ὁμοῖοι,
βάλλετέ μοι τόξοισι τὸν ἱμερόεντα Φιλῖνον,
βάλλετ', ἐπεὶ τὸν ξεῖνον ὁ δύσμορος οὐκ ἐλεεῖ μευ.
120 καὶ δὴ μὰν ἀπίοιο πεπαίτερος, αἱ δὲ γυναῖκες,
'αἰαῖ,' φαντί, 'Φιλῖνε, τό τοι καλὸν ἄνθος ἀπορρεῖ.'
μηκέτι τοι φρουρέωμες ἐπὶ προθύροισιν, Ἄρατε,
μηδὲ πόδας τρίβωμες· ὁ δ' ὄρθριος ἄλλον ἀλέκτωρ
κοκκύσδων νάρκαισιν ἀνιαραῖσι διδοίη·
εἷς δ' ἀπὸ τᾶσδε, φέριστε, Μόλων ἄγχοιτο παλαί-
125   στρας.
ἄμμιν δ' ἀσυχία τε μέλοι, γραῖά τε παρείη
ἅτις ἐπιφθύζοισα τὰ μὴ καλὰ νόσφιν ἐρύκοι."

      Τόσσ' ἐφάμαν· ὁ δέ μοι τὸ λαγωβόλον, ἁδὺ
          γελάσσας
ὡς πάρος, ἐκ Μοισᾶν ξεινήιον ὤπασεν ἦμεν.
130 χὠ μὲν ἀποκλίνας ἐπ' ἀριστερὰ τὰν ἐπὶ Πύξας

---

116 Οἰκοῦντα Hecker: οἰκεῦντα vel -τες M

---

38 Hyetis: unknown. Byblis, daughter of Miletus, fell in love
with her brother Caunus, killed herself, and was transformed
into a spring (Ov. Met. 9.663–65), which according to Pausanias
(7.5.10) was to be seen at Miletus, a city with a well-known sanc-
tuary of Aphrodite (cf. Id. 28.4). Oecus, a nearby town in Caria,
was founded by Miletus (Parth. Amat. narr. 11); it too had a
temple of Aphrodite (schol. Dionys. Per. 825). Dione was the
mother of Aphrodite (cf. Idd. 15.106, 17.36), but the name later
at least came to be used of Aphrodite herself.

sweet spring of Hyetis and Byblis, and Oecus, the steep abode of golden-haired Dione;[38] please wound the handsome Philinus for me with your arrows, wound him, for the wretch feels no pity for my friend. And indeed he is riper than a pear,[39] and the women are saying, "What a pity, Philinus: the fair flower of youth is slipping away from you!" We ought not to be keeping guard outside doors, Aratus, or pacing up and down:[40] let the crowing cock bring horrible stiffness[41] to someone else in the mornings—let Molon, and no one else, be throttled in that school of wrestling, my friend.[42] We should avoid anxiety and have an old woman who can spit to ward off all unpleasantness.'"[43]

When I had concluded, Lycidas laughed aloud as before and gave me his stick as a gift to mark the Muses' favor.[44] Then he turned to the left and set off on the road to Pyxa,[45]

[39] I.e., he is maturing quickly and is scarcely worth pursuing any longer.

[40] For the watching at the door, cf. p. 59. It is not quite clear whether Simichidas includes himself in the advice to give up on love affairs (cf. 97) or whether he refers to his having accompanied Aratus on the *kômos* to Philinus' house in the past.

[41] From sleeping in doorways.

[42] Wrestling schools were places where attractive boys could be encountered, and *erôs* is often described with wrestling imagery. Molon is probably a rival lover of Philinus.

[43] On apotropaic spitting see on p. 111 n. 16.

[44] Or, "as a gift from the Muses." There is an allusion to the Muses' gift of a staff to Hesiod as token of his investiture as a poet (*Theog.* 30–31).

[45] A deme southwest of Cos town, which according to the scholia had a temple of Apollo.

εἷρφ' ὁδόν· αὐτὰρ ἐγών τε καὶ Εὔκριτος ἐς Φρασι-
    δάμω
στραφθέντες χὠ καλὸς Ἀμύντιχος ἔν τε βαθείαις
ἁδείας σχοίνοιο χαμευνίσιν ἐκλίνθημες
ἔν τε νεοτμάτοισι γεγαθότες οἰναρέοισι.
135 πολλαὶ δ' ἄμμιν ὕπερθε κατὰ κρατὸς δονέοντο
αἴγειροι πτελέαι τε· τὸ δ' ἐγγύθεν ἱερὸν ὕδωρ
Νυμφᾶν ἐξ ἄντροιο κατειβόμενον κελάρυζε.
τοὶ δὲ ποτὶ σκιαραῖς ὀροδαμνίσιν αἰθαλίωνες
τέττιγες λαλαγεῦντες ἔχον πόνον· ἁ δ' ὀλολυγών
140 τηλόθεν ἐν πυκιναῖσι βάτων τρύζεσκεν ἀκάνθαις·
ἄειδον κόρυδοι καὶ ἀκανθίδες, ἔστενε τρυγών,
πωτῶντο ξουθαὶ περὶ πίδακας ἀμφὶ μέλισσαι.
πάντ' ὦσδεν θέρεος μάλα πίονος, ὦσδε δ' ὀπώρας.
ὄχναι μὲν πὰρ ποσσί, παρὰ πλευραῖσι δὲ μᾶλα
145 δαψιλέως ἁμῖν ἐκυλίνδετο, τοὶ δ' ἐκέχυντο·
ὄρπακες βραβίλοισι καταβρίθοντες ἔραζε·
τετράενες δὲ πίθων ἀπελύετο κρατὸς ἄλειφαρ.
Νύμφαι Κασταλίδες Παρνάσιον αἶπος ἔχοισαι,
ἀρά γέ πᾳ τοιόνδε Φόλω κατὰ λάινον ἄντρον
150 κρατῆρ' Ἡρακλῆι γέρων ἐστάσατο Χίρων;
ἀρά γέ πᾳ τῆνον τὸν ποιμένα τὸν ποτ' Ἀνάπῳ,

---

46 As the weather cooled in late summer, the vine leaves were
stripped away to promote ripening of the grapes.

47 It was debated in antiquity whether *ololugôn* meant a frog
or a sort of bird. The nightingale, which is sometimes said to sing
in dense thickets (cf. *Epit. Bion.* 9), may be meant here; but
nightingales sing when other birds are silent.

while Eucritus and I and the handsome lad Amyntas hap-
pily laid ourselves down on deep couches of sweet rush
and newly cut vine leaves.[46] Many a poplar and elm mur-
mured above our heads; trickling down from a cave of the
nymphs, a sacred spring plashed nearby; on the shady
branches the dusky cicadas worked hard at their song;
far off in the dense brambles the tree frog[47] kept up its
crooning; linnets and finches sang; doves were cooing, and
humming bees were flying around the spring. Everywhere
was the smell of rich harvest, the smell of gathered fruits.
Pears rolled plentifully at our feet and apples by our side,
and the branches weighed down with sloes were bent to
the ground. Wine jars were opened which had been sealed
for four years. Nymphs of Castalia who dwell on Mt. Par-
nassus,[48] could it have been a bowl like this that old Chiron
provided for Heracles in Pholus' rocky cave?[49] Could it
have been nectar like this which set that famous shepherd
by the river Anapus dancing among his sheepfolds—the

[48] Castalia is a spring below Mt. Parnassus at Delphi; these
Nymphs are therefore associated with Apollo, god of poetry, and
are invoked instead of the Muses. They are to be distinguished
from the local Nymphs mentioned in lines 137 and 154.

[49] According to ps.-Apollodorus, the Centaur Pholus enter-
tained Heracles with a wine so fragrant that it attracted the other
Centaurs, and in a drunken brawl Pholus was killed (2.5.4). The-
ocritus seems to follow a version in which Chiron too (himself a
Centaur) was present; in ps.-Apollodorus he is not, but his cave
is subsequently the site of Heracles' revenge on the Centaurs, and
Chiron is accidentally killed at that time.

τὸν κρατερὸν Πολύφαμον, ὃς ὤρεσι νᾶας ἔβαλλε,
τοῖον νέκταρ ἔπεισε κατ᾽ αὔλια ποσσὶ χορεῦσαι,
οἷον δὴ τόκα πῶμα διεκρανάσατε, Νύμφαι,
155 βωμῷ πὰρ Δάματρος ἀλωίδος; ἃς ἐπὶ σωρῷ
αὖτις ἐγὼ πάξαιμι μέγα πτύον, ἃ δὲ γελάσσαι
δράγματα καὶ μάκωνας ἐν ἀμφοτέραισιν ἔχοισα.

152 νᾶας Heinsius: λᾶας M

mighty Polyphemus, who used to pelt ships with mountains?[50] Of such quality was the drink which you then mixed for us,[51] Nymphs, by the altar of Demeter, goddess of the threshing floor. May I plant my great winnowing shovel in her heap of grain once more,[52] while she smiles on us with favor, holding sheaves and poppies in her hands.[53]

[50] Polyphemus (cf. *Idd.* 6, 11), whom Theocritus makes a Sicilian (on the Anapus see on *Id.* 1.68). He was made drunk by Odysseus' strong wine (Hom. *Od.* 9.359, νέκταρος . . . ἀπορρώξ) and pelted his departing ship with a "mountain peak" (ibid. 481). In the Homeric account Polyphemus does not dance, but he may have done so in Philoxenus' poem (see p. 105).

[51] I.e., the Nymphs of the spring (136–37) provided water to mix with the wine. It is possible, however, that the meaning is "caused to well up," a miraculous spring of wine to complement Chalcon's action in lines 6–7.

[52] Symbolizing the end of the harvest. The close of the poem alludes to the close of Odysseus' wanderings: Tiresias tells him that he must set out carrying an oar, and when he is so far from the sea that someone mistakes the unfamiliar oar for a winnowing shovel, he must "plant" it in the earth and at last placate Poseidon with a sacrifice (Hom. *Od.* 11.119–37).

[53] I.e., her statue will be decorated in this way.

IDYLL 8

A *singing contest between Menalcas and Daphnis; each stakes a panpipe, and a goatherd is appointed judge. They sing in alternating quatrains in the elegiac meter followed by a set of eight hexameters each; these fall into couplets. Daphnis' voice is judged to be the sweeter. He is overjoyed at his victory, while Menalcas grieves.*

If, as seems probable, the last line means that Daphnis married a nymph, then the characters are the mythical Daphnis and Menalcas, and the setting is the remote past; this is suggested also by the words "as the story goes" (ὥς φαντι) in line 2. The poem will in that case record how Daphnis came to be the archetypal bucolic singer.

The majority of scholars believe the poem not to be by Theocritus. The opening lines seem to imitate the opening of Idyll 6 *and the argument about the stakes and the summoning of a judge to be derived from* Idyll 5. *The use of elegiacs is unique.*

Criticism

Fantuzzi, M. "Textual Misadventures of Daphnis: The Pseudo-Theocritean *Idyll* 8 and the Origins of the Bucolic 'Manner.'" In Harder, Regtuit, Wakker, *Genre*, 61–79.

Reed, J. D. "Idyll 6 and the Development of Bucolic After Theocritus." In Clauss and Cuypers, *Companion*, 238–50.

8

ΔΑΦΝΙΣ ΚΑΙ ΜΕΝΑΛΚΑΣ

Δάφνιδι τῷ χαρίεντι συνάντετο βουκολέοντι
μῆλα νέμων, ὡς φαντί, κατ' ὤρεα μακρὰ Μενάλκας.
ἄμφω τώγ' ἤστην πυρροτρίχω, ἄμφω ἀνάβω,
ἄμφω συρίσδεν δεδαημένω, ἄμφω ἀείδεν.
5 πρᾶτος δ' ὦν ποτὶ Δάφνιν ἰδὼν ἀγόρευε Μενάλκας·
"μυκητᾶν ἐπίουρε βοῶν Δάφνι, λῇς μοι ἀεῖσαι;
φαμί τυ νικασεῖν, ὅσσον θέλω αὐτὸς ἀείδων."
τὸν δ' ἄρα χὠ Δάφνις τοιῷδ' ἀπαμείβετο μύθῳ·
"ποιμὴν εἰροπόκων ὀίων, συρικτὰ Μενάλκα,
10 οὔποκα νικασεῖς μ', οὐδ' εἴ τι πάθοις τύγ' ἀείδων."

ΜΕΝΑΛΚΑΣ

χρῄσδεις ὦν ἐσιδεῖν; χρῄσδεις καταθεῖναι ἄεθλον;

ΔΑΦΝΙΣ

χρῄσδω τοῦτ' ἐσιδεῖν, χρῄσδω καταθεῖναι ἄεθλον.

ΜΕΝΑΛΚΑΣ

καὶ τί νυ θησεύμεσθ' ὅ κεν ἁμὶν ἄρκιον εἴη;

ΔΑΦΝΙΣ

μόσχον ἐγὼ θησῶ, τὺ δὲ θὲς ἰσομάτορα ἀμνόν.

13 καὶ τί νυ Legrand: καὶ τίνα m: ἀλλά τι m

IDYLL 8

As he pastured his sheep in the high mountains, Menalcas
—so the story goes—encountered the handsome Daphnis
herding his cattle. Both had reddish hair, both were still
boys; both were skillful pipers, both skillful singers. And
so on seeing Daphnis, Menalcas was first to speak: "Daph-
nis, guardian of the lowing cattle, will you sing with me? I
think I shall defeat you, if I sing for as long as I like."
Daphnis in turn replied with these words: "Shepherd of
the fleecy sheep, Menalcas the piper, you will never defeat
me, even if you do yourself a mischief by your singing."

MENALCAS
Would you like to see? Would you like to make a wager?

DAPHNIS
I *would* like to see; I *would* like to make a wager.

MENALCAS
And what can we wager that will be enough for us?

DAPHNIS
I'll put down a calf; you stake a lamb grown as big as its
mother.

ΜΕΝΑΛΚΑΣ

15 οὐ θησῶ ποκα ἀμνόν, ἐπεὶ χαλεπὸς ὁ πατήρ μευ
χἀ μάτηρ, τὰ δὲ μῆλα ποθέσπερα πάντ' ἀριθμεῦντι.

ΔΑΦΝΙΣ

ἀλλὰ τί μὰν θησεῖς; τί δὲ τὸ πλέον ἑξεῖ ὁ νικῶν;

ΜΕΝΑΛΚΑΣ

σύριγγ' ἃν ἐπόησα καλὰν ἔχω ἐννεάφωνον,
λευκὸν κηρὸν ἔχοισαν ἴσον κάτω ἶσον ἄνωθεν·
20 ταύταν κατθείην, τὰ δὲ τῶ πατρὸς οὐ καταθησῶ.

ΔΑΦΝΙΣ

ἦ μάν τοι κἠγὼ σύριγγ' ἔχω ἐννεάφωνον,
λευκὸν κηρὸν ἔχοισαν ἴσον κάτω ἶσον ἄνωθεν.
πρώαν νιν συνέπαξ'· ἔτι καὶ τὸν δάκτυλον ἀλγῶ
τοῦτον, ἐπεὶ κάλαμός με διασχισθεὶς διέτμαξεν.

ΜΕΝΑΛΚΑΣ

25 ἀλλὰ τίς ἄμμε κρινεῖ; τίς ἐπάκοος ἔσσεται ἀμέων;

ΔΑΦΝΙΣ

τῆνόν πως ἐνταῦθα τὸν αἰπόλον, ἤν, καλέσωμες,
ᾧ ποτὶ ταῖς ἐρίφοις ὁ κύων ὁ φάλαρος ὑλακτεῖ.

Χοἰ μὲν παῖδες ἄυσαν, ὁ δ' αἰπόλος ἦνθ' ὑπακούσας·
χοἰ μὲν παῖδες ἀείδεν, ὁ δ' αἰπόλος ἤθελε κρίνειν.
30 πρᾶτος δ' ὢν ἄειδε λαχὼν ἰυκτὰ Μενάλκας,
εἶτα δ' ἀμοιβαίαν ὑπελάμβανε Δάφνις ἀοιδάν
βουκολικάν· οὕτω δὲ Μενάλκας ἄρξατο πρᾶτος.

18 ἔχω Warton (cf. 21): ἐγὼ M

IDYLL 8

MENALCAS

I'll never wager a lamb: my father is strict and so is my
mother, and they count all the sheep every evening.

DAPHNIS

But what will you stake? What profit will the winner get?

MENALCAS

I have a fine pipe of nine reeds that I made: its white wax
is equal above and equal below.[1] I would wager that, but
I'll not wager what belongs to my father.

DAPHNIS

I too have a pipe of nine reeds with white wax equal above
and equal below. I made it the other day, and this finger is
still sore because a reed split and cut me.

MENALCAS

But who will be our judge? Who will listen to us?

DAPHNIS

Look, perhaps we can call that goatherd whose dog with a
white spot is barking near the kids.

The boys shouted, and the goatherd came when he heard
them; the boys wanted to sing, and the goatherd was will-
ing to judge. Loud-voiced Menalcas drew the lot for sing-
ing first; then in response Daphnis took up the pastoral
song. And this is how Menalcas first began:

---

[1] Meaning uncertain; Menalcas may mean that the wax hold-
ing the reeds together at top and bottom was carefully made
uniform in thickness.

---

28 ὑπακούσας Cobet: ἐπ- m: ἐπακοῦσαι m
29 ἀείδεν Gebauer: ἄειδον M

ΜΕΝΑΛΚΑΣ

ἄγκεα καὶ ποταμοί, θεῖον γένος, αἴ τι Μενάλκας
πήποχ᾽ ὁ συρικτὰς προσφιλὲς ᾆσε μέλος,
35 βόσκοιτ᾽ ἐκ ψυχᾶς τὰς ἀμνάδας· ἢν δέ ποκ᾽ ἔνθῃ
Δάφνις ἄγων δαμάλας, μηδὲν ἔλασσον ἔχοι.

ΔΑΦΝΙΣ

κρᾶναι καὶ βοτάναι, γλυκερὸν φυτόν, αἴπερ ὁμοῖον
μουσίσδει Δάφνις ταῖσιν ἀηδονίσι,
τοῦτο τὸ βουκόλιον πιαίνετε· κἤν τι Μενάλκας
40 τεῖδ᾽ ἀγάγῃ, χαίρων ἄφθονα πάντα νέμοι.

ΜΕΝΑΛΚΑΣ

45 ἔνθ᾽ ὄις, ἔνθ᾽ αἶγες διδυματόκοι, ἔνθα μέλισσαι
46 σμήνεα πληροῦσιν, καὶ δρύες ὑψίτεραι,
47 ἔνθ᾽ ὁ καλὸς Μίλων βαίνει ποσίν· αἰ δ᾽ ἂν ἀφέρπῃ,
44 χὠ ποιμὴν ξηρὸς τηνόθι χαἰ βοτάναι.

ΔΑΦΝΙΣ

41 παντᾷ ἔαρ, παντᾷ δὲ νομοί, παντᾷ δὲ γάλακτος
42 οὔθατα πιδῶσιν, καὶ τὰ νέα τράφεται,
43 ἔνθα καλὰ Ναῒς ἐπινίσσεται· αἰ δ᾽ ἂν ἀφέρπῃ,
48 χὠ τὰς βῶς βόσκων χαἰ βόες αὐότεραι.

ΜΕΝΑΛΚΑΣ

ὦ τράγε, τᾶν λευκᾶν αἰγῶν ἄνερ, ἐς βάθος ὕλας
50 μυρίον—αἰ σιμαὶ δεῦτ᾽ ἐφ᾽ ὕδωρ ἔριφοι—

36 ἄγων Ahlwardt: ἔχων M
41–43 et 45–47 trai. Bindemann
42 πιδῶσιν Ahrens: πηδ- m: πλήθουσιν m

140

IDYLL 8

MENALCAS

Glens and rivers, race divine, if ever Menalcas the piper
sang a song that pleased you, may you pasture his lambs
with goodwill; and if ever Daphnis comes with his heifers,
may he get no less.

DAPHNIS

Springs and pastures, sweet greenery, if Daphnis sings like
the nightingales, make fat this herd of his; and if Menalcas
should bring any animal here, may he happily find every-
thing in abundance.

MENALCAS

Here are sheep, here are goats that bear twins, here bees
fill their hives and the oak trees are taller, here the hand-
some Milon walks. But if he goes away, the shepherd and
the pasture there are both dry.

DAPHNIS

Everywhere is spring, everywhere are pastures, every-
where the udders yield abundant milk and the young ani-
mals are growing, wherever the pretty Nais comes; but if
she goes away, both the oxherd and his cattle are quite
dried up.

MENALCAS

Billy goat, husband of the white nannies, go into the mea-
sureless depths of the forest (come here to the water, you

---

43 ἔνθα καλὰ Ναῒς Meineke: ἔνθ᾽ ἁ καλὰ παῖς M
49 ἐς Wilamowitz: ὦ vel ὤ M
50 αἱ Wilamowitz: ὤ M

ἐν τήνῳ γὰρ τῆνος· ἴθ', ὦ κόλε, καὶ λέγε, "Μίλων,
ὁ Πρωτεὺς φώκας καὶ θεὸς ὢν ἔνεμεν."

ΔΑΦΝΙΣ

⟨ . . . . ⟩

ΜΕΝΑΛΚΑΣ

μή μοι γᾶν Πέλοπος, μή μοι Κροίσεια τάλαντα
εἴη ἔχειν, μηδὲ πρόσθε θέειν ἀνέμων·
55 ἀλλ' ὑπὸ τᾷ πέτρᾳ τᾷδ' ᾀσομαι ἀγκὰς ἔχων τυ,
σύννομα μῆλ' ἐσορῶν Σικελικάν τ' ἐς ἅλα.

ΔΑΦΝΙΣ

δένδρεσι μὲν χειμὼν φοβερὸν κακόν, ὕδασι δ'
αὐχμός,
ὄρνισιν δ' ὕσπλαγξ, ἀγροτέροις δὲ λίνα,
ἀνδρὶ δὲ παρθενικᾶς ἀπαλᾶς πόθος. ὦ πάτερ, ὦ Ζεῦ,
60 οὐ μόνος ἠράσθην· καὶ τὺ γυναικοφίλας.

Ταῦτα μὲν ὦν δι' ἀμοιβαίων οἱ παῖδες ἄεισαν,
τὰν πυμάταν δ' ᾠδὰν οὕτως ἐξᾶρχε Μενάλκας·

ΜΕΝΑΛΚΑΣ

φείδευ τᾶν ἐρίφων, φείδευ, λύκε, τᾶν τοκάδων μευ,
μηδ' ἀδίκει μ', ὅτι μικκὸς ἐὼν πολλαῖσιν ὁμαρτέω.

51 καλὲ schol. lemma
52 ὁ Meineke: ὡς M
post 52 lac. ind. Wuestemann
53 Κροίσεια Jortin: χρύσεια M
56 Σικελικάν τε Valckenaer: τὰν Σικ. m: τὰν Σικελὰν m

snub-nosed kids), for that's where he is. Go, stump-horn, and say, "Milon, Proteus herded his seals even though he was a god."[2]

DAPHNIS

⟨ . . . . ⟩[3]

MENALCAS

I should not like to have the land of Pelops or the wealth of Croesus,[4] or to outrun the winds; rather let me sing with you in my arms beneath this rock as I watch my flock grazing and look out over the Sicilian sea.

DAPHNIS

A gale is a fearful trouble for trees, a drought for water, a snare for birds, nets for wild game; and for a man, desire for a tender girl. Father Zeus, I am not the only one to have fallen in love: you too are a lover of women.[5]

That, then, is what the boys sang in response to each other; and this is how Menalcas started their final song:

MENALCAS

Spare my kids, wolf, and spare their mothers; don't harm me just because I am little and tend a big flock.

---

[2] Odysseus encountered the sea god Proteus as he herded his seals (Hom. *Od.* 4.435–570). Menalcas' point is that Milon should not disdain him because he is a goatherd. Both seals and goats smell bad (5.51–52; Hom. *Od.* 4.441).   [3] Four lines, containing a further address or invitation to Nais, are lost.

[4] Pelops, who gave his name to the Peloponnese, was like Croesus proverbially rich (Thuc. 1.9.2).

[5] This idea is a commonplace of erotic poetry (e.g., Theognis 1345–48; Ascl. *Anth. Pal.* 5.64.5–6, 167.5–6).

65 ὦ Λάμπουρε κύον, οὕτω βαθὺς ὕπνος ἔχει τυ;
οὐ χρὴ κοιμᾶσθαι βαθέως σὺν παιδὶ νέμοντα.
ταὶ δ' ὄιες, μηδ' ὕμμες ὀκνεῖθ' ἁπαλᾶς κορέσασθαι
ποίας· οὔτι καμεῖσθ' ὅκκα πάλιν ἅδε φύηται.
σίττα νέμεσθε νέμεσθε, τὰ δ' οὔθατα πλήσατε πᾶ-
    σαι,
70 ὡς τὸ μὲν ὥρνες ἔχωντι, τὸ δ' ἐς ταλάρως ἀποθῶμαι.

    Δεύτερος αὖ Δάφνις λιγυρῶς ἀνεβάλλετ' ἀείδεν·

        ΔΑΦΝΙΣ

κἤμ' ἐκ τῶ ἄντρω σύνοφρυς κόρα ἐχθὲς ἰδοῖσα
τὰς δαμάλας παρελᾶντα καλὸν καλὸν ἦμεν ἔφασκεν·
οὐ μὰν οὐδὲ λόγον ἐκρίθην ἄπο τὸν πικρὸν αὐτᾷ,
75 ἀλλὰ κάτω βλέψας τὰν ἀμετέραν ὁδὸν εἶρπον.
76 ἁδεῖ' ἁ φωνὰ τᾶς πόρτιος, ἁδὺ τὸ πνεῦμα,
78 ἁδὺ δὲ τῶ θέρεος παρ' ὕδωρ ῥέον αἰθριοκοιτεῖν.
    τᾷ δρυΐ ταὶ βάλανοι κόσμος, τᾷ μαλίδι μᾶλα,
80 τᾷ βοΐ δ' ἁ μόσχος, τῷ βουκόλῳ αἱ βόες αὐταί.

    Ὡς οἱ παῖδες ἄεισαν, ὁ δ' αἰπόλος ὧδ' ἀγόρευεν·
"ἁδύ τι τὸ στόμα τοι καὶ ἐφίμερος, ὦ Δάφνι, φωνά·

---

77 (= 9.7) damn. Valckenaer; habent pap., M

---

6 "Shiny tail."   7 Or, perhaps, "you will not suffer ‹for
your indulgence›, because it will grow again."
  8 To drain off the whey.
  9 Brows just touching in the middle were considered attrac-
tive (*Anacreontea* 16.15–17 West, vol. 2, pp. 182–85 Campbell;

144

IDYLL 8

My dog Lampurus,[6] are you sleeping so deeply? You shouldn't be resting while a boy is the shepherd.

You sheep, don't be afraid to eat your fill of the soft grass; it will grow again before you are tired.[7]

Hey! Feed and feed, and all of you fill your udders, so that the lambs can have some milk and I can put the rest into cheese crates.[8]

Daphnis, singing second, next struck up his clear song:

DAPHNIS

And as for me, a girl with brows that meet[9] noticed me yesterday from her cave as I drove my heifers past, and she kept saying, How handsome I was, how handsome!

But I gave no answer—not even a bitter one—but went on my way looking at the ground.[10]

Sweet is the lowing of the heifer, sweet is her breath,[11] and sweet it is in summer to rest outdoors by running water.[12]

Acorns grace the oak tree, apples the apple tree, the calf the cow, and the cows themselves the cowherd.

So the boys sang, and the goatherd spoke as follows: "Your voice is a sweet one, Daphnis, and your tone is lovely;

Philostr. *Imag.* 2.5.4), though the Cyclops' single long brow is not a good feature (11.31–32).

[10] A sign of modesty.

[11] Or, "the breeze."

[12] I.e.,—as the next couplet makes clear—Daphnis is right to ignore the girl and keep to his cattle.

145

κρέσσον μελπομένω τευ ἀκουέμεν ἢ μέλι λείχειν.
λάσδεο τὰς σύριγγας, ἐνίκασας γὰρ ἀείδων.

85 αἰ δέ τι λῇς με καὶ αὐτὸν ἅμ᾽ αἰπολέοντα διδάξαι,
τήναν τὰν μιτύλαν δωσῶ τὰ δίδακτρά τοι αἶγα,
ἅτις ὑπὲρ κεφαλᾶς αἰεὶ τὸν ἀμολγέα πληροῖ.”
ὡς μὲν ὁ παῖς ἐχάρη καὶ ἀνάλατο καὶ πλατάγησε
νικάσας, οὕτως ἐπὶ ματέρι νεβρὸς ἅλοιτο.

90 ὡς δὲ κατεσμύχθη καὶ ἀνετράπετο φρένα λύπᾳ
ὥτερος, οὕτω καὶ νύμφα δμαθεῖσ᾽ ἀκάχοιτο.
κἠκ τούτω πρᾶτος παρὰ ποιμέσι Δάφνις ἔγεντο,
καὶ νύμφαν ἄκραβος ἐὼν ἔτι Ναΐδα γᾶμεν.

91 δμαθεῖσ᾽ Ahrens: γαμηθεῖσ᾽ m: γαμε- m

listening to your songs is better than tasting honey. Take
the pipes;[13] you have won the contest in song. And if you
would like to teach me too, as I herd my goats, I will give
you as my fee that goat without horns[14] which always fills
the milk pail above the brim." At his victory the boy was
delighted and jumped for joy and clapped his hands, just
as a fawn might leap around its mother. The other boy
smoldered resentfully and began to grieve in his heart, just
as a girl would grieve when wedded.[15] From that time,
Daphnis came to be first among the herdsmen, and he
married the nymph Nais[16] while still a youth.

[13] His own and that of Menalcas (17).

[14] The meaning of this adjective is uncertain; "young" and
"last-born" have also been suggested.

[15] If the text is sound, this must be a reference to loss of virgin-
ity on the wedding night.

[16] Or, "Nais as his bride."

IDYLL 9

*The speaker invites Daphnis and Menalcas to sing. Each
performs a song of seven lines with a homely concluding
image. Using past tenses, the speaker says that he gave a
gift to each singer. He then pays his own debt to the Muses,
by singing the song that he sang on that same occasion.*

*Unless a proem is missing, the inconcinnity of tenses
seems intolerable; and Menalcas herds cattle in lines 3–5
but sheep and goats in lines 17–18. Scholars have dissected
the poem in various ways. It is possible that lines 7–13,
15–21, and 28–36 have one source, the rest another (or
others). At any rate, there is general agreement that no
part is likely to be by Theocritus. The opening of Daphnis'
song is derived from lines 1–3 of* Idyll 1, *the gift of a staff
(23) from* Id. 7.43.

9

Βουκολιάζεο, Δάφνι· τὺ δ᾽ ᾠδᾶς ἄρχεο πρᾶτος,
ᾠδᾶς ἄρχεο, Δάφνι, ἐφεψάσθω δὲ Μενάλκας,
μόσχως βουσὶν ὑφέντες, ἐπὶ στείραισι δὲ ταύρως.
χοὶ μὲν ἅμᾳ βόσκοιντο καὶ ἐν φύλλοισι πλανῷντο
5   μηδὲν ἀτιμαγελεῦντες· ἐμὶν δὲ τὺ βουκολιάζευ
ἐκ τόθεν, ἄλλοθε δ᾽ αὖτις ὑποκρίνοιτο Μενάλκας.

ΔΑΦΝΙΣ

ἁδὺ μὲν ἁ μόσχος γαρύεται, ἁδὺ δὲ χἀ βῶς,
ἁδὺ δὲ χἀ σῦριγξ χὠ βουκόλος, ἁδὺ δὲ κἠγών.
ἔστι δέ μοι παρ᾽ ὕδωρ ψυχρὸν στιβάς, ἐν δὲ
νένασται
10   λευκᾶν ἐκ δαμαλᾶν καλὰ δέρματα, τάς μοι ἁπάσας
λὶψ κόμαρον τρωγοίσας ἀπὸ σκοπιᾶς ἐτίναξε.
τῶ δὲ θέρευς φρύγοντος ἐγὼ τόσσον μελεδαίνω,
ὅσσον ἐρῶν τὸ πατρὸς μύθων καὶ ματρὸς ἀκούειν.

Οὕτω Δάφνις ἄεισεν ἐμίν, οὕτω δὲ Μενάλκας·

ΜΕΝΑΛΚΑΣ

15   Αἴτνα μᾶτερ ἐμά, κἠγὼ καλὸν ἄντρον ἐνοικέω
κοίλαις ἐν πέτραισιν· ἔχω δέ τοι ὅσσ᾽ ἐν ὀνείρῳ

6 ἐκ τόθεν Cholmeley: ἔκποθεν m: ἔμπο(σ)θεν m: ἔμπροσθεν
m: ἐν ποθ᾽ ἐν m   10 ἀπ᾽ ἄκρας m

IDYLL 9

Sing your country songs, Daphnis: you begin your song first, begin your song, Daphnis, and let Menalcas follow, when you have put the calves to the cows and the bulls to the unmated heifers. Let the bulls graze with them and range among the flowers and never stray from the herd. Sing me your country songs from there, and let Menalcas respond from where he is.

DAPHNIS

Sweetly lows the calf, and sweetly the cow; sweet sounds the pipe and the oxherd, and so do I.[1] I have a place to lie by the cool water, where are piled fine hides of white heifers who were all hurled from the cliff by the wind from Africa as they browsed on arbutus. I care as much about the parching heat of summer as a lover cares about the advice of his father and mother.

So Daphnis sang for me, and Menalcas sang as follows:

MENALCAS

Etna, my mother, *I* live in a fine cave among the hollow rocks, and I have the wealth of dreams—plenty of ewes,

---

[1] Oddly he speaks as if he is not himself an oxherd. Perhaps by "oxherd" he means himself, defining the word further with "that is, I."

φαίνονται, πολλὰς μὲν ὄις, πολλὰς δὲ χιμαίρας,
ὧν μοι πρὸς κεφαλᾷ καὶ πρὸς ποσὶ κώεα κεῖται.
ἐν πυρὶ δὲ δρυΐνῳ χόρια ζεῖ, ἐν πυρὶ δ' αὖαι
20 φαγοὶ χειμαίνοντος· ἔχω δέ τοι οὐδ' ὅσον ὥραν
χείματος ἢ νωδὸς καρύων ἀμύλοιο παρόντος.

Τοῖς μὲν ἐπεπλατάγησα καὶ αὐτίκα δῶρον ἔδωκα,
Δάφνιδι μὲν κορύναν, τάν μοι πατρὸς ἔτραφεν
ἀγρός,
αὐτοφυῆ, τὰν οὐδ' ἂν ἴσως μωμάσατο τέκτων,
25 τήνῳ δὲ στρόμβω καλὸν ὄστρακον, ᾧ κρέας αὐτός
σιτήθην πέτραισιν ἐν Ἰκαρίαισι δοκεύσας,
πέντε ταμὼν πέντ' οὔσιν· ὁ δ' ἐγκαναχήσατο κόχλῳ.

Βουκολικαὶ Μοῖσαι, μάλα χαίρετε, φαίνετε δ'
ᾠδάν
τάν ποκ' ἐγὼ τήνοισι παρὼν ἄεισα νομεῦσι·
30 μηκέτ' ἐπὶ γλώσσας ἄκρας ὀλοφυγγόνα φύσω.
"τέττιξ μὲν τέττιγι φίλος, μύρμακι δὲ μύρμαξ,
ἴρηκες δ' ἴρηξιν, ἐμὶν δ' ἁ Μοῖσα καὶ ᾠδά.
τᾶς μοι πᾶς εἴη πλεῖος δόμος. οὔτε γὰρ ὕπνος
οὔτ' ἔαρ ἐξαπίνας γλυκερώτερον, οὔτε μελίσσαις
35 ἄνθεα· τόσσον ἐμὶν Μοῖσαι φίλαι. οὓς γὰρ ὀρεῦντι
γαθεῦσαι τὼς δ' οὔτι ποτῷ δαλήσατο Κίρκα."

26 ὑκκαρίεσι m
30 φύσω Graefe: -ῆς M
36 γαθεῦσαι Brunck: -εῦσι(ν) M

plenty of nanny goats, whose fleeces lie at my head and feet. On my fire of oak logs, blood puddings boil, and in winter drying acorns roast. I care no more about winter than a toothless man cares about nuts when there is soft wheaten bread.

I applauded them and gave each a gift: to Daphnis a staff grown on my father's farm, naturally shaped, which not even a craftsman could find fault with, and to Menalcas a fine spiral shell; I spotted it on the Icarian rocks[2] and ate the flesh myself, cutting it into five portions for the five of us. And Menalcas blew a blast on his shell.

Muses of country singing, many greetings to you! Disclose the song which once I sang in the presence of those herdsmen. Let me no longer grow an ulcer on the tip of my tongue.[3] "The cicada is dear to the cicada, the ant to the ant, hawks to hawks, and to me the Muse and song; may my whole house be filled with it. Neither sheep nor spring's sudden arrival is sweeter, nor are flowers sweeter for the bees; that is how dear the Muses are to me. Those whom they regard with favor Circe never harms with her potions."

[2] The island of Icaros, or Icaria, is northwest of Cos. One manuscript has a reading that relates to the town of Hyccara on the northern coast of Sicily.

[3] According to an obscure note in the scholia, such an ulcer was said to be a punishment for not returning "a portion that one has set aside." The idea then seems to be that by recording his song the poet hereby discharges a longstanding obligation to his teachers, the Muses.

IDYLL 10

The poem begins as a dialogue, set in a harvest field, between two reapers. Bucaeus has fallen behind in his work because he is preoccupied with love for Bombyca. Milon teases him and encourages him to sing a song in her praise. Milon then performs a compilation of down-to-earth rustic themes, which he says are far more suitable for a working man.

This is another poem that examines the relationship between love and song. Milon is rough, cynical, and given to proverbial expressions and clichés. His belief that women are a dangerous distraction and his exhortations to work are reminiscent of Hesiod's attitude in the Works & Days; *love, which requires leisure, is a luxury that laborers cannot afford. (There is perhaps an implicit contrast with Theocritus' shepherds, whose duties allow free time.) Bucaeus meanwhile is besotted with a spindly girl of poor color: his song only confirms his blindness to her imperfections (18, 24–29). No resolution between these two attitudes is suggested.*

Criticism

Cairns, F. "Theocritus Idyll 10." *Hermes* 98 (1970): 38–44.

Hunter, *Archaeology,* 125–27.

Hunter, *Selection,* 199–215.

Hutchinson, *Hellenistic Poetry,* 173–78.

10

ΜΙΛΩΝ

Ἐργατίνα Βουκαῖε, τί νῦν, ᾤζυρέ, πεπόνθεις;
οὔτε τὸν ὄγμον ἄγειν ὀρθὸν δύνᾳ, ὡς τὸ πρὶν ἆγες,
οὔθ᾽ ἅμα λᾳοτομεῖς τῷ πλατίον, ἀλλ᾽ ἀπολείπῃ,
ὥσπερ ὄις ποίμνας ἇς τὸν πόδα κάκτος ἔτυψε.
5 ποῖός τις δείλαν τὺ καὶ ἐκ μέσω ἄματος ἐσσῇ,
ὃς νῦν ἀρχόμενος τᾶς αὔλακος οὐκ ἀποτρώγεις;

ΒΟΤΚΑΙΟΣ

Μίλων ὀψαμᾶτα, πέτρας ἀπόκομμ᾽ ἀτεράμνω,
οὐδαμά τοι συνέβα ποθέσαι τινὰ τῶν ἀπεόντων;

ΜΙΛΩΝ

οὐδαμά. τίς δὲ πόθος τῶν ἔκτοθεν ἐργάτᾳ ἀνδρί;

ΒΟΤΚΑΙΟΣ

10 οὐδαμά νυν συνέβα τοι ἀγρυπνῆσαι δι᾽ ἔρωτα;

ΜΙΛΩΝ

μηδέ γε συμβαίη· χαλεπὸν χορίω κύνα γεῦσαι.

---

[1] The Greek word is *kaktos*. According to Theophrastus this
was an edible Sicilian plant with spiny leaves (*Hist. pl.* 6.4.10);
various Hellenistic poets refer to it (e.g., Philitas Fr. 15 Light-
foot). Linnaeus borrowed the term for a plant found only in the
Americas.

IDYLL 10

MILON

Workman Bucaeus, what's wrong with you, my poor fellow? You can't drive your swathe straight as you used to drive it, and you don't reap alongside the next man; you are left behind, as a sheep is left by the flock when a thorn[1] has pricked its foot. What will you be like in the evening or even in the afternoon, if right now at the start you don't nibble away at your row?

BUCAEUS

Milon, you who reap till late, a chip off the unyielding stone, have you never happened to long for someone who is absent?

MILON

Never. What use to a laboring man is longing for things outside his work?

BUCAEUS

Has it never happened that you have lost sleep through love?

MILON

No; and may it not happen, either. It's bad that a dog should get a taste of guts.

ΒΟΥΚΑΙΟΣ

ἀλλ᾽ ἐγώ, ὦ Μίλων, ἔραμαι σχεδὸν ἑνδεκαταῖος.

ΜΙΛΩΝ

ἐκ πίθω ἀντλεῖς δῆλον· ἐγὼ δ᾽ ἔχω οὐδ᾽ ἅλις ὄξος.

ΒΟΥΚΑΙΟΣ

τοιγὰρ τὰ πρὸ θυρᾶν μοι ἀπὸ σπόρω ἄσκαλα πάντα.

ΜΙΛΩΝ

15   τίς δέ τυ τᾶν παίδων λυμαίνεται;

ΒΟΥΚΑΙΟΣ

ἁ Πολυβώτα,

ἁ πρᾶν ἀμάντεσσι παρ᾽ Ἱπποκίωνι ποταύλει.

ΜΙΛΩΝ

εὗρε θεὸς τὸν ἀλιτρόν· ἔχεις πάλαι ὧν ἐπεθύμεις·
μάντις τοι τὰν νύκτα χροΐξεῖται καλαμαία.

ΒΟΥΚΑΙΟΣ

μωμᾶσθαί μ᾽ ἄρχῃ τύ· τυφλὸς δ᾽ οὐκ αὐτὸς ὁ
        Πλοῦτος,

20   ἀλλὰ καὶ ὠφρόντιστος Ἔρως. μὴ δὴ μέγα μυθεῦ.

18 χροΐξεῖται Valckenaer: χρ. ἁ fere M

---

2 Sour wine from the bottom of the cask. He pretends that
Bucaeus has a life of luxury and can afford to indulge himself in
love.

3 He seems to refer to a vegetable garden of his own, sown
recently.

4 "Girl" might mean "slave" or "daughter."

BUCAEUS

But *I* have been in love for almost ten days, Milon.

MILON

Clearly you draw wine from the cask. *I* haven't even enough vinegar.[2]

BUCAEUS

That is why the ground in front of my door is all unhoed since it was sown.[3]

MILON

And which of the girls is troubling you?

BUCAEUS

Polybotas' girl,[4] the one who was playing for the reapers at Hippocion's place the other day.[5]

MILON

God finds out the wicked. You have what you've been longing for all this while. A praying mantis will hug you all night long.[6]

BUCAEUS

You're beginning to mock me. But Wealth is not the only blind god—heedless Love is blind, too. Don't you talk big.[7]

---

[5] She plays the *aulos* pipe, an instrument resembling an oboe (cf. 34).

[6] She is skinny, ugly, and perhaps vicious. But the ancients seem not to have known that the female mantis sometimes kills and eats the male in the act of mating.

[7] Wealth is traditionally blind (as for example in Aristophanes' play *Wealth*): he rewards the undeserving. Bucaeus warns that Eros is just as indiscriminate, so that Milon may be his next victim.

ΜΙΛΩΝ

οὐ μέγα μυθεῦμαι· τὺ μόνον κατάβαλλε τὸ λᾶον,
καί τι κόρας φιλικὸν μέλος ἀμβάλευ. ἅδιον οὕτως
ἐργαξῇ. καὶ μὰν πρότερόν ποκα μουσικὸς ἦσθα.

ΒΟΥΚΑΙΟΣ

Μοῖσαι Πιερίδες, συναείσατε τὰν ῥαδινάν μοι
25 παῖδ'· ὧν γάρ χ' ἅψησθε, θεαί, καλὰ πάντα ποεῖτε.

Βομβύκα χαρίεσσα, Σύραν καλέοντί τυ πάντες,
ἰσχνάν, ἁλιόκαυστον, ἐγὼ δὲ μόνος μελίχλωρον.
καὶ τὸ ἴον μέλαν ἐστί, καὶ ἁ γραπτὰ ὑάκινθος·
ἀλλ' ἔμπας ἐν τοῖς στεφάνοις τὰ πρᾶτα λέγονται.
30 ἁ αἲξ τὰν κύτισον, ὁ λύκος τὰν αἶγα διώκει,
ἁ γέρανος τὤροτρον· ἐγὼ δ' ἐπὶ τὶν μεμάνημαι.
αἴθε μοι ἦς ὅσσα Κροῖσόν ποκα φαντὶ πεπᾶσθαι·
χρύσεοι ἀμφότεροί κ' ἀνεκείμεθα τᾷ Ἀφροδίτᾳ,
τὼς αὐλὼς μὲν ἔχοισα καὶ ἢ ῥόδον ἢ τύγε μᾶλον,
35 σχῆμα δ' ἐγὼ καὶ καινὰς ἐπ' ἀμφοτέροισιν ἀμύκλας.
Βομβύκα χαρίεσσ', οἱ μὲν πόδες ἀστράγαλοί τευς,
ἁ φωνὰ δὲ τρύχνος· τὸν μὰν τρόπον οὐκ ἔχω εἰπεῖν.

---

8 The Muses, according to Hesiod, came from Pieria near Mt.
Olympus (*Op.* 1–2).

9 The *bombyx* is a sort of *aulos*: she is named after her art.

10 A pale complexion was admired in women.

11 An unidentified plant (not the modern hyacinth) whose
leaves had marks resembling the letters AI. Various myths ex-
plained them as standing for Aias (Ajax) or *aiai* (alas!).

12 The Linnaean *Cytisus* is broom, but κύτισος has been
identified as *Medicago arborea,* the moon trefoil or tree medick.

MILON

I'm not talking big. You just knock down the crop and strike up some love song for your girl. You'll work more happily in that way. At one time you used to be a good singer.

BUCAEUS

"Pierian Muses,[8] sing with me about the slender girl; for all things you touch, goddesses, you make beautiful.

Charming Bombyca,[9] everyone else calls you Syrian, thin and sun-scorched; [10] I alone call you the color of honey. The violet is dark, and the lettered hyacinth;[11] but they are still chosen first in garlands. The goat follows the trefoil,[12] the wolf follows the goat, the crane follows the plow; but it's for you that I am mad. If only I had as much as they say Croesus once owned: we should both be set up as golden statues to Aphrodite, you holding your pipes and a rose or an apple,[13] and I with new clothes and with new Amyclaean shoes on both feet.[14] Charming Bombyca, your feet are like knucklebones,[15] your voice is like nightshade;[16] and as for your character, I haven't power to describe it."[17]

[13] Tokens of love.　　　[14] A superior style of shoe named after the Spartan town Amyclae.

[15] These can be well molded, symmetrical, pleasingly shiny, swiftly moving. Bucaeus does not make clear which aspect he admires.

[16] The meaning is obscure. Nightshade induces sleep or madness, so that Bucaeus may mean that her voice lulls him to sleep or drives him mad with passion.

[17] He means that she is indescribably attractive; but the words also suggest that his powers of description are inadequate.

ΜΙΛΩΝ

ἦ καλὰς ἄμμε ποῶν ἐλελάθει Βοῦκος ἀοιδάς·
ὡς εὖ τὰν ἰδέαν τᾶς ἁρμονίας ἐμέτρησεν.
40 ὤμοι τῶ πώγωνος, ὃν ἀλιθίως ἀνέφυσα.
θᾶσαι δὴ καὶ ταῦτα τὰ τῶ θείω Λιτυέρσα.

Δάματερ πολύκαρπε, πολύσταχυ, τοῦτο τὸ
    λᾷον
εὔεργόν τ᾽ εἴη καὶ κάρπιμον ὅττι μάλιστα.
    σφίγγετ᾽, ἀμαλλοδέται, τὰ δράγματα, μὴ πα-
    ριών τις
45   εἴπῃ "σύκινοι ἄνδρες· ἀπώλετο χοῦτος ὁ μισθός."
    ἐς βορέαν ἄνεμον τᾶς κόρθυος ἁ τομὰ ὕμμιν
ἢ ζέφυρον βλεπέτω· πιαίνεται ὁ στάχυς οὕτως.
    σῖτον ἀλοιῶντας φεύγειν τὸ μεσαμβρινὸν
    ὕπνον·
ἐκ καλάμας ἄχυρον τελέθει τημόσδε μάλιστα·
50   ἄρχεσθαι δ᾽ ἀμῶντας ἐγειρομένω κορυδαλλῶ
καὶ λήγειν εὕδοντος, ἐλινῦσαι δὲ τὸ καῦμα.
    εὐκτὸς ὁ τῶ βατράχω, παῖδες, βίος· οὐ μελε-
    δαίνει
τὸν τὸ πιεῖν ἐγχεῦντα· πάρεστι γὰρ ἄφθονον
    αὐτῷ.

MILON

Truly we hadn't realized what lovely songs Bucaeus could make. How well he measured out the form of his tune![18] Alas for my beard, grown in vain! Now consider these verses of divine Lityerses.[19]

"Demeter abounding in fruit, abounding in grain, may this crop be easy to work and as plentiful as can be.

"Binders, tie up the sheaves, in case a passerby should say, 'The fellows are as weak as fig wood: these wages are wasted, too.'

"Let the cut end of your sheaf face the north wind or the west: in that way the ear grows rich.[20]

"Corn threshers should avoid a midday sleep: at that time the top comes most easily from the stalk.

"Reapers should begin when the lark awakens and stop when it goes to sleep, but should rest during the heat.

"The frog's life is a pleasant one, my lads; he doesn't care about someone pouring his drink—it's there for him in plenty.

[18] He fitted his song to an appropriate musical mode or harmony.

[19] Lityerses, son of Midas, was for the Phrygians the inventor of agriculture, and a reaping song was named after him (Apollod. *FGH* 244 F 149). Milon's song will be of this practical sort.

[20] Wheat and barley were harvested while still unripe.

κάλλιον, ὦ 'πιμελητὰ φιλάργυρε, τὸν φακὸν
  ἕψειν,
55 μὴ 'πιτάμῃς τὰν χεῖρα καταπρίων τὸ κύμινον.

ταῦτα χρὴ μοχθεῦντας ἐν ἁλίῳ ἄνδρας ἀείδειν,
τὸν δὲ τεόν, Βουκαῖε, πρέπει λιμηρὸν ἔρωτα
μυθίσδεν τᾷ ματρὶ κατ' εὐνὰν ὀρθρευοίσᾳ.

55 μὴ 'πιτάμῃς pap., testim., m: μή τι τάμῃς m

"Stingy steward, it's better to start boiling the beans: you'll cut your hand if you split the cumin seeds."[21]

This is what men who work outdoors should sing. And as for that starving love of yours, Bucaeus[22]—it's something you should tell your mother about as she lies in bed in the mornings.[23]

[21] Cumin was used for seasoning soup. The seeds are very small, and "splitting cumin" was proverbial for niggardliness (e.g., Ar. *Vesp.* 1357).

[22] "Starving," because lovers are traditionally thin and because if he does not reap he will have nothing to eat. Some translate "your half-starved girlfriend" (cf. 18, 27 on Bombyca's thinness).

[23] In Milon's view Bucaeus is a "mother's boy" who can afford to waste his time talking about love.

IDYLL 11

This poem depicts the courtship of the sea nymph Galatea by Polyphemus; Idyll 6 provides a sequel. The main part, a love song of the Cyclops, is framed by an address to Nicias, which wittily suggests that song provides a better and cheaper remedy for love than conventional medicine.

Nicias was a doctor and poet from Miletus. Idyll 13 is addressed to him, and 28 compliments his wife Theugenis; Epigram 8 mentions a dedication of his to the god of healing. Eight of his own epigrams survive (HE 2755–86). Two lines are extant from his response to this idyll: "It's true, Theocritus: Love has taught many men to be poets who were uninspired before" (SH 566).

The Cyclopean monody as an attempt to cure love is inspired by Philoxenus (PMG 821–22; cf. p. 105). Polyphemus' serenade is in parts clumsy and ill-judged. Nicias is a sophisticated reader able to relish the contrast between Polyphemus' words and reality. The Cyclops is made to utter allusions to events in the future as recounted by Homer (38, 51, 61, 79), and his view of his domestic and personal attractions is clearly misplaced. The cozy interior of his cave is destined to witness hideous cannibalism, his appearance to inspire terror in Odysseus and his men. He wavers between pathos and bathos, between lyricism and a childlike self-indulgence.

166

IDYLL 11

Criticism

Brooke, A. "Theocritus' Idyll 11: A Study in Pastoral." *Arethusa* 4 (1971): 73–81.

Fantuzzi, M. "Mythological Paradigms in the Bucolic Poetry of Theocritus." *PCPhS* 41 (1995): 16–35.

Goldhill, *Poet's Voice,* 249–56.

Holtsmark, E. B. "Poetry as Self-enlightenment: Theocritus 11." *TAPhA* 97 (1966): 253–59.

Hunter, *Selection,* 215–43.

Kutzko, D. "The Bemused Singer and Well-versed Audience: The Use of Polyphemus in Theocritus." *SIFC* ns 5 (2007): 73–114.

Payne, *Invention of Fiction,* 67–82.

Spofford, E. W. "Theocritus and Polyphemus." *AJPh* 90 (1969): 22–35.

11

Οὐδὲν ποττὸν ἔρωτα πεφύκει φάρμακον ἄλλο,
Νικία, οὔτ' ἔγχριστον, ἐμὶν δοκεῖ, οὔτ' ἐπίπαστον,
ἢ ταὶ Πιερίδες· κοῦφον δέ τι τοῦτο καὶ ἁδύ
γίνετ' ἐπ' ἀνθρώποις, εὑρεῖν δ' οὐ ῥᾴδιόν ἐστι.
5 γινώσκειν δ' οἶμαί τυ καλῶς ἰατρὸν ἐόντα
καὶ ταῖς ἐννέα δὴ πεφιλημένον ἔξοχα Μοίσαις.
οὕτω γοῦν ῥάιστα διᾶγ' ὁ Κύκλωψ ὁ παρ' ἁμῖν,
ὡρχαῖος Πολύφαμος, ὅκ' ἤρατο τᾶς Γαλατείας,
ἄρτι γενειάσδων περὶ τὸ στόμα τὼς κροτάφως τε.
10 ἤρατο δ' οὐ μάλοις οὐδὲ ῥόδῳ οὐδὲ κικίννοις,
ἀλλ' ὀρθαῖς μανίαις, ἁγεῖτο δὲ πάντα πάρεργα.
πολλάκι ταὶ ὄιες ποτὶ τωὔλιον αὐταὶ ἀπῆνθον
χλωρᾶς ἐκ βοτάνας· ὁ δὲ τὰν Γαλάτειαν ἀείδων
αὐτὸς ἐπ' ἀιόνος κατετάκετο φυκιοέσσας
15 ἐξ ἀοῦς, ἔχθιστον ἔχων ὑποκάρδιον ἕλκος,
Κύπριδος ἐκ μεγάλας τό οἱ ἥπατι πᾶξε βέλεμνον.

10 οὐδὲ ῥόδῳ Ziegler: οὐδὲ ῥόδοις m: οὐδ' αὖ ῥόδῳ m: οὐδ'
αὖ ῥόδοις m

---

[1] See on *Id.* 10.24.
[2] I.e., an exceptional poet. The allocation of particular arts to
particular Muses occurred after the time of Theocritus.

IDYLL 11

There is in nature no remedy for love, Nicias—neither an ointment, I believe, nor a powder—other than the Pierian Muses.[1] This remedy is a light and pleasant one for mortals, but it is not easy to find. I know that you are well aware of this, being both a doctor and an especial favorite of all nine Muses.[2] Our countryman the Cyclops,[3] Polyphemus of old, got on as easily as he could[4] in this way when he was in love with Galatea, the beard just sprouting round his mouth and temples. He loved not with apples or roses or locks of hair,[5] but with outright madness, and he thought everything else was less important. Often his sheep returned alone[6] to their fold from the green pasture while he, singing of Galatea, pined away alone on the weedy seashore from daybreak, having a most hateful wound deep in his heart, which an arrow from the great Cyprian goddess[7] had fixed in his liver.[8] But he discovered

---

[3] According to post-Homeric writers, the Cyclopes inhabited Sicily (Thuc. 6.2.1).

[4] The Greek has a medical flavor, as one speaks of a patient being "easier."

[5] Tokens of love.

[6] Or, "of their own accord."

[7] Aphrodite, born on the island of Cyprus (Hes. *Theog.* 190–200).

[8] Seat of the passions.

ἀλλὰ τὸ φάρμακον εὗρε, καθεζόμενος δ᾽ ἐπὶ πέτρας
ὑψηλᾶς ἐς πόντον ὁρῶν ἄειδε τοιαῦτα·

ˁΩ λευκὰ Γαλάτεια, τί τὸν φιλέοντ᾽ ἀποβάλλῃ,
20 λευκοτέρα πακτᾶς ποτιδεῖν, ἁπαλωτέρα ἀρνός,
μόσχω γαυροτέρα, φιαρωτέρα ὄμφακος ὠμᾶς;
φοιτῇς δ᾽ αὖθ᾽ οὕτως ὅκκα γλυκὺς ὕπνος ἔχῃ με,
οἴχῃ δ᾽ εὐθὺς ἰοῖσ᾽ ὅκκα γλυκὺς ὕπνος ἀνῇ με,
φεύγεις δ᾽ ὥσπερ ὄις πολιὸν λύκον ἀθρήσασα;
25 ἠράσθην μὲν ἔγωγε τεοῦς, κόρα, ἁνίκα πρᾶτον
ἦνθες ἐμᾷ σὺν ματρὶ θέλοισ᾽ ὑακίνθινα φύλλα
ἐξ ὄρεος δρέψασθαι, ἐγὼ δ᾽ ὁδὸν ἁγεμόνευον.
παύσασθαι δ᾽ ἐσιδών τυ καὶ ὕστερον οὐδ᾽ ἔτι πᾳ νῦν
ἐκ τήνω δύναμαι· τὶν δ᾽ οὐ μέλει, οὐ μὰ Δί᾽ οὐδέν.
30 γινώσκω, χαρίεσσα κόρα, τίνος οὕνεκα φεύγεις·
οὕνεκά μοι λασία μὲν ὀφρὺς ἐπὶ παντὶ μετώπῳ
ἐξ ὠτὸς τέταται ποτὶ θώτερον ὡς μία μακρά,
εἷς δ᾽ ὀφθαλμὸς ὕπεστι, πλατεῖα δὲ ῥὶς ἐπὶ χείλει.
ἀλλ᾽ οὗτος τοιοῦτος ἐὼν βοτὰ χίλια βόσκω,
35 κἠκ τούτων τὸ κράτιστον ἀμελγόμενος γάλα πίνω·
τυρὸς δ᾽ οὐ λείπει μ᾽ οὔτ᾽ ἐν θέρει οὔτ᾽ ἐν ὀπώρᾳ,
οὐ χειμῶνος ἄκρω· ταρσοὶ δ᾽ ὑπεραχθέες αἰεί.

---

33 ὕπεστι Winsem: ἔπ- m   34 οὕτως m: ωὗτὸς m

---

9 Critics have puzzled over the fact that song is said to be both
a symptom of and a remedy for Polyphemus' love. The word
translated "remedy" (*pharmakon*) can mean a drug good or bad.
The idea is perhaps that singing was a temporary alleviation for
his pain and that the treatment had to be repeated. But the very

the remedy;[9] and, sitting on a high rock, he would sing in this way as he gazed out to sea:

"O white Galatea, why do you reject one who loves you—whiter than curd to look on,[10] softer than the lamb, more skittish than the calf, sleeker than the unripe grape—and why do you visit in this way as soon as sweet sleep holds me, but go off, departing at once, when sweet sleep releases me, fleeing like a ewe that has seen the gray wolf?[11] I fell in love with you, girl, when first you came with my mother[12] to gather hyacinth flowers[13] from the hill, and I led the way. And having seen you, since that time I cannot afterward even now cease at all from love;[14] but you don't care—not at all, by Zeus.

"I know why you avoid me, lovely girl: it's because a long, single eyebrow stretches from one of my ears to the other, a shaggy brow over my whole forehead; and beneath it is a single eye, and a broad nostril above my lip. Yet, though I am so, I pasture a thousand sheep, and from them I draw and drink the finest milk. Cheese does not fail me in summer or autumn or at the end of winter:[15] my racks are al-

---

act of singing about Galatea may foster his love (cf. 80, "shepherded his love"). At any rate, by the end of his song he has gained some consolation.

[10] Cf. on *Id.* 10.26–27. Galatea is named from *gala* (milk).

[11] Perhaps a naive description of his dreams.

[12] Polyphemus was the son of Poseidon and the sea nymph Thoösa (Hom. *Od.* 1.68–73).   [13] Cf. on *Id.* 10.28.

[14] The Greek is clumsily redundant, perhaps characteristically Cyclopean.   [15] Or, perhaps, "in midwinter"; but shortages are more likely at the end of the season.

συρίσδεν δ' ὡς οὔτις ἐπίσταμαι ὧδε Κυκλώπων,
τίν, τὸ φίλον γλυκύμαλον, ἁμᾷ κἠμαυτὸν ἀείδων
40 πολλάκι νυκτὸς ἀωρί. τράφω δέ τοι ἕνδεκα νεβρώς,
πάσας μαννοφόρως, καὶ σκύμνως τέσσαρας ἄρκτων.
ἀλλ' ἀφίκευσο ποθ' ἁμέ, καὶ ἑξεῖς οὐδὲν ἔλασσον,
τὰν γλαυκὰν δὲ θάλασσαν ἔα ποτὶ χέρσον ὀρεχθεῖν·
ἅδιον ἐν τὤντρῳ παρ' ἐμὶν τὰν νύκτα διαξεῖς.
45 ἐντὶ δάφναι τηνεί, ἐντὶ ῥαδιναὶ κυπάρισσοι,
ἔστι μέλας κισσός, ἔστ' ἄμπελος ἁ γλυκύκαρπος,
ἔστι ψυχρὸν ὕδωρ, τό μοι ἁ πολυδένδρεος Αἴτνα
λευκᾶς ἐκ χιόνος ποτὸν ἀμβρόσιον προΐητι.
τίς κα τῶνδε θάλασσαν ἔχειν καὶ κύμαθ' ἕλοιτο;
50 αἰ δέ τοι αὐτὸς ἐγὼν δοκέω λασιώτερος ἦμεν,
ἐντὶ δρυὸς ξύλα μοι καὶ ὑπὸ σποδῷ ἀκάματον πῦρ·
καιόμενος δ' ὑπὸ τεῦς καὶ τὰν ψυχὰν ἀνεχοίμαν
καὶ τὸν ἕν' ὀφθαλμόν, τῶ μοι γλυκερώτερον οὐδέν.
ὤμοι, ὅτ' οὐκ ἔτεκέν μ' ἁ μάτηρ βράγχι' ἔχοντα,
55 ὡς κατέδυν ποτὶ τὶν καὶ τὰν χέρα τεῦς ἐφίλησα,
αἰ μὴ τὸ στόμα λῇς, ἔφερον δέ τοι ἢ κρίνα λευκά
ἢ μάκων' ἁπαλὰν ἐρυθρὰ πλαταγώνι' ἔχοισαν·
ἀλλὰ τὰ μὲν θέρεος, τὰ δὲ γίνεται ἐν χειμῶνι,
ὥστ' οὔ κά τοι ταῦτα φέρειν ἅμα πάντ' ἐδυνάθην.

49 κα Brunck: κἀν m: τὰν m: ἀν m   καὶ Ahrens: ἢ M
59 κά Wilamowitz: ἄν M

ways laden. I know how to pipe like no other[16] of the Cyclopes here, singing of you, my dear sweet apple, and of myself, often late into the night. I am rearing eleven fawns for you, all with collars, and four bear cubs.

"Come to me, and you will be no worse off; let the gray sea beat upon the shore. You will spend the night more pleasantly in the cave with me. There are laurels, there are slender cypresses, there is dark ivy, there is the sweet-fruited vine, there is cold water which wooded Etna produces for me from its white snow, a divine drink. Who would choose the sea and its waves instead of these things?

"Even if I seem rather too shaggy, I do have oak logs and undying fire under the ash; and in my burning love for you[17] I would yield up my soul and my single eye. I have no dearer possession than that.

"If only my mother had borne me with gills, so that I could have come down to you and kissed your hand (if you do not want me to kiss your mouth) and brought you white snowdrops[18] or the soft poppy with its red petals. But poppies grow in summer, snowdrops in winter, so that I couldn't have brought you these all together. As it is, my

[16] Lit., "no one" (*outis*), a covert reference to Odysseus' assumed name Outis (Nobody), which proves to be the undoing of Polyphemus at Hom. *Od.* 9.366–408. Cf. line 79, where the Cyclops claims not to be a "nobody," and 61 "some (*tis*) stranger."

[17] Lit., "burned by you." Some translate, "if you were to burn me," an invitation to Galatea to singe his superfluous hair; but the chain of thought seems to be akin to that of lines 30–34 (physical disadvantage, material advantage).

[18] Not certainly identified; perhaps "narcissi."

60 νῦν μάν, ὦ κόριον, νῦν αὐτίκα νεῖν γε μαθεῦμαι,
αἴ κά τις σὺν ναῒ πλέων ξένος ὧδ᾽ ἀφίκηται,
ὡς εἰδῶ τί ποχ᾽ ἁδὺ κατοικεῖν τὸν βυθὸν ὔμμιν.
ἐξένθοις, Γαλάτεια, καὶ ἐξενθοῖσα λάθοιο,
ὥσπερ ἐγὼ νῦν ὧδε καθήμενος, οἴκαδ᾽ ἀπενθεῖν·
65 ποιμαίνειν δ᾽ ἐθέλοις σὺν ἐμὶν ἅμα καὶ γάλ᾽ ἀμέλγειν
καὶ τυρὸν πᾶξαι τάμισον δριμεῖαν ἐνεῖσα.
ἁ μάτηρ ἀδικεῖ με μόνα, καὶ μέμφομαι αὐτᾷ·
οὐδὲν πήποχ᾽ ὅλως ποτὶ τὶν φίλον εἶπεν ὑπέρ μευ,
καὶ ταῦτ᾽ ἆμαρ ἐπ᾽ ἆμαρ ὁρεῦσά με λεπτύνοντα.
70 φασῶ τὰν κεφαλὰν καὶ τὼς πόδας ἀμφοτέρως μευ
σφύσδειν, ὡς ἀνιαθῇ, ἐπεὶ κἠγὼν ἀνιῶμαι.
ὦ Κύκλωψ Κύκλωψ, πᾷ τὰς φρένας ἐκπεπότασαι;
αἴ κ᾽ ἐνθὼν ταλάρως τε πλέκοις καὶ θαλλὸν ἀμάσας
ταῖς ἄρνεσσι φέροις, τάχα κα πολὺ μᾶλλον ἔχοις
νῶν.
75 τὰν παρεοῖσαν ἄμελγε· τί τὸν φεύγοντα διώκεις;
εὑρησεῖς Γαλάτειαν ἴσως καὶ καλλίον᾽ ἄλλαν.
πολλαὶ συμπαίσδεν με κόραι τὰν νύκτα κέλονται,
κιχλίζοντι δὲ πᾶσαι, ἐπεί κ᾽ αὐταῖς ὑπακούσω.
δῆλον ὅτ᾽ ἐν τᾷ γᾷ κἠγών τις φαίνομαι ἦμεν.
80 Οὕτω τοι Πολύφαμος ἐποίμαινεν τὸν ἔρωτα
μουσίσδων, ῥᾷον δὲ διᾶγ᾽ ἢ εἰ χρυσὸν ἔδωκεν.

60 αὐτίκα Paley: αὐτόγα m: τόγε m
69 λεπτύνοντα Meineke: λεπτὸν ἐόντα M
74 κα Ahrens: καὶ M

174

girl, I shall learn to swim without delay, if some stranger comes here sailing in a ship, so that I may find out how pleasant it is to you folk to live in the deep sea.

"Come out, Galatea; and, having come out, forget to go back home, just as I do now as I sit here. If only you wanted to tend the sheep in company with me and to do the milking and set the cheese by putting in keen rennet.

"Only my mother treats me badly, and it's her that I blame: she has never once said a kind word to you on my behalf, even though she sees me growing thinner by the day. I shall tell her that my head and both my feet are throbbing, so that she may suffer, since I am suffering too.

"O Cyclops, Cyclops, where have your wits flown? If you went and plaited wicker baskets[19] and cut down greenery and carried it to your lambs, you would have much more sense. Milk the sheep that's by you; why do you pursue someone who flees?[20] Maybe you'll find another Galatea who is even prettier. Many girls invite me to play with them through the night, and they all giggle when I take notice.[21] It's clear that on land I too am a somebody."

In this way Polyphemus shepherded his love with singing, and he did better than if he had spent money.[22]

---

[19] For draining cheese or curd.
[20] Proverbial expressions.
[21] Or, "when I answer them."
[22] I.e., than if he had paid a fee to a doctor such as Nicias.

IDYLL 12

A lover's fulsome welcome for a boy who has been absent for two days. After a lengthy series of comparisons, the speaker expresses the hope that their love will be celebrated by lovers in the future. After further praise of the boy, he concludes with a long description of a kissing contest at Megara.

Scholars who take Theocritus to be the speaker deprecate a self-consciously learned but misapplied antiquarianism. It seems more likely, however, that references to obscure cults, etymology, pimples and touchstones, the highly optimistic hope for eternal fame, and the disproportion of the opening and closing sections, are meant to characterize the speaker as an effusive, insecure, perhaps comic, figure akin to the speakers of Idylls 3 and 29: *his ambition is not matched by his ability.*

The poem is in Ionic dialect, not in the Doric of Theocritus' pastoral characters.

Criticism

Hunter, *Archaeology*, 40–41, 186–95.
Payne, *Invention of Fiction*, 100–113.

12

Ἤλυθες, ὦ φίλε κοῦρε· τρίτῃ σὺν νυκτὶ καὶ ἠοῖ
ἤλυθες· οἱ δὲ ποθεῦντες ἐν ἤματι γηράσκουσιν.
ὅσσον ἔαρ χειμῶνος, ὅσον μῆλον βραβίλοιο
ἥδιον, ὅσσον ὄις σφετέρης λασιωτέρη ἀρνός,
5 ὅσσον παρθενικὴ προφέρει τριγάμοιο γυναικός,
ὅσσον ἐλαφροτέρη μόσχου νεβρός, ὅσσον ἀηδών
συμπάντων λιγύφωνος ἀοιδοτάτη πετεηνῶν,
τόσσον ἔμ᾽ εὔφρηνας σὺ φανείς, σκιερὴν δ᾽ ὑπὸ φη-
        γόν
ἠελίου φρύγοντος ὁδοιπόρος ἔδραμον ὥς τις.
10 εἴθ᾽ ὁμαλοὶ πνεύσειαν ἐπ᾽ ἀμφοτέροισιν Ἔρωτες
νῶιν, ἐπεσσομένοις δὲ γενοίμεθα πᾶσιν ἀοιδή·
"δίω δή τινε τώδε μετὰ προτέροισι γενέσθην
φῶθ᾽, ὁ μὲν εἴσπνηλος, φαίη χ᾽ Ὠμυκλαϊάζων,
τὸν δ᾽ ἕτερον πάλιν, ὥς κεν ὁ Θεσσαλὸς εἴποι, ἀίτην.
15 ἀλλήλους δ᾽ ἐφίλησαν ἴσῳ ζυγῷ. ἦ ῥα τότ᾽ ἦσαν
χρύσειοι πάλιν ἄνδρες, ὅτ᾽ ἀντεφίλησ᾽ ὁ φιληθείς."
εἰ γὰρ τοῦτο, πάτερ Κρονίδη, πέλοι, εἰ γάρ, ἀγήρῳ

12 δίω Ahrens: δοιὼ M   μετὰ προτέροισι Taylor e
schol.: μετ᾽ ἀμφοτέροισι M

178

IDYLL 12

You have come, my dear lad, after two days and nights you have come; but those who feel longing grow old in a day. As summer is sweeter than winter, the apple than the sloe; as the ewe is fleecier than her lamb; as a girl surpasses a woman three times married; as a fawn is nimbler than a calf; as the nightingale with its clear song is the most tuneful of all winged creatures—just so your coming has cheered me, and I have hurried to you as a traveler hurries to a shady oak when the sun is scorching.

If only the Loves would breathe on us both equally, and we could become a subject for song for future lovers— "Outstanding were these two among men of the past, the one inspiring (as a man from Amyclae might say), the other receptive, as a Thessalian would call him.[1] They loved one another on equal terms.[2] It was a second golden age indeed when the beloved loved in return." Father Zeus and you unaging immortals, two hundred genera-

---

[1] According to the scholia this poem is in Ionic dialect, but the dialect of Amyclae (near Sparta) was Doric, and that of Thessaly a form of Aeolic. Why Amyclae in particular is mentioned is not clear. The Doric *eispnêlos* seems to mean "inspirer" (from πνεῖν, "breathe"; cf. 10, πνεύσειαν) and *aîtês* "hearer," one who receives inspiration.

[2] Lit., "in an equal yoke." The metaphor is probably from yoked cattle, but it may be from a balanced pair of scales.

ἀθάνατοι, γενεῆς δὲ διηκοσίῃσιν ἔπειτα
ἀγγείλειεν ἐμοί τις ἀνέξοδον εἰς Ἀχέροντα·
20 "ἡ σὴ νῦν φιλότης καὶ τοῦ χαρίεντος ἄιτεω
πᾶσι διὰ στόματος, μετὰ δ' ἠιθέοισι μάλιστα."
ἀλλ' ἤτοι τούτων μὲν ὑπέρτεροι Οὐρανίωνες·
ἔσσεται ὡς ἐθέλουσιν. ἐγὼ δέ σε τὸν καλὸν αἰνέων
ψεύδεα ῥινὸς ὕπερθεν ἀραιῆς οὐκ ἀναφύσω.
25 ἢν γὰρ καί τι δάκῃς, τὸ μὲν ἀβλαβὲς εὐθὺς ἔθηκας,
διπλάσιον δ' ὤνησας, ἔχων δ' ἐπίμετρον ἀπῆλθον.
Νισαῖοι Μεγαρῆες, ἀριστεύοντες ἐρετμοῖς,
ὄλβιοι οἰκείοιτε, τὸν Ἀττικὸν ὡς περίαλλα
ξεῖνον ἐτιμήσασθε, Διοκλέα τὸν φιλόπαιδα.
30 αἰεί οἱ περὶ τύμβον ἀολλέες εἴαρι πρώτῳ
κοῦροι ἐριδμαίνουσι φιλήματος ἄκρα φέρεσθαι·
ὃς δέ κε προσμάξῃ γλυκερώτερα χείλεσι χείλη,
βριθόμενος στεφάνοισιν ἑὴν ἐς μητέρ' ἀπῆλθεν.
ὄλβιος ὅστις παισὶ φιλήματα κεῖνα διαιτᾷ.
35 ἦ που τὸν χαροπὸν Γανυμήδεα πόλλ' ἐπιβῶται
Λυδίῃ ἶσον ἔχειν πέτρῃ στόμα, χρυσὸν ὁποίῃ
πεύθονται, μὴ φαῦλος, ἐτήτυμον ἀργυραμοιβοί.

23 ἔσσεται Meineke: ἔσσονθ' M

tions from now I should like someone to bring me news in Acheron, from where there is no return, "Your love and that of the handsome youth[3] are spoken of by everyone, and especially by the young men."

But it is the gods who control these matters: it will be as they wish. And when I praise your beauty I shall not grow any liar's pimples above my slender nose.[4] If you *are* sometimes snappish, you mend the hurt at once and give me a double pleasure, and I go away with a surfeit.

Nisaean Megarians,[5] oarsmen supreme, may you live in prosperity because you greatly honored the stranger from Attica, Diocles the lover of boys.[6] Always at the beginning of spring the lads gather round his tomb and compete for the prize in kissing; and whoever most sweetly presses lips on lips goes home to his mother loaded with garlands. Fortunate is he who judges those kisses for the boys. I daresay he utters many a prayer to bright Ganymede[7] that his mouth should be like the Lydian stone with which money changers test real gold to make sure it is not false.[8]

[3] The same rare Thessalian word is used as in line 14.

[4] According to the scholia, pimples on the nose betokened a liar.

[5] Nisaea was the port of Megara on the Saronic Gulf.

[6] Diocles died at Megara defending his lover in battle (schol. ad loc.)

[7] Archetype of desirable youth.

[8] The touchstone (Bacchyl. Fr. 14). When rubbed on it, pure and impure gold would make different traces. All kisses seem good to the judge, who will need divine help to find the best.

IDYLL 13

This poem, like Idyll 11, *begins with an address, didactic in tone, to Theocritus' friend Nicias, and it too deals with the power of Eros. It tells a story from the voyage of the Argonauts. Heracles' beloved companion Hylas goes to fetch water and is pulled by the nymphs into their pool. Heracles ranges far and wide in his search for the boy, and the Argonauts have to set sail without him.*

A version of the story is told by Theocritus' contemporary Apollonius of Rhodes at the end of Book 1 of the Argonautica. Apollonius' next episode, the tale of Amycus and Polydeuces, is treated by Theocritus in Idyll 22. *It therefore seems very likely that Theocritus is writing in response to Apollonius' section of narrative. In Apollonius an important function of the Hylas story is to remove Heracles from the Argonautic expedition, for which he has already been shown to be unsuited; the erotic nature of his relationship with Hylas is only hinted at. Theocritus brings Eros to the fore, has no mention of the Argonaut Polyphemus (who in Apollonius brings the news about Heracles), has the Argonauts more plausibly decide to leave without Heracles rather than fail to notice his absence, and pointedly states that he did eventually rejoin the expedition. The pool of the nymphs is given a lush*

*setting of a type familiar from the bucolic poems, but the
prominent similes are a gesture toward epic style.*

Criticism

Hunter, *Selection*, 261–89.

Mastronarde, D. J. "Theocritus' Idyll 13: Love and the
    Hero." *TAPhA* 99 (1968): 273–90.

Payne, *Invention of Fiction*, 82–91.

Van Erp Taalman Kip, A. M. "Intertextuality and Theocri-
    tus 13." In *Modern Critical Theory and Classical Lit-
    erature*, edited by I. J. F. de Jong and J. P. Sullivan,
    158–69. Leiden, 1994.

13

Οὐχ ἁμῖν τὸν Ἔρωτα μόνοις ἔτεχ', ὡς ἐδοκεῦμες,
Νικία, ᾧτινι τοῦτο θεῶν ποκα τέκνον ἔγεντο·
οὐχ ἁμῖν τὰ καλὰ πράτοις καλὰ φαίνεται ἦμεν,
οἳ θνατοὶ πελόμεσθα, τὸ δ' αὔριον οὐκ ἐσορῶμες·

5 ἀλλὰ καὶ Ἀμφιτρύωνος ὁ χαλκεοκάρδιος υἱός,
ὃς τὸν λῖν ὑπέμεινε τὸν ἄγριον, ἤρατο παιδός,
τοῦ χαρίεντος Ὕλα, τοῦ τὰν πλοκαμῖδα φορεῦντος,
καί νιν πάντ' ἐδίδασκε, πατὴρ ὡσεὶ φίλον υἱόν,
ὅσσα μαθὼν ἀγαθὸς καὶ ἀοίδιμος αὐτὸς ἔγεντο·

10 χωρὶς δ' οὐδέποκ' ἦς, οὔτ' εἰ μέσον ἆμαρ ὄροιτο,
οὔθ' ὁπόχ' ἁ λεύκιππος ἀνατρέχοι ἐς Διὸς Ἀώς,
οὔθ' ὁπόκ' ὀρτάλιχοι μινυροὶ ποτὶ κοῖτον ὁρῷεν,
σεισαμένας πτερὰ ματρὸς ἐπ' αἰθαλόεντι πετεύρῳ,
ὡς αὐτῷ κατὰ θυμὸν ὁ παῖς πεπονημένος εἴη,

15 αὐτῷ δ' εὖ ἕλκων ἐς ἀλαθινὸν ἄνδρ' ἀποβαίη.
ἀλλ' ὅτε τὸ χρύσειον ἔπλει μετὰ κῶας Ἰάσων
Αἰσονίδας, οἱ δ' αὐτῷ ἀριστῆες συνέποντο

10 οὔτ' Sauppe: οὐδ' M
11 ὁπόχ' Grafe: ὅκα M   ἀνατρέχοι Schaefer: -χει M
15 αὐτῷ δ' εὖ ἕλκων corrupta: αὐτῶ (adv.), αὐτῷ schol. vv. ll.

---

[1] The parentage of Eros was notoriously controversial (schol.
ad loc.; Pl. *Symp.* 178b).

[2] Heracles is often called son of Amphitryon, though he was

184

IDYLL 13

Not for us alone, Nicias, as we used to think, was Love
begotten by whichever of the gods was his father:[1] we are
not the first to admire beauty, we who are mortal and do
not know what tomorrow brings. The bronze-hearted son
of Amphitryon, too, who withstood the fierce lion,[2] loved
a boy, the graceful Hylas who still wore his hair long.[3] Just
as a father teaches his dear son, he taught him all the
knowledge that had made him fine and famous himself.
He was never apart from him—neither as midday came
on, nor when Dawn with her white steeds gallops up to
the house of Zeus,[4] nor at the time when piping chicks
look to their rest as their mother shakes her wings on her
smoke-darkened perch[5]—so that the boy might be trained
as he wished and turn out a true man in company with
him.[6]

Now when Jason son of Aeson was to set sail after the
Golden Fleece, and there came as his companions the best

fathered by Zeus on Amphitryon's wife, Alcmena (cf. *Id.* 24). He
could defeat the famous Nemean lion, but not love.

[3] A haircutting ritual commonly marked the transition to
adulthood (Euphor. *Anth. Pal.* 6.279).

[4] Dawn, like Night and the Sun, has a chariot (Hom. *Od.*
23.241–46; cf. Theoc. *Id.* 2.166). This epic-sounding line is un-
dercut by the following description.

[5] In the rafters of a house.

[6] The last words are probably corrupt.

πασᾶν ἐκ πολίων προλελεγμένοι ὧν ὄφελός τι,
ἵκετο χὠ ταλαεργὸς ἀνὴρ ἐς ἀφνειὸν Ἰωλκόν,
20 Ἀλκμήνας υἱὸς Μιδεάτιδος ἡρωίνας,
σὺν δ' αὐτῷ κατέβαινεν Ὕλας εὔεδρον ἐς Ἀργώ,
ἅτις κυανεᾶν οὐχ ἅψατο συνδρομάδων ναῦς,
ἀλλὰ διεξάιξε βαθὺν δ' εἰσέδραμε Φᾶσιν,
αἰετὸς ὥς, μέγα λαῖτμα, ἀφ' οὗ τότε χοιράδες ἔσταν.
25 Ἆμος δ' ἀντέλλοντι Πελειάδες, ἐσχατιαὶ δέ
ἄρνα νέον βόσκοντι, τετραμμένου εἴαρος ἤδη,
τᾶμος ναυτιλίας μιμνάσκετο θεῖος ἄωτος
ἡρώων, κοίλαν δὲ καθιδρυθέντες ἐς Ἀργώ
Ἑλλάσποντον ἵκοντο νότῳ τρίτον ἆμαρ ἀέντι,
30 εἴσω δ' ὅρμον ἔθεντο Προποντίδος, ἔνθα Κιανῶν
αὔλακας εὐρύνοντι βόες τρίβοντες ἄροτρα.
ἐκβάντες δ' ἐπὶ θῖνα κατὰ ζυγὰ δαῖτα πένοντο
δειελινοί, πολλοὶ δὲ μίαν στορέσαντο χαμεύναν.
λειμὼν πάρ σφιν ἔκειτο, μέγα στιβάδεσσιν ὄνειαρ,
35 ἔνθεν βούτομον ὀξὺ βαθύν τ' ἐτάμοντο κύπειρον.
κὤχεθ' Ὕλας ὁ ξανθὸς ὕδωρ ἐπιδόρπιον οἴσων

34 λ. πάρ σφιν ἔκειτο A. Griffiths (λ. σφιν παρέκειτο pap.):
λ. γάρ σφιν ἔκειτο M

---

[7] Her father was Electryon, king of Midea in the Argolid (*Id.*
24.1–2).   [8] The Argo set sail from Pagasae, harbor of Iolcus
in Thessaly.   [9] The Phasis, at the far end of the Black Sea,
was Argo's destination; the Clashing Rocks, fated to be fixed once
a ship passed through them (Ap. Rhod. 2.604–6) guarded the
entrance to the Black Sea from the Bosporus. This sequence
therefore covers the whole voyage from that point in a single

heroes of every city as need dictated, then the man of many labors, son of Alcmena princess of Midea,[7] came to wealthy Iolcus,[8] and Hylas went down with him to the well-benched Argo, which did not touch the dark Clashing Rocks but shot straight through and sped into the deep river Phasis like an eagle over a vast expanse; since when the rocks have stood fixed.[9]

At the time when the Pleiades rise[10] and, once spring has turned to summer, distant uplands pasture the young lambs, then that godlike band of heroes in their prime put their minds to seafaring. Taking their places in the hollow Argo, they arrived at the Hellespont after three days of southerly wind. They anchored within the Propontis, where the oxen of the Cians cut broad furrows as they wear down the plowshares.[11] They disembarked on the beach and in the evening prepared their meal in pairs, though they laid a single bed on the ground for them all; for there was a meadow of great use for bedding, where they cut sharp sedge and thick[12] galingale. Hylas of the golden hair went with a bronze vessel to fetch water for

sentence, with a notable compression of Apollonius' two books of narrative. But the immediate transition from Bosporus to Phasis and the unexpected recurrence to the Rocks have led scholars to suspect a textual problem.

[10] The reappearance of the Pleiades in the night sky in late May or early June and their disappearance in late October or early November marked the limits of the sailing season.

[11] Cius, on the southern coast of the Propontis, was according to Apollonius founded by the Argonaut Polyphemus (1.1321–23, 1345–47).

[12] Or, "tall."

αὐτῷ θ᾽ Ἡρακλῆι καὶ ἀστεμφεῖ Τελαμῶνι,
οἳ μίαν ἄμφω ἑταῖροι ἀεὶ δαίνυντο τράπεζαν,
χάλκεον ἄγγος ἔχων. τάχα δὲ κράναν ἐνόησεν
40 ἡμένῳ ἐν χώρῳ· περὶ δὲ θρύα πολλὰ πεφύκει,
κυάνεόν τε χελιδόνιον χλωρόν τ᾽ ἀδίαντον
καὶ θάλλοντα σέλινα καὶ εἰλιτενὴς ἄγρωστις.
ὕδατι δ᾽ ἐν μέσσῳ Νύμφαι χορὸν ἀρτίζοντο,
Νύμφαι ἀκοίμητοι, δειναὶ θεαὶ ἀγροιώταις,
45 Εὐνίκα καὶ Μαλὶς ἔαρ θ᾽ ὁρόωσα Νύχεια.
ἤτοι ὁ κοῦρος ἐπεῖχε ποτῷ πολυχανδέα κρωσσόν
βάψαι ἐπειγόμενος· ταὶ δ᾽ ἐν χερὶ πᾶσαι ἔφυσαν·
πασάων γὰρ ἔρως ἁπαλὰς φρένας ἐξεφόβησεν
Ἀργείῳ ἐπὶ παιδί. κατήριπε δ᾽ ἐς μέλαν ὕδωρ
50 ἀθρόος, ὡς ὅτε πυρσὸς ἀπ᾽ οὐρανοῦ ἤριπεν ἀστήρ
ἀθρόος ἐν πόντῳ, ναύτας δέ τις εἶπεν ἑταίροις
"κουφότερ᾽, ὦ παῖδες, ποιεῖσθ᾽ ὅπλα· πλευστικὸς
          οὖρος."
Νύμφαι μὲν σφετέροις ἐπὶ γούνασι κοῦρον ἔχοισαι
δακρυόεντ᾽ ἀγανοῖσι παρεψύχοντ᾽ ἐπέεσσιν·
55 Ἀμφιτρυωνιάδας δὲ ταρασσόμενος περὶ παιδί
ᾤχετο, Μαιωτιστὶ λαβὼν εὐκαμπέα τόξα
καὶ ῥόπαλον, τό οἱ αἰὲν ἐχάνδανε δεξιτερὰ χείρ.
τρὶς μὲν Ὕλαν ἄυσεν, ὅσον βαθὺς ἤρυγε λαιμός·

51 ναύτας Brunck: -ταις M

---

[13] Father of Ajax and uncle of Achilles. In Apollonius' account
he tries to make the Argonauts go back for Heracles when he is
accidentally left behind as he searches for Hylas (1.1289–1344).

the meal for Heracles himself and steadfast Telamon,[13] two comrades who always dined together. Soon he spotted a spring in a low-lying place; around it grew lush reed, dark celandine, green maidenhair, flourishing celery, and creeping dog's-tooth grass. In the pool the Nymphs were in their stately dance, the Nymphs that never rest, goddesses feared by the country people, Eunice and Malis and Nychea with springtime in her eyes. The boy reached down, eager to dip his large pitcher in the fresh water; but the Nymphs all clung to his hand, all their tender hearts stricken with love for the Argive boy.[14] He plummeted headlong into the dark water, just as a shooting star plummets headlong from the heavens to the sea, and a sailor says to the crew, "Make the tackle ready, lads: there's a wind for sailing."[15]

The Nymphs tried to console the weeping boy, holding him in their laps; but the son of Amphitryon, anxious about the lad, went off with his bow finely curved in Scythian style[16] and his club, which his right hand always gripped. Three times he called for Hylas,[17] as loud as his deep

In Apollonius it is Ancaeus, not Telamon, who is Heracles' rowing partner (1.397–98).   [14] In early epic Argive = Greek, and perhaps so here; Hylas is not elsewhere said to be from Argos.

[15] Shooting stars were thought to presage a wind from the quarter in which they appeared (Theophr. Fr. 6.1.13; Aratus *Phaen.* 926–29; Virg. *Geo.* 1.365–67).   [16] Lake Maeotis borders the land of the Scythians, whose bow was shaped of two curves with a short handle between.   [17] In the cult of Hylas at Cius, the priest would call Hylas' name three times, and each time an echo responded (Ant. Lib. 26 = Nic. Fr. 48 Schneider). Theocritus here supplies an etiological explanation for the threefold cry.

τρὶς δ᾽ ἄρ᾽ ὁ παῖς ὑπάκουσεν, ἀραιὰ δ᾽ ἵκετο φωνά
60 ἐξ ὕδατος, παρεὼν δὲ μάλα σχεδὸν εἴδετο πόρρω.
62 νεβροῦ φθεγξαμένας τις ἐν οὔρεσιν ὠμοφάγος λίς
ἐξ εὐνᾶς ἔσπευσεν ἑτοιμοτάταν ἐπὶ δαῖτα·
Ἡρακλέης τοιοῦτος ἐν ἀτρίπτοισιν ἀκάνθαις
65 παῖδα ποθῶν δεδόνητο, πολὺν δ᾽ ἐπελάμβανε χῶρον.
σχέτλιοι οἱ φιλέοντες, ἀλώμενος ὅσσ᾽ ἐμόγησεν
οὔρεα καὶ δρυμούς, τὰ δ᾽ Ἰάσονος ὕστερα πάντ᾽ ἦς.
ναῦς γέμεν ἄρμεν᾽ ἔχοισα μετάρσια τῶν παρεόντων,
ἱστία δ᾽ ἡμίθεοι μεσονύκτιον αὖτε καθαίρουν,
70 Ἡρακλῆα μένοντες. ὁ δ᾽ ᾇ πόδες ἆγον ἐχώρει
μαινόμενος· χαλεπὸς γὰρ ἔσω θεὸς ἧπαρ ἄμυσσεν.
οὕτω μὲν κάλλιστος Ὕλας μακάρων ἀριθμεῖται·
Ἡρακλέην δ᾽ ἥρωες ἐκερτόμεον λιπόναυταν,
οὕνεκεν ἡρώησε τριακοντάζυγον Ἀργώ,
75 πεζᾷ δ᾽ ἐς Κόλχους τε καὶ ἄξενον ἵκετο Φᾶσιν.

61 ὡς δ᾽ ὁπότ᾽ ἠυγένειος ἀπόπροθι λῖς ἐσακούσας om.
pap., m   68 γέμεν Hermann: μὲν M
69 αὖτε καθαίρουν Wordsworth: ἐξεκάθαιρον M

---

[18] Some manuscripts have a line (61) designed to provide a
typical introduction for the abrupt simile: "Just as when a bearded
lion hearing from afar. . . . " For the abruptness cf. *Idd.* 14.39,
17.9.   [19] The simile (a response to Ap. Rhod. 1.1243–49,
where Polyphemus is compared to a hungry lion as he searches
for Hylas) has been thought inappropriate, since the lion wishes
to kill the fawn but Heracles hopes to rescue the boy. It does
however convey the frenzy of love and its loss; and the thorns
suggest wounds within (cf. Bion, *Epit. Ad.* 19–24). A formal sim-

throat could bellow; three times the boy replied, but his voice came faintly from under the water, and though close by he seemed a long way off.[18] At a fawn's crying in the hills, a lion that eats raw meat rushes from its lair toward the meal that awaits; just so in the untrodden thickets of thorns Heracles was driven along in his agitation and desire for the boy,[19] and he covered a great deal of ground. How unhappy lovers are! Greatly he suffered[20] as he wandered the hills and thickets, and all Jason's business was left behind. The ship was laden with the crew who were present, and it had its tackle aloft, but while they waited for Heracles the heroes took down the sails again at midnight.[21] He in his madness went wherever his feet led him: a cruel god was breaking his heart.[22]

That is how the handsome Hylas came to be numbered among the blessed ones; but Heracles was mocked as a deserter by the Argonauts because he had abandoned the Argo with its thirty benches;[23] and it was on foot that he came to the Colchians and the inhospitable Phasis.[24]

ilarity between the two is that Heracles is to be imagined wearing his lion skin (cf. line 6).

[20] "Suffered" evokes his Labors.

[21] The text of lines 68–69 is very uncertain. Why they should have wished to sail at night is not made clear.

[22] Eros; lit., "was tearing his liver" (cf. *Id.* 11.16).

[23] Sixty-oared.

[24] Inhospitable (*axeinon*) because King Aeetes, who had the Fleece, opposed the Argonautic mission. The *Euxeinos*, Euxine, Black Sea, was also called Axeinos. In the *Argonautica* Heracles never reaches Colchis but is glimpsed in north Africa on the Argonauts' return journey (4.1477–80).

IDYLL 14

Aeschinas has quarreled with Cynisca and is advised by his friend Thyonichus to find employment as a mercenary. As in Idyll 15, *ordinary people praise Ptolemy's regime, and everyday life's little dramas are contrasted with regal generosity and culture; among his other qualifications, Ptolemy is* erotikos *(61). (He is also* philomousos, *"a lover of the Muses," hinting at patronage for the poet;* Idyll 17 *expands this theme.) The contrast reflects that between the genre of mime, evoked by the speakers' language and social status, and the epic meter, more suited to praise of Ptolemy. Aeschinas is characterized as a man-in-the-street by his use of clichéd proverbial expressions (9, 23, 38, 43, 46, 49, 51; though he employs epic-style similes at 32, 39–42) and by his circumstantial account of food (cf. Id. 15.115–18). The friend who mocks a lover (cf. Milon in Id. 10) was a common feature of New Comedy and so was the excitable reporting of a lovers' quarrel; no doubt mimes had similar scenes. Accounts of drinking parties, too, have a long literary history: Homer tells how the drunken Centaur Eurytion ran amok (Od. 21.295–304), and Plato's famous* Symposium *is riotously interrupted by Alcibiades (212c3). The conversion of Aeschinas from lover to soldier is related to the conceit, memorably elaborated by Ovid, that "every lover is a soldier" (Am. 1.9); and in this case it is perhaps implied that the king's enemies are a better object for violence than Cynisca.*

Criticism

Burton, *Theocritus's Urban Mimes,* passim.
Hunter, *Archaeology,* 110–16.

ΑΙΣΧΙΝΑΣ

Χαίρειν πολλὰ τὸν ἄνδρα Θυώνιχον.

ΘΤΩΝΙΧΟΣ

ἄλλα τοιαῦτα

Αἰσχίνᾳ. ὡς χρόνιος.

ΑΙΣΧΙΝΑΣ

χρόνιος.

ΘΤΩΝΙΧΟΣ

τί δέ τοι τὸ μέλημα;

ΑΙΣΧΙΝΑΣ

πράσσομες οὐχ ὡς λῷστα, Θυώνιχε.

ΘΤΩΝΙΧΟΣ

ταῦτ᾽ ἄρα λεπτός,

χὠ μύσταξ πολὺς οὗτος, αὐσταλέοι δὲ κίκιννοι.

5 τοιοῦτος πρώαν τις ἀφίκετο Πυθαγορικτάς,
ὠχρὸς κἀνυπόδητος· Ἀθαναῖος δ᾽ ἔφατ᾽ ἦμεν.

ΑΙΣΧΙΝΑΣ

ἤρατο μὰν καὶ τῆνος;

1 ἄλλα τοιαῦτα Reiske: ἀλλά τοι αὐτά M

IDYLL 14

AESCHINAS

A very good day to Sir Thyonichus.[1]

THYONICHUS

And the same to Aeschinas. What a long time it's been!

AESCHINAS

A long time indeed.

THYONICHUS

And what's the matter with you?

AESCHINAS

I'm not doing very well, Thyonichus.

THYONICHUS

So that's why you are thin and your mustache is such a size,
and your locks are in a mess. The other day there arrived
a Pythagorean who looked like that, pale and barefoot; he
said he was from Athens.[2]

AESCHINAS

And was he in love, too?

---

[1] Friendly raillery.

[2] The home of philosophy. Philosophers' asceticism and un-
concern for worldly things were popularly perceived as squalid
and sometimes as hypocritical self-neglect. Followers of a Py-
thagorean lifestyle often had no fixed abode.

ΘΥΩΝΙΧΟΣ

ἐμὶν δοκεῖ, ὀπτῶ ἀλεύρω.

ΑΙΣΧΙΝΑΣ

παίσδεις, ὠγάθ', ἔχων· ἐμὲ δ' ἁ χαρίεσσα Κυνίσκα
ὑβρίσδει· λασῶ δὲ μανείς ποκα, θρὶξ ἀνὰ μέσσον.

ΘΥΩΝΙΧΟΣ

10 τοιοῦτος μὲν ἀεὶ τύ, φίλ' Αἰσχίνα, ἀσυχᾷ ὀξύς,
πάντ' ἐθέλων κατὰ καιρόν· ὅμως δ' εἶπον τί τὸ καινόν.

ΑΙΣΧΙΝΑΣ

Ὡργεῖος κἠγὼν καὶ ὁ Θεσσαλὸς ἱπποδιώκτας
Ἄγις καὶ Κλεύνικος ἐπίνομες ὁ στρατιώτας
ἐν χώρῳ παρ' ἐμίν. δύο μὲν κατέκοψα νεοσσώς
15 θηλάζοντά τε χοῖρον, ἀνῷξα δὲ Βίβλινον αὐτοῖς
εὐώδη τετόρων ἐτέων σχεδὸν ὡς ἀπὸ λανῶ·
βολβός τις, κοχλίας, ἐξαιρέθη· ἦς πότος ἁδύς.
ἤδη δὲ προϊόντος ἔδοξ' ἐπιχεῖσθαι ἄκρατον
ὤτινος ἤθελ' ἕκαστος· ἔδει μόνον ὤτινος εἰπεῖν.
20 ἀμὲς μὲν φωνεῦντες ἐπίνομες, ὡς ἐδέδοκτο·
ἁ δ' οὐδὲν παρεόντος ἐμεῦ. τίν' ἔχειν με δοκεῖς νῶν;

10 ἀσυχᾷ Ahrens: ἄσυχα m: -ος m
13 Ἄγις pap., coni. Meineke: Ἄπις M

---

3 Lit., "wheaten flour" of high quality—not the unbaked bar-
ley cakes of the poor, with which a philosopher ought to be satis-
fied. Pythagoreans were notoriously vegetarian (cf. Antiphan. Fr.
133 K-A).
4 I.e., I can bear your jesting, but not her insolence.
5 Lit., "there's little in the middle" between me and madness.

IDYLL 14

THYONICHUS

I believe he was—with well-baked bread.[3]

AESCHINAS

You're having a joke, my friend; but the lovely Cynisca
treats me with insolence:[4] I shall go mad before I know it,
I'm a hair's breadth away.[5]

THYONICHUS

You're always like this, my dear Aeschinas—rather keen,
wanting everything just right. Still, tell me your news.

AESCHINAS

The man from Argos and I and Agis the Thessalian and
Cleunicus the soldier[6] were dining at my place in the
country. I'd jointed a brace of fowls and a sucking pig, and
I'd cracked open for them a Biblian wine four years old,
almost as fragrant as when it came from the press;[7] an
onion or two had been set out, snails—it was a pleasant
party. After a while we decided to propose a toast in neat
wine to whomever each of us wished; the only rule was
that each had to say the name out loud.[8] We all spoke a
name and drank, as agreed; but she said nothing, even
though I was right there.[9] How do you think I felt? As

---

[6] A mercenary.   [7] This type of wine is well spoken of by
Hesiod (*Op.* 589) and is discussed at length by Athenaeus (31a),
who says that it may have originated from Biblia in Thrace. But
there was another well-known wine called Byblian, from Byblis
in Phoenicia; and some manuscripts read *byblinon* here. Why
Aeschinas should have kept it for four years when it would have
tasted better when new is unclear.   [8] This was not always
done (cf. *Id.* 2.152); hence the stipulation.   [9] If she is pres-
ent at a symposium, Cynisca is probably a *hetaira*.

"οὐ φθεγξῇ; λύκον εἶδες;" ἔπαιξέ τις. "ὡς σοφός" εἶ-
πεν,
κἠφλέγετ'· εὐμαρέως κεν ἀπ' αὐτᾶς καὶ λύχνον ἆψας.
ἔστι Λύκος, Λύκος ἐστί, Λάβα τῶ γείτονος υἱός,
25 εὐμάκης, ἁπαλός, πολλοῖς δοκέων καλὸς ἦμεν·
τούτω τὸν κλύμενον κατεφρύγετο τῆνον ἔρωτα.
χἀμῖν τοῦτο δι' ὠτὸς ἔγεντό ποχ' ἀσυχᾷ οὕτως·
οὐ μὰν ἐξήταξα, μάταν εἰς ἄνδρα γενειῶν.
ἤδη δ' ὦν πόσιος τοὶ τέσσαρες ἐν βάθει ἦμες,
30 χὠ Λαρισαῖος "τὸν ἐμὸν Λύκον" ᾆδεν ἀπ' ἀρχᾶς,
Θεσσαλικόν τι μέλισμα, κακαὶ φρένες· ἁ δὲ Κυνίσκα
ἔκλαεν ἐξαπίνας θαλερώτερον ἢ παρὰ ματρί
παρθένος ἑξαετὴς κόλπω ἐπιθυμήσασα.
τᾶμος ἐγώ, τὸν ἴσαις τύ, Θυώνιχε, πὺξ ἐπὶ κόρρας
35 ἤλασα, κἄλλαν αὖθις. ἀνειρύσασα δὲ πέπλως
ἔξω ἀποίχετο θᾶσσον. "ἐμὸν κακόν, οὔ τοι ἀρέσκω;
ἄλλος τοι γλυκίων ὑποκόλπιος; ἄλλον ἰοῖσα
θάλπε φίλον. τήνῳ τεὰ δάκρυα; μᾶλα ῥεόντω."
μάστακα δοῖσα τέκνοισιν ὑπωροφίοισι χελιδών
40 ἄψορρον ταχινὰ πέτεται βίον ἄλλον ἀγείρειν·
ὠκυτέρα μαλακᾶς ἀπὸ δίφρακος ἔπτετο τήνα

26 κατεφρύγετο Pohlenz: καταφ[pap.: κατετάκετο M
38 τεὰ Ahrens: τὰ σὰ m: τὰ m   ῥεόντω Wilamowitz: ῥεό-
ντι pap., M   41 ἔπτετο Hunt:]το pap.: ἔδραμε M

10 English, "Has the cat got your tongue?" It was believed that
if a wolf saw you first, you would be struck dumb (Pl. *Resp.* 336d);

a joke someone said, "Aren't you going to speak? Have you seen a wolf?"[10] "How clever!" she said, and started to blush; you could easily have kindled a torch from her. It's Lycus,[11] Lycus it is, the son of my neighbor Labes; he's tall and lithe, and many people think he's handsome: she was being burned up with that famous love of hers for him. It had come to my ears, too, just on the quiet, but I didn't ask any questions—so much for having grown a man's beard![12] Anyhow, the four of us were deep in drink, and the man from Larisa[13] sang "My Wolf" from the beginning,[14] a Thracian song, the mischief maker, and Cynisca suddenly started crying more copiously than a girl of six beside her mother when she wants a cuddle. Then I—you know how I am, Thyonichus—I gave her a slap round the head, and then another. She gathered up her robe and made off pretty quickly. "You wretched girl, aren't you satisfied with me? Have you someone cuter to cuddle? Go and warm up your other boyfriend. Are your tears for him? Let them flow as big as apples!"[15] The swallow gives a morsel to her chicks and quickly flies off again to collect more food; even quicker than that Cynisca flew from her

so the comment is a short way of saying, "Have you seen a wolf ⟨that saw you first⟩?"   [11] The name Lycus means "Wolf."

[12] I.e., at my age I should have known better than to ignore the evidence.

[13] Agis the Thessalian (12–13); Larisa is a town in Thessaly.

[14] Probably "from beginning to end"; but he may mean that the relevant words, "My Wolf" (or, perhaps, "Wolf"), came at the beginning. Nothing is known of this song.

[15] Or, following the manuscripts and with different punctuation, "It's for him that your tears are flowing as big as apples!"

ἰθὺ δι' ἀμφιθύρω καὶ δικλίδος, ᾇ πόδες ἆγον.
αἶνός θην λέγεταί τις "ἔβα ποκὰ ταῦρος ἀν' ὕλαν."
εἴκατι· ταὶ δ' ὀκτώ, ταὶ δ' ἐννέα, ταὶ δὲ δέκ' ἄλλαι·
45 σάμερον ἑνδεκάτα· ποτίθες δύο, καὶ δύο μῆνες
ἐξ ὧ ἀπ' ἀλλάλων· οὐδ' εἰ Θρᾳκιστὶ κέκαρμαι
οἶδε. Λύκος νῦν πάντα, Λύκῳ καὶ νυκτὸς ἀνῷκται·
ἄμμες δ' οὔτε λόγω τινὸς ἄξιοι οὔτ' ἀριθμητοί,
δύστανοι Μεγαρῆες ἀτιμοτάτᾳ ἐνὶ μοίρᾳ.
50 κεἰ μὲν ἀποστέρξαιμι, τὰ πάντα κεν ἐς δέον ἔρποι.
νῦν δὲ πόθεν; μῦς, φαντί, Θυώνιχε, γεύμεθα πίσσας.
χὤτι τὸ φάρμακόν ἐστιν ἀμηχανέοντος ἔρωτος,
οὐκ οἶδα· πλὰν Σῖμος, ὁ τᾶς ἐπιχάλκω ἐρασθείς,
ἐκπλεύσας ὑγιὴς ἐπανῆνθ', ἐμὸς ἁλικιώτας.
55 πλευσεῦμαι κἠγὼν διαπόντιος· οὔτε κάκιστος
οὔτε πρᾶτος ἴσως, ὁμαλὸς δέ τις ὁ στρατιώτας.

ΘΥΩΝΙΧΟΣ

ὤφελε μὲν χωρεῖν κατὰ νῶν τεὸν ὧν ἐπεθύμεις,
Αἰσχίνα. εἰ δ' οὕτως ἄρα τοι δοκεῖ ὥστ' ἀποδαμεῖν,
μισθοδότας Πτολεμαῖος ἐλευθέρῳ οἷος ἄριστος.

---

43 ποκὰ ταῦρος Meineke: καὶ τ. m: κεν τ. m: κε τ. m:
κένταυρος pap.   53 ἐπιχάλκω pap. in ras., m: ὑπο- pap., m

---

16 The details of this fable, which is alluded to at Soph. *OT*
477–79, are not known. Like Cynisca, the bull once released will
have been hard to recapture.

17 He seems to be counting the number of days between
memorable events: 20 + 8 + 9 + 10 + 11 + 2 = 60 days = 2 months.

18 His hair is unkempt (4); but for all she knows he may have
adopted some outlandish style. In the *Iliad* Thracians have top-

200

cozy couch straight through the inner door and the outer door, wherever her feet led. There's a proverb that says, "A bull once went through a forest."[16] Twenty—and eight —and nine—and ten more—today's the eleventh—add two;[17] it's two months we've been apart, and she doesn't even know if I have hair like a Thracian.[18] It's all Lycus now; even at night her door's open for Lycus. But *I* am out of the reckoning and of no account, doomed to dishonor like the poor Megarians.[19] If I could fall out of love, everything would turn out for the best. But as it is, how can I? I'm like the proverbial mouse that's tasting pitch.[20] What the remedy is for hopeless love, I don't know; except that Simus, who was in love with that brassy[21] girl, sailed off abroad and came back cured—he's my age. *I*'ll sail off overseas, too. A soldier's life isn't the worst—or the best, perhaps; but it's decent enough.[22]

THYONICHUS

I wish your hopes were coming to pass, Aeschinas; but if you really think you should go abroad, Ptolemy does pay a free man very well indeed.

knots (4.533, ἀκρόκομοι). Scythians shaved their heads (Eur. *El.* 241), and "Thracian" perhaps loosely refers to them.

[19] The proud Megarians once asked the Delphic oracle which Greeks were best and were told that they themselves were inferior to all (Deinias, *FGH* 306 F 6, quoted by the scholia here; cf. Callim. *Epigr.* 11.5–6 G-P = *AP* 5.6.5–6).

[20] I.e., unable to free itself, having once stepped in.

[21] *Epichalkos* means "bronze-plated," and although the metaphor "brazen" is not elsewhere used to describe a person in Greek, it seems appropriate here. The alternative reading ὑπο-χάλκω would mean "counterfeit," i.e., "worthless."

[22] He will enlist as a mercenary.

ΑΙΣΧΙΝΑΣ

60 τἆλλα δ᾽ ἀνὴρ ποῖός τις;

ΘΤΩΝΙΧΟΣ

          . . . τοισιν ἄριστος·
εὐγνώμων, φιλόμουσος, ἐρωτικός, εἰς ἄκρον ἁδύς,
εἰδὼς τὸν φιλέοντα, τὸν οὐ φιλέοντ᾽ ἔτι μᾶλλον,
πολλοῖς πολλὰ διδούς, αἰτεύμενος οὐκ ἀνανεύων,
οἷα χρὴ βασιλῆ· αἰτεῖν δὲ δεῖ οὐκ ἐπὶ παντί,
65 Αἰσχίνα. ὥστ᾽ εἴ τοι κατὰ δεξιὸν ὦμον ἀρέσκει
λῶπος ἄκρον περονᾶσθαι, ἐπ᾽ ἀμφοτέροις δὲ βεβακώς
τολμασεῖς ἐπιόντα μένειν θρασὺν ἀσπιδιώταν,
ᾇ τάχος εἰς Αἴγυπτον. ἀπὸ κροτάφων πελόμεσθα
πάντες γηραλέοι, καὶ ἐπισχερὼ ἐς γένυν ἕρπει
70 λευκαίνων ὁ χρόνος· ποιεῖν τι δεῖ ἇς γόνυ χλωρόν.

          60 οἷός τ[pap.   τοῖσιν ἄριστος pap. altera: ἐλευθέρῳ
οἷος ἄρ. M

AESCHINAS

And what sort of a person is he in other ways?

THYONICHUS

He's excellent[23]—shrewd, cultured,[24] a noted lover,[25] extremely pleasant, a man who knows who his friends are, and knows his enemies even better; he's generous to many and doesn't refuse a request, just as a king should—but it's not right to make requests all the time, Aeschinas. So if you fancy pinning the end of your cloak over your right shoulder,[26] and if you dare to stand firm and wait for the charge of a bold armed fighter, then off with you to Egypt as quick as you can. We're all growing gray at the temples, and time's white mark is creeping gradually down our cheeks. We should be doing something while our knees are still nimble.

[23] The text is uncertain; it is very unlikely that the word ἄριστος should stand at the end of both line 59 and line 60. The whole of 60 ought perhaps to be given to Thyonichus (reading οἷος for ποῖος): "and in other respects he's ‹outstanding›."

[24] Lit., "a lover of the Muses" (cf. *Id.* 17.112–14)—relevant for Theocritus, less so for Thyonichus.

[25] Ptolemy erected public monuments to his mistresses (Ath. 576e–f).

[26] I.e., wearing it in military style, with the right arm kept free for fighting.

IDYLL 15

The setting for this poem is Alexandria; the city, its citizens, and its rulers take center stage. Gorgo visits her friend Praxinoa and persuades her to venture out to see a festival of Adonis organized by Arsinoe, wife of Ptolemy Philadelphus. The scene changes to the street, where the two women make their way eventfully to the palace. They hear a hymn to Adonis performed by a female singer, then set off for home.

Adonis, lover of Aphrodite, died young, gored in the thigh by a wild boar, but he came back to life each year. His cult existed in various forms in cities throughout the Greek world (see pp. 504–17); the women celebrated his beauty and privilege as lover of the goddess, and on the next day mourned his death. The royal presentation described here is designed as a popular attraction; there is a lavish representation of Aphrodite and her consort made of precious materials and perhaps a competition in singing.

The hymn to Adonis, which in real life would have been in lyric meter, serves to continue the ecphrastic description of the festival begun in the conversation of Gorgo and Praxinoa. Some have seen its eroticism as mawkish, its description of foodstuffs as disproportionate, its mythological allusions as clumsy. At any rate, it seems primarily to be aimed at a female audience, and it is performed by a woman. Whether it is a masterpiece, like Thyrsis' song in Idyll 1, *or a composition of questionable quality, like Bucaeus' performance in* Idyll 10, *is left for readers to judge. Gorgo and Praxinoa, whose admiration for verisimilitude (80–83) seems to align them with some aspects of Theocritean writing, are impressed.*

As in Idyll 14, *humor and irony are seen not to be incompatible with praise for the royal family. There is an implicit contrast between the humdrum lives of Gorgo and Praxinoa on one hand and the marriage of Ptolemy and Arsinoe and the divine union of Aphrodite and Adonis on the other: the two women's husbands are no Adonises, and Diocleidas' dinner (147–48) will not match the royal cuisine.*

Gorgo and Praxinoa are, like Theocritus, of Syracusan origin (90). Their struggle to enter the palace, which has some elements in common with epic descriptions of storming a fortress, has been interpreted as symbolizing Theocritus' struggle to gain Ptolemaic patronage, or as representing initial resistance to the reception of his novel genre and Doric dialect (87–88), or as showing that his mimetic verse has an equivocal relationship with more elevated poetry.

The scholia report that the poem is modeled on a mime of Sophron, now lost, titled Spectators at the Isthmian Festival *(Fr. 10 K-A). If this is so, Theocritus will perhaps have imitated Sophron's technique of supplying a description of a scene via a conversation. Tragedies will no doubt have had similar scenes (cf. Eur.* Ion *184–218); the Sicilian comic writer Epicharmus wrote a* Spectators, *in which bystanders commented on dedicated objects at the Pythian festival (Θεαροί; Fr. 68 K-A). The fourth mimiamb of The-*

ocritus' contemporary *Herodas* bears some relation to this poem. In it two women and their servants visit a temple of Asclepius and appraise the realistic works of art on display.

Criticism

Burton, *Theocritus's Urban Mimes,* passim.
Fantuzzi–Hunter, *Tradition and Innovation,* 371–77.
Goldhill, *Poet's Voice,* 274–77.
Hunter, *Archaeology,* 110–38.
Reed, J. D. "Arsinoe's Adonis and the Poetics of Ptolemaic Imperialism." *TAPhA* 130 (2000): 319–51.
Zanker, *Realism,* 9–24.

On Sophron

Hordern, J. H. *Sophron's Mimes: Text, Translation and Commentary.* Oxford, 2004.

On Adonis

LIMC 1.222–29.
Reed, J. D. "The Sexuality of Adonis." *ClAnt* 14 (1995): 317–47.

15

ΓΟΡΓΩ

Ἔνδοι Πραξινόα;

ΠΡΑΞΙΝΟΑ

     Γοργὼ φίλα, ὡς χρόνῳ. ἔνδοι.
θαῦμ᾽ ὅτι καὶ νῦν ἦνθες. ὅρη δρίφον, Εὐνόα, αὐτᾷ·
ἔμβαλε καὶ ποτίκρανον.

ΓΟΡΓΩ

     ἔχει κάλλιστα.

ΠΡΑΞΙΝΟΑ

           καθίζευ.

ΓΟΡΓΩ

ὦ τᾶς ἀλεμάτω ψυχᾶς· μόλις ὕμμιν ἐσώθην,
5 Πραξινόα, πολλῶ μὲν ὄχλω, πολλῶν δὲ τεθρίππων·
παντᾷ κρηπῖδες, παντᾷ χλαμυδηφόροι ἄνδρες·
ἁ δ᾽ ὁδὸς ἄτρυτος· τὺ δ᾽ ἑκαστέρω αἰὲν ἀποικεῖς.

ΠΡΑΞΙΝΟΑ

ταῦθ᾽ ὁ πάραρος τῆνος· ἐπ᾽ ἔσχατα γᾶς ἔλαβ᾽ ἐνθών
ἰλεόν, οὐκ οἴκησιν, ὅπως μὴ γείτονες ὦμες
10 ἀλλάλαις, ποτ᾽ ἔριν, φθονερὸν κακόν, αἰὲν ὁμοῖος.

---

[1] Four-horse chariots on their way to race (cf. 51–52).

IDYLL 15

GORGO

Is Praxinoa at home?

PRAXINOA

Gorgo, my dear—what a long time it's been. I *am* at home.
It's a wonder you've got here even now. Eunoa, see to a
chair for her, and put a cushion on it.

GORGO

It's fine as it is.

PRAXINOA

Do sit down.

GORGO

Oh, how flustered I am! I only just managed to get away
alive from that big crowd and all those chariots,[1] Praxinoa.
There are hobnailed shoes everywhere, men in cloaks ev-
erywhere, and the road is endless—you live further and
further away.[2]

PRAXINOA

That's my crazy husband's doing. He's come to the ends of
the earth and bought a hovel, not a house, just out of spite,
so that we can't be neighbors—he's a mean so-and-so, al-
ways the same.

[2] Either Gorgo has moved before or the journey seems longer
each time.

ΓΟΡΓΩ

μὴ λέγε τὸν τεὸν ἄνδρα, φίλα, Δίνωνα τοιαῦτα
τῶ μικκῶ παρεόντος· ὄρη, γύναι, ὡς ποθορῇ τυ.
θάρσει, Ζωπυρίων, γλυκερὸν τέκος· οὐ λέγει ἀπφῦν.

ΠΡΑΞΙΝΟΑ

αἰσθάνεται τὸ βρέφος, ναὶ τὰν πότνιαν.

ΓΟΡΓΩ

καλὸς ἀπφῦς.

ΠΡΑΞΙΝΟΑ

15 ἀπφῦς μὰν τῆνός γα πρόαν–λέγομες δὲ πρόαν θην
"πάππα, νίτρον καὶ φῦκος ἀπὸ σκανᾶς ἀγοράσ-
δειν"—
ἷκτο φέρων ἅλας ἄμμιν, ἀνὴρ τρισκαιδεκάπαχυς.

ΓΟΡΓΩ

χὦμὸς ταυτᾷ ἔχει· φθόρος ἀργυρίω Διοκλείδας·
ἑπταδράχμως κυνάδας, γραιᾶν ἀποτίλματα πηρᾶν,
πέντε πόκως ἔλαβ' ἐχθές, ἅπαν ῥύπον, ἔργον ἐπ'
20   ἔργῳ.
ἀλλ' ἴθι, τὦμπέχονον καὶ τὰν περονατρίδα λάζευ.
βᾶμες τῶ βασιλῆος ἐς ἀφνειῶ Πτολεμαίω
θασόμεναι τὸν Ἄδωνιν· ἀκούω χρῆμα καλόν τι
κοσμεῖν τὰν βασίλισσαν.

16 πάππα Wilamowitz: πάντα Μ   ἀγοράζειν Ahrens:
-σδων pap., Μ
18 ταυτᾷ Reiske: ταυτ' m: ταυτά γ' m

IDYLL 15

GORGO

Don't talk about your husband Dinon like that, my dear, in front of the little one. See how he's looking at you, woman! Cheer up, Zopyrion, my darling; she's not talking about daddy.

GORGO

Good heavens![3] The child understands!

GORGO

Nice daddy![4]

PRAXINOA

And yet that very daddy the other day—only the other day, I said to him, "Dad, go and buy some soda and red dye from the stall"[5]—and he came back here with salt, the great overgrown twit![6]

GORGO

My husband's that way inclined, too—Diocleidas just throws money away. Yesterday for seven drachmas he bought five fleeces that were like dog skins or hair plucked off old skin bags,[7] nothing but filth, work upon work.[8] But come on, get your dress and wrap. Let's go to the palace of rich king Ptolemy to see the Adonia. I hear that the queen is putting on a fine show.

---

[3] Lit., "By the Lady," i.e., Persephone. A women's oath.

[4] Addressed to the baby.

[5] Carbonate of soda was used as a detergent; red dye was used for making rouge or for coloring clothes.

[6] Lit., "thirteen cubits tall" (about 18 feet).

[7] Or, perhaps, "depilated hair from old women."

[8] I.e., impossible to use without long preparation.

THEOCRITUS

ΠΡΑΞΙΝΟΑ
                    ἐν ὀλβίῳ ὄλβια πάντα.
ΓΟΡΓΩ
25 ὧν ἴδες, ὧν εἴπαις κεν ἰδοῖσα τὺ τῷ μὴ ἰδόντι.
    ἕρπειν ὥρα κ᾽ εἴη.

ΠΡΑΞΙΝΟΑ
                    ἀεργοῖς αἰὲν ἑορτά.
    Εὐνόα, αἶρε τὸ νῆμα καὶ ἐς μέσον, αἰνόδρυπτε,
    θὲς πάλιν· αἱ γαλέαι μαλακῶς χρῄζοντι καθεύδειν.
    κινεῦ δή· φέρε θᾶσσον ὕδωρ. ὕδατος πρότερον δεῖ,
30 ἁ δὲ σμᾶμα φέρει. δὸς ὅμως. μὴ δὴ πολύ, λᾳστρί.
    ἔγχει ὕδωρ. δύστανε, τί μευ τὸ χιτώνιον ἄρδεις;
    παῦέ ποχ᾽· οἷα θεοῖς ἐδόκει, τοιαῦτα νένιμμαι.
    ἁ κλᾲξ τᾶς μεγάλας πεῖ λάρνακος; ὧδε φέρ᾽ αὐτάν.

ΓΟΡΓΩ
    Πραξινόα, μάλα τοι τὸ καταπτυχὲς ἐμπερόναμα
35 τοῦτο πρέπει· λέγε μοι, πόσσω κατέβα τοι ἀφ᾽ ἱστῶ;

ΠΡΑΞΙΝΟΑ
    μὴ μνάσῃς, Γοργοῖ· πλέον ἀργυρίω καθαρῶ μνᾶν
    ἢ δύο· τοῖς δ᾽ ἔργοις καὶ τὰν ψυχὰν ποτέθηκα.

ΓΟΡΓΩ
    ἀλλὰ κατὰ γνώμαν ἀπέβα τοι· τοῦτό κεν εἴπαις.

---

25 κεν Toup: καὶ m: αν pap.   30 δὲ σμᾶμα Hermann: δ᾽
ἐς νᾶμα M   λᾳστρι E. Schwartz: ἄπληστε pap., M
    32 παῦέ ποχ᾽· οἷα Ahrens: παῦε ὁκοῖα fere M
    37 ποτέθηκα pap., coni. Valckenaer: προτέθεικα M

212

PRAXINOA

It's a rich man's world.

GORGO

When you've seen it you'll be able to talk about what
you've seen with someone who hasn't. Time to be going.

PRAXINOA

Every day's a holiday for people with nothing to do.[9]
Eunoa, pick up that yarn; just you dare let it lie around
again like that, you rascal: cats[10] like soft beds. Get a move
on; be quick and bring me some water. Water's what I want
first, and she brings soap. Give it me anyway. Not so much,
you thief. Pour the water on. You idiot, why are you wet-
ting my dress? That'll do; I'm clean in the eyes of heaven.[11]
Where's the key to the big clothes chest? Bring it here.

GORGO

That full-length dress really suits you, Praxinoa; tell me,
how much did it cost you straight off the loom?[12]

PRAXINOA

Don't remind me, Gorgo. It cost more than two minae of
good money,[13] and I put my heart and soul into the work.

GORGO

But it's turned out a great success; that you *can* say.

[9] Another proverbial-sounding expression.

[10] Actually "weasels," used for mousing in Greece; or "mon-
gooses," which were used in Egypt.

[11] Lit., "I'm washed as much as seemed good to the gods."
Text and meaning uncertain.

[12] Before being made up, embroidered, etc.

[13] An extremely high price; perhaps exaggerated.

ΠΡΑΞΙΝΟΑ

τὤμπέχονον φέρε μοι καὶ τὰν θολίαν· κατὰ κόσμον
40 ἀμφίθες. οὐκ ἀξῶ τυ, τέκνον. Μορμώ, δάκνει ἵππος.
δάκρυ' ὅσσα θέλεις, χωλὸν δ' οὐ δεῖ τυ γενέσθαι.
ἔρπωμες. Φρυγία, τὸν μικκὸν παῖσδε λαβοῖσα,
τὰν κύν' ἔσω κάλεσον, τὰν αὐλείαν ἀπόκλαξον.

ὦ θεοί, ὅσσος ὄχλος. πῶς καὶ πόκα τοῦτο περᾶσαι
45 χρὴ τὸ κακόν; μύρμακες ἀνάριθμοι καὶ ἄμετροι.
πολλά τοι, ὦ Πτολεμαῖε, πεποίηται καλὰ ἔργα,
ἐξ ὦ ἐν ἀθανάτοις ὁ τεκών· οὐδεὶς κακοεργός
δαλεῖται τὸν ἰόντα παρέρπων Αἰγυπτιστί,
οἷα πρὶν ἐξ ἀπάτας κεκροτημένοι ἄνδρες ἔπαισδον,
50 ἀλλάλοις ὁμαλοί, κακὰ παίχνια, πάντες ἀραῖοι.
ἁδίστα Γοργώ, τί γενώμεθα; τοὶ πολεμισταί
ἵπποι τῶ βασιλῆος. ἄνερ φίλε, μή με πατήσῃς.
ὀρθὸς ἀνέστα ὁ πυρρός· ἴδ' ὡς ἄγριος. κυνοθαρσής
Εὐνόα, οὐ φευξῇ; διαχρησεῖται τὸν ἄγοντα.
55 ὠνάθην μεγάλως ὅτι μοι τὸ βρέφος μένει ἔνδον.

ΓΟΡΓΩ

θάρσει, Πραξινόα· καὶ δὴ γεγενήμεθ' ὄπισθεν,
τοὶ δ' ἔβαν ἐς χώραν.

---

50 ἀραῖοι Warton: αροιοι in αεργοι mut. pap.: ἐριοί M
51 γενώμεθα pap., coni. Schaefer: γενοίμεθα M

---

14 Perhaps a reference to the danger from horses in the streets
(cf. 5, 51–52); or, perhaps, some sudden movement to distract the
child.

IDYLL 15

PRAXINOA

Bring me my cloak and sun hat; put them on properly. I'm not going to take you, baby. Boo, the Bogeyman! Horses bite.[14] Cry as much as you like, but I'm not going to have you lamed. Let's be going. Phrygia, take baby and play with him, call the dog in, and lock the front door.

My God,[15] what a crowd! How are we ever to get through this lot? They're like ants—countless, innumerable. You've done plenty of good things since your father became a god,[16] Ptolemy. Nowadays no criminal sneaks up to you Egyptian style[17] as you're walking along and does you a mischief like the tricks those deceitful scoundrels used to play, nasty rascals all as bad as each other, curse the lot of them.

Gorgo, darling, what's to become of us? It's the king's horses equipped for war.[18] Please, sir, don't tread on me. That chestnut stallion reared up: look, it's out of control! Aren't you going to get out of the way, Eunoa, you reckless creature? He'll be the death of the man leading him. Thank goodness baby's safe at home.

GORGO

Don't worry, Praxinoa; we've got behind them now, and they've gone to their places.

[15] The scene has changed to the street.

[16] Ptolemy II's father, Ptolemy I Soter, died in 283 BC.

[17] Although she lives in Alexandria, Praxinoa is proud of her Greek ancestry (89–93) and suspicious of the native population.

[18] They are on their way to the hippodrome, where one of the races was for horses so equipped (schol.).

215

ΠΡΑΞΙΝΟΑ

καὐτὰ συναγείρομαι ἤδη.
ἵππον καὶ τὸν ψυχρὸν ὄφιν τὰ μάλιστα δεδοίκω
ἐκ παιδός. σπεύδωμες· ὄχλος πολὺς ἄμμιν ἐπιρρεῖ.

ΓΟΡΓΩ

60 ἐξ αὐλᾶς, ὦ μᾶτερ;

ΠΡΑΞΙΝΟΑ

ἐγών, τέκνα.

ΓΟΡΓΩ

εἶτα παρενθεῖν
εὐμαρές;

ΠΡΑΞΙΝΟΑ

ἐς Τροίαν πειρώμενοι ἦνθον Ἀχαιοί,
κάλλισται παίδων· πείρᾳ θην πάντα τελεῖται.

ΓΟΡΓΩ

χρησμὼς ἁ πρεσβῦτις ἀπῴχετο θεσπίξασα.

ΠΡΑΞΙΝΟΑ

πάντα γυναῖκες ἴσαντι, καὶ ὡς Ζεὺς ἀγάγεθ᾽ Ἥραν.

ΓΟΡΓΩ

65 θᾶσαι, Πραξινόα, περὶ τὰς θύρας ὅσσος ὅμιλος.

ΠΡΑΞΙΝΟΑ

θεσπέσιος. Γοργοῖ, δὸς τὰν χέρα μοι· λάβε καὶ τύ,
Εὐνόα, Εὐτυχίδος· πότεχ᾽ αὐτᾶς μὴ ἀποπλαγχθῇς.

---

19 I.e., in the way that the horses are organizing themselves.
20 Like an oracle, the old woman avoided a direct answer.

PRAXINOA

And I'm pulling myself together now, too.[19] I've had a phobia of horses—and nasty cold snakes—since I was a child. Let's get a move on; there's a big crowd flowing this way.

GORGO

Are you coming from the palace, mother?

OLD WOMAN

I am, my children.

GORGO

Is it easy to get in, then?

OLD WOMAN

The Greeks got into Troy by trying, my darlings; you can manage anything if you really try.

GORGO

The oracular old lady has gone off.[20]

PRAXINOA

Women know everything—even how Zeus married Hera.[21]

GORGO

Look, Praxinoa, what a crowd there is at the entrance!

PRAXINOA

Enormous! Give me your hand, Gorgo, and Eunoa take Eutychis':[22] keep hold of her so you don't get separated.

---

[21] Possibly a reference to their first night together, which is mentioned but without details at Hom. *Il.* 14.295–96.

[22] Gorgo's attendant.

THEOCRITUS

πᾶσαι ἅμ᾽ εἰσένθωμες· ἀπρὶξ ἔχευ, Εὐνόα, ἁμῶν.
οἴμοι δειλαία, δίχα μοι τὸ θερίστριον ἤδη
70 ἔσχισται, Γοργοῖ. ποττῶ Διός, εἴ τι γένοιο
εὐδαίμων, ὤνθρωπε, φυλάσσεο τὠμπέχονόν μευ.

ΞΕΝΟΣ
οὐκ ἐπ᾽ ἐμὶν μέν, ὅμως δὲ φυλάξομαι.

ΠΡΑΞΙΝΟΑ
ὄχλος ἀλαθέως·
ὠθεῦνθ᾽ ὥσπερ ὕες.

ΞΕΝΟΣ
θάρσει, γύναι· ἐν καλῷ εἰμές.

ΠΡΑΞΙΝΟΑ
κῆς ὥρας κἤπειτα, φίλ᾽ ἀνδρῶν, ἐν καλῷ εἴης,
75 ἄμμε περιστέλλων. χρηστῶ κοἰκτίρμονος ἀνδρός.
φλίβεται Εὐνόα ἄμμιν· ἄγ᾽, ὦ δειλὰ τύ, βιάζευ.
κάλλιστ᾽· 'ἔνδοι πᾶσαι', ὁ τὰν νυὸν εἶπ᾽ ἀποκλάξας.

ΓΟΡΓΩ
Πραξινόα, πόταγ᾽ ὧδε. τὰ ποικίλα πρᾶτον ἄθρησον,
λεπτὰ καὶ ὡς χαρίεντα· θεῶν περονάματα φασεῖς.

ΠΡΑΞΙΝΟΑ
80 πότνι᾽ Ἀθαναία, ποῖαί σφ᾽ ἐπόνασαν ἔριθοι,
ποῖοι ζωογράφοι τἀκριβέα γράμματ᾽ ἔγραψαν.
ὡς ἔτυμ᾽ ἑστάκαντι καὶ ὡς ἔτυμ᾽ ἐνδινεῦντι,

---

23 The word for "all" is feminine here, but Praxinoa may have
adapted to the present context a masculine pronoun; in which

218

Let's all go in together; keep very close to us, Eunoa. Oh dear, oh dear, my cloak has been ripped in two already, Gorgo. For God's sake, sir, if you hope to be happy, take care with my cloak.

MAN

There isn't much I can do, but I'll try.

PRAXINOA

It really is a mob; they're pushing and shoving like pigs.

MAN

Don't worry, ma'am; we're fine now.

PRAXINOA

And may you be fine for ever and a day, you dear man, for looking after us. What a nice, kind man! Our Eunoa's getting squashed. Come on, you wretch, push your way through. Very good. "All inside," as the man said when he locked in the bride.[23]

GORGO

Praxinoa, come here. First of all, look at the tapestries,[24] how finely woven and elegant they are—you would say they were fit for gods to wear.

PRAXINOA

Lady Athena, what skilled women weavers they must have been to make them, and what designers to draw out lines so exactly! The figures look real when they're standing still

case the scene she alludes to will be the ritual locking in of the bride and groom by the "best man" on their wedding night (cf. *Id.* 18.5–6).

   [24] The scene may be a room in the palace, a tent set up for the occasion, or out of doors.

ἔμψυχ᾽, οὐκ ἐνυφαντά. σοφόν τι χρῆμ᾽ ἄνθρωπος.
αὐτὸς δ᾽ ὡς θαητὸς ἐπ᾽ ἀργυρέας κατάκειται
85 κλισμῷ, πρᾶτον ἴουλον ἀπὸ κροτάφων καταβάλλων,
ὁ τριφίλητος Ἄδωνις, ὁ κἠν Ἀχέροντι φιληθείς.

ΕΤΕΡΟΣ ΞΕΝΟΣ

παύσασθ᾽, ὦ δύστανοι, ἀνάνυτα κωτίλλοισαι,
τρυγόνες· ἐκκναισεῦντι πλατειάσδοισαι ἅπαντα.

ΠΡΑΞΙΝΟΑ

μᾶ, πόθεν ὥνθρωπος; τί δὲ τίν, εἰ κωτίλαι εἰμές;
90 πασάμενος ἐπίτασσε· Συρακοσίαις ἐπιτάσσεις.
ὡς εἰδῇς καὶ τοῦτο, Κορίνθιαι εἰμὲς ἄνωθεν,
ὡς καὶ ὁ Βελλεροφῶν. Πελοποννασιστὶ λαλεῦμες,
Δωρίσδειν δ᾽ ἔξεστι, δοκῶ, τοῖς Δωριέεσσι.
μὴ φύῃ, Μελιτῶδες, ὃς ἁμῶν καρτερὸς εἴη,
95 πλὰν ἑνός. οὐκ ἀλέγω. μή μοι κενεὰν ἀπομάξῃς.

ΓΟΡΓΩ

σίγη, Πραξινόα· μέλλει τὸν Ἄδωνιν ἀείδειν
ἁ τᾶς Ἀργείας θυγάτηρ, πολύιδρις ἀοιδός,

---

25 Lit., "in Acheron," the river in the underworld; cf. 102.
Aphrodite still loves him. There may, however, be a reference to
the story that in the underworld he was the lover of Persephone
(cf. Bion, *Epit. Ad.* 96; ps.-Apollod. *Bibl.* 3.14.4).

26 But the man is made to speak Doric just as broad as that of
the women (cf. on *Id.* 18.48). Perhaps he is imitating and mocking
their dialect.

27 Syracuse was a Corinthian colony. In the *Iliad* the hero
Bellerophon is said to be grandson of Sisyphus, king of Ephyre

and real when they're moving, as if they're alive, not woven. How clever humans are! And he himself—how wonderful he is, reclining on his silver couch, with the first down spreading from his temples, thrice-loved Adonis, who is desired even in death.[25]

ANOTHER MAN

Hey, you wretched women, stop that endless chattering! You're like turtledoves. They wear you out with all their broad vowels.[26]

PRAXINOA

Ah! And where's this fellow from? What is it to you if we chatter? Give your orders where you're master. We're Syracusan women that you're giving your orders to. And just so that you know, we're Corinthians from way back, just like Bellerophon.[27] We talk Peloponnesian, and Dorians are allowed to speak in Doric, I believe. Persephone,[28] please don't let us have any master but the one.[29] I don't care about you; don't bother wasting your time.[30]

GORGO

Stop talking, Praxinoa; the Argive woman's daughter is going to sing the hymn to Adonis, that talented singer who

---

(6.152–55), which was thought to be the old name for Corinth (cf. on *Id.* 28.17).

[28] Invoked particularly by women (cf. 14). Here Praxinoa uses a rare cult title, Melitodes.

[29] Probably Ptolemy, not her husband.

[30] Lit., "don't level an empty pot," a proverbial expression: there is no point leveling off a container that is empty.

ἄτις καὶ πέρυσιν τὸν ἰάλεμον ἀρίστευσε.
φθεγξεῖταί τι, σάφ᾽ οἶδα, καλόν· διαχρέμπτεται ἤδη.

ΓΤΝΗ ΑΟΙΔΟΣ

100 Δέσποιν᾽, ἃ Γολγώς τε καὶ Ἰδάλιον ἐφίλησας
αἰπεινάν τ᾽ Ἔρυκα, χρυσῷ παίζοισ᾽ Ἀφροδίτα,
οἷόν τοι τὸν Ἄδωνιν ἀπ᾽ ἀενάω Ἀχέροντος
μηνὶ δυωδεκάτῳ μαλακαὶ πόδας ἄγαγον Ὧραι,
βάρδισται μακάρων Ὧραι φίλαι· ἀλλὰ ποθειναί
105 ἔρχονται πάντεσσι βροτοῖς αἰεί τι φέροισαι.
Κύπρι Διωναία, τὺ μὲν ἀθανάταν ἀπὸ θνατᾶς,
ἀνθρώπων ὡς μῦθος, ἐποίησας Βερενίκαν,
ἀμβροσίαν ἐς στῆθος ἀποστάξασα γυναικός·
τὶν δὲ χαριζομένα, πολυώνυμε καὶ πολύναε,
110 ἁ Βερενικεία θυγάτηρ Ἑλένᾳ εἰκυῖα
Ἀρσινόα πάντεσσι καλοῖς ἀτιτάλλει Ἄδωνιν.
πὰρ μέν οἱ ὥρια κεῖται, ὅσα δρυὸς ἄκρα φέροντι,
πὰρ δ᾽ ἁπαλοὶ κᾶποι πεφυλαγμένοι ἐν ταλαρίσκοις
ἀργυρέοις, Συρίῳ δὲ μύρῳ χρύσει᾽ ἀλάβαστρα,
115 εἴδατά θ᾽ ὅσσα γυναῖκες ἐπὶ πλαθάνῳ πονέονται

98 πέρυσιν pap., coni. Reiske: πέρχην m: σπέρχιν m
99 διαχρέμπτεται pap.: -θρυπτ- M
105 φέροισαι pap., coni. Hemsterhuis: φορ- M

---

31 The lament was sung on the final day of the festival; cf. Bion's version, pp. 506–17. "Did the best" suggests that there was a competition; but "did so well" is a possible translation. It is not clear why the singer's name is not given; perhaps Gorgo is being depicted as forgetful.

did best in the lament last year.[31] She'll give an excellent performance, I'm sure. She's just clearing her throat.

WOMAN SINGER

Lady who loves Golgi and Idalium and lofty Eryx,[32] golden Aphrodite,[33] see how the soft-footed Hours[34] have brought you Adonis from ever-flowing Acheron in the twelfth month, the dear Hours, most slow-moving of the blessed gods; their coming is desired by all mankind, and they always bring with them some gift.[35] Cyprian goddess, daughter of Dione,[36] it is said that you changed Berenice from mortal to immortal, with drops of ambrosia on her breast; and it is for your sake, goddess of many names and many shrines, that Berenice's daughter Arsinoe, beautiful as Helen, indulges Adonis with good things of every kind. He has beside him everything that the fruit trees bear in season, and delicate gardens enclosed in silver baskets,[37] and golden bottles of Syrian perfume; all the cakes, too, that women shape on their kneading boards when they

[32] Cult centers of Aphrodite. Golgi and Idalium are on her island of Cyprus; Mt. Eryx is in Sicily.

[33] Lit., "Aphrodite who plays with gold," if the text is sound. Aphrodite is often called "golden" (e.g., Hom. *Il.* 22.470), but the golden toys are mysterious.

[34] The seasons, which progress imperceptibly.

[35] Seasonal produce; cf. 112.

[36] Cf. 7.116n.

[37] The so-called gardens of Adonis were pots containing plants that grew quickly but soon died, symbolizing his glorious but brief life (Pl. *Phdr.* 276b). On the final day of the festival they were thrown into the sea (cf. 133–35). Here the containers are regally ornate.

ἄνθεα μίσγοισαι λευκῷ παντοῖα μαλεύρῳ,
ὅσσα τ᾽ ἀπὸ γλυκερῶ μέλιτος τά τ᾽ ἐν ὑγρῷ ἐλαίῳ.
πάντ᾽ αὐτῷ πετεηνὰ καὶ ἑρπετὰ τεῖδε πάρεστι·
χλωραὶ δὲ σκιάδες μαλακῷ βρίθοισαι ἀνήθῳ
120 δέδμανθ᾽· οἱ δέ τε κῶροι ὑπερπωτῶνται Ἔρωτες,
οἷοι ἀηδονιδῆες ἀεξομενᾶν ἐπὶ δένδρῳ
πωτῶνται πτερύγων πειρώμενοι ὄζον ἀπ᾽ ὄζω.
ὢ ἔβενος, ὢ χρυσός, ὢ ἐκ λευκῶ ἐλέφαντος
αἰετοὶ οἰνοχόον Κρονίδᾳ Διὶ παῖδα φέροντες,
125 πορφύρεοι δὲ τάπητες ἄνω μαλακώτεροι ὕπνω·
ἁ Μίλατος ἐρεῖ χὼ τὰν Σαμίαν καταβόσκων,
"ἔστρωται κλίνα τὠδώνιδι τῷ καλῷ ἄμμιν."
τὸν μὲν Κύπρις ἔχει, τὰν δ᾽ ὁ ῥοδόπαχυς Ἄδωνις.
ὀκτωκαιδεκετὴς ἢ ἐννεακαίδεχ᾽ ὁ γαμβρός·
130 οὐ κεντεῖ τὸ φίλημ᾽· ἔτι οἱ περὶ χείλεα πυρρά.
νῦν μὲν Κύπρις ἔχοισα τὸν αὐτᾶς χαιρέτω ἄνδρα·
ἀῶθεν δ᾽ ἄμμες νιν ἅμα δρόσῳ ἀθρόαι ἔξω
οἰσεῦμες ποτὶ κύματ᾽ ἐπ᾽ ἀιόνι πτύοντα,
λύσασαι δὲ κόμαν καὶ ἐπὶ σφυρὰ κόλπον ἀνεῖσαι
135 στήθεσι φαινομένοις λιγυρᾶς ἀρξεύμεθ᾽ ἀοιδᾶς.

119 βρίθοισαι Brunck: -θουσαι pap.: -θοντες M
121 δένδρῳ Wilamowitz: -ων M   127 ἄμμιν Gow: ἄλλα
pap., M   128 τὸν μὲν Rossbach: τὰν μὲν pap., M
135 ἀρξεύμεθ᾽ G. Kiessling: -ξουμεθ᾽ ex -ξωμεθ᾽ pap.: -ξώ-
μεθ᾽ M

---

38 This may continue the list of foodstuffs (animal-shaped
cakes, or cooked meats), but it is perhaps more likely to refer to
models of animals in the tableau.

224

mix colorings of every kind with refined wheat flour, and those they make using sweet honey and smooth oil. All creatures of the earth and air are here with him,[38] and green arbors have been built, festooned with soft dill; boyish Cupids fly overhead like young nightingales that in a tree test their fledgling wings flying from branch to branch.

O ebony, O gold, O eagles of white ivory bearing to Zeus son of Cronus a boy to pour his wine, and purple coverings above, softer than sleep![39] Miletus and the shepherd who pastures the land of Samos will say, "The couch for the fair Adonis has been prepared by us."[40] The Cyprian goddess is embracing him, and Adonis holds her in his rosy arms. The bridegroom is eighteen or nineteen years old, and his kiss does not scratch; down is still around his lips. Farewell now to Cypris as she embraces her man. Early in the morning, with the dew still on the ground, all of us together will carry him to the plashing waves by the sea,[41] and as we untie our hair and let fall our robes to our ankles to bare our breasts[42] we shall begin our shrill lament.

[39] These lines describe the ebony and gilt couch of Aphrodite and Adonis, the frame or legs of which are decorated with ivory figures of Zeus' eagles and Ganymede.

[40] Miletus and Samos will be able to boast of their contribution. Miletus was famous for wool (cf. *Id.* 28.12–13), though Samos seems not to have been; possibly the couch rather than its covers is in question. The manuscripts read not "by us" but "another (couch)," but emphasis on the recurrent nature of the ritual seems less apt here.   [41] Not part of the ritual in all cities.

[42] Actions of mourning. Bion's *Lament* is of the type promised here.

ἕρπεις, ὦ φίλ' Ἄδωνι, καὶ ἐνθάδε κῆς Ἀχέροντα
ἡμιθέων, ὡς φαντί, μονώτατος. οὔτ' Ἀγαμέμνων
τοῦτ' ἔπαθ' οὔτ' Αἴας ὁ μέγας, βαρυμάνιος ἥρως,
οὔθ' Ἕκτωρ, Ἑκάβας ὁ γεραίτατος εἴκατι παίδων,
140 οὐ Πατροκλῆς, οὐ Πύρρος ἀπὸ Τροίας ἐπανενθών,
οὔθ' οἱ ἔτι πρότεροι Λαπίθαι καὶ Δευκαλίωνες,
οὐ Πελοπηιάδαι τε καὶ Ἄργεος ἄκρα Πελασγοί.
ἵλαος, ὦ φίλ' Ἄδωνι, καὶ ἐς νέωτ'· εὐθυμεύσαις
καὶ νῦν ἦνθες, Ἄδωνι, καί, ὅκκ' ἀφίκῃ, φίλος ἥξεις.

ΓΟΡΓΩ

145 Πραξινόα, τὸ χρῆμα σοφώτατον ἀ θήλεια·
ὀλβία ὅσσα ἴσατι, πανολβία ὡς γλυκὺ φωνεῖ.
ὥρα ὅμως κῆς οἶκον. ἀνάριστος Διοκλείδας·
χὠνὴρ ὄξος ἅπαν, πεινᾶντι δὲ μηδὲ ποτένθῃς.
χαῖρε, Ἄδων ἀγαπατέ, καὶ ἐς χαίροντας ἀφικνεῦ.

143 ιλαος ω pap.: ἴλαθι νῦν M
145 σοφώτατον pap., coni. J.A. Hartung: -τερον M

226

Dear Adonis, you are the one and only hero, so they say,
who visits both Acheron and the world here above. Nei-
ther Agamemnon nor mighty Ajax, the wrathful hero,[43]
achieved this, nor Hector, eldest of Hecuba's twenty sons,
nor Patroclus, nor Pyrrhus,[44] though he got back from
Troy, nor in even earlier times the Lapiths and the sons
of Deucalion,[45] nor the descendants of Pelops,[46] nor the
Pelasgian leaders of Argos.[47] Look on us with favor next
year too, dear Adonis. Now we have received you joyfully,
Adonis, and you will be dear to us when you come again.

GORGO

Praxinoa, the woman's a marvel: she's lucky to know so
much, and even luckier that she has such a sweet voice.
Still, it's time to be going home. Diocleidas hasn't had his
lunch. The man's pure vinegar; when he's hungry, it's not
safe to go near him. Farewell, darling Adonis; I hope you'll
find *us* faring well when you come again.

[43] He was angry at the Greeks for not awarding him the arms
of Achilles.

[44] Pyrrhus is another name for Neoptolemus, son of Achilles.

[45] The Lapiths are mentioned as superior to the present gen-
eration at Hom. *Il.* 1.262–68. Deucalion and Pyrrha repopulated
the earth after the flood (Pl. *Ti.* 22a).

[46] Including the House of Atreus, a member of which, Aga-
memnon, has been singled out already.

[47] Probably the descendants of Aeacus, who ruled Homer's
"Pelasgian Argos," i.e., Thessaly (Hom. *Il.* 2.681); Pyrrhus has
already been singled out.

IDYLL 16

*In this poem Theocritus appeals for patronage to Hiero II,
king of Syracuse, who came to power circa 276 BC. In the
fifth century Hiero I had employed lyric poets to celebrate
his chariot victories at the games, and Theocritus' appeal
implies that Hiero II should match the generosity of his
predecessor. The poem, which has aptly been described as
a sampler of poetic talents, is an unusual mixture of opti-
mism and pessimism, humor and seriousness, the personal
and the public. The idea of* kleos *(fame) being conferred
by poets is familiar from early Greek epic and lyric. The-
ocritus treats this idea at some length before discussing
the best use of money. The closing passage prophecies
Hiero's future successes in war and the peaceful state of his
kingdom.*

*The opening lines are hymnic in tone, but a homely
anecdote follows: Theocritus claims that his Charites, or
Graces, often come home glumly to the chest in which they
lodge when they have been given a frosty reception by
patrons who could afford to be generous. Here he adapts
a story told of the lyric poet Simonides, a contemporary of
Pindar, who was notoriously keen on money: Simonides
said he had one chest for thanks (charites) and another
for cash and that he found only the cash box to be of any
real use (schol. Arg., pp. 325.15–326.3 Wendel, Stob. Ecl.*

3.10.38). The notion of the Graces going from house to house in hopes of patronage may refer to some lost poem of Simonides (who is mentioned in l. 44); it alludes also to the genre of begging songs, examples of which are known from the Lives of Homer *(ps.-Herod.* Life of Homer *33 = Epigr. 15; pp. 394–97 West, Loeb 496); from Phoenix of Colophon, a contemporary of Theocritus (CA p. 233); and from Athenaeus (360b–d, PMG 848). Pindar and others use the word* charis *to refer to the glory conferred by poetry. Theocritus dwells on its reciprocal nature: the Graces bestow* charis *on the honorand with their graceful poems as thanks* (charites) *for their being received graciously— that is, with* charis*—by patrons.*

Criticism

Austin, N. "Idyll 16: Theocritus and Simonides." *TAPhA* 98 (1967): 1–21.

Griffiths, *Theocritus at Court,* 9–48.

Hunter, *Archaeology,* 77–109.

Meincke, *Untersuchungen,* 31–84.

Merkelbach, R. "Bettelgedichte." *RhM* 95 (1952): 312–27.

16

Αἰεὶ τοῦτο Διὸς κούραις μέλει, αἰὲν ἀοιδοῖς,
ὑμνεῖν ἀθανάτους, ὑμνεῖν ἀγαθῶν κλέα ἀνδρῶν.
Μοῖσαι μὲν θεαὶ ἐντί, θεοὺς θεαὶ ἀείδοντι·
ἄμμες δὲ βροτοὶ οἶδε, βροτοὺς βροτοὶ ἀείδωμεν.

5 Τίς γὰρ τῶν ὁπόσοι γλαυκὰν ναίουσιν ὑπ’ ἠῶ
ἡμετέρας Χάριτας πετάσας ὑποδέξεται οἴκῳ
ἀσπασίως, οὐδ’ αὖθις ἀδωρήτους ἀποπέμψει;
αἱ δὲ σκυζόμεναι γυμνοῖς ποσὶν οἴκαδ’ ἴασι,
πολλά με τωθάζοισαι, ὅτ’ ἀλιθίην ὁδὸν ἦλθον,
10 ὀκνηραὶ δὲ πάλιν κενεᾶς ἐν πυθμένι χηλοῦ
ψυχροῖς ἐν γονάτεσσι κάρη μίμνοντι βαλοῖσαι,
ἔνθ’ αἰεί σφισιν ἕδρη, ἐπὴν ἄπρακτοι ἵκωνται.
τίς τῶν νῦν τοιόσδε; τίς εὖ εἰπόντα φιλήσει;
οὐκ οἶδ’· οὐ γὰρ ἔτ’ ἄνδρες ἐπ’ ἔργμασιν ὡς πάρος
    ἐσθλοῖς
15 αἰνεῖσθαι σπεύδοντι, νενίκηνται δ’ ὑπὸ κερδέων.
πᾶς δ’ ὑπὸ κόλπου χεῖρας ἔχων πόθεν οἴσεται ἀθρεῖ
ἄργυρον, οὐδέ κεν ἰὸν ἀποτρίψας τινὶ δοίη,
ἀλλ’ εὐθὺς μυθεῖται· "ἀπωτέρω ἢ γόνυ κνάμα·

---

[1] The Muses, daughters of Zeus and Memory (Hes. *Theog.*
76).

IDYLL 16

It is always the concern of the daughters of Zeus,[1] and always the concern of poets, to hymn the gods and to hymn the glorious deeds of good men. The Muses are goddesses, and goddesses sing of the gods; we here on earth are mortals; as mortals, let us sing of mortals.

Now who of all those who live beneath the bright daylight will open up his house to give a glad welcome to my Graces,[2] and will not send them away unrewarded? They come home then barefoot and glum, with many a complaint that their journey has been in vain; they stay cowering at the bottom of their box once more with their heads drooping on their chilly knees, in the place where they are always to be found after they have come back with no success. But who is hospitable nowadays? Who will be generous in return for praise? I do not know; men are no longer eager, as they once were, to be praised for their glorious deeds, but instead they are obsessed by profit. Each person keeps his hand in his pocket and is on the lookout for a chance to make money; he would not even rub off the rust and give it to someone, but has a ready excuse: "Charity begins at home";[3] "If only I had some money myself!";

---

[2] I.e., the graceful poems I can compose for patrons.
[3] Lit., "the knee is closer than the shin."

αὐτῷ μοί τι γένοιτο." "θεοὶ τιμῶσιν ἀοιδούς."

20 "τίς δέ κεν ἄλλου ἀκοῦσαι; ἅλις πάντεσσιν Ὅμηρος."
"οὗτος ἀοιδῶν λῷστος, ὃς ἐξ ἐμεῦ οἴσεται οὐδέν."

Δαιμόνιοι, τί δὲ κέρδος ὁ μυρίος ἔνδοθι χρυσός
κείμενος; οὐχ ἅδε πλούτου φρονέουσιν ὄνασις,
ἀλλὰ τὸ μὲν ψυχᾷ, τὸ δέ πού τινι δοῦναι ἀοιδῶν·

25 πολλοὺς εὖ ἔρξαι πηῶν, πολλοὺς δὲ καὶ ἄλλων
ἀνθρώπων, αἰεὶ δὲ θεοῖς ἐπιβώμια ῥέζειν,
μηδὲ ξεινοδόκον κακὸν ἔμμεναι ἀλλὰ τραπέζῃ
μειλίξαντ᾽ ἀποπέμψαι ἐπὴν ἐθέλωντι νέεσθαι,
Μοισάων δὲ μάλιστα τίειν ἱερὸς ὑποφήτας,

30 ὄφρα καὶ εἰν Ἀίδαο κεκρυμμένος ἐσθλὸς ἀκούσῃς,
μηδ᾽ ἀκλεὴς μύρηαι ἐπὶ ψυχροῦ Ἀχέροντος,
ὡσεί τις μακέλα τετυλωμένος ἔνδοθι χεῖρας
ἀχὴν ἐκ πατέρων πενίην ἀκτήμονα κλαίων.
πολλοὶ ἐν Ἀντιόχοιο δόμοις καὶ ἄνακτος Ἀλεύα

35 ἁρμαλιὴν ἔμμηνον ἐμετρήσαντο πενέσται·
πολλοὶ δὲ Σκοπάδαισιν ἐλαυνόμενοι ποτὶ σακούς
μόσχοι σὺν κεραῇσιν ἐμυκήσαντο βόεσσι·
μυρία δ᾽ ἂμ πεδίον Κραννώνιον ἐνδιάασκον
ποιμένες ἔκκριτα μῆλα φιλοξείνοισι Κρεώνδαις·

25 εὖ Kreussler: δ᾽ εὖ M

---

4 Allusion to an anecdote about Simonides, who was told by
the tyrant Scopas to seek half his fee from the Dioscuri, whom he
had praised in half of a poem commissioned as praise of Scopas.
The palace collapsed and killed Scopas, but the poet escaped,

"It's the gods who reward poets";[4] "Who would wish to listen to anyone else? Homer's enough for everyone"; "The best poet is the one who will get nothing from me."

Gentlemen, what does it profit you to have countless money lying idle at home? For men of good sense this is not the best way to benefit from wealth; instead, you should spend some of it on yourselves and perhaps give some to a poet; you should do well by many of your relatives and many other men, too; regularly sacrifice to the gods; not be bad hosts, but entertain guests at your table and then help them on their way when they wish to go; and above all you should honor the holy interpreters of the Muses, so that even hidden in Hades you may be well spoken of and not lament that you are without glory by the cold waters of Acheron[5] like a man whose palms are calloused by the mattock and who laments the penniless poverty of himself and his ancestors.

Many serfs had their monthly rations measured out in the palaces of Antiochus[6] and king Aleuas; many calves along with the horned cows bellowed as they were driven to the cattle pens of the Scopads; and countless excellent sheep were tended by shepherds in the plain of Crannon for the hospitable descendants of Creon. But they had no plea-

---

having been summoned outside by "two men" (Cic. *De or.* 2.352, Callim. Fr. 64.11).

[5] A river in the underworld.

[6] Antiochus, Aleuas, Scopas of Crannon, and his father (Creon) ruled in Thessaly in the time of Simonides ("the bard of Ceos," 44) and commissioned poetry from him (*PMG* 528, 542, etc.).

40 ἀλλ' οὔ σφιν τῶν ἦδος, ἐπεὶ γλυκὺν ἐξεκένωσαν
θυμὸν ἐς εὐρεῖαν σχεδίαν στυγνοῖο γέροντος·
ἄμναστοι δὲ τὰ πολλὰ καὶ ὄλβια τῆνα λιπόντες
δειλοῖς ἐν νεκύεσσι μακροὺς αἰῶνας ἔκειντο,
εἰ μὴ θεῖος ἀοιδὸς ὁ Κήιος αἰόλα φωνέων
βάρβιτον ἐς πολύχορδον ἐν ἀνδράσι θῆκ' ὀνο-
45   μαστούς
ὁπλοτέροις· τιμὰς δὲ καὶ ὠκέες ἔλλαχον ἵπποι,
οἵ σφισιν ἐξ ἱερῶν στεφανηφόροι ἦλθον ἀγώνων.
τίς δ' ἂν ἀριστῆας Λυκίων ποτέ, τίς κομόωντας
Πριαμίδας ἢ θῆλυν ἀπὸ χροιᾶς Κύκνον ἔγνω,
50 εἰ μὴ φυλόπιδας προτέρων ὕμνησαν ἀοιδοί;
οὐδ' Ὀδυσεὺς ἑκατόν τε καὶ εἴκοσι μῆνας ἀλαθείς
πάντας ἐπ' ἀνθρώπους, Ἀίδαν τ' εἰς ἔσχατον ἐλθών
ζωός, καὶ σπήλυγγα φυγὼν ὀλοοῖο Κύκλωπος,
δηναιὸν κλέος ἔσχεν, ἐσιγάθη δ' ἂν ὑφορβός
55 Εὔμαιος καὶ βουσὶ Φιλοίτιος ἀμφ' ἀγελαίαις
ἔργον ἔχων αὐτός τε περίσπλαγχνος Λαέρτης,
εἰ μή σφεας ὤνασαν Ἰάονος ἀνδρὸς ἀοιδαί.

41 στυγνοῖο γέροντος Hemsterhuis: στυγνοῦ ἀχέροντος M

---

7 Lit., "emptied out their sweet spirits."

8 Charon, ferryman of the dead. For "the old man" the manuscripts read "Acheron" (cf. 31), which may be right.

9 Lyric poets such as Simonides, Pindar, and Bacchylides celebrated victories of their patrons' charioteers at the Olympic and other games.

10 Allies of the Trojans in the *Iliad* and in other epic poems, now lost. Glaucus and Sarpedon were Lycians (Hom. *Il.* 2.876).

sure from these things once they had breathed their last[7] on the grim old man's broad raft:[8] leaving behind those many blessings, they would have lain unremembered for long ages among the wretched dead if the inspired bard of Ceos, with his varied songs performed on a lyre of many strings, had not made them famous among later generations; and even swift horses which came back from the holy games bringing them crowns of victory had their share of glory.[9] Who would ever have known of the leaders of the Lycians[10] or the long-haired sons of Priam[11] or Cycnus, whose complexion was like a girl's,[12] if poets had not celebrated the battles of men of old? Odysseus, who wandered for six score months all through the world, and went to farthest Hades[13] while still alive, and escaped from the cave of the terrible Cyclops, would not have had long-lasting fame, and Eumaeus the swineherd and Philoetius who looked after the herding of cattle, and greathearted Laertes himself would have been unknown if the songs of the Ionian bard had not benefitted them.[14]

[11] In the *Iliad* it is the Greeks, not the Trojans, who are long-haired; but in poems now lost the Trojans may have been so described.

[12] Cycnus, a son of Poseidon, was killed by Achilles when the Greeks landed at Troy. The story was told in the *Cypria* (Arg. 10 West), an epic poem now lost. He was named Cycnus (Swan) because of his white skin.

[13] Hades is described as bordering the world's end at Hom. *Od.* 11.13–22.

[14] Laertes is Odysseus' father, Eumaeus and Philoetius loyal servants who helped Odysseus kill the suitors. Homer's birthplace was disputed, but he was generally thought to have been from the coast of Ionia.

Ἐκ Μοισᾶν ἀγαθὸν κλέος ἔρχεται ἀνθρώποισι,
χρήματα δὲ ζώοντες ἀμαλδύνουσι θανόντων.

60 ἀλλ᾽ ἶσος γὰρ ὁ μόχθος ἐπ᾽ ἠόνι κύματα μετρεῖν
ὅσσ᾽ ἄνεμος χέρσονδε μετὰ γλαυκᾶς ἁλὸς ὠθεῖ,
ἢ ὕδατι νίζειν θολερὰν διαειδέι πλίνθον,
καὶ φιλοκερδείῃ βεβλαμμένον ἄνδρα παρελθεῖν.
χαιρέτω ὅστις τοῖος, ἀνήριθμος δέ οἱ εἴη

65 ἄργυρος, αἰεὶ δὲ πλεόνων ἔχοι ἵμερος αὐτόν·
αὐτὰρ ἐγὼ τιμήν τε καὶ ἀνθρώπων φιλότητα
πολλῶν ἡμιόνων τε καὶ ἵππων πρόσθεν ἑλοίμαν.
δίζημαι δ᾽ ὅτινι θνατῶν κεχαρισμένος ἔλθω
σὺν Μοίσαις· χαλεπαὶ γὰρ ὁδοὶ τελέθουσιν ἀοιδοῖς

70 κουράων ἀπάνευθε Διὸς μέγα βουλεύοντος.
οὔπω μῆνας ἄγων ἔκαμ᾽ οὐρανὸς οὐδ᾽ ἐνιαυτούς·
πολλοὶ κινήσουσιν ἔτι τροχὸν ἅματος ἵπποι·
ἔσσεται οὗτος ἀνὴρ ὃς ἐμεῦ κεχρήσετ᾽ ἀοιδοῦ,
ῥέξας ἢ Ἀχιλεὺς ὅσσον μέγας ἢ βαρὺς Αἴας

75 ἐν πεδίῳ Σιμόεντος, ὅθι Φρυγὸς ἠρίον Ἴλου.
ἤδη νῦν Φοίνικες ὑπ᾽ ἠελίῳ δύνοντι
οἰκεῦντες Λιβύας ἄκρον σφυρὸν ἐρρίγασιν·
ἤδη βαστάζουσι Συρακόσιοι μέσα δοῦρα,
ἀχθόμενοι σακέεσσι βραχίονας ἰτεΐνοισιν·

---

72 ἅματος Wilamowitz: ἅρμ- M

---

15 A proverb (Ter. *Phorm.* 186; Apost. 14.34).
16 Hardly diplomatic when addressed to Hiero, whose ancestors took pride in their successes in chariot racing.
17 See on *Id.* 13.11.

From the Muses men gain a good reputation; the living use up what the dead bequeath. But it is as much effort to count on the beach the waves which the wind and gray sea drive landward, or to wash clean a muddy brick in clear water,[15] as to prevail on a man corrupted by greed. I will have nothing to do with such a man; may he have money without limit, and may desire for more constantly possess him. I for my part should prefer to have honor and the affection of others rather than plentiful mules and horses.[16]

I am in search of a mortal man to receive me with good grace when I arrive in the Muses' company (the road is a hard one for poets unaccompanied by the daughters of Zeus the great counselor). The heavens have not yet tired of bringing in the months and years, and the steeds of day will often yet put in motion the wheels of their chariot;[17] there shall be a man who shall have need of me as his poet,[18] when he has achieved as much as great Achilles or grim Ajax on the plain of Simois where the tomb of Phrygian Ilus stands.[19] Already the Phoenicians beneath the setting sun, who inhabit the farthest edge of Libya, tremble with fear;[20] already the Syracusans grasp their spears by the middle and load their arms with their wicker

[18] The language is solemnly oracular.

[19] The Simois flowed through the Trojan ("Phrygian") plain, in which stood the grave mound of Ilus, son of Dardanus (Hom. *Il.* 10.415, 11.371–72, etc.).

[20] The Carthaginians, who challenged the Syracusans for dominance of western Sicily, were from the coast of Tunisia, west of Sicily.

80 ἐν δ᾽ αὐτοῖς Ἱέρων προτέροις ἴσος ἡρώεσσι
    ζώννυται, ἵππειαι δὲ κόρυν σκιάουσιν ἔθειραι.
    αἳ γάρ, Ζεῦ κύδιστε πάτερ καὶ πότνι᾽ Ἀθάνα
    κούρη θ᾽ ἣ σὺν μητρὶ πολυκλήρων Ἐφυραίων
    εἴληχας μέγα ἄστυ παρ᾽ ὕδασι Λυσιμελείας,

85 ἐχθροὺς ἐκ νάσοιο κακαὶ πέμψειαν ἀνάγκαι
    Σαρδόνιον κατὰ κῦμα φίλων μόρον ἀγγέλλοντας
    τέκνοις ἠδ᾽ ἀλόχοισιν, ἀριθμητοὺς ἀπὸ πολλῶν.
    ἄστεα δὲ προτέροισι πάλιν ναίοιτο πολίταις,
    δυσμενέων ὅσα χεῖρες ἐλωβήσαντο κατ᾽ ἄκρας·

90 ἀγροὺς δ᾽ ἐργάζοιντο τεθαλότας· αἱ δ᾽ ἀνάριθμοι
    μήλων χιλιάδες βοτάνᾳ διαπιανθεῖσαι
    ἂμ πεδίον βληχῶντο, βόες δ᾽ ἀγεληδὸν ἐς αὖλιν
    ἐρχόμεναι σκνιφαῖον ἐπισπεύδοιεν ὁδίταν·
    νειοὶ δ᾽ ἐκπονέοιντο ποτὶ σπόρον, ἁνίκα τέττιξ

95 ποιμένας ἐνδίους πεφυλαγμένος ὑψόθι δένδρων
    ἀχεῖ ἐν ἀκρεμόνεσσιν· ἀράχνια δ᾽ εἰς ὅπλ᾽ ἀράχναι
    λεπτὰ διαστήσαιντο, βοᾶς δ᾽ ἔτι μηδ᾽ ὄνομ᾽ εἴη.
    ὑψηλὸν δ᾽ Ἱέρωνι κλέος φορέοιεν ἀοιδοί
    καὶ πόντου Σκυθικοῖο πέραν καὶ ὅθι πλατὺ τεῖχος

100 ἀσφάλτῳ δήσασα Σεμίραμις ἐμβασίλευεν.

---

21 I.e., a wicker frame supporting an outer layer of metal.

22 The opening line of this prayer echoes the Homeric "Father Zeus, Athena, and Apollo" (Hom. Il. 2.371, etc.); in general, it alludes to Pindar's prayer for Hiero I in his first Pythian ode (67–80).

23 Demeter and Persephone, who were associated with Sicily.

24 Syracuse, founded from Corinth (Ephyra; cf. 15.91). Lysimelea was a nearby lake or marsh (Thuc. 7.53.2).

shields;[21] and among them Hiero prepares himself like the warriors of old, a horsehair crest shadowing his helmet. Most honored father Zeus,[22] and Lady Athena, and you, maiden who together with your mother[23] have as your lot the great city of the wealthy Ephyreans by the waters of Lysimelea[24]—may stern necessity drive the enemy from this island over the Sardinian Sea[25] bearing news to wives and children of the deaths of men dear to them, a small number of messengers from a great army. May all those towns utterly ravaged by the hands of the enemy be settled once more by their former citizens. May they cultivate fields that flourish; may countless thousands of sheep, fattened on their pastures, bleat over the plain; may oxen heading for their byres hasten on his way the man traveling at dusk;[26] may the fallow land be made ready for sowing, while high in the trees the cicada, keeping watch over the shepherds in the heat of the day, chirps up in the branches; may spiders stretch their fine-spun webs over armor; and may the battle cry no longer exist even in name. May poets carry the lofty fame of Hiero beyond the Scythian sea[27] and where Semiramis used to reign within the broad walls she had built using pitch for mortar.[28] I am

[25] The sea north of Sicily—not an obvious escape route if the battle is to take place in the west of the island.

[26] Seeing them prompts him to seek shelter for the night. His being out so late is evidence of peace and stability.

[27] Either the Black Sea or Lake Maeotis (Sea of Azov).

[28] Babylon, famous for its brick walls cemented with bitumen (Hdt. 1.179). Some accounts made Semiramis the builder (Ctesias, *FGH* 688 F 1 = Diod. Sic. 2.7–9); Herodotus does not (1.184).

εἷς μὲν ἐγώ, πολλοὺς δὲ Διὸς φιλέοντι καὶ ἄλλους
θυγατέρες, τοῖς πᾶσι μέλοι Σικελὴν Ἀρέθοισαν
ὑμνεῖν σὺν λαοῖσι καὶ αἰχμητὴν Ἱέρωνα.
ὦ Ἐτεόκλειοι Χάριτες θεαί, ὦ Μινύειον
105 Ὀρχομενὸν φιλέοισαι ἀπεχθόμενόν ποτε Θήβαις,
ἄκλητος μὲν ἔγωγε μένοιμί κεν, ἐς δὲ καλεύντων
θαρσήσας Μοίσαισι σὺν ἁμετέραισιν ἴοιμ' ἄν.
καλλείψω δ' οὐδ' ὔμμε· τί γὰρ Χαρίτων ἀγαπητόν
ἀνθρώποις ἀπάνευθεν; ἀεὶ Χαρίτεσσιν ἄμ' εἴην.

107 ἴοιμ' ἄν Wilamowitz: ἰοίμαν M

only one poet, and the daughters of Zeus[29] love many others too. May they all have reason to celebrate Sicilian Arethusa[30] together with her people and Hiero the warrior. O Graces, goddesses favored by Eteocles, O you who love Minyan Orchomenus which in the past was hated by Thebes,[31] if I am not summoned I shall stay at home, but when I am invited I shall go confidently in company with my Muses. You, too, I shall not leave behind. Without the Graces what is there for mankind to desire? May I always be with the Graces.

[29] The Muses.

[30] On the famous spring Arethusa, see on *Id.* 1.117.

[31] An allusion to Pindar's fourteenth *Olympian Ode.* Eteocles, a king of Orchomenus in Boeotia, first set up the cult of the Graces (schol. ad loc., Hes. Fr. 71 M-W); the Minyans were an ancient race who lived in the area (Hom. *Il.* 2.511, *Od.* 11.284). For centuries the town had fought for supremacy with neighboring Thebes, which had the upper hand in the fourth century but was destroyed by Alexander in 335 BC.

IDYLL 17

*This encomium of Ptolemy II employs the traditional for-
mat of a hymn to present the king as a heroic figure. It
treats conventional topics for praise (parents, birth, terri-
tory and wealth, harmonious marriage), and includes an
indirect plea for reward or patronage (112–20). The begin-
ning and end in particular have characteristics of a hymn,
and the poem as a whole reflects on Ptolemy's status be-
tween heaven and earth by aligning him with heroic fig-
ures from the past.*

The Homeric Hymn to Apollo *told how various islands
were afraid to allow Leto to give birth and how Delos
spoke bravely in offering her refuge in return for being
honored in later times by her son Apollo. Theocritus has
the island of Cos, Ptolemy's birthplace, make a similar
speech of welcome to the future man-god, and the parallel
with Delos is drawn explicitly (66–67). There are notable
similarities to Callimachus' roughly contemporary* Hymn
to Zeus, *which links the god's birth with praise of Ptolemy,
mentions the eagle as bird of Zeus, and closes with a refer-
ence to* aretê *(virtue).*

Criticism

Griffiths, *Theocritus at Court*, 71–79.
Hunter, R. *Theocritus: Encomium of Ptolemy Philadel-
    phus.* Berkeley, 2003.
Meincke, *Untersuchungen*, 85–155.

17

Ἐκ Διὸς ἀρχώμεσθα καὶ ἐς Δία λήγετε Μοῖσαι,
ἀθανάτων τὸν ἄριστον, ἐπὴν μνασθῶμεν ἀοιδᾶς·
ἀνδρῶν δ᾽ αὖ Πτολεμαῖος ἐνὶ πρώτοισι λεγέσθω
καὶ πύματος καὶ μέσσος· ὃ γὰρ προφερέστατος ἀν-
δρῶν.
5 ἥρωες, τοὶ πρόσθεν ἀφ᾽ ἡμιθέων ἐγένοντο,
ῥέξαντες καλὰ ἔργα σοφῶν ἐκύρησαν ἀοιδῶν·
αὐτὰρ ἐγὼ Πτολεμαῖον ἐπιστάμενος καλὰ εἰπεῖν
ὑμνήσαιμ᾽· ὕμνοι δὲ καὶ ἀθανάτων γέρας αὐτῶν.
Ἴδαν ἐς πολύδενδρον ἀνὴρ ὑλατόμος ἐλθών
10 παπταίνει, παρεόντος ἅδην, πόθεν ἄρξεται ἔργου.
τί πρῶτον καταλέξω; ἐπεὶ πάρα μυρία εἰπεῖν
οἷσι θεοὶ τὸν ἄριστον ἐτίμησαν βασιλήων.

Ἐκ πατέρων οἷος μὲν ἔην τελέσαι μέγα ἔργον
Λαγείδας Πτολεμαῖος, ὅτε φρεσὶν ἐγκατάθοιτο
15 βουλάν, ἃν οὐκ ἄλλος ἀνὴρ οἷός τε νοῆσαι.
τῆνον καὶ μακάρεσσι πατὴρ ὁμότιμον ἔθηκεν
ἀθανάτοις, καί οἱ χρύσεος θρόνος ἐν Διὸς οἴκῳ

2 μνασθῶμεν ἀοιδᾶς Latte:]εν αοιδης pap.: ἀείδωμεν ἀοι-
δαῖς M
17 θρόνος Bergk: δόμος M

IDYLL 17

From Zeus let us begin, Muses, and with Zeus you should end whenever we are minded to sing,[1] since he is best of the immortals; but of men let Ptolemy be mentioned first and last and in the middle, since of men he is the most excellent. Past heroes, the sons of demigods, found skillful poets to celebrate their fine deeds,[2] but my skill in praise will make a hymn for Ptolemy: hymns are an honor given even to the immortals themselves. When a woodcutter comes to forested Ida[3] he looks everywhere in all that abundance for a place to begin his task. What should be my first subject? Countless are the ways in which I could tell how the gods have honored the best of kings.

Ptolemy son of Lagus[4] inherited the power to accomplish any great deed when once he stored up in his mind a plan such as no other man could have devised. The Father[5] made him equal in honor even to the blessed immortals, and he has his own golden throne in the house of Zeus.[6]

---

[1] "Minded to": text uncertain. The first three words quote the opening of Aratus' *Phaenomena,* a didactic poem on astronomy probably written not long before. The unusual move from "us" to "you" within this sentence sets off the quotation syntactically.

[2] Homer and other early epic poets.　　[3] Mt. Ida near Troy is called "wooded" by Homer (*Il.* 21.449).　　[4] Ptolemy I Soter, father of Ptolemy II Philadelphus.　　[5] Zeus, father of the gods.　　[6] After his death Soter was deified (cf. 15.47).

δέδμηται· παρὰ δ' αὐτὸν Ἀλέξανδρος φίλα εἰδώς
ἑδριάει, Πέρσαισι βαρὺς θεὸς αἰολομίτρας.
20 ἀντία δ' Ἡρακλῆος ἕδρα κενταυροφόνοιο
ἵδρυται στερεοῖο τετυγμένα ἐξ ἀδάμαντος·
ἔνθα σὺν ἄλλοισιν θαλίας ἔχει Οὐρανίδῃσι,
χαίρων υἱωνῶν περιώσιον υἱωνοῖσιν,
ὅττι σφεων Κρονίδης μελέων ἐξείλετο γῆρας,
25 ἀθάνατοι δὲ καλεῦνται ἑοὶ νέποδες γεγαῶτες.
ἄμφω γὰρ πρόγονός σφιν ὁ καρτερὸς Ἡρακλείδας,
ἀμφότεροι δ' ἀριθμεῦνται ἐς ἔσχατον Ἡρακλῆα.
τῷ καὶ ἐπεὶ δαίτηθεν ἴοι κεκορημένος ἤδη
νέκταρος εὐόδμοιο φίλας ἐς δῶμ' ἀλόχοιο,
30 τῷ μὲν τόξον ἔδωκεν ὑπωλένιόν τε φαρέτραν,
τῷ δὲ σιδάρειον σκύταλον κεχαραγμένον ὄζοις·
οἳ δ' εἰς ἀμβρόσιον θάλαμον λευκοσφύρου Ἥβας
ὅπλα καὶ αὐτὸν ἄγουσι γενειήταν Διὸς υἱόν.

25 ἑοὶ Heinsius: θεοὶ M

---

7 The diadem, a ribbon or band worn high on the head, was a
symbol of kingship adopted by Alexander from Dionysus, or, per-
haps, from the Persians whom he conquered. It was taken up by
the Ptolemies and other Hellenistic kings. Soter had been one of
Alexander's generals. He founded a cult of Alexander at Alexan-
dria and kept the body there. Soter represented himself as a de-
scendant of the royal house of Macedon and, through his mother
Arsinoe, as related to Heracles and Dionysus (Satyrus, *FGH* 631
F 1); hence Heracles' prominence in the following lines.

8 In the cave of Pholus: see on *Id.* 7.149–50. The Centaurs
represent destruction and uncivilized violence.

At his side, regarding him with favor, sits Alexander, destroyer of the Persians, a god, wearing his colorful diadem.[7] Facing them is set the chair of Heracles, slayer of the Centaurs,[8] made from hard adamant;[9] there he feasts in company with the other gods of heaven, greatly rejoicing in his children's children, because the son of Cronus has removed old age from their limbs[10] and they, who are his descendants, are called immortals: the mighty son of Heracles[11] is ancestor of them both,[12] and both trace back their lineage as far as Heracles. And so when he leaves the feast, replete now with fragrant nectar, for the house of his dear wife, he hands to one of them his bow and quiver that hangs down below his arm, and to the other his iron club with its knotted surface;[13] and they conduct the weapons and the bearded[14] son of Zeus himself to the ambrosial bedchamber of white-ankled Hebe.[15]

[9] Adamant means "unconquerable," and so is appropriate for Heracles' chair.

[10] Alexander died young, and so will never reach old age; Ptolemy, who died at an advanced age, will be restored to youth in his divinized state.

[11] Probably a reference to Caranus, legendary founder of the royal house of Macedon ten generations after Heracles (Satyrus loc. cit.).   [12] Alexander and Ptolemy.

[13] Replicating the knots in a wooden club, such as Heracles is more usually said to carry.

[14] I.e., older than Alexander and Soter; older too than Youth.

[15] Hebe ("Youth") is Heracles' wife, but here she has her own house on Olympus. The procession described here, with Heracles having drunk his fill, evokes the familiar bands of revelers ("comasts") who would escort a friend to the house of his mistress (cf. *Id.* 3).

Οἷα δ᾽ ἐν πινυταῖσι περικλειτὰ Βερενίκα
35 ἔπρεπε θηλυτέρῃς, ὄφελος μέγα γειναμένοισι.
τᾷ μὲν Κύπρον ἔχοισα Διώνας πότνια κούρα
κόλπον ἐς εὐώδη ῥαδινὰς ἐσεμάξατο χεῖρας·
τῷ οὔπω τινὰ φαντὶ ἁδεῖν τόσον ἀνδρὶ γυναικῶν
ὅσσον περ Πτολεμαῖος ἑὴν ἐφίλησεν ἄκοιτιν.
40 ἦ μὰν ἀντεφιλεῖτο πολὺ πλέον. ὧδέ κε παισί
θαρσήσας σφετέροισιν ἐπιτρέποι οἶκον ἅπαντα,
ὁππότε κεν φιλέων βαίνῃ λέχος ἐς φιλεούσης·
ἀστόργου δὲ γυναικὸς ἐπ᾽ ἀλλοτρίῳ νόος αἰεί,
ῥηίδιοι δὲ γοναί, τέκνα δ᾽ οὐ ποτεοικότα πατρί.
45 κάλλει ἀριστεύοισα θεάων πότν᾽ Ἀφροδίτα,
σοὶ τήνα μεμέλητο· σέθεν δ᾽ ἕνεκεν Βερενίκα
εὐειδὴς Ἀχέροντα πολύστονον οὐκ ἐπέρασεν,
ἀλλά μιν ἁρπάξασα, πάροιθ᾽ ἐπὶ νῆα κατελθεῖν
κυανέαν καὶ στυγνὸν ἀεὶ πορθμῆα καμόντων,
50 ἐς ναὸν κατέθηκας, ἑᾶς δ᾽ ἀπεδάσσαο τιμᾶς.
πᾶσιν δ᾽ ἤπιος ἥδε βροτοῖς μαλακοὺς μὲν ἔρωτας
προσπνείει, κούφας δὲ διδοῖ ποθέοντι μερίμνας.

Ἀργεία κυάνοφρυ, σὺ λαοφόνον Διομήδεα

---

16 Berenice was Soter's third wife, he her second husband.
Their son Ptolemy II, addressee of this poem, married his full
sister Arsinoe and acquired the title Philadelphus ("Sister-lover").

17 Perhaps a political reference. She was daughter of a certain
Magas and by her first husband mother of Magas I of Cyrene.

18 See on *Id.* 15.106.

19 Perhaps an allusion to the fact that Ptolemy chose to share
the throne with his son Philadelphus (285 BC).

IDYLL 17

As for renowned Berenice[16]—how she stood out among women of good sense, a great asset to her parents![17] The revered daughter of Dione, the Cyprian goddess,[18] pressed her slender hands upon Berenice's fragrant breast. For that reason, it is said, no woman has ever pleased her husband so much as Ptolemy loved his wife; and indeed she loved him far more deeply in return. When a loving husband sleeps with a loving wife in this way, he can with confidence hand on his whole estate to his children,[19] but a woman without affection is constantly thinking of another man and gives birth easily[20] to children who bear no resemblance to their father. Aphrodite, queen of goddesses, first in beauty,[21] you cared for this woman, and it was due to you that the lovely Berenice did not cross over Acheron, the river of lamentation: you snatched her up before she came to the black boat and its ever-grim ferryman,[22] placed her[23] in your temple, and granted her a share in your own honors. Kind to all mortals, she inspires gentle passions, and the cares that she bestows on a yearning lover are light ones.[24]

Dark-browed lady of Argos, uniting with Tydeus, the man

[20] Contrast lines 60–61. "Easily" seems to imply that for promiscuous women birth is frequent and routine; though a similar birthrate might be expected for an amorous married couple.

[21] Or, "Queen Aphrodite, first among goddesses in beauty."

[22] Charon.

[23] I.e., an image of her; the two were to be worshipped in tandem.

[24] Or, less likely, "she lightens the cares of a yearning lover."

μισγομένα Τυδῆι τέκες, Καλυδωνίῳ ἀνδρί,
55 ἀλλὰ Θέτις βαθύκολπος ἀκοντιστὰν Ἀχιλῆα
Αἰακίδᾳ Πηλῆι· σὲ δ', αἰχμητὰ Πτολεμαῖε,
αἰχμητᾷ Πτολεμαίῳ ἀρίζηλος Βερενίκα.
καί σε Κόως ἀτίταλλε βρέφος νεογιλλὸν ἐόντα,
δεξαμένα παρὰ ματρὸς ὅτε πρώταν ἴδες ἀῶ.
60 ἔνθα γὰρ Εἰλείθυιαν ἐβώσατο λυσίζωνον
Ἀντιγόνας θυγάτηρ βεβαρημένα ὠδίνεσσιν·
ἣ δέ οἱ εὐμενέοισα παρίστατο, κὰδ δ' ἄρα πάντων
νωδυνίαν κατέχευε μελῶν· ὃ δὲ πατρὶ ἐοικὼς
παῖς ἀγαπητὸς ἔγεντο. Κόως δ' ὀλόλυξεν ἰδοῖσα,
65 φᾶ δὲ καθαπτομένα βρέφεος χείρεσσι φίλησιν·
"ὄλβιε κοῦρε γένοιο, τίοις δέ με τόσσον ὅσον περ
Δῆλον ἐτίμησεν κυανάμπυκα Φοῖβος Ἀπόλλων·
ἐν δὲ μιᾷ τιμᾷ Τρίοπον καταθεῖο κολώναν,
ἶσον Δωριέεσσι νέμων γέρας ἐγγὺς ἐοῦσιν·
70 ἶσον καὶ Ῥήναιαν ἄναξ ἐφίλησεν Ἀπόλλων."
ὣς ἄρα νᾶσος ἔειπεν· ὃ δ' ὑψόθεν ἔκλαγε φωνᾷ

---

54 Καλυδωνίῳ ἀνδρί Hiller: -ιον ἄνδρα M

---

25 Tydeus, son of the king of Calydon in Aetolia, lived in exile at Argos and married Deipyle, daughter of the Argive king Adrastus (ps.-Apollod. *Bibl.* 1.8.5). Diomedes is prominent in the *Iliad*.

26 Perhaps an allusion to her now being a star in the heavens.

27 Ptolemy Philadelphus, born on the island of Cos in 308 BC.

28 A Macedonian noblewoman, mother of Berenice.

29 Goddess of childbirth. Taking off the girdle was a preliminary to giving birth.

250

from Calydon, you bore slaughterous Diomedes,[25] and deep-bosomed Thetis bore to Peleus, son of Aeacus, the spearman Achilles; you, warrior Ptolemy, glorious Berenice[26] bore to warrior Ptolemy. Cos received you from your mother when first you saw the light of day, and cared for you as a newborn infant.[27] It was there that the daughter of Antigone,[28] oppressed by the pains of labor, called on Eileithyia, the looser of girdles;[29] and she obligingly stood beside her and poured down painlessness on all her limbs; and he was born, the image of his father,[30] a child to delight his parents. Cos gave a joyful cry when she saw him;[31] she took hold of the child with loving hands and said, "Blessed may you be, my boy, and may you honor me as much as Phoebus Apollo honored dark-circled[32] Delos. And may you hold in the same honor the Triopian hill,[33] granting equal favor to the Dorians who live nearby; Lord Apollo loved Rhenaea with equal affection."[34] So the island spoke; and high above a great eagle shrieked

[30] Cf. lines 40–44.

[31] I.e., the eponymous nymph of the island.

[32] Lit., "with dark headdress" of the personified island, and so perhaps referring to the dark surrounding sea.

[33] On the Cnidian promontory opposite the southern part of Cos; a festival of the Dorians was held at its temple of Apollo (Hdt. 1.144.1), and Ptolemy treated the area with favor.

[34] I.e., no less than he loved Delos. Rhenaea, an island close to Delos, Apollo's birthplace, was equally favored by the god, and Cos hopes that his favor will similarly extend to herself. In the 520s the tyrant Polycrates formally dedicated Rhenaea to Apollo and linked it to Delos with a chain (Thuc. 1.13.6, 3.104.2).

251

ἐς τρὶς ἀπὸ νεφέων μέγας αἰετός, αἴσιος ὄρνις.
Ζηνός που τόδε σᾶμα· Διὶ Κρονίωνι μέλοντι
αἰδοῖοι βασιλῆες, ὁ δ᾽ ἔξοχος ὅν κε φιλήσῃ
75 γεινόμενον τὰ πρῶτα· πολὺς δέ οἱ ὄλβος ὀπαδεῖ,
πολλᾶς δὲ κρατέει γαίας, πολλᾶς δὲ θαλάσσας.

Μύριαι ἄπειροί τε καὶ ἔθνεα μυρία φωτῶν
λήιον ἀλδήσκουσιν ὀφελλόμεναι Διὸς ὄμβρῳ,
ἀλλ᾽ οὔτις τόσα φύει ὅσα χθαμαλὰ Αἴγυπτος,
80 Νεῖλος ἀναβλύζων διερὰν ὅτε βώλακα θρύπτει,
οὐδέ τις ἄστεα τόσσα βροτῶν ἔχει ἔργα δαέντων.
τρεῖς μέν οἱ πολίων ἑκατοντάδες ἐνδέδμηνται,
τρεῖς δ᾽ ἄρα χιλιάδες τρισσαῖς ἐπὶ μυριάδεσσι,
δοιαὶ δὲ τριάδες, μετὰ δέ σφισιν ἐννεάδες τρεῖς·
85 τῶν πάντων Πτολεμαῖος ἀγήνωρ ἐμβασιλεύει.
καὶ μὴν Φοινίκας ἀποτέμνεται Ἀρραβίας τε
καὶ Συρίας Λιβύας τε κελαινῶν τ᾽ Αἰθιοπήων·
Παμφύλοισί τε πᾶσι καὶ αἰχμηταῖς Κιλίκεσσι
σαμαίνει, Λυκίοις τε φιλοπτολέμοισί τε Καρσί
90 καὶ νάσοις Κυκλάδεσσιν, ἐπεί οἱ νᾶες ἄρισται
πόντον ἐπιπλώοντι, θάλασσα δὲ πᾶσα καὶ αἶα
καὶ ποταμοὶ κελάδοντες ἀνάσσονται Πτολεμαίῳ,
πολλοὶ δ᾽ ἱππῆες, πολλοὶ δέ μιν ἀσπιδιῶται
χαλκῷ μαρμαίροντι σεσαγμένοι ἀμφαγέρονται.

74 αἰδοῖοι pap., coni. Casaubon: -οῖο m: -οίου m
88 Παμφύλοισί Schrader: -ίοισί M

three times from the clouds, an auspicious omen.[35] This no doubt was a sign from Zeus: revered kings are watched over by Zeus son of Cronus, and that king is preeminent whom Zeus has loved from the moment of his birth. Great prosperity attends him, and great is the expanse of land, great the expanse of sea that he rules.

Countless lands and countless peoples raise their crops with the aid of rain from Zeus, but none of them produces as much as the lowlands of Egypt when the Nile in flood soaks and breaks up the soil, and none has so many cities of skilled craftsmen. Three hundred cities are built there, and three thousand in addition to three times ten thousand, and twice three, and thrice nine besides;[36] of all these lord Ptolemy is king. More: he takes a share of Phoenicia,[37] of Arabia, of Syria and Libya and of the dark-skinned Ethiopians; he rules over all the Pamphylians, the spearmen of Cilicia, the Lycians, and those keen warriors the Carians, and the islands of the Cyclades, since the best ships that sail the seas are his. The entire land and sea and all the roaring rivers are ruled by Ptolemy; many cavalrymen and many shield-bearing warriors loaded with flashing bronze attend him.

[35] The bird of Zeus ratifies the island's prayer. In iconography the eagle was associated particularly with the Ptolemies.

[36] This number (33,333) is expressed ingeniously and with a hint of mystic or ritual repetition, but it accords with the figure given by historians (more than 30,000 according to Diod. Sic. 1.31.7–8; cf. schol. Hom. *Il.* 9.383).

[37] The following list of lands directly or indirectly under Ptolemy's control seems to depict him as a new Alexander; it may also be connected with developments in the First Syrian War (ca. 276–271 BC) between Ptolemy and Antiochus.

95 Ὄλβῳ μὲν πάντας κε καταβρίθοι βασιλῆας·
   τόσσον ἐπ᾽ ἆμαρ ἕκαστον ἐς ἀφνεὸν ἔρχεται οἶκον
   πάντοθε. λαοὶ δ᾽ ἔργα περιστέλλουσιν ἕκηλοι·
   οὐ γάρ τις δηίων πολυκήτεα Νεῖλον ὑπερβὰς
   πεζὸς ἐν ἀλλοτρίαισι βοὰν ἐστάσατο κώμαις,
100 οὐδέ τις αἰγιαλόνδε θοᾶς ἐξήλατο ναὸς
   θωρηχθεὶς ἐπὶ βουσὶν ἀνάρσιος Αἰγυπτίῃσιν·
   τοῖος ἀνὴρ πλατέεσσιν ἐνίδρυται πεδίοισι
   ξανθοκόμας Πτολεμαῖος, ἐπιστάμενος δόρυ πάλλειν,
   ᾧ ἐπίπαγχυ μέλει πατρώια πάντα φυλάσσειν
105 οἷ᾽ ἀγαθῷ βασιλῆι, τὰ δὲ κτεατίζεται αὐτός.
   οὐ μὰν ἀχρεῖός γε δόμῳ ἐνὶ πίονι χρυσὸς
   μυρμάκων ἅτε πλοῦτος ἀεὶ κέχυται μογεόντων·
   ἀλλὰ πολὺν μὲν ἔχοντι θεῶν ἐρικυδέες οἶκοι,
   αἰὲν ἀπαρχομένοιο σὺν ἄλλοισιν γεράεσσι,
110 πολλὸν δ᾽ ἰφθίμοισι δεδώρηται βασιλεῦσι,
   πολλὸν δὲ πτολίεσσι, πολὺν δ᾽ ἀγαθοῖσιν ἑταίροις.
   οὐδὲ Διωνύσου τις ἀνὴρ ἱεροὺς κατ᾽ ἀγῶνας
   ἵκετ᾽ ἐπιστάμενος λιγυρὰν ἀναμέλψαι ἀοιδάν,
   ᾧ οὐ δωτίναν ἀντάξιον ὤπασε τέχνας.
115 Μουσάων δ᾽ ὑποφῆται ἀείδοντι Πτολεμαῖον
   ἀντ᾽ εὐεργεσίης. τί δὲ κάλλιον ἀνδρί κεν εἴη
   ὀλβίῳ ἢ κλέος ἐσθλὸν ἐν ἀνθρώποισιν ἀρέσθαι;
   τοῦτο καὶ Ἀτρεΐδαισι μένει· τὰ δὲ μυρία τῆνα

---

38 The crocodile and the hippopotamus.

39 Subject kings, or foreign rulers, whom he graciously con-
ciliates with lavish gifts.

In wealth he could outweigh all other kings, so much comes daily to his rich store from every direction. His people work their land undisturbed: no enemy passes over the Nile, teeming with its huge creatures,[38] to raise on land the war cry in villages not his own, and no one leaps ashore in armor from his swift ship to raid the cattle of Egypt: fair-haired Ptolemy, skilled at wielding the spear, is established in those broad plains. As a good king should, he is most concerned to keep safe his ancestral lands, and he acquires more himself. Not that gold is piled up uselessly in his rich palace like the stores of worker ants: much of it is in the glorious houses of the gods, since he constantly makes thank-offerings and gives other gifts, and much of it has been granted to mighty kings,[39] much to cities, and much to his brave companions.[40] No one skilled at performing a tuneful song comes to the sacred competitions of Dionysus without receiving a gift worthy of his art,[41] and those interpreters of the Muses celebrate Ptolemy in return for his good works. For a man of substance what could be finer than to win renown among mankind? That is in store for the sons of Atreus, too, while all that countless

[40] Called *hetairoi* rather than the usual word *philoi* as a reference to the *hetairoi* of the kings of Macedon, and especially of Alexander.

[41] Ptolemy funded festivals, such as the Ptolemaea, to commemorate Soter, at which poets could compete, and the guild called Artists of Dionysus as well as poetic victors at these games were granted some exemptions from tax. Cf. *Id.* 2.100–144.

ὅσσα μέγαν Πριάμοιο δόμον κτεάτισσαν ἑλόντες
120 ἀέρι πᾳ κέκρυπται, ὅθεν πάλιν οὐκέτι νόστος.

Μοῦνος ὅδε προτέρων τε καὶ ὧν ἔτι θερμὰ κονία
στειβομένα καθύπερθε ποδῶν ἐκμάσσεται ἴχνη,
ματρὶ φίλᾳ καὶ πατρὶ θυώδεας εἴσατο ναούς·
ἐν δ᾽ αὐτοὺς χρυσῷ περικαλλέας ἠδ᾽ ἐλέφαντι
125 ἵδρυται πάντεσσιν ἐπιχθονίοισιν ἀρωγούς.
πολλὰ δὲ πιανθέντα βοῶν ὅγε μηρία καίει
μησὶ περιπλομένοισιν ἐρευθομένων ἐπὶ βωμῶν,
αὐτός τ᾽ ἰφθίμα τ᾽ ἄλοχος, τᾶς οὔτις ἀρείων
νυμφίον ἐν μεγάροισι γυνὰ περιβάλλετ᾽ ἀγοστῷ,
130 ἐκ θυμοῦ στέργοισα κασίγνητόν τε πόσιν τε.
ὧδε καὶ ἀθανάτων ἱερὸς γάμος ἐξετελέσθη
οὓς τέκετο κρείουσα Ῥέα βασιλῆας Ὀλύμπου·
ἓν δὲ λέχος στόρνυσιν ἰαύειν Ζηνὶ καὶ Ἥρῃ
χεῖρας φοιβήσασα μύροις ἔτι παρθένος Ἶρις.

Χαῖρε, ἄναξ Πτολεμαῖε· σέθεν δ᾽ ἐγὼ ἶσα καὶ ἄλ-
135 λων
μνάσομαι ἡμιθέων, δοκέω δ᾽ ἔπος οὐκ ἀπόβλητον
φθέγξομαι ἐσσομένοις· ἀρετήν γε μὲν ἐκ Διὸς αἰτεῦ.

121 τε καὶ ὧν Briggs: τεκέων m: τοκέων m

---

42 In Hades; in irretrievable obscurity. For the idea that only
renown truly survives death, cf. *Id.* 16.34–57.

43 After their deaths Soter and Berenice were worshipped
under the cult title *Theoi sôtêres* (Savior Gods); probably "help"
is an allusion to this.

wealth which they gained in capturing the great palace of Priam is hidden somewhere in darkness from which there is no return.[42]

This man, alone of men of the past and of those whose steps' fresh imprint the trodden earth still bears on its surface, has founded fragrant shrines to his dear mother and father, and he has installed them there, resplendent in gold and ivory, to bring help to all mankind.[43] Each month[44] he burns many fat thighs of oxen on the bloodred altars, both himself and his noble wife. No better wife embraces her husband in his halls, and she loves her brother, her husband, with all her heart. In this way, too, was accomplished the sacred marriage of the immortals whom queen Rhea bore to the rulers of Olympus: it is one bed that Iris, still a virgin,[45] prepares for Zeus and Hera to sleep in, having cleansed her hands with perfumes.

Farewell, lord Ptolemy! I shall make mention of you just as much as of the other demigods,[46] and I think my account will not be rejected by future generations. As for virtue, you should request that from Zeus.

[44] Or, "as the year proceeds"; but probably monthly sacrifices to the Savior Gods are meant.

[45] In poetry Iris is the gods' messenger; in art she is associated with marriage processions. For Zeus and Hera each night is special like the first, and Iris prepares the bed accordingly. Her being "still a virgin" perhaps alludes to a custom that marriage beds were prepared by virgins, but there is no other evidence for this.

[46] The poem closes in the style of a hymn to a god (cf. *Idd.* 15.149, 22.214), and the bold address to Ptolemy as a demigod is of a part with this. Theocritus does however mention Zeus at the very end, as he undertook to do at the beginning.

IDYLL 18

The epithalamium, a song performed at the bedroom door of a newly married couple, was a traditional feature of weddings. Here Theocritus re-creates the epithalamium performed at the marriage of Helen and Menelaus at Sparta. Although the tone of the girls' song is conventionally joyous and filled with optimism, their innocent good wishes for future prosperity and mutual love seem to defy readers to ignore subsequent events.

An ancient source states, "In it certain things have been taken from the first book of Stesichorus' Helen" (Arg. p. 331.13 Wendel = Stesich. Fr. 189, vol. 3, pp. 90–91 Campbell). In that poem Stesichorus criticized Helen for eloping with Paris and bringing about the Trojan War.

It is likely that this epithalamium contains allusions to passages in similar poems by Sappho, some of which were in hexameters; surviving fragments include similes praising the bride and groom, and ribald banter (Frr. 104–17a Campbell). The tree cult described in lines 43–48, an antiquarian detail of a type familiar from other Hellenistic poets (and cf. Id. 7.106–14), marks the future divinization of Helen, so that the closing "Farewell" (49) evokes not only the end of a wedding song but also the formal close of a hymn (cf. Idd. 17.135, 22.214).

IDYLL 18

Criticism

Griffiths, *Theocritus at Court*, 86–90.

Hunter, *Archaeology*, 149–66.

Lane, N. "Some Illusive Puns in Theocritus, *Idyll* 18 Gow." *QUCC* 83 (2006): 23–26.

Morrison, *Narrator*, 239–42.

Stern, J. "Theocritus' *Epithalamium for Helen*." *RBPh* 56 (1978): 29–37.

18

Ἔν ποκ᾽ ἄρα Σπάρτᾳ ξανθότριχι πὰρ Μενελάῳ
παρθενικαὶ θάλλοντα κόμαις ὑάκινθον ἔχοισαι
πρόσθε νεογράπτω θαλάμω χορὸν ἐστάσαντο,
δώδεκα ταὶ πρᾶται πόλιος, μέγα χρῆμα Λακαινᾶν,
5 ἁνίκα Τυνδαρίδα κατεκλάξατο τὰν ἀγαπατάν
μναστεύσας Ἑλέναν ὁ νεώτερος Ἀτρέος υἱῶν.
ἄειδον δ᾽ ἅμα πᾶσαι ἐς ἓν μέλος ἐγκροτέοισαι
ποσσὶ περιπλέκτοις, ὑπὸ δ᾽ ἴαχε δῶμ᾽ ὑμεναίῳ·

Οὕτω δὴ πρωιζὰ κατέδραθες, ὦ φίλε γαμβρέ;
10 ἦ ῥά τις ἐσσὶ λίαν βαρυγούνατος; ἦ ῥα φίλυπνος;
ἦ ῥα πολύν τιν᾽ ἔπινες, ὅκ᾽ εἰς εὐνὰν κατεβάλλευ;
εὕδειν μὰν σπεύδοντα καθ᾽ ὥραν αὐτὸν ἐχρῆν τυ,
παῖδα δ᾽ ἐᾶν σὺν παισὶ φιλοστόργῳ παρὰ ματρί
παίσδειν ἐς βαθὺν ὄρθρον, ἐπεὶ καὶ ἔνας καὶ ἐς ἀῶ
15 κῆς ἔτος ἐξ ἔτεος, Μενέλαε, τεὰ νυὸς ἅδε.

ὄλβιε γάμβρ᾽, ἀγαθός τις ἐπέπταρεν ἐρχομένῳ τοι
ἐς Σπάρταν ἅπερ ὦλλοι ἀριστέες, ὡς ἀνύσαιο·

---

1 The word translated "then" (*ara*) is unexpected in an open-
ing line. A proem may be lost; or Theocritus may have wished to
give the effect of a lively narrator or of a fragmentary narrative
(cf. p. 340 on *Id.* 25).

2 In Homer Menelaus is regularly called *xanthos* (fair-haired).

IDYLL 18

Once upon a time, then,[1] at the palace of fair-haired[2] Menelaus in Sparta, girls with hyacinth blooms in their hair prepared to dance before the freshly painted bridal chamber (there were twelve of them, the most distinguished in the city, a fine sample of Spartan womanhood). When after his successful courtship the younger of Atreus' sons locked in his beloved Helen, daughter of Tyndareus, they all sang in unison, keeping time with their intricate steps, and the palace echoed to the sound of the wedding hymn.

"Have you fallen asleep so early, dear bridegroom?[3] Are your limbs just too heavy? Is sleep what you desire? Or were you far gone in drink when you were put to bed? If you were keen to go to sleep early you should have slept alone and left the girl to play deep into the night with the other girls at her loving mother's side, for she will be your bride the day after next and the day that dawns after that, and all the years to come.[4]

"Lucky bridegroom, a good man sneezed as omen of your success as you came to Sparta with the other princely

---

[3] Innuendo and ribald joking were a feature of marriage songs.

[4] I.e., if you were tired there was no need to have married her today.

μῶνος ἐν ἡμιθέοις Κρονίδαν Δία πενθερὸν ἑξεῖς.
Ζανός τοι θυγάτηρ ὑπὸ τὰν μίαν ἵκετο χλαῖναν,
20   οἵα Ἀχαιιάδων γαῖαν πατεῖ οὐδεμί᾽ ἄλλα·
ἦ μέγα κά τι τέκοιτ᾽, εἰ ματέρι τίκτοι ὁμοῖον.
ἄμμες δ᾽ αἱ πᾶσαι συνομάλικες, αἷς δρόμος ωὑτός
χρισαμέναις ἀνδριστὶ παρ᾽ Εὐρώταο λοετροῖς,
τετράκις ἑξήκοντα κόραι, θῆλυς νεολαία,
25   τᾶν οὐδ᾽ ἅτις ἄμωμος ἐπεί χ᾽ Ἑλένᾳ παρισωθῇ.

Ἀὼς ἀντέλλοισα καλὸν διέφανε πρόσωπον,
πότνια Νύξ, τό τε λευκὸν ἔαρ χειμῶνος ἀνέντος·
ὧδε καὶ ἁ χρυσέα Ἑλένα διεφαίνετ᾽ ἐν ἁμῖν.
πιείρᾳ μεγάλᾳ ἅτ᾽ ἀνέδραμε κόσμος ἀρούρᾳ
30   ἢ κάπῳ κυπάρισσος, ἢ ἅρματι Θεσσαλὸς ἵππος,
ὧδε καὶ ἁ ῥοδόχρως Ἑλένα Λακεδαίμονι κόσμος·
οὐδέ τις ἐκ ταλάρω πανίσδεται ἔργα τοιαῦτα,
οὐδ᾽ ἐνὶ δαιδαλέῳ πυκινώτερον ἄτριον ἱστῷ
κερκίδι συμπλέξασα μακρῶν ἔταμ᾽ ἐκ κελεόντων.
35   οὐ μὰν οὐδὲ λύραν τις ἐπίσταται ὧδε κροτῆσαι

26 διέφανε Ahrens: -φαινε M
27 τό τε Kaibel: ἅτε pap., M

---

⁵ Or, perhaps, "sneezed as you came to accomplish what the other princes came to accomplish." Menelaus was chosen by Helen, or in some accounts by her father, from a large number of suitors (ps.-Apollod. *Bibl.* 3.10.8; Hes. Frr. 196–204 M-W; Hyg. 81; Stesich.). On lucky sneezes cf. *Id.* 7.96.   ⁶ Helen being daughter of Zeus and Leda.   ⁷ Achaean = Greek.

⁸ Spartan girls famously exercised in the same way as the boys and men.

⁹ The reason for this number is not known. Perhaps each of

suitors:[5] you alone among heroes will have Zeus son of
Cronus as father-in-law.[6] You are sharing a bed with Zeus'
daughter, an Achaean girl[7] like no other who walks the
earth; a child of hers will indeed be great if it resembles
its mother. We, the whole company of her friends equal in
age, who run together and anoint ourselves in the same
way as men[8] at the bathing places of the river Eurotas, a
young group of four times sixty girls[9]—not one of us is
faultless in comparison with Helen.[10]

"Beautiful is the face revealed by Dawn when she rises,
lady Night,[11] and beautiful is bright spring at the end of
winter; just so did golden Helen stand out among us. As a
tall cypress rises high to adorn some fertile field or garden,
or as a Thracian horse[12] adorns its chariot, just so is rosy
Helen the ornament of Sparta. No one winds from her
basket yarn as good as hers, or at the patterned loom cuts
from the tall beams a closer weft once she has woven it
with her shuttle;[13] no one knows so well how to strike

the twelve chorus members speaks on behalf of a division of the
city.   [10] It may not be coincidental that the poem twice con-
ceals *paris* within longer words: here "in comparison with" is
parisôthê, and at line 30 "cypress" is *kyparissos*.

[11] The song takes place at bedtime, and the singers are re-
spectful of night as they praise the dawn.

[12] A famous breed (cf. Soph. *El.* 703; *Anth. Pal.* 9.21; Varro
Rust. 2.7.6; Luc. 6. 397ff.).

[13] The basket contains spun thread, which is wound on a bob-
bin; this is enclosed in a shuttle, which passes between the hori-
zontal warp threads to form the fabric, whose quality is judged by
the closeness of its weaving. The vertical loom beams support a
horizontal beam, to which the warp threads are attached; once
the work is completed, the fabric is cut away.

Ἄρτεμιν ἀείδοισα καὶ εὐρύστερνον Ἀθάναν

ὡς Ἑλένα, τᾶς πάντες ἐπ᾽ ὄμμασιν ἵμεροι ἐντί.

ὦ καλά, ὦ χαρίεσσα κόρα, τὺ μὲν οἰκέτις ἤδη.

ἄμμες δ᾽ ἐς δρόμον ἦρι καὶ ἐς λειμώνια φύλλα

40 ἑρψεῦμες στεφάνως δρεψεύμεναι ἁδὺ πνέοντας,

πολλὰ τεοῦς, Ἑλένα, μεμναμέναι ὡς γαλαθηναί

ἄρνες γειναμένας οἶος μαστὸν ποθέοισαι.

πρᾶταί τοι στέφανον λωτῶ χαμαὶ αὐξομένοιο

πλέξασαι σκιερὰν καταθήσομεν ἐς πλατάνιστον·

45 πρᾶται δ᾽ ἀργυρέας ἐξ ὄλπιδος ὑγρὸν ἄλειφαρ

λαζύμεναι σταξεῦμες ὑπὸ σκιερὰν πλατάνιστον·

γράμματα δ᾽ ἐν φλοιῷ γεγράψεται, ὡς παριών τις

ἀννείμῃ Δωριστί· "σέβευ μ᾽· Ἑλένας φυτόν εἰμι."

Χαίροις, ὦ νύμφα· χαίροις, εὐπένθερε γαμβρέ.

50 Λατὼ μὲν δοίη, Λατὼ κουροτρόφος, ὕμμιν

εὐτεκνίαν, Κύπρις δέ, θεὰ Κύπρις, ἶσον ἔρασθαι

ἀλλάλων, Ζεὺς δέ, Κρονίδας Ζεύς, ἄφθιτον ὄλβον,

ὡς ἐξ εὐπατριδᾶν εἰς εὐπατρίδας πάλιν ἔνθῃ.

εὕδετ᾽ ἐς ἀλλάλων στέρνον φιλότατα πνέοντες

55 καὶ πόθον· ἐγρέσθαι δὲ πρὸς ἀῶ μὴ ᾽πιλάθησθε.

νεύμεθα κἄμμες ἐς ὄρθρον, ἐπεί κα πρᾶτος ἀοιδός

---

[14] Both, being virgin goddesses, are suitable for celebration by a girl. Athena's epithet alludes to her warlike qualities, relevant for the manly exercise described in lines 22–23.

[15] The simile seems inappropriate, since the girls are the same age as Helen. There may be a cultic reference, as in the following lines.

up the lyre in celebration of Artemis and broad-breasted Athena as Helen, in whose eyes is every form of desire.[14]

"Beautiful and gracious girl, now you are a housewife. But we shall go early tomorrow to the running course and the flower meadows to gather fragrant garlands, and we shall have many thoughts of you, Helen, as suckling lambs miss the udder of the ewe that bore them.[15] We shall be the first to plait for you a garland of low-growing trefoil and to set it on a shady plane tree;[16] and we shall be the first to take smooth oil from its silver flask and let it drip beneath that shady plane. In the bark there will be an inscription, so that a passerby may read in Dorian style,[17] 'Revere me: I am Helen's tree.'

"Farewell, bride; farewell, groom, fortunate in your wife's father. May Leto—that good mother Leto—grant to you both fine children,[18] Cypris—the goddess Cypris—mutual love, and Zeus—Zeus the son of Cronus—endless prosperity, and that it may pass again from noble fathers to noble sons.

"Sleep, breathing love and desire into each other's breasts, and do not forget to wake at dawn.[19] We too shall come

[16] These lines describe a tree cult of Helen at Sparta, for which there is no other evidence.

[17] Meaning uncertain. The whole poem is in Doric dialect, and the inscription is no different. Possibly the phrase should be part of the inscription ("revere me in Dorian style"), with reference to some aspect of the cult.

[18] Leto, as mother of Artemis and Apollo, had the best children possible.

[19] A conventional wish (cf. *Id.* 24.7–9).

ἐξ εὐνᾶς κελαδήσῃ ἀνασχὼν εὔτριχα δειράν.
Ὑμὴν ὦ Ὑμέναιε, γάμῳ ἐπὶ τῷδε χαρείης.

back in the morning,[20] when after roosting the first cock
raises his feathered neck and crows.

"Hymen o Hymenaeus,[21] may you take pleasure in this
marriage."

[20] They will sing the *diegertikon* (waking-up song).
[21] God of marriage.

IDYLL 19

A brief anecdote about Eros. Stung by a bee, he complains to his mother, who points out the irony of the situation. The poem plays on the common idea that Eros' great power to harm is belied by his childish appearance (cf. Moschus 1, Bion Fr. 13).

The poem is very unlikely to be by Theocritus: it is attributed to him in a single manuscript that is of no independent value. There are some similarities to poem 35 in the collection of Anacreontea (Greek Lyric, vol. 2, pp. 206–9 Campbell), where Eros is told by his mother that a bee-sting is nothing in comparison with the pangs of love.

19

Τὸν κλέπταν ποτ' Ἔρωτα κακὰ κέντασε μέλισσα
κηρίον ἐκ σίμβλων συλεύμενον, ἄκρα δὲ χειρῶν
δάκτυλα πάνθ' ὑπένυξεν. ὁ δ' ἄλγεε καὶ χέρ' ἐφύση
καὶ τὰν γᾶν ἐπάταξε καὶ ἄλατο, τᾷ δ' Ἀφροδίτᾳ
5 δεῖξεν τὰν ὀδύναν, καὶ μέμφετο ὅττι γε τυτθόν
θηρίον ἐντὶ μέλισσα καὶ ἁλίκα τραύματα ποιεῖ.
χἀ μάτηρ γελάσασα· "τὺ δ' οὐκ ἴσος ἐσσὶ μελίσ-
         σαις,
ὃς τυτθὸς μὲν ἔεις τὰ δὲ τραύματα ἁλίκα ποιεῖς;"

7 τὺ Stephanus: τί M
8 ὃς Valckenaer: χὠ M   ἔεις Wilamowitz: ἔης M

270

IDYLL 19

A cruel bee once stung the thief Eros as he was plundering honey from the hives, and it made all his fingertips tingle. In pain, he blew on his hand, stamped on the ground, and jumped about, and he showed his wound to Aphrodite, complaining that such a small creature as a bee should inflict such wounds. His mother laughed and said, "Aren't you just like the bees, so small and yet so wounding?"

IDYLL 20

In this unhappy clash of the urban and the rustic, an oxherd tells how Eunica, a woman from the town, scorned to kiss him. He claims to be attractive to country women, lists oxherds loved by goddesses, and hopes that Eunica may have no one at all to love her.

The poem begins with the fastidious Eunica insulting her lover and ends with his wishing her ill for the future. It has features in common with the "renunciation of love" motif familiar from Latin poetry (e.g., Catull. 8; Tib. 1.9; Hor. Epod. 15, odes 3.26; Ov. Am. 3.11. Cf. Theoc. Id. 30; Maced. Anth. Pal. 5.245). The oxherd's proud self-consolation is inspired by Polyphemus in Idyll 11 *and by the rustic singer of* Idyll 3, *who cites examples from mythology.*

The author is very unlikely to be Theocritus.

Criticism

Fantuzzi, M. "The Importance of Being *Boukolos*: Ps.-Theocr. 20." In Paschalis, *Pastoral Palimpsests*, 13–35.
Kirsten, *Junge Hirten*, 89–137.

20

Εὐνίκα μ᾽ ἐγέλαξε θέλοντά μιν ἁδὺ φιλᾶσαι
καί μ᾽ ἐπικερτομέοισα τάδ᾽ ἔννεπεν· "ἔρρ᾽ ἀπ᾽ ἐμεῖο.
βουκόλος ὢν ἐθέλεις με κύσαι, τάλαν; οὐ μεμάθηκα
ἀγροίκως φιλέειν, ἀλλ᾽ ἀστικὰ χείλεα θλίβειν.
μὴ τύγε μευ κύσσῃς τὸ καλὸν στόμα μηδ᾽ ἐν
5   ὀνείροις.
οἷα βλέπεις, ὁπποῖα λαλεῖς, ὡς ἄγρια παίσδεις.
[ὡς τρυφερὸν καλέεις, ὡς κωτίλα ῥήματα φράσδεις·
ὡς μαλακὸν τὸ γένειον ἔχεις, ὡς ἀδέα χαίταν.]
χείλεά τοι νοσέοντι, χέρες δέ τοι ἐντὶ μέλαιναι,
10   καὶ κακὸν ἐξόσδεις. ἀπ᾽ ἐμεῦ φύγε μή με μολύνῃς."
τοιάδε μυθίζοισα τρὶς εἰς ἑὸν ἔπτυσε κόλπον,
καί μ᾽ ἀπὸ τᾶς κεφαλᾶς ποτὶ τὼ πόδε συνεχὲς εἶδεν
χείλεσι μυχθίζοισα καὶ ὄμμασι λοξὰ βλέποισα,
καὶ πολὺ τᾷ μορφᾷ θηλύνετο, καί τι σεσαρός
15   καὶ σοβαρόν μ᾽ ἐγέλαξεν. ἐμοὶ δ᾽ ἄφαρ ἔζεσεν αἷμα,
καὶ χρόα φοινίχθην ὑπὸ τῶλγεος ὡς ῥόδον ἔρσᾳ.
χἀ μὲν ἔβα με λιποῖσα, φέρω δ᾽ ὑποκάρδιον ὀργάν,
ὅττι με τὸν χαρίεντα κακὰ μωμήσαθ᾽ ἑταίρα.
ποιμένες, εἴπατέ μοι τὸ κρήγυον· οὐ καλὸς ἐμμί;
20   ἀρά τις ἐξαπίνας με θεὸς βροτὸν ἄλλον ἔτευξε;
καὶ γὰρ ἐμοὶ τὸ πάροιθεν ἐπάνθεεν ἁδύ τι κάλλος

          . . . .

IDYLL 20

Eunica laughed at me when I wanted a sweet kiss, and in a mocking tone she said, "Get away from me! Do you, an oxherd, want to kiss me, you poor thing? I've not learned to kiss country bumpkins, but to press townsmen's lips with mine. Don't you kiss my pretty mouth, even in your dreams! How you stare! How you prate! How roughly you flirt! [How softly you address me! What lively words you speak! How soft your beard is! How fragrant your hair![1]] Your lips are infected, your hands are filthy, and you stink. Get away from me, in case you make me dirty!" With these words she spat three times in her bosom,[2] tut-tutting and looking askance; she gave herself a ladylike air and laughed at me with a smile of contempt. Straightaway my blood boiled, and I blushed at the insult like a rose in the dew. She went off and left me, and I bear anger in my heart because this dirty slut made fun of me although I'm a handsome fellow. Shepherds, tell me the truth: am I not good-looking? Has some god suddenly made a different man of me? In the past beauty bloomed upon me ‹. . . . . .›[3]

[1] These two lines, unless they are clumsily ironic, do not fit the tone of what precedes and follows. Probably they are from another poem.   [2] Cf. *Id.* 6.39.

[3] Probably a line is missing, in which he mentioned his beard.

---

21 lac. post hunc v. ind. Hermann

ὡς κισσὸς ποτὶ πρέμνον, ἐμὰν δ᾽ ἐπύκαζεν ὑπήναν,
χαῖται δ᾽ οἷα σέλινα περὶ κροτάφοισι κέχυντο,
καὶ λευκὸν τὸ μέτωπον ἐπ᾽ ὀφρύσι λάμπε μελαίναις·
25 ὄμματά μοι γλαυκᾶς χαροπώτερα πολλὸν Ἀθάνας,
τὸ στόμα δ᾽ αὖ πακτᾶς ἀπαλώτερον, ἐκ στομάτων δέ
ἔρρεέ μοι φωνὰ γλυκερωτέρα ἢ μέλι κηρῶ.
ἁδὺ δέ μοι τὸ μέλισμα, καὶ ἢν σύριγγι μελίσδω,
κἢν αὐλῷ λαλέω, κἢν δώνακι, κἢν πλαγιαύλῳ.
30 καὶ πᾶσαι καλόν με κατ᾽ ὤρεα φαντὶ γυναῖκες,
καὶ πᾶσαί με φιλεῦντι· τὰ δ᾽ ἀστικά μ᾽ οὐκ ἐφίλασεν,
ἀλλ᾽ ὅτι βουκόλος ἐμμὶ παρέδραμε κοὔποτ᾽ ἀκούει
[χὠ καλὸς Διόνυσος ἐν ἄγκεσι πόρτιν ἐλαύνει].
οὐκ ἔγνω δ᾽ ὅτι Κύπρις ἐπ᾽ ἀνέρι μήνατο βούτᾳ
35 καὶ Φρυγίοις ἐνόμευσεν ἐν ὤρεσι, καὶ τὸν Ἄδωνιν
ἐν δρυμοῖσι φίλασε καὶ ἐν δρυμοῖσιν ἔκλαυσεν.
Ἐνδυμίων δὲ τίς ἦν; οὐ βουκόλος; ὅν γε Σελάνα
βουκολέοντα φίλασεν, ἀπ᾽ Οὐλύμπω δὲ μολοῖσα
Λάτμιον ἂν νάπος ἦλθε, καὶ εἰς ὁμὰ παιδὶ κάθευδε.
40 καὶ τύ, Ῥέα, κλαίεις τὸν βουκόλον. οὐχὶ δὲ καὶ τύ,
ὦ Κρονίδα, διὰ παῖδα βοηνόμον ὄρνις ἐπλάγχθης;
Εὐνίκα δὲ μόνα τὸν βουκόλον οὐκ ἐφίλασεν,

26 ἀπαλώτερον Valckenaer: γλυκερώτερον M
33 secl. Meineke
35 καὶ τὸν Wassenberg: αὐτὸν M
39 καὶ εἰς ὁμὰ Vossius: κεἰς ἐμὰ m: καὶ εἰς ἑὰ m

like ivy upon a tree stump, and thickly covered my chin,
and the hair curled round my temples like parsley, and my
forehead gleamed white above my dark brows; my eyes
were much brighter than gray-eyed Athena's, my mouth
was softer than curd, and from it my voice would flow
more sweet than honey from the comb. And my music
making is sweet, whether I play on the panpipe or trill on
the pipe, the reed, or the cross flute.[4] All the women in the
hills say I'm handsome, and they all kiss me. But this city
creature hasn't kissed me; because I'm an oxherd she has
passed me by and never takes notice of me. [The fair god
Dionysus, too, herds heifers in the valleys.[5]] Doesn't she
know that the Cyprian goddess was madly in love with an
oxherding man and pastured herds on the hills of Phrygia
and loved Adonis in the thickets and lamented him in the
thickets?[6] What was Endymion? Wasn't he an oxherd? Se-
lene fell in love with him as he herded his cattle; she came
from Olympus to the Latmian grove and slept with the
lad.[7] You too, Rhea, weep for your oxherd.[8] And did not
you, son of Cronus, soar aloft as a bird because of an ox-
herding boy?[9] Eunica alone has not felt love for her herds-

[4] Held transversely like a modern flute.

[5] No lover is mentioned, and the line seems out of place here.
The reference to Dionysus' herding must be to a myth not now
known.

[6] On Aphrodite and Adonis see pp. 205, 504–17.

[7] See on *Id.* 3.49–51.

[8] Cybele (Rhea) loved Attis, who was killed by a boar (Hdt.
1.34–35) or, in some versions, castrated (Ov. *Fasti* 4.221–44).

[9] In the guise of an eagle, Zeus carried off Ganymede as he
herded his cattle near Troy (Ov. *Met.* 10.155–61).

ἁ Κυβέλας κρέσσων καὶ Κύπριδος ἠδὲ Σελάνας.
μηκέτι μηδ᾽ ἅ, Κύπρι, τὸν ἀδέα μήτε κατ᾽ ἄστυ
45 μήτ᾽ ἐν ὄρει φιλέοι, μώνα δ᾽ ἀνὰ νύκτα καθεύδοι.

45 φιλέοι Ahrens: -έοις M   καθεύδοι Ahrens: -δοις M

man—she's greater than Cybele, the Cyprian and Selene. Cypris, may she never make love with her sweetheart either in town or in the hills; may she sleep all night alone.

IDYLL 21

Two old fishermen are resting in a lonely hut. Asphalion recounts his dream of catching a golden fish and hopes that he will become rich, but his companion responds that only hard work can keep him from starving.

This poem seems to be inspired by works of Theocritus, but it is probably not by him.

A five-line introduction addressed to a certain Diophantus sets out the moral of the story, that poverty is the stimulus to hard work and that the poor do not sleep easy. Similar are the moralizing passages addressed to Nicias that introduce Idylls *11 and 13. A fisherman is part of the world depicted on the cup in* Idyll *1. The poverty of Theocritus' Muses is a theme of* Idyll *16. Poor fishermen and the tools of their trade figure in epigrams by Leonidas of Tarentum, a contemporary of Theocritus (Anth. Pal. 6.4, 7.295, 504). Hard work is extolled by Milon in* Idyll *10. Penelope's account of her dream and its interpretation by the disguised Odysseus is the first of several such scenes in Greek literature (Hom. Od. 19.535–58; Callim. Fr. 2; Herod. 8; Mosch. 2.1–27).*

Criticism

Belloni, L. *[Teocrito] I pescatori.* Como, 2004.
Kirsten, *Junge Hirten,* 139–212.

281

21

Ἀ πενία, Διόφαντε, μόνα τὰς τέχνας ἐγείρει·
αὗτα τῷ μόχθοιο διδάσκαλος, οὐδὲ γὰρ εὕδειν
ἀνδράσιν ἐργατίναισι κακαὶ παρέχοντι μέριμναι·
κἂν ὀλίγον νυκτός τις ἐπιβρίσσησι, τὸν ὕπνον
5 αἰφνίδιον θορυβεῦντι ἐφιστάμεναι μελεδῶναι.

Ἰχθύος ἀγρευτῆρες ὁμῶς δύο κεῖντο γέροντες
στρωσάμενοι βρύον αὖον ὑπὸ πλεκταῖς καλύβαισι,
κεκλιμένοι τοίχῳ τῷ φυλλίνῳ· ἐγγύθι δ' αὐτοῖν
κεῖτο τὰ ταῖν χειροῖν ἀθλήματα, τοὶ καλαθίσκοι,
10 τοὶ κάλαμοι, τἄγκιστρα, τὰ φυκιόεντα δέλητα,
ὁρμιαὶ κύρτοι τε καὶ ἐκ σχοίνων λαβύρινθοι,
μήρινθοι κῶπαί τε γέρων τ' ἐπ' ἐρείσμασι λέμβος·
νέρθεν τᾶς κεφαλᾶς φορμὸς βραχύς, εἵματα, πῖλοι.
οὗτος τοῖς ἁλιεῦσιν ὁ πᾶς πόρος, οὗτος ὁ πλοῦτος·
15 οὐ κλεῖδ', οὐχὶ θύραν ἔχον, οὐ κύνα· πάντα περισσά
ταῦτ' ἐδόκει τήνοις· ἁ γὰρ πενία σφας ἐτήρει.
οὐδεὶς δ' ἐν μέσσῳ γείτων πέλεν, ἁ δὲ παρ' αὐτᾷ

2 αὗτα Meineke: αὐτὰ M
4 ἐπιβρίσσησι Reiske: -βησέησι m: -έεισι m
10 δέλητα Briggs: τε λήγα M
12 κῶπαί Stroth: κῶά M
14 πόρος Koehler: πόνος M

IDYLL 21

Poverty alone, Diophantus,[1] promotes skilled work: she is toil's tutor, because care and anxiety make it impossible for laboring men to sleep; and if one of them does nod off for a while, pressing worries suddenly disturb his rest.

Two old fishermen were lying down together on a bed of dried seaweed which they had strewn in their plaited hut, and they were reclining against the leafy wall.[2] Near them lay the tools of their trade—baskets, rods, hooks, seaweed-covered bait, lines, weels, traps made from rushes, cords, oars, an old boat on props, a little mat for a pillow, their clothes, their caps. This was the fishermen's only resource, their only wealth; they had no key, no door, no guard dog: all these things seemed unnecessary to them, because poverty was their safeguard. There was no neighbor anywhere near, and right up to their hut the sea chafed and

---

[1] A common name. Probably a friend of the poet.
[2] It is a temporary hut of plaited branches with the leaves still attached.

---

15 οὐ κλεῖδ' Bücheler: οὐδεὶς δ' M   οὐχὶ θύραν Briggs: οὐ χύθραν m: οὐ κύθραν m   ἔχον Kaibel: εἶχ' M
16 ταῦτ' Meineke: πάντ' M   ἁ γὰρ Reiske: ἄγρα M   ἐτήρει Ahrens: ἐτέρη M
17 πέλεν, ἁ Reiske: πενία M   αὐτᾳ Campbell: -τήν M

θλιβομέναν καλύβᾳ τραφερὰν προσέναχε θάλασσα.
κοὔπω τὸν μέσατον δρόμον ἄννεν ἅρμα Σελάνας,
20 τοὺς δ' ἁλιεῖς ἤγειρε φίλος πόνος, ἐκ βλεφάρων δέ
ὕπνον ἀπωσάμενοι σφετέραις φρεσὶν ἤρεθον αὐδάν.

ΑΣΦΑΛΙΩΝ

ψεύδοντ', ὦ φίλε, πάντες ὅσοι τὰς νύκτας ἔφασκον
τῶ θέρεος μινύθειν, ὅκα τἄματα μακρὰ φέροντι.
ἤδη μυρί' ἐσεῖδον ὀνείρατα, κοὐδέπω ἀώς.
25 μὴ λαθόμην τί τὸ χρῆμα χρόνου ταὶ νύκτες ἔχοντι;

ΕΤΑΙΡΟΣ

Ἀσφαλίων, μέμφῃ τὸ καλὸν θέρος; οὐ γὰρ ὁ καιρός
αὐτομάτως παρέβα τὸν ἐὸν δρόμον, ἀλλὰ τὸν ὕπνον
ἁ φροντὶς κόπτοισα μακρὰν τὰν νύκτα ποιεῖ τοι.

ΑΣΦΑΛΙΩΝ

ἆρ' ἔμαθες κρίνειν ποκ' ἐνύπνια; χρηστὰ γὰρ εἶδον.
30 οὔ σε θέλω τὠμῶ φαντάσματος ἦμεν ἄμοιρον.

ΕΤΑΙΡΟΣ

ὡς καὶ τὰν ἄγραν, τὠνείρατα πάντα μερίζευ.
εἰ γὰρ κεικάξω κατὰ τὸν νόον, οὗτος ἄριστος
ἐστὶν ὀνειροκρίτας, ὁ διδάσκαλός ἐστι παρ' ᾧ νοῦς.

18 καλύβᾳ Campbell: -βαν M
22 ψεύδοντ', ὦ Briggs: ψεύδοντο m: -ται m
25 χρόνου ταὶ Martinus: χρόνον δ' αἱ M
28 ποιεῖ τοι Hermann: ποιεῦντι M
32 εἰ γὰρ κεικάξω Wilamowitz: οὐ γὰρ νικάξῃ M

lapped against the land.[3] The chariot of the moon had not
yet run half its course[4] when their customary labor awak-
ened the fishermen;[5] and when they had rid their eyes of
sleep, their thoughts led them to start talking.

ASPHALION

Those people were liars, my friend, who used to say that
in summer the nights grow shorter as they usher in longer
days. I've had countless dreams already, and it's not yet
dawn. Surely I haven't forgotten how extremely long the
nights are?[6]

COMPANION

Do you find fault with the fair summer, Asphalion?[7] It's
not that the due time has decided to go beyond its proper
course, but that worry has cut short your sleep and made
the night seem long.

ASPHALION

Did you ever learn how to interpret dreams? I've had
some good ones.

COMPANION

Share out all your dreams, just as you do with your catch.
Even if I am to make an intelligent guess, the best dream
interpreter is the one taught by common sense. Besides,

[3] Text desperately corrupt.

[4] I.e., before midnight, apparently. But the moon's course
does not measure out the night as the sun's does the day.

[5] This does not seem to fit with Asphalion's opening words or
with the idea that anxiety disrupts sleep.

[6] Text and sense uncertain.

[7] A servant of Menelaus has this name at Hom. *Od.* 4.216.
Asphaleus is a cult title of the sea god Poseidon (Paus. 7.21.7).

ἄλλως καὶ σχολά ἐστι· τί γὰρ ποιεῖν ἂν ἔχοι τις
35 κείμενος ἐν φύλλοις ποτὶ κύματι μηδὲ καθεύδων;
ἀλλ᾽ ὄνος ἐν ῥάμνῳ τό τε λύχνιον ἐν πρυτανείῳ·
φαντὶ γὰρ ἀγρυπνίαν τάδ᾽ ἔχειν. † λέγεο ποτε νυκτός
ὄψιν τά τις ἔσσεο δὲ λέγει μάννεν ἑταίρῳ. †

ΑΣΦΑΛΙΩΝ

δειλινὸν ὡς κατέδαρθον ἐπ᾽ εἰναλίοισι πόνοισιν
40 (οὐκ ἦν μὰν πολύσιτος, ἐπεὶ δειπνεῦντες ἐν ὥρᾳ,
εἰ μέμνῃ, τᾶς γαστρὸς ἐφειδόμεθ᾽), εἶδον ἐμαυτόν
ἐν πέτρᾳ βεβαῶτα, καθεζόμενος δ᾽ ἐδόκευον
ἰχθύας, ἐκ καλάμω δὲ πλάνον κατέσειον ἐδωδάν.
καί τις τῶν τραφερῶν ὠρέξατο· καὶ γὰρ ἐν ὕπνοις
45 πᾶσα κύων † ἄρτον † μαντεύεται, ἰχθύα κἠγών.
χὠ μὲν τὠγκίστρῳ ποτεφύετο, καὶ ῥέεν αἷμα·
τὸν κάλαμον δ᾽ ὑπὸ τῶ κινήματος ἀγκύλον εἶχον.
τὼ χέρε τεινόμενος, περικλώμενος, εὗρον ἀγῶνα
πῶς ἀνέλω μέγαν ἰχθὺν ἀφαυροτέροισι σιδάροις·
50 εἶθ᾽ ὑπομιμνάσκων τῶ τρώματος ἠρέμα νύξα,
καὶ νύξας ἐχάλαξα, καὶ οὐ φεύγοντος ἔτεινα.
ἤνυσα δ᾽ ὦν τὸν ἄεθλον, ἀνείλκυσα χρύσεον ἰχθύν,

36 τε Haupt: δὲ M   37 ἀγρυπνίαν Reiske: ἄγραν
M   τάδ᾽ Ahrens: τόδ᾽ M   39 ἐπ᾽ Wakefield: ἐν M
42 βεβαῶτα Stephanus: μεμα- M
43 καλάμω Valckenaer: -μων M
48 περικλώμενος Hermann: -νον m: περὶ κνώδαλον m
50 ἠρέμα Eldik: ἆρ᾽ ἐμὲ M   νύξα Kiessling: -ας M
51 νύξας ἐχάλαξα Briggs, Hermann: νύξαι χαλέξας M
52 ἤνυσα δ᾽ ὦν Scaliger: ἠνυσιδὼν M

we've plenty of time; for what is a man to do lying on a bed
of leaves by the sea if he can't sleep? The donkey in the
thorn bush and the lamp in the town hall[8]—these are said
not to sleep. Tell me about the vision you had in the night.[9]

ASPHALION

I fell asleep early after my hard work at sea. (I hadn't eaten
a great deal, either;[10] if you remember, we didn't eat late
and were sparing with our stomachs.) I saw myself upon a
rock, and as I sat there I was watching for fish and dangling
from my rod the bait that lures them. A plump one nibbled
at it—for just as all sleeping dogs dream of their hunting,[11]
I dream of fish. Then he was hooked, and his blood flowed;
and the rod bent under the strain as I held it. Stretching
out my arms and bending over, I found I had trouble in
landing the great fish with my feeble implements. Then I
gave him a light prod to remind him of the wound, and
after that I gave him slack, then tightened the line when
he didn't try to get away. So I won the fight and landed
the golden fish covered all over with golden scales. I be-

---

[8] Proverbial expressions otherwise unknown. The town hall
(Prytaneum) housed the ever-burning hearth of the goddess Hes-
tia, but why this should be said to be a lamp is unclear.

[9] The manuscripts have gibberish here, but the basic sense
seems clear.

[10] Dreams resulting from indigestion were said not to be sig-
nificant (Artem. 1.7; Cic. *Div.* 1.60).

[11] "Hunting": the manuscripts have "bread." It is uncertain
what word should be restored.

παντᾷ τοι χρυσῷ πεπυκασμένον· εἷλέ με δεῖμα
μήτι Ποσειδάωνι πέλοι πεφιλημένος ἰχθύς,
55 ἢ τάχα τᾶς γλαυκᾶς κειμήλιον Ἀμφιτρίτας.
ἠρέμα δ᾽ αὐτὸν ἐγὼν ἐκ τὠγκίστρω ἀπέλυσα,
μή ποκα τῶ στόματος τἀγκίστρια χρυσὸν ἔχοιεν.
† καὶ τὸν μὲν πιστεύσασα καλά γε τὸν ἠπήρατον, †
ὤμοσα δ᾽ οὐκέτι λοιπὸν ὑπὲρ πελάγους πόδα θεῖναι,
60 ἀλλὰ μενεῖν ἐπὶ γᾶς καὶ τῶ χρυσῷ βασιλεύσειν.
ταῦτά με κἠξήγειρε, τὺ δ᾽, ὦ ξένε, λοιπὸν ἔρειδε
τὰν γνώμαν· ὅρκον γὰρ ἐγὼ τὸν ἐπώμοσα ταρβῶ.

ΕΤΑΙΡΟΣ

μὴ σύγε, μὴ τρέσσῃς· οὐκ ὤμοσας· οὐδὲ γὰρ ἰχθύν
χρύσεον ὡς ἴδες εἷλες, ἴσα δ᾽ ἦν ψεύδεσιν ὄψις.
65 εἰ δ᾽ ὕπαρ οὐ κνώσσων τὰ πελώρια ταῦτα ματεύσεις,
ἐλπὶς τῶν ὕπνων· ζάτει τὸν σάρκινον ἰχθύν,
μὴ σὺ θάνῃς λιμῷ καὶ τοῖς χρυσοῖσιν ὀνείροις.

53 εἷλέ Legrand: εἷχέ M
63 μὴ¹ Haupt: καὶ M
64 εἷλες Meineke: εὗρες M   ἦν Ahrens: ἐν M   ὄψις
Ahrens: -εις M
65 τὰ πελώρια Headlam: τὺ τὰ χωρία m: τοῦτο χωρία m

came afraid in case the fish was a favorite of Poseidon's, or maybe was the property of sea-green Amphitrite.[12] Gently I released him from the hook so that the barbs wouldn't retain gold from his mouth[13]—and I swore never again to venture on the sea, but to stay on land and be lord of my gold. At that I awoke; and now, my friend,[14] apply your mind to the matter, for I'm frightened by the oath I swore.

COMPANION

Don't you be afraid. You didn't swear an oath any more than you caught the golden fish you saw: the vision was nothing but lies. But if you are going to look for these amazing fish when you are awake, not in your slumbers, there is hope in your dreams. Look for a fish of flesh and blood, or you'll die of hunger and your golden dreams.

[12] A marine goddess.

[13] The text of line 58 is corrupt beyond conjecture.

[14] This word is normally used of a "guest-friend" who lives at a distance, and its application here to a fellow worker is odd.

IDYLL 22

A hymn to the Dioscuri, with twin inset narratives. The first tells how during the Argonautic expedition Polydeuces encountered the brutish king Amycus and defeated him in boxing. The second relates Castor's duel with Lynceus after he and Polydeuces had carried off girls whom Lynceus and his brother Idas were to marry.

Idyll 13 *treats the story of Hylas, the final episode of the first book of Apollonius'* Argonautica; *the story of Polydeuces and Amycus opens Book 2. The fact that the episodes are contiguous suggests that Theocritus' poems form a response to Apollonius' epic narrative. In both idylls the luxuriant country setting is emphasized, and contrasted with the threat it contains. The dialogue between Polydeuces and Amycus is in stichomythia, which is not a feature of epic but is typical of Theocritus' bucolic hexameters. In Apollonius, Amycus is killed; in Theocritus, he is shown mercy. Castor, however, is victorious in his fight with Lynceus, although an earlier version of the story had him killed (*Cypria Arg. 3 West; *Pind.* Nem. 10). *The first episode illustrates the moral and benign aspect of divine power and the second its amoral destruction of those unfortunate enough to oppose it. Such formal contrasts are familiar from inset songs in the bucolic poems.*

IDYLL 22

Criticism

Griffiths, F. T. "Theocritus' Silent Dioscuri." *GRBS* 17 (1976): 353–67.

Hunter, *Archaeology,* 44–76.

Hutchinson, *Hellenistic Poetry,* 162–67.

Köhnken, A. *Apollonios Rhodios und Theokrit* = *Hypomnemata* 12. Göttingen, 1965.

Sens, A. *Theocritus: Dioscuri (Idyll 22).* Göttingen, 1997.

22

Ὑμνέομεν Λήδας τε καὶ αἰγιόχου Διὸς υἱώ,
Κάστορα καὶ φοβερὸν Πολυδεύκεα πὺξ ἐρεθίζειν
χεῖρας ἐπιζεύξαντα μέσας βοέοισιν ἱμᾶσιν.
ὑμνέομεν καὶ δὶς καὶ τὸ τρίτον ἄρσενα τέκνα
5 κούρης Θεστιάδος, Λακεδαιμονίους δύ᾽ ἀδελφούς,
ἀνθρώπων σωτῆρας ἐπὶ ξυροῦ ἤδη ἐόντων,
ἵππων θ᾽ αἱματόεντα ταρασσομένων καθ᾽ ὅμιλον,
νηῶν θ᾽ αἳ δύνοντα καὶ οὐρανὸν εἰσανιόντα
ἄστρα βιαζόμεναι χαλεποῖς ἐνέκυρσαν ἀήταις.
10 οἳ δέ σφεων κατὰ πρύμναν ἀείραντες μέγα κῦμα
ἠὲ καὶ ἐκ πρῴρηθεν ἢ ὅππῃ θυμὸς ἑκάστου
εἰς κοίλην ἔρριψαν, ἀνέρρηξαν δ᾽ ἄρα τοίχους
ἀμφοτέρους· κρέμαται δὲ σὺν ἱστίῳ ἄρμενα πάντα
εἰκῇ ἀποκλασθέντα· πολὺς δ᾽ ἐξ οὐρανοῦ ὄμβρος
15 νυκτὸς ἐφερπούσης· παταγεῖ δ᾽ εὐρεῖα θάλασσα
κοπτομένη πνοιαῖς τε καὶ ἀρρήκτοισι χαλάζαις.
ἀλλ᾽ ἔμπης ὑμεῖς γε καὶ ἐκ βυθοῦ ἕλκετε νῆας
αὐτοῖσιν ναύτῃσιν ὀιομένοις θανέεσθαι·
αἶψα δ᾽ ἀπολήγουσ᾽ ἄνεμοι, λιπαρὴ δὲ γαλήνη

---

1 Lit., "yoked": there is a verbal play with "ox."
2 The ancient form of boxing glove (cf. 80–81); the fingers
were left free.

IDYLL 22

We celebrate the two sons of Leda and aegis-bearing Zeus, Castor and Polydeuces, who is a terrifying opponent to challenge in boxing when his palms are bound[1] with strips of ox hide.[2] Twice and three times[3] we celebrate the male children of Thestius' daughter, twin sons born in Sparta,[4] saviors of men whose lives are on a razor's edge, of horses panicking in the bloody tumult of battle, and of ships which, with no regard for the stars that rise and set in the heavens,[5] encounter stormy winds. These raise a great wave ahead or astern or from whatever quarter they will,[6] cast it into the hold and break open both sides of the ship; the mast and all the tackle are smashed and hang in disarray; as night approaches, a great downpour comes from the sky; and the broad sea roars, lashed by the blasts and by ceaseless hail. But even then you raise from the very depths ships together with their crews, who thought they would die: the winds cease at once, and there is an oily

[3] The reference is unclear. Perhaps "again and again"; or the separate sections of this poem may be meant.

[4] Thestius, father of Leda and Althaea, was king of Aetolia (Paus. 3.13.8); Leda was married to Tyndareus, king of Sparta.

[5] The sailing season was marked by the rising and setting of the Pleiades (cf. *Id.* 13.25); but at any time of year the stars' being obscured could presage bad weather.

[6] The winds are personified, as often.

20 ἂμ πέλαγος· νεφέλαι δὲ διέδραμον ἄλλυδις ἄλλαι·
ἐκ δ᾽ Ἄρκτοι τ᾽ ἐφάνησαν Ὄνων τ᾽ ἀνὰ μέσσον
ἀμαυρή
Φάτνη, σημαίνουσα τὰ πρὸς πλόον εὔδια πάντα.
ὦ ἄμφω θνητοῖσι βοηθόοι, ὦ φίλοι ἄμφω,
ἱππῆες κιθαρισταὶ ἀεθλητῆρες ἀοιδοί,
25 Κάστορος ἢ πρώτου Πολυδεύκεος ἄρξομ᾽ ἀείδειν;
ἀμφοτέρους ὑμνέων Πολυδεύκεα πρῶτον ἀείσω.

Ἡ μὲν ἄρα προφυγοῦσα πέτρας εἰς ἓν ξυνιούσας
Ἀργὼ καὶ νιφόεντος ἀταρτηρὸν στόμα Πόντου,
Βέβρυκας εἰσαφίκανε θεῶν φίλα τέκνα φέρουσα.
30 ἔνθα μιᾶς πολλοὶ κατὰ κλίμακος ἀμφοτέρων ἒξ
τοίχων ἄνδρες ἔβαινον Ἰησονίης ἀπὸ νηός·
ἐκβάντες δ᾽ ἐπὶ θῖνα βαθὺν καὶ ὑπήνεμον ἀκτήν
εὐνάς τ᾽ ἐστόρνυντο πυρεῖά τε χερσὶν ἐνώμων.
Κάστωρ δ᾽ αἰολόπωλος ὅ τ᾽ οἰνωπὸς Πολυδεύκης
35 ἄμφω ἐρημάζεσκον ἀποπλαγχθέντες ἑταίρων,
παντοίην ἐν ὄρει θηεύμενοι ἄγριον ὕλην.
εὗρον δ᾽ ἀέναον κρήνην ὑπὸ λισσάδι πέτρῃ,
ὕδατι πεπληθυῖαν ἀκηράτῳ· αἱ δ᾽ ὑπένερθε
λάλλαι κρυστάλλῳ ἠδ᾽ ἀργύρῳ ἰνδάλλοντο

---

37 δ᾽ ἀέναον κρήνην Eust. ad Dionys. Per. 1055: ἀένναον
κράναν M   39 λάλλαι Ruhnken: ἄλλαι M

---

7 The Manger is a hazy patch of light in the constellation
Cancer; its being invisible was thought to portend bad weather
(Aratus *Phaen.* 892–908). The Great Bear (Ursa Major) was used
by sailors as a guide to north.

calm upon the sea; the clouds scatter this way and that; the Bears become visible, and between the Asses the Manger can just be made out, a sign that all is set fair for sailing.[7] Rescuers of mortals both, both dearly loved, horsemen, lyre players, athletes, singers,[8] shall I begin my song with Castor or with Polydeuces first?[9] I shall hymn both, but Polydeuces first.

The Argo, then, having escaped the rocks that clashed together and the grim mouth of the wintry Black Sea,[10] arrived at the land of the Bebryces[11] with her crew of heroes, dear sons of the gods. There the many men disembarked by a single ladder from both sides of Jason's ship.[12] Stepping down on the deep sand and the sheltered shore, they spread their places to lie and wielded the fire sticks in their hands.[13] Castor rider of swift horses and swarthy Polydeuces were wandering apart from their comrades and viewing the varied wild woodland on the mountainside. Beneath a smooth rock they found an ever-flowing spring abounding in pure water; under the water the pebbles in the depths were like crystal or silver. Nearby

[8] Lyre playing and singing are not elsewhere said to be accomplishments of the Dioscuri.

[9] It is conventional in hymns for the poet to deliberate how to begin.

[10] See on *Id.* 13.24.

[11] A Thracian tribe already extinct by the time of Theocritus.

[12] "Many" and "single" are pointedly juxtaposed, but the point is not clear. The ship has two rows of benches, with two rowers at each.

[13] A spark is generated by rotating a stick of hard wood in a hole in a piece of softer wood.

40 ἐκ βυθοῦ· ὑψηλαὶ δὲ πεφύκεσαν ἀγχόθι πεῦκαι
λεῦκαί τε πλάτανοί τε καὶ ἀκρόκομοι κυπάρισσοι
ἄνθεά τ' εὐώδη, λασίαις φίλα ἔργα μελίσσαις,
ὅσσ' ἔαρος λήγοντος ἐπιβρύει ἂν λειμῶνας.
ἔνθα δ' ἀνὴρ ὑπέροπλος ἐνήμενος ἐνδιάασκε,
45 δεινὸς ἰδεῖν, σκληρῇσι τεθλασμένος οὔατα πυγμαῖς·
στήθεα δ' ἐσφαίρωτο πελώρια καὶ πλατὺ νῶτον
σαρκὶ σιδηρείῃ, σφυρήλατος οἷα κολοσσός·
ἐν δὲ μύες στερεοῖσι βραχίοσιν ἄκρον ὑπ' ὦμον
ἕστασαν ἠΰτε πέτροι ὀλοίτροχοι οὕστε κυλίνδων
50 χειμάρρους ποταμὸς μεγάλαις περιέξεσε δίναις·
αὐτὰρ ὑπὲρ νώτοιο καὶ αὐχένος ἠωρεῖτο
ἄκρων δέρμα λέοντος ἀφημμένον ἐκ ποδεώνων.
τὸν πρότερος προσέειπεν ἀεθλοφόρος Πολυδεύκης.

ΠΟΛΤΔΕΤΚΗΣ

χαῖρε, ξεῖν', ὅτις ἐσσί. τίνες βροτοί, ὧν ὅδε χῶρος;

ΑΜΤΚΟΣ

55 χαίρω πῶς, ὅτε τ' ἄνδρας ὁρῶ τοὺς μὴ πρὶν ὄπωπα;

ΠΟΛΤΔΕΤΚΗΣ

θάρσει· μήτ' ἀδίκους μήτ' ἐξ ἀδίκων φάθι λεύσσειν.

ΑΜΤΚΟΣ

θαρσέω, κοὐκ ἐκ σεῦ με διδάσκεσθαι τόδ' ἔοικεν.

---

14 The detailed description of Amycus is a hideous comple-
ment to the preceding sylvan scene.

grew tall pines, white poplars, plane trees, cypresses with leafy tops, and fragrant flowers, welcome work for the rough-haired bees, every sort that grow abundantly in the meadows at the close of spring. There in the open sat a mighty man,[14] terrible to look on. His ears had been pulped by hard blows; his monstrous chest and broad back swelled out with flesh hard as iron, like a colossal statue that has been shaped by hammering; on his tough arms below the shoulder the muscles stood out like smooth boulders which a winter torrent has rolled along and polished in its powerful eddies. Over his back and neck was suspended a lion skin fastened by the paws. The champion Polydeuces was first to speak:[15]

POLYDEUCES

Good day,[16] stranger, whoever you are. What people's land is this?

AMYCUS

How can it be a good day, when I see men I have never seen before?

POLYDEUCES

Have no fear. Be sure the men you see are neither lawless nor sons of lawless parents.

AMYCUS

I have no fear—and it is not right that I should learn that from you.

---

[15] The verbal sparring begins. Dialogue of this form is not found elsewhere in epic narrative poetry. The rural setting is however similar to that in Theocritus' bucolic poems, where such conversations are normal.

[16] "Hello" in Greek is literally "rejoice."

ΠΟΛΥΔΕΥΚΗΣ

ἄγριος εἶ, πρὸς πάντα παλίγκοτος ἠδ᾽ ὑπερόπτης;

ΑΜΥΚΟΣ

τοιόσδ᾽ οἷον ὁρᾷς· τῆς σῆς γε μὲν οὐκ ἐπιβαίνω.

ΠΟΛΥΔΕΥΚΗΣ

60 ἔλθοις, καὶ ξενίων κε τυχὼν πάλιν οἴκαδ᾽ ἱκάνοις.

ΑΜΥΚΟΣ

μήτε σύ με ξείνιζε, τά τ᾽ ἐξ ἐμεῦ οὐκ ἐν ἑτοίμῳ.

ΠΟΛΥΔΕΥΚΗΣ

δαιμόνι᾽, οὐδ᾽ ἂν τοῦδε πιεῖν ὕδατος σύγε δοίης;

ΑΜΥΚΟΣ

γνώσεαι, εἴ σευ δίψος ἀνειμένα χείλεα τέρσει.

ΠΟΛΥΔΕΥΚΗΣ

ἄργυρος ἢ τίς ὁ μισθός—ἐρεῖς;—ᾧ κέν σε πίθοιμεν;

ΑΜΥΚΟΣ

65 εἷς ἑνὶ χεῖρας ἄειρον ἐναντίος ἀνδρὶ καταστάς.

ΠΟΛΥΔΕΥΚΗΣ

πυγμάχος ἢ καὶ ποσσὶ θένων σκέλος, † ὄμματα δ᾽
    ὀρθά; †

58 ἠδ᾽ Hemsterhuis: ἢ M
60 κε Ahrens: γε M

IDYLL 22

POLYDEUCES
Are you a savage, angry and suspicious at everything?

AMYCUS
I am just as you see. *I* am not trespassing on *your* land.

POLYDEUCES
Come there, and you will return home with guest gifts.[17]

AMYCUS
I want no gifts; and I have none ready for you.

POLYDEUCES
Will you not even give us a drink of this water, good sir?

AMYCUS
You will find that out when thirst is parching your blistered[18] lips.

POLYDEUCES
Do you want payment in silver? Or will you tell us with what fee we can persuade you?

AMYCUS
Raise your fists in single combat, one to one.

POLYDEUCES
In boxing? Or is tripping allowed, and eye gouging?[19]

---

[17] Amycus is in some respects like the Odyssean Cyclops, and in that episode hospitality and guest gifts are an important theme.

[18] Or, perhaps, "gaping," in expectation of a drink.

[19] The manuscripts have "eyes straight ahead," but that makes no sense. Gouging was allowed in the all-in pancratium (Ar. *Pax* 897–98; Philostr. *Imag.* 2.6.3), and it is plausibly conjectured here (ὄμμα τ᾽ ὀρύσσων Platt).

ΑΜΥΚΟΣ

πὺξ διατεινάμενος σφετέρης μὴ φείδεο τέχνης.

ΠΟΛΥΔΕΥΚΗΣ

τίς γάρ, ὅτῳ χεῖρας καὶ ἐμοὺς συνερείσω ἱμάντας;

ΑΜΥΚΟΣ

ἐγγὺς ὁρᾷς· οὐ γύννις ἐὼν κεκλήσεθ᾽ ὁ πύκτης.

ΠΟΛΥΔΕΥΚΗΣ

70 ἦ καὶ ἄεθλον ἑτοῖμον ἐφ᾽ ᾧ δηρισόμεθ᾽ ἄμφω;

ΑΜΥΚΟΣ

σὸς μὲν ἐγώ, σὺ δ᾽ ἐμὸς κεκλήσεαι, αἴ κε κρατήσω.

ΠΟΛΥΔΕΥΚΗΣ

ὀρνίθων φοινικολόφων τοιοίδε κυδοιμοί.

ΑΜΥΚΟΣ

εἴτ᾽ οὖν ὀρνίθεσσιν ἐοικότες εἴτε λέουσι
γινόμεθ᾽, οὐκ ἄλλῳ κε μαχεσσαίμεσθ᾽ ἐπ᾽ ἀέθλῳ.

75 Ἦ ῥ᾽ Ἄμυκος καὶ κόχλον ἑλὼν μυκήσατο κοῖλον.
οἱ δὲ θοῶς συνάγερθεν ὑπὸ σκιερὰς πλατανίστους
κόχλου φυσηθέντος ἀεὶ Βέβρυκες κομόωντες.
ὣς δ᾽ αὔτως ἥρωας ἰὼν ἐκαλέσσατο πάντας
Μαγνήσσης ἀπὸ νηὸς ὑπείροχος ἐν δαῒ Κάστωρ.
80 οἱ δ᾽ ἐπεὶ οὖν σπείρῃσιν ἐκαρτύναντο βοείαις
χεῖρας καὶ περὶ γυῖα μακροὺς εἵλιξαν ἱμάντας,

74 κε Hermann: γε m: om. m

---

[20] The end of the line is doubtful.

AMYCUS

Box as well as you can; don't stint on your skill.

POLYDEUCES

And who is the man I am to fight with my gloved fists?

AMYCUS

You see him near you. He is no woman; he will be called "The Boxer."[20]

POLYDEUCES

Is there a prize here, too, that we can both fight for?

AMYCUS

If I win, you will be my property; if you win, I shall belong to you.

POLYDEUCES

Combat of that sort is for scarlet-crested fighting cocks.[21]

AMYCUS

Whether we shall be like fighting cocks or lions, this is the only prize we are to fight for.

With these words Amycus took a hollow shell and blew into it, and at the sound of its blast the Bebryces, whose hair is always worn long, promptly gathered together under the shady plane trees. Likewise Castor the noted warrior went and summoned all the heroes from the Magnesian ship.[22]

When they had strengthened their hands with thongs of ox hide and wound long straps around their forearms, they

[21] The loser in a cock fight was called *doulos*, "slave" (Ar. *Av.* 70). [22] The Argo was built at Pagasae and launched at Iolcus in Thessalian Magnesia.

ἐς μέσσον σύναγον φόνον ἀλλήλοισι πνέοντες.
ἔνθα πολὺς σφισι μόχθος ἐπειγομένοισιν ἐτύχθη,
ὁππότερος κατὰ νῶτα λάβοι φάος ἠελίοιο.
85 ἰδρείῃ μέγαν ἄνδρα παρήλυθες, ὦ Πολύδευκες,
βάλλετο δ' ἀκτίνεσσιν ἅπαν Ἀμύκοιο πρόσωπον.
αὐτὰρ ὅγ' ἐν θυμῷ κεχολωμένος ἵετο πρόσσω,
χερσὶ τιτυσκόμενος. τοῦ δ' ἄκρον τύψε γένειον
Τυνδαρίδης ἐπιόντος· ὀρίνθη δὲ πλέον ἢ πρίν,
90 σὺν δὲ μάχην ἐτάραξε, πολὺς δ' ἐπέκειτο νενευκὼς
ἐς γαῖαν. Βέβρυκες δ' ἐπαύτεον, οἱ δ' ἑτέρωθεν
ἥρωες κρατερὸν Πολυδεύκεα θαρσύνεσκον,
δειδιότες μή πώς μιν ἐπιβρίσας δαμάσειε
χώρῳ ἐνὶ στεινῷ Τιτυῷ ἐναλίγκιος ἀνήρ.
95 ἤτοι ὅγ' ἔνθα καὶ ἔνθα παριστάμενος Διὸς υἱὸς
ἀμφοτέρῃσιν ἄμυσσεν ἀμοιβαδίς, ἔσχεθε δ' ὁρμῆς
παῖδα Ποσειδάωνος ὑπερφίαλόν περ ἐόντα.
ἔστη δὲ πληγαῖς μεθύων, ἐκ δ' ἔπτυσεν αἷμα
φοίνιον· οἱ δ' ἅμα πάντες ἀριστῆες κελάδησαν,
100 ὡς ἴδον ἕλκεα λυγρὰ περὶ στόμα τε γναθμούς τε·
ὄμματα δ' οἰδήσαντος ἀπεστείνωτο προσώπου.
τὸν μὲν ἄναξ ἐτάρασσεν ἐτώσια χερσὶ προδεικνὺς
πάντοθεν· ἀλλ' ὅτε δή μιν ἀμηχανέοντ' ἐνόησε,
μέσσης ῥινὸς ὕπερθε κατ' ὀφρύος ἤλασε πυγμῇ,
105 πᾶν δ' ἀπέσυρε μέτωπον ἐς ὀστέον. αὐτὰρ ὁ πληγεὶς
ὕπτιος ἐν φύλλοισι τεθηλόσιν ἐξετανύσθη.
Ἔνθα μάχη δριμεῖα πάλιν γένετ' ὀρθωθέντος,
ἀλλήλους δ' ὄλεκον στερεοῖς θείνοντες ἱμᾶσιν.

squared up in the clear ring, breathing slaughter against each other. Then they spent much effort in settling which of them should get the sun at his back. Polydeuces, you outwitted the big man, and Amycus' whole face was dazzled. Full of fury, he charged forward, fists flailing. The son of Tyndareus hit him right on the chin as he advanced. He grew even angrier and mixed up the fight, rushing in head down. The Bebryces were cheering, and on the other side the heroes kept encouraging mighty Polydeuces, fearing that in that confined space the adversary huge as Tityus[23] would keep pressing and defeat him. The son of Zeus, with nimble footwork, kept cutting[24] him with left and right hands in turn, and he put a stop to the charge of the son of Poseidon, mighty though he was; he stood still, reeling from the blows, and spat out crimson blood. All the heroes shouted out together when they saw the serious damage to his mouth and jaws; and his eyes had closed up as his face swelled. Lord Polydeuces[25] confused him with feinting blows from all sides. When he saw that he was quite helpless, he struck him with his fist down on to his brow above the nose, and skinned his whole forehead to the bone. With this blow he was stretched out on his back among the leaves and flowers.

Then, once he had stood up, there was again a bitter contest, and they set to striking each other with the hard

[23] The gigantic Tityus suffered eternal punishment in the underworld for attempting to rape Leto (Hom. *Od.* 11.576–81).

[24] The leather strips had sharp edges.

[25] *Anax* (lord) may allude to the cult title of the Dioscuri *anake* or *wanakes*. Cf. 135.

ἀλλ' ὁ μὲν ἐς στῆθός τε καὶ ἔξω χεῖρας ἐνώμα
110 αὐχένος ἀρχηγὸς Βεβρύκων· ὁ δ' ἀεικέσι πληγαῖς
πᾶν συνέφυρε πρόσωπον ἀνίκητος Πολυδεύκης.
σάρκες δ' ᾧ μὲν ἱδρῶτι συνίζανον, ἐκ μεγάλου δέ
αἶψ' ὀλίγος γένετ' ἀνδρός· ὁ δ' αἰεὶ πάσσονα γυῖα
αὐξομένου φορέεσκε πόνου καὶ χροιῇ ἀμείνω.
115 Πῶς γὰρ δὴ Διὸς υἱὸς ἀδηφάγον ἄνδρα καθεῖλεν;
εἰπέ, θεά, σὺ γὰρ οἶσθα· ἐγὼ δ' ἑτέρων ὑποφήτης
φθέγξομαι ὅσσ' ἐθέλεις σὺ καὶ ὅππως τοι φίλον
αὐτῇ.
  Ἤτοι ὅγε ῥέξαι τι λιλαιόμενος μέγα ἔργον
σκαιῇ μὲν σκαιὴν Πολυδεύκεος ἔλλαβε χεῖρα,
120 δοχμὸς ἀπὸ προβολῆς κλινθείς, ἑτέρῳ δ' ἐπιβαίνων
δεξιτερῆς ἤνεγκεν ἀπὸ λαγόνος πλατὺ γυῖον.
καί κε τυχὼν ἔβλαψεν Ἀμυκλαίων βασιλῆα·
ἀλλ' ὅγ' ὑπεξανέδυ κεφαλῇ, στιβαρῇ δ' ἅμα χειρί
πλῆξεν ὑπὸ σκαιὸν κρόταφον καὶ ἐπέμπεσεν ὤμῳ·
125 ἐκ δ' ἐχύθη μέλαν αἷμα θοῶς κροτάφοιο χανόντος·
λαιῇ δὲ στόμα κόψε, πυκνοὶ δ' ἀράβησαν ὀδόντες·
αἰεὶ δ' ὀξυτέρῳ πιτύλῳ δηλεῖτο πρόσωπον,
μέχρι συνηλοίησε παρήια. πᾶς δ' ἐπὶ γαίῃ
κεῖτ' ἀλλοφρονέων καὶ ἀνέσχεθε νεῖκος ἀπαυδῶν

112 ᾧ Reiske: οἱ m: αἱ m
114 αὐξομένου Meineke: ἁπτομένου M   ἀμείνω Toup:
-ων M
120 ἑτέρῳ Toup: -ρῃ m: -ρᾳ m
128 ἐπὶ γαίῃ Ahrens: ἐπὶ γαῖαν m: ἐνὶ γαίῃ m

leather thongs. The leader of the Bebryces aimed his
punches at the chest and below the neck, but champion
Polydeuces made a mess of his whole face with disfiguring
blows. His flesh began to collapse as he sweated, and the
once mighty man quickly became puny, while Polydeuces'
limbs kept growing fitter and looking healthier as he in-
creased his efforts.

And how did the son of Zeus bring down his gluttonous
opponent? Tell me, goddess, for you know. Interpreting
for others, I shall utter what you wish in the manner you
prefer.[26]

Amycus, eager to make a knockout blow, seized hold of
Polydeuces' left arm with his left, bending to one side in
his defensive stance; coming forward with his right foot,
he delivered an uppercut with his broad fist. If the punch
had connected, he would have done serious harm to the
prince of Amyclae,[27] but Polydeuces swayed his head out
of the way and at the same time with his stout fist struck
his opponent under the left temple with his full weight;[28]
a gaping cut opened up at the temple, and the dark blood
gushed out. Then with left jabs[29] he made cuts around the
mouth, and Amycus' firmly fixed teeth rattled. All the time
he was messing up the face with a sharp rain of blows,
until at last he had pounded his cheeks to a pulp. Barely
conscious, Amycus measured his length on the ground

[26] The poet is the Muses' mouthpiece or interpreter: cf.
221–23; *Idd.* 16.29, 17.115.   [27] Amyclae near Sparta, of
which Tyndareus was king.   [28] Lit., "and fell on with his
shoulder" or (less likely) "and attacked Amycus' shoulder."
[29] By this time Amycus has released Polydeuces' left hand.

130 ἀμφοτέρας ἅμα χεῖρας, ἐπεὶ θανάτου σχεδὸν ἦεν.
τὸν μὲν ἄρα κρατέων περ ἀτάσθαλον οὐδὲν ἔρεξας,
ὦ πύκτη Πολύδευκες· ὄμοσσε δέ τοι μέγαν ὅρκον,
ὃν πατέρ' ἐκ πόντοιο Ποσειδάωνα κικλήσκων,
μήποτ' ἔτι ξείνοισιν ἑκὼν ἀνιηρὸς ἔσεσθαι.

Καὶ σὺ μὲν ὕμνησαί μοι, ἄναξ· σὲ δέ, Κάστορ,
135 ἀείσω,
Τυνδαρίδη ταχύπωλε, δορυσσόε, χαλκεοθώρηξ.

Τὼ μὲν ἀναρπάξαντε δύω φερέτην Διὸς υἱώ
δοιὰς Λευκίπποιο κόρας· δισσὼ δ' ἄρα τώγε
ἐσσυμένως ἐδίωκον ἀδελφεὼ υἷ' Ἀφαρῆος,
140 γαμβρὼ μελλογάμω, Λυγκεὺς καὶ ὁ καρτερὸς Ἴδας.
ἀλλ' ὅτε τύμβον ἵκανον ἀποφθιμένου Ἀφαρῆος,
ἐκ δίφρων ἅμα πάντες ἐπ' ἀλλήλοισιν ὄρουσαν
ἔγχεσι καὶ κοίλοισι βαρυνόμενοι σακέεσσι.
Λυγκεὺς δ' ἀρ μετέειπεν, ὑπὲκ κόρυθος μέγ' ἀύσας,
145 "δαιμόνιοι, τί μάχης ἱμείρετε; πῶς δ' ἐπὶ νύμφαις
ἀλλοτρίαις χαλεποί, γυμναὶ δ' ἐν χερσὶ μάχαιραι;
ἡμῖν τοι Λεύκιππος ἑὰς ἔδνωσε θύγατρας
τάσδε πολὺ προτέροις· ἡμῖν γάμος οὗτος ἐν ὅρκῳ.
ὑμεῖς δ' οὐ κατὰ κόσμον ἐπ' ἀλλοτρίοισι λέχεσσι
150 βουσὶ καὶ ἡμιόνοισι καὶ ἄλλοισι κτεάτεσσιν
ἄνδρα παρετρέψασθε, γάμον δ' ἐκλέψατε δώροις.
ἦ μὴν πολλάκις ὔμμιν ἐνώπιον ἀμφοτέροισιν

with his brain scrambled; close to death, he held up both hands and submitted. But although you had won, boxer Polydeuces,[30] you did not humiliate him further, but made him swear a solemn oath, invoking his father Poseidon from the sea, that he would never again willingly be troublesome to strangers.

Now that I have hymned you, lord, I shall celebrate you, Castor, son of Tyndareus, swift horseman, spear fighter, wearer of the bronze breastplate.[31]

The twin sons of Zeus had seized and were carrying off the two daughters of Leucippus; in hot pursuit were two brothers, sons of Aphareus, Lynceus and mighty Idas, bridegrooms who had been about to marry the girls. When they reached the tomb of the dead Aphareus, they all leaped from their chariots and went at each other, bearing the weight of swords and hollow shields. Shouting from beneath his helmet, Lynceus addressed them: "Sirs, why are you keen to fight? Why are you causing trouble about other men's brides? Why do you have drawn swords in your hands? Leucippus engaged these daughters of his to us long since; our marriage has been settled by oaths. It is quite wrong that to get other men's wives you should have turned him away from our agreement with cattle and mules and other property, and should have obtained marriage through underhand bribery.[32] I am a man of few

---

[30] Polydeuces now has the title boasted of by Amycus in line 69.   [31] The list of epithets is characteristic of hymns.

[32] The details alluded to here are not known from elsewhere; Theocritus expects his readers to know them.

αὐτὸς ἐγὼ τάδ' ἔειπα καὶ οὐ πολύμυθος ἐών περ·
'οὐχ οὕτω, φίλοι ἄνδρες, ἀριστήεσσιν ἔοικε
155 μνηστεύειν ἀλόχους, αἷς νυμφίοι ἤδη ἕτοιμοι.
πολλή τοι Σπάρτη, πολλὴ δ' ἱππήλατος Ἦλις
Ἀρκαδίη τ' εὔμηλος Ἀχαιῶν τε πτολίεθρα
Μεσσήνη τε καὶ Ἄργος ἅπασά τε Σισυφὶς ἀκτή·
ἔνθα κόραι τοκέεσσιν ὑπὸ σφετέροισι τρέφονται
160 μυρίαι οὔτε φυῆς ἐπιδευέες οὔτε νόοιο,
τάων εὐμαρὲς ὕμμιν ὀπυιέμεν ἅς κ' ἐθέλητε·
ὡς ἀγαθοῖς πολέες βούλοιντό κε πενθεροὶ εἶναι,
ὑμεῖς δ' ἐν πάντεσσι διάκριτοι ἡρώεσσι,
καὶ πατέρες καὶ ἄνωθεν ἅπαν πατρώιον αἷμα.
165 ἀλλά, φίλοι, τοῦτον μὲν ἐάσατε πρὸς τέλος ἐλθεῖν
ἄμμι γάμον· σφῶν δ' ἄλλον ἐπιφραζώμεθα πάντες.'
ἴσκον τοιάδε πολλά, τὰ δ' εἰς ὑγρὸν ᾤχετο κῦμα
πνοιὴ ἔχουσ' ἀνέμοιο, χάρις δ' οὐχ ἕσπετο μύθοις·
σφὼ γὰρ ἀκηλήτω καὶ ἀπηνέες. ἀλλ' ἔτι καὶ νῦν
170 πείθεσθ'· ἄμφω δ' ἄμμιν ἀνεψιὼ ἐκ πατρός ἐστον.
εἰ δ' ὑμῖν κραδίη πόλεμον ποθεῖ, αἵματι δὲ χρή
νεῖκος ἀναρρήξαντας ὁμοίιον ἔγχεα λοῦσαι,
Ἴδας μὲν καὶ ὅμαιμος ἑός, κρατερὸς Πολυδεύκης,
χεῖρας ἐρωήσουσιν ἀποσχομένω ὑσμίνης·
175 νῶι δ', ἐγὼ Κάστωρ τε, διακρινώμεθ' Ἄρηι,
ὁπλοτέρω γεγαῶτε. γονεῦσι δὲ μὴ πολὺ πένθος
ἡμετέροισι λίπωμεν. ἅλις νέκυς ἐξ ἑνὸς οἴκου

161 ὀπυιέμεν Wordsworth: -ειν M
173 ἑός Voss: ἐμός M
175 Κάστωρ m: Λυγκεύς m

words, but I have myself said many times to you both
to your faces, 'Dear friends, it is not right for heroes to
woo in this way brides who have grooms already arranged.
Sparta is a broad land, and so are Elis with its horse riders,
Arcadia where sheep can graze, the cities of Achaea, Mes-
sene and Argos, and the whole Sisyphean shore.[33] In those
places parents are bringing up countless girls not lacking
beauty or good sense, and you could easily marry which-
ever of them you like; for many men would wish to have
fine sons-in-law, and you are outstanding among heroes, as
are your ancestors and your father's bloodline.[34] Friends,
let this marriage of ours be completed; and let us see about
a different marriage for you.' I spoke such words many a
time, but the wind's breath took them and carried them
off to the wet waves of the sea, and they found no favor
with you, for you are not to be won over or compelled. But
there is still time to be persuaded; you are both our cous-
ins on our father's side. If however your hearts are set on
war and we must let loose evil conflict and drench our
spears in blood, Idas and his[35] kinsman mighty Polydeuces
shall hold back and not take part in the fight; let Lynceus
and I, who are the younger pair, settle the matter by com-
bat and not leave behind great grief for our parents. One
corpse from one house is enough; those who are left

[33] Sisyphus was from Corinth (Hom. *Il.* 6.152–53). These are
all places in the Peloponnese.

[34] He speaks as if Tyndareus, not Zeus, is their father.

[35] All the manuscripts have "my" for "his," and one manu-
script has "Castor" for "Lynceus." Wilamowitz suggested that
lines 171–80 are the conclusion of a defense speech by Castor,
the beginning of which is lost. In that case the word translated
"kinsman" (ὅμαιμος) would have its usual meaning, "brother."

εἷς· ἀτὰρ ὧλλοι πάντας εὐφρανέουσιν ἑταίρους,
νυμφίοι ἀντὶ νεκρῶν, ὑμεναιώσουσι δὲ κούρας
180 τάσδ᾽. ὀλίγῳ τοι ἔοικε κακῷ μέγα νεῖκος ἀναιρεῖν.”
εἶπε, τὰ δ᾽ οὐκ ἄρ᾽ ἔμελλε θεὸς μεταμώνια θήσειν.
τὼ μὲν γὰρ ποτὶ γαῖαν ἀπ᾽ ὤμων τεύχε᾽ ἔθεντο,
ὣ γενεῇ προφέρεσκον· ὁ δ᾽ εἰς μέσον ἤλυθε Λυγκεύς,
σείων καρτερὸν ἔγχος ὑπ᾽ ἀσπίδος ἄντυγα πρώτην·
185 ὣς δ᾽ αὔτως ἄκρας ἐτινάξατο δούρατος ἀκμάς
Κάστωρ· ἀμφοτέροις δὲ λόφων ἐπένευον ἔθειραι.
ἔγχεσι μὲν πρώτιστα τιτυσκόμενοι πόνον εἶχον
ἀλλήλων, εἴ πού τι χροὸς γυμνωθὲν ἴδοιεν.
ἀλλ᾽ ἤτοι τὰ μὲν ἄκρα πάρος τινὰ δηλήσασθαι
190 δοῦρ᾽ ἐάγη, σακέεσσιν ἐνὶ δεινοῖσι παγέντα.
τὼ δ᾽ ἄορ ἐκ κολεοῖο ἐρυσσαμένω φόνον αὖτις
τεῦχον ἐπ᾽ ἀλλήλοισι· μάχης δ᾽ οὐ γίνετ᾽ ἐρωή.
πολλὰ μὲν εἰς σάκος εὐρὺ καὶ ἱππόκομον τρυφάλειαν
Κάστωρ, πολλὰ δ᾽ ἔνυξεν ἀκριβὴς ὄμμασι Λυγκεύς
195 τοῖο σάκος, φοίνικα δ᾽ ὅσον λόφον ἵκετ᾽ ἀκωκή.
τοῦ μὲν ἄκρην ἐκόλουσεν ἐπὶ σκαιὸν γόνυ χεῖρα
φάσγανον ὀξὺ φέροντος ὑπεξαναβὰς ποδὶ Κάστωρ
σκαιῷ· ὁ δὲ πληγεὶς ξίφος ἔκβαλεν, αἶψα δὲ φεύγειν
ὡρμήθη ποτὶ σῆμα πατρός, τόθι καρτερὸς Ἴδας
200 κεκλιμένος θηεῖτο μάχην ἐμφύλιον ἀνδρῶν.
ἀλλὰ μεταΐξας πλατὺ φάσγανον ὧσε διαπρό
Τυνδαρίδης λαγόνος τε καὶ ὀμφαλοῦ· ἔγκατα δ᾽ εἴσω

178 πάντας Ald. ed. 2: -τες M
183 ὣ Ahrens: οἷ m: τοι m

310

will gladden all their comrades, bridegrooms instead of corpses, and will marry these girls.[36] It is best to end a great strife with a small loss."

So he spoke; and his words were not destined to be in vain. The elder two removed the armor from their shoulders and placed it on the ground. Lynceus stepped forward, brandishing his mighty spear beneath the outermost rim of his shield, while Castor wielded a pair of pointed spears; the plumes nodded on each man's crested helmet. First of all they stabbed at each other with their spears, striving to spot some unprotected part of the body; but before the spear points could cause a wound they stuck fast in their doughty shields. Drawing their swords from their scabbards, they once again devised death for each other, and there was no respite in the fighting. Castor dealt many blows on the broad shield and horsehair plume, sharp-eyed Lynceus[37] many on Castor's shield, but his sword point only touched the crimson crest. Then, as Lynceus brought his sharp sword down toward the left knee, Castor stepped back and chopped off his fingers. Wounded, he dropped his sword and immediately moved to flee to his father's tomb, where mighty Idas lay[38] watching the fight between kin. Rushing after him, the son of Tyndareus

[36] In fact there will be three left to marry two girls. Either the text is corrupt or Theocritus has committed an oversight, or Castor speaks as if both duelists will sacrifice themselves.

[37] Lynceus, named after the lynx, was proverbially keen sighted (Pind. *Nem.* 10.62–63; Ar. *Plut.* 210).

[38] Perhaps leaning against the grave marker (207, στήλην) rather than lying down.

THEOCRITUS

χαλκὸς ἄφαρ διέχευεν· ὁ δ' ἐς στόμα κεῖτο νενευκώς
Λυγκεύς, κὰδ δ' ἄρα οἱ βλεφάρων βαρὺς ἔδραμεν
ὕπνος.
205 οὐ μὰν οὐδὲ τὸν ἄλλον ἐφ' ἑστίῃ εἶδε πατρῴῃ
παίδων Λαοκόωσα φίλον γάμον ἐκτελέσαντα.
ἦ γὰρ ὅγε στήλην Ἀφαρηίου ἐξανέχουσαν
τύμβου ἀναρρήξας ταχέως Μεσσήνιος Ἴδας
μέλλε κασιγνήτοιο βαλεῖν σφετέροιο φονῆα·
210 ἀλλὰ Ζεὺς ἐπάμυνε, χερῶν δέ οἱ ἔκβαλε τυκτὴν
μάρμαρον, αὐτὸν δὲ φλογέῳ συνέφλεξε κεραυνῷ.

Οὕτω Τυνδαρίδαις πολεμιζέμεν οὐκ ἐν ἐλαφρῷ·
αὐτοί τε κρατέουσι καὶ ἐκ κρατέοντος ἔφυσαν.
χαίρετε, Λήδας τέκνα, καὶ ἡμετέροις κλέος ὕμνοις
215 ἐσθλὸν ἀεὶ πέμποιτε. φίλοι δέ τε πάντες ἀοιδοὶ
Τυνδαρίδαις Ἑλένη τε καὶ ἄλλοις ἡρώεσσιν,
Ἴλιον οἳ διέπερσαν ἀρήγοντες Μενελάῳ.
ὑμῖν κῦδος, ἄνακτες, ἐμήσατο Χῖος ἀοιδός,
ὑμνήσας Πριάμοιο πόλιν καὶ νῆας Ἀχαιῶν
220 Ἰλιάδας τε μάχας Ἀχιλῆά τε πύργον αὐτῆς·
ὑμῖν αὖ καὶ ἐγὼ λιγεῶν μειλίγματα Μουσέων,
οἷ' αὐταὶ παρέχουσι καὶ ὡς ἐμὸς οἶκος ὑπάρχει,
τοῖα φέρω. γεράων δὲ θεοῖς κάλλιστον ἀοιδαί.

---

39 This name is not given by other sources, who call the
mother Arene or Polydora (schol. Ap. Rhod. 1.151 = FGH 3
F 127, 16 F 2).   40 Aphareus ruled from Thalamae in Messenia, according to Pausanias (3.1.4; cf. 4.31.11).
41 Zeus.   42 Hymns traditionally close with the poet bid-

thrust his broad blade into his flank and out through the navel. The bronze sword filleted his innards at once; his head dropped, he fell on his face, and heavy sleep swept down upon his eyelids. But Laocoösa[39] did not see even her other son accomplish his marriage at the family hearth; for Messenian Idas[40] quickly tore up the gravestone that stood on Aphareus' tomb and was about to hurl it at the killer of his brother; but Zeus came to his aid, dashed the worked stone from his hands, and consumed him with the fiery thunderbolt.

It is no easy matter, then, to fight against the Tyndaridae: mighty themselves, they are sons of a mighty father.[41] Farewell, children of Leda;[42] may you always confer fair fame on my hymns. All bards are dear to the Tyndaridae, to Helen[43] and to the rest of the heroes who helped Menelaus to sack Troy. The Chian bard[44] devised fame for you, lords, when he hymned the city of Priam, the ships of the Greeks, the fighting at Troy, and Achilles, that tower of strength in battle.[45] I too bring you such pleasant offerings as my resources can provide: for the gods, songs are the best gift of honor.

ding the god farewell. This closing passage is an elaboration of the customary valediction.   [43] Helen, daughter of Leda and Zeus, is sister of the Dioscuri.   [44] Homer (cf. *Id.* 7.47).

[45] The Dioscuri are hardly mentioned in the *Iliad*, and it is puzzling that Theocritus should say that Homer gives them renown. But "lords" can scarcely refer to the rest of the heroes (216), since the word is used elsewhere with reference to their special title in cult (102, 135); and the poem should end with the Dioscuri.

IDYLL 23

A locked-out lover laments a boy's hard-heartedness and hangs himself outside the street door. The boy ignores the corpse and goes as usual to the baths, where a statue of Eros topples over and kills him.

The poem contains themes well known from ancient love poetry. It is a lesson in the nature of Eros (4–5, 62–63), as are Idylls 11 and 13 and Bion Fr. 13. The locked-out lover's song, or lament, is common (cf. Id. 3). Poetic lovers often threaten suicide, though they less often carry out the threat. Similar imagery is used in the tale of Iphis and Anaxarete in Book 14 of Ovid's Metamorphoses: he hangs himself at her door, and as she watches his funeral she is turned to stone, "which had long existed in her hard heart" (758).

Hardness is the organizing theme. The boy is unyielding and "stony-hearted" (1, 6, 20, 48). The lover hangs himself from the stone lintel and asks for an inscription to be carved on a stone wall. His stepping off his stone into oblivion is paralleled by the boy's dive from the stone pedestal and the stone statue's toppling on the boy.

The text is uncertain in many places. The numerous verbal reminiscences of Theocritus, Bion, and Moschus suggest that the poem is later than the second century BC.

IDYLL 23

Criticism

Copley, F. O. "The Suicide-Paraclausithyron: A Study of Pseudo-Theocritus, Idyll XXIII." *TAPhA* 71 (1940): 52–61.

Effe, B. *Theokrit und die griechische Bukolik.* Darmstadt, 1986, 328–39.

Hunter, R. L. "The Sense of an Author: Theocritus and [Theocritus]." In *The Classical Commentary: History, Practice, Theory, edited by* R. K. Gibson and C. S. Kraus, 100–105 = *Mnemosyne Supplement* 232. Leiden, 2002.

Myers, K. S. *Ovid:* Metamorphoses *Book XIV.* Cambridge, 2009, 180–91.

Radici Colace, P. "La tecnica compositiva dell' 'EPA-ΣTHΣ pseudo-Teocriteo (Idillio XXIII)." *GIF* ns 2 (1971): 325–46.

23

Ἀνήρ τις πολύφιλτρος ἀπηνέος ἤρατ᾽ ἐφάβω,
τὰν μορφὰν ἀγαθῶ, τὸν δὲ τρόπον οὐκέθ᾽ ὁμοίω·
μίσει τὸν φιλέοντα καὶ οὐδὲ ἓν ἄμερον εἶχε,
κοὔκ ἤδει τὸν Ἔρωτα τίς ἦν θεός, ἁλίκα τόξα
5 χερσὶ κρατεῖ, χὼς πικρὰ βέλη ποτικάρδια βάλλει·
πάντα δὲ κἂν μύθοισι καὶ ἐν προσόδοισιν ἀτειρής.
οὐδέ τι τῶν πυρσῶν παραμύθιον, οὐκ ἀμάρυγμα
χείλεος, οὐκ ὄσσων λιπαρὸν σέλας, οὐ ῥόδα μάλων,
οὐ λόγος, οὐχὶ φίλαμα, τὸ κουφίζει τὸν ἔρωτα.
10 οἷα δὲ θὴρ ὑλαῖος ὑποπτεύῃσι κυναγώς,
οὕτως † πάντ᾽ ἐποίει ποτὶ τὸν βροτόν †· ἄγρια δ᾽
    αὐτῷ
χείλεα καὶ κῶραι δεινὸν † βλέπον εἶχεν ἀνάγκαν †·
τᾷ δὲ χολᾷ τὸ πρόσωπον ἀμείβετο, φεῦγε δ᾽ ἀπὸ
    χρώς
ὕβριν † τᾶς ὀργᾶς † περικείμενον. ἀλλὰ καὶ οὕτως
15 ἦν καλός· ἐξ ὀργᾶς δ᾽ ἐρεθίζετο μᾶλλον ἐραστάς.
λοίσθιον οὐκ ἤνεικε τόσαν φλόγα τᾶς Κυθερείας,
ἀλλ᾽ ἐνθὼν ἔκλαιε ποτὶ στυγνοῖσι μελάθροις,
καὶ κύσε τὰν φλιάν, οὕτω δ᾽ ἀντέλλετο φωνά·

5 χὼς Warton: πῶς M   ποτικάρδια Stephanus: ποτὶ
παιδία M   8 ῥόδα μάλων Ahrens: ῥοδομάλλον M
14 περικείμενον Wakefield: -ος M

IDYLL 23

A man liable to love fell for a cruel youth fine of figure but
without morals to match, who detested his lover and had
not a single kind feeling. He did not know what sort of god
Love is, what a bow he wields in his hands, or how painful
are the arrows he shoots at the heart: in speech and be-
havior alike he would not yield at all. There was no conso-
lation for love's fires, no flashing smile about his lips, no
bright glance from his eyes, no blush on his cheeks,[1] no
word, no kiss to make the passion easier to bear. He would
glare at his lover as a wild beast in the woods glares at
the hunters.[2] His lips were cruel and his eyes had a terri-
ble look.[3] His face would turn pale with anger, and his
skin changed color as he showed his arrogance.[4] Even so,
he was good looking, and his lover was provoked even
more by his angry behavior. At last he could not bear the
flames of Cytherea.[5] He went and wept at the unwelcom-
ing house and kissed its doorpost, and his voice arose with

---

[1] A blush would indicate that he loved in return but was too
modest to say so.   [2] Lit., "he did everything to the mortal."
The text is corrupt.   [3] "Necessity" concludes the line, which
makes no sense.   [4] Hopelessly corrupt.   [5] Aphrodite.

---

15 ἦν Heinsius: ἡ M   ἐξ ὀργᾶς δ' Stephanus: δ' ἐξόρ-
πασ' M   16 ἤνεικε Stephanus: ἔνι καὶ M   τόσαν
φλόγα τᾶς Eldick: τὸ σαμφαότατος M
18 ἀνετέλλετο Edmonds: -τέλοντο M   φωνά Legrand:
-ναί M

"ἄγριε παῖ καὶ στυγνέ, κακᾶς ἀνάθρεμμα λεαίνας,
20 λάινε παῖ καὶ ἔρωτος ἀνάξιε, δῶρά τοι ἦνθον
λοίσθια ταῦτα φέρων, τὸν ἐμὸν βρόχον· οὐκέτι γάρ
σε,
κῶρε, θέλω λυπεῖν ποχ᾽ ὁρώμενος, ἀλλὰ βαδίζω
ἔνθα τύ μευ κατέκρινας, ὅπῃ λόγος ἦμεν ἀτερπέων
ξυνὸν τοῖσιν ἐρῶσι τὸ φάρμακον, ἔνθα τὸ λᾶθος.
25 ἀλλὰ καὶ ἢν ὅλον αὐτὸ λαβὼν ποτὶ χεῖλος ἀμέλξω,
οὐδ᾽ οὕτως σβέσσω τὸν ἐμὸν πόθον. ἄρτι δὲ χαίρειν
τοῖσι τεοῖς προθύροις ἐπιβάλλομαι. οἶδα τὸ μέλλον.
καὶ τὸ ῥόδον καλόν ἐστι, καὶ ὁ χρόνος αὐτὸ μαραίνει·
29 καὶ τὸ ἴον καλόν ἐστιν ἐν εἴαρι, καὶ ταχὺ γηρᾷ·
32 καὶ κάλλος καλόν ἐστι τὸ παιδικόν, ἀλλ᾽ ὀλίγον ζῇ.
ἥξει καιρὸς ἐκεῖνος ὁπάνικα καὶ τὺ φιλάσεις,
ἁνίκα τὰν κραδίαν ὀπτεύμενος ἁλμυρὰ κλαύσεις.
35 ἀλλὰ τύ, παῖ, καὶ τοῦτο πανύστατον ἁδύ τι ῥέξον·
ὁππόταν ἐξενθὼν ἀρταμένον ἐν προθύροισι
τοῖσι τεοῖσιν ἴδῃς τὸν τλάμονα, μή με παρένθῃς,
στᾶθι δὲ καὶ βραχὺ κλαῦσον, ἐπισπείσας δὲ τὸ
δάκρυ
λῦσον τᾶς σχοίνω με καὶ ἀμφίθες ἐκ ῥεθέων σῶν
40 εἵματα καὶ κρύψον με, τὸ δ᾽ αὖ πύματόν με φίλασον·
κἂν νεκρῷ χάρισαι τεὰ χείλεα. μή με φοβαθῇς·

22 λυπεῖν Fritzsche: -πῃς M   23 ἀτερπέων Meineke:
ἀταρπῶν M   26 οὐδ᾽ οὕτως Briggs: οὐδὲ τῶς M   πόθον
Boninus, Callierges: χόλον M
30–31 λευκὸν τὸ κρίνον ἐστί, μαραίνεται ἁνίκα πίπτει· ἁ
δὲ χιὼν λευκά, καὶ τάκεται ἁνίκα † παχθῇ secl. Haupt.
41 τεὰ Gallavotti: τὰ m: τὰ σὰ m

these words: "Cruel and sullen boy, reared by a savage lioness; stony-hearted boy unworthy of love—I have come to you bringing this last gift, my noose.[6] I do not want you to be troubled with the sight of me any longer, lad; I am going where you have condemned me to go, to a place where they say is the universal remedy for lovers' sufferings—oblivion. But if I put that remedy to my lips and drink it all, I shall not even then quench my desire. Now at last I begin to take pleasure in this door of yours.[7] I know what will happen to you. The rose is fair, too, but time withers it; the violet is fair, too, in the spring, but it quickly ages;[8] fair, too, is a boy's beauty, but it lasts a short time. A moment will arrive when you too are a lover, when your heart is on fire and you weep salt tears.

"But do me this one last sweet favor, my lad. When you come out and see my wretched body hanging in your doorway, do not pass me by; stop and weep a while, and after your libation of tears release me from the rope, put on me the clothes that your body has worn, cover me up, and give me a final kiss: dead though I be, grace me with your lips. You have nothing to fear from me: I cannot detain you:[9]

---

[6] A hideous mockery of the custom of hanging a garland at the beloved's door.

[7] I.e., I used to suffer by being shut out, but now I realize you will be punished. The text is again likely to be corrupt.

[8] The transmitted text here has two lines that are probably from another poem: "The lily is white, but it withers when it droops; snow is white, but it melts once it is sprinkled on the ground." The words "droops" and "sprinkled" are probably corrupt.

[9] "Detain" is a conjecture; the word is missing in the manuscripts.

οὐ δύναμαι κατέχειν σε· ἀπαλλάξεις με φιλάσας.
χῶμα δέ μοι κοίλανον ὅ μευ κρύψει τὸν ἔρωτα,
κἦν ἀπίῃς, τόδε μοι τρὶς ἐπαύσον· 'ὦ φίλε, κεῖσαι·'
ἢν δὲ θέλῃς, καὶ τοῦτο· 'καλὸς δέ μοι ὤλεθ' ἑταῖρος.'
γράψον καὶ τόδε γράμμα τὸ σοῖς τοίχοισι χαράσσω·
'τοῦτον ἔρως ἔκτεινεν· ὁδοιπόρε, μὴ παροδεύσῃς,
ἀλλὰ στὰς τόδε λέξον· "ἀπηνέα εἶχεν ἑταῖρον."'"

Ὧδ' εἰπὼν λίθον εἷλεν † ἐρεισάμενος δ' ἐπὶ τοίχῳ
ἄχρι μέσων ὁδῶν †, φοβερὸν λίθον, ἅπτετ' ἀπ' αὐτῶ
τὰν λεπτὰν σχοινίδα, βρόχον δ' ἐπέβαλλε τραχήλῳ,
τὰν ἕδραν δ' ἐκύλισεν ὑπὲκ ποδός, ἠδ' ἐκρεμάσθη
νεκρός. ὁ δ' αὖτ' ᾤξε θύρας καὶ τὸν νεκρὸν εἶδεν
φλιᾶς ἐξ ἰδίας ἀρταμένον, οὐδ' ἐλυγίχθη
τὰν ψυχάν, οὐ κλαῦσε νέον φόνον, ἀλλ' ἐπὶ νεκρῷ
εἵματα πάντ' ἐμίανεν ἐφαβικά, βαῖνε δ' ἐς ἄθλως
γυμνασίων, καὶ ἔκηλα φίλων ἐπεμαίετο λουτρῶν,
καὶ ποτὶ τὸν θεὸν ἦνθε τὸν ὕβρισε· λαϊνέας δέ
ἵπτατ' ἀπὸ κρηπῖδος ἐς ὕδατα· τῷ δ' ἐφύπερθεν
ἄλατο καὶ τὤγαλμα, κακὸν δ' ἔκτεινεν ἔφαβον·
νᾶμα δ' ἐφοινίχθη, παιδὸς δ' ἐπενάχετο φωνά·
"χαίρετε τοὶ φιλέοντες· ὁ γὰρ μισῶν ἐφονεύθη.
στέργετε δ' οἱ μισεῦντες· ὁ γὰρ θεὸς οἶδε δικάζειν."

42 κατέχειν Wilamowitz: εἶν M   ἀπαλλάξεις Meineke:
διαλλ- M   44 ἐπαύσον ed. Ald.: ὄπ- M   45 θέλῃς
Ahrens: λῃς M   46 τὸ σοῖς τοίχοισι Schaefer: τόσοις (σ)
τίχοισι M   χαράσσω Wilamowitz: -ξω M
    51 ἐπέβαλλε Briggs: ἔβαλλε M   54 φλιᾶς Meineke:
αὐλᾶς M   57 ἔκηλα Wilamowitz: λε M

one kiss, and you will be rid of me. Hollow out for me a grave to bury my love; as you depart, cry out three times, 'There you lie, my friend,' and, if you like, these words too: 'My fair companion is no more.' The inscription should be the words I am writing on your house wall: 'Love was the death of this man. Wayfarer, do not pass by; stop and say, "His companion was cruel."'"

With these words he took a stone, placed it on the threshold, fastened his slender rope above the door,[10] put the noose round his neck, kicked away the support from under his feet, and hung there a corpse.

The boy opened the doors and saw the corpse hanging from his own lintel, but his heart was not abashed, nor did he lament the death just done; he made all his boyish clothing unclean by touching the body[11] and went off to his contests at the wrestling school. Without a care he made for the baths that he loved and approached the god he had dishonored. He leaped from the pedestal into the water; but at the same time the statue leaped from above and killed the wicked youth. The water turned red, and over it floated the voice of the boy: "Rejoice, you lovers: he who hated love is killed. Be kind, you who hate love: the god knows how to dispense justice."

[10] "Placed . . . door": this must have been something like the sense, but the text is irrecoverably corrupt.

[11] I.e., ritually unclean; the text is again uncertain.

IDYLL 24

The first part of the poem tells how the baby Heracles strangled two snakes sent by Hera to kill him and how Tiresias foretold the child's great destiny. Here Theocritus retells a story from the lyric poet Pindar, who in his first Nemean Ode *(ca. 476 BC) related most of the same facts more briefly (and yet more briefly in* Paean 20 = S 1 Rutherford, *fragments of which survive). Theocritus dwells more than Pindar does on domestic aspects of the episode, such as the shield-cradle, the lullaby, the serving women, and the scene in the bedroom.*

In the second section, an Education of Heracles, the young hero's tutors are enumerated. In all surviving manuscripts the poem breaks off at line 140, but a papyrus preserves scraps of some thirty lines more. A marginal note mentions that the poem concluded with a prayer for victory. It may therefore have been entered, or have been written as if entered, for a competition in poetry.

The competition could have been one held by Ptolemy II Philadelphus, a keen patron of the arts, who claimed descent from Heracles (Id. 17.27). The detail of the shield-cradle, which is not in Pindar's version, has been taken to symbolize the new uses to which Theocritus is putting the meter of martial epic; but it may also refer to a story that

322

Ptolemy I Soter had been exposed in a shield by his father when he was born (Suda λ 25).

Criticism

Effe, B. "Die Destruktion der Tradition: Theokrits mythologische Gedichte." *RhM* 121 (1978): 48–77.

Fantuzzi–Hunter, *Tradition and Innovation,* 201–10, 255–66.

Stephens, S. *Seeing Double: Intercultural Poetics in Ptolemaic Alexandria.* Berkeley, 2003, 123–46.

Stern, J. "Theocritus' *Idyll* 24." *AJPh* 95 (1974): 348–61.

Ἡρακλέα δεκάμηνον ἐόντα ποχ' ἁ Μιδεᾶτις
Ἀλκμήνα καὶ νυκτὶ νεώτερον Ἰφικλῆα,
ἀμφοτέρους λούσασα καὶ ἐμπλήσασα γάλακτος,
χαλκείαν κατέθηκεν ἐς ἀσπίδα, τὰν Πτερελάου
5 Ἀμφιτρύων καλὸν ὅπλον ἀπεσκύλευσε πεσόντος.
ἁπτομένα δὲ γυνὰ κεφαλᾶς μυθήσατο παίδων·
"εὕδετ', ἐμὰ βρέφεα, γλυκερὸν καὶ ἐγέρσιμον ὕπνον·
εὕδετ', ἐμὰ ψυχά, δύ' ἀδελφεοί, εὔσοα τέκνα·
ὄλβιοι εὐνάζοισθε καὶ ὄλβιοι ἀῶ ἵκοισθε."
10 ὣς φαμένα δίνησε σάκος μέγα· τοὺς δ' ἕλεν ὕπνος.
ἇμος δὲ στρέφεται μεσονύκτιον ἐς δύσιν Ἄρκτος
Ὠρίωνα κατ' αὐτόν, ὁ δ' ἀμφαίνει μέγαν ὦμον,
τᾶμος ἄρ' αἰνὰ πέλωρα δύω πολυμήχανος Ἥρα,
κυανέαις φρίσσοντας ὑπὸ σπείραισι δράκοντας,
15 ὦρσεν ἐπὶ πλατὺν οὐδόν, ὅθι σταθμὰ κοῖλα θυράων

10 ἕλεν pap.: ἔλαβ' M

---

[1] See on Id. 13.20.   [2] Alcmena conceived the twins on
successive nights; Zeus (disguised as Amphitryon) fathered Her-
acles, Amphitryon Iphicles. Theocritus follows the version of the
myth in which they were born a day apart (cf. ps.-Apollod. 2.4.8);
Pindar has them born together (Nem. 1.36) and sets the episode
immediately after their birth.

IDYLL 24

Once upon a time Midean Alcmena[1] bathed and fed full with milk the ten-month-old Heracles and Iphicles, who was younger by one night,[2] and placed them both in a bronze shield, a fine piece of armor which Amphitryon had stripped from the body of Pterelaus.[3] She put her hands on the children's heads and said, "Sleep sweetly, my babies, and wake at last; sleep safely, children, my two souls, twin brothers. Rest happy, and happy reach the dawn." With these words she rocked[4] the great shield, and sleep came over them.

But at the time when the Bear at midnight turns its course to the west opposite to Orion, who reveals his huge shoulder,[5] Hera contrived to send two terrible and monstrous snakes, rippling with dark coils, across the broad thresh-

[3] Pterelaus, ruler of the west Greek island of Taphos, was killed by Amphitryon (ps.-Apollod. *Bibl.* 2.4.6). Heracles was conceived on the night before he returned from this expedition.

[4] The verb δινᾶν can be used of the wielding of a shield in battle.

[5] Obscure. The lines describe a time of year, probably mid-February, when Orion is just visible above the horizon (see Gow's note), but the context seems to demand that a time of day, midnight, should be defined here. Some aspect of the cult of Heracles or of the Ptolemies may perhaps lie behind this unexpected detail.

οἴκου, ἀπειλήσασα φαγεῖν βρέφος Ἡρακλῆα.
τὼ δ' ἐξειλυσθέντες ἐπὶ χθονὶ γαστέρας ἄμφω
αἱμοβόρους ἐκύλιον· ἀπ' ὀφθαλμῶν δὲ κακὸν πῦρ
ἐρχομένοις λάμπεσκε, βαρὺν δ' ἐξέπτυον ἰόν.
20 ἀλλ' ὅτε δὴ παίδων λιχμώμενοι ἐγγύθεν ἦνθον,
καὶ τότ' ἄρ' ἐξέγροντο, Διὸς νοέοντος ἅπαντα,
Ἀλκμήνας φίλα τέκνα, φάος δ' ἀνὰ οἶκον ἐτύχθη.
ἤτοι ὅγ' εὐθὺς ἄυσεν, ὅπως κακὰ θηρί' ἀνέγνω
κοίλου ὑπὲρ σάκεος καὶ ἀναιδέας εἶδεν ὀδόντας,
25 Ἰφικλέης, οὔλαν δὲ ποσὶν διελάκτισε χλαῖναν
φευγέμεν ὁρμαίνων· ὁ δ' ἐναντίος ἵετο χερσίν
Ἡρακλέης, ἄμφω δὲ βαρεῖ ἐνεδήσατο δεσμῷ,
δραξάμενος φάρυγος, τόθι φάρμακα λυγρὰ τέτυκται
οὐλομένοις ὀφίεσσι, τὰ καὶ θεοὶ ἐχθαίροντι.
30 τὼ δ' αὖτε σπείραισιν ἑλισσέσθην περὶ παῖδα
ὀψίγονον, γαλαθηνὸν ὑπὸ τροφῷ, αἰὲν ἄδακρυν·
ἂψ δὲ πάλιν διέλυον, ἐπεὶ μογέοιεν, ἀκάνθας
δεσμοῦ ἀναγκαίου πειρώμενοι ἔκλυσιν εὑρεῖν.
Ἀλκμήνα δ' ἄκουσε βοᾶς καὶ ἐπέγρετο πράτα·
35 "ἄνσταθ', Ἀμφιτρύων· ἐμὲ γὰρ δέος ἴσχει ὀκνηρόν·
ἄνστα, μηδὲ πόδεσσι τεοῖς ὑπὸ σάνδαλα θείης.
οὐκ ἀίεις, παίδων ὁ νεώτερος ὅσσον ἀυτεῖ;
ἦ οὐ νοέεις ὅτι νυκτὸς ἀωρί που, οἱ δέ τε τοῖχοι
πάντες ἀριφραδέες καθαρᾶς ἅπερ ἠριγενείας;

26 ἵετο Meineke: εἴχετο m: εἶλετο m
31 ἄδακρυν Xylander: -ρυ M
39 ἅπερ Briggs: ἄτερ M: δ' ἀ[pap.

old where stood the paneled doors[6] of the palace, urging them on to devour the baby Heracles. Uncoiling, they both twisted their blood-gorging bellies along the ground; as they moved, their eyes glinted with a wicked gleam, and they were spitting out deadly venom. Flicking their tongues, they came near the boys; but then Alcmena's dear children awoke: Zeus was aware of everything, and light was created throughout the palace.[7] Iphicles cried out at once when he caught sight of the grim creatures over the rim of the hollow shield, and he kicked at his woolen blankets in his efforts to get away; but Heracles made a grab at them and bound both in a powerful bond, seizing them by the neck, where baneful snakes produce their venom, which even the gods abhor. With their coils they then twisted themselves around the child, that favorite son,[8] still fed at his nurse's breast, who never wept;[9] and when they were exhausted they would uncoil their backbones again as they sought release from his fatal grip.

Alcmena heard the cry and was the first to wake: "Get up, Amphitryon; I feel timid and fearful. Get up, and do not wait to put sandals on your feet. Don't you hear what a noise our younger boy is making? Don't you notice that it is the middle of the night, surely, yet the walls are all plain to see, just as in[10] the clear light of dawn? I feel some

[6] Lit., "hollow doorposts." Probably σταθμὰ κοῖλα refers to the architectural term κοιλόσταθμος, which seems to mean lattices, panels, or coving.   [7] Zeus makes the light so that Heracles can see the serpents, and to rouse the household.

[8] Lit., "late-born." There may be an allusion to Hera's attempts to retard his birth (Ov. *Met.* 9.297–301; Ant. Lib. 29).

[9] Presaging his later fortitude.

[10] Or (reading ἄτερ), "without."

40 ἔστι τί μοι κατὰ δῶμα νεώτερον, ἔστι, φίλ᾽ ἀνδρῶν."
ὣς φάθ᾽· ὃ δ᾽ ἐξ εὐνᾶς ἀλόχῳ κατέβαινε πιθήσας·
δαιδάλεον δ᾽ ὥρμασε μετὰ ξίφος, ὅ οἱ ὕπερθεν
κλιντῆρος κεδρίνου περὶ πασσάλῳ αἰὲν ἄωρτο.
ἤτοι ὅγ᾽ ὠριγνᾶτο νεοκλώστου τελαμῶνος,
45 κουφίζων ἑτέρᾳ κολεόν, μέγα λώτινον ἔργον.
ἀμφιλαφὴς δ᾽ ἄρα παστὰς ἐνεπλήσθη πάλιν ὄρφνας.
δμῶας δὴ τότ᾽ ἄυσεν ὕπνον βαρὺν ἐκφυσῶντας·
"οἴσετε πῦρ ὅτι θᾶσσον ἀπ᾽ ἐσχαρεῶνος ἑλόντες,
δμῶες ἐμοί, στιβαροὺς δὲ θυρᾶν ἀνακόψατ᾽ ὀχῆας."
50 "ἄνστατε, δμῶες ταλασίφρονες· αὐτὸς ἀυτεῖ,"
ἦ ῥα γυνὰ Φοίνισσα μύλαις ἔπι κοῖτον ἔχουσα.
οἱ δ᾽ αἶψα προγένοντο λύχνοις ἅμα δαιομένοισι
δμῶες· ἐνεπλήσθη δὲ δόμος σπεύδοντος ἑκάστου.
ἤτοι ἄρ᾽ ὡς εἶδονθ᾽ ὑποτίτθιον Ἡρακλῆα
55 θῆρε δύω χείρεσσιν ἀπρὶξ ἁπαλαῖσιν ἔχοντα,
ἐκπλήγδην ἰάχησαν· ὃ δ᾽ ἐς πατέρ᾽ Ἀμφιτρύωνα
ἑρπετὰ δεικανάασκεν, ἐπάλλετο δ᾽ ὑψόθι χαίρων
κουροσύνᾳ, γελάσας δὲ πάρος κατέθηκε ποδοῖν
πατρὸς ἑοῦ θανάτῳ κεκαρωμένα δεινὰ πέλωρα.
60 Ἀλκμήνα μὲν ἔπειτα ποτὶ σφέτερον βάλε κόλπον
ξηρὸν ὑπαὶ δείους ἀκράχολον Ἰφικλῆα·
Ἀμφιτρύων δὲ τὸν ἄλλον ὑπ᾽ ἀμνείαν θέτο χλαῖναν
παῖδα, πάλιν δ᾽ ἐς λέκτρον ἰὼν ἐμνάσατο κοίτου.

Ὄρνιχες τρίτον ἄρτι τὸν ἔσχατον ὄρθρον ἄειδον,
65 Τειρεσίαν τόκα μάντιν ἀλαθέα πάντα λέγοντα
Ἀλκμήνα καλέσασα χρέος κατέλεξε νεοχμόν,
καί νιν ὑποκρίνεσθαι ὅπως τελέεσθαι ἔμελλεν

threat in the house, I do indeed, my dear husband." So she spoke. Obeying his wife, he got down from the bed. He made for his ornate sword, which always hung on a peg above his cedarwood couch, and reached for the newly woven baldric as he lifted with his other hand the scabbard, a great work made from lotus wood. The spacious room was again plunged in darkness. Then he called to the slaves, who were sound asleep and breathing deeply: "Fetch a light from the hearth as quickly as you can, slaves, and knock back the strong door bolts!"[11] "Get up, stouthearted slaves! Himself is calling!" cried a Phoenician woman who slept at the mill.[12] The slaves appeared at once as soon as their lamps were alight, and the palace was filled with them as they all bustled about. When they saw the baby Heracles gripping the pair of creatures in his tender hands, they cried out in astonishment. He showed the serpents to his father Amphitryon, leaped high in youthful joy, and with a laugh laid before his father's feet the terrible creatures in the sleep of death. Then Alcmena held in her lap Iphicles, who was in the extremity of fear and rigid with terror. Amphitryon placed the other child under his lambswool blanket, went back to bed, and thought of sleep.

Just after the third cockcrow heralding daybreak, Alcmena summoned Tiresias, the seer whose every word is truthful, recounted to him the strange occurrence, and asked him

[11] Probably those securing the children's room.

[12] Among the querns where corn was ground by hand. Cf. Hom. *Od.* 20.105–10, where twelve women sleep at the mill in Odysseus' palace.

ἠνώγει· "μηδ' εἴ τι θεοὶ νοέοντι πονηρόν,
αἰδόμενός με κρύπτε· καὶ ὡς οὐκ ἔστιν ἀλύξαι
70 ἀνθρώποις ὅ τι Μοῖρα κατὰ κλωστῆρος ἐπείγει.
μάντι Εὐηρείδα, μάλα τοι φρονέοντα διδάσκω."
τόσσ' ἔλεγεν βασίλεια· ὁ δ' ἀνταμείβετο τοίοις·
"θάρσει, ἀριστοτόκεια γύναι, Περσήιον αἷμα,
θάρσει· μελλόντων δὲ τὸ λώιον ἐν φρεσὶ θέσθαι.
ναὶ γὰρ ἐμῶν γλυκὺ φέγγος ἀποιχόμενον πάλαι ὄσ-
75   σων,
πολλαὶ Ἀχαιιάδων μαλακὸν περὶ γούνατι νῆμα
χειρὶ κατατρίψουσιν ἀκρέσπερον ἀείδοισαι
Ἀλκμήναν ὀνομαστί, σέβας δ' ἔσῃ Ἀργείαισι.
τοῖος ἀνὴρ ὅδε μέλλει ἐς οὐρανὸν ἄστρα φέροντα
80 ἀμβαίνειν τεὸς υἱός, ἀπὸ στέρνων πλατὺς ἥρως,
οὗ καὶ θηρία πάντα καὶ ἀνέρες ἥσσονες ἄλλοι.
δώδεκά οἱ τελέσαντι πεπρωμένον ἐν Διὸς οἰκεῖν
μόχθους, θνητὰ δὲ πάντα πυρὰ Τραχίνιος ἕξει·
γαμβρὸς δ' ἀθανάτων κεκλήσεται, οἳ τάδ' ἐπῶρσαν
85 κνώδαλα φωλεύοντα βρέφος διαδηλήσασθαι.

72 τοίοις Briggs: -ως m: -ος m
75 ἐμῶν Edmonds: -ὸν M
82 οἰκεῖν Callierges: -κῆν pap., m: -κῆς m

13 Meaning uncertain. κλωστήρ, here translated "distaff,"
usually means "yarn."   14 Tiresias was son of Eueres and the
nymph Chariclo (Callim. *Hymn* 5.81).

15 Alcmena's father, Electryon, was son of Perseus and An-
dromeda (ps.-Apollod. *Bibl.* 2.4.5).

330

to explain what the outcome would be. "And if the gods are planning something bad, do not hide it on account of your regard for me. Mortals cannot escape what Fate quickly spins from her distaff, even if they know what is to come.[13] Prophet, son of Eueres,[14] I am teaching you what you well know already." So spoke the queen, and he replied with these words: "Take heart, mother of noble children, descendant of Perseus,[15] take heart, and store up in your mind the better part of what is to come.[16] By the sweet light long gone from these eyes of mine,[17] many of the women of Greece, as by hand they rub the soft yarn on their knees at nightfall, will celebrate the name of Alcmena in song, and among Argive women you shall be honored. This son of yours, when he is a broad-chested man, is destined to ascend to the starry sky, and he will be mightier than all beasts and all other men. It is fated that when he has accomplished twelve labors he will live in the house of Zeus, while a pyre on Mt. Trachis will hold his mortal remains;[18] he will be called son-in-law of the gods,[19] who roused these monsters from their lairs to de-

---

[16] He does not dwell on the Labors, and he omits to mention Heracles' murder of his mortal wife, Megara, together with their children, his agonizing death, etc.   [17] Tiresias gained the gift of prophecy in compensation for his loss of sight, which (according to the version followed by Callimachus in the *Hymn to Athena*) came about when he accidentally saw Artemis bathing. Cf. ps.-Apollod. *Bibl.* 3.6.7 for other versions.

[18] His mortal part, inherited from his mother, will be burned away. See Soph. *Trach.* 1191–215.

[19] After his assumption to Olympus, he married Hebe (Youth), daughter of Zeus and Hera (Hes. *Theog.* 922, 950–55; Theoc. *Id.* 17.32–33).

ἔσται δὴ τοῦτ' ἆμαρ ὁπηνίκα νεβρὸν ἐν εὐνᾷ
καρχαρόδων σίνεσθαι ἰδὼν λύκος οὐκ ἐθελήσει.
ἀλλά, γύναι, πῦρ μέν τοι ὑπὸ σποδῷ εὔτυκον ἔστω,
κάγκανα δ' ἀσπαλάθου ξύλ' ἑτοιμάσατ' ἢ παλιούρου

90 ἢ βάτου ἢ ἀνέμῳ δεδονημένον αὖον ἄχερδον·
καῖε δὲ τώδ' ἀγρίαισιν ἐπὶ σχίζαισι δράκοντε
νυκτὶ μέσᾳ, ὅκα παῖδα κανεῖν τεὸν ἤθελον αὐτοί.
ἦρι δὲ συλλέξασα κόνιν πυρὸς ἀμφιπόλων τις
ῥιψάτω, εὖ μάλα πᾶσαν ὑπὲρ ποταμοῖο φέρουσα

95 ῥωγάδας ἐς πέτρας, ὑπερούριον, ἂψ δὲ νεέσθω
ἄστρεπτος. καθαρῷ δὲ πυρώσατε δῶμα θεείῳ
πρᾶτον, ἔπειτα δ' ἅλεσσι μεμιγμένον, ὡς νενόμισται,
θαλλῷ ἐπιρραίνειν ἐστεμμένῳ ἀβλαβὲς ὕδωρ·
Ζηνὶ δ' ἐπιρρέξαι καθυπερτέρῳ ἄρσενα χοῖρον,

100 δυσμενέων αἰεὶ καθυπέρτεροι ὡς τελέθοιτε."
φῆ, καὶ ἐρωήσας ἐλεφάντινον ᾤχετο δίφρον
Τειρεσίας πολλοῖσι βαρύς περ ἐὼν ἐνιαυτοῖς.

Ἡρακλέης δ' ὑπὸ ματρὶ νέον φυτὸν ὣς ἐν ἀλωᾷ
ἐτρέφετ', Ἀργείου κεκλημένος Ἀμφιτρύωνος.

105 γράμματα μὲν τὸν παῖδα γέρων Λίνος ἐξεδίδαξεν,
υἱὸς Ἀπόλλωνος μελεδωνεὺς ἄγρυπνος ἥρως·

86–87 secl. Dahl   98 ἐστεμμένῳ Schaefer: -ον M

---

[20] It was in fact only Hera who sent the snakes (13); Tiresias suggests that it was the gods in general.

[21] This sentence, which seems more appropriate to a description of the Golden Age, is probably an interpolation.

[22] To kindle the wood that the slaves are to collect.

332

stroy your baby.[20] A day shall come when the sharp-
toothed wolf shall see the fawn in its bed and not wish to
harm it.[21] But have fire ready under the ashes,[22] my lady;
and the rest of you collect dry sticks of thorn trees, spiny
shrubs, bramble or dry wild pear beaten by the wind. Burn
these two serpents on the wild firewood at midnight, the
very time when *they* meant to kill your son. At dawn let
one of your maids gather up the ashes, carry them across
the river, throw them all on the jagged rocks beyond our
boundaries, and return without looking back.[23] Fumigate
the palace with cleansing sulfur first of all, and then—as
is the normal practice—use a living branch trimmed with
wool to sprinkle a mixture of salt and pure water; and sac-
rifice a young male pig to lord Zeus so that you may for
ever lord it over your enemies." With these words Tiresias
left the ivory seat and departed, afflicted though he was
with the weight of many years.

Like a young sapling in an orchard Heracles was brought
up by his mother, and he was called the son of Amphi-
tryon, the Argive.[24] Old Linus,[25] the hero, son of Apollo,

[23] To avoid pollution or harm from the evil ritually cast out.
Cf. Ap. Rhod. 3.1038; Virg. *Ecl.* 8.102.

[24] Amphitryon was from Tiryns, which was associated with—
and eventually conquered by—Argos. "Was called" may hint at
the fact, not referred to elsewhere in the poem, that Amphitryon
was not his parent.

[25] Linus is said to have adapted the Phoenician alphabet to
Greek (Diod. Sic. 3.67.1). A more familiar story has him trying to
teach Heracles to play the lyre and being killed by his recalcitrant
pupil (ps.-Apollod. *Bibl.* 2.4.9).

τόξον δ᾽ ἐντανύσαι καὶ ἐπὶ σκοπὸν εἶναι ὀιστόν
Εὔρυτος ἐκ πατέρων μεγάλαις ἀφνειὸς ἀρούραις.
αὐτὰρ ἀοιδὸν ἔθηκε καὶ ἄμφω χεῖρας ἔπλασσεν
110 πυξίνᾳ ἐν φόρμιγγι Φιλαμμονίδας Εὔμολπος.
ὅσσα δ᾽ ἀπὸ σκελέων ἑδροστρόφοι Ἀργόθεν ἄνδρες
ἀλλάλους σφάλλοντι παλαίσμασιν, ὅσσα τε πύκται
δεινοὶ ἐν ἱμάντεσσιν ἅ τ᾽ ἐς γαῖαν προπεσόντες
πάμμαχοι ἐξεύροντο σοφίσματα σύμφορα τέχνᾳ,
115 πάντ᾽ ἔμαθ᾽ Ἑρμείαο διδασκόμενος παρὰ παιδί
Ἁρπαλύκῳ Πανοπῆι, τὸν οὐδ᾽ ἂν τηλόθε λεύσσων
θαρσαλέως τις ἔμεινεν ἀεθλεύοντ᾽ ἐν ἀγῶνι·
τοῖον ἐπισκύνιον βλοσυρῷ ἐπέκειτο προσώπῳ.
ἵππους δ᾽ ἐξελάσασθαι ὑφ᾽ ἅρματι καὶ περὶ νύσσαν
120 ἀσφαλέως κάμπτοντα τροχοῦ σύριγγα φυλάξαι
Ἀμφιτρύων ὃν παῖδα φίλα φρονέων ἐδίδαξεν
αὐτός, ἐπεὶ μάλα πολλὰ θοῶν ἐξήρατ᾽ ἀγώνων
Ἄργει ἐν ἱπποβότῳ κειμήλια, καί οἱ ἀαγεῖς
δίφροι ἐφ᾽ ὧν ἐπέβαινε χρόνῳ διέλυσαν ἱμάντας.
125 δούρατι δὲ προβολαίῳ ὑπ᾽ ἀσπίδι ὦμον ἔχοντα
ἀνδρὸς ὀρέξασθαι ξιφέων τ᾽ ἀνέχεσθαι ἀμυχμόν,
κοσμῆσαί τε φάλαγγα λόχον τ᾽ ἀναμετρήσασθαι
δυσμενέων ἐπιόντα, καὶ ἱππήεσσι κελεῦσαι,

116 τηλόθε pap., coni. Ahrens: -όθι M
125 ὦμον Cholmeley: νῶτον pap., M

---

26 Eurytus is mentioned in the *Odyssey* as a notable bowman who was killed when he challenged Apollo to a contest in archery (8.224–25); cf. ps.-Apollod. *Bibl.* 2.4.9.   27 This Eumolpus ("Fine Singer") is not mentioned elsewhere. Philammon was a

watchful guardian, taught the boy to read and write. Eurytus,[26] wealthy in inherited land, taught him to draw the bow and shoot an arrow at the target, while Eumolpus son of Philammon[27] made him a singer and formed his hands to the shape of the boxwood lyre. As for the moves by which Argive men in wrestling twist their hips and throw each other with their legs, and the techniques of boxers deft with the gloves,[28] and the artful skills of pancratiasts when they fight on the ground—all these he was taught by Harpalycus of Panopeus, a son of Hermes;[29] even seeing him from a distance, one would have become nervous to meet him in a contest, such was the scowling brow that extended over his grim face. Amphitryon himself carefully taught his son how to drive out his chariot horses and guard against striking the nave of the wheel in safely rounding the turning post; he had carried off many prizes from the swift races in Argos, the land where horses graze, and the chariots in which he rode remained undamaged until with age their leather straps grew slack.[30] Castor son of Hippalus taught him to keep his shoulder behind his shield with his spear in a defensive posture and to aim a blow at his opponent, to bear wounds inflicted by swords, to put the ranks in good order, to take the measure of an opposing enemy, and to issue commands to the cavalry—

son of Apollo (Pherec. *FGH* 3 F 26, 120).   [28] Lit., "thongs," strips of leather wrapped around the palm and fingers: see *Id.* 22.80–81.   [29] Panopeus was a town in Phocis. Harpalycus is not known in connection with Heracles, but ps.-Apollod. *Bibl.* 2.4.9 says that the wrestling teacher's name was Autolycus. This is perhaps the same Autolycus who was grandfather of Odysseus and son of Hermes (Pherecydes, *FGH* 3 F 120).   [30] These seem to have formed the bodywork (cf. Hom. *Il.* 5.727–28).

Κάστωρ Ἱππαλίδας δέδαεν, φυγὰς Ἄργεος ἐνθών,
130 οὗ ποκα κλᾶρον ἅπαντα καὶ οἰνόπεδον μέγα Τυδεύς
ναῖε παρ᾽ Ἀδρήστοιο λαβὼν ἱππήλατον Ἄργος·
Κάστορι δ᾽ οὔτις ὁμοῖος ἐν ἡμιθέοις πολεμιστής
ἄλλος ἔην πρὶν γῆρας ἀποτρῖψαι νεότητα.
Ὧδε μὲν Ἡρακλῆα φίλα παιδεύσατο μάτηρ.
135 εὐνὰ δ᾽ ἧς τῷ παιδὶ τετυγμένα ἀγχόθι πατρός
δέρμα λεόντειον μάλα οἱ κεχαρισμένον αὐτῷ,
δεῖπνον δὲ κρέα τ᾽ ὀπτὰ καὶ ἐν κανέῳ μέγας ἄρτος
Δωρικός· ἀσφαλέως κε φυτοσκάφον ἄνδρα κορέσσαι·
αὐτὰρ ἐπ᾽ ἄματι τυννὸν ἄνευ πυρὸς αἴνυτο δόρπον.
140 εἵματα δ᾽ οὐκ ἀσκητὰ μέσας ὑπὲρ ἔννυτο κνάμας.
. . . .] . . υ . . . νε . [. . . . .] . ελω [
. . . . . .] . ι· ποσον τι ρ ϋ[
. . . . . .] .ναμον εχ [
. . . . . .]ς· εν χροϊ κα [
145 . . . .]ψας· το δε κα [
. . . .]εν ξεινου[
. . . .]δεω . [
. . . .] . ε . [
. . . .] . ρ . [
150 . . . .] σα . [
. . . .′.]ντα . [
. . . .]λε θυρα[
. . . .]ιρον δε[
. . . .]ληα δι .[
155 . . . .]ον ι . [

Desunt vv. circiter xii.

Castor, who came as an exile from Argos. Tydeus once received Castor's whole estate and vineyard from Adrastus, and lived in Argos, the land of horses.[31] Among the demigods Castor had no equal as a warrior until old age wore away his youth.

That is how his dear mother had Heracles educated. The boy's bed was a lion skin placed near his father, and he took great delight in it.[32] For dinner he had roast meat and a big Dorian loaf in a basket[33] easily large enough to satisfy a laborer, but during the day he would take a small, uncooked meal.[34] His simple garment was worn above the knee.

---

[31] In the *Iliad* Tydeus is said to have fled Calydon after a murder; having come to Argos he was purified by Adrastus, whose daughter he married. Homer mentions his large estates in Argos (*Il.* 14.119–24); Theocritus' lines suggest that these were confiscated from Castor by Adrastus.

[32] Perhaps presaging his Labor with the Nemean Lion.

[33] Probably a coarse, manly sort of bread.

[34] Wittily ameliorating his notorious gluttony.

---

137 δὲ Stephanus: τε M

168 . . . .] . ạ . . . ων   μ . [. . . . .]υμπον
    . . . .] . δ᾽ ἐριῶπιδα [. . . . .]ς
170 . . . .]ταν ομοπατ[. . . . .]λᾶι.
    . . . .]κα . οχθε θε[. . . . .]θνητος
    . . . .] . [.] ạοιδον αṇọ[. . . . .]τυνεικὼς

(168) . . . . Olympus

(171) . . . . mortal

(172) . . . . bard . . . .

IDYLL 25

The background story is Heracles' Labor of cleansing the Augean Stables. There are three distinct scenes. The first is a dialogue between Heracles and a countryman who provides information about King Augeas; Heracles is menaced by the farm dogs. In the second, Heracles goes with Augeas and his son Phyleus to view the vast herds of cattle; he has to repel an attack by the bull Phaethon. In the third, Heracles tells Phyleus how he killed the Nemean Lion.

It is possible that the three sections are fragments of a longer poem, but it is more likely that they are an experiment in discontinuous narration: the first and third include dialogue, and in each Heracles confronts a dangerous animal. It is curious that the cleansing of the byres is not mentioned; though the magnitude of the task is indicated by a lengthy description of the innumerable herds. Instead of that Labor, the story of the Nemean Lion is told at length (and perhaps the Labor of capturing the Cretan Bull is hinted at in the encounter with Phaethon).

The subject matter and description of landscape may have led to the poem's inclusion among works of Theocritus, but the testimony of the few manuscripts that attribute it to him is not to be relied on; linguistic evidence suggests some other author of a similar date. The garrulously helpful countryman owes something to Eumaeus in the Odys-

sey, *but three Callimachean characters are perhaps relevant: in related episodes of Book 1 of the* Aetia, *Heracles asked a Lindian farmer and a certain Theiodamas for food and in each case killed one of their oxen when they refused (Frr. 22, 25d Harder), and in Book 3 he lodged and conversed with the poor man Molorchus during his mission against the Nemean Lion (Frr. 54b–i).*

Criticism

Fantuzzi–Hunter, *Tradition and Innovation*, 210–15.

Gutzwiller, *Hellenistic Epyllion*, 30–38.

Hunter, R. "Before and after Epic: Theocritus (?), *Idyll* 25." In Harder, Regtuit, and Wakker, *Genre*, 115–32.

Kurz, A. *Le Corpus Theocriteum et Homère. Un problème d'authenticité (Idylle 25).* Bern, 1982.

Serrao, G. *Il carme XXV del Corpus Teocriteo = Quaderni della RCCM* 4 (1962).

Schmitz, T. A. "Herakles in Bits and Pieces: *Id.* 25 in the *Corpus Theocriteum.*" In Baumbach and Bär, *Companion*, 259–82.

Zanker, G. "Pictorial Description as a Supplement for Narrative. The Labor of Augeas' Stables in the *Heracles Leontophonos.*" *AJPh* 117 (1996): 411–23.

Τὸν δ' ὁ γέρων προσέειπε βοῶν ἐπίουρος ἀροτρεύς,
παυσάμενος ἔργοιο τό οἱ μετὰ χερσὶν ἔκειτο·
"ἔκ τοι, ξεῖνε, πρόφρων μυθήσομαι ὅσσ' ἐρεείνεις,
Ἑρμέω ἀζόμενος δεινὴν ὄπιν εἰνοδίοιο·
5 τὸν γάρ φασι μέγιστον ἐπουρανίων κεχολῶσθαι,
εἴ κεν ὁδοῦ ζαχρεῖον ἀνήνηταί τις ὁδίτην.
ποίμναι μὲν βασιλῆος ἐΰτριχες Αὐγείαο
οὐ πᾶσαι βόσκονται ἴαν βόσιν οὐδ' ἕνα χῶρον·
ἀλλ' αἱ μέν ῥα νέμονται ἐπ' ὄχθαις ἀμφ' Ἐλισοῦ-
ντος,
10 αἱ δ' ἱερὸν θείοιο παρὰ ῥόον Ἀλφειοῖο,
αἱ δ' ἐπὶ Βουπρασίου πολυβότρυος, αἱ δὲ καὶ ὧδε·
χωρὶς δὲ σηκοί σφι τετυγμένοι εἰσὶν ἑκάσταις.
αὐτὰρ βουκολίοισι περιπλήθουσί περ ἔμπης
πάντεσσιν νομοὶ ὧδε τεθηλότες αἰὲν ἔασι
15 Μηνίου ἂμ μέγα τῖφος, ἐπεὶ μελιηδέα ποίην
λειμῶνες θαλέθουσιν ὑπόδροσοι εἰαμεναί τε
εἰς ἅλις, ἥ ῥα βόεσσι μένος κεραῇσιν ἀέξει.
αὐλις δέ σφισιν ἥδε τεῆς ἐπὶ δεξιὰ χειρός
φαίνεται εὖ μάλα πᾶσι πέρην ποταμοῖο ῥέοντος

19 πᾶσι Meineke: πᾶσα M

IDYLL 25

And[1] the old plowman, guardian of the cattle, stopped the work he had in hand and replied, "Stranger, I shall be happy to tell you whatever you ask, out of reverence for the awesome power of Hermes protector of travelers, who they say is most angry of all the gods if someone refuses to help a traveler who needs to find his way. The fleecy flocks of King Augeas do not graze in a single pasture or in a single place: some feed on the banks on each side of the river Helisous, others by the holy streams of divine Alpheus,[2] others in wine-producing Buprasium, and others in this area; and separate sheepfolds are made for each flock. As for the cattle, in spite of their teeming numbers there are always lush pasture lands for them all here by the great lake of Menius;[3] the dewy fields and water meadows produce in abundance honey-sweet grass which makes the horned cattle grow strong. The byres for them all can be seen on your right beyond the flowing river:[4]

[1] "And" and "replied" imply a preceding narrative. Some scholars feel that a passage is missing, others that the poem experiments with an effect of fragmentation (cf. on *Id.* 18.1). In some manuscripts this first section is titled Ἡρακλῆς πρὸς ἀγροῖκον (Heracles and the Countryman).

[2] Rivers in Elis (ps.-Apollod. *Bibl.* 2.5.5). Heracles diverted the Alpheus to purge Augeas' byres.

[3] The river of the town of Elis (Paus. 6.26.1). Pausanias says this was the river with which the byres were cleansed (5.1.10).

[4] Another glance toward the cleansing.

20 κείνῃ, ὅθι πλατάνιστοι ἐπηεταναὶ πεφύασι
χλωρή τ᾽ ἀγριέλαιος, Ἀπόλλωνος νομίοιο
ἱερὸν ἁγνόν, ξεῖνε, τελειοτάτοιο θεοῖο.
εὐθὺς δὲ σταθμοὶ περιμήκεες ἀγροιώταις
δέδμηνθ᾽, οἳ βασιλῆι πολὺν καὶ ἀθέσφατον ὄλβον
25 ῥυόμεθ᾽ ἐνδυκέως, τριπόλοις σπόρον ἐν νειοῖσιν
ἔσθ᾽ ὅτε βάλλοντες καὶ τετραπόλοισιν ὁμοίως.
οὔρους μὴν ἴσασι φυτοσκάφοι οἱ πολύεργοι,
ἐς ληνοὺς δ᾽ ἱκνεῦνται ἐπὴν θέρος ὥριον ἔλθῃ.
πᾶν γὰρ δὴ πεδίον τόδ᾽ ἐπίφρονος Αὐγείαο,
30 πυροφόροι τε γύαι καὶ ἀλωαὶ δενδρήεσσαι,
μέχρις ἐπ᾽ ἐσχατιὰς πολυπίδακος Ἀκρωρείης,
ἃς ἡμεῖς ἔργοισιν ἐποιχόμεθα πρόπαν ἦμαρ,
ἡ δίκη οἰκήων οἷσιν βίος ἔπλετ᾽ ἐπ᾽ ἀγροῦ.
ἀλλὰ σύ πέρ μοι ἔνισπε, τό τοι καὶ κέρδιον αὐτῷ
35 ἔσσεται, οὗτινος ὧδε κεχρημένος εἰλήλουθας.
ἠέ τι Αὐγείην ἢ καὶ δμώων τινὰ κείνου
δίζεαι οἵ οἱ ἔασιν; ἐγὼ δέ κέ τοι σάφα εἰδὼς
πάντα μάλ᾽ ἐξείποιμ᾽, ἐπεὶ οὐ σέ γέ φημι κακῶν ἔξ
ἔμμεναι οὐδὲ κακοῖσιν ἐοικότα φύμεναι αὐτόν,
40 οἷόν τοι μέγα εἶδος ἐπιπρέπει. ἦ ῥά νυ παῖδες
ἀθανάτων τοιοίδε μετὰ θνητοῖσιν ἔασι."
    Τὸν δ᾽ ἀπαμειβόμενος προσέφη Διὸς ἄλκιμος υἱός·
"ναί, γέρον, Αὐγείην ἐθέλοιμί κεν ἀρχὸν Ἐπειῶν
εἰσιδέειν· τοῦ γάρ με καὶ ἤγαγεν ἐνθάδε χρειώ.
45 εἰ δ᾽ ὁ μὲν ἂρ κατὰ ἄστυ μένει παρὰ οἷσι πολίταις

dense plane trees are growing there, and green wild olives, forming a holy shrine, stranger, for Apollo of the flocks,[5] a god of perfect power. Nearby are built the extensive lodgings for the country people who carefully look after our king's vast estate, sowing the seed on the fallow land that has been plowed three or four times.[6] The distant parts[7] of his property are known to the laborers who tend his trees, though they come in to the winepresses[8] when the summer season arrives. The whole of this plain belongs to wise Augeas, all the land that bears barley and the wooded orchards, as far as distant Acrorea with its many springs; it is there that we busy ourselves all day with our tasks, as is right and proper for serfs who get their livelihood in the country. But do tell me—it will be to your advantage— whom have you come to see? Is it Augeas or one of his servants? I have the knowledge and can tell you everything. *You*, I think, are not from a baseborn family and you do not have a humble look yourself, so imposing is your presence. Children of the gods stand out among mortals just as you do."

The valiant son of Zeus spoke in reply: "Yes, old man; it is Augeas, leader of the Epeans,[9] that I should like to see; in fact, it is my need to see him that has brought me here. If he is in residence in town among the citizens and is taking

---

[5] A well-known title of Apollo in cult.

[6] Land left fallow for a year was turned as often as possible (Hes. *Op.* 462–63).

[7] Sc., in case you wish to know about them.

[8] Centrally located, near the palace.

[9] The Epeans were an ancient people of Elis (Hom. *Il.* 2.615–19), where Augeas was king.

δήμου κηδόμενος, διὰ δὲ κρίνουσι θέμιστας,
δμώων δή τινα, πρέσβυ, σύ μοι φράσον ἡγεμονεύ-
      σας,
ὅστις ἐπ᾽ ἀγρῶν τῶνδε γεραίτατος αἰσυμνήτης,
ᾧ κε τὸ μὲν εἴποιμι, τὸ δ᾽ ἐκ φαμένοιο πυθοίμην.

50 ἄλλου δ᾽ ἄλλον ἔθηκε θεὸς ἐπιδευέα φωτῶν."
      Τὸν δ᾽ ὁ γέρων ἐξαῦτις ἀμείβετο δῖος ἀροτρεύς
"ἀθανάτων, ὦ ξεῖνε, φραδῇ τινὸς ἐνθάδ᾽ ἱκάνεις,
ὥς τοι πᾶν ὃ θέλεις αἶψα χρέος ἐκτετέλεσται.
ὧδε γὰρ Αὐγείης, υἱὸς φίλος Ἡελίοιο,

55 σφωιτέρῳ σὺν παιδί, βίῃ Φυλῆος ἀγαυοῦ,
χθιζός γ᾽ εἰλήλουθεν ἀπ᾽ ἄστεος ἤμασι πολλοῖς
κτῆσιν ἐποψόμενος, ἥ οἱ νήριθμος ἐπ᾽ ἀγρῶν.
ὥς που καὶ βασιλεῦσιν ἐείδεται ἐν φρεσὶν ᾖσιν
αὐτοῖς κηδομένοισι σαώτερος ἔμμεναι οἶκος.

60 ἀλλ᾽ ἴομεν μάλα πρός μιν· ἐγὼ δέ τοι ἡγεμονεύσω
αὖλιν ἐφ᾽ ἡμετέρην, ἵνα κεν τέτμοιμεν ἄνακτα."
      Ὣς εἰπὼν ἡγεῖτο, νόῳ δ᾽ ὅγε πόλλ᾽ ἐμενοίνα,
δέρμα τε θηρὸς ὁρῶν χειροπληθῆ τε κορύνην,
ὁππόθεν ὁ ξεῖνος· μεμόνει δέ μιν αἰὲν ἔρεσθαι·

65 ἂψ δ᾽ ὄκνῳ ποτὶ χεῖλος ἐλάμβανε μῦθον ἰόντα,
μή τί οἱ οὐ κατὰ καιρὸν ἔπος προτιμυθήσαιτο
σπερχομένου· χαλεπὸν δ᾽ ἑτέρου νόον ἴδμεναι ἀνδρός.
τοὺς δὲ κύνας προσιόντας ἀπόπροθεν αἶψ᾽ ἐνόησαν,
ἀμφότερον ὀδμῇ τε χροὸς δούπῳ τε ποδοῖιν·

64 μεμόνει Buttmann: μέμονε m: μέμοινε m: μέμαεν m

346

care of his people as they administer justice, then lead on,
old man, and point out one of his servants, the most senior
bailiff on this estate, so that I may tell him what I have to
say, and find out his answer. God has made mortals depend
on one another."[10]

The godlike[11] plowman answered him in return, "Stranger,
some god must have prompted your coming: everything
that you want has come to pass at once. Only yesterday
Augeas, the dear child of Helius, together with his son, the
glorious and valiant Phyleus, came here from the city for
a lengthy[12] inspection of the property he has in the coun-
try. Kings no doubt think their estates best safeguarded
when they take an interest themselves. We shall go to
him:[13] I shall lead you to my farm, where we can meet the
king."

With these words he led the way. As he looked at the lion
skin and the mighty club, he kept wondering where the
stranger might be from; he kept wanting to ask him, too,
but he would restrain himself just as the words were on
his lips, not wanting to obtrude on a man intent on his
purpose—it is hard to know someone else's mind. The
dogs sensed them from a distance as soon as they ap-
proached, by both their scent and the sound of their foot-

---

[10] Picking up the old man's closing words (40–41). Heracles
ends by affirming that even he must rely on others.

[11] Imitating Homer's epithet "godlike" for the swineherd Eu-
maeus in the *Odyssey*. The following scene evokes Odysseus'
arrival at the hut of Eumaeus in Book 14.

[12] Lit., "in many days." Or, perhaps, "came here after an ab-
sence of many days."   [13] Or, "Let us go. . . . "

70 θεσπέσιον δ᾽ ὑλάοντες ἐπέδραμον ἄλλοθεν ἄλλος
Ἀμφιτρυωνιάδῃ Ἡρακλέι· τὸν δὲ γέροντα
ἀχρεῖον κλάζον τε περίσσαινόν θ᾽ ἑτέρωθεν.
τοὺς μὲν ὅγε λάεσσιν ἀπὸ χθονὸς ὅσσον ἀείρων
φευγέμεν ἂψ ὀπίσω δειδίσσετο, τρηχὺ δὲ φωνῇ
75 ἠπείλει μάλα πᾶσιν, ἐρητύσασκε δ᾽ ὑλαγμοῦ,
χαίρων ἐν φρεσὶν ᾗσιν, ὁθούνεκεν αὖλιν ἔρυντο
αὐτοῦ γ᾽ οὐ παρεόντος· ἔπος δ᾽ ὅγε τοῖον ἔειπεν·
"ὢ πόποι, οἷον τοῦτο θεοὶ ποίησαν ἄνακτες
θηρίον ἀνθρώποισι μετέμμεναι, ὡς ἐπιμηθές.
80 εἴ οἱ καὶ φρένες ὧδε νοήμονες ἔνδοθεν ἦσαν,
ᾔδει δ᾽ ᾧ τε χρὴ χαλεπαινέμεν ᾧ τε καὶ οὐκί,
οὐκ ἄν οἱ θηρῶν τις ἐδήρισεν περὶ τιμῆς·
νῦν δὲ λίην ζάκοτόν τε καὶ ἀρρηνὲς γένετ᾽ αὔτως."
ἦ ῥα, καὶ ἐσσυμένως ποτὶ ταύλιον ἷξον ἰόντες.

85 Ἥλιος μὲν ἔπειτα ποτὶ ζόφον ἔτραπεν ἵππους
δείελον ἦμαρ ἄγων· τὰ δ᾽ ἐπήλυθε πίονα μῆλα
ἐκ βοτάνης ἀνιόντα μετ᾽ αὔλιά τε σηκούς τε.
αὐτὰρ ἔπειτα βόες μάλα μυρίαι ἄλλαι ἐπ᾽ ἄλλαις
ἐρχόμεναι φαίνονθ᾽ ὡσεὶ νέφη ὑδατόεντα,
90 ἄσσα τ᾽ ἐν οὐρανῷ εἶσιν ἐλαυνόμενα προτέρωσε
ἠὲ Νότοιο βίῃ ἠὲ Θρῃκὸς Βορέαο·
τῶν μέν τ᾽ οὔτις ἀριθμὸς ἐν ἠέρι γίνετ᾽ ἰόντων,
οὐδ᾽ ἄνυσις· τόσα γάρ τε μετὰ προτέροισι κυλίνδει
ἲς ἀνέμου, τὰ δέ τ᾽ ἄλλα κορύσσεται αὖτις ἐπ᾽ ἄλλοις·

steps. Barking furiously, they ran up to Heracles son of Amphitryon, while from all directions they barked excitedly[14] at the old man and fawned on him. Just by picking up some stones from the ground he scared them so that they fled back again, and by threatening them all in a harsh voice he stopped their barking; but inwardly he was glad that they guarded his house while he was away. His words were these: "My, what a creature this is that the gods our masters have made live among us, and how lacking in forethought! If their intelligence matched their keenness and they knew whom they should quarrel with and whom not, no other animal would be able to compete with their reputation; but as it is they are just too bad-tempered and aggressive." He spoke, and at a brisk pace they came to the farmstead.

The sun[15] then turned his chariot to the west, bringing in the late afternoon, and the fat flocks came up from pasture to reach their farms and pens. After that, countless cattle in thousands upon thousands came into view, like clouds full of rain that pass through the sky driven onward by the force of the south wind or of Thracian Boreas; innumerable, they pass ceaselessly above, so many does the wind's power roll along behind those in front; and more and more pile on, one after another. Just so many herds constantly

---

[14] Lit., "uselessly," "needlessly." [15] In some manuscripts this part has the title Ἐπιπώλησις (The Inspection). Probably by now Heracles has introduced himself to the king.

---

72 κλάζον τε Reiske: κλάζοντε m: ἀλαζόν τε m
85 ἔτραπεν m: ἔτραφεν m: ἤγαγεν m

THEOCRITUS

τόσσ' αἰεὶ μετόπισθε βοῶν ἐπὶ βουκόλι' ἤει.
πᾶν δ' ἄρ' ἐνεπλήσθη πεδίον, πᾶσαι δὲ κέλευθοι
ληΐδος ἐρχομένης, στείνοντο δὲ πίονες ἀγροὶ
μυκηθμῷ, σηκοὶ δὲ βοῶν ῥεῖα πλήσθησαν
εἰλιπόδων, οἶες δὲ κατ' αὐλὰς ηὐλίζοντο.
100 ἔνθα μὲν οὔτις ἔκηλος ἀπειρεσίων περ ἐόντων
εἱστήκει παρὰ βουσὶν ἀνὴρ κεχρημένος ἔργου·
ἀλλ' ὃ μὲν ἀμφὶ πόδεσσιν ἐϋτμήτοισιν ἱμᾶσι
καλοπέδιλ' ἀράρισκε παρασταδὸν ἐγγὺς ἀμέλγειν·
ἄλλος δ' αὖ νέα τέκνα φίλας ὑπὸ μητέρας ἵει
105 πινέμεναι λιαροῖο μεμαότα πάγχυ γάλακτος·
ἄλλος ἀμόλγιον εἶχ', ἄλλος τρέφε πίονα τυρόν,
ἄλλος ἐσῆγεν ἔσω ταύρους δίχα θηλειάων.
Αὐγείης δ' ἐπὶ πάντας ἰὼν θηεῖτο βοαύλους,
ἥντινά οἱ κτεάνων κομιδὴν ἐτίθεντο νομῆες,
110 σὺν δ' υἱός τε βίη τε βαρύφρονος Ἡρακλῆος
ὡμάρτευν βασιλῆι διερχομένῳ μέγαν ὄλβον.
ἔνθα καὶ ἄρρηκτόν περ ἔχων ἐν στήθεσι θυμὸν
Ἀμφιτρυωνιάδης καὶ ἀρηρότα νωλεμὲς αἰεὶ
ἐκπάγλως θαύμαζε θεοῦ τόγε μυρίον ἔδνον
115 εἰσορόων. οὐ γάρ κεν ἔφασκέ τις οὐδὲ ἐώλπει
ἀνδρὸς ληΐδ' ἑνὸς τόσσην ἔμεν οὐδὲ δέκ' ἄλλων
οἵτε πολύρρηνες πάντων ἔσαν ἐκ βασιλήων.
Ἥλιος δ' ᾧ παιδὶ τόγ' ἔξοχον ὤπασε δῶρον,
ἀφνειὸν μήλοις περὶ πάντων ἔμμεναι ἀνδρῶν,

103 παρασταδὸν Stephanus: περιστ- m: παριστ- m
114 θεοῦ Wilamowitz: -ων M   τόγε Cal.: τότε M

350

kept coming on behind those in front. All the plain, all the paths were filled with the advancing cattle, and the fertile fields were crowded[16] with their bellowing; the stalls were soon filled with shambling cattle, and the sheep settled in their folds.

Then not a single man, though their numbers were countless, stood idly by the cattle with no task to perform. One would fit clogs to his feet with well-cut leather straps so that he could walk around the animals while milking;[17] another would set the young calves, eager to drink the warm milk, under their mothers; another would hold a bucket, another would set rich cheese, and another would bring in the bulls separately from the cows. Augeas went to inspect all the stalls to see what care the shepherds took of his possessions, and in company with the king as he surveyed his great wealth went his son and the mighty and resolute Heracles. Then the son of Amphitryon, though the spirit in his breast was unbreakable and always firmly fixed, was filled with amazement when he saw the immense gift of the god. No one would have thought or imagined that the cattle of one man could be so many, or even of ten men endowed with flocks beyond all other kings. Helius had granted this splendid gift to his son, that he should be richer in cattle than all other men, and he

---

[16] Lit., "straitened," "made narrow," easy to understand of cattle but less easy of bellowing. Possibly the verb *stenoô* is used (uniquely) for *stenô*, so that the meaning is "echoed with their bellowing."   [17] These "clogs" may however be hobbles put on the cows to prevent them moving ("fitted hobbles on their feet so as to be able to stand close to them while milking").

120 καὶ ῥά οἱ αὐτὸς ὄφελλε διαμπερέως βοτὰ πάντα
    ἐς τέλος. οὐ μὲν γάρ τις ἐπήλυθε νοῦσος ἐκείνου
    βουκολίοις, αἵτ' ἔργα καταφθείρουσι νομήων,
    αἰεὶ δὲ πλέονες κερααὶ βόες, αἰὲν ἀμείνους
    ἐξ ἔτεος γίνοντο μάλ' εἰς ἔτος· ἦ γὰρ ἅπασαι

125 ζωοτόκοι τ' ἦσαν περιώσια θηλυτόκοι τε.
    ταῖς δὲ τριηκόσιοι ταῦροι συνάμ' ἐστιχόωντο
    κνήμαργοί θ' ἕλικές τε, διηκόσιοί γε μὲν ἄλλοι
    φοίνικες· πάντες δ' ἐπιβήτορες οἵγ' ἔσαν ἤδη.
    ἄλλοι δ' αὖ μετὰ τοῖσι δυώδεκα βουκολέοντο

130 ἱεροὶ Ἡελίου· χροιὴν δ' ἔσαν ἠύτε κύκνοι
    ἀργησταί, πᾶσιν δὲ μετέπρεπον εἰλιπόδεσσιν·
    οἳ καὶ ἀτιμαγέλαι βόσκοντ' ἐριθηλέα ποίην
    ἐν νομῷ· ὧδ' ἔκπαγλον ἐπὶ σφίσι γαυριόωντο.
    καὶ ῥ' ὁπότ' ἐκ λασίοιο θοοὶ προγενοίατο θῆρες

135 ἐς πεδίον δρυμοῖο βοῶν ἕνεκ' ἀγροτεράων,
    πρῶτοι τοίγε μάχηνδε κατὰ χροὸς ἤισαν ὀδμήν,
    δεινὸν δ' ἐβρυχῶντο φόνον λεύσσοντε προσώπῳ.
    τῶν μέν τε προφέρεσκε βίηφί τε καὶ σθένεϊ ᾧ
    ἠδ' ὑπεροπλίῃ Φαέθων μέγας, ὅν ῥα βοτῆρες

140 ἀστέρι πάντες ἔισκον, ὁθούνεκα πολλὸν ἐν ἄλλοις
    βουσὶν ἰὼν λάμπεσκεν, ἀρίζηλος δ' ἐτέτυκτο.
    ὃς δή τοι σκύλος αὖον ἰδὼν χαροποῖο λέοντος
    αὐτῷ ἔπειτ' ἐπόρουσεν εὐσκόπῳ Ἡρακλῆι
    χρίμψασθαι ποτὶ πλευρὰ κάρη στιβαρόν τε μέτωπον.

145 τοῦ μὲν ἄναξ προσιόντος ἐδράξατο χειρὶ παχείῃ
    σκαιοῦ ἄφαρ κέραος, κατὰ δ' αὐχένα νέρθ' ἐπὶ γαίης
    κλάσσε βαρύν περ ἐόντα, πάλιν δέ μιν ὦσεν ὀπίσσω

himself continually kept strong all the stock throughout
their lives. No disease visited his herds of the sort that ruin
shepherds' efforts: his horned cattle were always increas-
ing and improving from year to year; and all the cows had
female calves without a single still birth. Ranged with the
cows were three hundred black bulls with white legs and
two hundred others with tawny hides; these were already
all of mating age. Besides these, twelve others were graz-
ing, sacred to Helius,[18] white in color like swans, and they
stood out among the rest of the shambling cattle. They
grazed on the rich grass in their pasture apart from the
herds, so great was their confidence in their own strength.
When swift wild beasts came from the rough woodland
into the plain heading for the cattle out at pasture, these
bulls would scent them and rush to battle with terrific
bellowing and murderous looks. Huge Phaethon[19] stood
out among them for his power, strength and aggression;
the herdsmen all said he was like a star, because as he went
among the other cattle he shone out brightly and was clear
to see. When he caught sight of the dry skin of the grim
lion, he hurtled toward Heracles—who was not off his
guard—to strike his powerful head and brow against his
ribs. But as he approached, the hero instantly seized hold
of the left horn with his stout hand and in spite of its
weight bent the neck down to the ground, pushing him
backward by pressing with his shoulder, while the muscles,

[18] Probably their number represents the months of the year.
[19] "Shining," epithet of the Sun, and so suitable for an animal
sacred to him.

ὤμῳ ἐπιβρίσας· ὁ δέ οἱ περὶ νεῦρα τανυσθεὶς
μυῶν ἐξ ὑπάτοιο βραχίονος ὀρθὸς ἀνέστη.
150 θαύμαζον δ᾽ αὐτός τε ἄναξ υἱός τε δαΐφρων
Φυλεὺς οἵ τ᾽ ἐπὶ βουσὶ κορωνίσι βουκόλοι ἄνδρες,
Ἀμφιτρυωνιάδαο βίην ὑπέροπλον ἰδόντες.

Τὼ δ᾽ εἰς ἄστυ λιπόντε καταυτόθι πίονας ἀγροὺς
ἐστιχέτην, Φυλεύς τε βίη θ᾽ Ἡρακληείη.
155 λαοφόρου δ᾽ ἐπέβησαν ὅθι πρώτιστα κελεύθου,
λεπτὴν καρπαλίμοισι τρίβον ποσὶν ἐξανύσαντες
ἥ ῥα δι᾽ ἀμπελεῶνος ἀπὸ σταθμῶν τετάνυστο
οὔτι λίην ἀρίσημος ἐν ὕλῃ χλωρῇ ἐούσῃ,
τῇ μὲν ἄρα προσέειπε Διὸς γόνον ὑψίστοιο
160 Αὐγείω φίλος υἱὸς ἔθεν μετόπισθεν ἰόντα,
ἦκα παρακλίνας κεφαλὴν κατὰ δεξιὸν ὦμον·
"ξεῖνε, πάλαι τινὰ πάγχυ σέθεν πέρι μῦθον ἀκούσας,
εἰ περὶ σεῦ, σφετέρῃσιν ἐνὶ φρεσὶ βάλλομαι ἄρτι.
ἤλυθε γὰρ στείχων τις ἀπ᾽ Ἄργεος—ἦν νέος ἀκμήν—
165 ἐνθάδ᾽ Ἀχαιὸς ἀνὴρ Ἑλίκης ἐξ ἀγχιάλοιο,
ὃς δή τοι μυθεῖτο καὶ ἐν πλεόνεσσιν Ἐπειῶν
οὕνεκεν Ἀργείων τις ἔθεν παρεόντος ὄλεσσε
θηρίον, αἰνολέοντα, κακὸν τέρας ἀγροιώταις,
κοίλην αὖλιν ἔχοντα Διὸς Νεμέοιο παρ᾽ ἄλσος.
170 'οὐκ οἶδ᾽ ἀτρεκέως ἢ Ἄργεος ἐξ ἱεροῖο
αὐτόθεν ἢ Τίρυνθα νέμων πόλιν ἠὲ Μυκήνην.'

163 εἰ περὶ σεῦ Wilamowitz: ὡσεί περ m: ὡς εἴπερ m
164 ἦν Legrand: ὡς M

354

stretched over his sinews, stood out tautly at the top of his arm. The king himself and his wise son Phyleus and the herdsmen of the horned cattle were amazed to see the vast power of the son of Amphitryon.

Then[20] Phyleus and the mighty Heracles left the fertile fields and made for the city. As soon as they had set foot on the path, passing with swift steps over the narrow way which stretched from the cattle pens through a vineyard and which was not easy to make out in the greenery,[21] there the dear son of Augeas, turning his head a little to one side over his right shoulder, addressed the son of Zeus most high, who was walking behind him: "Stranger, I heard long ago a tale about you—I have just been reminding myself of it. When I was still quite young there arrived here an Achaean man from the coastal town of Helice,[22] traveling from Argos. He told many of the Epeans besides myself how he had been present when an Argive man had killed a wild beast, a terrible lion, a scourge of the country people, which had its hollow lair by the sacred grove of Zeus at Nemea.[23] 'I do not know for sure whether he was from holy Argos itself or whether he lived in the city of Tiryns or in Mycenae,' he said; and, if

[20] The third scene, which has no title in the manuscripts, begins here. The reason for Phyleus and Heracles traveling together is not explained. They may be going into exile: according to ps.-Apollodorus, Augeas banished them both when Phyleus took the side of Heracles in a quarrel about payment for the cleansing (2.5.5).   [21] It is not clear why the path should not be easy to make out or what greenery is meant.

[22] A town on the Corinthian Gulf, on the coast of northern Achaea.   [23] A town east of Elis.

ὣς κεῖνος ἀγόρευε· γένος δέ μιν εἶναι ἔφασκεν,
εἰ ἐτεόν περ ἐγὼ μιμνήσκομαι, ἐκ Περσῆος.
ἔλπομαι οὐχ ἕτερον τόδε τλήμεναι Αἰγιαλήων
175 ἠὲ σέ, δέρμα δὲ θηρὸς ἀριφραδέως ἀγορεύει
χειρῶν καρτερὸν ἔργον, ὅ τοι περὶ πλευρὰ καλύπτει.
εἴπ' ἄγε νῦν μοι πρῶτον, ἵνα γνώω κατὰ θυμόν,
ἥρως, εἴτ' ἐτύμως μαντεύομαι εἴτε καὶ οὐκί,
εἰ σύγ' ἐκεῖνος ὃν ἧμιν ἀκουόντεσσιν ἔειπεν
180 οὔξ Ἑλίκηθεν Ἀχαιός, ἐγὼ δέ σε φράζομαι ὀρθῶς.
εἰπὲ δ' ὅπως ὀλοὸν τόδε θηρίον αὐτὸς ἔπεφνες,
ὅππως τ' εὔυδρον Νεμέης εἰσήλυθε χῶρον·
οὐ μὲν γάρ κε τοσόνδε κατ' Ἀπίδα κνώδαλον εὕροις
ἱμείρων ἰδέειν, ἐπεὶ οὐ μάλα τηλίκα βόσκει,
185 ἀλλ' ἄρκτους τε σύας τε λύκων τ' ὀλοφώιον ἔθνος.
τῷ καὶ θαυμάζεσκον ἀκούοντες τότε μῦθον·
οἱ δέ νυ καὶ ψεύδεσθαι ὁδοιπόρον ἀνέρ' ἔφαντο
γλώσσης μαψιδίοιο χαριζόμενον παρεοῦσιν."
Ὣς εἰπὼν μέσσης ἐξηρώησε κελεύθου
190 Φυλεύς, ὄφρα κίουσιν ἅμα σφίσιν ἄρκιος εἴη
καί ῥά τε ῥηίτερον φαμένου κλύοι Ἡρακλῆος,
ὅς μιν ὁμαρτήσας τοίῳ προσελέξατο μύθῳ·
"ὦ Αὐγηιάδη, τὸ μὲν ὅττι με πρῶτον ἀνήρευ,
αὐτὸς καὶ μάλα ῥεῖα κατὰ στάθμην ἐνόησας.
195 ἀμφὶ δέ σοι τὰ ἕκαστα λέγοιμί κε τοῦδε πελώρου
ὅππως ἐκράανθεν, ἐπεὶ λελίησαι ἀκούειν,

185 ἔθνος Van Lennep: ἔρνος M

356

I remember rightly, he told us that the man was descended from Perseus.[24] I do not think that any of the Aegialeis[25] other than you could have had such daring; and the animal skin that covers your sides clearly bears witness to the deed your hands have done. Come, tell me now, hero, first of all—so that I may know for sure whether or not I am guessing correctly—whether you are the man whose tale the Achaean from Helice told us, and whether I recognize you rightly. He told us how you killed this dreadful creature on your own, and how it had come to the well-watered country of Nemea. Certainly in the Apian land[26] you could never find such a monstrous beast even if you felt the urge to see one: Apia does not maintain creatures of such a size, but only bears, boars and the destructive race of wolves. For that reason those who heard the story were amazed at the time, and some even said that the traveler was lying just to please his audience with empty talk."

With these words Phyleus moved aside from the middle of the path so that there could be room for them both to walk together and he could hear more easily what Heracles had to say. Heracles came by his side and addressed him with these words: "Son of Augeas, as for your first question, you have easily and accurately found the answer yourself. I shall give you an account in detail of what happened with this[27] beast, since you are keen to hear the

[24] Cf. *Id.* 24.73n.   [25] Aegialeia (Coastal Land) is an old term for Achaea (Paus. 5.1.1, 7.1.1); here it seems to be used less specifically for "Greek" (cf. Euphor. Fr. 83 Lightfoot).

[26] Old word for the Peloponnese.

[27] He indicates his lion skin.

νόσφιν γ᾿ ἢ ὅθεν ἦλθε· τὸ γὰρ πολέων περ ἐόντων
Ἀργείων οὐδείς κεν ἔχοι σάφα μυθήσασθαι·
οἷον δ᾿ ἀθανάτων τιν᾿ ἐίσκομεν ἀνδράσι πῆμα
200 ἱρῶν μηνίσαντα Φορωνήεσσιν ἐφεῖναι.
πάντας γὰρ πίσηας ἐπικλύζων ποταμὸς ὣς
λὶς ἄμοτον κεράιζε, μάλιστα δὲ Βεμβιναίους,
οἳ ἔθεν ἀγχόμοροι ναῖον ἄτλητα παθόντες.
τὸν μὲν ἐμοὶ πρώτιστα τελεῖν ἐπέταξεν ἄεθλον
205 Εὐρυσθεύς, κτεῖναι δέ μ᾿ ἐφίετο θηρίον αἰνόν.
αὐτὰρ ἐγὼ κέρας ὑγρὸν ἑλὼν κοίλην τε φαρέτρην
ἰῶν ἐμπλείην νεόμην, ἑτέρηφι δὲ βάκτρον
εὐπαγὲς αὐτόφλοιον ἐπηρεφέος κοτίνοιο
ἔμμητρον, τὸ μὲν αὐτὸς ὑπὸ ζαθέῳ Ἑλικῶνι
210 εὑρὼν σὺν πυκινῇσιν ὁλοσχερὲς ἔσπασα ῥίζαις.
αὐτὰρ ἐπεὶ τὸν χῶρον ὅθι λὶς ἦεν ἵκανον,
δὴ τότε τόξον ἑλὼν στρεπτὴν ἐπέλασσα κορώνῃ
νευρειήν, περὶ δ᾿ ἰὸν ἐχέστονον εἶθαρ ἔβησα.
πάντῃ δ᾿ ὄσσε φέρων ὀλοὸν τέρας ἐσκοπίαζον,
215 εἴ μιν ἐσαθρήσαιμι πάρος γ᾿ ἐμὲ κεῖνον ἰδέσθαι.
ἤματος ἦν τὸ μεσηγύ, καὶ οὐδέπω ἴχνια τοῖο
φρασθῆναι δυνάμην οὐδ᾿ ὠρυθμοῖο πυθέσθαι.
οὐδὲ μὲν ἀνθρώπων τις ἔην ἐπὶ βουσὶ καὶ ἔργοις
φαινόμενος σπορίμοιο δι᾿ αὔλακος ὅντιν᾿ ἐροίμην,
220 ἀλλὰ κατὰ σταθμοὺς χλωρὸν δέος εἶχεν ἕκαστον.
οὐ μὴν πρὶν πόδας ἔσχον ὄρος τανύφυλλον ἐρευνῶν

212 στρεπτὴν Brodaeus: -τῇ M
216 οὐδέπω C. Hartung: οὐδ᾿ ὅπῃ m: οὐδενὸς m

story; but I cannot tell you where it came from. The Argives may be many, but none of them could give you a satisfactory account: we can only guess that one of the immortal gods was angry about sacrifices and let it loose upon the people of Phoroneus.[28] Like a river in flood, the lion continually ravaged those who lived in the lowlands, and especially the people of Bembina,[29] who lived nearby and whose sufferings were intolerable. That was the first task which Eurystheus commanded me to perform: he ordered me to kill the dreadful creature. Off I went, taking my supple bow and my hollow quiver full of arrows, and in the other hand my club of spreading wild olive, solid, unseasoned, not stripped of its bark, which I had found myself under holy Helicon[30] and had pulled up whole with its mass of roots. When I reached the place where the lion was, I took my bow, fitted the twisted string into the notch, and placed on it at once a grief-bringing arrow. Casting my eyes in every direction, I kept looking out for the dreadful monster in the hope that I might see him before he saw me.

"It was the middle of the day, and I had not yet been able to spot his tracks or hear his roar; in all that cultivated land there was not a single person herding cattle or farming whom I could ask: pale fear kept each man penned at home. But I did not slacken my pace as I searched the leafy mountainside until I spotted him and immediately

[28] The Argive Phoroneus was grandfather of Argos, after whom the area was named (Paus. 2.16.1).

[29] A village near Nemea (Str. 8.6.19; Steph. Byz. s.v.).

[30] A mountain in southwestern Boeotia, sacred to the Muses.

πρὶν ἰδέειν ἀλκῆς τε μεταυτίκα πειρηθῆναι.
ἤτοι ὃ μὲν σήραγγα προδείελος ἔστιχεν εἰς ἥν,
βεβρωκὼς κρειῶν τε καὶ αἵματος, ἀμφὶ δὲ χαίτας
225 αὐχμηρὰς πεπάλακτο φόνῳ χαροπόν τε πρόσωπον
στήθεά τε, γλώσσῃ δὲ περιλιχμᾶτο γένειον.
αὐτὰρ ἐγὼ θάμνοισιν ἄφαρ σκιεροῖσιν ἐκρύφθην
ἐν τρίβῳ ὑλήεντι δεδεγμένος ὁππόθ' ἵκοιτο,
καὶ βάλον ἆσσον ἰόντος ἀριστερὸν εἰς κενεῶνα
230 τηυσίως· οὐ γάρ τι βέλος διὰ σαρκὸς ὄλισθεν
ὀκριόεν, χλωρῇ δὲ παλίσσυτον ἔμπεσε ποίῃ.
αὐτὰρ ὁ κρᾶτα δαφοινὸν ἀπὸ χθονὸς ὦκ' ἐπάειρε
θαμβήσας, πάντῃ δὲ διέδρακεν ὀφθαλμοῖσι
σκεπτόμενος, λαμυροὺς δὲ χανὼν ὑπέδειξεν ὀδόντας.
235 τῷ δ' ἐγὼ ἄλλον ὀιστὸν ἀπὸ νευρῆς προΐαλλον,
ἀσχαλόων ὅ μοι ὁ πρὶν ἐτώσιος ἔκφυγε χειρός·
μεσσηγὺς δ' ἔβαλον στηθέων, ὅθι πνεύμονος ἕδρη.
ἀλλ' οὐδ' ὣς ὑπὸ βύρσαν ἔδυ πολυώδυνος ἰός,
ἀλλ' ἔπεσε προπάροιθε ποδῶν ἀνεμώλιος αὔτως.
240 τὸ τρίτον αὖ μέλλεσκον ἀσώμενος ἐν φρεσὶν αἰνῶς
αὐερύειν· ὁ δέ μ' εἶδε περιγληνώμενος ὄσσοις
θὴρ ἄμοτος, μακρὴν δὲ περ' ἰγνύῃσιν ἕλιξε
κέρκον, ἄφαρ δὲ μάχης ἐμνήσατο· πᾶς δέ οἱ αὐχὴν
θυμοῦ ἐνεπλήσθη, πυρσαὶ δ' ἔφριξαν ἔθειραι
245 σκυζομένῳ, κυρτὴ δὲ ῥάχις γένετ' ἠΰτε τόξον,
πάντοθεν εἰλυθέντος ὑπὸ λαγόνας τε καὶ ἰξύν.
ὡς δ' ὅταν ἁρματοπηγὸς ἀνὴρ πολέων ἴδρις ἔργων
ὄρπηκας κάμπτῃσιν ἐρινεοῦ εὐκεάτοιο,
θάλψας ἐν πυρὶ πρῶτον, ἐπαξονίῳ κύκλα δίφρῳ·

made test of my strength.[31] Just before evening he was
making for his cave after a meal of blood and flesh; his
shaggy hide, his grim face and his chest were spattered
with gore, and he was licking his chops with his tongue.
For my part, I quickly hid in shady undergrowth on a
woodland path and lay in wait for him to approach. When
he came near I shot him in the left flank—in vain, since
my sharp arrow did not pierce his flesh, but fell back on
the green grass. Shocked, he quickly raised his gory head
from the ground and glared in every direction, and open-
ing his mouth he showed his ravening teeth. I launched
another arrow at him from my bowstring, annoyed that the
first had left my hand in vain. I hit him in the middle of
his chest, the seat of the lungs, but even then the cruel
arrow did not penetrate his hide, falling at his feet harm-
lessly and in vain. Feeling very much aggrieved, I was
about to draw my bow for the third time when the savage
brute, casting his eyes all around, caught sight of me and
coiled his long tail around his hindquarters; he intended
to fight at once. His whole neck swelled with anger, his
tawny mane bristled with fury, and his back bent like a bow
as he crouched and gathered all the strength in his flanks
and loins. As when a chariot builder expert in many skills
first warms in the fire and then bends shoots of the wild

---

[31] Or, less likely, "his strength."

---

236 ὅ μοι ὁ Hermann: ὅτι μοι m: ὅς μοι m: ὥς μοι m

250 τοῦ μὲν ὑπὲκ χειρῶν ἔφυγεν τανύφλοιος ἐρινός
    καμπτόμενος, τηλοῦ δὲ μιῇ πήδησε σὺν ὁρμῇ·
    ὡς ἐπ᾽ ἐμοὶ λῖς αἰνὸς ἀπόπροθεν ἀθρόος ἆλτο
    μαιμώων χροὸς ἆσαι· ἐγὼ δ᾽ ἑτέρηφι βέλεμνα
    χειρὶ προεσχεθόμην καὶ ἀπ᾽ ὤμων δίπλακα λώπην,
255 τῇ δ᾽ ἑτέρῃ ῥόπαλον κόρσης ὕπερ αὖον ἀείρας
    ἤλασα κὰκ κεφαλῆς, διὰ δ᾽ ἄνδιχα τρηχὺν ἔαξα
    αὐτοῦ ἐπὶ λασίοιο καρήατος ἀγριέλαιον
    θηρὸς ἀμαιμακέτοιο. πέσεν δ᾽ ὅγε πρὶν ἔμ᾽ ἱκέσθαι
    ὑψόθεν ἐν γαίῃ καὶ ἐπὶ τρομεροῖς ποσὶν ἔστη
260 νευστάζων κεφαλῇ· περὶ γὰρ σκότος ὄσσε οἱ ἄμφω
    ἦλθε, βίῃ σεισθέντος ἐν ὀστέῳ ἐγκεφάλοιο.
    τὸν μὲν ἐγὼν ὀδύνῃσι παραφρονέοντα βαρείαις
    νωσάμενος, πρὶν αὖτις ὑπότροπον ἀμπνυνθῆναι,
    αὐχένος ἀρρήκτοιο παρ᾽ ἰνίον ἤλασα προφθάς,
265 ῥίψας τόξον ἔραζε πολύρραπτόν τε φαρέτρην·
    ἤγχον δ᾽ ἐγκρατέως στιβαρὰς σὺν χεῖρας ἐρείσας
    ἐξόπιθεν, μὴ σάρκας ἀποδρύψῃ ὀνύχεσσι,
    πρὸς δ᾽ οὖδας πτέρνῃσι πόδας στερεῶς ἐπίεζον
    οὐραίους ἐπιβάς, μηροῖσί τε πλεύρ᾽ ἐφύλασσον,
270 μέχρι οὗ ἐξετάνυσσα βραχίοσιν ὀρθὸν ἀείρας
    ἄπνευστον, ψυχὴν δὲ πελώριος ἔλλαβεν Ἅιδης.
    καὶ τότε δὴ βούλευον ὅπως λασιαύχενα βύρσαν
    θηρὸς τεθνειῶτος ἀπὸ μελέων ἐρυσαίμην,

264 aut ἤλασα aut προφθὰς corruptum
269 μηροῖσί τε πλεύρ᾽ Briggs: πλευροῖσί τε μῆρ᾽ fere M
270 οὗ J. Hartung: οἱ m: om. m

fig, which splits easily, to make felloes to fit on the axle of
a chariot; and the smooth-barked fig in bending slips from
his grasp and with a single bound leaps far away: just so
the dreadful lion leaped headlong at me from a distance,
eager to get his fill of my flesh. I held my arrows and the
double cloak from my shoulders in front of me with one
hand, and raising my seasoned[32] club above his temple
with the other I brought it down on his skull, and there
and then I broke that hard piece of wild olive clean in
two on the stubborn beast's shaggy head. Before he could
reach me he fell in mid-leap to the ground, and stood
unsteadily on his feet; his head was dizzy, since the brain
within his skull had been shaken by the blow, and darkness
had come upon both his eyes. When I realized that the
pain was so bad that he could not think straight, I made
the first move before he could recover and attack again: I
seized[33] him by the scruff of his powerful neck, letting my
bow and stitched quiver fall to the ground; then, clasping
my strong hands together, I strangled him as hard as I
could from behind, in case he should lacerate me with his
claws. I stood on his rear feet and pressed them down hard
with my heels on the ground while keeping control of his
flanks with my thighs, until I was able to raise his lifeless
body in my arms and lay it out, as dread Hades took his
spirit.

"Next I pondered how I could strip the shaggy hide from
the body of the creature now that it was dead. The task

[32] Lit., "dry." This seems to contradict lines 207–8.
[33] ἤλασα (struck) seems inappropriate; "seized" is the mean-
ing required. The word is probably corrupt.

ἀργαλέον μάλα μόχθον, ἐπεὶ οὐκ ἔσκε σιδήρῳ
275 τμητὴ οὐδὲ λίθοις πειρωμένῳ οὐδὲ μὲν ἄλλῃ.
ἔνθα μοι ἀθανάτων τις ἐπὶ φρεσὶ θῆκε νοῆσαι
αὐτοῖς δέρμα λέοντος ἀνασχίζειν ὀνύχεσσι.
τοῖσι θοῶς ἀπέδειρα, καὶ ἀμφεθέμην μελέεσσιν
ἕρκος ἐνναλίου ταμεσίχροος ἰωχμοῖο.
280 οὗτός τοι Νεμέου γένετ᾽, ὦ φίλε, θηρὸς ὄλεθρος,
πολλὰ πάρος μήλοις τε καὶ ἀνδράσι κήδεα θέντος."

275 ἄλλῃ Wordsworth: ὕλῃ M

was a difficult one, because the hide could not be cut by someone using iron, stone or any other material.[34] Then some god made me think of cutting the lion's skin with its own claws. With these I quickly stripped it off and wrapped it round myself as protection from flesh wounds in the heat of battle.

"That, my friend, is how the destruction of the beast of Nemea came about—but not before he had caused great suffering to men and flocks."

[34] Text doubtful.

IDYLL 26

The first part of the poem briefly—perfunctorily—tells how Pentheus, king of Thebes, went to spy on the Maenads as they performed their rituals and how in consequence he was torn to pieces by his mother and aunts. In the second part the narrator disclaims any sympathy for Pentheus and hails Dionysus and his mother, Semele.

The story is familiar from the Bacchae *of Euripides, whose account Theocritus follows by and large. Like* Idylls *15–18, 22, and 24, the poem has hymnic elements. Its pious narrator and his tale against offending the god have features in common with the speakers and myths of the fifth and sixth* Hymns *of Callimachus. The detailed description of ritual action at the beginning, and the puzzling reference to punishment of children aged nine or ten, may be evidence that the poem was—or purports to have been—composed for performance at a festival of Dionysus; it will in that case have been spoken by the leader of a chorus.*

Criticism

Cairns, F. "Theocritus, *Idyll 26*." *PCPhS* 38 (1992): 1–38.

Cusset, C. *Les Bacchantes de Théocrite: texte, corps et morceaux.* Paris, 2001.

Hutchinson, *Hellenistic Poetry*, 160–62.

Vollgraff, W. "Le Péan delphique à Dionysos." *BCH* 48 (1924): 125–77.

26

Ἰνὼ καὐτονόα χἀ μαλοπάραυος Ἀγαύα
τρεῖς θιάσως ἐς ὄρος τρεῖς ἄγαγον αὐταὶ ἐοῖσαι.
χαῖ μὲν ἀμερξάμεναι λασίας δρυὸς ἄγρια φύλλα,
κισσόν τε ζώοντα καὶ ἀσφόδελον τὸν ὑπὲρ γᾶς,
5 ἐν καθαρῷ λειμῶνι κάμον δυοκαίδεκα βωμώς,
τὼς τρεῖς τᾷ Σεμέλᾳ, τὼς ἐννέα τῷ Διονύσῳ.
ἱερὰ δ᾽ ἐκ κίστας πεπονᾱμένα χερσὶν ἑλοῖσαι
εὐφάμως κατέθεντο νεοδρέπτων ἐπὶ βωμῶν,
ὡς ἐδίδαξ᾽, ὡς αὐτὸς ἐθυμάρει Διόνυσος.
10 Πενθεὺς δ᾽ ἀλιβάτω πέτρας ἄπο πάντ᾽ ἐθεώρει,
σχῖνον ἐς ἀρχαίαν καταδύς, ἐπιχώριον ἔρνος.
Αὐτονόα πράτα νιν ἀνέκραγε δεινὸν ἰδοῖσα,
σὺν δ᾽ ἐτάραξε ποσὶν μανιώδεος ὄργια Βάκχω,
ἐξαπίνας ἐπιοῖσα, τά τ᾽ οὐχ ὁρέοντι βέβαλοι.
15 μαίνετο μέν τ᾽ αὐτά, μαίνοντο δ᾽ ἄρ᾽ εὐθὺ καὶ ἄλλαι.
Πενθεὺς μὲν φεῦγεν πεφοβημένος, αἱ δ᾽ ἐδίωκον,
πέπλως ἐκ ζωστῆρος ἐς ἰγνύαν ἐρύσαισαι.
Πενθεὺς μὲν τόδ᾽ ἔειπε· "τίνος κέχρησθε, γυναῖκες";
Αὐτονόα τόδ᾽ ἔειπε· "τάχα γνώσῃ πρὶν ἀκοῦσαι."

14 τ᾽ Meineke: δ᾽ pap., M   15 ἄλλαι Ahrens: ἄλλαι M

---

[1] Or, less likely, "apple-cheeked."   [2] Mt. Cithaeron.

IDYLL 26

Ino, Autonoe and white-cheeked[1] Agave, themselves three in number, led three groups of worshippers to the mountain.[2] Some of them cut wild greenery from the densely growing oak trees, living ivy and asphodel that grows above ground,[3] and made up twelve altars in a pure meadow, three to Semele and nine to Dionysus. Taking from their box the sacred objects made with care,[4] they laid them reverently upon the altars of freshly gathered foliage, just as Dionysus himself had taught them, and just as he preferred.

Pentheus observed everything from a high rock, hidden in a mastich bush, a plant that grew in those parts. Autonoe, the first to see him, gave a dreadful yell and with a sudden movement kicked over[5] the sacred objects of frenzied Bacchus, which the profane may not see. She became frenzied herself, and at once the others too became frenzied. Pentheus fled in terror and they pursued him, hitching up their robes into their belts knee-high. Pentheus spoke: "What do you want, women?" Autonoe spoke: "You will know soon enough, and before we tell you." The

---

[3] Meaning uncertain. It is unlikely that a contrast is intended with the asphodel meadows of the underworld.

[4] Or, perhaps, "carefully molded offerings," like the shaped cakes carried in the *kistê* at the Thesmophoric festival (Ar. *Thesm.* 284–85). [5] Deliberately, it seems, so as to hide them from Pentheus' sight.

20 μάτηρ μὲν κεφαλὰν μυκήσατο παιδὸς ἑλοῖσα,
ὅσσον περ τοκάδος τελέθει μύκημα λεαίνας·
Ἰνὼ δ' ἐξέρρηξε σὺν ὠμοπλάτᾳ μέγαν ὦμον,
λὰξ ἐπὶ γαστέρα βᾶσα, καὶ Αὐτονόας ῥυθμὸς ωὑτός·
αἱ δ' ἄλλαι τὰ περισσὰ κρεανομέοντο γυναῖκες,

25 ἐς Θήβας δ' ἀφίκοντο πεφυρμέναι αἵματι πᾶσαι,
ἐξ ὄρεος πένθημα καὶ οὐ Πενθῆα φέροισαι.

Οὐκ ἀλέγω· μηδ' ἄλλος ἀπεχθομένῳ Διονύσῳ
φροντίζοι, μηδ' εἰ χαλεπώτερα τῶνδε μογήσαι,
εἴη δ' ἐνναετὴς ἢ καὶ δεκάτῳ ἐπιβαίνοι·

30 αὐτὸς δ' εὐαγέοιμι καὶ εὐαγέεσσιν ἅδοιμι.
ἐκ Διὸς αἰγιόχω τιμὰν ἔχει αἰετὸς οὕτως.
εὐσεβέων παίδεσσι τὰ λώια, δυσσεβέων δ' οὔ.

Χαίροι μὲν Διόνυσος, ὃν ἐν Δρακάνῳ νιφόεντι
Ζεὺς ὕπατος μεγάλαν ἐπιγουνίδα κάτθετο λύσας·

35 χαίροι δ' εὐειδὴς Σεμέλα καὶ ἀδελφεαὶ αὑτᾶς,
Καδμεῖαι πολλαῖς μεμελημέναι ἡρωίναις,
αἳ τόδε ἔργον ἔρεξαν ὀρίναντος Διονύσω
οὐκ ἐπιμωματόν. μηδεὶς τὰ θεῶν ὀνόσαιτο.

---

27 ἀπεχθομένῳ Ahrens: -νος pap.: -ναι M
28 τῶνδε μογήσαι pap., coni. Ahrens: τῶν δ' ἐμόγησε M

---

[6] I.e., she pulled off his other arm. [7] In the *Bacchae* Dionysus says to Pentheus, "Your name suits calamity" (508; cf. 367–68). [8] There must be some point to this specificity. Scholars have suggested allusion to a notorious recent death or a link with rules prescribing the age of participants in Dionysiac ritual. [9] Meaning uncertain. There may be an allusion to the story that the eagle was once a boy who attended Zeus in his

mother gave a roar like a lioness with cubs as she carried off her son's head; Ino tore off his great shoulder, shoulder blade and all, by setting her foot on his stomach; and Autonoe set to work in the same way.[6] The other women butchered what was left and returned to Thebes all smeared with blood, bearing back from the mountain not Pentheus but lamentation (*penthêma*).[7]

This is no concern of mine; nor should anyone else care about an enemy of Dionysus, even if he suffered a worse fate than this, even if he were nine years old or just embarking on his tenth.[8] May I myself act piously, and may my actions please the pious. The eagle gains honor in this way from Zeus who bears the aegis.[9] It is to the children of the pious, not to those of the impious, that good things come.

Farewell to Dionysus, for whom on snowy Dracanus[10] mighty Zeus opened up his own great thigh and placed him inside.[11] Farewell, too, to beautiful Semele and her sisters, daughters of Cadmus, much admired by women of that time,[12] who carried out this deed impelled by Dionysus, so that they are not to be blamed. Let no one criticize the actions of the gods.

---

childhood (Serv. on Virg. *Aen.* 1.394).   [10] Dracanus or Dracanum is listed as one of the god's supposed birthplaces at *Homeric Hymn to Dionysus* 1ff., where the word seems to refer to an island west of the Chersonese. A hill on the island of Icaros (west of Samos) and a promontory on Cos had the same name.

[11] Zeus sewed the fetus into his own thigh when Dionysus' mother Semele was smitten by a thunderbolt sent by jealous Hera (Eur. *Bacch.* 6ff., 286ff.).   [12] Lit., "heroines."

IDYLL 27

A girl, probably called Acrotime, at first rejects Daphnis'
courtship but is soon persuaded of his sincerity. She agrees
to go with him to see his home in a glade. There, reluc-
tantly on her part, they have intercourse, which both take
to be the beginning of marriage; this is confirmed by the
narrator in a short coda.

The opening lines of dialogue, in which Daphnis stole a
kiss, are lost; they will have been preceded by a brief in-
troduction to match the coda. The poem begins, like Idyll
21, with a repulse, but in this case the suitor is successful.
The dramatic dialogue is in stichomythia, a form familiar
from singing contests, here converted to roles in courtship
and seduction. As in Idylls 3, 7, 15, and 25, a change of
scene is to be inferred.

The names Daphnis, Menalcas, and Lycidas are from
Theocritus, and there are some verbal borrowings, but the
poem is unlikely to be by him. The text is corrupt in several
places; the name Acrotime itself is a conjecture.

Criticism

Kirsten, *Junge Hirten*, 33–87.

. . . .

27

ΚΟΡΗ
τὰν πινυτὰν Ἑλέναν Πάρις ἥρπασε βουκόλος ἄλλος.

ΔΑΦΝΙΣ
μᾶλλον ἑκοῖσ᾽ Ἑλένα τὸν βουκόλον ἔσχε φιλεῦσα.

ΚΟΡΗ
μὴ καυχῶ, σατυρίσκε· κενὸν τὸ φίλαμα λέγουσιν.

ΔΑΦΝΙΣ
ἔστι καὶ ἐν κενεοῖσι φιλάμασιν ἁδέα τέρψις.

ΚΟΡΗ
5 τὸ στόμα μευ πλύνω καὶ ἀποπτύω τὸ φίλαμα.

ΔΑΦΝΙΣ
πλύνεις χείλεα σεῖο; δίδου πάλιν, ὄφρα φιλάσω.

ΚΟΡΗ
καλόν σοι δαμάλας φιλέειν, οὐκ ἄζυγα κώραν.

ΔΑΦΝΙΣ
μὴ καυχῶ· τάχα γάρ σε παρέρχεται ὡς ὄναρ ἥβη.

2 ἑκοῖσ᾽ Ahrens: ἑδοῖς M   ἔσχε Hermann: ἐστὶ M

---

[1] Text uncertain.   [2] Borrowed from *Id.* 3.20.

IDYLL 27

. . . .

GIRL

Another oxherd, Paris, carried off Helen, a woman of good sense.

DAPHNIS

Not so; Helen captivated that oxherd on purpose with a kiss.[1]

GIRL

Don't be too confident, you little satyr. They say a kiss is an empty thing.

DAPHNIS

There is sweet pleasure even in empty kisses.[2]

GIRL

I'm wiping my mouth and spitting out your kiss.

DAPHNIS

You're wiping your lips? Give them to me again, so I can kiss them.

GIRL

You ought to be kissing your calves, not an unwedded girl.

DAPHNIS

Don't be too confident; your youth is passing quickly, like a dream.

ΚΟΡΗ

εἰ δέ τι γηράσκω τόδε που μέλι καὶ γάλα πίνω.

ΔΑΦΝΙΣ

10 ἁ σταφυλὶς σταφὶς ἔσται· ὁ νῦν ῥόδον, αὖον ὀλεῖται.

ΚΟΡΗ

19 μὴ 'πιβάλῃς τὴν χεῖρα. καὶ εἰσέτι; χεῖλος ἀμύξω.

ΔΑΦΝΙΣ

11 δεῦρ' ὑπὸ τὰς κοτίνους, ἵνα σοί τινα μῦθον ἐνίψω.

ΚΟΡΗ

οὐκ ἐθέλω· καὶ πρίν με παρήπαφες ἀδέι μύθῳ.

ΔΑΦΝΙΣ

δεῦρ' ὑπὸ τὰς πτελέας ἵν' ἐμᾶς σύριγγος ἀκούσῃς.

ΚΟΡΗ

τὴν σαυτοῦ φρένα τέρψον· ὀιζύον οὐδὲν ἀρέσκει.

ΔΑΦΝΙΣ

15 φεῦ φεῦ, τᾶς Παφίας χόλον ἄζεο καὶ σύγε, κώρα.

ΚΟΡΗ

χαιρέτω ἁ Παφία· μόνον ἵλαος Ἄρτεμις εἴη.

ΔΑΦΝΙΣ

μὴ λέγε, μὴ βάλλῃ σε καὶ ἐς λίνον ἄλλυτον ἔνθῃς.

10 ἔσται· ὁ νῦν Ribbeck: ἐστὶ καὶ οὐ M
19 huc trai. Ribbeck
14 ὀιζύον Hermann: ὀίζυον M   ἀρέσκει Stephanus:
-κη M

IDYLL 27

GIRL

I may be growing older, but at least I have milk and honey to drink.

DAPHNIS

The grape will become a raisin, and the rose will soon wither and die.

GIRL

Don't touch me! Are you still at it? I'll scratch your lip.

DAPHNIS

Come here under the wild olive trees; I want to tell you something.

GIRL

Not likely! You tricked me before with your talk.

DAPHNIS

Come here under the elms and listen to my piping.

GIRL

Pipe to satisfy yourself. I don't like anything dismal.

DAPHNIS

Ah! You too should beware the anger of the Paphian goddess, my girl.[3]

GIRL

I have no need for the Paphian if only Artemis favors me.

DAPHNIS

Don't say so, in case she shoots you and you go into a net you can't escape.[4]

---

[3] Sc., though you think you are not at risk. Aphrodite was born at Paphos in Cyprus.

[4] These should really be alternatives, if "shoots" is a reference to Aphrodite's arrows (for which cf. *Id.* 11.16).

ΚΟΡΗ

18 βαλλέτω ὡς ἐθέλει· πάλιν Ἄρτεμις ἄμμιν ἀρήγει.

ΔΑΦΝΙΣ

20 οὐ φεύγεις τὸν Ἔρωτα, τὸν οὐ φύγε παρθένος ἄλλη.

ΚΟΡΗ

φεύγω ναὶ τὸν Πᾶνα· σὺ δὲ ζυγὸν αἰὲν ἀείραις.

ΔΑΦΝΙΣ

δειμαίνω μὴ δή σε κακωτέρω ἀνέρι δώσει.

ΚΟΡΗ

πολλοί μ' ἐμνώοντο, νόῳ δ' ἐμῷ οὔτις ἔαδε.

ΔΑΦΝΙΣ

εἷς καὶ ἐγὼ πολλῶν μνηστὴρ τεὸς ἐνθάδ' ἱκάνω.

ΚΟΡΗ

25 καὶ τί, φίλος, ῥέξαιμι; γάμοι πλήθουσιν ἀνίας.

ΔΑΦΝΙΣ

οὐκ ὀδύνην, οὐκ ἄλγος ἔχει γάμος, ἀλλὰ χορείην.

ΚΟΡΗ

ναὶ μάν φασι γυναῖκας ἑοὺς τρομέειν παρακοίτας.

ΔΑΦΝΙΣ

μᾶλλον ἀεὶ κρατέουσι. τίνα τρομέουσι γυναῖκες;

ΚΟΡΗ

ὠδίνειν τρομέω· χαλεπὸν βέλος Εἰληθυίης.

18 ἐθέλει Valckenaer: -λῃς M   ἀρήγει Schaefer: -γῃ M
21 ἀείραις Ahrens: -ρες M
22 δώσει Schaefer: -σω M
23 νόῳ δ' ἐμῷ Fritzsche: νόον δ' ἐμὸν M

IDYLL 27

GIRL

Let her shoot me as she likes; Artemis is my defender, I tell you.

DAPHNIS

You can't escape Love: no girl ever did.

GIRL

I can, by Pan; but may you always be under his yoke.

DAPHNIS

I'm afraid he will present you to a worse man than me.

GIRL

I've had many suitors, but none took my fancy.

DAPHNIS

I too have come here as one of your many suitors.

GIRL

What am I to do, my friend?[5] Marriages are full of trouble.

DAPHNIS

A marriage has no grief or trouble: it has dancing![6]

GIRL

And they say wives are afraid of their husbands.

DAPHNIS

No, wives are always in charge. Whom do wives have to fear?

GIRL

I'm afraid of the pain of childbirth: sharp are the arrows of Eileithyia.[7]

---

[5] Now that he has shown honorable intentions she addresses him more civilly. [6] He chooses to understand "marriages" as "weddings" rather than "wedlock." [7] Goddess of childbirth. This and the following line allude to Hom. *Il.* 11.269–71.

ΔΑΦΝΙΣ

30 ἀλλὰ τεῇ βασίλεια μογοστόκος Ἄρτεμίς ἐστιν.

ΚΟΡΗ

ἀλλὰ τεκεῖν τρομέω, μὴ καὶ χρόα καλὸν ὀλέσσω.

ΔΑΦΝΙΣ

ἢν δὲ τέκῃς φίλα τέκνα, νέον φάος ὄψεαι ἥβας.

ΚΟΡΗ

καὶ τί μοι ἕδνον ἄγεις γάμου ἄξιον, ἢν ἐπινεύσω;

ΔΑΦΝΙΣ

πᾶσαν τὴν ἀγέλαν, πάντ᾽ ἄλσεα καὶ νομὸν ἑξεῖς.

ΚΟΡΗ

35 ὄμνυε μὴ μετὰ λέκτρα λιπὼν ἀέκουσαν ἀπενθεῖν.

ΔΑΦΝΙΣ

οὐ μαυτὸν τὸν Πᾶνα, καὶ ἢν ἐθέλῃς με διῶξαι.

ΚΟΡΗ

τεύχεις μοι θαλάμους, τεύχεις καὶ δῶμα καὶ αὐλάς;

ΔΑΦΝΙΣ

τεύχω σοι θαλάμους· τὰ δὲ πώεα καλὰ νομεύω.

ΚΟΡΗ

πατρὶ δὲ γηραλέῳ τίνα μάν, τίνα μῦθον ἐνίψω;

ΔΑΦΝΙΣ

40 αἰνήσει σέο λέκτρον ἐπὴν ἐμὸν οὔνομ᾽ ἀκούσῃ.

32 ἥβας Ahrens: υἷας M
35 ἀπενθεῖν Ziegler: -ένθης M
39 μάν Ahrens: μέν m: κεν m

IDYLL 27

DAPHNIS

But Artemis, that queen of yours, eases the pains of labor.

GIRL

But my fear of giving birth is in case I lose my good looks.

DAPHNIS

As a mother of dear children, you will see a new bright youthfulness.

GIRL

If I should consent, what gift do you bring worthy of my hand?

DAPHNIS

You shall have my whole herd, and all my glades and pastureland.

GIRL

Swear that when we have slept together you will not go away and leave me against my will.

DAPHNIS

By Pan I will not, even if you want to drive me off.

GIRL

Will you build me my own chamber? Will you build me a house and sheep pens?

DAPHNIS

I will build you a chamber; and I'll pasture your fair flocks.

GIRL

How, O how shall I tell my old father?

DAPHNIS

He will consent to your marriage when he hears my name.

ΚΟΡΗ

οὔνομα σὸν λέγε τῆνο· καὶ οὔνομα πολλάκι τέρπει.

ΔΑΦΝΙΣ

Δάφνις ἐγώ, Λυκίδας δὲ πατήρ, μήτηρ δὲ Νομαίη.

ΚΟΡΗ

ἐξ εὐηγενέων· ἀλλ' οὐ σέθεν εἰμὶ χερείων.

ΔΑΦΝΙΣ

οἶδ'· Ἀκροτίμη ἐσσί, πατὴρ δέ τοί ἐστι Μενάλκας.

ΚΟΡΗ

45 δεῖξον ἐμοὶ τεὸν ἄλσος, ὅπη σέθεν ἵσταται αὖλις.

ΔΑΦΝΙΣ

δεῦρ' ἴδε πῶς ἀνθεῦσιν ἐμαὶ ῥαδιναὶ κυπάρισσοι.

ΚΟΡΗ

αἶγες ἐμαί, βόσκεσθε· τὰ βουκόλω ἔργα νοήσω.

ΔΑΦΝΙΣ

ταῦροι, καλὰ νέμεσθ', ἵνα παρθένῳ ἄλσεα δείξω.

ΚΟΡΗ

τί ῥέζεις, σατυρίσκε; τί δ' ἔνδοθεν ἅψαο μαζῶν;

ΔΑΦΝΙΣ

50 μᾶλα τεὰ πράτιστα τάδε χνοάοντα διδάξω.

ΚΟΡΗ

ναρκῶ, ναὶ τὸν Πᾶνα. τεὴν πάλιν ἔξελε χεῖρα.

44 οἶδ' Jacobs: οὐδ' M   Ἀκροτίμη Edmonds: ἄκρα
τιμὴ M   45 τεὸν Wilamowitz: ἔθον M: ἔθεν M
48 ἵνα παρθένῳ ἄλσεα Stephanus: ἵν' ἄλσεα παρθένι M

GIRL

Tell me what that name is; often just a name can give delight.

DAPHNIS

I am Daphnis. My father is Lycidas, my mother Nomaea.[8]

GIRL

You are well born. But I am no less so.

DAPHNIS

I know it. You are Acrotime, and your father is Menalcas.

GIRL

Show me the glade where you spend the night.

DAPHNIS

Come and see how my slender cypresses are growing.

GIRL

Keep feeding, goats; I'm going to look at the oxherd's farm.

DAPHNIS

Graze well, bulls, so that I can show my glades to this girl.

GIRL

What are you doing, you little satyr? Why have you touched my breasts inside my robe?

DAPHNIS

I'll teach my first lesson to these downy apples of yours.

GIRL

I feel faint, by Pan. Take your hand out of there!

[8] "Pasturer." Not otherwise known.

ΔΑΦΝΙΣ

θάρσει, κῶρα φίλα. τί μοι ἔτρεμες; ὡς μάλα δειλά.

ΚΟΡΗ

βάλλεις εἰς ἀμάραν με καὶ εἵματα καλὰ μιαίνεις.

ΔΑΦΝΙΣ

ἀλλ' ὑπὸ σοὺς πέπλους ἁπαλὸν νάκος ἠνίδε βάλλω.

ΚΟΡΗ

55   φεῦ φεῦ, καὶ τὰν μίτραν ἀπέσχισας. ἐς τί δ' ἔλυσας;

ΔΑΦΝΙΣ

τᾷ Παφίᾳ πράτιστον ἐγὼ τόδε δῶρον ὀπάζω.

ΚΟΡΗ

μίμνε, τάλαν· τάχα τίς τοι ἐπέρχεται· ἦχον ἀκούω.

ΔΑΦΝΙΣ

ἀλλήλαις λαλέουσι τεὸν γάμον αἱ κυπάρισσοι.

ΚΟΡΗ

ἀμπεχόνην ποίησας ἐμὴν ῥάκος· εἰμὶ δὲ γυμνά.

ΔΑΦΝΙΣ

60   ἄλλην ἀμπεχόνην τῆς σῆς τοι μείζονα δώσω.

ΚΟΡΗ

φῄς μοι πάντα δόμεν· τάχα δ' ὕστερον οὐδ' ἅλα
        δοίης.

ΔΑΦΝΙΣ

αἴθ' αὐτὰν δυνάμαν καὶ τὰν ψυχὰν ἐπιβάλλειν.

55 ἀπέσχισας Scaliger: ἀπέστιχες M
59 ἀμπεχόνην . . . ἐμὴν Hermann: τἀμπέχονον . . . ἐμὸν M

384

IDYLL 27

DAPHNIS

Be brave, my dear. Why ever are you trembling? How nervous you are!

GIRL

You're throwing me into the ditch and dirtying my nice clothes.

DAPHNIS

But look, I'm throwing a soft fleece under your robes.

GIRL

Oh, you've torn my girdle too. Why have you undone it?

DAPHNIS

I give it as a first offering to the Paphian goddess.

GIRL

Stop, for goodness' sake! Someone's coming. I hear a sound.

DAPHNIS

It's the cypresses chattering together about your wedding.

GIRL

You've torn my shawl to shreds; I'm naked.

DAPHNIS

I'll give you another shawl bigger than yours.

GIRL

You promise to give me everything; but maybe you'll soon not even give me salt.[9]

DAPHNIS

If only I could add my soul itself to the gifts.

---

[9] I.e., deny even basic hospitality. Cf. Hom. *Od.* 17.455–57.

ΚΟΡΗ

Ἄρτεμι, μὴ νεμέσα σέο ῥήμασιν οὐκέτι πιστῇ.

ΔΑΦΝΙΣ

ῥέξω πόρτιν Ἔρωτι καὶ αὐτᾷ βοῦν Ἀφροδίτᾳ.

ΚΟΡΗ

65 παρθένος ἔνθα βέβηκα, γυνὴ δ᾽ εἰς οἶκον ἀφέρπω.

ΔΑΦΝΙΣ

ἀλλὰ γυνὴ μήτηρ τεκέων τροφός, οὐκέτι κώρα.

᾽Ως οἱ μὲν χλοεροῖσιν ἰαινόμενοι μελέεσσιν
ἀλλήλοις ψιθύριζον. ἄννστο δὲ φώριος εὐνή.
χἠ μὲν ἀνεγρομένη πάλιν ἔστιχε μᾶλα νομεύειν
70 ὄμμασιν αἰδομένοις—κραδίη δέ οἱ ἔνδον ἰάνθη—
ὃς δ᾽ ἐπὶ ταυρείας ἀγέλας κεχαρημένος εὐνᾶς.

Δέχνυσο τὰν σύριγγα τεὰν πάλιν, ὄλβιε ποιμάν,
τῶν δ᾽ αὖ ποιμενίων ἑτέραν σκεψώμεθα μολπάν.

65 ἀφέρπω Ahrens: -πη M: -ψω M
68 ἄννστο δὲ Meineke: ἀνίστατο M: ἀνίστα M
69 πάλιν ἔστιχε Wilamowitz: γε διέστιχε M
70 αἰδομένοις Hermann: -νη M
post 71 ἤιε(ν) m
72–73 om. m
72 τεὰν Ahrens: -ῶν M
73 δ᾽ αὖ Legrand: καὶ M   ποιμενίων Ahrens: ποιμαι-
γνίων M

IDYLL 27

GIRL
Artemis, please don't be angry if I no longer obey your commands.

DAPHNIS
I shall sacrifice a heifer to Eros and a cow to Aphrodite herself.

GIRL
I came here a virgin; I go home a wife.

DAPHNIS
Wife, mother and nurse of children, a girl no longer.

In this way they whispered to each other as they took pleasure in their young bodies; and their secret union was accomplished. She arose and went back to pasture her sheep with a shamefaced look, though in her heart she was happy, while he, rejoicing at their union, went off to his herds of cattle.

Take back your pipe again, blessed shepherd, and let us compose another pastoral song.[10]

---

[10] The text is very uncertain. As the beginning of the poem is lost, it is not possible to determine who is the shepherd addressed or the reason for his having lent his pipe. The poem would conclude satisfactorily with lines 67–71, and it may be that 72–73 are out of place.

IDYLL 28

Theocritus is about to set sail from Syracuse to Miletus, bearing with him an ivory distaff as a gift for Theugenis, the wife of his friend the poet and doctor Nicias (addressee of Idylls *11 and 13). The poem is imagined as accompanying the gift. The Aeolic dialect and sixteen-syllable meter (×× –∪∪– –∪∪– –∪∪– ×) evoke the Lesbian poets Sappho and Alcaeus, and it is possible that they composed poems, now lost, on similar themes. But the same meter was particularly associated with Theocritus' older contemporary Asclepiades (cf.* Id. *7.39–41), and at any rate among extant literature the poem seems most closely allied with dedicatory epigrams, which commonly name their recipient, describe the dedicated object, and give a reason for the gift (cf.* Theoc. *Epigrr. 1, 2, 8, 10, 12, 13). Because the distaff is the addressee, Theugenis and her excellent management of the household can be praised indirectly. As the distaff is a precious and finely wrought object, so* The Distaff *is a carefully crafted and exotic piece of workmanship. Composed by a Dorian in Aeolic dialect and bound for an Ionian destination, it is wittily characterized as an emigrant, setting out from Sicily to make its home in Miletus (21). Both the distaff and the poem will bring distinction to Theugenis.*

IDYLL 28

Criticism

Cairns, F. "The Distaff of Theugenis—Theocritus *Idyll* 28." *ARCA* 2 (1976): 293–30.

Fassino, M., and L. Prauscello. "Memoria ritmica e memoria poetica. Saffo e Alceo in Teocrito Idilli 28–30 tra ἀρχαιολογία metrica e innovazione alessandrina." *MD* 46 (2001): 9–37.

Hopkinson, *Hellenistic Anthology*, 172–77.

28

Γλαύκας, ὦ φιλέριθ᾽ ἀλακάτα, δῶρον Ἀθανάας
γύναιξιν νόος οἰκωφελίας αἶσιν ἐπάβολος,
θέρσεισ᾽ ἄμμιν ὑμάρτη πόλιν ἐς Νείλεος ἀγλάαν,
ὅππα Κύπριδος ἶρον καλάμω χλῶρον ὑπ᾽ ἀπάλω.
5 τυίδε γὰρ πλόον εὐάνεμον αἰτήμεθα πὰρ Δίος,
ὅππως ξέννον ἔμον τέρψομ᾽ ἴδων κἀντιφιληθέω,
Νικίαν, Χαρίτων ἱμεροφώνων ἴερον φύτον,
καὶ σὲ τὰν ἐλέφαντος πολυμόχθω γεγενημέναν
δῶρον Νικίαας εἰς ἀλόχω χέρρας ὀπάσσομεν,
10 σὺν τᾶ πόλλα μὲν ἔργ᾽ ἐκτελέσῃς ἀνδρείοις πέπλοις,
πόλλα δ᾽ οἶα γύναικες φορέοισ᾽ ὑδάτινα βράκη.
δὶς γὰρ μάτερες ἄρνων μαλάκοις ἐν βοτάνᾳ πόκοις
πέξαιντ᾽ αὐτοέτει, Θευγένιδός γ᾽ ἔννεκ᾽ ἐυσφύρω·
οὕτως ἀνυσίεργος, φιλέει δ᾽ ὄσσα σαόφρονες.
15 οὐ γὰρ εἰς ἀκίρας οὐδ᾽ ἐς ἀέργω κεν ἐβολλόμαν
ὄπασσαί σε δόμοις, ἀμμετέρας ἔσσαν ἀπὺ χθόνος.
καὶ γάρ τοι πάτρις ἂν ὢξ Ἐφύρας κτίσσε ποτ᾽ Ἀρ-
χίας,
νάσω Τρινακρίας μύελον, ἄνδρων δοκίμων πόλιν.

5 τυίδε pap., coni. Hermann: τὺ δὲ M
6 κἀντιφιληθέω Lobel: -λήσω M

IDYLL 28

Distaff, friend of spinners, gift of gray-eyed Athena to women whose minds are skilled in running the household, come with me boldly to the splendid city of Neleus,[1] where the precinct of Aphrodite lies green in its soft rushes. I ask Zeus for fair winds for my voyage there, so that I may see my friend with pleasure and be welcomed by him in return—my friend Nicias, holy offshoot of the lovely voiced Graces[2]—and so that I may bestow you, made out of ivory with great care, as a gift into the hands of Nicias' wife, with whom you will create many pieces of work for men's robes and many flowing garments such as women wear. The mothers of lambs in the pastures might be shorn of their soft fleeces twice each year so far as fair-ankled Theugenis is concerned,[3] so industrious is she, so prudent in behavior. I would not have liked to give you into the house of a weak or idle woman, since you are from my own country: your home town is that which Archias of Ephyra once founded,[4] marrow of the Trinacrian island,[5]

---

[1] Legendary founder of Miletus.

[2] I.e., Nicias' poetry is charming and graceful.

[3] The periphrasis for sheep and the dignified epithet for Theugenis are gently humorous.

[4] Syracuse, on the "three-promontoried" island of Sicily (Trinacria), was founded in 734 BC by Archias from Corinth, the original name of which was Ephyra.   [5] Marrow was prized as a toothsome tidbit, so that the word may suggest both a delicacy and an innermost vital force, "lifeblood."

νῦν μὰν οἶκον ἔχοισ᾽ ἄνερος ὃς πόλλ᾽ ἐδάη σόφα
20 ἀνθρώποισι νόσοις φάρμακα λύγραις ἀπαλάλκεμεν,
οἰκήσῃς κατὰ Μίλλατον ἐράνναν πεδ᾽ Ἰαόνων,
ὡς εὐαλάκατος Θεύγενις ἐν δαμότισιν πέλῃ,
καί οἱ μνᾶστιν ἀεὶ τῶ φιλαοίδω παρέχῃς ξένω.
κῆνο γάρ τις ἔρει τῶπος ἰδὼν σ᾽· "ἦ μεγάλα χάρις
25 δώρῳ σὺν ὀλίγῳ· πάντα δὲ τίματα τὰ πὰρ φίλων."

24 τῶπος ἰδων Wordsworth: τῶ ποσείδων fere M

392

a city of famous men. Now, sharing the home of a man who knows many wise drugs for averting dangerous maladies from humankind, you make your home with Ionians in lovely Miletus, so that Theugenis may be famous for her distaff among her townswomen, and you may always give her remembrance of her friend. Someone will say when they see you, "Indeed great goodwill goes with this slight gift;[6] and all things that come from friends are precious."

[6] Or, less likely, "The gift may be small, but it has great charm."

IDYLL 29

A man tries to persuade a boy to love no one else but him. The setting is a symposium in town. The poem begins with a famous quotation from Alcaeus, a lyric poet from Lesbos contemporary with Sappho (late 7th/early 6th century BC). It is likely that if more of his verse survived other allusions would be revealed. The speaker's moralizing is self-interested and conventional, but whether his tone is earnest or desperate is hard to tell. The dialect is Aeolic in imitation of Alcaeus, and the meter is one of those used by him (×× –∪∪ –∪∪ –∪×).

Criticism

Hunter, *Archaeology*, 171–81.
Morrison, *Narrator*, 250–52, 259–60.

29

"Οἶνος, ὦ φίλε παῖ," λέγεται, "καὶ ἀλάθεα"·
κἄμμε χρὴ μεθύοντας ἀλάθεας ἔμμεναι.
κἄγω μὲν τὰ φρένων ἐρέω κέατ' ἐν μύχῳ·
οὐκ ὄλας φιλέην μ' ἐθέλησθ' ἀπὺ καρδίας.
5 γινώσκω· τὸ γὰρ αἴμισυ τὰς ζοΐας ἔχω
ζὰ τὰν σὰν ἰδέαν, τὸ δὲ λοῖπον ἀπώλετο·
κὦταν μὲν σὺ θέλῃς, μακάρεσσιν ἴσαν ἄγω
ἀμέραν· ὄτα δ' οὐκ ἐθέλῃς σύ, μάλ' ἐν σκότῳ.
πῶς ταῦτ' ἄρμενα, τὸν φιλέοντ' ὀνίαις δίδων;
10 ἀλλ' αἴ μοί τι πίθοιο νέος προγενεστέρῳ,
τῷ κε λώιον αὖτος ἔχων ἔμ' ἐπαινέσαις.
πόησαι καλίαν μίαν ἐνν ἔνι δενδρίῳ,
ὄππυι μηδὲν ἀπίξεται ἄγριον ὄρπετον.
νῦν δὲ τῶδε μὲν ἄματος ἄλλον ἔχῃς κλάδον,
15 ἄλλον δ' αὔριον, ἐξ ἀτέρω δ' ἄτερον μάτης·
καὶ μέν σευ τὸ κάλον τις ἴδων ῥέθος αἰνέσαι,
τῷ δ' εὐθὺς πλέον ἢ τριέτης ἐγένευ φίλος,
τὸν πρῶτον δὲ φίλεντα τρίταιον ἐθήκαο·
† ἄνδρων τῶν ὑπερανορέων δοκέης πνέην·
20 φίλη δ', ἆς κε ζόης, τὸν ὔμοιον ἔχην ἄει. †
αἰ γὰρ ὦδε πόης, ἄγαθος μὲν ἀκούσεαι
ἐξ ἄστων· ὁ δέ τοί κ' Ἔρος οὐ χαλέπως ἔχοι,

IDYLL 29

"Wine and truth, my dear lad," as they say;[1] and we too ought to be truthful now that we are drunk. I'll tell you what thought is lying deep in my mind: that you are not willing to love me with all your heart. I know it: because of your beauty I keep hold of only half my life, and the rest is lost to me. When you are willing, I pass my days like a god, but when you are not I live in darkness. How can it be right to make your lover miserable? You are young; if only you would take your elder's advice, you would keep me more securely and thank me too. Make one nest in a single tree, in a place where no fierce snake can come:[2] as it is, you are to be found on one branch today and on another tomorrow, and you are for ever seeking a new place to settle. No sooner does someone praise your handsome face than to him you become like a friend of three years' standing, while he who loved you first is treated like an acquaintance of three days. You seem to aspire to the company of proud men when you ought to have a single life-long friend similar to yourself.[3] If you behave in that way you will have a good name among the citizens, and Love will not treat you harshly—Love who easily masters the

---

[1] A proverb said to have originated with Alcaeus (Pl. *Symp.* 217e and schol.; Alc. Fr. 366 Voigt): *in vino veritas.*

[2] I.e., as your only lover I could offer security.

[3] Text and sense very uncertain.

ὃς ἀνδρῶν φρένας εὐμαρέως ὑπαδάμναται
κάμε μόλθακον ἐξ ἐπόησε σιδαρίῳ.
25 ἀλλὰ πὲρρ ἀπάλω στύματός σε πεδέρχομαι
ὀμνάσθην ὅτι πέρρυσιν ἦσθα νεώτερος,
κὤτι γηράλεοι πέλομεν πρὶν ἀπύπτυσαι
καὶ ῥύσσοι, νεότατα δ' ἔχην παλινάγρετον
οὐκ ἔστι· πτέρυγας γὰρ ἐπωμαδίαις φόρει,
30 κάμμες βαρδύτεροι τὰ ποτήμενα συλλάβην.
ταῦτα χρή σε νόεντα πέλην ποτιμώτερον
καί μοι τὠραμένῳ συνέραν ἀδόλως σέθεν,
ὅππως, ἄνικα τὰν γέννν ἀνδρεΐαν ἔχῃς,
ἀλλάλοισι πελώμεθ' Ἀχιλλέιοι φίλοι.
35 αἰ δὲ ταῦτα φέρην ἀνέμοισιν ἐπιτρέπῃς,
ἐν θύμῳ δὲ λέγῃς "τί με, δαιμόνι', ἐννόχλης;"
νῦν μὲν κἀπὶ τὰ χρύσια μᾶλ' ἔνεκεν σέθεν
βαίην καὶ φύλακον νεκύων πεδὰ Κέρβερον,
τότα δ' οὐδὲ κάλεντος ἐπ' αὐλέίαις θύραις
40 προμόλοιμί κε, παυσάμενος χαλέπω πόθω.

31 σε νόεντα Bücheler: νοέοντα M

minds of men and has softened me who was hard as iron. By your soft lips, I ask you to remember that a year ago you were younger, that we grow old and wrinkled in the twinkling of an eye,[4] and that we cannot get our youth back again: it has wings on its shoulders, and we are too slow to catch things that can fly. You should think of this and be pleasanter toward me, and love me as guilelessly as I love you, so that when you are a man[5] we may be friends to each other like Achilles and Patroclus.[6] But if you consign my words to be carried away by the winds and say to yourself, "Why are you pestering me, sir?"—as it is, I would fetch the Golden Apples for you or bring back Cerberus, guard dog of the dead[7]—but in that case, I would not come to my courtyard door even if you called, and my cruel desire would be at an end.

[4] Lit., "before a man can spit."

[5] Lit., "when you have a manly cheek," i.e., a beard.

[6] Lit., "be Achillean friends to each other."

[7] The hardest of Heracles' Labors were to obtain the golden apples of the Hesperides and to bring Cerberus to the upper world.

IDYLL 30

A man in love with a boy vainly tries to argue himself out of his passion; he begins with resistance but ends with resignation.

The exhortatory address to one's soul is conventional, the soul's reply less so. Varied imagery is used to characterize youth and desire.

Dialect and meter are the same as in Idyll 28.

Criticism

Hunter, *Archaeology,* 181–86.
Hutchinson, *Hellenistic Poetry,* 167–70.

Ὤιαι τῶ χαλέπω καὶνομόρω τῶδε νοσήματος·
τετόρταιος ἔχει παῖδος ἔρος μῆνά με δεύτερον,
κάλω μὲν μετρίως, ἀλλ᾽ ὅποσον τῷ πόδι περρέχει
τὰς γᾶς, τοῦτο χάρις, ταῖς δὲ παραύαις γλύκυ μει-
    δίαι.
καὶ νῦν μὲν τὸ κάκον ταῖς μὲν ἔχει ταῖς δ᾽ ὀν‹ίησί
5   με›,
τάχα δ᾽ οὐδ᾽ ὅσον ὕπνω ᾽πιτύχην ἔσσετ᾽ ἐρωία.
ἔχθες γὰρ παρίων ἔδρακε λέπτ᾽ ἄμμε δι᾽ ὀφρύων,
αἰδέσθεις προσίδην ἄντιος, ἠρεύθετο δὲ χρόα·
ἔμεθεν δὲ πλέον τὰς κραδίας ὦρος ἐδράξατο·
10 εἰς οἶκον δ᾽ ἀπέβαν ἕλκος ἔχων καὶνο‹ν ἐν ἥπατι›.
πόλλα δ᾽ εἰσκαλέσαις θῦμον ἐμαύτῳ διελεξάμαν·
"τί δῆτ᾽ αὖτε πόης; ἀλοσύνας τί ἔσχατον ἔσσεται;
λεύκαις οὐκέτ᾽ ἴσαισθ᾽ ὅττι φόρης ἐν κροτάφοις τρί-
    χας;
ὦρα τοι φρονέην· μὴ ‹οὔτ›ι νέος τὰν ἰδέαν πέλων
15 πάντ᾽ ἔρδ᾽ ὅσσαπερ οἱ τῶν ἐτέων ἄρτι γεγεύμενοι.

2 με Bergk: om. M   3 πόδι Bücheler: παιδὶ M
4 μειδίᾳ Bergk: μειδίαμα M   5 ὀνίησί με Gow: οὐ M
7 λέπτ᾽ ἄμμε δι᾽ ὀφρύων Bergk: λεπτὰ μελιφρύγων M
9 κραδίας ὦρος Bergk: καρδία σωρός M
10 καῖνον ἐν ἥπατι Kraushaar: καὶ τὸ M

Alas for this cruel and fateful malady of mine! For two months now I have been in the grip of a quartan passion[1] for a boy; he is only moderately handsome, but from top to toe he's a complete charmer, with a sweet smile on his cheeks. At present the fever grips me on some days and abates on others, but soon there will not be enough respite even for me to get to sleep. Yesterday as he passed he stole a quick glance at me from beneath his eyelids, too shy to look at me directly, and blushed; love seized my heart even more, and I went home with a fresh wound inside me.[2] I called up my soul and had a long debate: "What are you up to again? When will there be an end to your folly? Have you forgotten that you have gray hair at your temples? It's high time to show sense: you are not young in looks, and you should not keep behaving like those just getting a taste

---

[1] I.e., he suffers intermittently. A quartan fever is one that recurs every four days.

[2] Lit., "liver": cf. *Id.* 11.16. (The word is a conjecture, the end of the line being lost.)

---

11 διελεξάμαν Bergk: διέλυξε M

12 δῆτ' αὖτε πόης Kraushaar: δὴ ταῦτ' ἐπόης M

13 οὐκέτ' ἰσαισθ' Gow: οὐκ ἐπίσθησθ' M   τρίχας Fritzsche: τρία M   14 φρονέην Hoffmann: φρονέεσιν M   οὔτι νέος Bergk: . . . ινέος M

καὶ μὰν ἄλλο σε λάθει· τὸ δ' ἄρ' ἧς λώιον ἔμμεναι
ξέννον τῶν χαλέπων παῖδος ἐρώ‹των προγενέστε-
ρον›.
τῷ μὲν γὰρ βίος ἔρπει ἴσα γόννοις ἐλάφω θόας,
χαλάσει δ' ἀτέρᾳ ποντοπόρην αὔριον ἄρμενα·
20 τὸ δ' αὖτε γλυκέρας ἄνθεμον ἄβας πεδ' ὑμαλίκων
μένει. τῷ δ' ὁ πόθος καὶ τὸν ἔσω μύελον ἐσθίει
ὀμμιμνασκομένω, πόλλα δ' ὅραι νύκτος ἐνύπνια,
παύσασθαι δ' ἐνίαυτος χαλέπας οὐκ ἴ‹κανος νόσω›."
ταῦτα κάτερα πόλλα πρὸς ἔμον θῡμὸν ἐμεμψάμαν·
25 ὃ δὲ τοῦτ' ἔφατ'· "ὅττις δοκίμοι τὸν δολομάχανον
νικάσην Ἔρον, οὗτος δοκίμοι τοῖς ὑπὲρ ἀμμέων
εὔρην βραϊδίως ἄστερας ὁππόσσακιν ἔννεα.
καὶ νῦν, εἴτ' ἐθέλω, χρή με μάκρον σχόντα τὸν ἄμ-
φενα
ἔλκην τὸν ζύγον, εἴτ' οὐκ ἐθέλω· ταῦτα γάρ, ὤγαθε,
30 βόλλεται θέος ὃς καὶ Δίος ἔσφαλε μέγαν νόον
καὔτας Κυπρογενήας· ἔμε μάν, φύλλον ἐπάμερον
σμίκρας δεύμενον αὔρας, ὀνέλων ὦκα φόρει ‹πνόᾳ›."

17 ἐρώτων suppl. H. Fritzsche, προγενέστερον Wilamowitz
(-ῳ Bergk): ἔραν nec plura M
  18 ἔρπει Bergk: ἔρπερω M   γόννοις Bücheler: γόνοις
M   θόας Bergk: θοαῖς M
  19 χαλάσει Ahrens: δλάσει M   ἄρμενα Ahrens: ἀμέ-
ραν M
  20 τὸ δ' Wilamowitz: τω δ pap.: οὐδ' M
  23 χαλέπας οὐκ ἴκανος νόσω Bergk: οὐ χαλεπαὶ οὐχὶ M
  25 ἔφατ' ὅττις δοκίμοι Bergk: ἔφτ' ὅτις δοκεῖ μοι M

404

for life. And you are forgetting another thing: for an older man it's better to be a stranger to the cruel love of boys. A boy's life moves along like the running of a swift deer; the next day he will cast off and sail elsewhere; the flowering of his sweet youth is spent with his companions. But as for his lover, desire gnaws at his inmost marrow as he reminisces; at night he often dreams, and a year is not enough to put a stop to his cruel malady." With these and many other things I reproached my heart; but the answer came, "Whoever believes he can defeat crafty Love believes also that he can easily discover how many times nine are the stars above. Willing or unwilling, I must now stretch out my neck and drag at the yoke:[3] that, my friend, is the will of the god who can upset the great mind of Zeus and of Aphrodite herself. As for me, he swiftly takes me up and carries me away like a short-lived leaf which needs only the slightest breeze."

[3] At *Id.* 12.15 lovers are pictured as contented yoke fellows, but here the emphasis is on the thankless drudgery of the unloved lover.

---

26 δοκίμοι τοὶς ὑπὲρ ἀμμέων Bergk: δοκεῖ μοι τᾶς ὑπὲρ ἄμμ' M

29 ὤγαθε Th. Fritzsche: ὦ γα θέος M

31 φύλλον Th. Fritzsche: φίλον M

32 ὀνέλων Ahrens: ὁ μέλλων M ὦκα Ahrens: αἴκα M πνόᾳ suppl. Legrand: om. M

IDYLL 31

On a papyrus of about AD 500 (P. Antinoe), Idyll 30 is followed by these fragments of a poem not found in any manuscript. It is likely to have been another lyric in Aeolic dialect addressed to a boy.

Ναυκλαρω φ[
Σμικραναι̣[
ουτος κανδρ[
συ δε τω Διος [
5 τι̣ το καλλο[. . . . .] . κο̣δ̣[.] .α̣[
[. . . . .] . . [.] . [. . . . . . .] . . . . χο̣σ . . τ̣ο̣[
[. . . . .] . εων αμφι̣[
[. . . . .] . ει̣α̣[.] εχει χωτα.[
[. . . . .] . [.]μω δ' ολ̣[
10 [. . . . .]α̣κ̣α̣ρων κάρτα̣ [
[. . . . .] . πινα
[. . . . .]σει και [
                                    ]

Desunt vv. circiter xiii.

                              ]
                              ]τ̣ον
                              ]χες
                              ]ρον
                              ]σον
                              ]αλλευ
                                ]υτον
                              ]χατα

IDYLL 31

Ship's captain . . . .

Small . . . .

This . . . .

But you . . . . of Zeus . . . .

Beauty . . . .

ΑΠΟΣΠΑΣΜΑΤΑ

1 Eust. p. 620.29

ἀδελφὴ δέ ἐστιν Ἄρεως ἡ Ἥβη, ὡς καὶ Θεόκριτος μυθολογεῖ.

2 *Etym. Magn.* p. 290.52 s.v. δυσί

καὶ αὐτὸ δὲ τὸ δύο εὕρηται κλινόμενον. καὶ παρὰ τὸ δύο δυσὶν ἀντιφέρεσθαι, ὡς παρὰ Θεοκρίτῳ.

3 Ath. 284A

Θεόκριτος δ᾽ ὁ Συρακόσιος ἐν τῷ ἐπιγραφομένῃ Βερε-νίκῃ τὸν λεῦκον ὀνομαζόμενον ἰχθὺν ἱερὸν καλεῖ διὰ τούτων·

  κεἴ τις ἀνὴρ αἰτεῖται ἐπαγροσύνην τε καὶ ὄλβον,
  ἐξ ἁλὸς ᾧ ζωή, τὰ δὲ δίκτυα κείνῳ ἄροτρα,

FRAGMENTS

1 Eustathius

Hebe is a sister of Ares, as Theocritus recounts.[1]

[1] Heracles was married to Hebe; possibly this was mentioned in the lost closing lines of *Id.* 24.

2 *Etymologicum Magnum*

In fact the word "two" is declinable, and from it "two compete against twain," as in Theocritus.[1]

[1] The sense is not quite clear, and the quotation may in fact be an inexact reminiscence of Aratus *Phaen.* 468, δύω δυσὶν ἀντιφέρονται. Alternatively, it may be from the lost passage after *Id.* 22.170, where Castor proposes a duel between the two sets of brothers.

3 Athenaeus, *Scholars at Dinner*

Theocritus of Syracuse in his poem entitled *Berenice*[1] refers to the so-called white fish as sacred, in the following passage: "And if anyone who makes his living from the sea, whose nets are his plows, asks for good fishing and pros-

[1] Probably the deified Berenice, wife of Ptolemy I (cf. *Idd.* 15.106–8; 17.45–50, 123); she may well be the "goddess" (3) to whom the fish is to be sacrificed.

411

σφάζων ἀκρόνυχος ταύτῃ θεῷ ἱερὸν ἰχθύν
ὃν λεῦκον καλέουσιν, ὃ γάρ θ᾽ ἱερώτατος ἄλλων,
5   καί κε λίνα στήσαιτο καὶ ἐξερύσαιτο θαλάσσης
ἔμπλεα.

perity, and at nightfall slaughters for this goddess a sacred fish, one men refer to as white because it is the most sacred fish of all, his nets would be taut and he would pull them out of the sea full."

EPIGRAMS

In the archaic and classical periods, epigrams were used for funerary, dedicatory, and celebratory inscriptions. Poets of the generation before Theocritus were perhaps the first to compose literary, nonfunctional epigrams. They broadened the range of subject matter to include topics familiar from lyric poetry and drinking songs: love, sex, humor, the symposium. Far the greater part are composed in elegiac couplets or iambic trimeters.

Twenty-four epigrams are attributed to Theocritus. Six have a rural setting, and most of these feature Daphnis or Thyrsis. Most of the rest are fictitious epitaphs or descriptions of statues. The variety of meters in poems 17 to 24 is very unusual, another aspect perhaps of Theocritus' experimentation with form. The epitaphs on poets are of particular interest.

Criticism

Baumbach, M., A. Petrovic, and I. Petrovic, eds. *Archaic and Classical Greek Epigram.* Cambridge, 2010.

Bing, P. "Theocritus' Epigrams on the Statues of Ancient Poets." *A&A* 34 (1988): 117–23.

Bing, P., and J. S. Bruss. *Brill's Companion to Hellenistic Epigram down to Philip.* Leiden, 2007.

Dihle, A., ed. *L'Épigramme grecque.* Geneva, 1968.

Garrison, D. H. *Mild Frenzy: A Reading of the Hellenistic Love Epigram.* Wiesbaden, 1978.

Gow, A. S. F. and D. L. Page. *The Greek Anthology: Hellenistic Epigrams,* 1.183–91, 2.525–37. Cambridge, 1965.

Gutzwiller, K. *Poetic Garlands: Hellenistic Epigrams in Context.* Berkeley, 1998.

Harder, M. A., R. F. Regtuit, and G. C. Wakker, eds. *Hellenistic Epigrams.* Leuven, 2002.

Rossi, L. *The Epigrams Ascribed to Theocritus: A Method of Approach.* Leuven, 2001.

Tarán, S. L. *The Art of Variation in the Hellenistic Epigram.* Leiden, 1979.

ΕΠΙΓΡΑΜΜΑΤΑ

1 AP 6.336

Τὰ ῥόδα τὰ δροσόεντα καὶ ἁ κατάπυκνος ἐκείνα
ἕρπυλλος κεῖται ταῖς Ἑλικωνιάσιν·
ταὶ δὲ μελάμφυλλοι δάφναι τίν, Πύθιε Παιάν,
Δελφὶς ἐπεὶ πέτρα τοῦτό τοι ἀγλάισεν·
5 βωμὸν δ᾽ αἱμάξει κεραὸς τράγος οὗτος ὁ μαλός
τερμίνθου τρώγων ἔσχατον ἀκρεμόνα.

2 AP 6.177

Δάφνις ὁ λευκόχρως, ὁ καλᾷ σύριγγι μελίσδων
βουκολικοὺς ὕμνους, ἄνθετο Πανὶ τάδε,
τοὺς τρητοὺς δόνακας, τὸ λαγωβόλον, ὀξὺν ἄκοντα,
νεβρίδα, τὰν πήραν ᾇ ποκ᾽ ἐμαλοφόρει.

EPIGRAMS

1[1] *Greek Anthology*

The roses covered in dew and that thickly growing thyme
are reserved for the Muses of Helicon, but the dark-leaved
bays are for you, Pythian god of healing: this is the plant
with which the cliffs of Delphi pay you honor.[2] This white,
horned billy goat that is nibbling the end of a branch of
terebinth will shed his blood on your altar.

> [1] Perhaps an inscription for a landscape painting.
> [2] Apollo, also god of poetry. Pythian = Delphian.

2[1] *Greek Anthology*

Fair-skinned Daphnis, performer of country songs on his
fine pipe, has made these dedications to Pan: his pierced
reeds,[2] his throwing stick, a sharp spear, a fawn skin, and
the knapsack in which he used to carry apples.[3]

> [1] Daphnis dedicates his gear. The *Greek Anthology* contains
> many such fictitious dedicatory epigrams. The assumption must
> be that Daphnis is giving up the hunt; "fair-skinned" perhaps
> implies that he is no longer spending his time out in the sun.
> "Pierced reeds" probably refers to a pipe, not to fowlers' reeds
> (for which see Bion Fr. 13).
> [2] Not the pipe (*syrinx*) of line 1, but the double pipes pierced
> with holes for the stops.
> [3] Lunch; or tokens of love.

417

THEOCRITUS

3 AP 9.338

Εὕδεις φυλλοστρῶτι πέδῳ, Δάφνι, σῶμα κεκμακός
ἀμπαύων, στάλικες δ᾽ ἀρτιπαγεῖς ἀν᾽ ὄρη·
ἀγρεύει δέ τυ Πὰν καὶ ὁ τὸν κροκόεντα Πρίηπος
κισσὸν ἐφ᾽ ἱμερτῷ κρατὶ καθαπτόμενος,
5 ἄντρον ἔσω στείχοντες ὁμόρροθοι. ἀλλὰ τὺ φεῦγε,
φεῦγε μεθεὶς ὕπνου κῶμα † καταγρόμενον.

4 AP 9.437

Τήναν τὰν λαύραν τόθι ταὶ δρύες, αἰπόλε, κάμψας
σύκινον εὑρήσεις ἀρτιγλυφὲς ξόανον
ἀσκελὲς αὐτόφλοιον ἀνούατον, ἀλλὰ φάλητι
παιδογόνῳ δυνατὸν Κύπριδος ἔργα τελεῖν.
5 σακὸς δ᾽ εὐίερος περιδέδρομεν, ἀέναον δέ

3 ἀσκελὲς Jahn: τρισκελὲς Μ

418

3[1] *Greek Anthology*

You are asleep on a couch of leaves on the ground, Daphnis, resting your weary body, and your stakes have just been set up in the hills;[2] but Pan is on your trail, and Priapus, who is fastening yellow ivy on his lovely brows,[3] and they are both coming into your cave with some purpose. Get away; cast off the deep sleep that is overcoming you and get away.[4]

[1] This, like *Epigr.* 1, is or purports to be a description of a picture. Daphnis is about to be surprised by two lustful deities: the hunter hunted.

[2] I.e., he is tired after setting up his hunter's nets.

[3] On Priapus see on *Id.* 1.81. "Lovely" is surprising, perhaps humorous.

[4] "Overcoming you" is probably not what the poet wrote; perhaps "just beginning" (κ_αταρχόμενον_ Toup).

4[1] *Greek Anthology*

Follow that lane by the oak trees, goatherd, and you will find a newly carved statue of figwood.[2] It is legless and earless, and the bark has not been removed, but it does have a fertile phallus that can do the business of Aphrodite. A sacred precinct surrounds it, and an ever-flowing

[1] This poem is abnormally long for an epigram, but it has elements characteristic of many such poems: the giving of directions; the set-piece description of a pleasant spot, with elegant compound adjectives; the invitation to sit; the vow to a god. The conclusion is humorous and unexpected: it turns out that the vow does not represent the preferred outcome.

[2] Statues of Priapus were often little more than wooden pillars with crude head and phallus.

ῥεῖθρον ἀπὸ σπιλάδων πάντοσε τηλεθάει
δάφναις καὶ μύρτοισι καὶ εὐώδει κυπαρίσσῳ,
ἔνθα πέριξ κέχυται βοτρυόπαις ἕλικι
ἄμπελος, εἰαρινοὶ δὲ λιγυφθόγγοισιν ἀοιδαῖς
10   κόσσυφοι ἀχεῦσιν ποικιλότραυλα μέλη.
ξουθαὶ δ᾽ ἀδονίδες μινυρίσμασιν ἀνταχεῦσι
    μέλπουσαι στόμασιν τὰν μελίγαρυν ὄπα.
ἕζεο δὴ τηνεὶ καὶ τῷ χαρίεντι Πριήπῳ
    εὔχε᾽ ἀποστέρξαι τοὺς Δάφνιδός με πόθους,
15   κεὐθὺς ἐπιρρέξειν χίμαρον καλόν. ἢν δ᾽ ἀνανεύσῃ,
    τοῦδε τυχὼν ἐθέλω τρισσὰ θύη τελέσαι·
ῥέξω γὰρ δαμάλαν, λάσιον τράγον, ἄρνα τὸν ἴσχω
    σακίταν. ἀίοι δ᾽ εὐμενέως ὁ θεός.

5 AP 9.433

Λῆς ποτὶ τᾶν Νυμφᾶν διδύμοις αὐλοῖσιν ἀεῖσαι
    ἁδύ τί μοι; κἠγὼ πακτίδ᾽ ἀειράμενος
ἀρξεῦμαί τι κρέκειν, ὁ δὲ βουκόλος ἄμμιγα θέλξει
    Δάφνις κηροδέτῳ πνεύματι μελπόμενος.
5   ἐγγὺς δὲ στάντες λασίας δρυὸς ἄντρου ὄπισθεν
    Πᾶνα τὸν αἰγιβάταν ὀρφανίσωμες ὕπνου.

6 AP 9.432

Ἀ δείλαιε τὺ Θύρσι, τί τὸ πλέον εἰ κατατάξεις
    δάκρυσι διγλήνους ὦπας ὀδυρόμενος;

spring coming out of the rocks is everywhere lush with laurels, myrtles and fragrant cypress. Around it a vine bearing clusters of grapes spreads its tendrils; in spring the blackbirds utter their varied songs with clear-voiced music, and in response tuneful nightingales utter their warbling as from their throats they sound their honeyed voices. Sit down there and pray the gracious god Priapus that I may fall out of love with Daphnis in return for a fine kid being sacrificed to him without delay. But if he refuses[3]—I am willing to make him three offerings in return for success with Daphnis: I will sacrifice a heifer, a shaggy billy goat, and a stall-fed lamb that I have. May the god listen favorably to your prayer.

[3] Cf. *Id.* 7.109–14: we expect the god to be threatened.

5[1] *Greek Anthology*

By the Nymphs, are you willing[2] to play something sweet for me on the double pipes? I will pick up my lyre and begin to play, and Daphnis the oxherd will provide a charming accompaniment with the breath of his reeds bound with wax.[3] Let's stand by the leafy oak behind the cave and deprive goats' mate Pan of sleep.[4]

[1] The reader is invited to join in bucolic music.
[2] From *Id.* 1.12.
[3] I.e., the syrinx (cf. *Id.* 1.129).
[4] An allusion to the siesta of Pan as described at *Id.* 1.15–18.

6[1] *Greek Anthology*

Ah, poor Thyrsis, what is the use of having your two eyes dissolve in tears, and of lamenting so? Your kid is gone,

οἴχεται ἁ χίμαρος, τὸ καλὸν τέκος, οἴχετ᾽ ἐς Ἀιδαν·
τραχὺς γὰρ χαλαῖς ἀμφεπίαξε λύκος.
5 αἱ δὲ κύνες κλαγγεῦντι· τί τὸ πλέον, ἀνίκα τήνας
ὀστίον οὐδὲ τέφρα λείπεται οἰχομένας;

7 AP 7.659

Νήπιον υἱὸν ἔλειπες, ἐν ἁλικίᾳ δὲ καὶ αὐτός,
Εὐρύμεδον, τύμβου τοῦδε θανὼν ἔτυχες.
σοὶ μὲν ἕδρα θείοισι μετ᾽ ἀνδράσι· τὸν δὲ πολῖται
τιμασεῦντι πατρὸς μνώμενοι ὡς ἀγαθοῦ.

8 AP 6.337

Ἦλθε καὶ ἐς Μίλητον ὁ τοῦ Παιήονος υἱός,
ἰητῆρι νόσων ἀνδρὶ συνοισόμενος
Νικίᾳ, ὅς μιν ἐπ᾽ ἦμαρ ἀεὶ θυέεσσιν ἱκνεῖται,
καὶ τόδ᾽ ἀπ᾽ εὐώδους γλύψατ᾽ ἄγαλμα κέδρου,
5 Ἠετίωνι χάριν γλαφυρᾶς χερὸς ἄκρον ὑποστάς
μισθόν· ὁ δ᾽ εἰς ἔργον πᾶσαν ἀφῆκε τέχνην.

your lovely pet, gone to Hades;[2] a cruel wolf has gripped her in its claws. Your dogs are barking; but what is the use of that when she is gone and neither bone nor ash is left of her?

[1] Thyrsis and his pet kid.

[2] The tone of "gone to Hades" and "neither bone nor ash" (6) is for the reader to determine; both are suited to human, not animal, death. They may elevate the kid; or they may imply that Thyrsis is overreacting.

7[1] *Greek Anthology*

The son you have left behind is very young, Eurymedon, and you yourself have encountered this tomb, dying in your prime. You have a place among the blessed dead; but the citizens will treat your son with honor, recognizing that he had a noble father.

[1] Epitaph for Eurymedon; cf. no. 15.

8[1] *Greek Anthology*

The son of the Healer has come to Miletus, too, as associate with a man who cures illnesses—Nicias, who every day without fail prays to him with offerings and has had this statue carved from fragrant cedarwood. He agreed to pay Eetion a high price on account of his skilled craftsmanship, and Eetion put all his art into the work.

[1] On a wooden statue of Asclepius, son of Apollo and god of physicians, made by a certain Eetion for Theocritus' friend Nicias (cf. *Idd.* 11 and 28).

9 AP 7.660

Ξεῖνε, Συρακόσιός τοι ἀνὴρ τόδ᾽ ἐφίεται Ὄρθων·
χειμερίας μεθύων μηδαμὰ νυκτὸς ἴοις.
καὶ γὰρ ἐγὼ τοιοῦτον ἔχω πότμον, ἀντὶ δὲ πολλᾶς
πατρίδος ὀθνείαν κεῖμαι ἐφεσσάμενος.

10 AP 6.338

Ὑμῖν τοῦτο, θεαί, κεχαρισμένον ἐννέα πάσαις
τὤγαλμα Ξενοκλῆς θῆκε τὸ μαρμάρινον,
μουσικός· οὐχ ἑτέρως τις ἐρεῖ. σοφίῃ δ᾽ ἐπὶ τῇδε
αἶνον ἔχων Μουσέων οὐκ ἐπιλανθάνεται.

11 AP 7.661

Εὐσθένεος τὸ μνῆμα· φυσιγνώμων † ὁ σοφιστής
δεινὸς ἀπ᾽ ὀφθαλμοῦ καὶ τὸ νόημα μαθεῖν.
εὖ μιν ἔθαψαν ἑταῖροι ἐπὶ ξείνης ξένον ὄντα,
χὐμνοθέτης αὐτοῖς δαιμονίως φίλος ἦν.
5 πάντων ὧν ἐπέοικε λάχεν τεθνεὼς ὁ σοφιστής·
καίπερ ἄκικυς ἐὼν εἶχ᾽ ἄρα κηδεμόνας.

5 ἐπέοικε λάχεν Legrand: ἐπέοικεν ἔχει M

9 *Greek Anthology*

Stranger, here is the advice of Orthon from Syracuse: never go out drunk on stormy nights. That is how I met my fate; and I lie clad in foreign soil rather than in my famous fatherland.[1]

[1] "Famous" or "great"; but the Greek word, πολλῆς, sounds awkward and should probably be changed so that the phrase is "native land."

10 *Greek Anthology*

Xenocles set up this marble image to please all nine of you, goddesses, since he is a talented musician, and no one says otherwise. Having gained a good reputation for this skill, he is not unmindful of the Muses.[1]

[1] The Muses made him *mousikos* (3), a musician.

11 *Greek Anthology*

This is the gravestone of Eusthenes, an expert physiognomer[1] skilled in reading a man's character from his face. His companions gave him a decent burial, a foreigner in a foreign land, and the poet was a firm friend of theirs.[2] In death this master of his profession got all proper rites: though strengthless,[3] he had men to care for him.

[1] "Expert" seems to be the sense required, but the words ὁ σοφιστής, which recur at the end of line 5, are out of place.

[2] Text uncertain; perhaps "of his" (αὐτῷ Hecker).

[3] Eusthenes means "of good strength."

12 AP 6.339

Δαμομένης ὁ χοραγός, ὁ τὸν τρίποδ᾽, ὦ Διόνυσε,
  καὶ σὲ τὸν ἅδιστον θεῶν μακάρων ἀναθείς,
μέτριος ἦν ἐν πᾶσι, χορῷ δ᾽ ἐκτάσατο νίκαν
  ἀνδρῶν, καὶ τὸ καλὸν καὶ τὸ προσῆκον ὁρῶν.

13 AP 6.340

Ἁ Κύπρις οὐ πάνδαμος. ἱλάσκεο τὰν θεὸν εἰπών
  οὐρανίαν, ἁγνᾶς ἄνθεμα Χρυσογόνας
οἴκῳ ἐν Ἀμφικλέους, ᾧ καὶ τέκνα καὶ βίον εἶχε
  ξυνόν· ἀεὶ δέ σφιν λώιον εἰς ἔτος ἦν
5 ἐκ σέθεν ἀρχομένοις, ὦ πότνια· κηδόμενοι γάρ
  ἀθανάτων αὐτοὶ πλεῖον ἔχουσι βροτοί.

EPIGRAMS

12 *Greek Anthology*

Damomenes the chorus trainer, who dedicated this tripod and your statue, Dionysus,[1] sweetest of the blessed gods, used good measure in everything[2] and won the prize for the men's chorus, since he provided a fitting and attractive performance.

[1] He has won the prize for a men's chorus at a festival of Dionysus and in thanks has dedicated a tripod and an image of the god.

[2] *Metrios* (measured) is elaborated in the following lines, but there is probably a reference to choric *meter.* "In everything (*pâsi*)": most manuscripts have "among the boys (*paisi*)"; the meaning would then be that he did moderately with a chorus of boys but won in the men's competition.

13 *Greek Anthology*

This[1] is not Aphrodite of the People; when you pray to the goddess, you should address her as Heavenly. She was set up here by the chaste Chrysogona in the house of Amphicles, with whom she shared her children and her life.[2] By making first sacrifices to you, Lady,[3] they flourished more each year. Mortals do better when they have care for the gods.

[1] An inscription for a statue of Aphrodite Urania, a common cult title of the goddess. The contrast between this and the title *Pandêmos* (of the whole people [= promiscuous]), is discussed for example at Plato, *Symposium* 180d. The dedicatee's chastity makes that unsuitable.   [2] "Shared" suggests that she is dead (and that the inscription has been added to the statue after her death), or perhaps that her husband is dead.

[3] Perhaps daily sacrifices before this statue. There may also be a suggestion that chastity makes for a harmonious marriage.

14 AP 9.435

Ἀστοῖς καὶ ξείνοισιν ἴσον νέμει ἥδε τράπεζα·
θεὶς ἀνελεῦ ψήφου πρὸς λόγον ἑλκομένης.
ἄλλος τις πρόφασιν λεγέτω· τὰ δ᾽ ὀθνεῖα Κάικος
χρήματα καὶ νυκτὸς βουλομένοις ἀριθμεῖ.

15 AP 7.658

Γνώσομαι εἴ τι νέμεις ἀγαθοῖς πλέον ἢ καὶ ὁ δειλός
ἐκ σέθεν ὡσαύτως ἶσον, ὁδοιπόρ᾽, ἔχει.
"χαιρέτω οὗτος ὁ τύμβος," ἐρεῖς, "ἐπεὶ Εὐρυμέδοντος
κεῖται τῆς ἱερῆς κοῦφος ὑπὲρ κεφαλῆς."

16 AP 7.662

Ἡ παῖς ᾤχετ᾽ ἄωρος ἐν ἑβδόμῳ ἥδ᾽ ἐνιαυτῷ
εἰς Ἀίδην πολλῆς ἡλικίης προτέρη,
δειλαίη, ποθέουσα τὸν εἰκοσάμηνον ἀδελφόν,
νήπιον ἀστόργου γευσάμενον θανάτου.
5 αἰαῖ ἐλεινὰ παθοῦσα Περιστερή, ὡς ἐν ἑτοίμῳ
ἀνθρώποις δαίμων θῆκε τὰ λυγρότατα.

---

[1] Or (less likely) "before most girls of the same age." But "most" (πολλῆς) may be corrupt.

14 *Greek Anthology*

This bank[1] offers the same rate to natives and foreigners alike. Deposit your money, and withdraw it according to a strict reckoning. Others may make excuses, but Caicus transacts foreign business even at night for those who need it.[2]

[1] A poem to be displayed outside a bank. Such signs have been found at Pompeii and elsewhere.

[2] It is perhaps also implied that Caicus is so honest that one can trust him even in the dark.

15 *Greek Anthology*

Traveler, I shall now learn whether you respect good men more or whether you treat bad men just the same. You will say,[1] "Bless this tomb, because it lies lightly[2] over the holy head of Eurymedon."

[1] Sc., if you do indeed prefer good men to bad.

[2] A variation on the prayer that earth should lie lightly on a dead person.

16 *Greek Anthology*

This girl went to Hades untimely in her seventh year, before she had lived out most of her life;[1] poor child, she was pining for her brother,[2] who tasted cruel death as an infant aged twenty months. Ah, Peristere,[3] your suffering is pitiful. How near to mortals god has placed the most grievous unhappiness!

[2] It is implied that she wished to be reunited with him.

[3] Presumably the mother; the children's names are to be imagined as inscribed on the tomb.

17 AP 9.599

Θᾶσαι τὸν ἀνδριάντα τοῦτον, ὦ ξένε,
  σπουδᾷ, καὶ λέγ' ἐπὴν ἐς οἶκον ἔνθῃς·
"Ἀνακρέοντος εἰκόν' εἶδον ἐν Τέῳ
  τῶν πρόσθ' εἴ τι περισσὸν ᾠδοποιῶν."
5 προσθεὶς δὲ χὤτι τοῖς νέοισιν ἄδετο,
  ἐρεῖς ἀτρεκέως ὅλον τὸν ἄνδρα.

18 AP 9.600

Ἅ τε φωνὰ Δώριος χὡνὴρ ὁ τὰν κωμῳδίαν
  εὑρὼν Ἐπίχαρμος.
ὦ Βάκχε, χάλκεόν νιν ἀντ' ἀλαθινοῦ
  τὶν ὧδ' ἀνέθηκαν
5 τοὶ Συρακούσσαις ἐνίδρυνται, πελωρίστᾳ πόλει,
  οἷ' ἄνδρα πολίταν.
σοφῶν ἔοικε ῥημάτων μεμναμένους
  τελεῖν ἐπίχειρα·
πολλὰ γὰρ ποττὰν ζόαν τοῖς παισὶν εἶπε χρήσιμα.
10 μεγάλα χάρις αὐτῷ.

6 ἄνδρα πολίταν Wordsworth: -ρὶ -ίτᾳ m: -ρὶ -ῖται
m   7 σοφῶν ἔοικε Kaibel: σωρὸν γὰρ εἶχε vel σωρὸν
εἶχε M

---

[1] A metrically experimental piece. Lines 1, 5, and 9 are tro-
chaic tetrameters (–∪–× –∪–× –∪–× –∪∩); lines 3 and 7 are iam-
bic trimeters (see on no. 17); and lines 2, 4, 6, 8, and 10 are forms
of reizianum (×–∪∪–× or ∪∪–∪∪–×).

EPIGRAMS

17[1] *Greek Anthology*

Look carefully at this statue, stranger, and when you reach home say, "In Teos I saw an image of Anacreon, who was preeminent among the lyric poets of old."[2] If you add that he took pleasure in young lads, you will describe the whole man exactly.

---

[1] The meter is iambic trimeters (×–∪–×–∪–×–∪∩) alternating with phalaecian hendecasyllables (×– –∪∪–∪–∪–∩). The combination is not found elsewhere, and so far as is known it was not used by Anacreon.

[2] Anacreon of Teos (near Ephesus in Ionia), a lyric poet of the sixth century, famous for his erotic and sympotic compositions. This is one of a number of epigrams in the *Greek Anthology* that celebrate or commemorate him (*Anth. Pal.* 7.23–33; *Anth. Plan.* 306–9).

18[1] *Greek Anthology*

The dialect is Dorian, and so is the man: Epicharmus, the inventor of comedy.[2] Those who inhabit Syracuse, an awesome city, have set him up here for you, Bacchus,[3] a bronze image of his real self, since he was their fellow citizen. It is fitting that those who remember his wise words[4] should recompense him: he expressed a great deal of useful guidance for young lives. He deserves great thanks.

---

[2] Epicharmus (fl. early fifth century), from Doric-speaking Sicily, was regarded by some as the first comic poet. Collections of maxims culled from writings attributed to him were in circulation (cf. line 9).

[3] Dionysus, god of drama.

[4] Text uncertain. The manuscript reading is "heap of words."

19 AP 13.3

Ὁ μουσοποιὸς ἐνθάδ᾽ Ἱππῶναξ κεῖται.
εἰ μὲν πονηρός, μὴ προσέρχευ τῷ τύμβῳ·
εἰ δ᾽ ἐσσὶ κρήγυός τε καὶ παρὰ χρηστῶν,
θαρσέων καθίζευ, κἢν θέλῃς ἀπόβριξον.

20 AP 7.663

Ὁ μικκὸς τόδ᾽ ἔτευξε τᾷ Θραΐσσᾳ
Μήδειος τὸ μνᾶμ᾽ ἐπὶ τᾷ ὁδῷ κἠπέγραψε Κλείτας.
ἕξει τὰν χάριν ἁ γυνὰ ἀντὶ τήνων
ὧν τὸν κῶρον ἔθρεψε· τί μάν; ἔτι χρησίμα καλεῖται.

21 AP 7.664

Ἀρχίλοχον καὶ στᾶθι καὶ εἴσιδε τὸν πάλαι ποιητάν
τὸν τῶν ἰάμβων, οὗ τὸ μυρίον κλέος
διῆλθε κἠπὶ νύκτα καὶ ποτ᾽ ἀῶ.
ἦ ῥά νιν αἱ Μοῖσαι καὶ ὁ Δάλιος ἠγάπευν Ἀπόλ-
λων,
5   ὡς ἐμμελής τ᾽ ἐγένετο κἠπιδέξιος
ἔπεά τε ποιεῖν πρὸς λύραν τ᾽ ἀείδειν.

---

1 For a statue of Archilochus, a seventh-century poet from Paros renowned for his invective and for metrical experimentation. This poem, like no. 18, is in stanzas of three lines: archilochian (see on no. 20) plus iambic trimeter (see on no. 17) plus iambic trimeter catalectic (∪–∪– ×–∪– ∪–∩).

EPIGRAMS

19 *Greek Anthology*

Here lies the poet Hipponax.[1] If you are a rascal, don't come near the tomb; but if you are honest and from decent people, sit down with confidence and, if you like, take a nap.

[1] Hipponax, a sixth-century Ephesian poet notorious for his obscenity and violent personal attacks. He wrote mostly in the scazon meter, an iambic trimeter with heavy penultimate syllable. This epigram is in scazons, and imitates his Ionic dialect.

20[1] *Greek Anthology*

Little Medeius had this memorial built by the roadside for his Thracian nurse[2] with an inscription saying that it was for Cleita. The woman will have proper thanks for looking after the boy. And why? Because she will still be called "loyal."[3]

[1] The meter is Phalaecian hendecasyllables (see on no. 17) alternating with archilochians ($- - \underset{\smile\smile}{} - \cup\cup - \cup\cup - \cup - \cup - \cap$).

[2] Cf. *Id.* 2.70. She is a slave from Thrace.

[3] The family called her loyal in life, and the same adjective describes her in the inscription.

21[1] *Greek Anthology*

Stop and look on Archilochus the old-time poet and writer of iambics, whose infinite fame has spread east and west.[2] He was indeed a favorite of the Muses and of Delian Apollo, being so musical and skilled at making poetry and performing it on the lyre.

[2] Lit., "to the night and to the dawn," where the sun rises and sets.

433

22 AP 9.598

Τὸν τοῦ Ζανὸς ὅδ᾽ ὑμὶν υἱὸν ὠνήρ
τὸν λεοντομάχαν, τὸν ὀξύχειρα,
πρᾶτος τῶν ἐπάνωθε μουσοποιῶν
Πείσανδρος συνέγραψεν οὐκ Καμίρου,
5 χὤσσους ἐξεπόνασεν εἶπ᾽ ἀέθλους.
τοῦτον δ᾽ αὐτὸν ὁ δᾶμος, ὡς σάφ᾽ εἰδῇς,
ἔστασ᾽ ἐνθάδε χάλκεον ποήσας
πολλοῖς μησὶν ὄπισθε κἠνιαυτοῖς.

23 AP 7.262

Αὐδήσει τὸ γράμμα, τί σᾶμά τε καὶ τίς ὑπ᾽ αὐτῷ.
Γλαύκης εἰμὶ τάφος τῆς ὀνομαζομένης.

24 AP 9.436

Ἀρχαῖα τὠπόλλωνι τἀναθήματα
ὑπῆρχεν· ἡ βάσις δὲ τοῖς μὲν εἴκοσι,
τοῖς δ᾽ ἑπτά, τοῖς δὲ πέντε, τοῖς δὲ δώδεκα,
τοῖς δὲ διηκοσίοισι νεωτέρη ἤδ᾽ ἐνιαυτοῖς·
5 τοσσόσδ᾽ ἀριθμὸς ἐξέβη μετρούμενος.

1 τὠπόλλωνι τἀναθήματα Wilamowitz: -ωνος τὰν. ταῦτα
M   5 τοσσόσδ᾽ ἀριθμὸς Wilamowitz: τοσσόσδε γάρ
νιν M

1 The text of lines 1 and 5 is uncertain. Unless line 1 was
originally a hexameter, the metrical scheme is three iambic trim-
eters, a hexameter, and another iambic trimeter, an asymmetry
almost unique among literary epigrams.

22 *Greek Anthology*

This man, Pisander of Camirus,[1] was the first of the old-time poets to write about the son of Zeus, the lion slayer, good at using his hands, and about all the Labors that he accomplished. You should know that many months—many years—later the people set up this likeness of him here in bronze.

[1] Pisander, a poet of the seventh or sixth century from Camirus on the island of Rhodes, wrote an epic on Heracles. The meter of this epigram is scazons (cf. no. 19); Pisander used hexameters.

23 *Greek Anthology*

The inscription will tell what monument this is and who lies beneath it. I am the tomb of the celebrated Glauce.[1]

[1] Or perhaps "of the woman called Glauce." A famous lyre player of this name is mentioned at *Id.* 4.31, but the epigram provides no identifying details. The heading in the manuscript says that Glauce is a *hetaira*, but that may be a guess.

24[1] *Greek Anthology*

Long ago the offerings were already Apollo's,[2] but the pedestal is more recent by twenty years for these, by seven for these, by five for these, by twelve for these, and by two hundred for these: such turned out to be the figure when a reckoning was made.

[2] An inscription for five offerings to Apollo newly gathered together on a single base. A note in the manuscript says that they are from Syracuse.

25 AP 7.534

Ἄνθρωπε, ζωῆς περιφείδεο μηδὲ παρ' ὥρην
  ναυτίλος ἴσθι· καὶ ὡς οὐ πολὺς ἀνδρὶ βίος.
δείλαιε Κλεόνικε, σὺ δ' εἰς λιπαρὴν Θάσον ἐλθεῖν
  ἠπείγευ Κοίλης ἔμπορος ἐκ Συρίης,
5 ἔμπορος, ὦ Κλεόνικε· δύσιν δ' ὑπὸ Πλειάδος αὐτὴν
  ποντοπορῶν αὐτῇ Πλειάδι συγκατέδυς.

5 ὑπὸ Πλειάδος Graefe: ὑποπληάδων M   6 ποντο-
πορῶν αὐτῇ Pierson: -πόρῳ ναύτῃ M

EPIGRAMS

25[1] *Greek Anthology*

Mortal, take care of your life and do not go to sea at the wrong time; life is short as it is. Poor Cleonicus, as a merchant going from Hollow Syria you were in a hurry to reach fair Thasos.[2] As a merchant,[3] Cleonicus—and as you made your voyage just before the setting of the Pleiads, your own star set with the Pleiads themselves.[4]

[1] The Planudean Anthology cites only the first couplet, and attributes it to Theocritus, but the Palatine Anthology gives the whole poem to an Automedon of Aetolia.

[2] Hollow Syria: Phoenicia and Palestine. Thasos: an island off the coast of Thrace.

[3] I.e., (probably) as a mere merchant: your hope of profit was not worth the risk.

[4] See on *Id.* 13.25.

26 = T 9

27 = T 8

MOSCHUS

TESTIMONIA

1 *Suda* s.v. Μόσχος, μ 1278

Μόσχος, Συρακούσιος, γραμματικός, Ἀριστάρχου γνώριμος. οὗτός ἐστιν ὁ δεύτερος ποιητὴς μετὰ Θεόκριτον, τὸν τῶν βουκολικῶν δραμάτων ποιητήν. ἔγραψε καὶ αὐτός.

2 Vid. Theoc. T 1

cf. Σ *Anth. Pal.* 9.440 οὗτος ὁ Μόσχος ποιητής ἐστι τῶν καλουμένων βουκολικῶν ποιημάτων, ὧν πρῶτος Θεόκριτος, δεύτερος αὐτὸς ὁ Μόσχος, τρίτος Βίων Σμυρναῖος.

3 Ath. 485e

Μόσχος δ' ἐν ἐξηγήσει Ῥοδιακῶν Λέξεων κεραμεοῦν ἀγγεῖόν φησιν αὐτὸ εἶναι, ἐοικὸς ταῖς λεγομέναις πτωματίσιν, ἐκπεταλώτερον δέ.

TESTIMONIA

1 *Suda* s.v. Moschus

Moschus of Syracuse, scholar, acquaintance of Aristar-chus.[1] He is second after Theocritus, the poet of bucolic mimes. He composed some of these himself.

[1] Famous scholar and head of the Alexandrian library in the second century BC.

2 Scholiast on the *Greek Anthology*

This Moschus is a composer of so-called bucolic verse. Theocritus was first, Moschus himself second, and Bion of Smyrna third.

3 Athenaeus, *Scholars at Dinner*

Moschus in the explanatory notes to the *Rhodian Vocabu-lary* says that it (the *lepastê*) is a ceramic vessel that re-sembles what are referred to as *ptômatides,* but that it has a more extended shape.

441

EROS THE RUNAWAY

Aphrodite makes public proclamation against Eros, as if he is a dangerous runaway slave, and promises a reward. The "wanted man" is described at length in terms allegorical of his nature: he seems a mere child, but his power is universal.

An epigram by Meleager (1st c. BC) is a similar proclamation against Eros (Anth. Pal. 5.177).

ΕΡΩΣ ΔΡΑΠΕΤΗΣ

Ἁ Κύπρις τὸν Ἔρωτα τὸν υἱέα μακρὸν ἐβώστρει·
"ὅστις ἐνὶ τριόδοισι πλανώμενον εἶδεν Ἔρωτα,
δραπετίδας ἐμός ἐστιν· ὁ μανύσας γέρας ἑξεῖ.
μισθός τοι τὸ φίλημα τὸ Κύπριδος· ἢν δ' ἀγάγῃς νιν,
5 οὐ γυμνὸν τὸ φίλημα, τὺ δ', ὦ ξένε, καὶ πλέον ἑξεῖς.
ἔστι δ' ὁ παῖς περίσαμος· ἐν εἴκοσι πᾶσι μάθοις νιν.
χρῶτα μὲν οὐ λευκὸς πυρὶ δ' εἴκελος· ὄμματα δ' αὐτῷ
δριμύλα καὶ φλογόεντα· κακαὶ φρένες, ἁδὺ λάλημα·
οὐ γὰρ ἴσον νοέει καὶ φθέγγεται· ὡς μέλι φωνά,
10 ὡς δὲ χολὰ νόος ἐστίν· ἀνάμερος, ἠπεροπευτάς,
οὐδὲν ἀλαθεύων, δόλιον βρέφος, ἄγρια παίσδων.
εὐπλόκαμον τὸ κάρανον, ἔχει δ' ἰταμὸν τὸ μέτωπον.
μικκύλα μὲν τήνῳ τὰ χερύδρια, μακρὰ δὲ βάλλει·
βάλλει κεἰς Ἀχέροντα καὶ εἰς Ἀΐδεω βασίλεια.
15 γυμνὸς ὅλος τό γε σῶμα, νόος δέ οἱ εὖ πεπύκασται,
καὶ πτερόεις ὡς ὄρνις ἐφίπταται ἄλλον ἐπ' ἄλλῳ,
ἀνέρας ἠδὲ γυναῖκας, ἐπὶ σπλάγχνοις δὲ κάθηται.
τόξον ἔχει μάλα βαιόν, ὑπὲρ τόξῳ δὲ βέλεμνον—
τυτθὸν μὲν τὸ βέλεμνον, ἐς αἰθέρα δ' ἄχρι φο-
ρεῖται—
20 καὶ χρύσεον περὶ νῶτα φαρέτριον, ἔνδοθι δ' ἐντί

14 βασίλεια Wilamowitz: -ῆα M

444

EROS THE RUNAWAY

Cypris made public proclamation about her son Eros: "If anyone has seen Eros loitering on street corners, he is a runaway from me, and anyone giving information about him shall have a reward. The reward shall be a kiss from Cypris; but if you bring him along with you, my friend, you shall have more than just a bare kiss. The boy is easy to recognize; twenty words are enough to describe him.[1] His skin is not white, but like fire; his eyes are piercing and bright as flame; his intentions are wicked but his chatter is sweet, for his thoughts do not match his words: his voice is like honey, his mind like gall. He is a savage, a deceiver, a complete liar, a wily brat whose play is all cruel. He has a pretty head of hair, but a bold forehead. His hands are little, but they can shoot a long way: they can shoot even as far as Acheron and the halls of Hades. His body is stark naked but his mind is well covered, and like a winged bird he flits from one person to another, men and women alike, and settles in their hearts. He has a little bow, and on the bow an arrow; the arrow is tiny, but it reaches sky-high. On his back he has a small golden quiver, and in it are the

[1] Or, perhaps, "You would know him among twenty."

τοὶ πικροὶ κάλαμοι τοῖς πολλάκι κἀμὲ τιτρώσκει.
πάντα μὲν ἄγρια ταῦτα· πολὺ πλέον ἁ δαῒς αὐτῶ·
βαιὰ λαμπὰς ἐοῖσα τὸν ἅλιον αὐτὸν ἀναίθει.
ἢν τύγ' ἕλῃς τῆνον, δήσας ἄγε μηδ' ἐλεήσῃς,
25   κἢν ποτίδῃς κλαίοντα, φυλάσσεο μή σε πλανάσῃ·
κἢν γελάῃ, τύ νιν ἕλκε, καὶ ἢν ἐθέλῃ σε φιλῆσαι,
φεῦγε· κακὸν τὸ φίλημα· τὰ χείλεα φάρμακον ἐντί.
ἢν δὲ λέγῃ, 'λάβε ταῦτα· χαρίζομαι ὅσσα μοι ὅπλα,'
μὴ τὺ θίγῃς πλάνα δῶρα, τὰ γὰρ πυρὶ πάντα βέβα-
πται."

22 πλέον ἁ δαῒς Wilamowitz: πλέονα δ' ἀεὶ m: πλέον δέει m:
πλέον δέ οἱ m
29 post h. v. in quibusdam codd. sequitur v. subditivus (?) αἲ
αἲ καὶ τὸ σίδαρον, ὃ τὸν πυρόεντα καθέξει

keen shafts with which he wounds even me. All this equipment is harmful, but even more so is his torch: it is a little light, but it can set the Sun himself on fire.[2]

"If you should catch this boy, tie him up and have no pity. If you see him crying, take care not to be tricked. If he laughs, keep pulling him along, and if he wants to kiss you, don't let him: his kiss is dangerous, his lips poison. If he says, 'Take these: I make you a gift of all my weapons,' do not touch those treacherous gifts, for they have all been tempered in the fire."[3]

[2] Allegorical of the intensity of burning passion; and also suggesting that the sun god, like everyone else, can be made to fall in love.

[3] The arrows would normally be tempered by being plunged in water, but those of Eros are tempered in fire; that is, they inflict burning passion.

EUROPA

The Europa *promises to be an etiological poem on the name of Europe (1–15), but it in fact consists of an elegant and witty narrative recounting the abduction of the girl Europa by Zeus disguised as a bull. Four tableaux make up the story: Europa in bed, in the meadow, crossing the sea on the bull's back, and canonized as mother of Zeus' children. The poem is framed by prophecy: Europa's prophetic dream at the start, which marks her awakening sexuality, is complemented by Zeus' forecast of her future at the close. Within this frame stand two naïve speeches of Europa (21–27, 135–52), each ending with a prayer; and within this inner frame are two set-piece descriptions, of her flower basket and of her passage across the sea (37–62, 115–30). The latter description is directly inspired by contemporary paintings and mosaics; the former purports to reproduce in words a real work of art.*

The myth of Europa had been treated by, among others, Hesiod, Stesichorus, Simonides, and Bacchylides, but it is not known whether Moschus is indebted to any particular source. The dream and the basket are probably his own invention. The poem contains many verbal reminiscences of Homer.

448

Criticism

Bühler, W. *Die Europa des Moschos: Text, Übersetzung und Kommentar = Hermes Einzelschrift* 13. Wiesbaden, 1960.

Campbell, M. *Moschus:* Europa. Hildesheim, 1991.

Gutzwiller, *Hellenistic Epyllion,* 63–73.

Hopkinson, *Hellenistic Anthology,* 200–215.

Smart, J. "Intertextual Dynamics in Moschus' *Europa*." *Arethusa* 45 (2012): 43–55.

ΜΟΣΧΟΥ ΕΥΡΩΠΗ

Εὐρώπῃ ποτὲ Κύπρις ἐπὶ γλυκὺν ἧκεν ὄνειρον,
νυκτὸς ὅτε τρίτατον λάχος ἵσταται ἐγγύθι δ᾽ ἠώς,
ὕπνος ὅτε γλυκίων μέλιτος βλεφάροισιν ἐφίζων
λυσιμελὴς πεδάᾳ μαλακῷ κατὰ φάεα δεσμῷ,
5 εὖτε καὶ ἀτρεκέων ποιμαίνεται ἔθνος ὀνείρων.
τῆμος ὑπωροφίοισιν ἐνὶ κνώσσουσα δόμοισι
Φοίνικος θυγάτηρ ἔτι παρθένος Εὐρώπεια
ὤϊσατ᾽ ἠπείρους δοιὰς περὶ εἷο μάχεσθαι,
Ἀσίδα τ᾽ ἀντιπέρην τε· φυὴν δ᾽ ἔχον οἷα γυναῖκες.
10 τῶν δ᾽ ἣ μὲν ξείνης μορφὴν ἔχεν, ἣ δ᾽ ἄρ᾽ ἐῴκει
ἐνδαπίῃ, καὶ μᾶλλον ἑῆς περιέσχετο κούρης,
φάσκεν δ᾽ ὥς μιν ἔτικτε καὶ ὡς ἀτίτηλέ μιν αὐτή.
ἡ δ᾽ ἑτέρη κρατερῇσι βιωομένη παλάμῃσιν
εἴρυεν οὐκ ἀέκουσαν, ἐπεὶ φάτο μόρσιμον εἷο
15 ἐκ Διὸς αἰγιόχου γέρας ἔμμεναι Εὐρώπειαν.

14 εἷο Ahrens: εἶναι M

---

[1] Aphrodite, born on the island of Cyprus (Hes. *Theog.* 191–200). [2] Dreams seen just before daybreak were thought to be true ones (Pl. *Resp.* 572a).

[3] The women's quarters were usually upstairs.

[4] Phoenix gave his name to Phoenicia, where the poem is set.

[5] Europe is of course not named: the poem is an etiology of how it came to be so called. Europa's dream and her trip to the

450

EUROPA

Cypris[1] once sent upon Europa a sweet dream. At the time when the third part of night begins and dawn is near; when limb-loosening sleep, sweeter than honey, sits on the eyelids and binds the eyes with a soft bond; and when the herd of true dreams goes afield[2]—at that time, as she slumbered in her upper chamber,[3] Europa, daughter of Phoenix,[4] still a virgin, thought she saw two continents contend for her, Asia and the land opposite;[5] and they had the form of women.[6] Of these, one had the appearance of a foreigner, while the other resembled a native woman and clung more and more to her daughter, and kept saying that she had herself borne and reared her. But the other, using the force of her strong hands, drew her not unwillingly along, for she said it was fated by Zeus who bears the aegis[7] that Europa should be her prize.

seashore are inspired by two famous passages in which a girl travels with her handmaidens to an erotic encounter: (1) Nausicaa's dream and trip to the seashore in *Odyssey* 6; (2) Medea's dream and her ride to meet Jason in Book 3 of Apollonius' *Argonautica*.

[6] The personification is inspired by lines 181–87 of Aeschylus' *Persae*, where the Persian queen Atossa sees Europe and Asia as two women in native dress; cf. Soph. Fr. 881 Lloyd-Jones.

[7] A traditional epithet of Zeus in Homer. The aegis was either a tasseled goatskin or a shield covered in goat hide (*aix* = goat). On it were depicted personifications of Strife and other horrors (*Il.* 5.738–42).

ἢ δ' ἀπὸ μὲν στρωτῶν λεχέων θόρε δειμαίνουσα,
παλλομένη κραδίην· τὸ γὰρ ὡς ὕπαρ εἶδεν ὄνειρον.
ἑζομένη δ' ἐπὶ δηρὸν ἀκὴν ἔχεν, ἀμφοτέρας δέ
εἰσέτι πεπταμένοισιν ἐν ὄμμασιν εἶχε γυναῖκας.
20 ὀψὲ δὲ δειμαλέην ἀνενείκατο παρθένος αὐδήν·
"τίς μοι τοιάδε φάσματ' ἐπουρανίων προΐηλεν;
ποῖοί με στρωτῶν λεχέων ὕπερ ἐν θαλάμοισιν
ἡδὺ μάλα κνώσσουσαν ἀνεπτοίησαν ὄνειροι;
τίς δ' ἦν ἡ ξείνη τὴν εἴσιδον ὑπνώουσα;
25 ὥς μ' ἔλαβε κραδίην κείνης πόθος, ὥς με καὶ αὐτή
ἀσπασίως ὑπέδεκτο καὶ ὡς σφετέρην ἴδε παῖδα.
ἀλλά μοι εἰς ἀγαθὸν μάκαρες κρήνειαν ὄνειρον."

Ὥς εἰποῦσ' ἀνόρουσε, φίλας δ' ἐπεδίζεθ' ἑταίρας
ἥλικας οἰέτεας θυμήρεας εὐπατερείας
30 τῆσιν ἀεὶ συνάθυρεν ὅτ' ἐς χορὸν ἐντύνοιτο
ἢ ὅτε φαιδρύνοιτο χρόα προχοῇσιν ἀναύρων
ἢ ὁπότ' ἐκ λειμῶνος εὔπνοα λείρι' ἀμέργοι.
αἱ δέ οἱ αἶψα φάανθεν, ἔχον δ' ἐν χερσὶν ἑκάστη
ἀνθοδόκον τάλαρον· ποτὶ δὲ λειμῶνας ἔβαινον
35 ἀγχιάλους, ὅθι τ' αἰὲν ὁμιλαδὸν ἠγερέθοντο
τερπόμεναι ῥοδέῃ τε φυῇ καὶ κύματος ἠχῇ.
αὐτὴ δὲ χρύσεον τάλαρον φέρεν Εὐρώπεια.

27 κρήνειαν Wakefield: κρίν- M
32 ἀμέργοι Meineke: -σοι M

8 I.e., covered with bedclothes.
9 The verb can also imply sexual excitement.
10 A dangerous venue. Europa stands in a long line of girls who are themselves plucked in flower meadows by gods. Perse-

Europa leaped in fright from her covered bed,[8] her heart pounding; she had experienced the dream as if it were real. Sitting down, she kept a long time silent; and still she kept a vision of both women before her now open eyes. At last the girl raised her frightened voice: "Which of the gods in heaven has sent such visions upon me? What sort of dreams appearing above my covered bed have scared me[9] as I slept so sweetly in my chamber? Who was the foreign woman whom I saw as I slept? How love for her seized my heart! How joyfully she herself welcomed me and looked on me as her own child! May the blessed gods bring this dream to fulfillment for me with a good result!"

With these words she leaped up and looked for her dear companions, girls of the same age, born in the same year, dear to her heart and from noble fathers, with whom she always played when she entered the dance, or when she washed her body in the streams of rivers, or when she plucked fragrant lilies from the meadow. And at once they appeared to her; and each held in her hands a basket for flowers; and they went to the meadows near the sea,[10] where they always gathered together in groups, delighting in the growing roses and in the sound of the waves. Europa herself carried a golden basket,[11] a thing to admire,

phone is the best-known example (*Hymn. Hom. Cer.* 1–18, 406–33); cf. Eur. *Ion* 887–96 (Creusa), *Hel.* 214–51 (Helen).

[11] The basket is linked both thematically and genealogically with its owner. Set-piece descriptions, or "ecphraseis," of works of art are a feature of Greek poetry, the originary text being the description of Achilles' shield, made by Hephaestus, at Hom. *Il.* 18.478–608. Here Moschus seems to be directly indebted to Theocritus' description of the rustic cup at *Id.* 1.27–56.

θηητόν, μέγα θαῦμα, μέγαν πόνον Ἡφαίστοιο
ὃν Λιβύῃ πόρε δῶρον ὅτ' ἐς λέχος Ἐννοσιγαίου
40 ἤιεν· ἡ δὲ πόρεν περικαλλέι Τηλεφαάσσῃ,
ἥτε οἱ αἵματος ἔσκεν· ἀνύμφῳ δ' Εὐρωπείῃ
μήτηρ Τηλεφάασσα περικλυτὸν ὤπασε δῶρον.
ἐν τῷ δαίδαλα πολλὰ τετεύχατο μαρμαίροντα·
ἐν μὲν ἔην χρυσοῖο τετυγμένη Ἰναχὶς Ἰώ
45 εἰσέτι πόρτις ἐοῦσα, φυὴν δ' οὐκ εἶχε γυναίην.
φοιταλέη δὲ πόδεσσιν ἐφ' ἁλμυρὰ βαῖνε κέλευθα
νηχομένῃ ἰκέλη, κυάνου δ' ἐτέτυκτο θάλασσα·
δοιοῦ δ' ἕστασαν ὑψοῦ ἐπ' ὀφρύσιν αἰγιαλοῖο
φῶτες ἀολλήδην θηεῦντο δὲ ποντοπόρον βοῦν.
50 ἐν δ' ἦν Ζεὺς Κρονίδης ἐπαφώμενος ἠρέμα χερσί
πόρτιος Ἰναχίης τήν θ' ἑπταπόρῳ παρὰ Νείλῳ
ἐκ βοὸς εὐκεράοιο πάλιν μετάμειβε γυναῖκα.
ἀργύρεος μὲν ἔην Νείλου ῥόος, ἡ δ' ἄρα πόρτις
χαλκείη, χρυσοῦ δὲ τετυγμένος αὐτὸς ἔην Ζεύς.
55 ἀμφὶ δὲ δινήεντος ὑπὸ στεφάνην ταλάροιο
Ἑρμείης ἤσκητο, πέλας δέ οἱ ἐκτετάνυστο

47 κυάνου Meineke: -νη M   48 δοιοῦ Hermann: -οὶ
M   ὀφρύσιν m, coni. Hermann: -ύι m: -ύος m
51 Ἰναχίης· τὴν Pierson: εἰναλίης τὴν m: εἶναι ληιστὴν
m: ἐς καλλίστην m

---

[12] The lineage of the basket is indebted to the impressive
pedigree of Agamemnon's scepter, another work of Hephaestus,
at Hom. *Il.* 2.102–8. The basket belonged to Europa's grand-
mother Libye, who was raped by a god (the Earthshaker Posei-

a great wonder, a great work of Hephaestus, which he gave as a gift to Libya when she went to the bed of the Earth-shaker.[12] She gave it to the beautiful Telephassa, who was of her blood; and Telephassa, mother of Europa, presented it as a splendid gift to Europa when she was still unmarried. On it were wrought many elaborate designs that gleamed brightly: there was Io, daughter of Inachus,[13] wrought of gold, still a heifer; and she did not have the form of a woman. She went wandering with her feet on the briny paths as if swimming, and the sea was wrought of blue enamel. High up on the cliffs[14] of either shore stood people in crowds who gazed on the seagoing cow. There was Zeus, son of Cronus, touching lightly with his hands the heifer, daughter of Inachus, which by the seven-branched Nile he was changing back from a well-horned cow to a woman. The stream of the Nile was of silver, and the heifer of bronze, and Zeus himself was wrought of gold. All around, under the rim of the rounded basket, Hermes was depicted, and near him Argus was stretched

don) and gave her name to Libya; and it depicted the rape by a god of Libye's grandmother Io, who gave her name to Ionia. Europa inherits both the basket and the experiences depicted on it.

[13] Io was a priestess of Hera. Zeus desired her and changed her into a cow to escape Hera's notice, but Hera requested the cow as a gift and set many-eyed Argus to watch over her. Argus was killed by Hermes, and the peacock arose from his blood; in revenge Hera tormented the cow with a gadfly, which drove her to Egypt via the Bosporus and the Ionian Sea. There Zeus touched her and restored her true form; from the touch she conceived Epaphus (*epaphan* = touch).

[14] Lit., "brows."

Ἄργος ἀκοιμήτοισι κεκασμένος ὀφθαλμοῖσι.
τοῖο δὲ φοινήεντος ἀφ᾽ αἵματος ἐξανέτελλεν
ὄρνις ἀγαλλόμενος πτερύγων πολυανθέι χροιῇ,
60 τὰς ὅ γ᾽ ἀναπλώσας ὡσεί τέ τις ὠκύαλος νηῦς
χρυσείου ταλάροιο περίσκεπε χείλεα ταρσοῖς.
τοῖος ἔην τάλαρος περικαλλέος Εὐρωπείης.

Αἳ δ᾽ ἐπεὶ οὖν λειμῶνας ἐς ἀνθεμόεντας ἵκανον,
ἄλλη ἐπ᾽ ἀλλοίοισι τότ᾽ ἄνθεσι θυμὸν ἔτερπον.
65 τῶν ἣ μὲν νάρκισσον ἐύπνοον, ἣ δ᾽ ὑάκινθον,
ἣ δ᾽ ἴον, ἣ δ᾽ ἕρπυλλον ἀπαίνυτο· πολλὰ δ᾽ ἔραζε
λειμώνων ἐαροτρεφέων θαλέθεσκε πέτηλα.
αἳ δ᾽ αὖτε ξανθοῖο κρόκου θυόεσσαν ἔθειραν
δρέπτον ἐριδμαίνουσαι· ἀτὰρ μέσσῃσιν ἄνασσα
70 ἀγλαΐην πυρσοῖο ῥόδου χείρεσσι λέγουσα
οἷά περ ἐν Χαρίτεσσι διέπρεπεν Ἀφρογένεια.

Οὐ μὲν δηρὸν ἔμελλεν ἐπ᾽ ἄνθεσι θυμὸν ἰαίνειν,
οὐδ᾽ ἄρα παρθενίην μίτρην ἄχραντον ἔρυσθαι.
ἦ γὰρ δὴ Κρονίδης ὥς μιν φράσαθ᾽ ὣς ἐόλητο
75 θυμὸν ἀνωίστοισιν ὑποδμηθεὶς βελέεσσι
Κύπριδος, ἣ μούνη δύναται καὶ Ζῆνα δαμάσσαι.
δὴ γὰρ ἀλευόμενός τε χόλον ζηλήμονος Ἥρης

60 τὰς ὅγ᾽ Maas: ταρσὸν M

---

[15] Lit., "many-flowered," and so particularly suitable for a basket used for gathering flowers.

[16] The shields of Achilles and Heracles have Ocean around their edges (Hom. *Il.* 18.607–8; Hes. [*Sc.*] 314–17), and Theocritus' rustic beaker is bordered with acanthus (*Id.* 1.55). Here the

out, endowed with unsleeping eyes. From his crimson blood arose a bird, exulting in the many-hued[15] color of its wings: spreading them out like a sea-swift ship it covered the lip of the golden basket with its tail.[16] Such was the basket of beauteous Europa.

Now when they reached the flower meadows one girl delighted her heart with one flower, one with another. One of them picked the fragrant narcissus, another the hyacinth,[17] another the violet, another thyme; for on the ground many flowers of the meadows nourished in spring were blooming. Others again competed to gather fragrant tresses[18] of golden saffron. But in their midst the princess, plucking with her hands the splendor of a flame-red rose,[19] stood out like the foam-born goddess among the Graces.[20]

Not for long was she to please her heart with the flowers or keep her virgin girdle undefiled.[21] No sooner had the son of Cronus noticed her than he was in turmoil in his heart, overcome by the unexpected arrows of Cypris, who alone can overcome even Zeus. Indeed, to avoid the anger of jealous Hera and wishing to deceive the girl's simple

arrangement is less clear; perhaps the peacock's eyed tail spreads round the rim of the basket.

[17] See on Theoc. *Id.* 10.28.

[18] A poeticism for flowers.

[19] The act symbolizes her own ravishment.

[20] Aphrodite, born from the foam (*aphros*) produced when Cronus cast into the sea the genitals of his castrated father, Uranus (Hes. *Theog.* 154–206). The simile is inspired by Hom. *Od.* 6.102–9, where Nausicaa among her handmaidens is compared to Artemis with her band of nymphs.

[21] I.e., removed by a man.

παρθενικῆς τ᾽ ἐθέλων ἀταλὸν νόον ἐξαπατῆσαι
κρύψε θεὸν καὶ τρέψε δέμας καὶ γείνετο ταῦρος,
80 οὐχ οἷος σταθμοῖς ἐνιφέρβεται, οὐδὲ μὲν οἷος
ὦλκα διατμήγει σύρων εὐκαμπὲς ἄροτρον,
οὐδ᾽ οἷος ποίμνης ἔπι βόσκεται, οὐδὲ μὲν οἷος
μάστι ὑποδμηθεὶς ἐρύει πολύφορτον ἀπήνην.
τοῦ δή τοι τὸ μὲν ἄλλο δέμας ξανθόχροον ἔσκε,
85 κύκλος δ᾽ ἀργύφεος μέσσῳ μάρμαιρε μετώπῳ,
ὄσσε δ᾽ ὑπογλαύσσεσκε καὶ ἵμερον ἀστράπτεσκεν.
ἶσά τ᾽ ἐπ᾽ ἀλλήλοισι κέρα ἀνέτελλε καρήνου
ἄντυγος ἡμιτόμου κεραῆς ἄτε κύκλα σελήνης.
ἤλυθε δ᾽ ἐς λειμῶνα καὶ οὐκ ἐφόβησε φαανθεὶς
90 παρθενικάς, πάσῃσι δ᾽ ἔρως γένετ᾽ ἐγγὺς ἱκέσθαι
ψαῦσαί θ᾽ ἱμερτοῖο βοὸς τοῦ τ᾽ ἄμβροτος ὀδμή
τηλόθι καὶ λειμῶνος ἐκαίνυτο λαρὸν ἀυτμήν.
στῆ δὲ ποδῶν προπάροιθεν ἀμύμονος Εὐρωπείης
καί οἱ λιχμάζεσκε δέρην, κατέθελγε δὲ κούρην.
95 ἣ δέ μιν ἀμφαφάασκε καὶ ἠρέμα χείρεσιν ἀφρὸν
πολλὸν ἀπὸ στομάτων ἀπομόργνυτο καὶ κύσε
      ταῦρον.
αὐτὰρ ὃ μειλίχιον μυκήσατο· φαῖο κεν αὐλοῦ
Μυγδονίου γλυκὺν ἦχον ἀνηπύοντος ἀκούειν·
ὤκλασε δὲ πρὸ ποδοῖιν ἐδέρκετο δ᾽ Εὐρώπειαν
100 αὐχέν᾽ ἐπιστρέψας καί οἱ πλατὺ δείκνυε νῶτον.
ἣ δὲ βαθυπλοκάμοισι μετέννεπε παρθενικῇσι·

83 μάστι Ahrens: ὅστις M   91 τ᾽ Gow: δ᾽ m: γ᾽ m: om. m
97 φαῖο Meineke: φαῖέ m: φαίης m

458

mind, he hid his godhead, altered his shape, and became a bull—not such a bull as feeds in the stall, nor such as cuts a furrow, dragging the well-bent plow, nor such as grazes in charge of the herds, nor such as pulls a heavily laden wagon, subdued by the whip.[22] The rest of his body was golden colored; but a silvery circle gleamed in the middle of his forehead, and his eyes shone brightly from underneath and shot forth desire like lightning; his matching horns rose from his head like crescents of the horned moon when its rim is cut in half.[23] He went into the meadow and did not frighten the girls when he appeared: a desire arose in them all to come near and touch the lovely bull, whose divine fragrance from far off exceeded even the sweet scent of the meadow. He stopped before the feet of noble Europa, licked her neck, and charmed the girl. She stroked him gently, and with her hands wiped away the mass of foam from his mouth, and she kissed the bull.[24] He lowed gently—you would have said you heard the sweet sound of a Mygdonian[25] flute playing—and knelt before her feet and gazed at Europa as he turned his neck, and showed her his broad back. And she said to the girls

[22] Or "yoke," if ζεύγλη (Bühler) is preferred.

[23] I.e., like two crescent moons, each of which is like a half-rim of the moon.

[24] The phrasing is perhaps sexually suggestive.

[25] Mygdonia was part of Phrygia, and the Phrygian *aulos* was known for its low note.

"δεῦθ', ἑτάραι φίλιαι καὶ ὁμήλικες, ὄφρ' ἐπὶ τῷδε
ἑζόμεναι ταύρῳ τερπώμεθα· δὴ γὰρ ἁπάσας
νῶτον ὑποστορέσας ἀναδέξεται οἷά τ' ἐνηὴς
105 πρηΰς τ' εἰσιδέειν καὶ μείλιχος· οὐδέ τι ταύροις
ἄλλοισι προσέοικε, νόος δέ οἱ ἠΰτε φωτὸς
αἴσιμος ἀμφιθέει, μούνης δ' ἐπιδεύεται αὐδῆς."
    Ὣς φαμένη νώτοισιν ἐφίζανε μειδιόωσα,
αἱ δ' ἄλλαι μέλλεσκον, ἄφαρ δ' ἀνεπήλατο ταῦρος,
110 ἣν θέλεν ἁρπάξας, ὠκὺς δ' ἐπὶ πόντον ἵκανεν.
ἡ δὲ μεταστρεφθεῖσα φίλας καλέεσκεν ἑταίρας
χεῖρας ὀρεγνυμένη, ταὶ δ' οὐκ ἐδύναντο κιχάνειν.
ἀκτάων δ' ἐπιβὰς πρόσσω θέεν ἠΰτε δελφίς,
χηλαῖς ἀβρεκτοῖσιν ἐπ' εὐρέα κύματα βαίνων.
115 ἡ δὲ τότ' ἐρχομένοιο γαληνιάασκε θάλασσα,
κήτεα δ' ἀμφὶς ἄταλλε Διὸς προπάροιθε ποδοῖιν,
γηθόσυνος δ' ὑπὲρ οἶδμα κυβίστεε βυσσόθε δελφίς.
Νηρεΐδες δ' ἀνέδυσαν ὑπὲξ ἁλός, αἱ δ' ἄρα πᾶσαι
κητείοις νώτοισιν ἐφήμεναι ἐστιχόωντο.
120 καὶ δ' αὐτὸς βαρύδουπος ὑπεὶρ ἅλα Ἐννοσίγαιος
κῦμα κατιθύνων ἁλίης ἡγεῖτο κελεύθου
αὐτοκασιγνήτῳ· τοὶ δ' ἀμφί μιν ἠγερέθοντο
Τρίτωνες, πόντοιο βαρύθροοι αὐλητῆρες,
κόχλοισιν ταναοῖς γάμιον μέλος ἠπύοντες.
125 ἡ δ' ἄρ' ἐφεζομένη Ζηνὸς βοέοις ἐπὶ νώτοις
τῇ μὲν ἔχεν ταύρου δολιχὸν κέρας, ἐν χερὶ δ' ἄλλῃ
εἴρυε πορφυρέην πέπλου πτύχα ὄφρα κε μή μιν
δεύοι ἐφελκόμενον πολιῆς ἁλὸς ἄσπετον ὕδωρ.
κολπώθη δ' ὤμοισι πέπλος βαθὺς Εὐρωπείης

with their deep tresses, "Come here, dear companions, girls of my age, so that we may enjoy ourselves sitting on this bull: making a couch of his back, he will take us all, so mild and gentle and tame is he to look on;[26] nor is he at all like other bulls, but a sensible mind like a man's surrounds him, and he lacks only speech." With these words she sat smiling on his back, and the others were about to do so, but the bull leaped up suddenly, having gained the girl he wanted, and arrived swiftly at the sea. She turned round and kept calling her dear companions, stretching out her hands; but they could not reach her. Crossing the beach, he sped onward like a dolphin, going over the wide waves with hooves unwetted. Then the sea became calm as he went along, and the sea beasts played all around before the feet of Zeus, and the dolphin somersaulted joyfully over the swell out of the deep. The Nereids rose from the sea, and all moved in ranks sitting on the backs of sea beasts. And above the surface the deep-roaring Earth-shaker himself was leader of the sea path for his brother, smoothing the waves; and around him were gathered the Tritons,[27] deep-sounding musicians of the sea, playing a wedding song on their tapering shells. And she, sitting on the back of the bull Zeus, with one hand held a long horn of the bull, and with the other gathered up the purple folds of her robe so that the gray sea's great waters might not wet it trailing along. The deep robe of Europa bellied out

---

[26] Or perhaps, "as one would expect ($o\hat{i}\acute{a}\ \tau\epsilon$) from a bull so mild. . . ."   [27] Sea-divinities with human bodies and fish tails, companions of Poseidon.

---

127 $\pi\acute{\epsilon}\pi\lambda o\upsilon$ Bühler: $\kappa\acute{o}\lambda\pi o\upsilon$ M

130 ἱστίον οἷά τε νηὸς ἐλαφρίζεσκε δὲ κούρην.
ἡ δ' ὅτε δὴ γαίης ἄπο πατρίδος ἦεν ἄνευθεν,
φαίνετο δ' οὔτ' ἀκτή τις ἁλίρροθος οὔτ' ὄρος αἰπύ,
ἀλλ' ἀὴρ μὲν ὕπερθεν ἔνερθε δὲ πόντος ἀπείρων,
ἀμφί ἑ παπτήνασα τόσην ἀνενείκατο φωνήν·

135 "πῇ με φέρεις θεόταυρε; τίς ἔπλεο; πῶς δὲ κέλευθα
ἀργαλέ' εἰλιπόδεσσι διέρχεαι οὐδὲ θάλασσαν
δειμαίνεις; νηυσὶν γὰρ ἐπίδρομός ἐστι θάλασσα
ὠκυάλοις, ταῦροι δ' ἁλίην τρομέουσιν ἀταρπόν.
ποῖον σοὶ ποτὸν ἡδύ, τίς ἐξ ἁλὸς ἔσσετ' ἐδωδή;

140 ἦ ἄρα τις θεὸς ἐσσί; θεοῖς γ' ἐπεοικότα ῥέξεις.
οὔθ' ἅλιοι δελφῖνες ἐπὶ χθονὸς οὔτε τι ταῦροι
ἐν πόντῳ στιχόωσι, σὺ δὲ χθόνα καὶ κατὰ πόντον
ἄτρομος ἀίσσεις, χηλαὶ δέ τοί εἰσιν ἐρετμά.
ἦ τάχα καὶ γλαυκῆς ὑπὲρ ἠέρος ὑψόσ' ἀερθεὶς

145 εἴκελος αἰψηροῖσι πετήσεαι οἰωνοῖσιν.
ὤμοι ἐγὼ μέγα δή τι δυσάμμορος, ἥ ῥά τε δῶμα
πατρὸς ἀποπρολιποῦσα καὶ ἑσπομένη βοῒ τῷδε
ξείνην ναυτιλίην ἐφέπω καὶ πλάζομαι οἴη.
ἀλλὰ σύ μοι, μεδέων πολιῆς ἁλὸς Ἐννοσίγαιε,

150 ἵλαος ἀντιάσειας, ὃν ἔλπομαι εἰσοράασθαι
τόνδε κατιθύνοντα πλόον προκέλευθον ἐμεῖο·
οὐκ ἀθεεὶ γὰρ ταῦτα διέρχομαι ὑγρὰ κέλευθα."

Ὣς φάτο· τὴν δ' ὧδε προσεφώνεεν ἠύκερως βοῦς·
"θάρσει παρθενική· μὴ δείδιθι πόντιον οἶδμα.

155 αὐτός τοι Ζεύς εἰμι, κεἰ ἐγγύθεν εἴδομαι εἶναι
ταῦρος, ἐπεὶ δύναμαί γε φανήμεναι ὅττι θέλοιμι.
σὸς δὲ πόθος μ' ἀνέηκε τόσην ἅλα μετρήσασθαι

462

round her like the sail of a ship, and it bore the girl up
lightly. But when she was far from her homeland, and
neither a sea-sounding shore nor a high mountain was to
be seen, but air above and the boundless sea below, gazing
around she spoke these words: "Where are you carrying
me, godlike bull? Who are you? And how do you pass over
ways hard for shambling cattle, and do not fear the sea?
The sea is passable for swift ships, but bulls fear a briny
path. What sweet drink, what food will there be for you
from the sea? Are you then some god? At any rate, you do
things fitting gods. Seagoing dolphins do not go on land,
and bulls do not go at all on the sea; but you speed fear-
lessly over land and sea, and hooves are oars for you. Soon,
I daresay, rising high above the clear sky, you will fly like
the swift birds. Alas! How very unlucky I am! Leaving my
father's house and going with this bull, I make a strange
foreign voyage and wander alone. But may you, ruler of
the gray sea, Earthshaker, receive me kindly; I suspect I
see you directing this voyage and leading the way for me;
not without some god do I pass over these watery ways."

So she spoke; and the horned bull addressed her with
these words: "Take courage, my girl; do not fear the sea
swell. I am Zeus himself, even if at close quarters I seem
to be a bull, since I can take whatever appearance I might
wish. Love for you made me cross so much sea in the shape

---

136 ἀργαλέ᾽ εἰλιπόδεσσι Ahrens: ἀργαλέοισι πόδεσσι
m: -έην π. m
140 γ᾽ Edmonds: δ᾽ M
155 κεἰ Wakefield: καὶ M

ταύρῳ ἐειδόμενον. Κρήτη δέ σε δέξεται ἤδη
ἥ μ' ἔθρεψε καὶ αὐτόν, ὅπῃ νυμφήια σεῖο
160 ἔσσεται· ἐξ ἐμέθεν δὲ κλυτοὺς φιτύσεαι υἷας
οἳ σκηπτοῦχοι ἅπαντες ἐπιχθονίοισιν ἔσονται."
    Ὣς φάτο· καὶ τετέλεστο τά περ φάτο. φαίνετο
        μὲν δή
Κρήτη, Ζεὺς δὲ πάλιν σφετέρην ἀνελάζετο μορφήν
λῦσε δέ οἱ μίτρην, καί οἱ λέχος ἔντυον Ὧραι.
165 ἡ δὲ πάρος κούρη Ζηνὸς γένετ' αὐτίκα νύμφη,
καὶ Κρονίδῃ τέκε τέκνα καὶ αὐτίκα γίνετο μήτηρ.

of a bull. Crete, where I myself was reared,[28] will soon receive you; there your marriage will take place; and from me you shall bear famous sons[29] who shall all be rulers over men."

So he spoke; and what he said was brought to pass. Crete indeed came in sight, and Zeus took on his own shape again and loosened her girdle, and the Hours[30] prepared her bed. And she who was formerly a girl at once became the bride of Zeus, and she bore children to the son of Cronus and at once became a mother.[31]

---

[28] Most ancient accounts agreed that Zeus was brought up, if not actually born, in Crete, away from the murderous designs of his father, Cronus (see, e.g., Callim. *Hymn* 1).

[29] Minos, Rhadmanthys, and Sarpedon, according to ps.-Apollod. *Bibl.* 3.1.1; Hes. Fr. 140 M-W. They were kings of Crete, the islands, and Lycia, respectively.

[30] Goddesses of charm and beauty, associated with Aphrodite.

[31] The ending is abrupt, and the repetition of "became" and "at once" seems odd. Some critics have felt that the poem is incomplete, since there is no mention of the naming of Europe. It seems more likely, however, that Moschus is indulging in word-play and emphasizing the immediacy and lack of delay that are characteristic of divine actions (e.g., Pind. *Pyth.* 9.66–70; Callim. *Hymn* 1.50, 56).

LAMENT FOR BION

This poem echoes Bion's Lament for Adonis *in lamenting Bion's death; there are echoes, too, of the story of Daphnis and nature's lament for him in the first idyll of Theocritus. The poet seems to be Italian, or to claim that Bion had links with Italy, and to have been made heir to Bion's song (94–97); he cannot then be Moschus, who was probably several decades older than Bion. The poem is notable for its self-conscious learning: famous lamenters of myth and towns associated with famous poets are introduced, and no doubt there are more references to Bion's poetry than can now be detected.*

Criticism

Manakidou, F. P. "ΕΠΙΤΑΦΙΟΣ ΑΔΩΝΙΔΟΣ and ΕΠΙ-ΤΑΦΙΟΣ ΒΙΩΝΟΣ: Remarks on Their Generic Form and Content." *MD* 37 (1997): 27–58.

Maria di Nino, M. "Le 'Verità nascoste.' Consapevola appartenenzo a un genere, autoinvestitura e bugie metapoetiche in [Mosco] III." *Philologus* 153 (2009): 86–108.

Mumprecht, V. *Epitaphios Bionos: Text, Übersetzung, Kommentar.* Zürich, 1964.

Payne, *Invention of Fiction*, 156–58.

[ΜΟΣΧΟΥ] ΕΠΙΤΑΦΙΟΣ ΒΙΩΝΟΣ

Αἴλινά μοι στοναχεῖτε νάπαι καὶ Δώριον ὕδωρ,
καὶ ποταμοὶ κλαίοιτε τὸν ἱμερόεντα Βίωνα.
νῦν φυτά μοι μύρεσθε καὶ ἄλσεα νῦν γοάοισθε,
ἄνθεα νῦν στυγνοῖσιν ἀποπνείοιτε κορύμβοις·
5 νῦν ῥόδα φοινίσσεσθε τὰ πένθιμα, νῦν ἀνεμῶναι,
νῦν ὑάκινθε λάλει τὰ σὰ γράμματα καὶ πλέον αἰαῖ
λάμβανε τοῖς πετάλοισι· καλὸς τέθνακε μελικτάς.

ἄρχετε Σικελικαί, τῶ πένθεος ἄρχετε, Μοῖσαι.

ἀδόνες αἱ πυκινοῖσιν ὀδυρόμεναι ποτὶ φύλλοις
10 νάμασι τοῖς Σικελοῖς ἀγγείλατε τᾶς Ἀρεθοίσας
ὅττι Βίων τέθνακεν ὁ βουκόλος, ὅττι σὺν αὐτῷ
καὶ τὸ μέλος τέθνακε καὶ ὤλετο Δωρὶς ἀοιδά.

ἄρχετε Σικελικαί, τῶ πένθεος ἄρχετε, Μοῖσαι.

Στρυμόνιοι μύρεσθε παρ' ὕδασιν αἴλινα κύκνοι,
15 καὶ γοεροῖς στομάτεσσι μελίσδετε πένθιμον ᾠδάν
†οἵαν ὑμετέροις ποτὶ χείλεσι γῆρας ἀείδει.†

5 ἀνεμῶναι Valckenaer: -να M
16 γῆρας ἀείδει Wilamowitz: γῆρυς ἄειδεν M

LAMENT FOR BION

Cry woe, you glades and you Dorian waters; you rivers, weep for the lovely Bion. Lament now, you plants that grow; moan now, you groves; you flowers, breathe your last, your clusters withered; you roses and anemones, bloom red now in mourning; you hyacinth, make your letters speak and take on your leaves more cries of woe:[1] the fine singer is dead.

Begin, Sicilian Muses, begin your grieving song.

You nightingales that lament among the dense foliage, bear news to the Sicilian streams of Arethusa[2] that Bion the oxherd is dead; that with him song too has died, and Dorian minstrelsy has perished.

Begin, Sicilian Muses, begin your grieving song.

You swans of Strymon, cry woe beside your waters;[3] with your lamenting voices sing a dirge such as old age produces from your throats.[4] Say once more to the daughters

---

[1] See on Theoc. *Id.* 10.28.   [2] Cf. Theoc. *Id.* 1.117.

[3] The river Strymon in Thrace (Bistonia), whose waters bore along the still singing head of Orpheus when he was torn to pieces by the daughters of Oeagrus, king of Thrace (Phan. *CA* Fr.1; Ov. *Met.* 5.577–641).   [4] The swan was said to sing beautifully just before its death. The text of this line is however uncertain.

εἴπατε δ᾽ αὖ κούραις Οἰαγρίσιν, εἴπατε πάσαις
Βιστονίαις Νύμφαισιν, "ἀπώλετο Δώριος Ὀρφεύς."

ἄρχετε Σικελικαί, τῶ πένθεος ἄρχετε, Μοῖσαι.

20 κεῖνος ὁ ταῖς ἀγέλαισιν ἐράσμιος οὐκέτι μέλπει,
οὐκέτ᾽ ἐρημαίαισιν ὑπὸ δρυσὶν ἥμενος ᾄδει,
ἀλλὰ παρὰ Πλουτῆι μέλος Ληθαῖον ἀείδει.
ὤρεα δ᾽ ἐστὶν ἄφωνα, καὶ αἱ βόες αἱ ποτὶ ταύροις
πλαζόμεναι γοάοντι καὶ οὐκ ἐθέλοντι νέμεσθαι.

25 ἄρχετε Σικελικαί, τῶ πένθεος ἄρχετε, Μοῖσαι.

σεῖο, Βίων, ἔκλαυσε ταχὺν μόρον αὐτὸς Ἀπόλλων,
καὶ Σάτυροι μύροντο μελάγχλαινοί τε Πρίηποι·
καὶ Πᾶνες στοναχεῦντο τὸ σὸν μέλος, αἵ τε καθ᾽ ὕλαν
Κρανίδες ὠδύραντο, καὶ ὕδατα δάκρυα γέντο·
30 Ἀχὼ δ᾽ ἐν πέτραισιν ὀδύρεται ὅττι σιωπῇ
κοὐκέτι μιμεῖται τὰ σὰ χείλεα, σῷ δ᾽ ἐπ᾽ ὀλέθρῳ
δένδρεα καρπὸν ἔριψε τὰ δ᾽ ἄνθεα πάντ᾽ ἐμαράνθη·
μάλων οὐκ ἔρρευσε καλὸν γλάγος, οὐ μέλι σίμβλων,
κάτθανε δ᾽ ἐν κηρῷ λυπεύμενον, οὐκέτι γὰρ δεῖ
35 τῶ μέλιτος τῶ σῶ τεθνακότος αὐτὸ τρυγᾶσθαι.

28 στοναχεῦντο Wakefield: -τι M

470

of Oeagrus, say to all the Nymphs of Bistonia, "The Dorian Orpheus is dead."

Begin, Sicilian Muses, begin your grieving song.

He who used to delight the herds sings no more; no more does he perform his songs sitting beneath the lone oak trees: now he sings a song of Lethe[5] in the house of Pluto. The mountains are silent; the cows that range with the bulls are lamenting, and will not graze.

Begin, Sicilian Muses, begin your grieving song.

Apollo himself lamented your early death, Bion; the Satyrs keened, and the Priapi, clad in black;[6] the Pans grieved for your minstrelsy; in the woods nymphs of the spring lamented, and their water was turned to tears. Echo laments among the rocks because she is silent and can imitate the sounds from your lips no more. To honor your death, the trees have dropped their fruit and every flower has withered; fair milk has ceased to flow from the flocks, and honey from the hives; it perished for grief in the comb: there is no more need to gather it, now that your honey has died away.[7]

[5] The underworld's River of Forgetfulness. Pluto = Hades.

[6] Mourning garb. But the idea of Priapi dressed in black— dressed at all—is curious, and the idea of a collection of these, like Pans and Satyrs, is unique to this passage.

[7] I.e., his honey-sweet song.

ἄρχετε Σικελικαί, τῶ πένθεος ἄρχετε, Μοῖσαι.

οὐ τόσον εἰναλίαισι παρ᾽ ᾀόσι μύρατο Σειρήν,
οὐδὲ τόσον ποκ᾽ ἄεισεν ἐνὶ σκοπέλοισιν Ἀηδών,
οὐδὲ τόσον θρήνησεν ἀν᾽ ὤρεα μακρὰ Χελιδών,
40 Ἀλκυόνος δ᾽ οὐ τόσσον ἐπ᾽ ἄλγεσιν ἴαχε Κῆυξ,
42 οὐδὲ τόσον γλαυκοῖς ἐνὶ κύμασι Κηρύλος ᾆδεν,
41 οὐ τόσον ἀῴοισιν ἐν ἄγκεσι παῖδα τὸν Ἀοῦς
ἱπτάμενος περὶ σᾶμα κινύρατο Μέμνονος ὄρνις,
ὅσσον ἀποφθιμένοιο κατωδύραντο Βίωνος—

45 ἄρχετε Σικελικαί, τῶ πένθεος ἄρχετε, Μοῖσαι—

ἀδονίδες πᾶσαί τε χελιδόνες, ἅς ποκ᾽ ἔτερπεν,
ἃς λαλέειν ἐδίδασκε· καθεζόμεναι δ᾽ ἐπὶ πρέμνοις
ἀντίον ἀλλάλαισιν ἐκώκυον, αἱ δ᾽ ὑπεφώνευν·
"ὄρνιθες λυπεῖσθ᾽ αἱ πενθάδες; ἀλλὰ καὶ ἄμμες."

50 ἄρχετε Σικελικαί, τῶ πένθεος ἄρχετε, Μοῖσαι.

τίς ποτὶ σᾷ σύριγγι μελίξεται, ὦ τριπόθητε;

37 Σειρήν Bücheler: δε/γε/σε πρίν m: δελφίν m
49 λυπεῖσθ᾽ αἱ Ahrens: -εῦσθαι m: -εῦσθε m: -εῖσθε m

8 The Sirens were handmaidens of Persephone who were metamorphosed into part birds when she was abducted by Hades (Ap. Rhod. 4.895–903; Ov. *Met.* 5.551–63). Their song is here taken to be a lament for the lost Persephone.

9 Philomela and Procne, daughters of Pandion, were transformed into a nightingale (*aêdôn*) and a swallow (*chelidôn*), which

Begin, Sicilian Muses, begin your grieving song.

Not so much did the Siren lament on the seashore;[8] not so much did Aëdon once sing on the crags; not so much did Chelidon wail in the high hills;[9] not so much did Ceyx call aloud at the sufferings of Alcyone;[10] not so much did Cerylus sing on the green waves;[11] not so much did the bird of Memnon lament for the son of Eos in the eastern valleys as it flew around his tomb,[12] as much as there lamented for the death of Bion—

Begin, Sicilian Muses, begin your grieving song—

all the nightingales and swallows which he used to delight and teach to sing. Perched on the branches, they sang dirges across to each other, and in answer came the cry, "Do you mournful birds lament? We do just the same."[13]

Begin, Sicilian Muses, begin your grieving song.

We miss you so much! Who will make music on your pipe?

continued to lament their cruel fates (Soph. Frr. 581–93 Lloyd-Jones; Ov. *Met.* 6.424–674; ps.-Apollod. *Bibl.* 3.14.8).

[10] Ceyx and his wife, Alcyone, were transformed into birds whose cries were taken to be laments (Hom. *Il.* 9.563; cf. Lucian *Halcyon* 1; Ov. *Met.* 11.410–748; ps.-Apollod. *Bibl.* 1.7.4).

[11] Cerylus is otherwise unknown.

[12] In the Trojan War Memnon was killed by Achilles, and the smoke from his pyre was transformed into lamenting birds (Ov. *Met.* 13.576–622).

[13] Sense and text uncertain. "Mournful birds" probably refers to the birds of myth cataloged above, and not to real birds sitting opposite.

τίς δ' ἐπὶ σοῖς καλάμοις θήσει στόμα; τίς θρασὺς
    οὕτως;
εἰσέτι γὰρ πνείει τὰ σὰ χείλεα καὶ τὸ σὸν ἄσθμα,
ἀχὼ δ' ἐν δονάκεσσι τεᾶς ἔτι βόσκετ' ἀοιδᾶς.
55 Πανὶ φέρω τὸ μέλισμα; τάχ' ἂν καὶ κεῖνος ἐρεῖσαι
τὸ στόμα δειμαίνοι μὴ δεύτερα σεῖο φέρηται.

ἄρχετε Σικελικαί, τῶ πένθεος ἄρχετε, Μοῖσαι.

κλαίει καὶ Γαλάτεια τὸ σὸν μέλος, ἅν ποκ' ἔτερπες
ἑζομέναν μετὰ σεῖο παρ' ἀιόνεσσι θαλάσσας·
60 οὐ γὰρ ἴσον Κύκλωπι μελίσδεο. τὸν μὲν ἔφευγεν
ἁ καλὰ Γαλάτεια, σὲ δ' ἅδιον ἔβλεπεν ἅλμας,
καὶ νῦν λασαμένα τῶ κύματος ἐν ψαμάθοισιν
ἔζετ' ἐρημαίαισι, βόας δ' ἔτι σεῖο νομεύει.

ἄρχετε Σικελικαί, τῶ πένθεος ἄρχετε, Μοῖσαι.

65 πάντα τοι, ὦ βούτα, συγκάτθανε δῶρα τὰ Μοισᾶν,
παρθενικᾶν ἐρόεντα φιλήματα, χείλεα παίδων,
καὶ στυγνοὶ περὶ σῶμα τεὸν κλαίουσιν Ἔρωτες,
χὰ Κύπρις φιλέει σε πολὺ πλέον ἢ τὸ φίλημα
τὸ πρῴαν τὸν Ἄδωνιν ἀποθνάσκοντα φίλησεν.

69a ἄρχετε Σικελικαί, τῶ πένθεος ἄρχετε, Μοῖσαι.

70 τοῦτό τοι, ὦ ποταμῶν λιγυρώτατε, δεύτερον ἄλγος,
τοῦτο, Μέλη, νέον ἄλγος. ἀπώλετο πρᾶν τοι Ὅμηρος,

54 ἔτι βόσκετ' Brunck: ἐπιβ- M
68 χὰ J. A. Hartung: ἁ M

Who will set his lips to your flute of reeds? Who would dare? Your lips, your breath still breathe in them, and the sound of your song is still kept up in those reeds. Shall I take your pipe to Pan? Even he, I think, would be afraid to put it to his lips in case he should take second place to you.

Begin, Sicilian Muses, begin your grieving song.

Galatea, too, weeps for your music—Galatea, whom you used to delight as she sat with you on the seashore; for you sang nothing like the Cyclops.[14] The lovely Galatea would avoid him, but you were a more welcome sight to her than the sea. Now she has forgotten the waves: she sits on the empty beach and still tends your cattle.

Begin, Sicilian Muses, begin your grieving song.

Every gift of the Muses died along with you, dear ox-herd—the delightful kisses of girls, the lips of boys—and round your corpse gloomy Loves make their lament, and Cypris plies you with many more kisses than she did Adonis, lately dead.[15]

Begin, Sicilian Muse, begin your grieving song.

This is a second grief, a fresh grief, for you, Meles, most musical of rivers.[16] It is not long since the death of your

14 Probably an allusion to some lost poem of Bion on the Cyclops and Galatea; cf. Bion Fr. 16.

15 An allusion to Bion's *Lament for Adonis* (pp. 504–17).

16 Meles: a river near Smyrna, birthplace of Bion. Homer was said to have been born in the vicinity, or to have been the son of Meles and a nymph (*Contest of Homer and Hesiod* 2 West).

τῆνο τὸ Καλλιόπας γλυκερὸν στόμα, καί σε λέγοντι
μύρασθαι καλὸν υἷα πολυκλαύτοισι ῥεέθροις,
πᾶσαν δὲ πλῆσαι φωνᾶς ἅλα· νῦν πάλιν ἄλλον
75   υἱέα δακρύεις καινῷ δ᾽ ἐπὶ πένθεϊ τάκῃ.
ἀμφότεροι παγαῖς πεφιλημένοι· ὃς μὲν ἔπινε
Παγασίδος κράνας, ὁ δ᾽ ἔχεν πόμα τᾶς Ἀρεθοίσας.
χὢ μὲν Τυνδαρέοιο καλὰν ἄεισε θύγατρα
καὶ Θέτιδος μέγαν υἷα καὶ Ἀτρείδαν Μενέλαον,
80   κεῖνος δ᾽ οὐ πολέμους, οὐ δάκρυα, Πᾶνα δ᾽ ἔμελπε
καὶ βούτας ἐλίγαινε καὶ ἀείδων ἐνόμευε
καὶ σύριγγας ἔτευχε καὶ ἁδέα πόρτιν ἄμελγε
καὶ παίδων ἐδίδασκε φιλήματα καὶ τὸν Ἔρωτα
ἔτρεφεν ἐν κόλποισι καὶ ἤρεθε τὰν Ἀφροδίταν.

85   ἄρχετε Σικελικαί, τῶ πένθεος ἄρχετε, Μοῖσαι.

πᾶσα, Βίων, θρηνεῖ σε κλυτὰ πόλις, ἄστεα πάντα.
Ἄσκρα μὲν γοάει σε πολὺ πλέον Ἡσιόδοιο·
Πίνδαρον οὐ ποθέοντι τόσον Βοιωτίδες ὕλαι·
οὐ τόσον Ἀλκαίῳ περιμύρατο Λέσβος ἐραννά,
90   οὐδὲ τόσον τὸν ἀοιδὸν ὀδύρατο Τήιον ἄστυ·
σὲ πλέον Ἀρχιλόχοιο ποθεῖ Πάρος, ἀντὶ δὲ Σαπφοῦς
εἰσέτι σεῦ τὸ μέλισμα κινύρεται ἁ Μιτυλήνα.
.   .   .   .
ἐν δὲ Συρακοσίοισι Θεόκριτος· αὐτὰρ ἐγώ τοι

73 μύρασθαι Meineke: -εσθαι M
74 δὲ πλῆσαι Schaefer: δ᾽ ἔπλησε M
93 ante h. v. lac. stat. Musurus

476

poet Homer, sweet mouthpiece of Calliope;[17] they say that
from your lamenting waters you made moan for your fine
son, and the whole sea was filled with the sound of your
voice. Now you weep again for another son and dis-
solve with fresh grief. Both were dear to springs: the one
used to drink from Pegasus' fountain,[18] and Arethusa was
source for the other. One sang of the beautiful daughter
of Tyndareus,[19] of Thetis' great son[20] and of Menelaus son
of Atreus; the other celebrated not wars and tears but Pan
and oxherds, and he sang as he pastured his flocks. He
made panpipes, milked his sweet heifers, and taught about
the kisses of boys; he kept Love close by him and provoked
Aphrodite.[21]

Begin, Sicilian Muses, begin your grieving song.

Every famous city, every town laments you, Bion. Ascra
groans for you much more than for Hesiod; the woods of
Boeotia do not yearn for Pindar so much as for you; lovely
Lesbos did not grieve so much for Alcaeus, nor the town
of Teos for its own poet;[22] Paros missed you more than
Archilochus; Mitylene still mourns for your music, and not
for Sappho's.

. . . .[23]

and Theocritus among the Syracusans. But the dirge I sing

[17] Muse of epic poetry.

[18] Hippocrene, created by a blow from the hoof of Pegasus
(Ovid, *Met.* 5.256ff.); it was on Mt. Helicon in Boeotia, where
Hesiod encountered the Muses (*Theog.* 22–34).

[19] Helen.　　[20] Achilles.　　[21] Cf. Bion Fr. 14.

[22] Anacreon.　　[23] Some lines are missing.

Αὐσονικᾶς ὀδύνας μέλπω μέλος, οὐ ξένος ᾠδᾶς
95 βουκολικᾶς, ἀλλ᾽ ἅντε διδάξαο σεῖο μαθητάς
κλαρονόμος μοίσας τᾶς Δωρίδος, ᾇ με γεραίρων
ἄλλοις μὲν τεὸν ὄλβον ἐμοὶ δ᾽ ἀπέλειπες ἀοιδάν.

ἄρχετε Σικελικαί, τῶ πένθεος ἄρχετε, Μοῖσαι.

αἰαῖ ταὶ μαλάχαι μέν, ἐπὰν κατὰ κᾶπον ὄλωνται,
100 ἠδὲ τὰ χλωρὰ σέλινα τό τ᾽ εὐθαλὲς οὖλον ἄνηθον
ὕστερον αὖ ζώοντι καὶ εἰς ἔτος ἄλλο φύοντι·
ἄμμες δ᾽ οἱ μεγάλοι καὶ καρτεροί, οἱ σοφοὶ ἄνδρες,
ὁππότε πρᾶτα θάνωμες, ἀνάκοοι ἐν χθονὶ κοίλᾳ
εὕδομες εὖ μάλα μακρὸν ἀτέρμονα νήγρετον ὕπνον.
105 καὶ σὺ μὲν ὧν σιγᾷ πεπυκασμένος ἔσσεαι ἐν γᾷ,
ταῖς Νύμφαισι δ᾽ ἔδοξεν ἀεὶ τὸν βάτραχον ᾄδειν.
ταῖς δ᾽ ἐγὼ οὐ φθονέοιμι, τὸ γὰρ μέλος οὐ καλὸν
ᾄδει.

ἄρχετε Σικελικαί, τῶ πένθεος ἄρχετε, Μοῖσαι.

φάρμακον ἦλθε, Βίων, ποτὶ σὸν στόμα, φάρμακον
ἦδες.
110 τοιούτοις χείλεσσι ποτέδραμε κοὐκ ἐγλυκάνθη;
τίς δὲ βροτὸς τοσσοῦτον ἀνάμερος ἢ κεράσαι τοι
ἢ δοῦναι καλέοντι τὸ φάρμακον; ἢ φύγεν ᾠδάν.

ἄρχετε Σικελικαί, τῶ πένθεος ἄρχετε, Μοῖσαι.

ἀλλὰ Δίκα κίχε πάντας· ἐγὼ δ᾽ ἐπὶ πένθεϊ τῷδε

for you expresses the grief of Italy. I am no stranger to bucolic song: I have inherited that Dorian Muse which you taught your pupils; that was your bequest to me when you left your wealth to others but to me your song.

Begin, Sicilian Muses, begin your grieving song.

Alas! When garden mallows die back, or green parsley, or the flourishing curly anise, they live again and grow another year; but we men, great and strong and wise, as soon as we die, unhearing in the hollow earth we sleep a long, an endless, an unwaking sleep. And so you, surrounded by silence, will be in the earth, while the Nymphs deem it right for the frog to croak for ever. But I feel no envy: that song is not a good one.

Begin, Sicilian Muses, begin your grieving song.

Poison came to your lips, Bion: you ate poison.[24] How could it approach such lips and not turn to sweetness? Who was so inhuman as to mix that poison for you, or to supply it at your request? He escapes my song.[25]

Begin, Sicilian Muses, begin your grieving song.

But Justice[26] catches up with every man. Even so, I shed

---

[24] The story is unknown.   [25] Text and meaning uncertain.
[26] Reference unknown. Perhaps "Death" (ἀλλ' Ἀίδας Schmitz) should be read.

---

102 καρτεροὶ, οἱ Briggs: καρτεροὶ m: καρτερικοὶ m
105 ὧν Wakefield: ἐν M
107 ταῖς Meineke: τοῖς vel τῷ M

115   δακρυχέων τεὸν οἶτον ὀδύρομαι. εἰ δυνάμαν δέ,
     ὡς Ὀρφεὺς καταβὰς ποτὶ Τάρταρον, ὥς ποκ' Ὀδυσ-
        σεύς,
     ὡς πάρος Ἀλκείδας, κἠγὼ τάχ' ἂν ἐς δόμον ἦλθον
     Πλουτέος ὥς κέ σ' ἴδοιμι καί, εἰ Πλουτῆι μελίσδῃ,
     ὡς ἂν ἀκουσαίμαν τί μελίσδεαι. ἀλλ' ἄγε Κώρᾳ
120   Σικελικόν τι λίγαινε καὶ ἁδύ τι βουκολιάζευ·
     καὶ κείνα Σικελά, καὶ ἐν Αἰτναίαισιν ἔπαιζεν
     ᾀόσι, καὶ μέλος οἶδε τὸ Δώριον· οὐκ ἀγέραστος
     ἐσσεῖθ' ἁ μολπά, χὡς Ὀρφέι πρόσθεν ἔδωκεν
     ἁδέα φορμίζοντι παλίσσυτον Εὐρυδίκειαν,
125   καὶ σέ, Βίων, πέμψει τοῖς ὤρεσιν. εἰ δέ τι κἠγών
     συρίσδων δυνάμαν, παρὰ Πλουτέι κ' αὐτὸς ἄειδον.

    118 κέ σ' Schaefer: κεν M
    119 ἀλλ' ἄγε Wilamowitz: ἀλλ' ἐπί m: ἀλλὰ πᾶσα m: καὶ
πᾶσα m: καὶ παρά m
    121 Σικελά, καὶ Teucher: σικελικὰ m: -κὰ καὶ m: -καῖσιν m

tears at this sad event and lament your death. Had it been possible, I would have gone down to Tartarus and maybe entered the halls of Hades like Orpheus,[27] like Odysseus once did,[28] like Alcides,[29] in order to see you and, if you sing for Pluto, to hear what song it is. But come, play for the Maiden[30] some Sicilian song, some sweet country melody. She too is a Sicilian who used to play on the shores of Etna, and she knows the Dorian mode. Your song will not go unrewarded; just as she once gave back Eurydice to Orpheus for his sweet lyre playing, so she will restore you, Bion, to your hills. And if my piping had any power, I would myself have played for Pluto.

[27] Who went to fetch Eurydice.

[28] In Book 11 of the *Odyssey*.

[29] "Descendant of Alcaeus" = Heracles, who went to Hades to fetch Cerberus. Alcaeus was father of Amphitryon, husband of Heracles' mother, Alcmena (cf. Theoc. *Id.* 24).

[30] Persephone, abducted by Hades from Sicily, according to the most popular tradition (e.g., Cic. *Verr.* 4.106ff.).

MEGARA

A pair of laments. Megara, wife of Heracles, tells how she witnessed the murder of her children by their maddened father and regrets that his Labors mean that he is rarely at home. Alcmena, her mother-in-law, echoes these lamentations and gives a detailed account of an ill-omened dream about Heracles and Iphicles.

In treating the familiar story of Heracles from an original perspective—Heracles' effect on two female relatives— the poem is reminiscent of Idd. *24 and [25]. The extended laments are perhaps inspired by those of Hecuba, Helen, and Andromache in Books 22 and 24 of the* Iliad. *Both women employ elaborate epic-style similes; there are resemblances, too, to the dialogue of tragedy.*

The author is unknown. Only one manuscript includes the poem among Moschus' works; several place it next to Id. *[25].*

Criticism

Breitenstein, T. *Recherches sur le poème* Mégara. Copenhagen, 1966.
Vaughn, J. W. *The* Megara *(Moschus IV). Text, translation, and commentary.* Bern, 1976.

[ΜΟΣΧΟΥ] ΜΕΓΑΡΑ

"Μῆτερ ἐμή, τίφθ' ὧδε φίλον κατὰ θυμὸν ἰάπτεις
ἐκπάγλως ἀχέουσα, τὸ πρὶν δέ τοι οὐκέτ' ἔρευθος
σῴζετ' ἐπὶ ῥεθέεσσι; τί μοι τόσον ἠνίησαι;
ἦ ῥ' ὅ τοι ἄλγεα πάσχει ἀπείριτα φαίδιμος υἱός
5 ἀνδρὸς ὑπ' οὐτιδανοῖο, λέων ὡσεί θ' ὑπὸ νεβροῦ;
ὤμοι ἐγώ, τί νυ δή με θεοὶ τόσον ἠτίμησαν
ἀθάνατοι; τί νύ μ' ὧδε κακῇ γονέες τέκον αἴσῃ;
δύσμορος, ἥτ' ἐπεὶ ἀνδρὸς ἀμύμονος ἐς λέχος ἦλθον,
τὸν μὲν ἐγὼ τίεσκον ἴσον φαέεσσιν ἐμοῖσιν
10 ἠδ' ἔτι νῦν σέβομαί τε καὶ αἰδέομαι κατὰ θυμόν,
τοῦ δ' οὔτις γένετ' ἄλλος ἀποτμότερος ζωόντων
οὐδὲ τόσων σφετέρῃσιν ἐγεύσατο φροντίσι κηδέων.
σχέτλιος, ὃς τόξοισιν, ἅ οἱ πόρεν αὐτὸς Ἀπόλλων
ἠέ τινος Κηρῶν ἢ Ἐρινύος αἰνὰ βέλεμνα,
15 παῖδας ἑοὺς κατέπεφνε καὶ ἐκ φίλον εἵλετο θυμὸν
μαινόμενος κατὰ οἶκον, ὃ δ' ἔμπλεος ἔσκε φόνοιο.
τοὺς μὲν ἐγὼ δύστηνος ἐμοῖς ἴδον ὀφθαλμοῖσι
βαλλομένους ὑπὸ πατρί, τό τ' οὐδ' ὄναρ ἤλυθεν
    ἄλλῳ,
οὐδέ σφιν δυνάμην ἀδινὸν καλέουσιν ἀρῆξαι
20 μητέρ' ἐήν, ἐπεὶ ἐγγὺς ἀνίκητον κακὸν ἦεν.

18 τ' Gow: δ' M

484

MEGARA

"Mother,[1] why are you breaking your heart in this way with
excessive grief? Why have your cheeks lost their color?
Why are you so sad? Is it because your famous son is
undergoing troubles without end at the command of a
worthless man,[2] like a lion controlled by a fawn? Alas, why
have the immortal gods treated me with such dishonor?
Why did my parents bring me into a life fated to be so
wretched? I am so unfortunate! I came to the marriage
bed of a glorious husband; I valued him as much as my
own eyes, and I still revere and honor him in my heart. Yet
no living man has had such a miserable lot or tasted so
many sorrows in his mind. The luckless man! With the
arrows given him by Apollo—hideous weapons of some
doom or Fury—rushing in madness through his own
house he slaughtered his children and robbed them of life,
and the place was drenched in gore. It was my terrible lot
to see with my own eyes our children being shot by their
father, a thing no one else has even dreamed of, and I
could not help them as they kept calling for their mother,
for the evil was so close and irresistible. Just as a bird la-

[1] In fact she is Megara's mother-in-law; but μήτηρ was used
as a respectful form of address from a young to an older woman.
[2] Eurystheus, king of Tiryns, who ordered Heracles to per-
form the Labors.

ὡς δ᾽ ὄρνις δύρηται ἐπὶ σφετέροισι νεοσσοῖς
ὀλλυμένοις, οὕς τ᾽ αἰνὸς ὄφις ἔτι νηπιάχοντας
θάμνοις ἐν πυκινοῖσι κατεσθίει, ἡ δὲ κατ᾽ αὐτούς
25 πωτᾶται κλάζουσα μάλα λιγὺ πότνια μήτηρ,
οὐδ᾽ ἄρ᾽ ἔχει τέκνοισιν ἐπαρκέσαι, ἦ γὰρ οἱ αὐτῇ
ἆσσον ἴμεν μέγα τάρβος ἀμειλίκτοιο πελώρου—
ὣς ἐγὼ αἰνοτόκεια φίλον γόνον αἰάζουσα
μαινομένοισι πόδεσσι δόμον κάτα πολλὸν ἐφοίτων.
30 ὥς γ᾽ ὄφελον μετὰ παισὶν ἅμα θνήσκουσα καὶ αὐτή
κεῖσθαι φαρμακόεντα δι᾽ ἥπατος ἰὸν ἔχουσα,
Ἄρτεμι, θηλυτέρῃσι μέγα κρείουσα γυναιξί·
τῷ χ᾽ ἡμᾶς κλαύσαντε φίλησ᾽ ἐν χερσὶ τοκῆες
πολλοῖς σὺν κτερέεσσι πυρῆς ἐπέβησαν ὁμοίης,
35 καί κεν ἕνα χρύσειον ἐς ὀστέα κρωσσὸν ἁπάντων
λέξαντες κατέθαψαν ὅθι πρῶτον γενόμεσθα.
νῦν δ᾽ οἱ μὲν Θήβην ἱπποτρόφον ἐνναίουσιν
Ἀονίου πεδίοιο βαθεῖαν βῶλον ἀροῦντες,
αὐτὰρ ἐγὼ Τίρυνθα κάτα κραναὴν πόλιν Ἥρης
40 πολλοῖσιν δύστηνος ἰάπτομαι ἄλγεσιν ἦτορ
αἰὲν ὁμῶς, δακρύων δὲ πάρεστί μοι οὐδ᾽ ἵ᾽ ἐρωή.
ἀλλὰ πόσιν μὲν ὁρῶ παῦρον χρόνον ὀφθαλμοῖσιν
οἴκῳ ἐν ἡμετέρῳ, πολέων γάρ οἱ ἔργον ἑτοῖμον
μόχθων, τοὺς ἐπὶ γαῖαν ἀλώμενος ἠδὲ θάλασσαν
45 μοχθίζει πέτρης ὅγ᾽ ἔχων νόον ἠὲ σιδήρου
καρτερὸν ἐν στήθεσσι· σὺ δ᾽ ἠΰτε λείβεαι ὕδωρ,

---

[3] The simile may be inspired by Eur. HF 71, 974, 1039–41,
where bird similes are used to describe Megara's protective be-

ments for her murdered chicks which, still nestlings, a foul serpent is devouring in the dense thicket; the mother flutters around them with piercing cries, but she cannot come to help her children, for she is in terror of going near the grim creature[3]—just so I, their wretched mother, ranged everywhere through the house with maddened steps, lamenting my dear children. Artemis, you who have great power over women of flesh and blood, I do so wish that I had lain dead along with my children, shot through the heart with a poisoned arrow.[4] Then my lamenting parents would have taken us in their arms and placed us all on the same pyre with many funeral offerings, and gathering up our bones into one golden urn they would have buried us in the land of our birth. But they are living in Thebes, with its many horses, and they plow the deep soil of the Aonian plain,[5] while here in Tiryns, Hera's rocky city,[6] I am wretched and heartbroken with the same sorrows over and over, and I do not have a single respite from my weeping.

"It is rarely that I set eyes on my husband at home; he is often called away to perform the Labors which he ranges the world to carry out with a steady determination[7] in his heart. And as for you, in floods of tears you weep all the

---

havior and the murder of her children. In Euripides, however, Megara too is killed, and the Labors take place before the murders.   [4] The text is suspect here: (1) Women often wish for death from the "gentle arrows of Artemis" (e.g., Hom. *Od.* 20.61–62); (2) there is no other evidence for Heracles having used poisoned arrows against his family.   [5] Aonia = Boeotia.

[6] The Heraeum, a famous temple of the goddess, was nearby.

[7] Lit., "having a mind of stone or iron."

487

νύκτας τε κλαίουσα καὶ ἐκ Διὸς ἥμαθ᾽ ὁπόσσα.
ἄλλος μὰν οὐκ ἄν τις εὐφρήναι με παραστάς
κηδεμόνων· οὐ γάρ σφε δόμων κατὰ τεῖχος ἐέργει,
καὶ λίην πάντες γε πέρην πιτυώδεος Ἰσθμοῦ
50 ναίουσ᾽, οὐδέ μοί ἐστι πρὸς ὅντινά κε βλέψασα
οἷα γυνὴ πανάποτμος ἀναψύξαιμι φίλον κῆρ
νόσφι γε δὴ Πύρρης συνομαίμονος· ἢ δὲ καὶ αὐτή
ἀμφὶ πόσει σφετέρῳ πλέον ἄχνυται Ἰφικλῆι,
σῷ υἱεῖ· πάντων γὰρ οἰζυρώτατα τέκνα
55 γείνασθαί σε θεῷ τε καὶ ἀνέρι θνητῷ ἔολπα.”

    Ὣς ἄρ᾽ ἔφη· τὰ δέ οἱ θαλερώτερα δάκρυα μήλων
κόλπον ἐς ἱμερόεντα κατὰ βλεφάρων ἐχέοντο
μνησαμένη τέκνων τε καὶ ὧν μετέπειτα τοκήων.
ὣς δ᾽ αὔτως δακρύοισι παρήια λεύκ᾽ ἐδίαινεν
60 Ἀλκμήνη· βαρὺ δ᾽ ἧγε καὶ ἐκ θυμοῦ στενάχουσα
μύθοισιν πυκινοῖσι φίλην νυὸν ὧδε μετηύδα·
“δαιμονίη παίδων, τί νύ τοι φρεσὶν ἔμπεσε τοῦτο
πευκαλίμης; πῶς ἄμμ᾽ ἐθέλεις ὀροθυνέμεν ἄμφω
κήδε᾽ ἄλαστα λέγουσα τά τ᾽ οὐ νῦν πρῶτα κέκλαυται;
65 ἦ οὐχ ἅλις, οἷς ἐχόμεσθα τὸ δεύτατον, αἰὲν ἐπ᾽ ἦμαρ
γινομένοις; μάλα μέν γε φιλοθρηνής κέ τις εἴη
ὅστις ἀριθμηθεῖσιν ἐφ᾽ ἡμετέροις ἀχέεσσι
θαρσοίη· τοιῆσδ᾽ ἐκυρήσαμεν ἐκ θεοῦ αἴσης.
καὶ δ᾽ αὐτὴν ὁρόω σε, φίλον τέκος, ἀτρύτοισιν
70 ἄλγεσι μοχθίζουσαν· ἐπιγνώμων δέ τοί εἰμι

67 ἀριθμηθεῖσιν Wilamowitz: -μήσειεν Μ
68 θαρσοίη Hermann: θάρσει· οὐ Μ

488

days and nights Zeus sends. There is no other relative of mine to support and comfort me; it is not a house wall that separates them from me, but they all live far beyond the pine-clad Isthmus, and there is no one for me, unfortunate woman, to look to for reviving my spirits, apart from my sister Pyrrha; and she has more grief about her husband Iphicles, your son.[8] It seems that to god and man alike you have borne the most unfortunate of children."

So she spoke; and tears as big as apples[9] poured down from her eyes into her lovely bosom as she thought of her children and next of her parents. Alcmena likewise drenched her white cheeks with tears. With a deep and heartfelt groan she addressed her dear daughter-in-law with these words of wisdom: "My dear child, what is this notion that has occurred to your prudent mind? How is it that you wish to upset us both by speaking of cares we cannot forget? This is not the first time we have wept over them. Are not those miseries enough which we endure from day to day?[10] It would be a person truly in love with lamentation who did not lose heart in reckoning the sum of our griefs, such is the fate allotted us by heaven. I see you yourself, dear child, laboring under endless sorrows, and I can forgive your grief,[11] since one can have enough even of good

---

[8] Alcmena was mother of Heracles by Zeus and of Iphicles by her mortal husband, Amphitryon: cf. Theoc. *Id.* 24. The brothers were awarded Megara and her sister by their father, Creon, as compensation for their freeing Thebes from the domination of Erginus (ps.-Apollod. *Bibl.* 2.4.11).

[9] Cf. Theoc. *Id.* 14.38 (and 32 for θαλερώτερον).

[10] The text and meaning of lines 65–68 are uncertain.

[11] Text uncertain. Perhaps, "I advise you to rest" (ἀσχαλάαν Sitzler); but that too strains the Greek.

ἀγχαλάαν, ὅτε δή γε καὶ εὐφροσύνης κόρος ἐστί.
καί σε μάλ᾽ ἐκπάγλως ὀλοφύρομαι ἠδ᾽ ἐλεαίρω
οὕνεκεν ἡμετέροιο λυγροῦ μετὰ δαίμονος ἔσχες
ὅς θ᾽ ἡμῖν ἐφύπερθε κάρης βαρὺς αἰωρεῖται.
75 ἴστω γὰρ Κούρη τε καὶ εὐέανος Δημήτηρ,
ἅς κε μέγα βλαφθείς τις ἑκὼν ἐπίορκον ὀμόσσαι
†δυσμενέων†, μηδέν σε χερειότερον φρεσὶν ᾖσι
στέργειν ⟨μ᾽⟩ ἢ εἴπερ μοι ὑπὲκ νηδυιόφιν ἦλθες
καί μοι τηλυγέτη ἐνὶ δώμασι παρθένος ἦσθα·
80 οὐδ᾽ αὐτήν γέ νυ πάμπαν ἔολπά σε τοῦτό γε λήθειν.
τῷ μή μ᾽ ἐξείπῃς ποτ᾽, ἐμὸν θάλος, ὥς σευ ἀκηδέω,
μηδ᾽ εἴ κ᾽ ἠυκόμου Νιόβης πυκινώτερα κλαίω.
οὐδὲν γὰρ νεμεσητὸν ὑπὲρ τέκνου γοάασθαι
μητέρι δυσπαθέοντος· ἐπεὶ δέκα μῆνας ἔκαμνον
85 †πρὶν καί πέρ τ᾽ ἰδέειν μιν, ἐμῷ ὑπὸ ἥπατ᾽ ἔχουσα,†
καί με πυλάρταο σχεδὸν ἤγαγεν Ἀιδωνῆος,
ὧδέ ἑ δυστοκέουσα κακὰς ὠδῖνας ἀνέτλην.
νῦν δέ μοι οἴχεται υἱὸς ἐπ᾽ ἀλλοτρίης νέον ἆθλον
ἐκτελέων, οὐδ᾽ οἶδα δυσάμμορος εἴτε μιν αὖτις
90 ἐνθάδε νοστήσανθ᾽ ὑποδέξομαι εἴτε καὶ οὐκί.
  "πρὸς δ᾽ ἔτι μ᾽ ἐπτοίησε διὰ γλυκὺν αἰνὸς ὄνειρος
ὕπνον, δειμαίνω δὲ παλίγκοτον ὄψιν ἰδοῦσα
ἐκπάγλως μή μοί τι τέκνοις ἀποθύμιον ἕρπῃ.

76 ὀμόσσαι Brunck: -σσῃ M
78 μ᾽ add. Hermann: om. M
88 υἱὸς Valckenaer: οἷος M
93 ἕρπῃ Hermann: ἔρδοι M

cheer. I grieve for you and pity you very much because you have a part in the ghastly doom which hangs heavy over the heads of our family. I call to witness the Maiden[12] and Demeter of the fair robes—an oath which only a real madman[13] would be willing to break—that in my heart I love you no less than if you had been born from my womb and were the favorite daughter of my house; you yourself are not unaware of that, I think. So never say that I do not care for you, my darling, even if I weep faster than Niobe of the beautiful hair.[14] A mother should not be blamed for lamenting a child who is in trouble; after all, I suffered for ten months carrying him inside me before I cast eyes on him,[15] and he almost brought me to Aidoneus, Warden of the Gate,[16] so terrible were the pains I suffered at his birth. And now my son has gone to carry out a new task in a foreign land, and in my wretchedness I cannot tell whether or no he will return and I shall welcome him here once more.

"And that is not all. A horrible dream frightened me as I was sleeping sweetly, and the sight of that threatening vision makes me extremely fearful that some accident is

---

[12] Persephone. Only women swore by Demeter and her daughter. [13] The text has "one of my enemies" as the subject, but "enemies" seems to be corrupt.

[14] So called at Hom. *Il.* 24.602. Apollo and Artemis killed her children as punishment for her boastfulness; constantly weeping, she was metamorphosed into a dripping rock.

[15] The text of line 85 is corrupt, but there is clearly a reference to the story of Heracles' birth, which was retarded by Hera (Hom. *Il.* 19.119; Ov. *Met.* 9.285–315).

[16] Hades, who keeps guard at the gates of the underworld.

εἴσατο γάρ μοι ἔχων μακέλην εὐεργέα χερσί
95 παῖς ἐμὸς ἀμφοτέρῃσι, βίῃ Ἡρακληείῃ,
τῇ μεγάλῃ ἐλάχαινε, δεδεγμένος ὡς ἐπὶ μισθῷ,
τάφρον τηλεθάοντος ἐπ᾽ ἐσχατιῇ τινος ἀγροῦ
γυμνὸς ἄτερ χλαίνης τε καὶ εὐμίτροιο χιτῶνος.
αὐτὰρ ἐπειδὴ παντὸς ἀφίκετο πρὸς τέλος ἔργου
100 καρτερὸν οἰνοφόροιο πονεύμενος ἔρκος ἀλωῆς,
ἤτοι ὃ λίστρον ἔμελλεν ἐπὶ προύχοντος ἐρείσας
ἀνδήρου καταδῦναι ἃ καὶ πάρος εἵματα ἔστο·
ἐξαπίνης δ᾽ ἀνέλαμψεν ὑπὲρ καπέτοιο βαθείης
πῦρ ἄμοτον, περὶ δ᾽ αὐτὸν ἀθέσφατος εἰλεῖτο φλόξ.
105 αὐτὰρ ὅγ᾽ αἰὲν ὄπισθε θοοῖς ἀνεχάζετο ποσσίν
ἐκφυγέειν μεμαὼς ὀλοὸν μένος Ἡφαίστοιο·
αἰεὶ δὲ προπάροιθεν ἑοῦ χροὸς ἠύτε γέρρον
νώμασκεν μακέλην, περὶ δ᾽ ὄμμασιν ἔνθα καὶ ἔνθα
πάπταινεν μὴ δή μιν ἐπιφλέξῃ δήιον πῦρ.
110 τῷ μὲν ἀοσσῆσαι λελιημένος, ὥς μοι ἔικτο,
Ἰφικλέης μεγάθυμος ἐπ᾽ οὔδεϊ κάππεσ᾽ ὀλισθών
πρὶν ἐλθεῖν, οὐδ᾽ ὀρθὸς ἀναστῆναι δύνατ᾽ αὖτις,
ἀλλ᾽ ἀστεμφὲς ἔκειτο, γέρων ὡσεῖτ᾽ ἀμενηνός
ὄντε καὶ οὐκ ἐθέλοντα βιήσατο γῆρας ἀτερπές
115 καππεσέειν, κεῖται δ᾽ ὅγ᾽ ἐπὶ χθονὸς ἔμπεδον αὔτως
εἰσόκε τις χειρός μιν ἀνειρύσῃ παριόντων
αἰδεσθεὶς ὄπιδα προτέρην πολιοῖο γενείου.
ὣς ἐν γῇ λελίαστο σακεσπάλος Ἰφικλέης,
αὐτὰρ ἐγὼ κλαίεσκον ἀμηχανέοντας ὁρῶσα
120 παῖδας ἐμούς, μέχρι δή μοι ἀπέσσυτο νήδυμος ὕπνος
ὀφθαλμῶν ἠὼς δὲ παραυτίκα φαινόλις ἦλθε.

about to happen to my children. The mighty Heracles, my son, appeared to me; he was holding in both hands a trusty spade and digging, like a hired laborer, a big ditch along the edge of a fertile field, having stripped off his cloak and well-girded tunic. When he reached the end of the task of laboring at a stout defense for that area of vines, he was about to rest his spade on the bank of earth and dress himself again, when suddenly raging fire blazed out over that deep trench and indescribable flames rolled all around him. All the time he kept moving backward with quick steps as he strove to escape the destructive power of Hephaestus, and all the time he kept wielding the spade in front of his body like a shield as he glanced this way and that in case the hostile fire should burn him up. Then I dreamed that brave Iphicles, eager to help him, slipped and fell on the ground before he could reach him; he could not raise himself again, but lay there helplessly like a feeble old man whom joyless age has forced to fall, much against his will; he lies there on the ground until some passerby lifts him up out of respect for the reverence once felt for his gray beard.[17] Iphicles, wielding his shield, lay just so on the ground, and I was crying at the sight of my sons helpless, until sweet sleep fled from my eyes and bright dawn instantly appeared.

[17] The dream seems to portend Heracles' death on the pyre (cf. on Theoc. *Id.* 24.83) and (though this happened earlier) Iphicles' death while helping his brother in battle (ps.-Apollod. *Bibl.* 2.7.3; Paus. 8.14.9–10).

τοῖα, φίλη, μοι ὄνειρα διὰ φρένας ἐπτοίησαν
παννυχίη· τὰ δὲ πάντα πρὸς Εὐρυσθῆα τρέποιτο
οἴκου ἀφ' ἡμετέροιο, γένοιτο δὲ μάντις ἐκείνῳ
125   θυμὸς ἐμός, μηδ' ἄλλο παρὲκ τελέσειέ τι δαίμων."

"These, my dear, were the dreams that so startled me all night long. I hope they may all be turned against Eurystheus and away from our house![18] May my heart's foreboding apply to him, and may heaven bring about nothing else but that!"

[18] For the formal language of "turning away" (*apopompê*), cf. Theoc. 6.23–24.

ΜΟΣΧΟΤ ΑΠΟΣΠΑΣΜΑΤΑ

1 Stob. 4.17.19

Τὰν ἅλα τὰν γλαυκὰν ὅταν ὤνεμος ἀτρέμα βάλλῃ,
τὰν φρένα τὰν δειλὰν ἐρεθίζομαι, οὐδ' ἔτι μοι γᾶ
ἐντὶ φίλα, ποθίει δὲ πολὺ πλέον ἁ μεγάλα μ' ἅλς.
ἀλλ' ὅταν ἀχήσῃ πολιὸς βυθὸς ἁ δὲ θάλασσα
5 κυρτὸν ἐπαφρίζῃ τὰ δὲ κύματα μακρὰ μεμήνῃ,
ἐς χθόνα παπταίνω καὶ δένδρεα τὰν δ' ἅλα φεύγω,
γᾶ δέ μοι ἀσπαστά, χἁ δάσκιος εὔαδεν ὕλα
ἔνθα καὶ ἢν πνεύσῃ πολὺς ὤνεμος ἁ πίτυς ᾄδει.
ἦ κακὸν ὁ γριπεὺς ζώει βίον, ᾧ δόμος ἁ ναῦς,
10 καὶ πόνος ἐντὶ θάλασσα, καὶ ἰχθύες ἁ πλάνος ἄγρα.
αὐτὰρ ἐμοὶ γλυκὺς ὕπνος ὑπὸ πλατάνῳ βαθυφύλλῳ,
καὶ παγᾶς φιλέοιμι τὸν ἐγγύθεν ἆχον ἀκούειν
ἃ τέρπει ψοφέοισα τὸν ἄγρυπνον, οὐχὶ ταράσσει.

1 βάλλῃ Stephanus: βάλοι M   2 μοι γᾶ Bosius:
μοῖσα M   3 πλέον ἁ μεγάλα μ' ἅλς Edmonds: πλέονα
μεγάλαν ἅλα M   7 χἁ Stephanus: τάχα M   13 ἄγρυ-
πνον Gow: ἀγροῖκον M

2 Stob. 4.20.29

Ἤρατο Πὰν Ἀχῶς τᾶς γείτονος, ἤρατο δ' Ἀχώ
σκιρτατᾶ Σατύρω, Σάτυρος δ' ἐπεμήνατο Λύδᾳ.
ὡς Ἀχὼ τὸν Πᾶνα, τόσον Σάτυρος φλέγεν Ἀχώ

FRAGMENTS

1 Stobaeus

When the wind falls gently on the blue sea, my timid heart plucks up courage; I no longer love the land, and the great sea has much more appeal. But when the gray deep roars and the foaming sea swells and the waves grow long and wild, then I turn my gaze toward the land and the trees, and I avoid the sea; the earth is welcome to me and the shady wood is pleasant, where the pine tree sings even when the wind is high. The fisherman's life is truly a wretched one: his boat is his house, the sea his toil, the fish his moving prey. But I should like to sleep sweetly under a leafy plane tree and enjoy listening to the plash of a spring whose sound delights, and does not disturb, the sleepless.[1]

[1] Perhaps a complete poem.

2 Stobaeus

Pan loved his neighbor Echo, Echo loved a frisky Satyr, and the Satyr was mad for Lyda. Echo inflamed the heart of Pan just as much as the Satyr did Echo's and Lyda

καὶ Λύδα Σατυρίσκον· Ἔρως δ' ἐσμύχετ' ἀμοιβά.
5 ὅσσον γὰρ τήνων τις ἐμίσεε τὸν φιλέοντα,
τόσσον ὁμῶς φιλέων ἠχθαίρετο, πάσχε δ' ἃ ποίει.
ταῦτα λέγω πᾶσιν τὰ διδάγματα τοῖς ἀνεράστοις·
στέργετε τὼς φιλέοντας ἵν' ἢν φιλέητε φιλῆσθε.

3 Stob. 4.20.55

Ἀλφειὸς μετὰ Πῖσαν ἐπὴν κατὰ πόντον ὁδεύῃ,
ἔρχεται εἰς Ἀρέθοισαν ἄγων κοτινηφόρον ὕδωρ,
ἕδνα φέρων καλὰ φύλλα καὶ ἄνθεα καὶ κόνιν ἱράν,
καὶ βαθὺς ἐμβαίνει τοῖς κύμασι τὰν δὲ θάλασσαν
5 νέρθεν ὑποτροχάει, κοὐ μίγνυται ὕδασιν ὕδωρ,
ἁ δ' οὐκ οἶδε θάλασσα διερχομένω ποταμοῖο.
κῶρος δεινοθέτας κακομάχανος αἰνὰ διδάσκων
καὶ ποταμὸν διὰ φίλτρον Ἔρως ἐδίδαξε κολυμβῆν.

4 APlan. 4.200

ΕΙΣ ΕΡΩΤΑ ΑΡΟΤΡΙΩΝΤΑ

Λαμπάδα θεὶς καὶ τόξα βοηλάτιν εἵλετο ῥάβδον
οὖλος Ἔρως, πήρην δ' εἶχε κατωμαδίην,
καὶ ζεύξας ταλαεργὸν ὑπὸ ζυγὸν αὐχένα ταύρων
ἔσπειρεν Δηοῦς αὔλακα πυροφόρον·
5 εἶπε δ' ἄνω βλέψας αὐτῷ Διί, "πλῆσον ἀρούρας
μή σε τὸν Εὐρώπης βοῦν ὑπ' ἄροτρα βάλω."

---

[1] Epigram on a picture of Eros plowing. On Zeus' transformation into a bull to seduce Europa, see Moschus 2.

the Satyr's, and their love kept smoldering turn and turn about. A beloved who hated a lover was detested just as much, causing and suffering the same pains. Here is my lesson for all those who are not in love: be kind to those who love you, so that when you are in love you may be loved in return.

3 Stobaeus

When Alpheüs leaves Pisa and makes his journey by sea,[1] he brings to Arethusa his water that produces the wild-olive trees,[2] and he bears as bridal gifts fair leaves and flowers and sacred dust;[3] he plunges deep into the waves and moves along beneath the sea, not mingling his water with its water. That rascally, impudent Eros, teacher of mischief, by his spells has even taught a river how to dive.

[1] Alpheüs, the river at Olympia, was said to pass under the sea as a stream of fresh water and to emerge near Syracuse in Sicily as a spring, Arethusa. See Ovid, *Met.* 5.572–641.

[2] Olympia was famous for these; at the Olympic Games the victors' crowns were of wild olive.

[3] From the racecourse at Olympia, part of the sacred site.

4 Planudean Anthology

On Eros Plowing

Cruel Eros set aside his torch and his arrows, shouldered a knapsack, and took up an ox goad; he put under the yoke the necks of working oxen and began to sow Demeter's furrows for a crop of wheat. Looking up, he cried to great Zeus himself, "Give me a full crop or I'll put you to my plow, bull of Europa."[1]

BION

TESTIMONIA

1 Vid. Theoc. T 1.

2 Vid. Mosch. T 2.

TESTIMONIA

1 See Theoc. T 1.

2 See Mosch. T 2.

THE LAMENT FOR ADONIS

The Lament for Adonis, *though in part set in the country-side, is probably inspired by the Adonis song at Theocritus* Id. *15.100–144 (an "urban" idyll). There in a static scene, Aphrodite and Adonis are celebrated as happy lovers; here Bion dwells on the gory death of Adonis and the goddess's lament for him. There are several changes of scene (Aphrodite's bed, Adonis in the hills, Aphrodite and the dying Adonis, Aphrodite's palace), and the emphasis is on speech and movement. On a formal level the poem owes much to those hymns of Callimachus (to Apollo, Athena, and Demeter) in which details supplied in passing by an anonymous "master of ceremonies" figure (here a female celebrant) allow readers to construct for themselves a dramatic context.*

The poem is a hexameter version of the ritual lament uttered on the day of mourning at the Adonia festival (see p. 205). In real life this may have been in rhythmic prose or may have consisted in ritual cries and exclamations. Sappho appears to have composed a Lament for Adonis *in lyric meter (Fr. 140 Voigt); and the lyric lament for performance at wakes was well established as a literary form by the sixth century. Such works had a stately and consolatory tone. Bion, by contrast, aims to reproduce the strident effect and heightened eroticism of an exotic foreign festival; hence the extraordinary amount of repetition, alliteration, and assonance, which suggest rapid movement and animation. The refrain is perhaps inspired by the lament for Daphnis in Theocritus Id. 1, and it represents the repeated interjections of woe characteristic of Greek laments. Antiphony and antithesis are found throughout: the focus is alternately on Aphrodite and Adonis, while the poet varies themes of praise and reproach, life and death, past happiness and present grief.*

Criticism

Alexiou, M. *The Ritual Lament in Greek Tradition.* 2nd ed. Lanham, MD, 2002.

Fantuzzi, *M. Bionis Smyrnaei* Adonidis Epitaphium. Liverpool, 1985.

Hopkinson, *Hellenistic Anthology,* 215–26.

Reed, J. D. *Bion of Smyrna: The Fragments and the* Adonis. Cambridge, 1997.

ΕΠΙΤΑΦΙΟΣ ΑΔΩΝΙΔΟΣ

Αἰάζω τὸν Ἄδωνιν, "ἀπώλετο καλὸς Ἄδωνις"·
"ὤλετο καλὸς Ἄδωνις," ἐπαιάζουσιν Ἔρωτες.

μηκέτι πορφυρέοις ἐνὶ φάρεσι Κύπρι κάθευδε·
ἔγρεο, δειλαία, κυανόστολα καὶ πλατάγησον
5 στήθεα καὶ λέγε πᾶσιν, "ἀπώλετο καλὸς Ἄδωνις."

αἰάζω τὸν Ἄδωνιν· ἐπαιάζουσιν Ἔρωτες.

κεῖται καλὸς Ἄδωνις ἐν ὤρεσι μηρὸν ὀδόντι,
λευκῷ λευκὸν ὀδόντι τυπείς, καὶ Κύπριν ἀνιῇ
λεπτὸν ἀποψύχων· τὸ δέ οἱ μέλαν εἴβεται αἷμα
10 χιονέας κατὰ σαρκός, ὑπ' ὀφρύσι δ' ὄμματα ναρκῇ,
καὶ τὸ ῥόδον φεύγει τῶ χείλεος· ἀμφὶ δὲ τήνῳ
θνᾴσκει καὶ τὸ φίλημα, τὸ μήποτε Κύπρις ἀποίσει.
Κύπριδι μὲν τὸ φίλημα καὶ οὐ ζώοντος ἀρέσκει,
ἀλλ' οὐκ οἶδεν Ἄδωνις ὅ νιν θνᾴσκοντα φίλησεν.

15 αἰάζω τὸν Ἄδωνιν· ἐπαιάζουσιν Ἔρωτες.

ἄγριον ἄγριον ἕλκος ἔχει κατὰ μηρὸν Ἄδωνις,
μεῖζον δ' ἁ Κυθέρεια φέρει ποτικάρδιον ἕλκος.

4 κυανόστολα Wilamowitz: -στόλε M
7 ἐν Ameis: ἐπ' M

THE LAMENT FOR ADONIS

I wail for Adonis: "Fair Adonis is dead." "Fair Adonis is dead," wail the Loves in answer.

Sleep no more in your purple sheets, Cypris: rouse yourself, unhappy goddess, and beat your breast robed in black, and say to everyone, "Fair Adonis is dead."

I wail for Adonis; the Loves wail in answer. Fair Adonis lies on the hills, wounded in his thigh with a tusk, wounded in his white thigh with a white tusk, and he grieves Cypris as he breathes his last faint breath. His dark blood drips over his snow-white flesh, and under his brows his eyes grow dim; the rosy hue flees from his lip, and around it dies the kiss, too, which Cypris will never carry off again.[1] Even when he is not alive his kiss pleases Cypris; but Adonis does not know that she kissed him when he was dead.

I wail for Adonis; the Loves wail in answer. Adonis has a cruel, cruel wound in his thigh; but greater is the wound Cytherea[2] has in her heart. Around that boy his own

[1] He is unconscious and cannot give her a kiss to "take away."
[2] A title of Aphrodite, who had a temple on the island of Cythera (cf. 35).

τῆνον μὲν περὶ παῖδα φίλοι κύνες ὠρύονται
καὶ Νύμφαι κλαίουσιν Ὀρειάδες· ἁ δ' Ἀφροδίτα
20 λυσαμένα πλοκαμῖδας ἀνὰ δρυμὼς ἀλάληται
πενθαλέα νήπλεκτος ἀσάνδαλος, αἱ δὲ βάτοι νιν
ἐρχομέναν κείροντι καὶ ἱερὸν αἷμα δρέπονται·
ὀξὺ δὲ κωκύοισα δι' ἄγκεα μακρὰ φορεῖται
Ἀσσύριον βοόωσα πόσιν, καὶ πολλὰ καλεῦσα.
25 ἀμφὶ δέ νιν μέλαν αἷμα παρ' ὀμφαλὸν ἀωρεῖτο,
στήθεα δ' ἐκ μηρῶν φοινίσσετο, τοὶ δ' ὑπὸ μαζοὶ
χιόνεοι τὸ πάροιθεν Ἀδώνιδι πορφύροντο.

"αἰαῖ τὰν Κυθέρειαν," ἐπαιάζουσιν Ἔρωτες.

ὤλεσε τὸν καλὸν ἄνδρα, σὺν ὤλεσεν ἱερὸν εἶδος.
30 Κύπριδι μὲν καλὸν εἶδος ὅτε ζώεσκεν Ἄδωνις,
κάτθανε δ' ἁ μορφὰ σὺν Ἀδώνιδι. "τὰν Κύπριν αἰαῖ"
ὤρεα πάντα λέγοντι, καὶ αἱ δρύες "αἲ τὸν Ἄδωνιν"·
καὶ ποταμοὶ κλαίοντι τὰ πένθεα τᾶς Ἀφροδίτας,
καὶ παγαὶ τὸν Ἄδωνιν ἐν ὤρεσι δακρύοντι,

18 ὠρύονται Hermann (ὠρύσαντο iam m): ὠδύραντο M
24 πολλὰ Hermann: παῖδα M

---

[3] The mountain nymphs of Cyprus, patronesses of the hunt, by whom, according to some accounts, Adonis was reared (cf. Ov. *Met.* 10.512–14).

[4] The ritual dishevelment of mourning.

[5] Her wounds correspond to those of Adonis (16); there is perhaps also an allusion to the self-laceration practiced by mourning women.

hounds howl and the mountain nymphs weep;[3] but Aphrodite, her tresses loosed, roams grief-stricken among the thickets with her hair unbraided, barefoot;[4] the brambles tear her as she goes and draw her sacred blood.[5] Wailing loudly, she moves through the long glens, crying out for her Assyrian husband and calling him many times.[6] But round his navel was floating the dark blood, and his chest grew red with blood from his thighs, and Adonis' breasts, once snow-white, grew dark.[7]

"Woe for Cytherea," wail the Loves in answer. She has lost her handsome lord, and with him she has lost her holy beauty. Cypris had beauty when Adonis was living, but her loveliness died with Adonis. "Woe for Cypris," say all the hills, and the oaks say, "Woe for Adonis."[8] The rivers lament Aphrodite's suffering, the springs in the hills are weeping for Adonis, from grief the flowers turn red,[9] and

[6] Text uncertain. Other possibilities are "uttering the Assyrian cry, calling for her husband and boy" and "crying out for her Assyrian husband and calling him her boy." But in this context "boy" seems odd.   [7] Adonis seems to be lying with his thigh higher than his head and chest, so that the blood flows from the wound over the upper part of his body. The pose is improbable, and the "floating" blood is a very strange expression. If the conjectures $\epsilon \hat{\imath} \mu a$ and $\chi \epsilon \iota \rho \hat{\omega} \nu$ are adopted, the whole sentence can be made to refer to Aphrodite: "around her the dark robe floated at her navel, and her chest was made scarlet by her hands, and her breasts, snow-white before, grew crimson for Adonis."

[8] The so-called pathetic fallacy: natural country sounds (echoing hills, rustling leaves, etc.) are taken to be made purposely and in sympathy with a human event.   [9] Or perhaps "turn brown," withering in sympathy. Roses are specified at line 66, but not here.

35 ἄνθεα δ' ἐξ ὀδύνας ἐρυθαίνεται, ἁ δὲ Κυθήρα
πάντας ἀνὰ κναμώς, ἀνὰ πᾶν νάπος οἰκτρὸν ἀείδει,

"αἰαῖ τὰν Κυθέρειαν· ἀπώλετο καλὸς Ἄδωνις"·

Ἀχὼ δ' ἀντεβόασεν, "ἀπώλετο καλὸς Ἄδωνις."
Κύπριδος αἰνὸν ἔρωτα τίς οὐκ ἔκλαυσεν ἂν αἰαῖ;

40   ὡς ἴδεν, ὡς ἐνόησεν Ἀδώνιδος ἄσχετον ἕλκος,
ὡς ἴδε φοίνιον αἷμα μαραινομένῳ περὶ μηρῷ,
πάχεας ἀμπετάσασα κινύρετο, "μεῖνον Ἄδωνι,
δύσποτμε μεῖνον Ἄδωνι, πανύστατον ὥς σε κιχείω,
ὥς σε περιπτύξω καὶ χείλεα χείλεσι μίξω.

45 ἔγρεο τυτθόν, Ἄδωνι, τὸ δ' αὖ πύματόν με φίλησον,
τοσσοῦτόν με φίλησον ὅσον ζώει τὸ φίλημα,
ἄχρις ἀποψύχῃς ἐς ἐμὸν στόμα, κεἰς ἐμὸν ἧπαρ
πνεῦμα τεὸν ῥεύσῃ, τὸ δέ σευ γλυκὺ φίλτρον ἀμέλξω,
ἐκ δὲ πίω τὸν ἔρωτα· φίλημα δὲ τοῦτο φυλάξω

50 ὡς αὐτὸν τὸν Ἄδωνιν, ἐπεὶ σύ με, δύσμορε, φεύγεις.
φεύγεις μακρόν, Ἄδωνι, καὶ ἔρχεαι εἰς Ἀχέροντα
πὰρ στυγνὸν βασιλῆα καὶ ἄγριον· ἁ δὲ τάλαινα
ζώω καὶ θεός ἐμμι καὶ οὐ δύναμαί σε διώκειν.
λάμβανε, Περσεφόνα, τὸν ἐμὸν πόσιν· ἐσσὶ γὰρ αὐτά
πολλὸν ἐμεῦ κρέσσων, τὸ δὲ πᾶν καλὸν ἐς σὲ

55   καταρρεῖ.
ἐμμὶ δ' ἐγὼ πανάποτμος, ἔχω δ' ἀκόρεστον ἀνίαν,

---

36 ἀνὰ πᾶν νάπος οἰκτρὸν Wakefield: ἀνάπαλιν ἀποσοι-
κτρὰν M   52 πὰρ Ameis: καὶ M
55 καταρρεῖ Stephanus: καὶ ἄρρει M

Cythera[10] sings pitifully through all her mountainsides and through every glade, "Woe for Cytherea: fair Adonis is dead"; and Echo made reply, "Fair Adonis is dead." Who would not have cried "Woe" for Cypris' woeful love?

When she saw,[11] when she beheld Adonis' unstaunchable wound, when she saw the red blood around his wasting thigh, she stretched out her arms and wailed, "Stay, Adonis, stay, ill-fated Adonis, so that I may possess you for the last time, so that I can embrace you and mingle lips with lips. Rouse yourself a little, Adonis, and kiss me for a final time; kiss me as much as your kiss has life, until you breathe your last into my mouth,[12] and your spirit flows into my heart, and I drain your sweet love. I will keep this kiss as if it were Adonis himself, since you flee me, ill-fated.[13] You flee far off, Adonis, and go your way to Acheron[14] to a king grim and cruel; but I live a wretched life and am a goddess and cannot go after you. Take my husband, Persephone: you are much greater than I, and every fair thing falls to you.[15] I am altogether unfortunate, and

10 I.e., the island, or its nymph, mourning in sympathy. Some have preferred to take *Kythêra* as a by-form of *Kythereia* (cf. *Adonis Dead* 1, 16, 22). Neither solution seems ideal.

11 The imaginary scene changes. After her distraught wanderings, she has found Adonis.

12 It was customary to catch a loved one's last breath as a way of continuing the union after death (cf. Virg. *Aen.* 4.684–85).

13 Flight and pursuit are common metaphors in courtship.

14 A river in the underworld.

15 Lit., "flows down to you"; the words are borrowed from Theoc. *Id.* 1.5.

καὶ κλαίω τὸν Ἄδωνιν, ὅ μοι θάνε, καί σε φοβεῦμαι.
θνᾴσκεις, ὦ τριπόθητε, πόθος δέ μοι ὡς ὄναρ ἔπτα,
χήρα δ' ἁ Κυθέρεια, κενοὶ δ' ἀνὰ δώματ' Ἔρωτες,
60 σοὶ δ' ἅμα κεστὸς ὄλωλε. τί γάρ, τολμηρέ, κυνάγεις;
καλὸς ἐὼν τί τοσοῦτον ἐμήναο θηρὶ παλαίειν";
ὧδ' ὀλοφύρατο Κύπρις· ἐπαιάζουσιν Ἔρωτες,

"αἰαῖ τὰν Κυθέρειαν, ἀπώλετο καλὸς Ἄδωνις."

δάκρυον ἁ Παφία τόσσον χέει ὅσσον Ἄδωνις
65 αἷμα χέει, τὰ δὲ πάντα ποτὶ χθονὶ γίνεται ἄνθη·
αἷμα ῥόδον τίκτει, τὰ δὲ δάκρυα τὰν ἀνεμώναν.

αἰάζω τὸν Ἄδωνιν, "ἀπώλετο καλὸς Ἄδωνις."

μηκέτ' ἐνὶ δρυμοῖσι τὸν ἀνέρα μύρεο, Κύπρι·
οὐκ ἀγαθὰ στιβάς ἐστιν Ἀδώνιδι φυλλὰς ἐρήμα.
70 λέκτρον ἔχοι, Κυθέρεια, τὸ σὸν νῦν νεκρὸς Ἄδωνις·
καὶ νέκυς ὢν καλός ἐστι, καλὸς νέκυς, οἷα καθεύδων.
κάτθεό νιν μαλακοῖς ἐνὶ φάρεσιν οἷς ἐνίαυεν
ὡς μετὰ τεῦς ἀνὰ νύκτα τὸν ἱερὸν ὕπνον ἐμόχθει·
παγχρυσέῳ κλιντῆρι πόθες καὶ στυγνὸν Ἄδωνιν,

61 τί τοσοῦτον Köchly: τοσοῦτον M   ἐμήναο Brunck:
ἔμηνας M   64 χέει d'Orville: ἐγχέει M
    69 οὐκ Ahrens: ἔστ' M
    70 ἔχοι Valckenaer: ἔχει M
    72 οἷς Stephanus: οἱ M
    73 ὡς Bücheler: τοῖς M   τεῦς Wilamowitz: σεῦ M
    74 παγχρυσέῳ Wilamowitz: -σῳ M   πόθες Platt: πόθει
m: ποθεῖ m

512

I have grief insatiable; I wail for Adonis because he is dead to me, and I detest you. Thrice-beloved one, you are dying, and my love[16] has flown like a dream; Cytherea is widowed, and the Loves are idle in my house. With you my charm has perished.[17] Why did you rashly go hunting? So handsome, why were you so mad as to struggle with a wild beast?"

With these words Cypris mourned; the Loves wailed in answer, "Woe for Cytherea: fair Adonis is dead."

The Paphian[18] sheds as many tears as Adonis sheds drops of blood, and all are turned to flowers on the ground: the blood bears roses, the tears anemones.[19] I wail for Adonis: "Fair Adonis is dead."

Weep no longer in the thickets for your husband, Cypris; a lonely bed of leaves is no good bed for Adonis. Let Adonis, now a corpse, have your couch, Cytherea: even as a corpse he is fair, a fair corpse, as if asleep. Lay him out on the soft sheets where he used to rest when with you he labored through the night in holy sleep.[20] Lay out Adonis, though he is a dreadful sight, on your couch[21] all of gold,

---

[16] Referring to Adonis, perhaps.   [17] The *kestos* was a belt of material with seductive powers (cf. *Il.* 14.214). She used it to charm Adonis, and so has no more use for it.

[18] Aphrodite had a famous temple at Paphos in Cyprus.

[19] Anemones were proverbially short-lived (cf. Ov. *Met.* 10.738–39).

[20] The text is probably corrupt. If this is a sexual euphemism, it sounds grotesque. His sleep is presumably called "holy" because he was with a goddess.

[21] But *klintêr* also means "bier."

βάλλε δέ νιν στεφάνοισι καὶ ἄνθεσι· πάντα σὺν
75   αὐτῷ·
ὡς τῆνος τέθνακε καὶ ἄνθεα πάντ' ἐμαράνθη.
ῥαῖνε δέ νιν Συρίοισιν ἀλείφασι, ῥαῖνε μύροισιν·
ὀλλύσθω μύρα πάντα· τὸ σὸν μύρον ὤλετ' Ἄδωνις.
    κέκλιται ἁβρὸς Ἄδωνις ἐν εἵμασι πορφυρέοισιν,
80   ἀμφὶ δέ νιν κλαίοντες ἀναστενάχουσιν Ἔρωτες
κειράμενοι χαίτας ἐπ' Ἀδώνιδι· χὠ μὲν ὀιστώς,
ὃς δ' ἐπὶ τόξον ἔβαλλεν, ὃ δὲ πτερόν, ὃς δὲ φαρέτραν·
χὠ μὲν ἔλυσε πέδιλον Ἀδώνιδος, οἳ δὲ λέβητι
χρυσείῳ φορέοισιν ὕδωρ, ὃ δὲ μηρία λούει,
85   ὃς δ' ὄπιθεν πτερύγεσσιν ἀναψύχει τὸν Ἄδωνιν.

"αἰαῖ τὰν Κυθέρειαν," ἐπαιάζουσιν Ἔρωτες.

ἔσβεσε λαμπάδα πᾶσαν ἐπὶ φλιαῖς Ὑμέναιος
καὶ στέφος ἐξεκέδασσε γαμήλιον· οὐκέτι δ' "ὑμήν
ὑμήν," οὐκέτ' ἄειδεν ἐὸν μέλος, ἀλλ' ἔλεγ', "αἰαῖ
90   αἰαῖ," καὶ "τὸν Ἄδωνιν" ἔτι πλέον ἢ "Ὑμέναιον."

75 δέ νιν Wassenbergh: δ' ἐνὶ M
77 Συρίοισιν Ruhnken: μύροισιν M
82 ἔβαλλεν, ὃ Wilamowitz: ἔβαιν' ὃς M
83 οἳ Graefe: ὃς M   86 αἰαῖ Van Lennep: αὐτὰν M
88 ἐξεκέδασσε Pierson: ἐξεπέτασσε M
89 ἄειδεν ἐὸν Köchly: ἀειδονέος M   ἀλλ' ἔλεγ' Maas:
ἄλλεται M   90 ἢ Higt: αἲ M

---

22 At the annual Adonis festival, the effigy on its bier was sprinkled with flowers and perfumes. Here the origin of the cus-

and strew him with garlands and flowers.[22] Let all things be with him.[23] When he died all the flowers withered, too. Sprinkle him with Syrian unguents,[24] sprinkle him with perfumes. Let all perfumes perish: Adonis, your perfume, has perished.

Delicate Adonis lies in purple garments,[25] and around him weeping wail the Loves, cutting their hair for Adonis. One casts on him his arrows, another his bow, another a wing feather, another his quiver.[26] One has loosed Adonis' sandal; others bring water in a golden bowl, another washes his thighs, another fans Adonis from behind with his wings. "Woe for Cytherea," cry the Loves in answer.

Hymenaeus put out all his torches at the doorposts and scattered his wedding garland:[27] no longer did he sing "Hymen, Hymen," no longer did he sing his own song, but he said, "Woe, woe" and "Woe for Adonis" even louder

tom is suggested: all flowers died with Adonis (76; cf. 35), and Adonis was Aphrodite's "perfume" or sweet favorite, so that all perfumes ought to be poured on him, too.

[23] Text probably corrupt. There is no verb expressed in the Greek.   [24] Syria was famous for its unguents, but the adjective is particularly apt here because of the Syrian origins of Adonis' family (cf. Ov. *Met.* 10.503–14).

[25] The setting changes. Adonis is lying on Aphrodite's couch. This was a popular scene in Greek and Roman art.

[26] Or ". . . another his bow, another his feathered quiver," if ὃς δ' εὔπτερον ἆγε φαρέτραν is read. The wing feather seems out of place; but "feathered quiver" is unlikely.

[27] Hymenaeus, god of marriage, had celebrated the lovers' union with torches, garlands, and wedding songs at the bedroom door. This joyful attitude now changes to one of grief.

αἱ Χάριτες κλαίοντι τὸν υἱέα τῶ Κινύραο,
"ὤλετο καλὸς Ἄδωνις" ἐν ἀλλάλαισι λέγοισαι,
"αἰαῖ" δ᾽ ὀξὺ λέγοντι πολὺ πλέον ἢ Παιῶνα.
χαὶ Μοῖραι τὸν Ἄδωνιν ἀνακλείοισιν ἐν Ἀΐδα
95 καί νιν ἐπαείδουσιν, ὃ δέ σφισιν οὐκ ἐπακούει·
οὐ μὰν οὐκ ἐθέλει, Κώρα δέ νιν οὐκ ἀπολύει.

λῆγε γόων Κυθέρεια τὸ σάμερον, ἴσχεο κομμῶν·
δεῖ σε πάλιν κλαῦσαι, πάλιν εἰς ἔτος ἄλλο δακρῦ-
σαι.

93 αἰαῖ Pierson: αὐτὰν M   Παιῶνα Ahrens: τὺ διώνα M
94 χαὶ Meineke: καὶ M   ἀνακλείοισιν Gow post
Ahrens: -κλαί- M   ἐν Ἀΐδα Briggs: ἄδωνιν M
97 κομμῶν Barth: κώμων M

than he had sung "Hymenaeus." The Graces weep for the son of Cinyras,[28] saying to each other, "Fair Adonis is dead"; and they cry "Woe" much louder than they once sang the paean.[29] The Fates call up Adonis, Adonis, and sing incantations for him, but he does not obey them—not that he is unwilling, but the Maiden will not let him go.[30]

Cease your wailing for today, Cytherea; stop your lamentations: you must lament again and weep again another year.

[28] Adonis was said by the Greeks to be the son of an incestuous union between Cinyras, a Syrian settler in Cyprus, and his daughter Myrrha, who was metamorphosed into a myrrh tree (Ov. *Met.* 10.298–518).

[29] A solemn choral performance associated with Apollo; as Apollo's attendants, the Graces, would have sung it at the wedding of Adonis and Aphrodite. The manuscripts read "much more than you, Dione" (for Dione = Aphrodite see on Theoc. *Id.* 7.116); but why should the Graces mourn much more than Aphrodite?

[30] Is she in love with him herself?

THE WEDDING SONG OF
ACHILLES AND DEIDAMIA

Like the sixth and eleventh idylls of Theocritus, to which it alludes (lines 2–3), this fragment combines a tale from mythology with a pastoral setting. Lycidas sings how the Greek army mustered for Troy while Achilles, disguised as a girl, courted and attempted to seduce Deidamia, daughter of Lycomedes, king of Scyros. (Thetis, mother of Achilles, had placed him there knowing that he would be killed if he fought at Troy.) The "wedding song" of the title (cf. Theoc. Id. 18) was presumably reported as part of the marriage celebrations.

The story was treated in the Scyrians of Euripides, now lost (Frr. 680–84 Collard and Cropp). It is twice referred to by Ovid (Ars Am. 1.681–704, Met. 13.162–70). The fullest extant account is in Statius' Achilleid. The hero's singing and wool working are traditional features of the story.

Criticism

Fantuzzi, M. "Achilles at Scyros, and One of His Fans: *The Epithalamium of Achilles and Deidamia.*" In Baumbach –Bär, *Companion,* 283–305.

Gutzwiller, *Hellenistic Epyllion,* 73–76.

[ΒΙΩΝΟΣ] ΕΠΙΘΑΛΑΜΙΟΣ ΑΧΙΛΛΕΩΣ
ΚΑΙ ΔΗΙΔΑΜΕΙΑΣ

ΜΥΡΣΩΝ

Λῆς νύ τί μοι, Λυκίδα, Σικελὸν μέλος ἁδὺ λιγαίνειν,
ἱμερόεν γλυκύθυμον ἐρωτικόν, οἷον ὁ Κύκλωψ
ἄεισεν Πολύφαμος ἐπ' ἠόνι ‹τᾷ› Γαλατείᾳ;

ΛΥΚΙΔΑΣ

κἠμοὶ συρίσδεν, Μύρσων, φίλον, ἀλλὰ τί μέλψω;

ΜΥΡΣΩΝ

5   Σκύριον ‹ὄν›, Λυκίδα, ζαλώμενος ᾆδες ἔρωτα,
λάθρια Πηλεΐδαο φιλάματα, λάθριον εὐνάν,
πῶς παῖς ἔσσατο φᾶρος, ὅπως δ' ἐψεύσατο μορφάν,
χὤπως ἐν κώραις Λυκομηδίσιν οὐκ ἀλεγοίσαις
ἠείδη κατὰ παστὸν Ἀχιλλέα Δηιδάμεια.

ΛΥΚΙΔΑΣ

10 ἅρπασε τὰν Ἑλέναν πόθ' ὁ βωκόλος, ἆγε δ' ἐς Ἴδαν,
Οἰνώνῃ κακὸν ἄλγος. ἐχώσατο ‹δ'› ἁ Λακεδαίμων

3 τᾷ add. Brunck: om. M   4 κἠμοὶ Brunck: κῆν μοι M
5 ὄν add. Ahrens: om. M   ζαλώμενος ᾆδες Ahrens:
ζαλῶν μένος ἁδὺς M   7 ἐψεύσατο Canter: ἔγευ- M
8 χὤπως ἐν Meineke: κῆν ὅπως m: κ. ὅπος m   οὐκ
ἀλεγοίσαις Ahrens: ὁ ἀπαλέγοισα M
9 ἠείδη Edmonds: ἀηδὴν M

THE WEDDING SONG OF ACHILLES
AND DEIDAMIA

MYRSON

Will you sing me some sweet Sicilian song, Lycidas—some
sweet and charming love song such as the Cyclops Poly-
phemus sang to Galatea on the seashore?

LYCIDAS

I too should like to pipe, Myrson. But what should be my
theme?

MYRSON

The Scyrian love story, Lycidas, which you used to sing to
great acclaim, about the secret kisses of Peleus' son and
his secret affair; how the lad put on a robe and donned a
disguise, and how among the carefree[1] daughters of Lyco-
medes Deidamia came to know Achilles in her bedcham-
ber.

LYCIDAS

"Once upon a time the oxherd[2] stole away Helen and took
her to Ida, a cause of great sorrow for Oenone. Sparta

---

[1] "Carefree" is a conjecture; the text is corrupt.

[2] Paris, who tended his cattle on Mt. Ida and then judged the
goddesses' beauty contest, Helen being his reward for giving the
prize to Aphrodite. At that time he was married to Oenone.

πάντα δὲ λαὸν ἄγειρεν Ἀχαϊκόν, οὐδέ τις Ἕλλην,
οὔτε Μυκηναίων οὔτ᾽ Ἤλιδος οὔτε Λακώνων,
μεῖνεν ἑὸν κατὰ δῶμα φυγὼν δύστανον Ἄρηα.
15 λάνθανε δ᾽ ἐν κώραις Λυκομηδίσι μοῦνος Ἀχιλλεύς,
εἴρια δ᾽ ἀνθ᾽ ὅπλων ἐδιδάσκετο, καὶ χερὶ λευκᾷ
παρθενικὸν κόρον εἶχεν, ἐφαίνετο δ᾽ ἠύτε κώρα·
καὶ γὰρ ἴσον τήναις θηλύνετο, καὶ τόσον ἄνθος
χιονέαις πόρφυρε παρηίσι, καὶ τὸ βάδισμα
20 παρθενικῆς ἐβάδιζε, κόμας δ᾽ ἐπύκαζε καλύπτρῃ.
θυμὸν δ᾽ ἀνέρος εἶχε καὶ ἀνέρος εἶχεν ἔρωτα·
ἐξ ἀοῦς δ᾽ ἐπὶ νύκτα παρίζετο Δηιδαμείᾳ,
καὶ ποτὲ μὲν τήνας ἐφίλει χέρα, πολλάκι δ᾽ αὐτᾶς
στάμονα καλὸν ἄειρε τὰ δαίδαλα δ᾽ ἄτρι᾽ ἐπήνει·
25 ἤσθιε δ᾽ οὐκ ἄλλᾳ σὺν ὁμάλικι, πάντα δ᾽ ἐποίει
σπεύδων κοινὸν ἐς ὕπνον. ἔλεξέ νυ καὶ λόγον αὐτᾷ·
"ἄλλαι μὲν κνώσσουσι σὺν ἀλλήλαισιν ἀδελφαί,
αὐτὰρ ἐγὼ μούνα, μούνα δὲ σύ, νύμφα, καθεύδεις.
αἱ δύο παρθενικαὶ συνομάλικες, αἱ δύο καλαί,
30 ἀλλὰ μόναι κατὰ λέκτρα καθεύδομες, ἁ δὲ πονηρά
†νύσσα† δολία με κακῶς ἀπὸ σεῖο μερίσδει.
οὐ γὰρ ἐγὼ σέο. . . . ."

14 φυγὼν δύστανον Bentley: φέρων δυσὶν ἁγνὸν m: φ. δισ-
σὶν ἀνὰν m   Ἄρηα Scaliger: ἄρνα M
    21 δ᾽ ἀνέρος Lennep: δ᾽ ἄρεος M
    22 παρίζετο Canter: μερ- M
    24 στάμονα Scaliger: στόμ᾽ ἀνὰ M   δαίδαλα δ᾽ ἄτρι᾽
Lennep: δ᾽ ἀδέα δάκρυ᾽ M
    26 αὐτᾷ Vrsinus: -τάν M

was enraged and mustered all the Achaean host;[3] not a single Greek, from Mycenae, Elis or Sparta, avoided the cruel war by staying at home. Achilles alone did not take part. He kept hidden among the daughters of Lycomedes, learned about wool working instead of arms, wielded a girl's broom[4] in his untanned hand, and looked just like a maiden: he behaved in a feminine way, he had a delicate blush like theirs on his snowy cheeks, he walked like a girl, and he kept his hair covered with a headdress. But he had a man's heart and a man's love: from morning till night he sat by Deidamia, at times kissing her hand, and often lifting up her warp threads to praise her intricate weaving. He would eat with no other companion, and he made every effort to persuade her to sleep with him; in fact he said to her, 'Other sisters sleep with one another, but I sleep alone and you sleep alone, my dear.[5] We are two beautiful girls of the same age, but we sleep alone in our beds; the wicked ⟨. . . .⟩ craftily keeps me apart from you. For I do not . . . you.'"

---

[3] Achaean = Greek.

[4] "Broom" is suspect (cf. however *Od.* 20.149); possibly "he did girls' work" (κόπον conjectured by Scaliger).

[5] The Greek word, *nympha*, usually means "bride," and reveals Achilles' intentions.

---

28 μούνα, μούνα Lennep: μούνα μίμνω M   δὲ σύ Hermann: σὺ δέ M

29 αἱ δύο Salmasius: αἱ δ᾽ ὑπὸ M

30 κατὰ Scaliger: καὶ M

ΒΙΩΝΟΣ ΑΠΟΣΠΑΣΜΑΤΑ

1 Strabo 1.5.7

ΕΙΣ ΥΑΚΙΝΘΟΝ

Ἀμφασία τὸν Φοῖβον ἕλεν τόσον ἄλγος ἔχοντα.
δίζετο φάρμακα πάντα σοφὰν δ᾽ ἐπεμαίετο τέχναν,
χρῖεν δ᾽ ἀμβροσίᾳ καὶ νέκταρι, χρῖεν ἅπασαν
ὠτειλάν· μοιραῖα δ᾽ ἀναλθέα τραύματα πάντα.

2 ἐπεμαίετο Crispinus: ἐπεβένετο m: ἐπεβώσετο vel -ατο
m   4 μοιραῖα Hermann: μοίραιαι vel -αισι M   τραύ-
ματα Hermann: φάρμακα M

2 Stob. 1.8.39

ΚΛΕΟΔΑΜΟΣ

Εἴαρος, ὦ Μύρσων, ἢ χείματος ἢ φθινοπώρω
ἢ θέρεος τί τοι ἁδύ; τί δὲ πλέον εὔχεαι ἐλθεῖν;
ἢ θέρος, ἀνίκα πάντα τελείεται ὅσσα μογεῦμες,
ἢ γλυκερὸν φθινόπωρον, ὅκ᾽ ἀνδράσι λιμὸς ἐλαφρά,
5 ἢ καὶ χεῖμα δύσεργον—ἐπεὶ καὶ χείματι πολλοί
θαλπόμενοι τέρπονται ἀεργίᾳ τε καὶ ὄκνῳ—

6 τέρπονται Grotius: θάλποντας M

524

FRAGMENTS

1 Stobaeus

Phoebus was speechless, such was his grief. He sought out all his remedies and brought to bear his wisdom and skill. With nectar and ambrosia he anointed, he anointed the wound thoroughly; but all wounds ordained by fate cannot be healed.[1]

[1] On Hyacinth, favorite of Apollo, who was killed accidentally by a discus thrown by the god. The fullest account is that of Ovid (*Met.* 10.162–219).

2 Stobaeus

CLEODAMUS[1]

In spring, winter, autumn and summer, Myrson, what is pleasing to you? And to which do you look forward the most? Summer, perhaps, when all our labors come to fruition? Or sweet autumn, when it is easy to deal with hunger? Or even winter, when it's hard to work—for in winter, too, many men keep themselves warm and enjoy a

[1] A dialogue, probably part of a longer poem, on the topic "Which season is best?"

ἤ τοι καλὸν ἔαρ πλέον εὔαδεν; εἰπὲ τί τοι φρήν
αἱρεῖται, λαλέειν γὰρ ἐπέτραπεν ἁ σχολὰ ἄμμιν.

ΜΥΡΣΩΝ

κρίνειν οὐκ ἐπέοικε θεήια ἔργα βροτοῖσι,
10 πάντα γὰρ ἱερὰ ταῦτα καὶ ἀδέα· σεῦ δὲ ἔκατι
ἐξερέω, Κλεόδαμε, τό μοι πέλεν ἅδιον ἄλλων.
οὐκ ἐθέλω θέρος ἦμεν, ἐπεὶ τόκα μ' ἅλιος ὀπτῇ·
οὐκ ἐθέλω φθινόπωρον, ἐπεὶ νόσον ὥρια τίκτει.
οὐ λῶ χεῖμα· φέρει νιφετόν, κρυμὼς δὲ φοβεῦμαι.
15 εἶαρ ἐμοὶ τριπόθητον ὅλῳ λυκάβαντι παρείη,
ἁνίκα μήτε κρύος μήθ' ἅλιος ἄμμε βαρύνει.
εἴαρι πάντα κύει, πάντ' εἴαρος ἀδέα βλαστεῖ,
χἀ νὺξ ἀνθρώποισιν ἴσα καὶ ὁμοίιος ἀώς.

7 εὔαδεν; εἰπὲ τί τοι φρήν Vrsinus: εὐαδ' ἐνεῖπε τοι τι φρὸν
M   14 οὐ λῶ Ameis: οὐλον M

3 Stob. 1.9.3

Μοίσας Ἔρως καλέοι, Μοῖσαι τὸν Ἔρωτα φέροιεν.
μολπὰν ταὶ Μοῖσαί μοι ἀεὶ ποθέοντι διδοῖεν,
τὰν γλυκερὰν μολπάν, τᾶς φάρμακον ἅδιον οὐδέν.

4 Stob. 3.29.52

Ἐκ θαμινᾶς ῥαθάμιγγος, ὅπως λόγος, αἰὲς ἰοίσας
χἀ λίθος ἐς ῥωχμὸν κοιλαίνεται.

526

lazy and idle life. Or do you prefer the lovely spring? Tell me your opinion, since leisure has given us time for a chat.

MYRSON

It is not for mortals to pass judgment on the works of the gods, which are all sweet and holy. But for your sake, Cleodamus, I shall speak out and say which season I think the sweetest. I do not wish for summer, because the sun burns me then. I do not wish for autumn, because that season produces disease. I have no wish to endure winter: I dread the frost and snow. But for spring I long intensely, and I wish it could be here the whole year round—no trouble then from frostbite or from sunburn. In spring everything is ready to give birth, in spring there is sweet growth of every sort, and we humans have days and nights that are matched and equal in length.

3 Stobaeus

Let Love summon the Muses, and let the Muses support me in my love.[1] May the Muses always provide me with song when I am filled with desire—sweet song, no remedy sweeter.[2]

[1] Or possibly, "remove my love."

[2] On song as a palliative or remedy (φάρμακον) for *erôs*, cf. Theoc. *Id.* 11.1–3, 80–81.

4 Stobaeus

It is said that water droplets, continually dripping, can hollow out a channel even in stone.[1]

[1] On perseverance; perhaps advice to a lover.

5 Stob. 3.29.53

Οὐ καλόν, ὦ φίλε, πάντα λόγον ποτὶ τέκτονα φοιτῆν,
μηδ᾽ ἐπὶ πάντ᾽ ἄλλω χρέος ἰσχέμεν· ἀλλὰ καὶ αὐτός
τεχνᾶσθαι σύριγγα, πέλει δέ τοι εὐμαρὲς ἔργον.

6 Stob. 4.1.8

Μηδὲ λίπῃς μ᾽ ἀγέραστον, †ἐπὴν χὠ Φοῖβος ἀείδειν
μισθὸν ἔδωκε†. τιμὰ δὲ τὰ πράγματα κρέσσονα ποιεῖ.

7 Stob. 4.16.14

Οὐκ οἶδ᾽, οὐδ᾽ ἐπέοικεν ἃ μὴ μάθομες πονέεσθαι.

8 Stob. 4.16.15

Εἴ μευ καλὰ πέλει τὰ μελύδρια, καὶ τάδε μῶνα
κῦδος ἐμοὶ θήσοντι τά μοι πάρος ὤπασε Μοῖσα·
εἰ δ᾽ οὐχ ἀδέα ταῦτα, τί μοι πολὺ πλείονα μοχθεῖν;
εἰ μὲν γὰρ βιότω διπλόον χρόνον ἄμμιν ἔδωκεν
5 ἢ Κρονίδας ἢ Μοῖρα πολύτροπος, ὥστ᾽ ἀνύεσθαι
τὸν μὲν ἐς εὐφροσύναν καὶ χάρματα τὸν δ᾽ ἐπὶ
μόχθῳ,
ἦν τάχα μοχθήσαντι ποθ᾽ ὕστερον ἐσθλὰ δέχεσθαι.
εἰ δὲ θεοὶ κατένευσαν ἕνα χρόνον ἐς βίον ἐλθεῖν
ἀνθρώποις, καὶ τόνδε βραχὺν καὶ μείονα πάντων,
10 ἐς πόσον, ἆ δειλοί, καμάτως κεῖς ἔργα πονεῦμες,

5 Stobaeus

My friend, it is not good to resort to a craftsman when you want something done, or always to be reliant on someone else. You should make the panpipe yourself: it's a simple job.

6 Stobaeus

Don't leave me unrewarded. Even Phoebus rewards singing,[1] and honor makes things better.

[1] The text is irremediably corrupt.

7 Stobaeus

I do not know how—nor is it right—to waste effort on matters about which we are ignorant.[1]

[1] Or perhaps punctuate "I do not know; nor is it right to . . . ," if the opening words are a reply to a question.

8 Stobaeus

If my ditties are pleasing, then those few that fate has so far granted me will secure my reputation. If they are not, what is the point of further effort? If the son of Cronus[1] or fickle fate had granted us two lifetimes—one to be passed without a view to pleasure and enjoyment, the other in labor—then perhaps it would be possible to labor first and have one's pleasure at some later time. But since it is the gods' will that mankind should have a single lifespan—brief and insignificant at that—how long, poor

ψυχὰν δ' ἄχρι τίνος ποτὶ κέρδεα καὶ ποτὶ τέχνας
βάλλομες ἱμείροντες ἀεὶ πολὺ πλείονος ὄλβω;
λαθόμεθ' ἢ ἄρα πάντες ὅτι θνατοὶ γενόμεσθα,
χὼς βραχὺν ἐκ Μοίρας λάχομες χρόνον;

9 Stob. 4.20.7

Ταὶ Μοῖσαι τὸν Ἔρωτα τὸν ἄγριον οὐ φοβέονται
ἐκ θυμῶ δὲ φιλεῦντι καὶ ἐκ ποδὸς αὐτῷ ἕπονται.
κἢν μὲν ἄρα ψυχάν τις ἔχων ἀνέραστον ἀείδῃ,
τῆνον ὑπεκφεύγοντι καὶ οὐκ ἐθέλοντι διδάσκειν·
5   ἢν δὲ νόον τις Ἔρωτι δονεύμενος ἁδὺ μελίσδῃ,
ἐς τῆνον μάλα πᾶσαι ἐπειγόμεναι προρέοντι.
μάρτυς ἐγὼν ὅτι μῦθος ὅδ' ἔπλετο πᾶσιν ἀλαθής·
ἢν μὲν γὰρ βροτὸν ἄλλον ἢ ἀθανάτων τινὰ μέλπω,
βαμβαίνει μοι γλῶσσα καὶ ὡς πάρος οὐκέτ' ἀείδει·
10   ἢν δ' αὖτ' ἐς τὸν Ἔρωτα καὶ ἐς Λυκίδαν τι μελίσδω,
καὶ τόκα μοι χαίροισα διὰ στόματος ῥέει αὐδά.

1 οὐ Gesner: ἢ M   2 ἐκ Gesner: ἠκ M   δὲ φι-
λεῦντι Valckenaer: φιλέοντι M   5 τις Brunck: τω M

10 Stob. 4.20.26

Ἁ μεγάλα μοι Κύπρις ἔθ' ὑπνώοντι παρέστα
νηπίαχον τὸν Ἔρωτα καλᾶς ἐκ χειρὸς ἄγοισα
ἐς χθόνα νευστάζοντα, τόσον δέ μοι ἔφρασε μῦθον·
"μέλπειν μοι, φίλε βοῦτα, λαβὼν τὸν Ἔρωτα δί-
        δασκε."

creatures, are we to struggle at wearisome work? How long are we to put our hearts and souls into working for gain, constantly eager to get more and more wealth? [2] It seems we have all forgotten that we are mortal, and how the span of life allotted us by fate is short.

[1] Zeus.

[2] This is a familiar theme of ancient philosophical diatribe and satire (e.g., Hor. *Sat.* 1.1).

9 Stobaeus

The Muses are not afraid of wild Eros: they love him deeply and attend him closely. If some poet sings without love in his soul, they are elusive and reluctant to teach him; but if someone sings sweetly in the throes of love, they rush forward keenly all together. I can bear witness that this tale is true in all cases. If I celebrate anyone else, god or mortal, my tongue trembles and no longer sings as it did before; but if I sing anything about Eros and Lycidas,[1] then song flows from my lips quite happily.

[1] The speaker is probably a shepherd in love with a certain Lycidas (for whom cf. Bion [2]; Theoc. *Id.* 7, [27].42).

10 Stobaeus

The great goddess Cypris appeared to me while I was still asleep. She was leading by her fair hand innocent young Eros, who kept his eyes fixed on the ground. This is what she said: "My dear herdsman, please take Eros and teach

5 ὡς λέγε· χὰ μὲν ἀπῆλθεν, ἐγὼ δ᾽ ὅσα βουκολίασδον,
  νήπιος ὡς ἐθέλοντα μαθεῖν, τὸν Ἔρωτα δίδασκον,
  ὡς εὗρεν πλαγίαυλον ὁ Πάν, ὡς αὐλὸν Ἀθάνα,
  ὡς χέλυν Ἑρμάων, κίθαριν ὡς ἁδὺς Ἀπόλλων.
  ταῦτά νιν ἐξεδίδασκον· ὁ δ᾽ οὐκ ἐμπάζετο μύθων,
10 ἀλλά μοι αὐτὸς ἄειδεν ἐρωτύλα, καί με δίδασκε
  θνατῶν ἀθανάτων τε πόθως καὶ ματέρος ἔργα.
  κἠγὼν ἐκλαθόμαν μὲν ὅσων τὸν Ἔρωτα δίδασκον,
  ὅσσα δ᾽ Ἔρως με δίδαξεν ἐρωτύλα πάντα διδάχθην.

11 Stob. 4.20.27

Ἕσπερε, τᾶς ἐρατᾶς χρύσεον φάος Ἀφρογενείας,
Ἕσπερε, κυανέας ἱερόν, φίλε, νυκτὸς ἄγαλμα,
τόσσον ἀφαυρότερος μήνας ὅσον ἔξοχος ἄστρων,
χαῖρε, φίλος, καί μοι ποτὶ ποιμένα κῶμον ἄγοντι
5 ἀντὶ σελαναίας τὺ δίδου φάος, ὥνεκα τήνα
σάμερον ἀρχομένα τάχιον δύεν. οὐκ ἐπὶ φωρὰν
ἔρχομαι οὐδ᾽ ἵνα νυκτὸς ὁδοιπορέοντας ἐνοχλέω,
ἀλλ᾽ ἐράω· καλὸν δέ γ᾽ ἐρασσαμένῳ συναρέσθαι.

  3 ἀφαυρότερος Vrsinus: -ρον M   7 ὁδοιπορέοντας
Gaisford: -οντα m: -οντ᾽ m

---

  [1] Hesperus, the Evening Star, was associated particularly with
Aphrodite (Pl. *Epin.* 987b; Arist. *Met.* 1073b31). Here she is
called Ἀφρογένεια (born from the foam), with reference to the
story of her birth (Hes. *Theog.* 195–98).

him to sing." With these words she went away, and assuming in my innocence that he did want to learn, I set about teaching Eros all my knowledge of country music: I taught him how Pan invented the cross pipe, Athena the double pipe, Hermes the lyre of tortoiseshell, and sweet Apollo the box lyre.[1] I tried to educate him in these things, but he paid no heed to my words. Instead, he would sing love songs of his own, and he taught me about the love affairs of mortals and immortals, and what his mother causes to happen. So I forgot all about what I was teaching Eros, and I learned instead all the love songs that Eros taught me.[2]

[1] A list of "first inventors." The story of Pan and the cross pipes is unattested except here; that of the *aulos* is best known from Ov. *Fasti* 6.695–710, and that of the lyre from *Hymn. Hom. Merc.* 20–67. As god of "sweet" music, Apollo was credited with many instruments, including the *cithara* (Plut. [*De mus.*] 14, 1135f).

[2] This may be a complete poem. The notion of inspiration coming from a god while the poet sleeps is a common one (cf. Callim. Fr. 2; Enn. *Ann.* Frr. 2–10 Skutsch; Persius *prol.* 1–3; Prop. 3.3; *Anacreontea* 1), as is that of the Preceptor of Love (ἐρωτοδιδάσκαλος).

11 Stobaeus

Hesperus, golden light of lovely Aphrodite,[1] Hesperus, my friend, sacred glory of dark night, less bright than the moon but unrivaled among the stars, hail, my friend, and as I go to serenade the shepherd provide me with light in place of the moon, who is new today and has set too early. I am not going thieving or to commit highway robbery: I am in love, and it is surely a good thing to help a lover in his loving.

12 Stob. 4.20.28

Ὄλβιοι ‹οἱ› φιλέοντες ἐπὴν ἴσον ἀντεράωνται.
ὄλβιος ἦν Θησεὺς τῶ Πειριθόω παρεόντος,
εἰ καὶ ἀμειλίκτοιο κατήλυθεν εἰς Ἀΐδαο·
ὄλβιος ἦν χαλεποῖσιν ἐν Ἀξείνοισιν Ὀρέστας
5   ὥνεκά οἱ ξυνὰς Πυλάδας ἄρητο κελεύθως·
ἦν μάκαρ Αἰακίδας ἑτάρω ζώοντος Ἀχιλλεύς·
ὄλβιος ἦν θνάσκων ὅ οἱ οὐ μόρον αἰνὸν ἄμυνεν.

5 ἄρητο Vrsinus: ἄρκτο m: ἄροιτο m   7 ὅ οἱ οὐ
Meineke: ὅτι οἱ M

13 Stob. 4.20.57

Ἰξευτὰς ἔτι κῶρος ἐν ἄλσεϊ δενδράεντι
ὄρνεα θηρεύων τὸν ὑπόπτερον εἶδεν Ἔρωτα
ἐσδόμενον πύξοιο ποτὶ κλάδον· ὡς δὲ νόησε,
χαίρων ὥνεκα δὴ μέγα φαίνετο τὦρνεον αὐτῷ,
5   τὼς καλάμως ἅμα πάντας ἐπ᾽ ἀλλάλοισι συνάπτων
τᾷ καὶ τᾷ τὸν Ἔρωτα μετάλμενον ἀμφεδόκευε.
χὠ παῖς, ἀσχαλάων ὅκα οἱ τέλος οὐδὲν ἀπάντη,
τὼς καλάμως ῥίψας ποτ᾽ ἀροτρέα πρέσβυν ἵκανεν
ὅς νιν τάνδε τέχναν ἐδιδάξατο, καὶ λέγεν αὐτῷ
10 καί οἱ δεῖξεν Ἔρωτα καθήμενον. αὐτὰρ ὁ πρέσβυς
μειδιάων κίνησε κάρη καὶ ἀμείβετο παῖδα·

12 Stobaeus

Blessed are those who love when they are loved equally in return. Blessed was Theseus when Pirithoüs was at his side, even though he went down to pitiless Hades.[1] Blessed was Orestes among the grim dwellers on the Black Sea, because Pylades had chosen to share his journey.[2] Blessed was Achilles, descendant of Aeacus, while his companion was alive; and he was blessed in dying, since he did not ward off his cruel fate.[3]

[1] Theseus and Pirithoüs tried to kidnap Persephone as wife for Pirithoüs, but Hades held them fast (hence "pitiless"). Theseus was rescued by Heracles. See Frazer on ps.-Apollod. *Bibl.* 2.5.12 and *Epit.* 1.23–24.

[2] The faithful Pylades accompanied Orestes on his mission to steal a statue of Artemis from Tauri on the coast of the Black Sea. The best-known treatment of the story is Euripides' *Iphigeneia in Tauris.*

[3] Achilles, grandson of Aeacus, was happy to follow his companion Patroclus to Hades.

13 Stobaeus

A fowler, still a boy, was hunting birds in a woodland grove and saw winged Eros sitting on a branch of a box tree. When he noticed him, he was excited because the bird seemed a good catch. Fastening all his rods together one to another he lay in wait for Eros,[1] who was hopping here and there. The boy grew annoyed when he met with no success. He threw away his rods and went to an old plowman who had taught him that skill; he told him the story and showed him Eros perched in the tree. The old man shook his head with a smile and answered the boy: "Stop

535

"φείδεο τᾶς θήρας, μηδ' ἐς τόδε τὤρνεον ἔρχευ.
φεῦγε μακράν· κακόν ἐντι τὸ θηρίον. ὄλβιος ἔσσῃ
εἰσόκε μή νιν ἕλῃς· ἢν δ' ἀνέρος ἐς μέτρον ἔλθῃς
15 οὗτος ὁ νῦν φεύγων καὶ ἀπάλμενος αὐτὸς ἀφ' αὐτῶ
ἐλθὼν ἐξαπίνας κεφαλὰν ἔπι σεῖο καθιξεῖ."

2 ὑπόπτερον Briggs: ἀπότροπον M   7 ὄκα Porson:
οὕνεχα M

14 Stob. 4.20.58

Ἄμερε Κυπρογένεια, Διὸς τέκος ἠὲ θαλάσσας,
τίπτε τόσον θνατοῖσι καὶ ἀθανάτοισι χαλέπτεις;
τυτθὸν ἔφαν. τί νυ τόσσον ἀπήχθεο καὶ τεῖν αὐτᾷ
ταλίκον ὡς πάντεσσι κακὸν τὸν Ἔρωτα τεκέσθαι,
5 ἄγριον, ἄστοργον, μορφᾷ νόον οὐδὲν ὁμοῖον;
ἐς τί δέ νιν πτανὸν καὶ ἑκαβόλον ὤπασας ἦμεν
ὡς μὴ πικρὸν ἐόντα δυναίμεθα τῆνον ἀλύξαι;

4 τεκέσθαι Hermann: τέκηαι m: τέκναι m

15 Stob. 4.21.3

Μορφὰ θηλυτέραισι πέλει καλόν, ἀνέρι δ' ἀλκά.

16 Stob. 4.46.17

Αὐτὰρ ἐγὼν βασεῦμαι ἐμὰν ὁδὸν ἐς τὸ κάταντες
τῆνο ποτὶ ψάμαθόν τε καὶ ἀιόνα ψιθυρίσδων,

your hunting and don't go near that bird; get far away from it; it's a dangerous creature. You will be happy so long as you don't catch him; but when you come to the measure of a man, this bird which now avoids you and has hopped away will suddenly come unbidden and land on your head."[2]

[1] The end of the first rod was coated with sticky birdlime made from mistletoe (ἰξός, viscus).
[2] Probably a complete poem. It is allegorical of the sudden onset of love, and like Fr. 10 it has a preceptor figure.

14 Stobaeus

Gentle Cyprian goddess, child of Zeus and of the sea,[1] why do you give so much trouble to mortals and to the immortal gods? That is only the half of it:[2] why were you so hateful to yourself that you gave birth to Eros, such a great bane to all, savage, uncaring, ill-matched in body and mind?[3] Why did you make him winged and far-shooting so that although he is so cruel we cannot avoid him?

[1] See on Mosch. 2.71.
[2] Lit., "I have said little."
[3] I.e., his appearance belies his character. Cf. Mosch. 1.6–23.

15 Stobaeus

Beauty is the glory of women, courage of men.

16 Stobaeus

But I shall go on my way down the hillside over there to the sandy seashore, whispering my song and imploring

537

λισσόμενος Γαλάτειαν ἀπηνέα· τὰς δὲ γλυκείας
ἐλπίδας ὑστατίῳ μέχρι γήραος οὐκ ἀπολειψῶ.

1 βασεῦμαι Vrsinus: βὰς εὖ καὶ M

17 Orion, *Anth.* 5.11

Πάντα θεῶ γ᾽ ἐθέλοντος ἀνύσιμα· πάντα βροτοῖσιν
ἐκ μακάρων ῥάιστα καὶ οὐκ ἀτέλεστα γένοιτο.

1 θεῶ γε Schneidewin: θεοῦ γὰρ M   ἀνύσιμα corrup-
tum?   2 ῥάιστα Ahrens: γὰρ ῥάστα M

cruel Galatea; and I will not abandon my sweet hopes even when I am advanced in age.[1]

[1] Part of a speech by the Cyclops Polyphemus. That Bion followed Theocritus in treating this subject is known from the *Lament for Bion,* lines 58–63.

17 Orion, Florilegium

If god so wills it, everything can be brought about; with the help of the blessed gods everything can be easy for mortals and not be unaccomplished.[1]

[1] The sense of this fragment seems clear, but the text is badly preserved.

ADONIS DEAD

ADONIS DEAD

The boar that gored Adonis is brought before Aphrodite and pleads that it was only trying to kiss him, an ingenious line of defense.

Only one independent manuscript preserves the poem; it is juxtaposed with Bion's Lament for Adonis, *to which it is clearly related in subject and Doric dialect (and cf., e.g.,* Lament *74, στυγνόν;* Ad. Dead *3, στυγνάν). The meter is catalectic iambic dimeters, or "hemiambs," (×–∪–∪–×). This meter is used in many of the* Anacreontea, *a collection of poems ranging in date from perhaps the second century BC to the sixth century AD; a majority treat love and drinking, topics associated with the sixth-century BC Ionian lyric poet Anacreon (see D. A. Campbell,* Greek Lyric, *vol. 2, pp. 162–257).*

ΕΙΣ ΝΕΚΡΟΝ ΑΔΩΝΙΝ

Ἄδωνιν ἡ Κυθήρη
ὡς εἶδε νεκρὸν ἤδη
στυγνὰν ἔχοντα χαίταν
ὠχράν τε τὰν παρειάν,
5   ἄγειν τὸν ὗν πρὸς αὐτάν
ἔταξε τὼς Ἔρωτας.
οἳ δ᾽ εὐθέως ποτανοί
πᾶσαν δραμόντες ὕλαν
στυγνὸν τὸν ὗν ἀνεῦρον,
10   δῆσαν δὲ καὶ πέδασαν.
χὠ μὲν βρόχῳ καθάψας
ἔσυρεν αἰχμάλωτον,
ὁ δ᾽ ἐξόπισθ᾽ ἐλαύνων
ἔτυπτε τοῖσι τόξοις·
15   ὁ θὴρ δ᾽ ἔβαινε δειλῶς,
φοβεῖτο γὰρ Κυθήρην.
τῷ δ᾽ εἶπεν Ἀφροδίτα,
"πάντων κάκιστε θηρῶν,
σὺ τόνδε μηρὸν ἴψω;
20   σύ μου τὸν ἄνδρ᾽ ἔτυψας;"
ὁ θὴρ δ᾽ ἔλεξεν ὧδε·

ADONIS DEAD

When Cythera[1] saw Adonis already dead, his hair disheveled and his cheeks pale, she commanded the Loves to bring the boar to her. They flew off directly, went quickly through the whole forest, found the grim[2] boar, and bound him in fetters. One of them put a noose around his neck and dragged him along a prisoner, and another drove him from behind by striking him with his bow. The creature walked on timidly, being afraid of Cythera. And Aphrodite said to him, "Foul beast, did you injure this thigh? Did you strike this man of mine?" The beast replied, "Cythera, I

[1] Aphrodite.
[2] Or, perhaps, "gloomy," "mournful."

---

10 δὲ Wilamowitz: τε M

"ὄμνυμί σοι, Κυθήρη,
αὐτάν σε καὶ τὸν ἄνδρα
καὶ ταῦτά μου τὰ δεσμά
25 καὶ τώσδε τὼς κυναγώς·
τὸν ἄνδρα τὸν καλόν σευ
οὐκ ἤθελον πατάξαι,
ἀλλ' ὡς ἄγαλμ' ἐσεῖδον
καὶ μὴ φέρων τὸ καῦμα
30 γυμνὸν τὸν εἶχε μηρόν
ἐμαινόμαν φιλᾶσαι.
†καί μευ κατεσίναζε·†
τούτους λαβοῦσα τέμνε,
τούτους κόλαζε, Κύπρι·
35 τί γὰρ φέρω περισσῶς
ἐρωτικοὺς ὀδόντας;
εἰ δ' οὐχί σοι τάδ' ἀρκεῖ,
καί ταῦτά μου τὰ χείλη·
τί γὰρ φιλεῖν ἐτόλμων;"
40 τὸν ἠλέησε Κύπρις
εἶπέν τε τοῖς Ἔρωσι
τὰ δεσμά οἱ 'πιλῦσαι.
ἐκ τῶδ' ἐπηκολούθει,
κἆς ὕλαν οὐκ ἔβαινε,
45 καὶ τῷ πυρὶ προσελθών
ἔκαιε τοὺς ὀδόντας.

swear by you yourself, by your man, by these fetters of mine, and by your hunters, that I did not mean to strike that handsome man of yours. When I saw his statuesque beauty my passion was unbearable and I was mad enough to kiss him on his thigh that was bare. Deal harshly with me;[3] take these tusks and cut them off and punish them, Cypris: why should I have tusks that are so extremely passionate? And if you are not satisfied with that, cut off these lips of mine, too: for why was I so bold as to try to kiss him?" Cypris felt pity for him and told the Loves to untie his bonds. After that he followed her and no longer went into the forest; approaching the fire, he burned his tusks.[4]

[3] Sense and text quite uncertain.
[4] "Tusks" is an emendation; the manuscript has "Loves."

---

44 κὰς ὕλαν Valckenaer: καὶ σύλαν M
45 τῷ Heinsius: τε M
46 ὀδόντας Faber: ἔρωτας M

P. RAINER 29801
(BUCOLIC FRAGMENT)

BUCOLIC FRAGMENT

*This fragment of a bucolic poem is preserved on two sides
of a leaf of papyrus dating from the late third century AD;
the date of the poem itself is uncertain, as is the order in
which the two parts should be read. If the order printed
here is correct, then Silenus addresses Pan and ironically
asks what has happened to his shepherd's pipe (13–21);
then Pan sets about making and testing a new pipe. It
seems that Dionysus is expecting Pan to perform in a com-
petition (4) and will be angry if he fails to do so (26).*

*It has been suggested that the poem is the source for
Virgil's sixth* Eclogue, *where Silenus is found in a country
setting; but he may have appeared in one of Moschus' or
Bion's lost bucolic poems.*

Criticism

Bernsdorff, H. *Das Fragmentum Bucolicum Vindobo-
nense (P.Vindob.Rainer 29801) = Hypomnemata* 123.
Göttingen, 1999.
Gallavotti, K. *RFIC* ns 19 (1942): 233–58.
Page, D. L. *GLP,* no. 123, pp. 502–7.

PAPYRUS VINDOBONENSIS
RAINER 29801

A

Desunt vv. 20

]κ‌αι. . . . . . .]. .ε[

]. .εν‌α[. . . . . . .]εων‌λ . [

] . ο‌κατ[. . . . .]αλλαμ[

]φωνον εφ . [.] . . το παρθ‌ε‌ν[

]α‌την, καμάτῳ δ᾿ ὕπο γού[νατα

] . ε χαμαὶ σ[. . . . . .] φίλῳ δ᾿ ἐφομάρτε‌ε[

[τὸν] δὲ ἰδὼν γ[.]λ‌ερο‌ν προσέφη Σιληνὸς[

[εἶπ]έ μοι, ὦ νομέων μέγα κοίρανε, πῶς ἁ‌[ν ἴοι τις

[αἰχ]μητὴς μενέχαρμος ἄτερ σακέων πολ[εμόνδε;

[πῶς δὲ] χορῶν ἐπ᾿ ἀγῶνας ἄνευ σύριγγος ἱκά[νοις;

[πῇ σ]οι πηκτὶς ἔβη, μηλοσκόπε; πῇ σεο φ[ωνή;

π[ῇ] μελέων κλέος εὐρύ, τὸ καὶ Διὸς οὔατ᾿ ἰα[ίνει;

ἦ ῥά σευ ὑπνώοντος ἀπειρεσίην μετὰ θο[ίνην

κλέψε τεὴν σύριγγα κατ᾿ οὔρεα Δάφνις ὁ βού[της

ἦ Λυκίδας ἢ Θύρσις, Ἀμύντιχος ἠὲ Μεν[άλκας;

κείνοις γὰρ κραδίην ἐπικαίεαι ἠιθέοισ[ιν.

ἦ[έ] μιν ἕδνον ἔδωκας ὀρεσσιπόλῳ τινὶ ν[ύμφῃ;

P. RAINER 29801
BUCOLIC FRAGMENT

(20 lines missing)

. . . stood by . . . girl . . . with weariness his knees . . . on
the ground . . . accompanied dear . . . At sight of him, Si-
lenus[1] addressed him merrily: "Tell me, great lord of shep-
herds, how could a doughty warrior go into battle without
his shield? And how could *you* come to the competition in   10
dance without your pipe? Where has your pipe[2] gone,
shepherd? Where is your voice? Where are your far-famed
songs which even Zeus delights to hear? Did Daphnis the
oxherd steal your pipe in the mountains while you took a
nap after a heavy meal[3]— or Lycidas or Thyrsis, Amynti-   15
chus or Menalcas? Those are the lads your heart burns for.
Or have you given it to some mountain nymph as a mar-

---

[1] A sort of Old Man of the Forest, crude and ugly but wise,
father of the Satyrs (cf. Eur. *Cyclops*).   [2] Or, less likely,
"lyre."   [3] Or, perhaps, "long hunt."

---

6 ἐφομάρτεε Collart: εφορμ- pap.
15 ἢ Λυκίδας ἢ Maas: ηλυδοσητοι pap.
16 κείνοις Maas: κεινος pap.   17 ἕδνον Maas: ενδον pap.

σὸν γὰρ ὑπὸ πτερύγεσσιν ἀεὶ φέρετ᾽ ἦτορ [
πάντῃ γὰρ γαμέεις, πάντῃ δέ σε . [. .]ρι . [
20 ἢ σὺ λαβὼν σύριγγα τε[. . .] . . φα[
δειμαίνων σατύροις[. . . .] . [
μή τι σε κερτομέωσιν, ἐπεὶ . . [
εὐύμνων προχέοις κεχρημέ[
μούνους δ᾽ ἀμφὶ νομῆας ἀίδριας ἐσσ[ι
25 οἵ σεο θάμβος ἔχουσι καὶ οὔν[ομ]α] ρι . [
πῶς δ᾽ οὔ τοι φόβος ἐστὶ μέγα[ς] μὴ β . [
οἷον ἄναυδον ἴδοιτο καὶ οὐκ ἀλέγ[οντα
καὶ λασίας σέο χεῖρας †αποδνει† . . . [
δῆσαι οἰοπόλοισιν ἐν οὔρεσιν[

B

Desunt vv. 20

```
                    ]ομεν[
                 ].ηλοισ[. . . . . .]νοιδ[
                 ]ν μεταχ[. . . . .]φαινετ[
                 ]ων σπευδ[. . . .]εκειν μ.[
5               ]ἐκ φηγοῖο λαβὼν εὐαν[θέα κηρόν
                  ]ν ἔθαλψεν ὑπ᾽ ἠελίοιο [βολαῖσι
                ] πωτᾶτο φιλόδροσος α[. . .] μέλισσα
                 ]ομευσε τὸ κηρίον ὠδίνουσα
            Διω]νύσοιο καρήατι, πίμπλατο δὲ δρῦς
10             ]ήεντος· ἐν ἀνθεμόεντι δὲ κηρῷ

                 ]υτρήτοις μέλι λείβετο[
```

554

riage gift? Your heart is constantly borne along under the
wings of . . . [4] You marry everywhere,[5] and everywhere . . .
or taking your pipe . . . afraid of the Satyrs . . . in case they   20
make fun of you when . . . you should pour out lacking . . .
songful . . . Only around the ignorant shepherds are you
. . . who are in awe of you and . . . your name . . . Why are   25
you not very afraid that . . . should see you alone without
a voice and unconcerned about . . . and tie up your shaggy
arms in the lonely hills?"

(20 lines missing)

taking wax, well made from flowers, from an oak tree . . .
he warmed it in the sun's rays . . . many a dew-loving[6] bee   5
flew . . . had . . . the wax with much effort . . . the head of
Dionysus, and the oak was filled . . . the wax, product of
flowers, . . . pierced . . . honey dripped . . . melted in the   10

[4] Meaning uncertain.

[5] "Marriage/marry" is too formal. Pan has casual liaisons and
gives presents as a matter of course.

[6] Bees carry water (Arist. *HA* 625b19; Ael. *NA* 1.10, 5.11; cf.
Callim. *Hymn* 2.110) in order to dilute the honey or cool the hive.

αὐγαῖς δ᾽ ἠε]λίοιο τακεὶς ὑπελύετο κηρός
      ] . . . λε ῥέειν ἀτάλαντος ἐλαίῳ
π]ηκτίδα πῆξε < >χρίσας λάσιος Πάν
15   ]νοιῆσιν, ὅπως μένοι ἔμπεδα κηρός.
      ]πρόσθεν ἀπ᾽ αἰθέρος ἵπτατο Περσεύς,
      ]ανε καὶ ἔκτισεν ἀγλαὸν ἄστυ
      ] . ιδ [. .]†ορωεν† κ[ε]κμηῶτες
            ]φιλω . [. . . .]†μοιατα† Βάκχαις
20   π]ερὶ Πανὸς ἐπήδα

            ]μένη ἐς χορὸν ἐλθεῖν
      χείλεσσι]ν ἐφήρμοσεν ἀκροτάτοισι
      ]φέηκε, θεοῦ δ᾽ ἐνιφυσιόωντος
      ἰσ]χυρὸν ὑπ᾽ ἄσθματος αὐχένος ἶνες
25   ]†εσνεχροισενενθεδατο† χρώς·
      καλά]αμοιο μελιζέμεν ἀρχόμενος Πάν
      ]βαιον ἐπῆιε χεῖλος ἀμείβων
      π]άλιν ἔπνεεν εὐρυτέροισιν

sun's rays, it became liquid . . . flow like oil . . . shaggy Pan
smeared it on his pipe to make it firm . . . so that the wax   15
should stay in place . . . formerly Perseus flew from the sky
. . . came and founded a glorious city[7] . . . wearied . . . the
Bacchae . . . leaped around Pan . . . to join the dance . . .   20
just touched his lyre with it . . . and as the god blew . . .
the sinews of his neck ‹stood out› with the powerful . . .
flesh . . . Pan, beginning to play . . . ranged over, moving   25
his lips . . . blew again with broader . . .

[7] The sudden reference to Perseus is puzzling. It has been
suggested that he was the subject of Pan's first song with the new
pipe or that Pan went off to Mycenae, a city founded by Perseus
(Paus. 2.15.4, 16.3).

PATTERN POEMS
(*TECHNOPAEGNIA*)

PATTERN POEMS

Perhaps because most are in Doric dialect, the pattern poems are transmitted in some manuscripts of the bucolic poets (they are also in Book 15 of the Greek Anthology*). Lines of differing lengths are used to produce a shape on the page. The idea may have come from dedications in prose carved on awkwardly shaped objects, but it seems unlikely that these verses were intended for inscription on real objects.*

The first known composer of pattern poems (later called Technopaegnia*) is Simias of Rhodes (fl. 290–270 BC), grammarian and poet, who published* On Rare Words *(Γλῶσσαι) in three books, and four books of poems in various meters (CA pp. 116–20).*

In Wings *each "wing" has six "feathers," i.e. lines, of decreasing length; the epic phrase "winged words" (ἔπεα πτερόεντα) is made real. The wings claim to belong to a grotesque statue of Eros, a bearded child, who speaks in the manner of a dedicatory epigram. The poem accounts for the statue's odd appearance. The text is corrupt, and the content of Eros' speech is not clear in every detail. Its theology is partly Orphic: this is the demiurge Eros, who took over governance of the world from Uranus and Ge. The statue thus represents an amalgam of Eros' attributes:*

560

he is ancient, hence bearded, but depicted in traditional Hellenistic fashion as a winged child.

The Ax *is composed in pairs of lines, each pair slightly shorter than the one before. The shape of a double ax head is formed when line 1 is written first, line 2 last, line 3 after line 1, line 4 before line 2, and so forth. The poem purports to be inscribed on an ax used by Epeus to make the Wooden Horse.*

The Egg *begins by elaborating the idea of the poet as nightingale: it is the product of his ingenuity. Hermes, the ingenious god, inspired him to devise it (1–8). The remainder of the poem is an enormous simile which compares the metrical feet and the god's swift movement to the swift feet of mountain fawns. Within the simile, words for "feet," "limbs," "number," "rhythm," and "measure" maintain the comparison. The* Egg *is in pairs of lines, each pair slightly longer than the last; it is not clear whether the two shortest lines should form the tips of an oval egg or whether they should be juxtaposed at the center, successive lines being placed around them so as to construct a spiral. Whichever arrangement is preferred, leaping eye-movements will weave the object anew each time it is read (cf. 3).*

The Panpipe *is in ten pairs of lines, each pair slightly shorter than the last, so as to form the shape of a panpipe of ten reeds. It claims to be inscribed on a pipe dedicated to Pan by Simichidas/Theocritus (12). Its simple message is expressed in riddlingly obscure language: here the reader must labor to construct meaning as well as shape. A contemporary taste for gratuitous obscurity is evident in the* Alexandra *of Lycophron, a 1,474-line iambic messenger speech packed with recondite vocabulary and allusions to little-known myths.*

The no less riddling Altar *of Dosiadas, whose date is not known, shares its Doric dialect and some recherché vocabulary with the* Panpipe *and refers to Paris by the name Theocritus. It claims to be the altar set up on the island of Lemnos by Jason on his way to fetch the Golden Fleece; near it at a later time Philoctetes was bitten by a snake and abandoned by the Greeks, before being taken to Troy by Odysseus and Diomedes.*

Besantinus' Altar, *in Ionic dialect, has vocabulary in common with Dosiadas'* Altar *and ends with an allusion to Philoctetes' wound. It states that, unlike other altars, it is not real but a creation of the Muses. Its obscure language is complemented by an acrostic, which spells out the words* Ὀλύμπιε, πολλοῖς ἔτεσι θύσειας *(Olympian, may you sacrifice in many years). This is likely to be a reference to the emperor Hadrian (AD 117–138), who took the title "Olympian" and was well disposed to poetry and the arts. The Greek name Besantinus given in the manuscript may be a corruption of Bestinus, i.e., L. Julius Vestinus, who is said to have supervised the education of Hadrian (IG 14.1085 = IGUR 62; cf. Suda o 835 s.v. Οὐηστῖνος).*

The meters of the poems are as follows:

Wings *and* Ax: *the longest lines are five choriambs (–∪∪–) plus ∪–×. Choriambs are removed one by one, until only ∪–× remains for the shortest lines.*

Egg *has a complex mixture of rhythms, including iambic, cretic, and dactylic elements.*

The Panpipe *is dactylic. The longest lines are pairs of hexameters (–∪∪ –∪∪ –∪∪ –∪∪ –∪∪ –∪); half a foot is removed for each succeeding pair, until only –∪∪– (a catalectic dimeter) remains.*

Altar (1) *is iambic. Lines 1–2 and 7–14 catalectic dimeter* (×–× ×–×), *3–4 trimeter* (×–∪– ×–∪– ×– –×), *5–6 catalectic trimeter with heavy penultimate syllable* (×–∪– ×–∪– ∪– –∪), *15–16 a shorter form* (– –∪–∪–∪– –), *and 17–18 apparently shortened catalectic tetrameter* (– –∪– ×–∪– ∪–∪–×).

Altar (2) *has mixed rhythms: 1–3 anacreontic* (∪∪–∪–∪–×), *4–6 trochaic tetrameter catalectic* (–∪–× –∪–× –∪–× –∪×), *10–20 iambic dimeter* (×–∪–×∪×), *21–23 anapestic dimeter* (–∪∪–∪∪–∪∪–), *and 24–26 choriambic trimeter plus* ∪–× (–∪∪– –∪∪– –∪∪– ∪–×).

Criticism

Ernst, U. *Carmen figuratum.* Cologne, 1991.

Higgins, D. *Pattern Poetry: Guide to an Unknown Literature.* New York, 1987.

Kwaspisz, J. *The Greek Figure Poems = Hellenistica Groningana* 19. Leuven, 2013.

Luz, C. *Technopaegnia: Formspiele in der griechische Dichtung = Mnemosyne Supplement* 324. Leiden, 2010, 327–53.

Strodel, S. *Zur Überlieferung und zum Verständnis der hellenistischen Technopaignien.* Frankfurt am Main, 2002.

ΣΙΜΙΟΥ ΠΤΕΡΥΓΕΣ ΕΡΩΤΟΣ

Λεῦσσέ με τὸν Γᾶς τε βαθυστέρνου ἄνακτ᾽ Ἀκμονίδαν τ᾽ ἄλλυδις ἑδράσαντα·
μηδὲ τρέσῃς, εἰ τόσος ὢν δάσκια βέβριθα λάχνᾳ γένεια.
τᾶμος ἐγὼ γὰρ γενόμαν, ἁνίκ᾽ ἔκραιν᾽ Ἀνάγκα,
πάντα δὲ τᾶς εἶκε φραδαῖσι λυγραῖς
5 ἑρπετά, πάνθ᾽ ὅσ᾽ ἕρπει
δι᾽ αἴθρας

Χάους τέ.
οὔτι γε Κύπριδος παῖς
ὠκυπέτας ἠδ᾽ Ἄρεος καλεῦμαι·
10 οὔτι γὰρ ἔκρανα βίᾳ, πραϋνόῳ δὲ πειθοῖ·
εἶκε δέ μοι Γαῖα Θαλάσσας τε μυχοὶ χάλκεος Οὐρανός τε·
τῶν δ᾽ ἐγὼ ἐκνοσφισάμαν ὠγύγιον σκᾶπτρον, ἔκρινον δὲ θεοῖς θέμιστας.

AP 15.24; Buc. codd. aliquot
2 βέβριθα λάχνᾳ Salmasius: βεβριθότα λαγνᾳ fere M
3 ἔκραιν᾽ Salmasius: ἔκριν᾽ M
4 δὲ τᾶς εἶκε Powell: δ᾽ ἐκ τᾶς εἶκε m: δ᾽ ἐκτάσει καὶ m
9 ἠδ᾽ Powell: δ᾽ M   Ἄρεος m: ἀέρος m: ἀέριος m
10 ἔκρανα Salmasius: ἔκρινα M   βίᾳ Stephanus:
βίας M   πραϋνόῳ Bergk: πραϋνῳ M
12 ἔκρινον Salmasius: ἔκραινον M

SIMIAS
THE WINGS

Behold me, the lord of deep-bosomed Earth, him who set
aside the son of Acmon.[1] Do not be shocked that a person
so small should have so bushy a beard. I was born when
Necessity held sway,[2] and all creatures of the land and of
the air yielded to her gloomy will. I am not to be called
the swift-flying son of Cypris and Ares,[3] for I did not gain
power by force, but by gentle persuasion. The earth, the
depths of the sea and the brazen vault of heaven[4] yielded
to me; I took for myself their ancient scepter and began to
lay down ordinances for the gods.

[1] Uranus (cf. 11–12).

[2] According to one version of the Orphic cosmogony, Time
and Necessity ruled jointly at the beginning of the world and were
parents of Chaos and Ether (cf. 6–7; Hes. *Theog.* 116–20). Here
Necessity seems to be overseer of the rule of Uranus and Earth
(Ge).

[3] Text uncertain. Perhaps "I am the son of Chaos, not of Cy-
pris and Ares."

[4] A Homeric expression (*Il.* 17.425).

ΣΙΜΙΟΥ ΠΕΛΕΚΥΣ

1   Ἀνδροθέᾳ δῶρον ὁ Φωκεὺς κρατερᾶς μηδοσύνας ἦρα τίνων Ἀθάνᾳ

3   τᾶμος ἐπεὶ τὰν ἱερὰν κηρὶ πυρίπνῳ πόλιν ἠθάλωσεν

5   οὐκ ἐνάριθμος γεγαὼς ἐν προμάχοις Ἀχαιῶν,

7   νῦν δ᾽ ἐς Ὁμήρειον ἔβα κέλευθον

9   τρὶς μάκαρ, ὃν σὺ θυμῷ

11   ὅδ᾽ ὄλβος

12   ἀεὶ πνεῖ.

10   ἵλαος ἀμφιδερχθῇς.

8   σὰν χάριν, ἁγνὰ πολύβουλε Παλλάς.

6   ἀλλ᾽ ἀπὸ κρανᾶν ἰθαρᾶν νᾶμα κόμιζε δυσκλής

4   Δαρδανιδᾶν, χρυσοβαφεῖς δ᾽ ἐστυφέλιξ᾽ ἐκ θεμέθλων ἄνακτας,

2   ὤπασ᾽ Ἐπειὸς πέλεκυν, τῷ ποκὰ πύργων θεοτεύκτων κατέρειψεν αἶπος

AP 15.22; Buc. codd. aliquot

SIMIAS
THE AX

Epeus of Phocis presented to Athena, the manly goddess, in gratitude for her sound advice,[1] the ax with which he once brought down the lofty god-built towers[2] at the time when he, with fire-breathing destruction, reduced to ashes the holy city of the Dardanids[3] and knocked its gilded lords from their secure seats. He was not numbered among the foremost Achaean fighters but, little known, he used to carry water from pure springs.[4] Now, however, he has gone along the road of Homer[5] thanks to you, wise and holy Pallas. Thrice blessed is he whom you look upon propitiously and with favor: good fortune of that sort lives for ever.

[1] Epeus made the Wooden Horse "with Athena's help" (Hom. *Od.* 8.493, 11.523).

[2] I.e., by using his ax to make the Horse he made it possible for Troy to be razed. The city was built by Laomedon with the help of Apollo (Hom. *Il.* 21.446–47).

[3] The Trojans, descendants of Dardanus.

[4] According to a legend later than Homer, Epeus acted as water carrier for the Greeks (Athen. 456f = Stesich. *PMG* 200).

[5] He has been celebrated in the *Odyssey* and has thereby gained fame, κλέος (~ 6 δυσκλεής).

ΣΙΜΙΟΥ ΡΟΔΙΟΥ ΩΙΟΝ
ΧΕΛΙΔΟΝΟΣ

1	Κωτίλας
3	τῆ τόδ' ἄτριον νέον
5	πρόφρων δὲ θυμῷ δέξο δὴ γὰρ ἁγνᾶς
7	τὸ μὲν θεῶν ἐριβόας Ἑρμᾶς ἔκαξε κάρυξ
9	ἄνωγε δ' ἐκ μέτρον μονοβάμονος με τὸν πύρουθ' ἀέξειν
11	θοῶς δ' ὑπερθεν οἰκὺ λέχριον ὄφρων νεῦμα ποδῶν σποράδων πιφαύσκειν
13	θοαῖς ὔτ' αἰόλαις νεβροῖς καὶ ἀλλάκτων, ὀρσιπόδων ἐλάφων τέκεσσι·
19	κᾶτ' ὄκα βοᾶς ἀκοὰν μεθέπων ὄγ' ἄφαρ λάσιον νυθοβόλων αὖ ὀρέων ἔσσυται ἄγκος·
20	ταῖς δὴ δαίμων κλυτὸς ἴστα θοῶσιν ὁδόν· δονέων ποσὶ πολύπλοκα μέθιε μέτρα μολπᾶς.
18	ῥίμφα πετρόκοιτον ἐκλιπὼν ὄρος· ματρὸς πλαγκτὸν μαιόμενος βαλιᾶς ἐλεῖν τέκος·
16	βλαχᾷ δ' οἰῶν πολυβότων αὖ ὀρέων νομὸν ἔβαν ταινοθύρων τ' <αὖ> ἄντρα Νυμφᾶν·
14	ταί τ' ἀμβρότῳ πόθῳ φίλας ματρὸς ῥόοισ' ἅμα μεθ' ἱμερόεντα μαζόν,
12	ἴχνεα θενῶν τὰν πανάιολον Πιερίδων μονόδουπον αὐδάν,
10	ἀριθμὸν εἰς ἄκραν δεκάδ' ὑχνίων κόσμον νέμοντα ῥυθμῶν,
8	φῦλ' ἐς βροτῶν ὑπὸ φίλας ἐλὼν πτερὼσι ματρός,
6	λέγεια νιν κάμ' ἀμφὶ ματρὸς ὡδῖς·
4	Δωρίας ἀηδόνος·
2	ματέρος

SIMIAS
THE EGG

Behold this fresh, finely woven product of a twittering
mother, a Dorian nightingale; accept it gladly, for it is
from the shrill labor pains of a holy mother. Hermes, loud-
voiced herald of the gods, took it from under its dear
mother's wings and gave it to the world, commanding me
to increase gradually the number of feet from the original
one foot up to ten at the end, while maintaining proper or-
der in the rhythm. Swiftly he demonstrated this, bringing
the quick, sidelong motion of spreading feet from above
and striking, as he went along, the varied but uniform tune
of the Muses. He plied his limbs as do swift, dappled
fawns, offspring of nimble-footed stags, which, out of im-
mortal longing for their dear mother, rush quickly to the
teat they long for, all hastening over the high hilltops with
nimble feet as they follow behind the loving mothers who
suckle them; bleating, they go through the mountain pas-
tures of flocks of grazing sheep and caves of slender-an-
kled Nymphs; then some savage beast, hearing their echo-
ing cries in the innermost recesses of his den, suddenly
leaves his rocky lair and bounds out, seeking to catch one
of the dappled mother's wandering offspring, and follow-
ing the sound of their cries he rushes rapidly through the
undergrowth of the snow-clad mountain valleys. It was
with feet as swift as theirs that the renowned god sped on
his course as he let fall the intricate measures of the song.

569

AP 15.27; Buc. codd. aliquot

1–4 ita Wilamowitz praeeunte Bergk: κ. μ. τί τόδ᾽ ᾠὸν νέον ἀγνᾶς ἀηδόνος δωρίας ἀγρίου m: κ. ἄτριον ματέρος δωρίας τῆ τόδ᾽ ᾠὸν νέον ἀγνᾶς ἀηδόνος m

5 ἀγνᾶς Salmasius: -νὰ M

6 κάμ᾽ ἀμφὶ Salmasius: κἀμφὶ M

8 πτεροῖσι Scaliger: πέτροισ(ι) M

9 με τὸν Koennecke: μέγαν M

10 ῥυθμῶν Bergk: -μόν m: -μῷ m

13 θοαῖς ἴσ᾽ Bergk: θοαῖσί τε M

15 πᾶσαι Wilamowitz: πάλαι M   κατ᾽ ἀρθμίας Salmasius: καταριθμίας m: -ρυθμ- m

16 βλαχᾷ Edmonds: -χαὶ m: λαχαὶ m   ἀν᾽ suppl. Salmasius: om. M

17 θαλαμᾶν Haeberlin: -οις m: om. m   μυχοιτάτοις Gow (-τῳ Wilamowitz): πουκότατον m: -ότητα m

18 πετρόκοιτον Salmasius: πτερόκ- m: περίκ- m

19 κᾆτ᾽ Wilamowitz: καὶ τάδ᾽ M   ὄγ᾽ ἄφαρ Bergk: ἄφαρ ὄγε M   λάσιον Salmasius: -ίων M   ἔσσυται ἄγκος Salmasius: ἔσσυτ᾽ ἀνάγκαις M

20 κλυτὸς Bergk: -ταῖς M   θοοῖσι Jacobs: θο m: θεοῖς m   ὁδὸν suppl. Gow: om. M   δονέων ποσὶ Jacobs: π. δ. m: π. πονέων m

ΘΕΟΚΡΙΤΟΥ ΣΥΡΙΓΞ

Οὐδενὸς εὐνάτειρα, Μακροπτολέμοιο δὲ μάτηρ,
μαίας ἀντιπέτροιο θοὸν τέκεν ἰθυντῆρα,
οὐχὶ Κεράσταν ὅν ποτε θρέψατο ταυροπάτωρ,
ἀλλ' οὗ πειλιπὲς αἶθε πάρος φρένα τέρμα σάκους,
5 οὔνομ' Ὄλον, δίζων, ὃς τᾶς Μέροπος πόθον
κούρας γηρυγόνας ἔχε τᾶς ἀνεμώδεος,
ὃς Μοίσᾳ λιγὺ πᾶξεν ἰοστεφάνῳ
ἕλκος, ἄγαλμα πόθοιο πυρισμαράγου,
ὃς σβέσεν ἀνορέαν ἰσαυδέα
10 παπποφόνου Τυρίας τ' ⟨ἐξήλασεν⟩,
ᾧ τόδε τυφλοφόρων ἐρατὸν
πᾶμα Πάρις θέτο Σιμιχίδας.
ψυχὰν ᾇ, βροτοβάμων,
στήτας οἶστρε Σαέττας,
15 κλωποπάτωρ, ἀπάτωρ,
λαρνακόγυιε,   χαρεὶς
ἁδὺ μελίσδοις
ἔλλοπι κούρᾳ
Καλλιόπᾳ
20 νηλεύστῳ.

AP 15.21; Buc. codd. aliquot
10 τ' ἐξήλασεν Haeberlin: τε m: τ' ἀφείλετο m
13 ᾇ Hecker: ἀεὶ m: ὦ m
16 χαρεὶς Hecker: χαίροις M

THEOCRITUS (?)
THE PANPIPE

The bedfellow of Nobody and mother of Far-war[1] gave birth to the swift director of the nurse who stood in for a stone,[2] not the Horned One who was once nurtured by a bull father,[3] but he whose mind was once set on fire by the p-lacking shield rim,[4] Whole by name, double in nature,[5] who loved the voice-dividing girl, swift as the wind and with human speech,[6] him who put together a shrill wound[7] for the violet-crowned Muse to represent his fiery love,[8] who extinguished the might that sounded like a man who murdered his grandfather, and drove it out of the Tyrian girl.[9] To him Paris son of Simichus dedicated the lovely possession of the carriers of blindness.[10] May it please your soul, man-treading gadfly of the Lydian woman,[11] son of a thief and son of no one, coffer limbed,[12] and may you play it sweetly to a girl who has no voice of her own but is an unseen Calliope.[13]

---

1 Penelope, whose husband Odysseus told the Cyclops that his name was Nobody; the name of their son, Telemachus, means "Far-fighting."

2 Pan, who according to some accounts was the son of Penelope and Hermes (Hdt. 2.145.4). As goat and god he is swift and "directs" goats, such as the one called Amalthea, which suckled Zeus on Crete; Cronus believed that he had succeeded in swallowing his son, but he had been given a stone instead.

3 Comatas, "Long-haired" (*keras,* "horn," is sometimes said to mean "hair"), who was fed by bees (Theoc. *Id.* 7.83–89), which

were thought to be born from the putrefying carcasses of oxen (Virg. *Geo.* 4.281–314).

4 Comatas was inflamed with love by Pitys (Longus 2.7.6); *itys* is the rim of a shield.

5 Pan means "All"; double because half-goat.

6 Pan loved Echo, here called *meropa* (human), which was said to mean "voice-dividing" (*meros,* "part," *ops,* "voice").

7 *Syrinx* (panpipe) also means a suppurating wound.

8 Pan pursued the nymph Syrinx, who was transformed into a reed (Longus 2.34.3; Ov. *Met.* 1.690–712); from it he made the first panpipe, in order to sing of his love.

9 Pan helped the Greeks defeat the Persians at Marathon by causing panic among them (Hdt. 6.105.2–3). Perseus, who accidentally killed his grandfather (ps.-Apollod. *Bibl.* 2.4.4), sounds like "Persian"; "the Tyrian girl" is Europa, abducted by Zeus from Tyre in Phoenicia, who gave her name to Europe (cf. Mosch. 2).

10 Theocritus (called Simichidas in *Id.* 7) means "Chosen by God," but here it is assumed to mean "chooser of a god"; Paris judges the famous beauty contest of the goddesses and stands for the name of the poet. "Carriers of blindness" (*typhlophorous*): *pêros* (blind) is a synonym of *typhlos,* and *pêra* means a countryman's knapsack; so "carriers of blindness" means "country people."

11 "Man-treading" (*brotobamona*) apparently refers to Paris' running over the mountain rocks, *brotos* being similar in meaning to *laos* (people), which sounds like *laas* (stone). (But the suggestion of Wilamowitz that *botobamona,* "mounter of goats," should be read is attractive; cf. Theoc. *Epigr.* 5.6 αἰγιβάτην). The "Lydian woman" may be Omphale, who according to the ancient commentary here was stung by love for Pan (hence, "gadfly").

12 Hermes, god of thieves, was said by some to be Pan's father. "Son of no one" may refer to his having numerous fathers (see on l. 1) or to stories that Odysseus was his father (schol. on Theoc.

Id. 1.123) or that he had none (schol. Luc. 3.402). "Coffer-limbed" (*larnakoguie*), because another word for *larnax* (coffer) is *chêlos,* which sounds like *chêlê* (hoof).

13 Echo, who can only repeat the words of others. Calliope means "Beautiful Voice." She is one of the Muses.

ΔΩΣΙΑΔΑ ΒΩΜΟΣ

Εἱμάρσενός με στήτας
πόσις, Μέροψ δίσαβος,
τεῦξ', οὐ σποδεύνας ἶνις Ἐμπούσας, μόρος
Τεύκροιο βούτα καὶ κυνὸς τεκνώματος,
5   Χρύσας δ' ἆιτας ἆμος ἐψάνδρα
τὸν γυιόχαλκον οὖρον ἔρραισεν,
ὃν ἀπάτωρ δίσευνος
μόγησε ματρόριπτος.
ἐμὸν δὲ τεῦγμ' ἀθρήσας
10   Θεοκρίτοιο   κτάντας
τριεσπέροιο   καύστας
θώυξεν   αἴν'   ἰύξας,
χάλεψε   γάρ   νιν   ἰῷ
σύργαστρος ἐκδυγήρας·
15   τὸν δ' αἰλινεῦντ' ἐν ἀμφικλύστῳ
Πανός τε ματρὸς εὐνέτας φώρ
δίζωος ἶνίς τ' ἀνδροβρῶτος, Ἰλοραιστᾶν
ἦρ' ἀρδίων, ἐς Τευκρίδ' ἄγαγον τρίπορθον.

AP 15.26; Bucol. codd. aliquot
5 δ' suppl. Valckenaer
12 αἴν' ἰύξας Salmasius: ἀνιύξας M
14 ἐκδυγήρας Salmasius: ἐκδὺς γῆρας M
15 αἰλινεῦντ' Hecker: ἀεὶ λινεῦντ' M: ἐλινύοντ' schol.

DOSIADAS
THE ALTAR

I was made by the husband of a woman who wore male attire, a twice-young mortal,[1] not that offspring of Empusa who went to bed in the ashes, nemesis of the Teucrian oxherd and the bitch's child,[2] but the friend of Chryse, when the husband-boiler smashed the bronze-limbed guard made by the fatherless, twice-married god hurled down by his mother.[3] When the murderer of Theocritus and burner of the product of three nights saw my structure, he uttered a terrible cry, receiving a poisonous bite from the creature that sheds old age and creeps upon its belly; but as he wailed aloud in that wave-washed place,[4] the thievish, twice-lived bedfellow of Pan's mother came with the offspring of a cannibal and took him to the thrice-sacked daughter of Teucer for the sake of his Ilus-smashing arrowheads.[5]

[1] Jason, husband of Medea who eloped with him from Colchis dressed as a man (schol. ad loc.); he is twice young because she rejuvenated him by boiling him in a cauldron (Pherecydes *EGM/FGH* 113 = Simon. *PMG* 548).   [2] Achilles, who according to some accounts was married to Medea in the Isles of the Blessed after his death (Lycophr. 798). His mother Thetis is riddlingly called Empusa because like her she could change shape at will (Pind. *Nem.* 4.59–64, Ov. *Met.* 11.229–65). She put her son Achilles in the fire to make him immortal (Ap. Rhod. 4.869–79). At Troy he killed Paris, who before the war tended his own cattle (Hom. *Il.* 24.29), and Hector, son of Hecuba; after the war she was transformed into a dog (Eur. *Hec.* 1265; cf. *Il.* 24.209–13).

³ Jason was a favorite of Athena; Chryse is a goddess sometimes identified with her (schol. Soph. *Phil.* 194) to whom he built an altar on the way to Colchis (Philostr. Jun. *Imag.* 17). Talos, bronze guardian of Crete, was destroyed by Medea when he pelted the Argo with rocks (Ap. Rhod. 4.1629–88). Talos had been made by the lame blacksmith-god Hephaestus, who married Aphrodite and Aglaia (Hes. *Theog.* 945–6) and who according to Hesiod was a virgin birth from Hera (ibid. 927–9), who cast him down from Olympus in disgust at his deformity (Hom. *Il.* 18.395–7).

⁴ Theocritus = Paris (cf. *Syrinx* 12). His killer is Philoctetes, who kindled Heracles' pyre and in return was given his bow, a talisman necessary for the fall of Troy (Soph. *Phil.* 113, 801–3). Philoctetes was bitten by a water-snake on the wave-washed island of Lemnos.

⁵ Odysseus and Diomedes took Philoctetes to Troy because they needed his arrows to capture the city. Odysseus is "thievish" because he stole the Palladium from Troy. Penelope was mother of Pan by Hermes (see on *Panpipe* 16). Odysseus was "twice-lived" because he came back from the underworld (*Od.* 11). The "cannibal" is Diomedes' father Tydeus, who ate the head of Melanippus (ps.-Apollod. *Bibl.* 3.6.8). "Teucris" is Troy/Ilium, sacked successively by Heracles (*Il.*5.640–43, 648–51), the Amazons (ibid. 3.188–89) and the Greeks. Ilus, son of Tros, was its founder (ps.-Apollod. *Bibl.* 3.12.3).

ΒΗΣΑΝΤΙΝΟΥ ΒΩΜΟΣ

Ὅλος οὔ με λιβρὸς ἱρῶν
Λιβάδεσσιν οἷα κάλχης
Ὑποφοινίῃσι τέγγει·
Μαύλιες δ' ὕπερθε πέτρης Ναξίης θοούμεναι
5   Παμάτων φείδοντο Πανός· οὐ στροβίλῳ λιγνύι
Ἰξὸς εὐώδης μελαίνει τρεχνέων με Νυσίων.
Ἐς γὰρ βωμὸν ὁρῇς με μήτε γλούρου
Πλίνθοις μήτ' Ἀλύβης παγέντα βώλοις,
Οὐδ' ὃν Κυνθογενὴς ἔτευξε φύτλη
10   Λαβόντε μηκάδων κέρα,
Λισσαῖσιν ἀμφὶ δειράσιν
Ὅσσαι νέμονται Κυνθίαις,
Ἰσόρροπος πέλοιτό μοι·
Σὺν οὐρανοῦ γὰρ ἐκγόνοις
15   Εἰνάς μ' ἔτευξε γηγενής,
Τάων ἀείζωον τέχνην
Ἔνευσε πάλμυς ἀφθίτων.
Σὺ δ', ὦ πιὼν κρήνηθεν, ἣν
Ἶνις κόλαψε Γοργόνος,
20   Θύοις τ' ἐπισπένδοις τ' ἐμοὶ
Ὑμηττιάδων πολὺ λαροτέρην
Σπονδὴν ἄδην. ἴθι δὴ θαρσέων
Ἐς ἐμὴν τεῦξιν· καθαρὸς γὰρ ἐγὼ
Ἰὸν ἱέντων τεράων οἷα κέκευθ' ἐκεῖνος,
25   Ἀμφὶ Νέαις Θρηικίαις ὃν σχεδόθεν Μυρίνης
Σοί, Τριπάτωρ, πορφυρέου φὼρ ἀνέθηκε κριοῦ.

BESANTINUS
THE ALTAR

The deep-red blood of sacrifices does not drench me with drops of gore dark as the ink of the cuttlefish; the knives sharpened on a Naxian whetstone[1] spare the possession of Pan;[2] the fragrant sap of Nysian branches[3] does not blacken me with its swirling smoke: behold, I am an altar made neither of gold ingots nor of nuggets from Alybe;[4] may I not weigh so much as the altar built by the twins born on Cynthus from the horns of bleating sheep that graze on the smooth ridges of Cynthus.[5] I was made, with the help of the children of heaven,[6] by a group of nine born on earth,[7] and the lord of the immortals granted that their art should live for ever. O you who drank from the fountain which the Gorgon's offspring struck forth,[8] may you sacrifice and offer upon me sufficient libations much sweeter than the daughters of Hymettus.[9] Approach this structure of mine with confidence: I am free from such poisonous creatures as hid near that altar set up at Thracian Neae near Myrine to you, Goddess of Three Fathers, by the thief of the purple ram.[10]

AP 15.25; Buc. unus cod.

2 κάλχης Edmonds: κάχλην M

3 πέτρῃ Ναξίῃ Edmonds: -ης -ας M

5 στροβίλῳ Salmasius: -λων M

7 μήτε γλούρου Bergk: μεταγχούρου m: μήτε ταγχ- m

10 λαβόντε Wilamowitz: -τα M

[1] The best sort: Pind. *Isthm.* 6.73.

[2] Herds of animals.

[3] Incense from Nysa in Arabia.

[4] Mentioned in the *Iliad* as a source of silver (2.857).

[5] Cynthus: a mountain on Delos, birthplace of Apollo and Artemis, where there was an altar of Apollo made from horns (Callim. *Hymn* 2.60).

[6] The Graces; or the three Heliconian Muses (*Anth. Plan.* 220).

[7] The nine Muses, daughters of Uranus and Ge, according to Alcman (*PMG* 67 = Diod. Sic. 4.7.1).

[8] The spring Hippocrene, fount of poetic inspiration, which welled up on Mt. Helicon when a rock was struck by the hoof of Pegasus, born of the Gorgon's blood (Hes. *Theog.* 281).

[9] The bees of Hymettus in Attica, whose honey was the best (Plin. *HN* 11.32).

[10] It was near the altar set up by Jason at Neae, an island near Myrine on Lemnos, that Philoctetes was bitten by a water snake (see on Dosiadas *Altar* 4–6, 13–14). Why Neae is called "Thracian" is not clear. The "Goddess of Three Fathers" is Athena, whose title Tritogeneia is here taken to mean "thrice begotten."

INDEX

Th. = Theocritus, M. = Moschus, B. = Bion; AD = The Wedding Song of Achilles and Deidamia, ADead = Adonis Dead, ER = Eros the Runaway, Eur = Europa, LA = Lament for Adonis, LB = Lament for Bion, Meg = Megara, PR = PRainer.

References without prefix are to the *Idylls* of Theocritus.

INDEX

INDEX

INDEX

INDEX